PRESEF
COACHING STOCK
OF BRITISH RAILWAYS

PART ONE - BR DESIGN STOCK

FIRST EDITION

Peter Hall & Peter Fox

ublished by Platform 5 Publishing Ltd., Wyvern House, Sark Road, Sheffield S2 4HG, ngland.

rinted in England by Alden Press, Osney Mead, Oxford OX2 0EF and BDC Printing Services td., Slack Lane, Derby, DE3 3FL.

3BN 1-872524-63-X.

The Keighley & Worth Valley Railway is one of the few railways regularly operating suburban coaches. BS No. 43345 has been extensively

Peter Graham

CONTENTS

Correction: The coach illustrated in the inside front cover picture is in fact 17041 not 14042.

PREFACE TO THE FIRST EDITION

Platform 5's companion to their essential guide to preserved locomotives and multiple units 'Preserved Locomotives of British Railways', has been awaited for many years. The ever increasing amount of preserved railway carriages now dictates more than one volume to do the subject justice Thus presented here is the first volume of the series which it is intended will eventually cover all preserved carriages, this first volume confining itself to British Rail design coaching stock.

This book represents the third attempt to tackle what is indeed a very difficult subject to compile to a high level of accuracy. The first book on the subject 'Preserved Railway Coaches' by Michael Harris was published in 1976. This valiant effort, only let down by a few niggling typographical errors, listed over 600 carriages. Few of those listed are however included here, as the preservation of British Railways standard coaches in 1976 was very much in its infancy. 1992 saw the publication of 'Preserved Railway Carriages' by John Lloyd and Murray Brown. This weighty tome tackled the subject differently by a numerical listing of all carriages known to have been preserved. Although considerable documental research had been undertaken, it was regrettably obvious that physical checking of the whereabouts of many vehicles was lacking. Another shortcoming in our opinion, was the lack of narrative regarding the different vehicles. Thus for other than number crunching aficionadoes, much of the content seemed lost to a wider audience.

Thus we offer our interpretation of the subject. No doubt readers will have their own opinions as to how successfully we have tackled the subject. We hope that readers will find that it is a considerable improvement on what has been published previously.

Peter Hall, Peter Fox, October 1994

INTRODUCTION

This book is being compiled during the period of greatest ownership change of rolling stock on Britain's railways since at least 1923, if not ever. Thus before proceeding further it is worthwhile explaining the ground rules used to decide which vehicles are and are not included within this title. Firstly, carriages owned by the three rolling stock leasing companies, Angel Train Company, Eversholt Leasing and Porterbrook Leasing are excluded if they are leased to one of the twenty-five train operating units/companies, as is Rail Express Systems coaching stock. Many of the passenger carrying carriages currently under the jurisdiction of the latter will transfer to the ownership of Flying Scotsman Railways in April 1995 but this is all in the future. Secondly, only carriages which have been in the ownership of, or operated under the jurisdiction of the British Railways Board are included. Thirdly only carriages built to British Railways designs are included, carriages built in the early days of British Railways perpetuating constituent companies' designs being excluded. These will however be covered in a future volume of this series. Fourthly, multiple unit stock is excluded whether or not the individual vehicle is powered or unpowered. Finally although the title suggests only 'preserved' vehicles are included, for completeness all vehicles still in existence are included, whatever their status, provided they obey rules one to four above.

It has however been found necessary to include several vehicles which do not strictly obey the above set of rules. Thus the 'Golden Arrow' Pullman cars are included as although built in the British Railways era their design is loosely based on earlier designs. Also included are the preserved Ferry Vans built as freight stock but to passenger stock designs. Similarly a couple of Inspection Saloons built to a freight lot are also included. Not included however in the main body of the book are the various carriages which have operated under the jurisdiction of British Rail and have been subsequently sold to overseas railway administrations for further use or preservation. Such carriages can be found listed separately in an appendix towards the back of this book. Readers requiring further information regarding these carriages are recommended to consult stock books covering the various overseas railway administrations.

The general format of the book is that passenger-carrying carriages are listed first followed by non-passenger carrying coaching stock. Within the passenger carrying section this is split into the four major designs so far represented in preservation, Pullman, Mark 1, Mark 2 and Mark 3. Within the various splits carriages are listed numerically by first number carried. During the life of many carriages extensive changes are made to the vehicle. Generally the rule has been to list carriages as built with subsequent conversion details given. However if a conversion is so substantial that a new lot number has been issued the carriage will be shown numerically by its latest lot rather than its original lot, details of its previous incarnations being given.

Information contained about the individual carriages listed herein can be split into two categories, historical and preservation. The historical information has been compiled from extensive research of both published works and notes compiled over many years. It is hoped that this information is as accurate as possible. However over the years much contradictory information has been published and it has often been difficult to establish without doubt the correct situation. Thus before criticising the authors for errors in this sphere readers should be sure of their sources of information. Remember that the mind is the best distorter of facts. Obviously however any historical correction or clarification regarding the carriages in this book would be gratefully received. The preservation information is principally compiled from regularly visiting the various sites mentioned and it is believed that information regarding locations is as up to date as is possible. It should however be emphasised that errors are possible in describing the locations due in the main to two factors. Firstly, although much of what is published regarding preserved coaching stock in enthusiast periodicals is accurate, on occasions, what is published is erroneous due to either poor interpretation of the facts or lack of knowledge leading to inaccurate assumptions by the journalists, it being apparent that many periodicals could be greatly improved by their journalists checking facts before going into print. The result of this is that in a few cases, especially with regard to recent developments which the authors have been unable to physically check, published information could be incorporated in good faith, only for it to be subsequently proved to be inaccurate. Secondly, movements of preserved carriages between sites are taking place on an almost daily basis and no official lists of transfers exist in this field. Thus if a movement between sites has taken place since our last visits it is possible that we have not become aware of it, thus the location shown may unknowingly be that where the vehicle was last confirmed as being located rather than where it can currently be found. It is believed however that such occurrences in this book can be counted on the fingers of one hand. The authors would of course welcome notification of these occurrences if they do in fact exist.

WITH GRATEFUL THANKS

Although much of this book is the result of considerable study and research of the subject by the authors over many years it would not have been possible without the help of many others. Thus, the authors whilst accepting the bouquets and reluctantly the brickbats for this tome would like to give credit for the assistance given by several people in particular.

Firstly we would like to thank David Morris for his computing consultancy and confusion in bringing our records into the 1990s, also for his chauffeuring over many years. Our thanks go to Peter Gardner for his navigation on many trips, this having added greatly to the mileage covered in researching this book, also to Graham Dawson for dealing with public relations in often difficult circumstances.

Several carriage enthusiasts have provided invaluable help through correspondence. In this respect special thanks are due to Dave Whittaker, Brian Cuttell, Charlie Cross, Andrew Barclay, Clive Warneford, David Rouse, Roger Harris, Terry Bye and especially Lee Taylor.

With the diversity of ownership of the carriages included herein much detective work has been necessary. Special thanks is thus given to those whom have freely given time and assistance when pestered, in particular Richard Gibbon (National Railway Museum), Neil Tyas (Lancastrian Carriage & Wagon), Tim Robbins (Venice Simplon Orient Express), Richard Edmondson (Queen of Scots Train), David Sinclair, Richard Oakley, Brian Halford, Tracey & Alan Lear, Charles Paget, Tom Tighe, Mike Warner, Ken Ryder and the many railway officers and volunteers around the country who have answered our many awkward questions both by letter and when visiting the sites.

Finally thanks to Roger Butcher for the help given in the departmental field which has led to the resolving of many a query and to all those we have forgotten to mention but whose help has been very much appreciated.

THE CURRENT PRESERVATION SCENE

Around 1300 carriages are listed in this volume, the vast majority of which have been purchased from the British Railways Board in the last twenty years. Excluding the consequences of the various railway sell-offs over the next few years this figure is not expected to rise significantly further, the supply of vehicles seemingly of interest to preservationists being almost exhausted.

It would be very fair to say that the impetus for the purchase of so many carriages has been to have something to operate the trains with on the ever expanding number of private railways, the term preserved railway being only loosely applicable in many cases. The result has obviously been that many carriages are quite literally run into the ground and then discarded to the ever lengthening queue of long term restoration projects, their place being taken by the latest acquisition, often still in its last state railway livery and moquette, thus hardly reflecting the hoped for 'romantic age of steam' atmosphere. During the compilation of notes for this book the authors have travelled many miles in the carriages listed and unfortunately the general impression is of tattiness and neglect. But perhaps that is what it was really like in the steam era and the higher standards of cleanliness and tidiness on many of the trains now running on Railtrack metals is indeed progress in the right direction, just as the public relations people tell us!

Several private railways, fortunately, are addressing this problem and producing some very nicely restored carriages often under conditions that direct the majority of funds and resources elsewhere. It would however certainly appear that a time bomb is slowly ticking away for the private railways and the problems that in recent years have created considerable difficulties for British Rail regarding for example door locks and distorted body shells will one day have to be addressed by the private railways. Then of course there is always asbestos!

Particularly on recent visits by the authors to various preservation sites the epidemic of health and safety paranoia is increasingly being contracted. One of the consequences of this is that for those whom visit such places to view the supposedly historical collection of rolling stock are increasingly being disappointed. Carriages often suffer more so in this respect, with access to view being increasingly restricted, whilst the railways continue to appeal to enthusiasts in particular, for funds to restore carriages which the same enthusiasts are refused access to view. Surely it is ironic that it is easier to view carriages in the countries of the former eastern bloc than it is in Britain's so-called railway museums. The consequence of this seemingly uncontrollable epidemic is that the authors have been increasingly made less welcome at many sights on recent visits. Is this what the enthusiast who have willingly contributed to preservation in the past had in mind or does commercialism now rule and gricers are as much a nuisance on private railways as they have been to generations of British Railways shedmasters?

MAIN-LINE RUNNING

Since the procedure of allocating private owner numbers to coaching stock passed to run on the main line was introduced by British Rail in 1974 a number of vehicles included in this book have been approved although some are no longer authorised. Those currently authorised can be conveniently grouped into three categories. Firstly those used by what could be considered industrial operators. Currently Nomix-Chipman and Schering operate weed killing trains using converted British Railways design carriages whilst the Ministry of Defence operate four Nuclear Flask Escort coaches which are normally found operating in pairs. Secondly there are the carriages, principally corridor brakes, used as support coaches for preserved steam and diesel locomotives passed for main line use. Thirdly there are the privately owned main line sets. It is in this field that expansion is likely as railway privatisation progresses, a number of recent purchases having been made with this intention in mind. Currently the main base for such operators is Steamtown Railway Centre, Carnforth, this being the base of 'The Statesman' set of Mark 2 Pullmans, the 'Pilkington K Glass' set of Mark 1 corridors and the 'Carnforth Maroon Set' which is in reality a pool currently consisting of eighteen Mark 1 and Mark 2 carriages formed as required. At the top end of the market are the Millerhill, Edinburgh based 'Royal Scotsman' set formed primarily of Metropolitan-Cammell Pullmans along with a couple of Mark 1s and an LNER saloon. The 'Queen of Scots' train currently operates with one Mark 1 Corridor Brake Second along with three much older carriages. Sea Containers Ltd by way of their Venice-Simplon Orient Express subsidiary operate two luxury sets, the 'VSOE Pullman' set which includes three of the Golden Arrow Pullmans a Mark 1 Corridor Brake Second and Bogie Ferry Van along with six older Pullman cars. The recently formed 'Ocean Liner Express' set currently contains three Mark 1 First Opens and a Gangwayed Brake Van along with a leased Restaurant Buffet and Mark 2 Corridor Brake First. This set is expected to be strengthened in the not too distant future. The only other main line set currently in use is the maroon liveried Scottish Railway Preservation Society set of nine Mark 1s based at Bo'ness. Lastly mention should be made of what is referred to as 'BN91' set. Until recently this consisted of six Mark 1s owned by Flying Scotsman Railways and a similar number leased from the Inter City Charter Unit. A recent change has seen the addition of a Mark 1 Corridor Brake Composite from the Flying Scotsman Railways reserve fleet, whilst it is understood a further three Mark 1 Tourist Second Opens currently at The Railway Age, Crewe are to be added shortly. However as Flying Scotsman Railways are in the process of acquiring the special trains unit it is expected that the two fleets will become merged. Finally mention should be made of an exception to the three categories so far mentioned. This is the recently converted Mark 1 Tourist Second Open which has been internally renovated in the style of a LMS club car. This carriage, 5067. is based at Steamtown Railway Centre, Carnforth and is normally used in conjunction with the 'The Statesman' set.

GUIDE TO THE LAYOUT

It is hoped that the layout used in this book is almost self explanatory, therefore avoiding the need to continually refer back to lists of abbreviations etc. It would however be probably worthwhile to make a few comments on the layout before continuing.

As previousy stated the order of the book is, Passenger Carrying Coaching Stock subdivided by Pullman, Mark 1, Mark 2 and Mark 3 followed by Non Passenger Carrying Coaching Stock. This main part of the book is followed by various pages giving additional information regarding carriages and locations. Within each section carriages are arranged numerically by first number carried. In the main the numbering of carriages has been well organised, grouping particular designs together, thus details of a particular vehicle type are given as a main heading along with its type code. This is followed by details of particular lots and the vehicles preserved within them.

Lot details given include the lot number, builder, month the particular lot was ordered and completed, diagram number, design code, seats and type of bogies fitted when built. Although this probably makes perfect sense to the majority of readers the following notes are given as added explanation.

Type Code

This is a standard code adopted by British Rail for the identification of coaching stock throughout the network. With a few exceptions, mainly non-passenger carrying types, this consists of codes of up to five letters. Codes and a description of them are given below:-

Bar	Bar Car	BPOT	Post Office Brake Tender Van
BCK	Corridor Brake Composite	BS	Brake Second
BFB	Bullion Bogie Flat	BSK	Corridor Brake Second
BFK	Corridor Brake First	BSO	Open Brake Second
BG	Gangwayed Full Brake	C	Composite
Booth	Booth Car	CCT	Covered Carriage Truck

8

CCTbogie	Bogie Covered Carriage Truck
CK	Corridor Composite
CL	Composite with Lavatory
ExhibVan	Exhibition Van
FK	Corridor First
FISH	Fish Van
FO	Open First
FRUIT D	Fruit Van
GUV	General Utility Van
HB	Horse Box
LFK	Corridor Lounge First
NPV	Newspaper Van
PB	Pullman Brake First
PC	Pullman Parlour First
PCV	Parcels Carrying Van
PK	Pullman First with Kitchen
POS	Post Office Sorting Van
POT	Post Office Tender Van
RB	Restaurant Buffet (with kitchen)
RF	Restaurant First (with kitchen)
RFO	First Class Restaurant
RG	Griddle Car
RK	Restaurant Kitchen
RKB	Restaurant Kitchen/Buffet
RMB	Open Second with Miniature Buffet
ROYAL	Royal Saloon
RSO	Second Class Restaurant
RU	Restaurant Unclassified (with kitchen)
RUO	Unclassified Restaurant
S	Second
SD	Saloon Discotheque
SK	Corridor Second
SLB	Bullion Van
SLC	Composite Sleeping Car
SLE	Convertible Sleeping Car
SLEP	Convertible Sleeping Car with Pantry
SLF	First Class Sleeping Car
SLO	Second Open with Lavatory
SLS	Second Class Sleeping Car (four berth)
SLST	Second Class Sleeping Car, twin-berth
SLSTP	Second Class Sleeping Car, twin-berth with Pantry
SO	Open Second
SO(NG)	Open Second (non-gangwayed)
TCV	Two Tier Car Carrier
TSO	Tourist Open Second

Lot Number

To coincide with the introduction of the first designs of British Railways coaching stock in 1950, a new range of order numbers was introduced commencing at '30001' and known as lot numbers was started. Subsequently all new orders for coaching stock and some conversions of existing vehicles, with the noteable exception of some Pullman cars, have been allocated a lot number. The highest lot number issued to date is 31143, however it is unclear whether this system will be perpetuated following the transfer of coaching stock assets to leasing companies which will ultimately become private companies competing in theory with all comers to lease stock to train operating companies.

Builder

The construction of the majority of the carriages took place at the former British Railways workshops at Ashford, Derby, Doncaster, Eastleigh, Earlestown, Faverdale, Lancing, Swindon, Wolverton and York, whilst in addition certain conversions took place at Stewarts Lane Carriage and Wagon Repair Shops. However, certain carriages were built by outside contractors. Where two builders are shown the first was responsible for the underframe, the second for the body work.

Ordered

This is the month in which the order for a particular lot of carriages was placed. It should however be noted that lots were not ordered in strict chronological order due in the main to contractual reasons and this also can create ambiguities with vehicles appearing to be ordered after they were built.

Completed

This is the month in which the order was officially completed, usually coinciding with the date on which the last vehicle of the lot entered service.

Original Diagram

This is the original British Railways diagram to which the particular vehicles were built. These are shown for all carriages for which they have been known to have been issued. However since the late 1970s new designs have been issued a Design Code instead.

New Diagram

Since the late 1970s all new designs of coaching stock have been issued a Design Code rather than a Diagram Number, similarly the majority of vehicles remaining at the time were retrospectively allocated a Design Code. The Design Code consists of seven alphanumeric characters. The first two characters are letters the first being either:- A - for locomotive hauled passenger carrying coaching stock. N - for locomotive hauled non passenger carrying coaching stock. The second letter designates the layout of the vehicle and varies for each of the above as follows:-

For first letter A (locomotive hauled passenger carrying coaching stock):-

A   Gangwayed Corridor | B   Gangwayed Corridor Brake

C	Gangwayed Open (2 + 2 seating)	L	Restaurant with Kitchen/As 'C' but with
D	Gangwayed Open (2 + 1 seating)		disabled person's toilet, Mk IV stock
E	Gangwayed Open Brake	M	Restaurant Open
G	Griddle	N	Miniature buffet
H	Buffet with Kitchen	P	Pullman Kitchen
I	As 'C' but fitted with drophead buckeye and	Q	Pullman Bar
	no gangway at one end	R	Pullman Brake
J	Restaurant Buffet with Kitchen	S	Sleeping Car
K	Kitchen Car	T	Royal Train Coach

For first letter N (locomotive hauled non passenger carrying coaching stock):-

A	Gangwayed Full Brake (BG)	T	Post Office Stowage Van (POT)
I	General Utility Van (GUV)	U	Brake and Post Office Sorting Van (BPOT)
J	Parcels Carrying Van (PCV)	V	Two tier Car Transporter (TCV)
L	Gangwayed Newspaper Van (PVG)	W	Bogie for Bullion (BFB)
P	Covered Carriage Truck (CCT)	Y	Exhibition Van (ExhibVan)
R	Fish Van (Fish)	Z	Driving Luggage Van (DLV)
S	Post Office Sorting Van (POS)		

These two letters are followed by three digits, the first of which designates the passenger accommodation as follows:

1	First	4	Unclassified
2	Second (now known as Standard)	5	None
3	Composite		

The subsequent two numbers indicate various detail variations.

These first five characters of the Design Code are referred to as the New Diagram and it is these which are shown in this book.

It should be noted that in certain cases vehicles which have remained in service into the 1980s are not shown as being allocated a New Diagram. Such vehicles have undergone conversion without the issue of new lot numbers and consequently the New Diagram ß   s no relation to the Diagram Number. Thus the New Diagrams have been omitted to avoid confusion.

Seats

This only applies to passenger carrying coaches with seated accommodation and is the amount and type of seats in the carriage when built. 'F' designates first class seats, 'S' designates second class seats now referred to as standard. Prior to 3rd June 1956 what is referred to as second class accommodation was referred to as third class accommodation with designation 'T', however throughout this book, in order to be consistent it is always referred to as second, 'U' designates unclassified accommodation, i.e. that not specifically designated for the use of first or second class passengers.

Bogies

This shows the type of bogies fitted to the carriage when first built. The various types of bogies used are:-

BR Mk I (BR1) - Standard double bolster leaf spring bogie. Generally 90 m.p.h. but certain vehicles, mainly BGs, were allowed to run at 100 m.p.h. with special maintenance. Weight: 6.1 t.

BR Mk I heavy duty (BR1 h.d.) - Similar to the BR1 but with a larger axle box and an extra stiffening plate welded along the top of the frame. Particularly used for catering carriages. Weight: 6.5 t

BR Mk II (BRII) - Later variant of BR1. Single bolster leaf spring bogie. Used on certain types of Non-passenger carrying coaching stock. Weight: 5.3 t.

BR Mk I Madison - Experimental development of the BR1 bogie with single centre bolster leaf spring. Fitted to certain Corridor Seconds of lot 30349. Not perpetuated in later designs. Weight: 5.6 t.

COMMONWEALTH - Heavy, cast steel coil spring bogie. 100 m.p.h. Note that there are many different variants of this type according to the weight of the vehicle. Weight: around 6.75 t.

B4 - Coil spring fabricated bogie. 100 m.p.h. Weight: 5.2 t.

B5 - Heavy duty version of B4. 100 m.p.h. Weight: 5.3 t.

BT10 - A fabricated bogie with air suspension. 125 m.p.h. Weight ?t. Fuller details concerning the various bogies employed can be found in the introduction to the various sections of this book.

Brakes

The universal braking system for passenger trains inherited by British Railways was by the vacuum system. This system being perpetuated with the Mark 1s which were, with the exception of one lot referred to elsewhere, all built with this system. The fitting of vacuum brakes continued into the early batches of Mark 2s, not being replaced by the air system until the appearance of the Mark 2A in late 1967. As the changeover to air braking has yet to be completed various modifications to carriage brake systems have been made. In the details for carriages included in this book, details of brakes are only given if a change of braking system has taken place since the carriage was built.

The above details are followed by information regarding changes made to the carriages in that particular lot along with and any other relevant information regarding their main line career. Details then follow of the individual vehicles.

Following the first number any subsequent capital stock numbers are given, followed by any departmental numbers. This is followed by the location of the vehicle and any other relevant information concerning its current status such as plated number, current number if not previously carried and certain other details which may be of interest to readers.

Renumbering

This has generally occurred due to either of two reasons, firstly when a carriage has been substantially altered and secondly as part of a general renumbering to avoid duplicate numbers on the British Rail TOPS computer system.

Departmental Numbers

When a carriage is transferred into departmental service it is normally allocated a new number. The majority of carriages in this book to which this has happened have been numbered into the DB97xxxx series. This series was first used at the end of 1966, the intention being that all service vehicles converted from condemned coaching stock would be so numbered. However, until 1970 this numbering series was little used as almost all service vehicles continued to be numbered into the various regional series, several such vehicles having been preserved which were numbered in the Western Region DW150xxx series, the Southern Region DS70xxx series and the Eastern Region DE32xxxx series. From 1970 the DB975xxx series began in earnest, although until 1979 some of the regional number series were still used. By the end of 1980 the DB975xxx series had been completed and as the DB976xxx series was in use for service vehicles converted from condemned freight stock, the series jumped to DB977000. When TOPS was first implemented in 1973 each departmental vehicle acquired a prefix indicating the department which owned it. No prefix indicated that it was a CCE vehicle, A was used for the CM&EE, C for BREL, K for S&T Engineer, L for CM&EE Electrical Construction, P for Shipping and Internal Services, R for Research, T for Traffic, X for Stores and Z for PRO & Publicity. Obviously certain vehicles changed prefix when responsibility for ownership changed and a number of anomalies inevitably occurred. Such prefixes have not been included in this book however it is hoped to include them in a future edition when further research into the subject has been undertaken. Certain vehicles when transferred to departmental service are designated as 'Internal Use Only', such vehicles being given a number in the 0xxxx series, this indicating that movement is restricted. A few such vehicles are featured in this book.

Location

The location where the carriage is normally to be found is given if known. Fuller details of UK locations including O.S. grid references are given under 'List of Locations'. It should however be noted that it is the intention of this book to record where individual carriages are rather than who owns them, thus it should not be assumed that a vehicle has any obligation to the site were it is located. In certain cases where carriages are located away from the site shown, such as for restoration, details are given of the current temporary whereabouts.

Plated number

Privately owned carriages authorised to run on the Railtrack network are allocated a private owner number and referred to as "plated". The number consists of an owner prefix followed by a five figure number in the 99xxx series. Carriages have to be passed by Railtrack each year and this is denoted by a white equilateral triangle painted on the solebar with the year painted in black. It should be noted that there are other carriages, not registered for running at the time of going to press, which also have private owner numbers allocated. Such carriages, especially those in use as locomotive support coaches, spend considerable time away from the location shown for them, thus it should not necessarily be assumed that such carriages will be seen on a visit to the location shown for them.

Details of departmental use of carriages is normally given at the end of each lot.

Finally it should be noted that the above explained presentation of information varies slightly for certain carriages due to the individuality of many carriages. However, the above explanations equally apply.

PULLMAN CAR COMPANY STOCK

Fifty four Pullman cars were constructed for use on Britain's Railways in the British Rail era. The ten 'Golden Arrow' cars of 1951 and the forty four 'Metro-Cammell' cars of 1960. The majority of these cars remain to this day, either preserved or seeing some other use.

GOLDEN ARROW CARS

Seven Pullman cars were constructed in 1951 by the Birmingham Railway Carriage and Wagon Company, in connection with the 'Festival of Britain'. This was in fact a revival of an order placed in 1938 which had not been progressed as a result of the onset of the Second World War. The underframes and bogies were of Gresley pattern and the bodies were of strong timber and galvanised steel construction, these perpetuating the straight sided design of earlier cars. However a noteable departure from tradition was that the oval shaped windows in the lavatories and pantries were changed to a rectangular shape. The interiors were a slightly modernised version of the traditional Pullman specification although in no way lacking the splendour of earlier cars. The cars were intended for use on the 'Golden Arrow', a boat train operating between London Victoria and Dover, and initially special workings in connection with the Festival of Britain. The first cars were previewed on 5th June 1951 and entered public service six days later. Three further cars were constructed at Preston Park in 1952 to augment those built the previous year, one of these 'PHOENIX' being in fact a new body on the pre-war chassis of 'RAINBOW (II)' which was burnt out at Micheldever on 15th August 1936 and mounted on Pullman bogies whilst the other two were mounted on Gresley bogies. Thus a total of ten 'Golden Arrow' cars, three parlour firsts, one parlour second, five parlour kitchen cars and a bar car were constructed. To augment the fleet five earlier cars, two parlour brake seconds (Car No. 36 & Car No. 208), one parlour brake first (MINERVA) and two parlour seconds (Car No. 34 & Car No. 35) were refurbished.

On 12th June 1961 steam locomotive haulage was replaced by electric haulage on the 'Golden Arrow' following completion of the electrification of the former South Eastern Railway main line, motive power being the new E5000 electric locomotives, later Class 71. This required the cars to be fitted with electric train heating. As the E5000 locomotives could only provide heating of 300 kW(400 amps) at the line voltage of 750 it was necessary to install such heaters in addition to those of the usual voltage on BR of 1000. However the heaters fitted were to UIC standards having an earth return via the track. In 1963 'PEGASUS' was withdrawn from the 'Golden Arrow' pool and transferred to the London Midland Region were it was put into the Euston-Glasgow night sleeper and rebranded as 'Nightcap Bar', continuing in use as such until the mid 1970s. On 14th June 1965 second class Pullman cars were withdrawn from the 'Golden Arrow' and replaced by BR standard coaches. The displaced cars found some use elsewhere, in particular on the 'Bournemouth Belle' train, but by the early 1970s some of the cars had been withdrawn with only 'PEGASUS' on the London Midland Region and 'PERSEUS', 'PHOENIX', 'ORION', 'CARINA' and 'CYGNUS', by now air-braked, in the 'Golden Arrow' pool remaining. These later five cars were withdrawn following the demise of the 'Golden Arrow' which last ran on Saturday 30th September 1972. Only two cars have not survived, both of which were early withdrawals, the sole second class car 303 which was scrapped by Birds at Long Marston and 'HERCULES' which saw a number of years service as a departmental vehicle awaiting conversion to a laboratory coach to be numbered DB975022, a conversion which was never carried out. It was broken up by British Rail at Clapham Junction Carriage & Wagon workshop in 1973. A number of chairs from 'HERCULES' continue in use at various houses and offices in the Sheffield and Deby areas.

Four of the surviving cars are in the hands of Sea Containers whom have restored three of them for use in their Venice-Simplon Orient Express mainline set, the fourth remaining in store for possible future use. 'ARIES' is a familiar site to travellers along the M62 motorway, from which it can be clearly seen, now serving as a static restaurant, as is 'ORION' now retired in Devon. 'AQUILLA' is part of the Colne Valley Railways dining train making frequent journeys up the short line at Castle Hedingham whilst 'PEGASUS' is on static display at Tyseley.

METROPOLITAN-CAMMELL CARS

By the end of the 1950s it became apparent that the 1928 built cars then in use on the Eastern Region were in need of replacement. Thus an order for 44 new cars was awarded to Metropolitan-Cammell (successor of the Metropolitan Carriage and Wagon Company). Delivery commenced in 1960 and was completed in 1961.

The British Railways standard Mk 1 design was modified to suit the traditions of the Pullman Car Company. The most obvious departure from the Mk 1 design were larger main windows and recessed inward opening flat doors. Commonwealth bogies were fitted. Five types of vehicle were constructed, thirteen firsts with kitchen, eight firsts without kitchen, fifteen seconds with kitchen, seven seconds without kitchen and one bar car. As no new brake vehicles were built 1928 brakes, suitably refurbished, continued in use for a number of years before being replaced by Mark I full brakes.

During the winter of 1967-8 the first class cars were refurbished and the seating increased by replacing single loose chairs of traditional pattern with fixed 2 + 1 seating as used on the Mark I Pullmans. During the period 1968-71 second class Pullman accommodation was progressively replaced with second class standard stock. This resulted in the displacement of the second class cars the seven with out kitchens being reclassified as open firsts and continued in use for several years on non-Pullman workings particularly in East Anglia. The Bar Car was transferred for use as a Nightcar Bar on West Coast Sleeping car services whilst the seconds with kitchen were stored and several saw no further use. Also at this time the cars remaining in use on Eastern Region Pullman services were fitted with Air-brakes whilst retaining their vacuum brakes. Cars converted being 311/13-21/24-31

Pullman services ceased on the East Coast main line on 5th May 1978. A few of the cars continued in service on Motorail and special workings for a few years longer. The last of these cars were withdrawn in 1980 although those which had been declassified to FOs continued in use until 1981

Although the majority of cars have survived for preservation the presence of blue asbestos used in their construction clouds the future of several of the cars. Fortunately a substantial number of the cars including those used in the 'Royal Scotsman Train' and by Flying Scotsman Railways have had the asbestos removed. The 'Royal Scotsman' cars have in effect been gutted and had completely new interiors installed some being used as sleeping cars. However the luxuriant standards of these vehicles does justice to their pedigree. Car 332 and Car 340 are used as static restaurants as is the body of 'STORK' whilst those on the North Yorkshire Moors Railway are being progressively brought back into use on that railway's dining train following removal of asbestos and prolonged restoration, 'ROBIN' being the first to return to service.

Of the cars not to survive, 312/22/30/34/36/38/39/41-45 were scrapped at Snailwell. Interestingly 330 was used after withdrawal as the staff coach for the commissioning of Romanian built Class 56 locomotives. 323 was converted to Laboratory Coach 14, DB975427 in 1975 and subsequently sold to Vic Berry Ltd. It has been suggested that this car may still survive in store with 314 rather than being broken up as reported in the railway press although this is thought doubtful. The authors would therefore be very interested to hear from any one whom could verify either story.

Note: Pullman Cars built after the ones referred to here were built for BR and not the Pullman Car Company, as by then it had been nationalised in order to solve a dispute regarding the introduction of new Pullman services on lines which had formerly been operated by BR catering staff.

PARLOUR FIRST   PFP

Builder: Birmingham Carriage & Wagon Company.
Built: 1951.   **Seats:** 32F.   **Bogies:** Gresley.
Notes: Air-braked.

301 PERSEUS   Venice-Simplon Orient Express   VSOE99530. 'VSOE' set

Builder: Pullman Car Company, Preston Park.
Built: 1952.   **Seats:** 26F.   **Bogies:** Pullman.
Notes: Underframe and bogies from car 176 'Rainbow (II)' the body of which was destroyed by
fire at Micheldever on 15/8/1936. Air-braked.

302 PHOENIX   Venice-Simplon Orient Express   VSOE99531. 'VSOE' set

PARLOUR FIRST WITH KITCHEN   PFK

Builder: Pullman Car Company, Preston Park.
Built: 1952.   **Seats:** 22F.   **Bogies:** Gresley.

304 ARIES   Yew Tree Inn, Thornham   Used as restaurant

Builder: Birmingham Carriage & Wagon Company.
Built: 1951.   **Seats:** 22F.   **Bogies:** Gresley.
Notes: 306/07 Air-braked.

305 AQUILLA   Colne Valley Railway
306 ORION   Peco Modelrama, Beer   Used as restaurant
307 CARINA   Venice-Simplon Orient Express

PARLOUR FIRST   PFP

Builder: Birmingham Carriage & Wagon Company.
Built: 1951.   **Seats:** 32F.   **Bogies:** Gresley.
Notes: Air-braked.

308 CYGNUS   Venice-Simplon Orient Express   VSOE99532. 'VSOE' set

BAR CAR   PBAR

Builder: Birmingham Carriage & Wagon Company.
Built: 1951.   **Seats:** 14F.   **Bogies:** Gresley.

310 PEGASUS   Birmingham Railway Museum

PARLOUR FIRST with KITCHEN   PFK

Builder: Metropolitan Cammell.
Built: 1960-61.   **Seats:** 20F.   **Bogies:** Commonwealth.
Notes: Refurbished 1967-68 and loose seating replaced with 26 fixed seats, Dual-braked. 314 con-
verted to CM&EE Staff Training Coach ADB975876 in 1979 and 316 & 320 to CCE Staff Coaches
DB975608 and DB975609 in 1976.

311 EAGLE   Steamtown Railway Centre, Carnforth   National Collection
313 FINCH   Great Scottish & Western Railway   GSWR99964. 'Royal Scotsman'set
314 HAWK   Vic Berry Ltd.
315 HERON   Great Central Railway
316 MAGPIE   Steamtown Railway Centre, Carnforth
317 RAVEN   Great Scottish & Western Railway   GSWR99967. 'Royal Scotsman'set
318 ROBIN   North Yorkshire Moors Railway
319 SNIPE   Great Scottish & Western Railway   GSWR99965. 'Royal Scotsman'set
320 STORK   Steam Rock Cafe, Muswell Hill   Body only remains
321 SWIFT   Northampton & Lamport Railway

PARLOUR FIRST   PFP

Builder: Metropolitan Cammell.
Built: 1960-61.   **Seats:** 24F.   **Bogies:** Commonwealth.

Notes: Refurbished 1967-68 and loose seating replaced with 29 fixed seats. Dual-braked.

324	AMBER	Great Scottish & Western Railway	GSWR99961. 'Royal Scotsman'set
325	AMETHYST	Strathspey Railway	SR No. 108
326	EMERALD	National Railway Museum	
327	GARNET	North Yorkshire Moors Railway	
328	OPAL	North Yorkshire Moors Railway	
329	PEARL	Great Scottish & Western Railway	GSWR99962. 'Royal Scotsman'set
331	TOPAZ	Great Scottish & Western Railway	GSWR99963. 'Royal Scotsman'set

PARLOUR SECOND WITH KITCHEN   PSK

Builder: Metropolitan Cammell.
Built: 1960-61.   **Seats:** 30S.   **Bogies:** Commonwealth.

Notes: 335 converted to CCE Staff Coach DB975584 in 1976 and preserved with dual brakes 333/46 restored with BR1 bogies.

332	CAR No. 332	Train Now Standing Restaurant, Pannal	Used as restaurant
333	CAR No. 333	Casterton Taverner Motor Inn, Stamford	'MAGNA
335	CAR No. 335	Flying Scotsman Railways, Bounds Green	
337	CAR No. 337	Great Central Railway	
340	CAR No. 340	Avon Causeway Hotel, Hurn	Used as restaurant
346	CAR No. 346	Casterton Taverner Motor Inn, Stamford	'CASTRA

PARLOUR SECOND   PSP

Builder: Metropolitan Cammell.
Built: 1960-61.   **Seats:** 42S.   **Bogies:** Commonwealth.

Preserved with dual brakes.

347	CAR No. 347	Flying Scotsman Railways, Bounds Green
348	CAR No. 348	Flying Scotsman Railways, Bounds Green
349	CAR No. 349	Flying Scotsman Railways, Bounds Green
350	CAR No. 350	Flying Scotsman Railways, Bounds Green
351	CAR No. 351	Flying Scotsman Railways, Bounds Green
352	CAR No. 352	Flying Scotsman Railways, Bounds Green
353	CAR No. 353	Flying Scotsman Railways, Bounds Green

BAR CAR   PBAR

Builder: Metropolitan Cammell.
Built: 1960-61.   **Seats:** 24S.   **Bogies:** Commonwealth.

Preserved with dual brakes.

354	HADRIAN BAR	Flying Scotsman Railways, Bounds Green

MARK I PASSENGER CARRYING COACHING STOCK

Many readers will already have read the highly recommended book 'British Railways Mark I Coaches' by Keith Parkin (available from Platform 5 mail order dept price £19.95 + £2 p & p (UK)) and those who have not are strongly recommended to do so. Thus rather than replicate what has already been written about the design and development of this universally applauded stock, notes are rather brief in this respect.

The semi-open composite 15000 and Corridor Brake Third 34095 (interestingly built to an LMS lot) were first displayed at Marylebone to the railway hierarchy on 18th September 1950. Regrettably neither of these two carriages survive. The first production examples appeared the following year and numerous examples of these have been preserved.

As the Mark I carriage was in production for well over a decade it was inevitable that a steady process of detail change to the original design would take place. One of the most significant developments during the period was in bogie design. The standard bogie used under Mark Is was the BR Mark I (BR1) based on a GWR design and its heavy duty version (BR1h.d.) which was used for various catering carriages. A later variant of this, the BR Mark II (BR2) was used on General Utility Vans which are described in a later section. Various developments in bogie design took place over the years and the majority of these are discussed in Keith Parkin's book. The result was that later builds of passenger carrying Mark 1s were built with Commonwealth bogies, Those so built being:

RF	310-342		FO	3076-3080, 3101-3151
RUO	1018-1057		TSO	4900-5069
RG	1100-1102		BSO	9363-9380
RB	1644-1699, 1739-1772		FK	13303-13360
RMB	1813-1837, 1853-1882		BFK	14013-14027
RU	1959-1991		CK	16153-16267
SLF	2105-2132		BCK	21236-21275
SLC	2428-2454		SK	25704-26217
SLSTP	2579-2691		BSK	35294-35499

Inevitably over the years various bogie changes have taken place for various reasons and these are detailed below:

1. Commonwealth removed by Southern Region and replaced with BR Mark 1 from carriages in 2) below.

RUO	1019
TSO	4900-4907, 4909-4916, 5024
CK	16198, 16200-16205, 16210, 16220, 16221
BCK	21263, 21264
SK	25907-25910, 25912-25918, 25920, 25944, 25946, 25948, 25953, 25972

1.1. BR1 subsequently replaced with Commonwealth.

TSO	4901, 4905, 4910, 4913, 5024

1.2. BR1 subsequently replaced with B4.

TSO	4902, 4909, 4915, 4916

2. BR Mark I removed by Southern Region and replaced with Commonwealth from carriages in (1) above.

FO	3068
TSO	3749, 3828, 3829, 3837, 3840, 3844, 3846, 3916, 3918, 3919, 3921, 3923, 3924, 3988, 3990-3994, 4058, 4059, 4062, 4063, 4065, 4066, 4072, 4076, 4376, 4381, 4389, 4392, 4393, 4436
CK	15563, 15567, 15568, 15570, 15572, 15891, 15896
BSK	34638, 34641, 34642, 34971, 35010, 35011

3. BR Mark 1 heavy duty replaced with Gresley.

RU	1926-1932, 1934-1937, 1939

3.1. Gresley subsequently replaced with Commonwealth.

RU   1927, 1930, 1931, 1934

4. BR Mark I heavy duty replaced with Commonwealth.

RB   1705-1713, 1725-1729, 1733, 1618-21
RMB   1838, 1841, 1842, 1845, 1846, 1848
RU   1913, 1917, 1921, 1922, 1951

5. BR Mark I replaced with Commonwealth

SLC   2424-2426
FO   3028, 3035

6. BR Mark I/BR Mark I heavy duty replaced with B4/B5

RFO	4-6, 9
RG	1103-1105
RSO	1001, 1008-1011, 1014-1017
RKB	1500-1569
RB	1700-1704, 1730-1732, 1734-1738
RMB	1803, 1805-1807, 1849-1852
RU	1904, 1923, 1924, 1933, 1941-1948, 1950, 1953, 1954, 1956-1958
SLF	2000-2104
SLC	2400-2423, 2427
SLSTP	2500-2578
ROYAL	499, 2900, 2901
FO	3000-3002, 3005, 3007-3018, 3020-3027, 3029-3034, 3036-3041, 3044-3055, 3059, 3063-3067, 3069-3073, 3075, 3085-3099, 3100
TSO	4437-4439, 4441, 4442, 4457, 4459, 4626, 4627, 4674, 4709-4716, 4718-4723, 4725, 4726, 4771, 4773-4775
SO	4820, 4822-4826, 4828, 4829
TSO	4833, 4837, 4840-4843, 4845-4863, 4865-4870, 4872-4899
BSO	9270, 9271, 9273, 9323-9326, 9328, 9333-9337, 9340, 9341
FK	13074, 13085, 13089, 13091, 13092, 13094, 13108, 13110, 13147, 13176, 13213, 13225-13230, 13232-13241, 13245, 13247, 13248, 13253-13264, 13266, 13268-13288, 13290-13299, 13300-13302
BFK	14000, 14001, 14012
CK	15616, 15768-15770, 15788, 15789, 15791, 15806, 15810, 15811, 15813, 15815, 15816, 15819, 15820, 15837, 15861-15870, 15886, 15887, 15897, 15910, 15912, 16009-16012, 16014, 16016, 16019-16024, 16026-16028, 16036, 16039, 16041-16046, 16085-16099, 16100-16107, 16112, 16117-16132, 16143
BCK	21071, 21072, 21085, 21128, 21129, 21139, 21173, 21175, 21182-21185, 21187-21194, 21212, 21213, 21215, 21216, 21219, 21222-21224, 21231-21235
SK	24544, 24719, 25060, 25097, 25101, 25167, 25230, 25595-25599, 25601-25605, 25607-25616, 25618, 25619, 25621-25627
BSK	34836-34840, 34842, 34843, 34846-34850, 34852, 34853, 34855-34857, 34859, 34860, 34862, 34864-34866, 34872, 34873, 34876-34906, 34908-34924, 34926-34933, 34992, 35024-35038, 35095, 35134, 35191-35204, 35207, 35209, 35210, 35242-35245, 35247-35250, 35274-35284, 35286-35293.

6.1. B4/B5 subsequently replaced with BT5

RKB   1524

7. BR Mark I replaced with BR Mark II Madison

SK   25346-25379, 25385, 25391, 25397, 25399

N.B. When 1106 and 1883 were built utilising RK underframes they were fitted with B5 bogies.

Various carriages have had their bogies changed after preservation and details of these changes can be found in the headings for individual lots.

Another development to later built carriages was the use of melamine interior panels in Second Class accommodation, carriages so panelled being Tourist Open Second 4840-5069, Open Brake Second 9363-9380, Corridor Composite 16108-16267, Corridor Brake Composite 21231-21275 and Corridor Brake Second 35274-35499.

The train braking system fitted to all Mark I carriages when built was vacuum braking. However in 1963 the Southern Region commenced the fitting of carriages used on continental boat trains with r-brakes. At the same time the Southern Region took delivery of the only lot of Mark Is to be fitted with air-brakes from new, these being Brake Corridor Composites 21263-21275, initially for use on uch workings. In addition a batch of twenty Mark 2 Corridor Firsts fitted with air-brakes were also elivered to the Southern Region at this time. The Southern Region soon expanded its air-braking rogram to cover the majority of its allocation by 1970. The above mentioned bogie swop on the outhern Region taking place in the late 1960's in order to provide carriages already fitted with air-rakes and used on Boat Trains with comparable ride characteristics to the newer stock.

urther conversions to air-braking were made from 1967 onwards as a consequence of the ntroduction of Mark 2A stock. Only a limited number of Mark IIa designs were constructed, thus in rder to form air-braked train sets various Mark I catering vehicles and open firsts in particular were tted with air-brakes. In the majority of cases the vacuum brakes were removed, however a number f carriages retained the vacuum system thus becoming dual braked.

full list of Mark I passenger carrying coaching stock fitted with air-brakes can be found as an ppendix to this book.

wo major projects took place to significantly develop passenger carrying coaching stock during the ark 1 era. The first of these occurred during 1957 when British Railways commissioned private ontractors and Doncaster works to produce fourteen prototype first and second class carriages. The terior layout and decor of these vehicles was left entirely to the builders who had to keep within e limits of the standard BR Mark I body shell. Eight of these were opens, four firsts and four seconds, vo of which were converted from existing carriages and six were corridors, three firsts and three econds. Two of the open firsts, 3081 and 3083 are preserved along with one of the converted open econds 3785. Regrettably none of the corridor carriages have been preserved.

he second major project was carried out with more thoroughness than the first. This was the highly ublicised XP64 train which appeared in 1964 consisting of eight carriages to the new design, three pen Seconds, two Corridor Firsts and two Corridor Seconds, these were augmented by four efurbished carriages to traditional design, Unclassified Restaurant 1991, Open First 3150 and Brake orridor Seconds 35411 and 35424. The XP64 carriages were mounted on the still relatively new 4 bogies whilst the refurbished Mark I's retained Commonwealth bogies. Pressure heating and entilation with floor level inlets and openable windows was fitted though with only steam as primary ergy source. The most distinctive feature was the door arrangement. A central cross vestibule as retained, however the only other external door was fitted to each coach side and these were agonally opposed across the coach. The doors themselves were given a jack-knife operation with double section door folding back upon itself. This could only be achieved with flat surfaces so the oors were inset. The doors, not surprisingly, proved too complicated for the rough and tumble of ervice and in 1970-71, after the set was dispersed, the coaches were rebuilt with standard flush tting outward opening doors, during overhaul at Wolverton. Five of the XP64 carriages have been eserved representing all three variants. Also preserved is the Unclassified Restaurant now onverted to a camping coach whilst the Open First continues in service.

CATERING CARRIAGES

our distinct phases of catering car construction occurred reflecting the substantial changes in ocieties changed attitude to refreshments whilst travelling.

he first phase consisted of carriages intended to be operated as part of two and three coach catering ets reflecting the tradition dating back to Edwardian days of offering substantial multi-course lunches nd dinners and requiring large kitchens for their preparation and large seating areas for their onsumption. The intention was to have two car sets comprising Restaurant First with Kitchen and estaurant Second Open and three car sets comprising a Full Kitchen Car flanked by Restaurant First pen and Restaurant Second Open. A total of forty carriages were constructed, five Restaurant First ith Kitchen, ten Full Kitchen, eleven Restaurant First Open and fourteen Restaurant Second Open. notable feature of the Open Restaurants which featured loose chairs was the lack of centre estibule doors. Regrettably this phase of construction is poorly represented in preservation with only vo of the Restaurant Second Opens 1012 & 1013 surviving in near original condition, the only eserved Mark Is built without centre doors. All may not however be lost as a Restaurant First Open nd three Restaurant Second Open's remain in departmental stock and may one day be saved for reservation. A couple of the Restaurant Firsts with Kitchen also survive but have been rebuilt as riddle Cars.

perating experience showed that general purpose open stock with fixed seating rather than the loose eating of the open restaurant cars was perfectly viable for dining purposes and consequently no urther Restaurant First Opens were constructed. However two further batches of Restaurant Open d appear, the first being a batch of four Seconds built in 1960 for the Scottish Region which had xed seating and were identical in all but name to the Open Seconds being built at the time. One of these, 1015, survives in preservation, however it has been converted to a camping coach. Unilaterally the Eastern Region continued to prefer to have specially designated stock for dining, which at least aids the public and probably also its own staff. Thus in 1961 a batch of forty loose-chaired Unclassified Restaurant Cars entered service with them. Regrettably none of these has been preserved, but a number remain in departmental service. The Eastern Region peculiarity continued ithis policy into the 1970s when many of the RUOs were replaced by Open Firsts which were renumbered and designated RUO, thirteen ''conversions'' taking place. Further Kitchen Cars and Restaurant Firsts with Kitchen were built but these were not intended to be part of sets. One Kitchen Car from these later builds has been preserved but due to a quirk in the British Railways numbering, details are included in the non passenger carrying coaching stock section. Two of the later Restaurant Firsts have been preserved, one however, 334, having been substantially rebuilt as a Restaurant Buffet prior to preservation although it still retains first class seating.

The second distinct phase of catering carriage construction commenced with the construction in 1956 of three prototype carriages, Kitchen Buffet 1546, Restaurant Buffet 1700 and Unclassified Restaurant 1900. These prototypes were obviously considered, with some minor modifications, to be suitable, substantial numbers of each being subsequently constructed. None of the prototypes survive in preservation, but a considerable number of their descendants do so with examples from the majority of lots preserved, although in several cases these have been substantially modified. At the same time a vehicle with a miniature buffet facility was developed. This was basically a Tourist Open Second with two seating bays removed and replaced by a well equipped buffet. Experience with the first twelve vehicles showed that further storage space was necessary and a store cupboard replaced a further four seats on later built examples, the first twelve subsequently being modified to have this facility. Not surprisingly these carriages have been particularly popular with preservationists and examples from all lots have been preserved. Two preserved of particular note are 1872 and 1873 which were equipped with control cables by the southern region to permit multiple working with 4-TC units. Another innovative design of this time was the Griddle Car. Three of these were completed in 1960, the original now forming part of the national collection. Subsequently three of the original Restaurant First with Kitchen were converted to this specification and as already mentioned two of these have been preserved in this form.

The third phase occurred in 1968 when two completely new prototype designs appeared built on the frames of withdarwn Kitchen Cars, Booth Car 1106 and Bar Car 1883, both of which are now preserved in this form. The Booth Car was a new and, so far, unique catering design. It was never easy for staff to serve meals along the aisle of normal dining cars. This car separated the serving and general passenger movement routes. The kitchen unit was central in order to separate drinkers and eaters. For the limited seating capacity to be viable a rapid turnover was necessary and meals were designed so as to be ordered, served and eaten within about 30 minutes, service being through a cut out between the staff corridor and tables. The Bar Car was an attempt at the 'good pub' ideal and from experience with Griddle Cars it was considered, as with the Booth Car, desirable to separate the bar and buffet sections. It would appear that neither design was considered very successful as no further carriages were constructed based on Booth Car or Bar Car. Indeed these were the last ''new'' Mark I catering carriages to be constructed.

Finally a fourth phase commenced in 1970 which involved an extensive program of modifications and rebuilding. This included rebuilding of the majority of Restaurant Firsts and substantially modifying Unclassified Restaurants. Later in the program extensive refurbishing took place on the Restaurant Buffets. Full details of these changes are given in Keith Parkin's book and it will be seen that the majority of Unclassified Restaurants and Restaurant Buffets now preserved were so treated.

By virtue of being initially numbered in the catering car series the only one of the three Mark 1 Roya Train Carriages so far preserved is considered here. The Royal Kitchen and Dining Car was completed in 1956 having been ordered in Coronation year. The kitchen end of 499 is fitted out similar tc contemporary standard catering vehicles with a staff compartment and lavatory, Kitchen and Pantry. From a vestibule at the other end a sliding door gives entry to a dining area the full width of the vehicle. Eight places could be set along a central table. Service was from side tables in a smaller compartment adjoining the pantry. If more dining space was needed two serving tables could be removed, the partition taken down and the dining compartment correspondingly enlarged. It was displaced from the Royal Train in 1989 being replaced by Mark III vehicle 2918 which took over its function, being relegated to the reserve fleet which in reality meant storage at Wolverton. Following display at Wolverton Works on 25th September 1993 when the general public, probably for the first time, were allowed access, the carriage has been put on display at the Midland Railway Centre. Although having not been used for several years the two other Mark I Royal Train carriages remain stored at Wolverton awaiting a decision as to their fate. It is hoped that they two will soon be on public display.

SLEEPING CARS

Three designs of sleeping cars were constructed, Sleeping First, Sleeping Composite and Sleeping Second. All cars had eleven compartments with either one or two sleeping berths dependent upon classification and an attendants compartment. Examples of each design have been preserved.

In 1971 modifications were made to several cars in order that they could be used for either first or second class passengers (one or two berths) and classified Sleeping either Class. Three of these converted cars have been preserved.

Use of blue asbestos in their construction has already resulted in several preserved examples being scrapped and it is possible that this fate may befall some of the others. Fortunately a few have had the asbestos removed prior to main line use and thus have a much brighter future.

GANGWAYED OPEN STOCK

Four designs of Open stock were produced, Open First, Open Second, Tourist Open Second and Brake Open Second. A particular failure of the preservation movement is that none of the first lot of Open First or the first two lots of Tourist Open Second have been acquired. These were unique along with the previously mentioned Restaurant Firsts and Seconds in not having a centre vestibule door. It is understood that such doors became a requirement on later batches as a result of safety recommendations. Indeed it appears that the fitting of these doors became necessary at rather short notice as the second lot of Open Firsts had them inserted into the centre seating bay, although these doors were sealed out of use for most of their life, with the legend 'No Entry' being applied on the outside and tables being fitted. Three of these are however preserved as part of Richard Oakley's project to operate a main line set of early Mark 1s. Subsequent builds had slightly reduced seating bay widths in order to accommodate the vestibule centre doors.

A significant change to the later lots was the use of fluorescent lighting in the main saloons instead of tungsten lighting. The carriages involved being Open First 3104-3151, Tourist Open Second 4830-5069 and Brake Open Second 9363-9380.

Not surprisingly the Open Firsts have been particularly popular for operators of main line sets with all but two of the later build from lots 30697 and 30717 included here having seen such use so far. A most welcome recent development has been the restoring of several of the Open Firsts formerly used by the Southern Region on Boat Trains, all of which are preserved, in the privately sponsored 'Ocean Liner Express' main line set.

The considerable number of Tourist Open Seconds preserved is probably not too much of a surprise considering that they are probably the most suitable carriage for use on the private railways of Britain. The most notable preserved, although it should really be considered under non gangwayed carriages is 4378 of which only the underframe is original. The original carriage bodywork was destroyed in the devastating Lewisham accident of 1957. In 1962 Eastleigh fitted a new reinforced plastic body built to a non-gangwayed second diagram. It initially saw use as DS70200 on the Lancing Works train. After a spell on the Hayling Island Branch for which it was renumbered 1000 it was transferred to the Clapham Junction-Kensington Olympia service in 1964. It was withdrawn in 1967 and remained in store for a long while before being preserved at the East Somerset Railway where it is regularly used to convey passengers. It will also be noted that several have found use as static restaurants and it would not be surprising that others may have had a similar fate and are still to be discovered by the authors. To date only a few Tourist Open Seconds have appeared in mainline sets, but as the majority of recent sales have gone to those with such aspirations, this situation is expected to change in the not too distant future.

Several of the preserved Brake Open Seconds were converted to what was branded 'Micro-Buffet', this involving the removal of one seating bay and replacing this by a counter with a space for a trolley. The adjacent toilet was also removed and converted into a steward's washing area/store. Eighteen of these conversions took place of which eight have been preserved. Considering how suitable the Brake Open Seconds were for private railways it seems surprising that so few have in fact been preserved compared with their corridor equivalents. Fortunately examples of the four lots built are preserved.

GANGWAYED CORRIDOR STOCK

Six designs of corridor stock were produced, Corridor First, Corridor Second, Corridor Composite, Brake Corridor First, Brake Corridor Second and Brake Corridor Composite. Three-aside seating was provided in each compartment, but the second class compartments on carriages delivered to the Western and Southern Regions did not have an armrest between seats and were consequently considered to have four a side seating. The seconds had eight compartments whilst the firsts and Composites had seven. The Brake Seconds and Firsts had four compartments whilst the Brake Composites had five.

A noteable conversion that does survive in preservation is one of the three corridor firsts converted at Eastleigh in 1967 to a Corridor Lounge First. These three conversions were considered as prototypes to gauge public reaction to the possibility of having a supplement paying 'luxury class' after the style of the LMS 'Club trains'. All the alterations were to the 'lounge' section leaving the remainder of the carriage unaltered with three first class compartments. In the space gained by the removal of four compartments, two lounges were built. Three fixed seats at each end of the lounges flanked four central seats mounted on swivels allowing a 360 rotation. All seats had armrests concealing ashtrays and light switches and adjustable headrest pillows. The ceiling was lower and almost flat and incorporated fluorescent tubes to give general lighting to the lounges and corridor. Directional lighting was provided above each seat by an individually switched spotlight. Tubular steam heating ran the length of the lounge body sides and corridor portions were given slotted covers to deflect incoming air. The preserved example, 14901, had a particularly interesting working history being used as part of the XP64 set for a number of years on 'Cheltenham Spa Express' workings.

During 1986-87 twenty-six Corridor Brake Seconds were converted to Courier Vehicles. These were intended for high security mail and parcels traffic which was accompanied en route. The toilet and adjacent compartment were retained for use of the travelling staff. The windows of the second compartment were plated over with a small ventilation grille near the top. The erstwhile third compartment side panels were completely removed and roller shutter doors, the full height of the sides, fitted. The fourth compartment window was plated over and the passenger door sealed. The majority of these have recently been withdrawn with several having been purchased by preservationists. It is expected that the majority of these will be utilised as main line support coaches for preserved locomotives operating on the Railtrack network. Following on from this it should be mentioned that the use of the Corridor Brakes as support coaches has been particularly popular with examples of all three designs being currently so used.

NON GANGWAYED STOCK

Standard designs of suburban stock appeared in 1954 and coincidentally coincided with the commencement of the mass production of diesel multiple units. A surprising variety of types was built involving compartment and open stock, with and without lavatories and on 57' and 63'6'' underframes. Most were designed around a compartment length of about 6'3'' with the toilet, if fitted, taking up the length of one bay. In the two composite designs an extra couple of inches extra was given to first class passengers and correspondingly taken from the seconds which were left with a rather tight 6'1'', the narrowest on locomotive-hauled BR stock.

None of the lavatory-less composites or Open Seconds have survived in preservation, but examples of other designs are represented. Regrettably preservation has not been kind to these vehicles, the large number of doors to be maintained requiring much effort, many that were initially preserved being broken up at the hands of preservationists. Some have however been restored and see regular use giving the general public and enthusiast alike an insight of what it was once like travelling on suburban trains.

RESTAURANT FIRST RF

Lot No.: 30013. **Builder:** Doncaster.   **Ordered:** 12/1950   **Completed:** 11/1952.
Diagram: 16.   **Seats:** 17F.   **Bogies:** BR Mk1 h.d.

Rebuilt as RG in 1965, diagram 31, Seats 30U, Bogies B5. 301 preserved with BR1 bogies.

301	1104	Battlefield Steam Railway	'JESSIE'
302	1105 DB975878	Watercress Line	

1105 converted to CCE Staff Coach in 1979.

Lot No.: 30633. **Builder:** Ashford/Swindon.   **Ordered:** 10/1959   **Completed:** 01/1962.
Diagram: 17.   **New diagram:** AL101.   **Seats:** 24F.   **Bogies:** Commonwealth.

334 rebuilt as RB in 1970, diagram 26, new diagram AJ404, seats 12U.

324		North Yorkshire Moors Railway	'CAR 324'
334	1779	Midland Railway Centre	

ROYAL DINING SALOON ROYAL

Lot No.: 30129. **Builder:** Wolverton.   **Ordered:** 11/1953   **Completed:** 10/1956.
Diagram: 201.   **New diagram:** AT502.   **Seats:** 8   **Bogies:** BR1.

Rebogied with B5s. Air braked.

99	2902	Midland Railway Centre

RESTAURANT CAR SECOND RSO

Lot No.: 30014. **Builder:** York.   **Ordered:** 12/1950   **Completed:** 09/1951.
Diagram: 56.   **Seats:** 48S.   **Bogies:** BR1.

Original design with no centre doors.

1012	DW150353	Great Central Railway	
1013	DB975323	Keighley & Worth Valley Railway	K&WVR No. 35

1012 converted to Cinema Coach in 1963 & 1013 to a Catering Training Coach in 1973. 1013 has been restored as a TSO containing 62S, but is still labelled 'Restaurant Car'.

Lot No.: 30526. **Builder:** Wolverton.   **Ordered:** 08/1958   **Completed:** 07/1960.
Diagram: 60.   **Seats:** 48S.   **Bogies:** BR1.

Built with fixed seating. Rebogied with B4s, preserved with BR1s.

1015	Dawlish Warren Camp Site	Camping Coach 'SWINDON'

GRIDDLE CAR RG

Lot No.: 30637. **Builder:** Ashford/Eastleigh.   **Ordered:** 10/1959   **Completed:** 09/1960.
Diagram: 30.   **New diagram:** AG401.   **Seats:** 26U.   **Bogies:** Commonwealth.

100	National Railway Museum	Stored at MoD Kineton

BOOTH CAR BOOTH

Lot No.: 30783. **Builder:** Derby.   **Ordered:** 02/1967   **Completed:** 04/1968.
Diagram: 32.   **New diagram:** AG404.   **Seats:** 20U.   **Bogies:** B5.

Built on frames of RK 80020, lot 30524, built Charles Roberts, ordered 07/1958, completed 04/1962.

106	Gwili Railway

KITCHEN BUFFET RKB

Lot No.: 30514. **Builder:** Cravens.   **Ordered:** 07/1958   **Completed:** 01/1961.
Diagram: 25.   **New diagram:** AH502.   **Bogies:** BR Mark 1 h.d.

Rebogied with B5s, 1526 restored with BR1s. 1525 Air-braked but restored with vacuum-brakes.

1525	Great Central Railway
1526	Great Central Railway

Lot No.: 30624. **Builder:** Cravens.   **Ordered:** 07/1959   **Completed:** 06/1961.
Diagram: 25.   **New diagram:** AH502.   **Bogies:** BR Mark 1 h.d.

Rebogied with B5s. Air braked.

1566	Bluebell Railway	
1569	Swindon & Cricklade Railway	'WESTERN GOURMET

RESTAURANT BUFFET   R⁵

Lot No.: 30628. **Builder:** Pressed Steel.   **Ordered:** 08/1959   **Completed:** 12/1961.
Diagram: 24.   **New diagram:** AJ402.   **Seats:** 23U.   **Bogies:** Commonwealth.

1646/51/54/57/65/94/95/96 rebuilt as RBR, new diagram AJ403, with polypropylene chairs.
Air-braked (1665 Dual-braked). 1694/95 restored with vacuum brakes.

1646	The Railway Age, Crewe	Stored at Basford Hall Yar
1651	Llangollen Railway	
1654	Scottish Industrial Railway Centre	
1657	Llangollen Railway	'ELEN
1665	Llangollen Railway	'GWAEDDAN
1668	Watercress Line	
1682	Severn Valley Railway	
1694	Paignton & Dartmouth Railway	'HELENA
1695	Great Central Railway	
1696	Venice-Simplon Orient Express	Ocean Liner Express Se

1696 is on loan from the Special Trains Unit.

Lot No.: 30512. **Builder:** BRCW.   **Ordered:** 06/1958   **Completed:** 01/1961.
Diagram: 24.   **New diagram:** AJ402.   **Seats:** 23U.   **Bogies:** BR Mark 1 h.d.

Rebogied with B5s. 1703 preserved with BR1 bogies. 1703 Air-braked. 1730 Dual-braked.

1703	East Lancashire Railway	
1730	Bo'ness & Kinneil Railway	SCR99818. SRPS Se

OPEN SECOND with MINIATURE BUFFET   RME

Lot No.: 30485. **Builder:** York.   **Ordered:** 06/1957   **Completed:** 03/1958.
Diagram: 97.   **New diagram:** AN201.   **Seats:** 48S.   **Bogies:** BR1.

Originally built without store cupboard but added 1972-77 and seating reduced to 44S
1803/05/06/07 rebogied with B4s, 1803/07 restored with BR1s. 1805/06/07 Air-braked, 1806/0
restored with vacuum brakes. 1806/07 saw use on Southern Region Boat Trains

1802	Midland Railway Centre	
1803	Dean Forest Railway	'HAZEL
1804	West Somerset Railway	'ARIES
1805	Swindon & Cricklade Railway	
1806	Watercress Line	
1807	Watercress Line	
1808	Gloucestershire-Warwickshire Railway	
1809	Colne Valley Railway	
1811	Gloucestershire-Warwickshire Railway	
1812	Lakeside Railway	

Lot No.: 30520. **Builder:** Wolverton.   **Ordered:** 07/1958   **Completed:** 12/1960.
Diagram: 99.   **New diagram:** AN203.   **Seats:** 44S.   **Bogies:** Commonwealth.
1824 preserved with Gresley bogies and 1836 preserved with BR1 bogies. 1813/15/16/33 Dua
braked.

1813		The Railway Age, Crewe	Stored at Basford Hall Ya
1815		Bere Ferrers Station Museum, Devon	
1816		East Lancashire Railway	
1818		Bluebell Railway	
1823		North Yorkshire Moors Railway	
1824		Keighley & Worth Valley Railway	K&WVR No. 2
1826		Embsay Steam Railway	YDR No.
1829	DB977098	Llangollen Railway	
1833		East Lancashire Railway	

835	DB977186	Peak Railway, Darley Dale
836		Keighley & Worth Valley Railway	K&WVR No. 27
837		East Lancashire Railway

829/35 converted to CCE Staff Coaches in 1982/83.

.ot No.: 30507. **Builder:** Wolverton. **Ordered:** 05/1958 **Completed:** 06/1960.
)iagram: 98. **New diagram:** AN202. **Seats:** 44S. **Bogies:** BR1.

838/45/48 rebogied with Commonwealths. 1851/52 rebogied with B5s, 1852 restored with BR1s.
838/45/48 Dual-braked.

838	Bluebell Railway
839	Steamport Railway Museum
840	Watercress Line
845	Chinnor & Princess Risborough Railway
848	East Lancashire Railway
851	Watercress Line
852	Great Central Railway

.ot No.: 30670. **Builder:** Wolverton. **Ordered:** 03/1960 **Completed:** 01/1962.
)iagram: 99. **New diagram:** AN203. **Seats:** 44S. **Bogies:** Commonwealth.

854/57/59/60/61/63/64 Dual-braked

854	Pontypool & Blaenavon Railway	
855	Severn Valley Railway	
856	Severn Valley Railway	
857	Embsay Steam Railway	
859	Bo'ness & Kinneil Railway	SCR99822. SRPS Set
860	Steamtown Railway Centre, Carnforth	
861	Flying Scotsman Railways, Bounds Green	FSS99132 BN91 Set
862	Midland Railway Centre	'THE WYVERN BAR'
863	Steamtown Railway Centre, Carnforth	RPR99245
864	Llangollen Railway	

859 was to be converted to a Class 90 Driver Training Coach DB977617 but the conversion was
cancelled. 1863 is expected to move to the Severn Valley Railway in the near future.

.ot No.: 30702. **Builder:** Wolverton. **Ordered:** 06/1961 **Completed:** 05/1962.
)iagram: 99. **New diagram:** AN203. **Seats:** 44S. **Bogies:** Commonwealth.

869/70/72/73/74/75/76/78/79/80/82 Air-braked, 1874 restored with Vacuum-brakes. 1872/73
vere adapted for use with Southern Region EMU stock, also seeing use on Southern Region Boat
Trains.

865	Swanage Railway	
866	Bo'ness & Kinneil Railway	'CAR No 1866'
869	Llangollen Railway	
870	Nomix-Chipman, Horsham	CC99019 Spray Coach
872	Nene Valley Railway	
873	Bodmin Steam Railway	
874	Bodmin Steam Railway	
875	East Lancashire Railway	'LADY MARGARET'
876	Gloucestershire-Warwickshire Railway	
878	Llangollen Railway	
879	Steamport Railway Museum	
880	East Lancashire Railway	
882	Steamtown Railway Centre, Carnforth	WDS99311. Carnforth Maroon Set

BAR CAR   BAR

.ot No.: 30784. **Builder:** Derby. **Ordered:** 02/1967 **Completed:** 04/1968.
)iagram: 100. **New diagram:** AN206. **Seats:** 36U. **Bogies:** B5.

Built on frames of RK 80021, lot 30524, built Charles Roberts, ordered 07/1958, completed 04/1962.
Air braked.

883	Severn Valley Railway	'LESLIE'

UNCLASSIFIED RESTAURANT RU

Lot No.: 30401. **Builder:** Ashford/Swindon. **Ordered:** 05/1956 **Completed:** 11/1957.
Diagram: 23. **New diagram:** AL401. **Seats:** 33U. **Bogies:** BR Mk1 h.d.
1909 rebuilt as RU(B), diagram 29, new diagram AJ407, seats 29U.

1908	Swanage Railway	
1909	West Somerset Railway	'ORION

Lot No.: 30476. **Builder:** Ashford/Swindon. **Ordered:** 05/1957 **Completed:** 12/1958.
Diagram: 23. **New diagram:** AL401. **Seats:** 33U. **Bogies:** BR Mk1 h.d.
Rebuilt as RU(B), diagram 29, new diagram AJ407, Commonwealth bogies, seats 29U.

Restored with BR1 bogies. Dual-braked.

1917	Dean Forest Railway

Lot No.: 30513. **Builder:** BRCW. **Ordered:** 06/1958 **Completed:** 01/1960.
Diagram: 23. **New diagram:** AL401. **Seats:** 33U. **Bogies:** BR Mk1 h.d.
1933 rebogied with B4/B5, remainder with Gresley's, 1927/30/31/34 subsequently rebogied with
Commonwealths. 1928 rebuilt as RB(S), diagram 27, new diagram AJ405, seats 23U.
1927/30/33/34 rebuilt as RU(B), diagram 29, new diagram AJ407, seats 29U.

1926	Steamtown Railway Centre, Carnforth	Body only remains
1927	Dawlish Warren Camp Site	Camping Coach 'LONDON
1928	Strathspey Railway	SR No. 10S
1929	Steamtown Railway Centre, Carnforth	Body only remains
1930	Dawlish Warren Camp Site	Camping Coach 'EXETER
1931	Dawlish Warren Camp Site	Camping Coach 'GLOUCESTER
1933	Avon Valley Railway	
1934	Dawlish Warren Camp Site	Camping Coach 'SWANSEA
1936	Strathspey Railway	SR No. 110 'CRAIGONERIE
1937	Swanage Railway	Stored at Horsham

1927/31/34 preserved with EMU Mk.4 bogies and 1930 with BR1/BR II bogies.

Lot No.: 30575. **Builder:** Ashford/Swindon. **Ordered:** 01/1959 **Completed:** 09/1960.
Diagram: 23. **New diagram:** AL401. **Seats:** 33U. **Bogies:** BR Mk1 h.d.
1946/47/53/54 rebogied with B4/B5 and rebuilt as RB(S), diagram 27, new diagram AJ405, seats
23U, subsequently rebuilt as RBR, new diagram AJ414. 1951 rebuilt as RU(B), diagram 29, new
diagram AJ407, Commonwealth bogies, seats 29U, preserved with EMU Mk.4 bogies. 1946/54
Air-braked. 1947/53 Dual-braked.

1946	Gloucestershire-Warwickshire Railway	
1947	Swanage Railway	Stored at Horsham
1949	Steamtown Railway Centre, Carnforth	
1951	Dawlish Warren Camp Site	Camping Coach 'NEWPORT
1953	Venice-Simplon Orient Express	
1954		Stored at Norwich
1955	Kent & East Sussex Railway	K&ESR No. 69 'DIANA

1954 is currently for sale. 1963 converted to RK by Keighley and Worth Valley Railway.

Lot No.: 30632. **Builder:** Ashford/Swindon. **Ordered:** 10/1959 **Completed:** 06/1961.
Diagram: 23. **New diagram:** AL401. **Seats:** 33U. **Bogies:** Commonwealth.
1963/87/91 rebuilt as diagram 23A, new diagram AL402, seats 29U, 1991 subsequently rebuilt
as RU(B), diagram 29, new diagram AJ407. 1961/62/65/69/70/73/81 rebuilt as RB(S), diagram
27, new diagram AJ405, seats 23U, then as RBR, new diagram AJ414
1961/62/63/65/69/70/73/81/87 air braked.

1961		Watercress Line	
1962		Great Central Railway	
1963	DB975948	Keighley & Worth Valley Railway	K&WVR No. 28
1965		Long Marston Military Railway	8805
1969		Embsay Steam Railway	
1970		Peak Railway, Darley Dale	
1973		Watercress Line	

1981		Battlefield Steam Railway	
1987	DB975982	Bluebell Railway	
1991		Dawlish Warren Camp Site	Camping Coach 'BRISTOL'

1991 was used as part of the XP64 train and has been preserved with EMU Mk.4 bogies. 1963 converted to Test Car 11 & 1987 to HST Barrier Coach in 1980.

FIRST CLASS SLEEPING CAR SLF

Lot No.: 30159. **Builder:** Wolverton.   **Ordered:** 04/1954   **Completed:** 12/1958.
Diagram: 1.   **New diagram:** AS101.   **Bogies:** BR1.
Rebogied with B5s. 11 Berths plus attendant's compartment. Transferred to Royal Train Stock in 19xx. Air braked.

2013	2908	Southall Railway Centre	

Lot No.: 30490. **Builder:** Metro-Cammell.   **Ordered:** 07/1957   **Completed:** 10/1959.
Diagram: 1.   **New diagram:** AS101.   **Bogies:** BR1.
Rebogied with B5s, restored with BR1s. 11 Berths plus attendant's compartment.

2080	Peak Railway, Darley Dale	

Lot No.: 30590. **Builder:** Metro-Cammell.   **Ordered:** 03/1959   **Completed:** 08/1960.
Diagram: 1.   **New diagram:** AS101.   **Bogies:** Commonwealth.
11 Berths plus attendant's compartment.

2108	Bluebell Railway	On loan from Queen of Scots
2110	Bluebell Railway	On loan from Queen of Scots

Lot No.: 30687. **Builder:** Wolverton.   **Ordered:** 06/1960   **Completed:** 07/1961.
Diagram: 1.   **New diagram:** AS101.   **Bogies:** Commonwealth.
11 Berths plus attendant's compartment. Restored with Air-brakes.

2127	Great Scottish & Western Railway	GSWR99887. Royal Scotsman Train

Lot No.: 30722. **Builder:** Wolverton.   **Ordered:** 08/1961   **Completed:** 06/1962.
Diagram: 1.   **New diagram:** AS101.   **Bogies:** Commonwealth.
11 Berths plus attendant's compartment. 2132 restored with BR1 bogies.

2131	Steamtown Railway Centre, Carnforth	
2132	Llangollen Railway	Numbered 2130

COMPOSITE SLEEPING CAR SLC

Lot No.: 30688. **Builder:** Wolverton.   **Ordered:** 06/1960   **Completed:** 08/1961.
Diagram: 5.   **New diagram:** AS301.   **Bogies:** Commonwealth.
17 Berths (5F 12S) plus attendant's compartment. Dual-braked.

2442	Bluebell Railway	On loan from Queen of Scots

SECOND CLASS SLEEPING CAR SLSTP

Lot No.: 30036. **Builder:** Doncaster.   **Ordered:** 03/1951   **Completed:** 11/1957.
Diagram: 10.   **New diagram:** AS201.   **Bogies:** BR1.
Rebogied with B5s, preserved with BR1s. 22 berths plus attendant's compartment. Transferred to Royal Train stock in 1982. Dual-braked.

2500	2909	Steamtown Railway Centre, Carnforth	

Lot No.: 30245. **Builder:** York/Doncaster.   **Ordered:** 05/1955   **Completed:** 11/1957.
Diagram: 10.   **New diagram:** AS201.   **Bogies:** BR1.
Rebogied with B5s. 22 Berths plus attendant's compartment. Converted to SLE in 1971.

2536	2815	Welshpool & Llanfair Railway	Body only remains

Lot No.: 30379. **Builder:** York/Doncaster.   **Ordered:** 03/1956   **Completed:** 08/1958.
Diagram: 10.   **New diagram:** AS201.   **Bogies:** BR1.

Rebogied with B5s. 22 Berths plus attendant's compartment.

2564	Swanage Railway
2573	Embsay Steam Railway

Lot No.: 30491. **Builder:** Metro-Cammell.   **Ordered:** 07/1957   **Completed:** 10/1959.
Diagram: 10.   **New diagram:** AS201.   **Bogies:** BR1.

Rebogied with B5s, restored with BR1s. 22 Berths plus attendant's compartment.

2574	Llangollen Railway

Lot No.: 30529. **Builder:** Wolverton.   **Ordered:** 08/1958   **Completed:** 01/1960.
Diagram: 10.   **New diagram:** AS201.   **Bogies:** Commonwealth.

22 Berths plus attendant's compartment

2586	East Lancashire Railway
2592	National Rifle Club, Bisley Camp
2599	Avon Valley Railway

Lot No.: 30586. **Builder:** Wolverton.   **Ordered:** 02/1959   **Completed:** 01/1961.
Diagram: 10.   **New diagram:** AS201.   **Bogies:** Commonwealth.

22 Berths plus attendant's compartment. Converted to SLE in 1971.

2612	2821	Bo'ness & Kinneil Railway
2613	2822	Bo'ness & Kinneil Railway

OPEN FIRST   FO

Lot No.: 30008. **Builder:** BRCW.   **Ordered:** 12/1950   **Completed:** 05/1954.
Diagram: 72.   **Seats:** 42F.   **Bogies:** BR1.

Rebogied with B4s, 3016 restored with BR1s. Unique to this lot is a door inserted into the centre seating bay. Air-braked.

3013	DB975653	R. Oakley, Brentford Rubbish Terminal	
3014	DB975658	R. Oakley, Brentford Rubbish Terminal	Stored at Booth-Roe Metals
3016	DB975650 6331	Steamtown Railway Centre, Carnforth	

Converted to HST Barrier Coaches in 1977-78, DB975650 subsequently returned to capital stock in 1990 as 6331.

Lot No.: 30091. **Builder:** Doncaster.   **Ordered:** 04/1953   **Completed:** 06/1954.
Diagram: 73.   **New diagram:** AD103.   **Seats:** 42F.   **Bogies:** BR1.

3045/51 rebogied with B4s. 3051 Air-braked.

3042		Great Central Railway
3045		Birmingham Railway Museum
3051	DB977492	Venice-Simplon Orient Express

3051 converted to Anglia Class 90 Driver Training Train Coach in 1987.

Lot No.: 30169. **Builder:** Doncaster.   **Ordered:** 05/1954   **Completed:** 08/1955.
Diagram: 73.   **New diagram:** AD103.   **Seats:** 42F.   **Bogies:** BR1.

3063 – 67/69/70 rebogied with B4s & 3068 with Commonwealths, 3065/67/70 restored with BR1s, 3068 restored with B4s. 3063 – 3070 Air-braked. 3064 – 70 were principally used on Southampton Boat Trains.

3058	DB975313	West Somerset Railway		'TAUNTON CIDER'
3060	DB975314	Gwili Railway		
3063		Venice-Simplon Orient Express		
3064	DB975607	Venice-Simplon Orient Express		
3065		Watercress Line		'ORCHID'
3066		Venice-Simplon Orient Express	VSOE99566. Ocean Liner Express Set	
3067		Watercress Line		
3068	DB975606	Venice-Simplon Orient Express	VSOE99568. Ocean Liner Express Set	
3069		Venice-Simplon Orient Express	VSOE99540. Ocean Liner Express Set	
3070		Watercress Line		'FERN'

3058/60 converted to Mobile Classroom Coaches in 1973 & 3064/68 to CM&EE Test Car 7 & Laboratory Coach 2 'Electra' in 1976. 3058 converted to buffet car by the West Somerset Rly.

Lot No.: 30242. **Builder:** York/Doncaster.   **Ordered:** 05/1955   **Completed:** 09/1956.
Diagram: 73.   **New diagram:** AD103.   **Seats:** 42F.   **Bogies:** BR1.

Rebogied with Commonwealths.

3079   DB975315   Great Central Railway

Converted to a Mobile Classroom Coach in 1973.

Lot No.: 30359. **Builder:** BRCW.   **Ordered:** 08/1956   **Completed:** 07/1957.
Diagram: 77.   **Seats:** 33F.   **Bogies:** BR1.

1957 prototype.

3081   South Devon Railway

Lot No.: 30372. **Builder:** Doncaster.   **Ordered:** 05/1957   **Completed:** 07/1957.
Diagram: 74.   **Seats:** 36F.   **Bogies:** BR1.

1957 prototype with rotatable seating.

3083   Severn Valley Railway

Lot No.: 30472. **Builder:** BRCW.   **Ordered:** 05/1957   **Completed:** 08/1959.
Diagram: 73.   **New diagram:** AD103.   **Seats:** 42F.   **Bogies:** BR1.

Rebogied with B4s. Air-braked.

3089	DB977351	Avon Valley Railway	Stored at Long Marston
3090		Swanage Railway	
3091	DB977352	Gloucestershire-Warwickshire Railway	
3092		Great Central Railway	
3094	042136	The Railway Age, Crewe	Stored at Basford Hall Yard

3089/91 converted to MTA Brake Force Runners in 1986.

Lot No.: 30576. **Builder:** BRCW.   **Ordered:** 01/1959   **Completed:** 10/1959.
Diagram: 73.   **New diagram:** AD103.   **Seats:** 42F.   **Bogies:** BR1.

Rebogied with B4s. 3096 restored with Dual-brakes.

3095		Great Central Railway	
3096		Bo'ness & Kinneil Railway	SCR99827. SRPS Set

Lot No.: 30648. **Builder:** Wolverton.   **Ordered:** 10/1959   **Completed:** 06/1961.
Diagram: 73.   **New diagram:** AD103.   **Seats:** 42F.   **Bogies:** Commonwealth.

3103   Severn Valley Railway

Lot No.: 30697. **Builder:** Swindon.   **Ordered:** 03/1961   **Completed:** 02/1963.
Diagram: 73.   **New diagram:** AD103.   **Seats:** 42F.   **Bogies:** Commonwealth.

Built with fluorescent lighting. 3128 converted to RUO in 1976, new diagram AM201 and to SO in 1981, new diagram AD204. 3122/28 Air-braked. 3105/06/09/10/12/13/17 restored with Dual-brakes.

3105		Steamtown Railway Centre, Carnforth	WDS99121. Carnforth Maroon Set
3106		Flying Scotsman Railways, Bounds Green	FSS99122. '122' BN91 Set
3108		West Somerset Railway	
3109		Flying Scotsman Railways, Bounds Green	FSS99123. '123' BN91 Set
3110		Flying Scotsman Railways, Bounds Green	FSS99124. '124' BN91 Set
3112		Flying Scotsman Railways, Bounds Green	FSS99357. '357' BN91 Set
3113		Steamtown Railway Centre, Carnforth	WDS99125. Carnforth Maroon Set
3116		Bluebell Railway	'DIANE'
3117		Steamtown Railway Centre, Carnforth	WDS99127. Carnforth Maroon Set
3122	042137	The Railway Age, Crewe	Stored at Basford Hall Yard
3125		Lavender Line, Isfield	'MANDY'
3126		Great Central Railway	
3128	1058 3600	Steamtown Railway Centre, Carnforth	GRAM99371.Carnforth Maroon Set

Lot No.: 30717. **Builder:** Swindon.   **Ordered:** 08/1961   **Completed:** 12/1963.
Diagram: 73.   **New diagram:** AD103.   **Seats:** 42F.   **Bogies:** Commonwealth.

Built with fluorescent lighting.

3130   Steamtown Railway Centre, Carnforth

OPEN SECOND SO

Lot No.: 30031. **Builder:** Derby. **Ordered:** 03/1951 **Completed:** 09/1954.
Diagram: 94. **New diagram:** AD201. **Seats:** 48S. **Bogies:** BR1.

3727 Gloucestershire-Warwickshire Railway

TOURIST OPEN SECOND TSO

Lot No.: 30043. **Builder:** Doncaster. **Ordered:** 04/1951 **Completed:** 12/1953.
Diagram: 93. **New diagram:** AC204. **Seats:** 64S. **Bogies:** BR1.

3749 rebogied with Commonwealths by Southern Region. 3738/45/46/48/49 Air-braked by Southern Region. 3738/45 restored with vacuum brakes.

3736	Birmingham Railway Museum	
3738	Watercress Line	
3743	Marsden Rattler Restaurant,South Shields	Used as Restaurant
3745	Avon Valley Railway	
3746	Avon Valley Railway	Stored at Long Marston
3748	Watercress Line	
3749	Avon Valley Railway	Stored at Long Marston
3753	Kent & East Sussex Railway	K&ESR No. 64

3749 was to be converted to Class 90 Driver Training Coach DB977623 but conversion was cancelled.

Lot No.: 30079. **Builder:** York. **Ordered:** 02/1953 **Completed:** 12/1953.
Diagram: 93. **New diagram:** AC204. **Seats:** 64S. **Bogies:** BR1.

3759 Air-braked by Southern Region. 3766 restored with Commonwealth bogies and Dual Brakes.

3759	Foster Yeoman, Isle of Grain	Used as Offices
3764	Swanage Railway	Numbered 1885
3766	Steamtown Railway Centre, Carnforth WDS99317. Carnforth Maroon Set	
3767	Glenfinnan Station Museum	
3769	Southall Railway Centre	
3771	East Lancashire Railway	

3764 has been converted to an RMB by the Swanage Railway.

Lot No.: 30043. **Builder:** Doncaster. **Ordered:** 04/1951 **Completed:** 12/1953.
Diagram: 93. **New diagram:** AC204. **Seats:** 64S. **Bogies:** BR1.
3785 is a 1957 prototype conversion.

3779	East Anglian Railway Museum	
3785	Battlefield Steam Railway	Body only remains

Lot No.: 30079. **Builder:** York. **Ordered:** 02/1953 **Completed:** 12/1953.
Diagram: 93. **New diagram:** AC204. **Seats:** 64S. **Bogies:** BR1.

3798	North Yorkshire Moors Railway	
3801	North Yorkshire Moors Railway	
3805	North Yorkshire Moors Railway	
3809	Midland Railway Centre	
3815	Avon Valley Railway	AD 3305

Lot No.: 30054. **Builder:** Ashford/Eastleigh. **Ordered:** 10/1951 **Completed:** 06/1954.
Diagram: 93. **New diagram:** AC204. **Seats:** 64S. **Bogies:** BR1.

3825 Peak Railway, Darley Dale

Lot No.: 30080. **Builder:** York. **Ordered:** 02/1953 **Completed:** 01/1954.
Diagram: 93. **New diagram:** AC204. **Seats:** 64S. **Bogies:** BR1.

3860	North Yorkshire Moors Railway	
3866	Alf Hall, Delph Station	Used as Offices
3868	North Norfolk Railway	
3872	North Yorkshire Moors Railway	
3881	Lakeside Railway	

Lot No.: 30086. **Builder:** Ashford/Eastleigh. **Ordered:** 04/1953 **Completed:** 01/1955.
Diagram: 93. **New diagram:** AC204. **Seats:** 64S. **Bogies:** BR1.

3918/19/24 rebogied with Commonwealths by Southern Region. 3918/19/24/25 Air-braked by Southern Region.

3906	Watercress Line
3918	Rushden Station Museum
3919	Northampton & Lamport Railway
3924	Coventry Railway Centre
3925	Conwy Valley Railway Museum
3948	North Yorkshire Moors Railway
3950	Llangollen Railway
3958	Elsecar at Barnsley, Elsecar
3960	Gloucestershire-Warwickshire Railway
3961	Southall Railway Centre
3962	Lakeside Railway

3919/24 were to be converted to Class 90 Driver Training Train Coaches DB977624/26 but conversion was cancelled.

Lot No.: 30090.	**Builder:** York.	**Ordered:** 04/1953	**Completed:** 03/1954.
Diagram: 93.	**New diagram:** AC204.	**Seats:** 64S.	**Bogies:** BR1.

3991 rebogied with Commonwealths by Southern Region. 3991 Air-braked by Southern Region.

3984	Audley End Miniature Railway	
3991	Avon Valley Railway	Stored at Long Marston

3991 was to be converted to Class 90 Driver Training Train Coach DB977627 but conversion was cancelled.

Lot No.: 30149.	**Builder:** Ashford/Swindon.	**Ordered:** 03/1954	**Completed:** 03/1957.
Diagram: 93.	**New diagram:** AC204.	**Seats:** 64S.	**Bogies:** BR1.

4058/66 rebogied with Commonwealths by Southern Region. 4035/55/58/66/74 Air-braked by Southern Region. 4035 was used on the 'Night Ferry' train.

4035	Avon Valley Railway	Stored at Long Marston
4037	Kent & East Sussex Railway	K&ESR No. 65
4039	West Somerset Railway	
4046	Pontypool & Blaenavon Railway	
4055	Swanage Railway	
4058	Avon Valley Railway	Stored at Long Marston
4066	Nomix-Chipman, Horsham	CC99017 Staff & Dormitory Coach
4074	Swanage Railway	
4079	Strathspey Railway	SR No. 111
4081	Paignton & Dartmouth Railway	

4058/66 were to be converted to Class 90 Driver Training Train Coaches DB977629/30 but conversion was cancelled.

Lot No.: 30171.	**Builder:** York.	**Ordered:** 05/1954	**Completed:** 01/1956.
Diagram: 93.	**New diagram:** AC204.	**Seats:** 64S.	**Bogies:** BR1.

4127	Strathspey Railway	SR No. 103 Believed Scrapped

Lot No.: 30172.	**Builder:** York.	**Ordered:** 05/1954	**Completed:** 04/1956.
Diagram: 93.	**New diagram:** AC204.	**Seats:** 64S.	**Bogies:** BR1.

4198		North Yorkshire Moors Railway	
4199		East Lancashire Railway	
4200		Nene Valley Railway	
4205		Paignton & Dartmouth Railway	
4207		North Yorkshire Moors Railway	
4215		Bo'ness & Kinneil Railway	
4218		Dean Forest Railway	
4223		Kingdom of Fife RPS	Stored at Methil Power Station
4224		Bo'ness & Kinneil Railway	
4232	DB977238	East Lancashire Railway	
4233		Paignton & Dartmouth Railway	
4236		Llangollen Railway	
4243		Llangollen Railway	
4249		Caledonian Railway	

| 4252 | North Yorkshire Moors Railway |
| 4255 | Lakeside Railway |

4232 converted to a Special Instruction Coach in 1984.

Lot No.: 30207. **Builder:** BRCW. **Ordered:** 01/1955 **Completed:** 10/1956.
Diagram: 93. **New diagram:** AC204. **Seats:** 64S. **Bogies:** BR1.

4260	West Somerset Railway	
4275	Woolacombe Station, Devon	Body only remain
4286	National Railway Museum	Currently for sal
4288	Woolacombe Station, Devon	Body only remain
4289	Woolacombe Station, Devon	Body only remain
4290	North Yorkshire Moors Railway	
4300	Dean Forest Railway	
4304	The Buffers Restaurant, Scholes	Number to be confirme
4306	Keighley & Worth Valley Railway	K&WVR No. 3
4316	Dean Forest Railway	
4317	Woolacombe Station, Devon	Body only remain
4325	Play Train, Huddersfield Station	'PENDRAGON PULLMAN
4328	Pullman Lodge Hotel & Restaurant, Seaburn	Public Bar 'CHRISTINA
4331	Gloucestershire-Warwickshire Railway	
4345	Severn Valley Railway	
4346	West Somerset Railway	
4349	Swanage Railway	
4350	East Lancashire Railway	
4354	Cheddleton Railway Centre	
4355 DB977412	North Norfolk Railway	Loaned from Avon Valley Railwa

4355 converted to a Special Instruction Coach in 1986.

OPEN SECOND SC

Lot No.: 30067. **Builder:** Eastleigh. **Ordered:** 05/1952 **Completed:** 02/1955.
Diagram: 94. **New diagram:** AD201. **Seats:** 48S. **Bogies:** BR1.

| 4362 | Great Central Railway |

Lot No.: 30121. **Builder:** Eastleigh. **Ordered:** 04/1953 **Completed:** 11/1955.
Diagram: 94. **New diagram:** AD201. **Seats:** 48S. **Bogies:** BR1.

4366	Midland Railway Centre
4371	East Lancashire Railway
4372	Peak Railway, Darley Dale

TOURIST OPEN SECOND TSC

Lot No.: 30219. **Builder:** Ashford/Swindon. **Ordered:** 03/1955 **Completed:** 09/1957.
Diagram: 93. **New diagram:** AC204. **Seats:** 64S. **Bogies:** BR1.

4392/93 rebogied with Commonwealths by Southern Region. 4378 body destroyed in 195
Lewisham accident, replacement nine compartment Second glass-reinforced plastic body fitted
1962. It saw use on the Lancing works train, Hayling Island branch & 'Kenny Belle'.

4378 DS70200 1000	East Somerset Railway	
4392	Cheddleton Railway Centre	
4393	Nomix-Chipman, Horsham	CC99018 Generator & Chemicals Sto
4399	Severn Valley Railway	
4406	Embsay Steam Railway	YDR No.
4410	Lakeside Railway	

4392/93 Air-braked by Southern Region. 4392/93 were to be converted to Class 90 Driver Trai
ing Train coaches DB977632/3 but conversion cancelled.

Lot No.: 30226. **Builder:** BRCW. **Ordered:** 04/1955 **Completed:** 01/1957.
Diagram: 93. **New diagram:** AC204. **Seats:** 64S. **Bogies:** BR1.

4416	Swanage Railway
4419	West Somerset Railway
4420	Gwili Railway
4422	Bo'ness & Kinneil Railway

4423	Watercress Line	
4424	Pleasurewood Hills Park, Lowestoft	Used as Cafeteria
4425	North Yorkshire Moors Railway	
4427	Leadburn Inn, Leadburn	Used as Restaurant
4435	West Somerset Railway	
4440 DB977175	Gloucestershire-Warwickshire Railway	
4449 DB977413	West Somerset Railway	
4455	North Yorkshire Moors Railway	
4460	Embsay Steam Railway	YDR No. 1
4466	Bo'ness & Kinneil Railway	
4467	Keighley & Worth Valley Railway	K&WVR No. 34
4472	Dean Forest Railway	

4440 converted to a Train Crew Training Coach in 1983. 4449 converted to a Special Instruction Coach in 1986.

OPEN SECOND   SO

Lot No.: 30227. **Builder:** BRCW.   **Ordered:** 04/1955   **Completed:** 04/1957.
Diagram: 94.   **New diagram:** AD201.   **Seats:** 48S.   **Bogies:** BR1.

4474	Orient Express Restaurant, Elsenham	Body only remains
4476	Peak Railway, Darley Dale	
4477	Strathspey Railway	SR No. 114 'CRAIGELLACHIE'
4480	Midland Railway Centre	
4484	Llangollen Railway	'BRANWEN'

TOURIST OPEN SECOND   TSO

Lot No.: 30243. **Builder:** York.   **Ordered:** 05/1955   **Completed:** 01/1957.
Diagram: 93.   **New diagram:** AC204.   **Seats:** 64S.   **Bogies:** BR1.
4627 rebogied with B4s.

4489	Bideford Station Museum	
4493	West Somerset Railway	
4494	Dalriada Steam Packet Company, Loch Awe	Used as Cafeteria
4495	Caledonian Railway	
4496	South Devon Railway	
4503	Llangollen Railway	
4507	Paignton & Dartmouth Railway	
4508	Birmingham Railway Museum	
4509	Severn Valley Railway	
4512	Colne Valley Railway	
4521	North Norfolk Railway	
4529	Bo'ness & Kinneil Railway	
4534	Midland Railway Centre	
4537	Midland Railway Centre	
4545	Severn Valley Railway	
4549	Watercress Line	
4550	Severn Valley Railway	
4562	East Somerset Railway	
4575	Embsay Steam Railway	YDR No. 8
4584	East Somerset Railway	
4588	Keighley & Worth Valley Railway	K&WVR No. 25 'JUBILEE BAR'
4593	Severn Valley Railway	
4597	North Yorkshire Moors Railway	
4599	West Somerset Railway	
4600	Watercress Line	
4602	West Somerset Railway	
4606	The Cedar Tree Restaurant, Nutbourne	Used as Restaurant
4610	Great Central Railway	
4614	Dean Forest Railway	
4615	Nene Valley Railway	Numbered 5079
4623	Peak Railway, Darley Dale	
4627	Nene Valley Railway	
4628	Colne Valley Railway	

| 4630 | Great Central Railway | |
| 4635 | Nene Valley Railway | Body only remains |

4588 converted to a bar car by the Keighley & Worth Valley Railway.

Lot No.: 30375. **Builder:** York.   **Ordered:** 06/1957   **Completed:** 10/1957.
Diagram: 93.   **New diagram:** AC204.   **Seats:** 64S.   **Bogies:** BR1.
4712 rebogied with B4s and restored with BR1s.

4640	Kent & East Sussex Railway	K&ESR No. 85
4641	East Somerset Railway	
4642	Paignton & Dartmouth Railway	'ISADORA'
4643	Llangollen Railway	
4647	East Lancashire Railway	
4651	North Norfolk Railway	
4654	Pontypool & Blaenavon Railway	Numbered 4256
4656	Watercress Line	
4660	West Somerset Railway	
4662	Great Central Railway	
4663	Sidings Hotel and Restaurant	Body only remains
4665	Paignton & Dartmouth Railway	
4666	Embsay Steam Railway	YDR No. 7
4667	Nene Valley Railway	
4668	Lavender Line, Isfield	'NATALIE'
4672	Platform Three Restaurant, Colwyn Bay	Used as Restaurant
4676	Caledonian Railway	
4677	Pontypool & Blaenavon Railway	
4686	Nene Valley Railway	
4690	Severn Valley Railway	
4702	Llangollen Railway	
4712	Watercress Line	

Lot No.: 30739. **Builder:** Derby.   **Ordered:** 01/1963   **Completed:** 06/1964.
Diagram: 91.   **New diagram:** AC202.   **Seats:** 64S.   **Bogies:** B4.
XP64 prototype stock.

| 4728 | North Yorkshire Moors Railway | |
| 4729 | Dean Forest Railway | |

Lot No.: 30375. **Builder:** York.   **Ordered:** 06/1957   **Completed:** 10/1957.
Diagram: 93.   **New diagram:** AC204.   **Seats:** 64S.   **Bogies:** BR1.

4774 rebogied with B4s.

4751	Marsden Rattler Restaurant,South Shields	Used as Restaurant
4754	COD Bicester Military Railway	WGT880
4755	Bogie Chain Public House, Wallsend	Number to be confirmed
4756	Paignton & Dartmouth Railway	
4758	Great Central Railway	
4760	Lakeside Railway	
4762	East Lancashire Railway	
4763	Paignton & Dartmouth Railway	
4764	Swindon & Cricklade Railway	
4766	Swindon & Cricklade Railway	
4767	East Lancashire Railway	
4772	Paignton & Dartmouth Railway	
4774	Keighley & Worth Valley Railway	K&WVR No. 3
4777	Strathspey Railway	SR No. 11

OPEN SECOND   SO

Lot No.: 30376. **Builder:** York.   **Ordered:** 03/1956   **Completed:** 12/1957.
Diagram: 94.   **New diagram:** AD201.   **Seats:** 48S.   **Bogies:** BR1.

4779	Llangollen Railway
4784	East Lancashire Railway
4785	South Devon Railway
4786	North Yorkshire Moors Railway
4787	Gloucestershire-Warwickshire Railway

4788	Great Central Railway	
4789	Llangollen Railway	'TANGWEN'
4790	Gloucestershire-Warwickshire Railway	
4794	Railway Inn, Whittlesea	Used as Restaurant
4795	Cheddleton Railway Centre	
4796	Llangollen Railway	'RHIANNON'
4798	Gloucestershire-Warwickshire Railway	
4799	Embsay Steam Railway	
4802	South Devon Railway	
4803	Swanage Railway	
4804	Midland Railway Centre	
4805	South Devon Railway	
4806	Gloucestershire-Warwickshire Railway	
4808	Llangollen Railway	'ANGHARAD'
4809	Caledonian Railway	

Lot No.: 30473. **Builder:** BRCW. **Ordered:** 05/1957 **Completed:** 05/1959.
Diagram: 94. **New diagram:** AD201. **Seats:** 48S. **Bogies:** BR1.
4822/23/24/28 rebogied with B4s.

4810	Colne Valley Railway	
4814	West Somerset Railway	'WHITBREAD BAR'
4816	Midland Railway Centre	
4817	North Yorkshire Moors Railway	
4822	The Railway Age, Crewe	Stored at Crewe Carriage Shed
4823	The Railway Age, Crewe	Stored at Crewe Carriage Shed
4824	Battlefield Steam Railway	
4828	The Railway Age, Crewe	Stored at Crewe Carriage Shed

4814 has been converted to a bar car by the West Somerset Railway.

TOURIST OPEN SECOND   TSO

Lot No.: 30506. **Builder:** Wolverton. **Ordered:** 05/1959 **Completed:** 12/1959.
Diagram: 89. **New diagram:** AC201. **Seats:** 64S. **Bogies:** BR1.
Built with fluorescent lighting. 4830/31/32/36 Dual-braked.

4830	Lavender Line, Isfield	
4831	Bo'ness & Kinneil Railway	SCR99824. SRPS Set
4832	Bo'ness & Kinneil Railway	
4836	Bo'ness & Kinneil Railway	SCR99831. SRPS Set
4839	North Yorkshire Moors Railway	

Lot No.: 30525. **Builder:** Wolverton. **Ordered:** 08/1958 **Completed:** 04/1960.
Diagram: 89. **New diagram:** AC201. **Seats:** 64S. **Bogies:** BR1.
Built with fluorescent lighting. 4840/43/56/57/62/67/84/85/86/91/95/99 rebogied with B4s. 4840
restored with BR1s. 4856 Dual-braked.

4840	Keighley & Worth Valley Railway	K&WVR No. 33
4843	North Norfolk Railway	
4844	Bo'ness & Kinneil Railway	
4856	Bo'ness & Kinneil Railway	SCR99829. SRPS Set
4857	Great Central Railway	
4862	Dean Forest Railway	
4864	Caledonian Railway	
4867	Buckinghamshire Railway Centre	
4871	Bo'ness & Kinneil Railway	
4884	West Somerset Railway	
4885	East Lancashire Railway	
4886	Steamport Railway Museum	
4891	The Railway Age, Crewe	Stored at Basford Hall Yard
4895	East Lancashire Railway	
4899	Swanage Railway	

Lot No.: 30646. **Builder:** Wolverton. **Ordered:** 10/1959 **Completed:** 05/1961.
Diagram: 89. **New diagram:** AC201. **Seats:** 64S. **Bogies:** Commonwealth.

Rebogied with BR1s by Southern Region, 4913 subsequently had Commonwealths refitted. 4912 restored with Commonwealth Bogies and Dual Brakes.

4900	Keighley & Worth Valley Railway	K&WVR No. 38
4903	Elsecar at Barnsley, Elsecar	
4904	Midland Railway Centre	
4906	Gwili Railway	
4907	East Somerset Railway	
4911	West Somerset Railway	
4912	Steamtown Railway Centre, Carnforth WDS99318. Carnforth Maroon Set	
4913	The Railway Age, Crewe	Stored at Basford Hall Yard
4914	Great Central Railway	

Lot No.: 30690. **Builder:** Wolverton.   **Ordered:** 06/1960   **Completed:** 04/1962.
Diagram: 89.   **New diagram:** AC201.   **Seats:** 64S.   **Bogies:** Commonwealth.

Built with fluorescent lighting. 5024 rebogied with BR1s by SR but subsequently had Commonwealths refitted. 4955 restored with BR1s. 4919/27/46/61/63/66/79/96, 5001/08/09/25/29/30/33/44 Air-braked. 5028 Dual-braked.

4918	Battlefield Steam Railway	
4919	Nene Valley Railway	
4921	Bluebell Railway	
4922	Great Central Railway	
4923	The Railway Age, Crewe	Stored at Basford Hall Yard
4927	The Railway Age, Crewe	Stored at Basford Hall Yard
4928	East Lancashire Railway	
4931	Steamtown Railway Centre, Carnforth	
4932	Steamtown Railway Centre, Carnforth	
4933	East Lancashire Railway	To be exported to U.S.A.
4937	East Lancashire Railway	
4941	Bluebell Railway	
4945	Swanage Railway	
4946	The Railway Age, Crewe	To be added to BN91 set
4947	The Railway Age, Crewe	Stored at Basford Hall Yard
4948	Great Central Railway	
4954	Steamtown Railway Centre, Carnforth	
4955	Keighley & Worth Valley Railway	
4957	Bluebell Railway	
4958	Steamtown Railway Centre, Carnforth	
4961	The Railway Age, Crewe	Stored at Basford Hall Yard
4962	South Devon Railway	
4963	Rail UK Ltd.	
4965	Great Central Railway	
4966	The Railway Age, Crewe	Stored at Basford Hall Yard
4974	Peak Railway, Darley Dale	
4976	South Yorkshire Railway	
4978	The Railway Age, Crewe	Stored at Basford Hall Yard
4979	The Railway Age, Crewe	Stored at Basford Hall Yard
4980	The Railway Age, Crewe	Stored at Basford Hall Yard
4981	The Railway Age, Crewe	Stored at Crewe Carriage Shed
4982	Great Central Railway	
4983	The Railway Age, Crewe	Stored at Basford Hall Yard
4989	The Railway Age, Crewe	Stored at Basford Hall Yard
4990	North Yorkshire Moors Railway	
4992	East Lancashire Railway	
4996	The Railway Age, Crewe	To be added to BN91 set
4997	Ystwth Valley Railway	Stored at Steamtown, Carnforth
5000	North Yorkshire Moors Railway	
5001	The Railway Age, Crewe	
5003	Embsay Steam Railway	
5008	The Railway Age, Crewe	To be added to BN91 set
5009	Rail UK Ltd.	
5024	West Somerset Railway	
5025	Rail UK Ltd.	
5028	Bo'ness & Kinneil Railway	
5029	Rail UK Ltd.	

5030	Rail UK Ltd.	
5031	East Lancashire Railway	
5033	Steamtown Railway Centre, Carnforth	
5034	Bluebell Railway	
5036	The Railway Age, Crewe	Stored at Crewe Carriage Shed
5044	Steamtown Railway Centre, Carnforth	

5034 converted for use as a dormitory coach.

Lot No.: 30724. **Builder:** York. **Ordered:** 08/1962 **Completed:** 12/1963.
Diagram: 89. **New diagram:** AC201. **Seats:** 64S. **Bogies:** Commonwealth.

Built with fluorescent lighting. 5067 restored with Air-brakes.

5045	Midland Railway Centre	
5049	Scottish Industrial Railway Centre	
5053	Strathspey Railway	SR No. 116
5054	Gloucestershire-Warwickshire Railway	
5055	Strathspey Railway	SR No. 117
5057	Strathspey Railway	SR No. 118
5060	Strathspey Railway	SR No. 119
5067	Steamtown Railway Centre, Carnforth	RFM99993 'LMS Club Car'

OPEN BRAKE SECOND   BSO

Lot No.: 30170. **Builder:** Doncaster. **Ordered:** 05/1954 **Completed:** 03/1956.
Diagram: 183. **New diagram:** AE201. **Seats:** 39S. **Bogies:** BR1.
9229/37/75/76 converted to BSOT, new diagram AE209, seats 31S in 1981. 9273 rebogied with B4s, restored with BR1s. 9208/25/27/29/37 Dual-braked.

9208	DB977134	Avon Valley Railway	Stored at Long Marston
9218		Lakeside Railway	
9220		Severn Valley Railway	
9225	DB977135	Northampton & Lamport Railway	
9227		Bo'ness & Kinneil Railway	SCR99821. SRPS Set
9229	9015	Swanage Railway	
9235		North Yorkshire Moors Railway	
9237	9016	Bo'ness & Kinneil Railway	
9241		East Somerset Railway	
9254		Kent & East Sussex Railway	K&ESR No. 75 'PETROS'
9267		North Yorkshire Moors Railway	
9269	DB975269 041332	Kent & East Sussex Railway	K&ESR No. 73
9273		Keighley & Worth Valley Railway	K&WVR No. 40
9274		North Yorkshire Moors Railway	
9275	9001	Paignton & Dartmouth Railway	
9276	9000	Peak Railway, Darley Dale	

9269 converted to a S&T Office Coach in 1973 and 9208/25 were converted to Stock Movement Brakes in 1983. 9016 was to be converted to Class 90 Driver Training Train Coach DB977634 but conversion was cancelled.

Lot No.: 30244. **Builder:** Doncaster. **Ordered:** 05/1955 **Completed:** 08/1956.
Diagram: 183. **New diagram:** AE201. **Seats:** 39S. **Bogies:** BR1.

9278		West Somerset Railway
9281		Midland Railway Centre
9300	DB977176	Midland Railway Centre
9315		Caledonian Railway
9316		Great Central Railway

9300 converted to a Train Crew Training Coach in 1983.

Lot No.: 30443. **Builder:** GRCW. **Ordered:** 01/1957 **Completed:** 01/1960.
Diagram: 183. **New diagram:** AE201. **Seats:** 39S. **Bogies:** BR1.

9356	East Lancashire Railway	
9362	Strathspey Railway	SR No.106

Lot No.: 30698. **Builder:** Wolverton. **Ordered:** 04/1961 **Completed:** 12/1963.
Diagram: 184. **New diagram:** AE202. **Seats:** 39S. **Bogies:** Commonwealth.
Built with fluorescent lighting. Converted to BSOT, new diagram AE210, seats 31S in 1980.

9369	9010	Dean Forest Railway	
9370	9011	Embsay Steam Railway	YDR No. 6
9377	9003	Watercress Line	
9380	9014	Llangollen Railway	'GWENHWYVAR'

CORRIDOR FIRST   FK

Lot No.: 30019. **Builder:** Swindon.   **Ordered:** 12/1950   **Completed:** 06/1952.
Diagram: 116.   **New diagram:** AA101.   **Seats:** 42F.   **Bogies:** BR1.

13043	North Yorkshire Moors Railway

Lot No.: 30089. **Builder:** Swindon.   **Ordered:** 04/1953   **Completed:** 11/1954.
Diagram: 116.   **New diagram:** AA101.   **Seats:** 42F.   **Bogies:** BR1.

13085/89/92 rebogied with B4s.

13085	Army Dogs School, Welby Lane Camp
13088	214 High Street, Burbage, Wiltshire
13089	Gloucestershire-Warwickshire Railway
13092	Northampton & Lamport Railway

Lot No.: 30107. **Builder:** Swindon.   **Ordered:** 04/1953   **Completed:** 12/1954.
Diagram: 116.   **New diagram:** AA101.   **Seats:** 42F.   **Bogies:** BR1.

13125	Battlefield Steam Railway

Lot No.: 30381. **Builder:** Ashford/Swindon.   **Ordered:** 04/1956   **Completed:** 07/1959.
Diagram: 116.   **New diagram:** AA101.   **Seats:** 42F.   **Bogies:** BR1.

13228/29/30/3/6/7 rebogied with B4s. 13228/29/30 Dual-braked.

13228		Bo'ness & Kinneil Railway
13229		Bo'ness & Kinneil Railway	SCR99826. SRPS Se
13230		Bo'ness & Kinneil Railway	SCR99828. SRPS Se
13231	DB977132	Avon Valley Railway
13233		Swindon & Cricklade Railway
13236		
13237		

13231 converted to a Special Instruction Coach in 1983.

Lot No.: 30667. **Builder:** Swindon.   **Ordered:** 03/1960   **Completed:** 09/1962.
Diagram: 116.   **New diagram:** AA101.   **Seats:** 42F.   **Bogies:** Commonwealth.

13349 converted to LFK in 1967, diagram 79, new diagram AZ101, seats 38F. 13317/21/23 restored with Dual-brakes.

13303		Swindon & Cricklade Railway
13308		Swanage Railway	Numbered 308. Stored at Horsham
13313		Great Central Railway
13314		Swanage Railway	Numbered 314. Stored at Horsham
13316		Swindon & Cricklade Railway
13317		Steamtown Railway Centre, Carnforth	WDS99303. Carnforth Maroon Se
13320		Steamtown Railway Centre, Carnforth
13321		Steamtown Railway Centre, Carnforth	WDS99316. Carnforth Maroon Se
13323		Steamtown Railway Centre, Carnforth	WDS99302. Carnforth Maroon Se
13324		Mangapp's Farm Railway Museum
13326		Gloucestershire-Warwickshire Railway
13328		Nene Valley Railway
13329		Gloucestershire-Warwickshire Railway
13331		The Railway Age, Crewe	Stored at Basford Hall Yar
13333		East Lancashire Railway
13335		
13337		Gloucestershire-Warwickshire Railway
13340		Llangollen Railway
13349	14901	Telford Railway Centre

Lot No.: 30738. **Builder:** Derby.   **Ordered:** 01/1963   **Completed:** 06/1964.
Diagram: 121.   **New diagram:** AA103.   **Seats:** 42F.   **Bogies:** B4.

XP64 prototype stock.

13407	Dean Forest Railway

CORRIDOR BRAKE FIRST   BFK

Lot No.: 30382. **Builder:** Ashford/Swindon.   **Ordered:** 04/1956   **Completed:** 02/1960.
Diagram: 161.   **New diagram:** AB101.   **Seats:** 24F.   **Bogies:** BR1.

14007 17007	Southall Railway Centre	
14010 17010	Kingdom of Fife RPS	Stored at Methil Power Station

Lot No.: 30668. **Builder:** Swindon.   **Ordered:** 03/1960   **Completed:** 12/1961.
Diagram: 161.   **New diagram:** AB101.   **Seats:** 24F.   **Bogies:** Commonwealth.

14013 17013	Southall Railway Centre	
14018 17018	Birmingham Railway Museum	
14019 17019	Keighley & Worth Valley Railway	COWS99792.
14021 17021	Southall Railway Centre	HLPG99421. 777 Support Coach

17021 was to be converted to S&T Staff Coach DB975592 but conversion was cancelled. 14019 is currently on loan to the North Eastern Locomotive Preservation Group for use as a support coach for locomotive 60532.

Lot No.: 30718. **Builder:** Swindon.   **Ordered:** 08/1961   **Completed:** 11/1963.
Diagram: 161.   **New diagram:** AB101.   **Seats:** 24F.   **Bogies:** Commonwealth.

14024 17024	Humberside Locomotive Group	
14025 17025	Steamtown Railway Centre, Carnforth	EAB99990. 46441 Support Coach
14026 17026	Great Central Railway	

CORRIDOR COMPOSITE   CK

Lot No.: 30005. **Builder:** Metro-Cammell.   **Ordered:** 12/1950   **Completed:** 10/1953.
Diagram: 126.   **New diagram:** AA301.   **Seats:** 24F 18S.   **Bogies:** BR1.

5096	Great Central Railway
5207	Cheddleton Railway Centre
5208	Cheddleton Railway Centre

Lot No.: 30033. **Builder:** Derby.   **Ordered:** 03/1951   **Completed:** 09/1953.
Diagram: 126.   **New diagram:** AA301.   **Seats:** 24F 18S.   **Bogies:** BR1.

5319	Buckinghamshire Railway Centre

Lot No.: 30075. **Builder:** Derby.   **Ordered:** 01/1953   **Completed:** 07/1954.
Diagram: 126.   **New diagram:** AA301.   **Seats:** 24F 18S.   **Bogies:** BR1.

5401	Strathspey Railway SR No. 101

Lot No.: 30135. **Builder:** Metro-Cammell.   **Ordered:** 01/1954   **Completed:** 07/1955.
Diagram: 128.   **New diagram:** AA302.   **Seats:** 24F 24S.   **Bogies:** BR1.

Air-braked by Southern Region.

5565	Didcot Railway Centre
5577	Didcot Railway Centre

Lot No.: 30139. **Builder:** BRCW.   **Ordered:** 01/1954   **Completed:** 07/1955.
Diagram: 128.   **New diagram:** AA302.   **Seats:** 24F 24S.   **Bogies:** BR1.

5611	Great Central Railway

Lot No.: 30158. **Builder:** Wolverton.   **Ordered:** 04/1954   **Completed:** 10/1956.
Diagram: 126.   **New diagram:** AA301.   **Seats:** 24F 18S.   **Bogies:** BR1.

5626 7626	Llangollen Railway
5632 7632	West Somerset Railway
5644 7644	South Devon Railway
5663 7663	Peak Railway, Darley Dale
5667 7667	Llangollen Railway
5673 7673	Swanage Railway
5674 7674	Llangollen Railway

Lot No.: 30179. **Builder:** Metro-Cammell.   **Ordered:** 07/1954   **Completed:** 02/1956.
Diagram: 126.   **New diagram:** AA301.   **Seats:** 24F 18S.   **Bogies:** BR1.

15709	North Yorkshire Moors Railway
15745 7745	North Yorkshire Moors Railway

Lot No.: 30221. **Builder:** Metro-Cammell. **Ordered:** 03/1955 **Completed:** 08/1956.
Diagram: 126. **New diagram:** AA301. **Seats:** 24F 18S. **Bogies:** BR1.

15829	Gwili Railway
15834 7834	Bo'ness & Kinneil Railway
15849	Cholsey & Wallingford Railway

Lot No.: 30317. **Builder:** Wolverton. **Ordered:** 10/1955 **Completed:** 01/1957.
Diagram: 126. **New diagram:** AA301. **Seats:** 24F 18S. **Bogies:** BR1.

15916 7916	East Lancashire Railway	
15927 7927	Kent & East Sussex Railway	K&ESR No. 8
15928 7928	East Lancashire Railway	
15931 7931	Llangollen Railway	
15932 7932	Sidings Hotel and Restaurant	Body only remain
15936 DB977101	ABB Transportation Ltd., York Works	Reduced to underfram
15939 7939	Colne Valley Railway	
15943 7943	Peak Railway, Darley Dale	
15952	Embsay Steam Railway	YDR No.
15960	Great Central Railway	
15961 7961	Kent & East Sussex Railway	K&ESR No. 8
15981	Colne Valley Railway	
15984 7984	Colne Valley Railway	

15936 converted to EMU Barrier Coach in 1982.

Lot No.: 30351. **Builder:** Wolverton. **Ordered:** 01/1956 **Completed:** 04/1957.
Diagram: 126. **New diagram:** AA301. **Seats:** 24F 18S. **Bogies:** BR1.

16012/19 rebogied with B4s, 16025 operated on Wegmann bogies for several years. 16012/1
preserved on BR1 bogies.

15989 DB977056	Gloucestershire-Warwickshire Railway
15997 DB977054	North Norfolk Railway
16012	Bodmin Steam Railway
16019	Northampton & Lamport Railway
16025	Great Central Railway

15989/97 converted to Test Train Coaches in 1981.

Lot No.: 30471. **Builder:** Metro-Cammell. **Ordered:** 05/1957 **Completed:** 04/1959.
Diagram: 126. **New diagram:** AA301. **Seats:** 24F 18S. **Bogies:** BR1.

16065 7065	Bodmin Steam Railway
16068 7068	Bodmin Steam Railway
16070 7070	Great Central Railway
16071 7071	Llangollen Railway
16083 7083	Watercress Line

Lot No.: 30665. **Builder:** Derby. **Ordered:** 03/1960 **Completed:** 06/1961.
Diagram: 126. **New diagram:** AA301. **Seats:** 24F 18S. **Bogies:** Commonwealth.

16153 7153	East Lancashire Railway	
16155 7155	Peak Railway, Darley Dale	
16156 7156	North Yorkshire Moors Railway	
16158 7158	Euroclad, Wentloog Corporate Park	
16160 7160	Schering Agriculture, Chesterton Junct.	SA99908. Generator & Store
16165 7165	Embsay Steam Railway	
16166 7166	Gloucestershire-Warwickshire Railway	
16167 7167	Venice-Simplon Orient Express	
16168 7168	Steamtown Railway Centre, Carnforth	
16169 7169	Severn Valley Railway	
16172 7172	Euroclad, Wentloog Corporate Park	
16187 7187	Steamtown Railway Centre, Carnforth	TRTS99714. Pilkington K Glass S
16188 7188	Euroclad, Wentloog Corporate Park	
16190 7190	Steamtown Railway Centre, Carnforth	
16191 7191	Steamtown Railway Centre, Carnforth	TRTS99719. Pilkington K Glass S
16195 7195	Gloucestershire-Warwickshire Railway	

6160 fitted with B4 bogies and Air-brakes when converted to Weedkilling train Generator & Stores oach. 16187/91 restored with dual brakes.

ot No.: 30666. **Builder:** Derby. **Ordered:** 03/1960 **Completed:** 06/1961.
iagram: 128. **New diagram:** AA302. **Seats:** 24F 24S. **Bogies:** Commonwealth.

6201/02/03/04/10/21 rebogied with BR1s by Southern Region. 16202 restored with Com-onwealths.

6201 7201	Bo'ness & Kinneil Railway		
6202	Severn Valley Railway		
6203 7203	Schering Agriculture, Chesterton Junct.	SA99907. Spray Coach
6204 7204	Plym Valley Railway		
6210 7210	Bluebell Railway		
6212 7212	Euroclad, Wentloog Corporate Park		
6221 7221	Gloucestershire-Warwickshire Railway		

6203 fitted with B4 bogies and Air-brakes when converted for use as Weedkilling Train Spray Coach.

ot No.: 30729. **Builder:** Derby. **Ordered:** 06/1962 **Completed:** 09/1963.
iagram: 126. **New diagram:** AA301. **Seats:** 24F 18S. **Bogies:** Commonwealth.

6235/37 preserved with BR1 bogies.

6232 7232	Severn Valley Railway
6233 7233	North Yorkshire Moors Railway
6235 7235	Buckinghamshire Railway Centre
6237 7237	Bodmin Steam Railway

ot No.: 30730. **Builder:** Derby. **Ordered:** 06/1962 **Completed:** 12/1963.
iagram: 126. **New diagram:** AA301. **Seats:** 24F 18S. **Bogies:** Commonwealth.

6263 7263	Bluebell Railway
6267	Severn Valley Railway

CORRIDOR BRAKE COMPOSITE　　　BCK

ot No.: 30132. **Builder:** Metro-Cammell. **Ordered:** 01/1954 **Completed:** 01/1955.
iagram: 171. **New diagram:** AB301. **Seats:** 12F 18S. **Bogies:** BR1.

1027	East Anglian Railway Museum
1031	Battlefield Steam Railway
1034	West Somerset Railway
1059	Midland Railway Centre

ot No.: 30185. **Builder:** Metro-Cammell. **Ordered:** 07/1954 **Completed:** 05/1956.
iagram: 171. **New diagram:** AB301. **Seats:** 12F 18S. **Bogies:** BR1.

1096 restored with Dual-brakes.

1092	Gloucestershire-Warwickshire Railway	
1096	Steamtown Railway Centre, Carnforth	SNG99080. 4498 Support Coach
1100	North Yorkshire Moors Railway	
1103	North Norfolk Railway	

ot No.: 30186. **Builder:** Metro-Cammell. **Ordered:** 07/1954 **Completed:** 05/1956.
iagram: 172. **New diagram:** AB302. **Seats:** 12F 24S. **Bogies:** BR1.
ebogied with B4s.

129	Dean Forest Railway

ot No.: 30424. **Builder:** Charles Roberts. **Ordered:** 10/1956 **Completed:** 01/1959.
iagram: 172. **New diagram:** AB302. **Seats:** 12F 24S. **Bogies:** BR1.
1184/87 rebogied with B4s, 21184 restored with BR1s.

1174	West Somerset Railway	'PHOENIX'
1184	Great Central Railway	
1187	Gwili Railway	

ot No.: 30425. **Builder:** Metro-Cammell. **Ordered:** 10/1956 **Completed:** 09/1958.
iagram: 171. **New diagram:** AB301. **Seats:** 12F 18S. **Bogies:** BR1.

1224 rebogied with B4s.

21205 DB977094	Swanage Railway	
21208	Watercress Line	
21214	Spa Valley Railway	
21224 DB977580	The Railway Age, Crewe	Stored at Basford Hall Yard

21205 converted to S&T Brake coach in 1982 & 21224 to a S&T Staff & Tool Coach in 1988.

Lot No.: 30574. **Builder:** GRCW.   **Ordered:** 01/1959   **Completed:** 08/1960.
Diagram: 171. **New diagram:** AB301.   **Seats:** 12F 18S.   **Bogies:** BR1.

Rebogied with B4s. 21234 underframe fitted with Leyland body in 1982, Seats 72S.

21232	Midland Railway Centre	MRC99040. 80080 Support Coach
21234 DB977091	East Kent Light Railway	

Lot No.: 30669. **Builder:** Swindon.   **Ordered:** 03/1960   **Completed:** 02/1962.
Diagram: 171. **New diagram:** AB301.   **Seats:** 12F 18S.   **Bogies:** Commonwealth.

21247 restored with BR1 bogies. 21245 restored with Dual-brakes.

21236	Eastleigh Railway Preservation Society	RPR99120. 828 Support Coach
21238	Bluebell Railway	
21240	North Yorkshire Moors Railway	
21242	Great Central Railway	
21245	Flying Scotsman Railways, Bounds Green	SLOA99356. BN91 Set
21247	Dean Forest Railway	
21249	Lavender Line, Isfield	'GEMMA'

21236 is on loan from the Severn Valley Railway. 21238 converted for use as a dormitory.

Lot No.: 30731. **Builder:** Derby.   **Ordered:** 08/1962   **Completed:** 12/1963.
Diagram: 171. **New diagram:** AB301.   **Seats:** 12F 18S.   **Bogies:** Commonwealth.

21256 restored with Dual-brakes.

21252	Watercress Line	
21254	Severn Valley Railway	
21256	Steamtown Railway Centre, Carnforth	WDS99304. Carnforth maroon set
21261	Embsay Steam Railway	YDR No. 3

Lot No.: 30732. **Builder:** Derby.   **Ordered:** 08/1962   **Completed:** 02/1964.
Diagram: 172. **New diagram:** AB302.   **Seats:** 12F 24S.   **Bogies:** Commonwealth.

Built with Air-brakes. 21272 became Vacuum-braked in 1973, restored with Dual-brakes.

21272	Flying Scotsman Railways, Bounds Green	FSS99129. '129' BN91 Set
21275	Nomix-Chipman, Horsham	CC99016 Staff, Store & Dormitory Coach

CORRIDOR SECOND   SK

Lot No.: 30002. **Builder:** Derby.   **Ordered:** 12/1950   **Completed:** 12/1951.
Diagram: 146. **New diagram:** AA201.   **Seats:** 48S.   **Bogies:** BR1.

24006	West Somerset Railway	
24049	Albert Loom Ltd., Spondon	Body only remains
24127	Swanage Railway	

Lot No.: 30020. **Builder:** Ashford/Eastleigh.   **Ordered:** 12/1950   **Completed:** 05/1952.
Diagram: 146. **New diagram:** AA201.   **Seats:** 48S.   **Bogies:** BR1.

24307	West Somerset Railway

Lot No.: 30007. **Builder:** BRCW.   **Ordered:** 12/1950   **Completed:** 06/1953.
Diagram: 146. **New diagram:** AA201.   **Seats:** 48S.   **Bogies:** BR1.

24396	The Anglers Arms, Weldon Bridge	Used as Restaurant

Lot No.: 30030. **Builder:** Derby.   **Ordered:** 03/1951   **Completed:** 12/1953.
Diagram: 146. **New diagram:** AA201.   **Seats:** 48S.   **Bogies:** BR1.

24421	Gloucestershire-Warwickshire Railway	
24434	Sidings Hotel and Restaurant	Body only remains

Lot No.: 30088. **Builder:** Swindon.   **Ordered:** 04/1953   **Completed:** 07/1954.
Diagram: 146. **New diagram:** AA201.   **Seats:** 48S.   **Bogies:** BR1.

24458   South Devon Railway

Lot No.: 30057. **Builder:** BRCW.   **Ordered:** 03/1952   **Completed:** 01/1954.
Diagram: 146.   **New diagram:** AA201.   **Seats:** 48S.   **Bogies:** BR1.

24576 DB977189   Northampton & Lamport Railway

24576 converted to a Train Crew Training Coach in 1983.

Lot No.: 30058. **Builder:** Cravens.   **Ordered:** 05/1952   **Completed:** 10/1953.
Diagram: 146.   **New diagram:** AA201.   **Seats:** 48S.   **Bogies:** BR1.

24676   Sidings Hotel and Restaurant   Body only remains
24677 DB977247   Fire Service Training Centre

24677 converted to Special Instruction Coach in 1984.

Lot No.: 30078. **Builder:** Swindon.   **Ordered:** 02/1953   **Completed:** 05/1954.
Diagram: 146.   **New diagram:** AA201.   **Seats:** 48S.   **Bogies:** BR1.

24778   Gloucestershire-Warwickshire Railway

Lot No.: 30137. **Builder:** BRCW.   **Ordered:** 01/1954   **Completed:** 01/1955.
Diagram: 146.   **New diagram:** AA201.   **Seats:** 48S.   **Bogies:** BR1.

24800   Avon Valley Railway   Reduced to Carflat B745120
24804   North Yorkshire Moors Railway
24808   North Yorkshire Moors Railway

Lot No.: 30153. **Builder:** Derby.   **Ordered:** 04/1954   **Completed:** 06/1956.
Diagram: 146.   **New diagram:** AA201.   **Seats:** 48S.   **Bogies:** BR1.

24825   Gwili Railway
24839   Severn Valley Railway
24843   Gwili Railway
24845   Severn Valley Railway
24899 DB977103   ABB Transportation Ltd., York Works   Reduced to underframe
24918   Cholsey & Wallingford Railway

24899 converted to EMU Barrier Coach in 1982. 24839/96 used for volunteer accommodation at Bridgnorth, Severn Valley Railway.

Lot No.: 30154. **Builder:** Derby.   **Ordered:** 04/1954   **Completed:** 06/1956.
Diagram: 146.   **New diagram:** AA201.   **Seats:** 48S.   **Bogies:** BR1.

24949   Gloucestershire-Warwickshire Railway
24959   East Anglian Railway Museum

Lot No.: 30208. **Builder:** Derby.   **Ordered:** 01/1955   **Completed:** 12/1956.
Diagram: 147.   **New diagram:** AA202.   **Seats:** 64S.   **Bogies:** BR1.

24977   Sidings Hotel and Restaurant   Body only remains
24984   North Yorkshire Moors Railway
24985   West Somerset Railway
24993   Buckinghamshire Railway Centre   Numbered 24493
24997   Nene Valley Railway
25020 18020   Gloucestershire-Warwickshire Railway
25032 18032   South Devon Railway
25040   Avon Valley Railway

Lot No.: 30155. **Builder:** Wolverton.   **Ordered:** 04/1954   **Completed:** 05/1956.
Diagram: 146.   **New diagram:** AA201.   **Seats:** 48S.   **Bogies:** BR1.

25142   North Yorkshire Moors Railway

Lot No.: 30230. **Builder:** Metro-Cammell.   **Ordered:** 04/1955   **Completed:** 11/1957.
Diagram: 147.   **New diagram:** AA202.   **Seats:** 64S.   **Bogies:** BR1.

25189 converted to Auto-buffet coach in 1962 but subsequently converted back to standard.

25189 18189   Great Central Railway
25225   Foxfield Light Railway
25231   Foxfield Light Railway
25236 DB977102   ABB Transportation Ltd., York Works   Reduced to underframe

25236 converted to EMU Barrier Coach in 1982.

Lot No.: 30231. **Builder:** Metro-Cammell.   **Ordered:** 04/1955   **Completed:** 04/1958.
Diagram: 146.   **New diagram:** AA201.   **Seats:** 48S.   **Bogies:** BR1.

25252 18252   The Carriages of Moy, Moy   Body only remains

Lot No.: 30349. **Builder:** Wolverton.   **Ordered:** 02/1956   **Completed:** 10/1957.
Diagram: 146.   **New diagram:** AA201.   **Seats:** 48S.   **Bogies:** BR1.

25346/47/55/62/64/66/85 rebogied with BRII bogies. 25307 preserved with BRII bogies.

25299	Avon Valley Railway	
25307	Paignton & Dartmouth Railway	'NINA'
25308 18308	West Somerset Railway	
25312	Great Central Railway	
25323 18323	West Somerset Railway	
25337	Lakeside Railway	
25341 18341	Gloucestershire-Warwickshire Railway	
25346	Severn Valley Railway	
25347	Nene Valley Railway	
25355 18355	South Devon Railway	
25362 18362	South Yorkshire Railway	
25364	Lakeside Railway	
25366 18366	Great Central Railway	
25385 18385	East Lancashire Railway	
25401 18401	Schering Agriculture, Chesterton Junct.	SA99909. Staff & Workshop

25401 rebogied with B4s and Air-braked when converted to Weedkilling Train Staff & Workshop Coach. 25347 is on loan from the Northampton and Lamport Railway.

Lot No.: 30350. **Builder:** Wolverton.   **Ordered:** 02/1956   **Completed:** 12/1957.
Diagram: 146.   **New diagram:** AA201.   **Seats:** 48S.   **Bogies:** BR1.

25417 18417	Llangollen Railway	
25421 18421	Llangollen Railway	
25424 18424	Swanage Railway	
25425 18425	Window Tech Systems Ltd., Kirk Sandall	Body only remains
25444 18444	Pontypool & Blaenavon Railway	
25446	Kent & East Sussex Railway	K&ESR No. 63
25451	Gloucestershire-Warwickshire Railway	
25454	West Somerset Railway	

Lot No.: 30374. **Builder:** York.   **Ordered:** 05/1958   **Completed:** 11/1958.
Diagram: 146.   **New diagram:** AA201.   **Seats:** 48S.   **Bogies:** BR1.

25472	Embsay Steam Railway	YDR No. 5
25488 18488	North Yorkshire Moors Railway	
25498	Severn Valley Railway	
25500	Buckinghamshire Railway Centre	
25501	Gloucestershire-Warwickshire Railway	

Lot No.: 30737. **Builder:** Derby.   **Ordered:** 01/1963   **Completed:** 06/1964.
Diagram: 152.   **New diagram:** AA206.   **Seats:** 48S.   **Bogies:** B4.
XP64 prototype stock.

25508	North Yorkshire Moors Railway
25509	Dean Forest Railway

Lot No.: 30426. **Builder:** Wolverton.   **Ordered:** 10/1956   **Completed:** 09/1958.
Diagram: 146.   **New diagram:** AA201.   **Seats:** 48S.   **Bogies:** BR1.

25646 converted to Exhibition Van at Doncaster in 1981, new diagram NY526. 25607/18/23 rebogied with B4s.

25560 18560	Bodmin Steam Railway	
25562 18562	South Yorkshire Railway	
25572 18572	Bodmin Steam Railway	
25574 18574	Schering Agriculture, Chesterton Junct.	SA99910. Dormitory Coach
25591 18591	Plym Valley Railway	
25594 18594	Severn Valley Railway	
25607 18607 DB977513	Foxfield Light Railway	
25618 18618	Gloucestershire-Warwickshire Railway	

25623	DB977100	ABB Transportation Ltd., York Works	Reduced to underframe
25631	18631	Gloucestershire-Warwickshire Railway	
25639		Nene Valley Railway	
25646	99636	Gloucestershire-Warwickshire Railway	
25686	18686	Severn Valley Railway	
25693	18693	South Devon Railway	
25697		Colne Valley Railway	
25700		North Yorkshire Moors Railway	

25623 converted to EMU Barrier Coach in 1982 & 18607 to a Driver Training Train Coach in 1987 1987. 25574 rebogied with B4s and Air-braked when converted to Weedkilling Train Dormitory Coach. 25594/686 used for volunteer accommodation on Severn Valley Railway.

Lot No.: 30685. **Builder:** Derby.   **Ordered:** 09/1960   **Completed:** 07/1962.
Diagram: 146.   **New diagram:** AA201.   **Seats:** 48S.   **Bogies:** Commonwealth.

25729/56/67/93, 25806/08/37/62 restored with dual brakes.

25706	18706		The Railway Age, Crewe	Stored at Crewe Carriage Shed
25711	18711		Great Central Railway	
25728	18728		Bluebell Railway	
25729	18729		Steamtown Railway Centre, Carnforth	WDS99314. Carnforth Maroon Set
25735	18735	DB977653	Avon Valley Railway	Stored at Long Marston
25743	18743		Gloucestershire-Warwickshire Railway	
25752	18752		Bluebell Railway	
25756	18756		Steamtown Railway Centre, Carnforth	TRTS99722. Pilkington K Glass Set
25767	18767		Steamtown Railway Centre, Carnforth	TRTS99710. Pilkington K Glass Set
25769	18769		Bluebell Railway	
25771	18771		Severn Valley Railway	
25776	18776		Bluebell Railway	
25778	18778		Bluebell Railway	
25788	18788		The Railway Age, Crewe	Stored at Crewe Carriage Shed
25792	18792		The Railway Age, Crewe	Stored at Crewe Carriage Shed
25795	18795		Bluebell Railway	
25806	18806		Steamtown Railway Centre, Carnforth	TRTS99721. Pilkington K Glass Set
25807	18807	DB977420	Llangollen Railway	
25808	18808		Steamtown Railway Centre, Carnforth	TRTS99716. Pilkington K Glass Set
25809	18809		The Railway Age, Crewe	Stored at Basford Hall Yard
25828	18828		East Lancashire Railway	
25832	18832		Spa Valley Railway	
25836			ABB Transportation Ltd., York Works	Reduced to underframe
25837	18837		Steamtown Railway Centre, Carnforth	TRTS99717. Pilkington K Glass Set
25843	18843		Spa Valley Railway	
25845	18845		Spa Valley Railway	
25853	18853		Bluebell Railway	
25856	18856		Bluebell Railway	
25857	18857		Spa Valley Railway	
25862	18862		Steamtown Railway Centre, Carnforth	TRTS99718. Pilkington K Glass Set
25869	18869		Swindon & Cricklade Railway	
25871	18871		Bluebell Railway	
25891	18891	DB977518	Foxfield Light Railway	
25893	18893		Steamtown Railway Centre, Carnforth	TRTS99712. Pilkington K Glass Set

18735/807 converted to Special Instruction coaches in 1989/86 & 18891 to a Driver Training Train Coach in 1987. 25776/95, 25853/56/71 converted for use as dormitory coaches.

Lot No.: 30686. **Builder:** Derby.   **Ordered:** 06/1960   **Completed:** 05/1962.
Diagram: 147.   **New diagram:** AA202.   **Seats:** 64S.   **Bogies:** Commonwealth.

25917 rebogied with BR1s by Southern Region. 25917 Air-braked by Southern Region. 25955 restored with Dual-brakes.

25911	18911	Bekonscot Model Village	Body only remains
25917	18917	East Somerset Railway	
25955	18955	Steamtown Railway Centre, Carnforth	WDS99315. Carnforth Maroon Set
25958	18958	The Railway Age, Crewe	Stored at Crewe Carriage Shed
25968	18968	The Railway Age, Crewe	Stored at Crewe Carriage Shed

Lot No.: 30719. **Builder:** Derby.   **Ordered:** 08/1961   **Completed:** 12/1962.
Diagram: 146.   **New diagram:** AA201.   **Seats:** 48S.   **Bogies:** Commonwealth.

26013 restored with Dual-brakes.

25994	18994	Bluebell Railway	
26012	19012	The Railway Age, Crewe	Stored at Crewe Carriage Shed
26013	19013	Steamtown Railway Centre, Carnforth TRTS99713. Pilkington K Glass Set	
26014	19014	Midland Railway Centre	
26025	19025	Peak Railway, Darley Dale	
26043	19043	Peak Railway, Darley Dale	
26049	19049	Peak Railway, Darley Dale	

25994 converted for use as a dormitory coach.

Lot No.: 30726. **Builder:** York.   **Ordered:** 09/1961   **Completed:** 11/1963.
Diagram: 146.   **New diagram:** AA201.   **Seats:** 48S.   **Bogies:** Commonwealth.

26157	19157	Peak Railway, Darley Dale	
26169	19169	Bluebell Railway	On loan from Queen of Scots
26193		Nene Valley Railway	
26208	19208	Bluebell Railway	On loan from Queen of Scots

26169/208 converted for use as sleeping cars.

CORRIDOR BRAKE SECOND   BSK

Lot No.: 30003. **Builder:** Derby.   **Ordered:** 12/1950   **Completed:** 10/1952.
Diagram: 181.   **New diagram:** AB201.   **Seats:** 24S.   **Bogies:** BR1.

34042   Solent Rigging Services, Shamrock Quay   Used as Offices

Lot No.: 30025. **Builder:** Wolverton.   **Ordered:** 12/1950   **Completed:** 05/1952.
Diagram: 181.   **New diagram:** AB201.   **Seats:** 24S.   **Bogies:** BR1.

34111   Avon Valley Railway   AD5318

Lot No.: 30021. **Builder:** Ashford/Eastleigh.   **Ordered:** 12/1950   **Completed:** 11/1952.
Diagram: 181.   **New diagram:** AB201.   **Seats:** 24S.   **Bogies:** BR1.

34255 DB975534   Midland Railway Centre

Converted to CCE Staff & Dormitory & Workshop Coach in 1970.

Lot No.: 30074. **Builder:** Wolverton.   **Ordered:** 01/1953   **Completed:** 06/1954.
Diagram: 181.   **New diagram:** AB201.   **Seats:** 24S.   **Bogies:** BR1.

34393   Great Central Railway

Lot No.: 30060. **Builder:** GRCW.   **Ordered:** 03/1952   **Completed:** 02/1954.
Diagram: 181.   **New diagram:** AB201.   **Seats:** 24S.   **Bogies:** BR1.

34460   Caerphilly Railway

Lot No.: 30095. **Builder:** Wolverton.   **Ordered:** 04/1953   **Completed:** 04/1955.
Diagram: 181.   **New diagram:** AB201.   **Seats:** 24S.   **Bogies:** BR1.

34584 converted to Exhibition Van in 1972 at Swindon, new diagram NY503. 34525 restored with Commonwealth bogies and Air-brakes.

34525		Great Scottish & Western Railway	GSWR99966. Royal Scotsman Train
34531	DB977410	Avon Valley Railway	Stored at Long Marston
34535		Paignton & Dartmouth Railway	
34537		Llangollen Railway	
34538		Llangollen Railway	
34539	DB975618	Caledonian Railway	
34540	DB977311	Swindon & Cricklade Railway	
34548	DB977437	Gloucestershire-Warwickshire Railway	
34550		Paignton & Dartmouth Railway	
34556		Venice-Simplon Orient Express	
34557		North Eastern Locomotive Pres. Group NELP99760. 62005 Support Coach	
34558		Embsay Steam Railway	
34562		Severn Valley Railway	
34584	99622	Llangollen Railway	'GWENABWY'

34531 converted to a Special Instruction Coach & 34548 to a S&T Staff & Tool Coach in 1986, 34540 to a CCE Staff Coach in 1985 and 34539 to a Diesel Locomotive Test Train Coach in 1977.

Lot No.: 30141. **Builder:** GRCW.	**Ordered:** 01/1954	**Completed:** 06/1955.
Diagram: 181. **New diagram:** AB201.	**Seats:** 24S.	**Bogies:** BR1.

34612	Lakeside Caravan Park, Exbridge	Body only remains

Lot No.: 30142. **Builder:** GRCW.	**Ordered:** 01/1954	**Completed:** 09/1955.
Diagram: 182. **New diagram:** AB202.	**Seats:** 32S.	**Bogies:** BR1.

34618	Watercress Line	
34620 DB975289	Bodmin Steam Railway	Reduced to underframe
34623	Colne Valley Railway	
34624	East Lancashire Railway	
34625	Midland Railway Centre	
34626	Madame Tussauds, Windsor & Eton Central	Body of GWR 233 on u/f
34627	Bodmin Steam Railway	

34620 converted to a S&T Staff & Tool Coach in 1973.

Lot No.: 30143. **Builder:** Charles Roberts.	**Ordered:** 01/1954	**Completed:** 06/1955.
Diagram: 182. **New diagram:** AB202.	**Seats:** 32S.	**Bogies:** BR1.

34644 Air-braked by Southern Region.

34634 DB975149	Swindon & Cricklade Railway	Body only remains
34644 DB977086	Solent Rigging Services, Shamrock Quay	Used as Offices

34634 converted to a BTU Tool Van in 1971, & 34644 to a Barrier Coach in 1982.

Lot No.: 30156. **Builder:** Wolverton.	**Ordered:** 04/1954	**Completed:** 10/1955.
Diagram: 181. **New diagram:** AB201.	**Seats:** 24S.	**Bogies:** BR1.

34665	Dean Forest Railway	
34666	East Lancashire Railway	5407 Support Coach
34671	Didcot Railway Centre	
34672	The Railway Age, Crewe	
34675 DB977500	South Yorkshire Railway	
34676	Gloucestershire-Warwickshire Railway	
34682 DB977301	Fire Service Training Centre	
34699	North Yorkshire Moors Railway	
34712	Northampton & Lamport Railway	
34738	Great Central Railway	
34742	Solent Rigging Services, Shamrock Quay	Used as Offices

34675/82 converted to Special Instruction Coaches 1987/85.

Lot No.: 30157. **Builder:** Wolverton.	**Ordered:** 04/1954	**Completed:** 12/1955.
Diagram: 182. **New diagram:** AB202.	**Seats:** 32S.	**Bogies:** BR1.

34756 DB975084	Plym Valley Railway
34769 DB975047	West Somerset Railway

34756 converted to a BTU Staff & Dormitory Coach in 1971 & 34769 to a S&T Contractor's Staff & Dormitory Coach in 1970.

Lot No.: 30225. **Builder:** Charles Roberts.	**Ordered:** 04/1955	**Completed:** 06/1957.
Diagram: 182. **New diagram:** AB202.	**Seats:** 32S.	**Bogies:** BR1.

34929 rebogied with B4s, but restored with BR1s.

34925	Venice-Simplon Orient Express
34929	Gloucestershire-Warwickshire Railway

Lot No.: 30229. **Builder:** Metro-Cammell.	**Ordered:** 04/1955	**Completed:** 04/1957.
Diagram: 182. **New diagram:** AB202.	**Seats:** 32S.	**Bogies:** BR1.

35011 rebogied with Commonwealths by Southern Region. 34991 restored with Commonwealth bogies. 34991, 35006/11 Air-braked by Southern Region.

34935	Nene Valley Railway
34937	Long Marston Military Railway
34941	Swindon & Cricklade Railway
34945	Plym Valley Railway

34947	Watercress Line	
34949	East Lancashire Railway	
34950	Long Marston Military Railway	
34951	Long Marston Military Railway	
34952	Venice-Simplon Orient Express	
34953	Battlefield Steam Railway	
34991	Venice-Simplon Orient Express	VSOE99538. 'BAGGAGE CAR No. !
35006 DB975660 6337	Gloucestershire-Warwickshire Railway	
35011 DB977588	London Underground Ltd.	
35012	Gwili Railway	

35006 converted to HST Barrier Coach in 1978, subsequently returned to capital stock in 199 as 6337. 35011 converted to a Brake Force Runner in 1988.

Lot No.: 30233. **Builder:** GRCW.   **Ordered:** 04/1955   **Completed:** 06/1957.
Diagram: 181.   **New diagram:** AB201.   **Seats:** 24S.   **Bogies:** BR1.

35043	Nene Valley Railway	
35059	Swanage Railway	
35069	Strathspey Railway	SR No. 11
35070	East Lancashire Railway	
35072	Paignton & Dartmouth Railway	'ANN/
35073	Steamtown Railway Centre, Carnforth	
35087 DB975455	North Eastern Locomotive Pres. Group	
35089	North Yorkshire Moors Railway	

35087 converted to BTU Staff & Tool Coach in 1975.

Lot No.: 30386. **Builder:** Charles Roberts.   **Ordered:** 05/1956   **Completed:** 06/1958.
Diagram: 181.   **New diagram:** AB201.   **Seats:** 24S.   **Bogies:** BR1.

35123	Bo'ness & Kinneil Railway	SPG99070. 44871 Support Coac
35128	Steamport Railway Museum	
35129 DB977426	South Yorkshire Railway	
35130	Bodmin Steam Railway	
35131	Midland Railway Centre	PES99090. 46201 Support Coac
35148 DB977334	North Norfolk Railway	
35153	COD Bicester Military Railway	MODA99150. Nuclear Flask Escort Coac
35158	Bulmers Railway Centre, Hereford	
35169	Colne Valley Railway	
35174	Avon Valley Railway	AD 531

35129 converted to a Special Instruction Coach in 1986, 35148 converted to Test Train Coac in 1986.

Lot No.: 30427. **Builder:** Wolverton.   **Ordered:** 10/1956   **Completed:** 04/1959.
Diagram: 181.   **New diagram:** AB201.   **Seats:** 24S.   **Bogies:** BR1.

35192/93/97, 35200/01/04/07/10/48 rebogied with B4s. 35197 & 35201 converted to Courie Vehicles in 1987, new diagram NN504, Dual-braked.

35185 DB977339	Venice-Simplon Orient Express	
35188 DB977330	Llangollen Railway	
35192	Buckinghamshire Railway Centre	
35193	Peak Railway, Darley Dale	
35197 80218	Bo'ness & Kinneil Railway	
35200	Peak Railway, Darley Dale	
35201 80219	Gloucestershire-Warwickshire Railway	
35204	Southall Railway Centre	
35207	Venice-Simplon Orient Express	
35210 DB977638	Lancastrian Carriage & Wagon, Heysham	To be scrappe
35212	COD Bicester Military Railway	MODA99151. Nuclear Flask Escort Coac
35215 DB975662	Glenfinnan Station Museum	
35219	Bulmers Railway Centre, Hereford	
35239	Nene Valley Railway	
35248	Nene Valley Railway	
35255	Avon Valley Railway	
35257	West Somerset Railway	
35270	Directors Saloon, Wymondham	

5185 converted to a MTA Brake Force Runner in 1986, 35188 to a Special Instruction Coach
า 1985, 35210 to a CCE Staff Coach in 1989 and 35215 to a CCE Staff & Dormitory Coach in 1978.

ot No.: 30573. Builder: GRCW.   **Ordered:** 01/1959   **Completed:** 05/1960.
iagram: 181.   **New diagram:** AB201.   **Seats:** 24S.   **Bogies:** BR1.

ebogied with B4s. 35276/91 converted to Courier Vehicles in 1987, new diagram NN504, Dual-braked.

5276 80220	Didcot Railway Centre	5029 Support Coach
5290	The Railway Age, Crewe	Stored at Basford Hall Yard
5291 80224		Stored at Old Oak Common CARMD

ot No.: 30699. Builder: Wolverton.   **Ordered:** 04/1961   **Completed:** 01/1963.
iagram: 181.   **New diagram:** AB201.   **Seats:** 24S.   **Bogies:** Commonwealth.

5296/97/99, 35304/15/16/23/27/28/31 converted to Courier vehicles in 1986-7, new diagram
N504, Dual-braked. 35322 restored with Dual-brakes. 35305 restored with BR1 bogies.

5296 80211	Flying Scotsman Railways, Bounds Green	
5297 80204	Midland Railway Centre	
5299 80217	North Yorkshire Moors Railway	
5304 80206	Bo'ness & Kinneil Railway	
5305	Elsecar at Barnsley, Elsecar	
5308	Gloucestershire-Warwickshire Railway	
5309	Lakeside Railway	
5314	East Lancashire Railway	
5315 80222	Severn Valley Railway	Currently for sale
5316 80213	Severn Valley Railway	RPR99244. SVR locomotives support coach
5322	Didcot Railway Centre	BLS99035. 70000 Support Coach
5323 80214	Flying Scotsman Railways, Bounds Green	
5326	South Devon Railway	
5327 80225	Southall Railway Centre	Stored at Old Oak Common CARMD
5328 80221	Bo'ness & Kinneil Railway	
5329	Watercress Line	
5330	Lakeside Railway	
5331 80223	Flying Scotsman Railways, Bounds Green	
5333	Didcot Railway Centre	SU99180. 6024 Support Coach
5334	Great Central Railway	
5337	Eastleigh Railway Preservation Society	
5340	Llangollen Railway	
5342	Llangollen Railway	
5343	Cheddleton Railway Centre	
5362	National Railway Museum	Friends of NRM Coach

5337 is on loan from the Severn Valley Railway.

ɔt No.: 30700. Builder: Wolverton.   **Ordered:** 04/1961   **Completed:** 01/1963.
iagram: 182.   **New diagram:** AB202.   **Seats:** 32S.   **Bogies:** Commonwealth.

5405   Bo'ness & Kinneil Railway

ɔt No.: 30721. Builder: Wolverton.   **Ordered:** 08/1961   **Completed:** 09/1963.
iagram: 181.   **New diagram:** AB201.   **Seats:** 24S.   **Bogies:** Commonwealth.
5407 restored with Dual-brakes.

5407	Queen of Scots Train	SHRC99886.
5414	Pleasurewood Hills Park, Lowestoft	Used as Cafeteria

ɔt No.: 30728. Builder: Wolverton.   **Ordered:** 04/1962   **Completed:** 02/1963.
iagram: 181.   **New diagram:** AB201.   **Seats:** 24S.   **Bogies:** Commonwealth.

5447	Southall Railway Centre
5448	Bluebell Railway
5449	North Yorkshire Moors Railway

ɔt No.: 30721. Builder: Wolverton.   **Ordered:** 08/1961   **Completed:** 09/1963.
iagram: 181.   **New diagram:** AB201.   **Seats:** 24S.   **Bogies:** Commonwealth.

5466 converted to Courier Vehicle in 1986, new diagram NN504, Dual-brakes. 35459/61/65
stored with Dual-brakes.

5451	Keighley & Worth Valley Railway	DRC99313. 45596 Support Coach
5455	East Lancashire Railway	To be exported to U.S.A.

35457	North Yorkshire Moors Railway	STOR99995. 44767 Support Coach
35459	Steamtown Railway Centre, Carnforth	TRTS99723. Pilkington K Glass Se
35461	Steamtown Railway Centre, Carnforth	TRTS99720. Pilkington K Glass Se
35463	Steamtown Railway Centre, Carnforth	WDS99312. 48151 Support Coach
35464	North Yorkshire Moors Railway	
35465	The Railway Age, Crewe	WR99991. D172 Support Coach
35466 80207	Southall Railway Centre. 35028 Support Coach	
35467	Severn Valley Railway	SVR99242. SVR locomotives support coach
35468	National Railway Museum	
35470		Stored at Oxley CARMI
35473	Cheddleton Railway Centre	
35475	Lancashire Fire Brigade, Washington Hall	Used as Classroom
35476	Midland Railway Centre	MRC99041. 46203 Support Coach
35478	COD Bicester Military Railway	MODA99152. Nuclear Flask Escort Coach
35481	COD Bicester Military Railway	MODA99153. Nuclear Flask Escort Coach
35486	Markinch Goods Depot	JBC99405. 60009 Support Coach
35494	Pontypool & Blaenavon Railway	

35470 is currently for sale

LAVATORY COMPOSITE   CL

Lot No.: 30094. **Builder:** Doncaster.   **Ordered:** 04/1953   **Completed:** 04/1955.
Diagram: 313.   **Seats:** 19F 42S.   **Bogies:** BR1.

43003	Keighley & Worth Valley Railway	K&WVR No. 3
43010	Stephenson Railway Museum	
43012	Northampton & Lamport Railway	
43024	Strathspey Railway	SR No. 10
43034	North Norfolk Railway	
43041	North Norfolk Railway	
43043	Great Central Railway	
43046	National Railway Museum	

BRAKE SECOND   BS

Lot No.: 30045. **Builder:** York.   **Ordered:** 04/1951   **Completed:** 03/1955.
Diagram: 371.   **Seats:** 72S.   **Bogies:** BR1.

43128	Keighley & Worth Valley Railway	K&WVR No. 2
43140	East Kent Light Railway	
43145	Keighley & Worth Valley Railway	K&WVR No. 3
43147	Northampton & Lamport Railway	
43157	East Anglian Railway Museum	

SECOND   S

Lot No.: 30051. **Builder:** Derby.   **Ordered:** 06/1951   **Completed:** 11/1955.
Diagram: 326.   **Seats:** 108S.   **Bogies:** BR1.

46097	Midland Railway Centre

Lot No.: 30038. **Builder:** Wolverton.   **Ordered:** 03/1951   **Completed:** 11/1954.
Diagram: 326.   **Seats:** 108S.   **Bogies:** BR1.

46116	Gloucestershire-Warwickshire Railway	
46130	Llangollen Railway	
46132	Gwili Railway	
46137	Swansea Vale Railway	
46139	Great Central Railway	
46141	Severn Valley Railway	
46142	Caledonian Railway	
46145	Keighley & Worth Valley Railway	Body of L&Y 47 on underfram
46147	North Norfolk Railway	
46157	Keighley & Worth Valley Railway	K&WVR No. 1

ot No.: 30098. **Builder:** Derby.   **Ordered:** 04/1953   **Completed:** 04/1955.
Diagram: 326.   **Seats:** 108S.   **Bogies:** BR1.

| 6218 | The Carriages of Moy, Moy | Body only remains |
| 6235 | Embsay Steam Railway | Reduced to underframe |

OPEN SECOND WITH LAVATORY   SLO

ot No.: 30092. **Builder:** Doncaster.   **Ordered:** 04/1953   **Completed:** 06/1955.
Diagram: 330.   **Seats:** 80S.   **Bogies:** BR1.

8001	Great Central Railway	
8004	Midland Railway Centre	
8011	Keighley & Worth Valley Railway	K&WVR No. 17
8015	Stephenson Railway Museum	
8018	Keighley & Worth Valley Railway	K&WVR No. 19
8026	North Norfolk Railway	Reduced to underframe

BRAKE SECOND   BS

ot No.: 30047. **Builder:** Swindon.   **Ordered:** 04/1951   **Completed:** 05/1955.
Diagram: 370.   **Bogies:** BR1.

| 3049 43264 | East Somerset Railway |
| 3051 43266 | Gwili Railway |

ot No.: 30087. **Builder:** York.   **Ordered:** 04/1953   **Completed:** 08/1955.
Diagram: 371.   **Seats:** 72S.   **Bogies:** BR1.

3086 43275	Cheddleton Railway Centre	ARMY 3034
3100 43289	East Somerset Railway	ARMY 5310
3111 43300	Cheddleton Railway Centre	
3156 43345	Keighley & Worth Valley Railway	K&WVR No. 10
3160 43349	Strathspey Railway	SR No. 104
3168 43357	North Norfolk Railway	
3170 43359	North Norfolk Railway	

ot No.: 30093. **Builder:** Doncaster.   **Ordered:** 04/1953   **Completed:** 12/1954.
Diagram: 371.   **Seats:** 72S.   **Bogies:** BR1.

3172 43172	Stephenson Railway Museum
3182 43182	Llangollen Railway
3186 43186	Midland Railway Centre
3190 43190	Buckinghamshire Railway Centre

MARK 2 PASSENGER CARRYING COACHING STOCK

The origins of Mark 2 carriages can be traced back to late 1958. At that time an order was placed with Swindon Works to design and build a potential successor to the BR Mark 1 carriage. The specification contained the desire to reduce the weight of the carriage by using new materials and design techniques. The most important feature of the resulting carriage was its monocoque body with no frame. The resulting carriage, corridor first W13252, appeared in 1963. Other features included pressure ventilation and tungsten lighting. It was mounted on the recently developed B4 bogie. The interior and window width however continued to reflect Mk 1 practice. This particular carriage, the only Mark 2 not to have been built at Derby, now forms part of the national collection and is currently stored at MoD Kineton, space at York currently being restricted due to rebuilding work, it was however on display as part of the National Railway Museum on Tour Exhibition held at Swindon in 1990.

Seventy production carriages followed in 1964 based on the prototype, the most significant difference being wider windows. These carriages, 13361-13406/13410-13433, perpetuated the Mark 1 interior with much use of wood. Special mention should be made of the twenty carriages, 13387 13406, delivered to the Southern Region. Unlike their contemporaries these did not have pressure ventilation and were fitted with air brakes rather than vacuum brakes. At this time the Southern Region was in the process of converting the majority of its locomotive hauled passenger trains to air-braking They entered service in Southern Green livery being intended for use on continental boat trains. One of these carriages, 13396, was selected for conversion as the prototype air-conditioned coach subsequently being renumbered DB975290 and it survives to this day at the Railway Technical Centre, Derby. Regrettably none of the other 1964 built carriages has survived into preservation, the use of blue asbestos in their construction contributing to their demise.

After completion of the first 71 carriages no further Mark 2s were built for two years. However, during this period further design work was undertaken by BR, before a further large build of new stock for the electrified services between Euston, Manchester and Liverpool due to start in April 1966. A total of 133 tourist open seconds were build for these LMR services. Although a number of new features from the XP64 design, new pattern seats and wide double glazed windows, were incorporated in these carriages, many traditional features, such as mid-body side doors and standard toilets were retained Essentially these coaches were an interim design. Even so, by the use of rich and attractive colours good illumination and the new type seat with ashtrays in the arm rests in the smoking areas, the coaches set a good standard of comfort for second class passengers. The carriages were pressure ventilated, had 64 seats and two toilets both located at one end of the coach. There were entrance doors at both ends and in the centre of the vehicle, which was divided by a cross vestibule. A further 26 carriages to this design were built for the Western Region. This batch was followed by 28 open seconds for the LMR with 48 seats on a two plus one layout rather than the two plus two layout of the tourist open seconds. These open seconds were intended to be used for serving meals from the adjoining restaurant car. Finally 64 brake carriages were constructed, 28 brake corridor firsts and 36 brake open seconds. Interestingly all 64 carriages used the same body shell resulting in the seconds having wider seat spacing and tables than is found in the tourist open seconds. The brake firsts retained the Mark 1 interiors with much use of wood as on the earlier corridor firsts, but aluminium window frames were fitted. In the mid 1980s eight of the BSOs had one seating bay removed and replaced with a buffet counter, the adjacent toilet being converted to a store room. These coaches were reclassified BSOT and mainly saw use in Scotland. Examples of all these designs can be found in preservation, whilst a small fleet of TSOs, BSOs and BSOTs remains in service in Scotland principally being used for peak summer season trains.

Also built for the LMR electrification were 29 Pullman cars, constructed during 1965. This special batch of cars, seven Pullman brakes, eight kitchens and fourteen saloons, were not part of the basic Mark 2 building programme, but the body shells, underframes, external profile and appearance were similar to the Mark 2 coaches although the layout and Pullman style amenities were of course exclusive to this special design. As more modern designs entered service these coaches were displaced from prestigious West Coast services, their vacuum brakes causing problems with drivers used to air-braked stock on other Inter-City services. One set was however later fitted with air-brakes and used for several years on charter trains. This set has now been fully restored and operates as ''The Statesman'' private train, the remainder having all been scrapped.

Other than the batch of twenty Corridor Firsts for the Southern Region, all Mark 2s built up to 1966 were vacuum braked and remained so throughout their operational lives with a few notable exceptions. In 1971 36 vehicles were transferred to Scotland for use on the Edinburgh-Glasgow push pull service introduced that year. These vehicles were modified with air operated disc brakes amongst other modifications and comprised twenty-two TSOs, seven BSOs and seven FKs. One, 9400, has survived for preservation and is currently at Errol Station, Tayside. In the early 1970s air-braked Mark 2s were introduced on the LMR electrified services on which demand for meal service was high and rather than unnecessarily air-brake Mark 2 Second Class Dining Cars ten of the Open Seconds were air-braked. One of these, 5255, has been saved for possible use in a main line set. Air-braked Motorail trains operated during the 1980s and although these were generally formed of Mark 1 stock, Mark II BFK 14042 was air-braked for use in such trains but has recently been scrapped. Further details regarding the individual carriages air-braked can be found in an appendix later in this book.

The next batch of coaches, designated Mark 2A, was a development of the basic Mark 2 vehicle, but with improvements in detail fittings. The Mark 2A design included many new features. Ergonomically designed seating, individual seat lights, greater sound and heat insulation, pressure ventilation, foot-operated toilet flush and hand basin spray which had been fully tested in the XP64 coaches were included as standard items. The first class coaches now also had interiors incorporating features developed from the XP64 prototypes including fluorescent lighting, aluminium trim and plastic covered head and arm rests. By 1967 developments in insulation had also made possible remarkable improvements in noise reduction within the vehicle; multi-thickness floors provided an effective barrier to noises from bogie, track and operation of vehicle brakes. A new design of vestibule end and gangway, incorporating foldaway end doors, gave a compact and much neater appearance as well as reducing noise and preventing draught. The Mark IIa designs included four types of vehicle, Tourist Open Second, Corridor First, Brake Open Second and Corridor Brake First, the latter two again sharing the same body shell thus giving wider tables and spacing between seats. However, so far as train working was concerned, the most important development included in the Mark 2A design was the decision by the BRB to commence a gradual changeover to air braking. For years British operators and engineers had debated the merits of air or vacuum brakes. Although air braking was already used extensively in this country for many years in self contained operating areas, the Southern electric and GE steam suburban being well known examples, because of the high cost of converting locomotives and the much larger fleet of passenger coaches previously in use, it was never a practical possibility during the heyday of steam. By the mid-1960s conditions obviously had changed; Inter City services were now covered by a smaller fleet of intensively used sets of stock working in fixed formations. Indeed, as previously mentioned the Southern Region had already embarked on the air-braking of much of its fleet of locomotive hauled passenger carrying coaching stock a few years earlier. Against this background the BRB decided to adopt air braking for all new stock. Apart from the first few vehicles, which started running in December 1967, all of the 289 Mark 2A vehicles entered service in 1968. First deliveries were to the ER for the East Coast Route during the early part of the year, followed by deliveries to the WR which gradually phased in the new sets on trains between Paddington, South Wales and Bristol.

A consequence of only a limited number of designs of Mark 2A vehicles was that a number of Mark 1 vehicles, particularly catering, were fitted with air brakes in order to operate in sets with them. However, by the late 1970s the tables had been turned and the cascade of Mark 2As on to lesser services resulted in a surplus of First Class vehicles, thus a program of conversion to vacuum braking was instigated in order that these vehicles could operate with older Second Class vehicles, the air-brakes being swapped with vacuum brakes from Gangwayed Brake Vans which were at the time being fitted with air-brakes. Air brakes were replaced with vacuum brakes on seventeen FKs and nineteen BFKs. Four of the BFKs were subsequently reclassified to BSKs and renumbered in order to redress an imbalance of accommodation on commuter trains out of Paddington. It is from these that many of the preserved examples are drawn, the vacuum brakes having been more favourable for use on private lines. In the mid 1980s a program of declassification was implemented in order to redress the over provision of First Class accommodation in the air-braked carriage fleet. Consequently twelve FKs were declassified and renumbered, subsequently two were reinstated to first class standards. Similarly in the early 1990s eight BFKs were similarly declassified and renumbered. Details of the individual carriages involved in these various changes to Mark 2A stock can be found in an appendix later in this book. A number of air-braked Mark 2As have been preserved mainly as static exhibits or as part of main line sets. An interesting conversion is that of TSO 5344 by the West Somerset Railway to vacuum braking in order to make it compatible with its other stock. A small fleet remains in service principally in use on secondary locomotive hauled services in North Wales and North West England and several of the vacuum braked BFKs are used in conjunction with Mark 2s in Scotland.

One experimental feature of the XP64 train, not adopted so far as a standard feature, was the wide door. The jack-knife door on the XP64 coaches was not entirely successful, but to meet the need for an improved wide door the BRB re-designed the doors during 1968 by providing a 3 ft wide door re-located at the end of the coach. Changes were also made to the layout of the open second; as a result of moving the doors to the extreme ends of the vehicle the toilets were rearranged with one at each end of the passenger saloon and the centre cross vestibule was removed. As the doors between the entrance vestibules and the passenger saloon had to be offset from centre to clear the toilet compartment, the adjacent seats at each end were singles, reducing the seating capacity to 62. This revised design was designated Mark 2B, a total of 111 vehicles being built of three types, Tourist Open Second, Corridor First and Corridor Brake First. All these vehicles were delivered to the Western Region apart from the first eleven Corridor Firsts which went to the Eastern Region for the East Coast Line. The wide door wrapping around the end of the coach became standard on all subsequent builds of hauled stock, but by the early 1990s it became apparent that the design had put unanticipated stress on the body structure requiring remedial action. This resulted in the earlier than intended elimination of Mark 2Bs and later Mark 2Cs from the passenger carrying fleet. Four of the brakes did however become part of the Royal Train fleet were they continue in use. As with the Mark 2As a surfeit of first class accommodation in the mid 1980s resulted in a programme of declassification with twenty FKs being so treated, four of these subsequently being reinstated to first class. A number of TSOs and FKs have been preserved generally as static exhibits or with the intention of forming mainline sets.

Experience during the summers of 1968 and 1969 showed that during spells of very hot weather, when it became necessary for passengers to open the sliding ventilation windows to lower the temperature in the coach, the noise level became unacceptable and all the progress made in soundproofing was wasted. A decision in favour of full air conditioning was made in 1969. As it was not possible to secure delivery of the electrical equipment before 1970 or early 1971, BR decided to implement the design changes necessary for the installation of full air conditioning in the next batch of stock and install the equipment when the vehicles returned to works for their first overhaul. This retrospective fitting did in reality never taking place. 250 vehicles designated Mark 2C were constructed to this specification to five designs, Tourist Open Second, Brake Open Second, Corridor First, Corridor Brake First and the first Mark 2 Open Firsts. The decision to build this later batch of 18 carriages resulted from the fact that during the late 1960s faster journey times had reduced the time available for meal service and on an increasing number of trains, particularly on journeys between Euston, Manchester and Liverpool, only one meal service was now possible. Accordingly arrangements were made for first class passengers to be served at their seats in Mark 1 open firsts. But as the new Mark 2A stock came into service the contrast between older Mark 1 vehicles and the new stock was particularly noticeable. In fact on the East Coast Main Line passengers in the new open seconds were enjoying a much quieter ride than those in the Mark 1 open firsts. The main feature of the new FOs was the Pullman type individually adjustable seats. The first of the coaches were delivered towards the end of 1970 and were allocated to the LMR, as were the other Mark 2Cs, in substitution for Mark 1 FOs on Anglo Scottish and Euston -Manchester or Liverpool trains. Note that the BSOs had a standard seat spacing with a separate bodyshell to the BFKs, unlike the Mark 2 and 2A variants. In the early 1980s thirty of the TSOs had a seating bay removed and replaced with a counter whilst the adjacent toilet was converted to a store room, the resultant coach classified TSOT being intended to provide a buffet service on secondary services where demand did not warrant provision of more extensive catering. A portable catering trolley could be accommodated behind the counter allowing change of trains en route by catering staff. As with early Mark 2 designs several first class carriages were declassified during the mid 1980s. This included all but one of the Open Firsts, twenty-seven Corridor Firsts and six Corridor Brake Firsts. Examples of all types have been preserved as with Mark 2Bs either for static use or with the intention of main line running.

The fully air-conditioned version of the Mark 2C appeared in 1971 designated Mark 2D with initial deliveries going to the ER and later deliveries to the LMR. Five types of Mark 2D were produced, Tourist Open Second, Brake Open Second, Corridor First, Corridor Brake First and Open First. The most obvious feature was the narrow tinted windows without any opening section. Another new feature, at least as far as every day stock was concerned, was public address equipment. Of particular interest was that Mark 2D was the last type of locomotive hauled stock to be built with compartments, all subsequent stock being open. Twenty of the TSOs were converted in the early 1980s to TSOTs in the same manner as applied to the Mark 2Cs. Subsequently five of these conversions were further modified by the removal of another seating bay and fitting a proper buffet counter with boiler and microwave oven, being referred to as RMBT. These conversions were initially intended for use on the enhanced North West-South East service via Kensington Olympia introduced in 1986, however as this service dwindled they found use on other Cross Country services. The inevitable over provision of first class accommodation resulted in thirty six Open Firsts being reseated as Tourist Open Seconds in the late 1980s being initially used on the remaining Inter City locomotive hauled services emanating from Paddington, but were soon utilised on other services. The Mark 2D design was developed as the Mark 2E which was lit entirely by fluorescent tubes, but its major difference was a smaller toilet which enabled the seating capacity to be restored to that of Mark 2A and earlier types. Three Types were produced Tourist Open Second, Brake Open Second and Open First with deliveries being made to the Western and London Midland Regions. The only significant conversion to Mark IIe took place in the early 1990s when six Open First had four seats removed and a toilet replaced with a pantry, microwave oven and serving table for use on sleeping car services to & from the West Country. To date the only vehicles of Mark 2D and Mark 2E designs preserved are for use in a mainline set based at Steamtown, Carnforth and one carriage, 5809, currently being used by ABB at Derby to develop he possibility of full scale refurbishment of vehicles still in service. A considerable number of these arriages remain in service principally on Cross Country services.

The final Mark 2 design, the Mark 2F was introduced in 1973 and incorporated various features being eveloped in connection with Mark 3 vehicles. These included plastic interior panels, Inter-City 70 eats and a modified air-conditioning system. As with Mark 2E three types were built, Tourist Open econd, Brake Open Second and Open First. An early conversion was that of TSO 5970 which in 1975 vas converted to a Self Service Buffet. However this coach was surprisingly withdrawn in 1982 and old to Northern Ireland Railways, the concept presumably having not been successful. By the mid 980s the reoccurring problem of over provision of first class accommodation in the carriage fleet esulted in forty seven Open Firsts being declassified as Open Seconds, the conversion consisting of emoval of headrests from the seats and renumbering. Subsequently thirty of these had a more ubstantial conversion which included the provision of mainly unidirectional seating, power operated liding doors and improved air-conditioning system, being reclassified as Tourist Second Open to eflect the increased seating capacity of seventy four. Of the other seventeen, 3297 (6426) & 3343 5441) have been scrapped following accidents, 3403 (6450) has returned to First Class status whilst leven have been converted to Buffet Open Firsts and three have been converted to Sleeper Reception 'ars. The Buffet Open First conversion consists of the removal of sixteen seats from one end of the oach and replacing these with a Buffet unit. Thirty two of these conversions have been made, eleven tilising the above mentioned Open Seconds the remainder utilising Open Firsts. The Sleeper eception Car consists of the replacement of the existing interior with a pantry, microwave cooking acilities, seating area for passengers, telephone booth and staff toilet. Nine of these conversions have een made, three utilising the above mentioned Open Seconds the remainder utilising Open Firsts. ourteen Brake Open Seconds were converted from 1979 onwards for use as Driving Trailers initially n the Edinburgh-Glasgow Queen Street line and later on services between Edinburgh/Glasgow and lorth East Scotland, transferring to East Anglian Inter City services when they were ousted by Class 58 'Sprinters' in Scotland. The majority of Mark 2F coaches remain in service on various Inter City randed services around England and Scotland.

PULLMAN FIRST WITH KITCHEN PK

Lot No.: 30755. **Builder:** Derby. **Ordered:** 11/1964 **Completed:** 04/1966.
Diagram: 15. **New diagram:** AP101. **Seats:** 18F. **Bogies:** B4.

504	Steamtown Railway Centre, Carnforth	MANC99678 'THE WHITE ROSE
506	Steamtown Railway Centre, Carnforth	MANC99679 'THE RED ROSE

PULLMAN PARLOUR FIRST PC

Lot No.: 30754. **Builder:** Derby. **Ordered:** 11/1964 **Completed:** 04/1966.
Diagram: 78. **New diagram:** AQ101. **Seats:** 36F. **Bogies:** B4.

546	Steamtown Railway Centre, Carnforth	MANC99670 'CITY OF MANCHESTER
548	Steamtown Railway Centre, Carnforth	MANC99671 'ELIZABETHAN
549	Steamtown Railway Centre, Carnforth	MANC99672 'PRINCE RUPERT
550	Steamtown Railway Centre, Carnforth	MANC99673 'GOLDEN ARROW
551	Steamtown Railway Centre, Carnforth	MANC99674 'CALEDONIAN
552	Steamtown Railway Centre, Carnforth	MANC99675 'SOUTHERN BELLE
553	Steamtown Railway Centre, Carnforth	MANC99676 'KING ARTHUR

PULLMAN BRAKE FIRST PE

Lot No.: 30753. **Builder:** Derby. **Ordered:** 11/1964 **Completed:** 04/1966.
Diagram: 85. **New diagram:** AR101. **Seats:** 30F. **Bogies:** B4.

586	Steamtown Railway Centre, Carnforth	MANC99677 'TALISMAN

OPEN FIRST FC

Lot No.: 30810. **Builder:** Derby. **Ordered:** 05/1969 **Completed:** 12/1970.
Diagram: 80. **New diagram:** AD104. **Seats:** 42F. **Bogies:** B4.

Mark 2C. Declassified to SO in 1982/3, new diagram AD205.

3152	6411 DB977547	London Underground LTD.	
3155	6415	Steamtown Railway Centre, Carnforth	Stored at RTC, Derb
3161	6414	North Yorkshire Moors Railway	
3167	6400	North Yorkshire Moors Railway	
3168	6412	Midland Railway Centre	

3152 converted to a Brake Force Runner in 1987.

Lot No.: 30843. **Builder:** Derby. **Ordered:** 04/1972 **Completed:** 02/1973.
Diagram: 82. **New diagram:** AD106. **Seats:** 42F. **Bogies:** B4.
Mark 2D.

3260	Steamtown Railway Centre, Carnforth

TOURIST OPEN SECOND TSC

Lot No.: 30751. **Builder:** Derby. **Ordered:** 10/1964 **Completed:** 06/1967.
Diagram: 88. **New diagram:** AC205. **Seats:** 64S. **Bogies:** B4.

5125	Watercress Line	
5136	Bodmin Steam Railway	
5141	Watercress Line	
5145	Caledonian Railway	
5149	Strathspey Railway	SR No. 1
5171	Watercress Line	
5175	The Railway Age, Crewe	
5181	Bodmin Steam Railway	
5188	Caledonian Railway	
5199	East Lancashire Railway	
5200	Watercress Line	
5211	Great Eastern Railway	
5216	East Lancashire Railway	
5219	Great Eastern Railway	

220	Llangollen Railway	
222	Watercress Line	
224	Ystwth Valley Railway	Stored at Steamtown, Carnforth
228	Strathspey Railway	SR No. 107

OPEN SECOND   SO

ot No.: 30752. **Builder**: Derby.   **Ordered**: 10/1964   **Completed**: 10/1966.
iagram: 87. **New diagram**: AD203.   **Seats**: 48S.   **Bogies**: B4.
255 Air-braked.

229	Northampton & Lamport Railway	
235	Peak Railway, Darley Dale	
236	Watercress Line	
237	Watercress Line	
238	East Lancashire Railway	
239	Watercress Line	
241	Greater Manchester Museum of Science & Industry	
243	Watercress Line	
249	Watercress Line	
255	Rail UK Ltd	Stored at Blackpool CS

TOURIST OPEN SECOND   TSO

ot No.: 30776. **Builder**: Derby.   **Ordered**: 01/1967   **Completed**: 04/1968.
iagram: 86. **New diagram**: AC206.   **Seats**: 64S.   **Bogies**: B4.
lark 2A. 5344 restored with Vacuum brakes.

273	024996	MoD CAD Kineton	
299		Steamtown Railway Centre, Carnforth	WDS99321 Carnforth Maroon Set
310		Donnington Park Race Track	Hospitality Suite
324		Buckinghamshire Railway Centre	Body only remains
333		Midland Railway Centre	
344		West Somerset Railway	

ot No.: 30787. **Builder**: Derby.   **Ordered**: 05/1967   **Completed**: 12/1968.
iagram: 86. **New diagram**: AC206.   **Seats**: 64S.   **Bogies**: B4.
lark 2A.

| 391 | | Rail UK Ltd | Stored at Blackpool CS |
| 421 | 024995 | MoD CAD Kineton | |

ot No.: 30791. **Builder**: Derby.   **Ordered**: 11/1967   **Completed**: 09/1969.
iagram: 105. **New diagram**: AC207. **Seats**: 62S.   **Bogies**: B4.
lark 2B.

438	Cheriton Exhibition Centre	
449	The Railway Age, Crewe	Stored at Basford Hall Yard
452	Pleasure Island, Lytham St. Annes	
453	Rail UK Ltd	Stored at Blackpool CS
455	National Railway Museum	
461	Midland Railway Centre	
462	The Railway Age, Crewe	Stored at Basford Hall Yard
463	Rail UK Ltd	Stored at Blackpool CS
464	The Railway Age, Crewe	Stored at Basford Hall Yard
476	Ridings Railtours	
487	Rail UK Ltd	Stored at Blackpool CS
494	The Railway Age, Crewe	Stored at Basford Hall Yard

ot No.: 30795. **Builder**: Derby.   **Ordered**: 05/1969   **Completed**: 11/1970.
iagram: 106. **New diagram**: AC208. **Seats**: 62S.   **Bogies**: B4.
lark 2C. 5547/58/63/68/5603 converted to TSOT in 1980-1, new diagram AG201, seats 54S.

524	Eureka, National Childrens Museum	
526	East Lancashire Railway	Half of body removed & grounded
533	Ridings Railtours	
536	Great Eastern Railway	

5541		Cheriton Exhibition Centre	
5547	6501	RFS Engineering Ltd, Doncaster	
5558	6521	RFS Engineering Ltd, Doncaster	
5563	6527	RFS Engineering Ltd, Doncaster	
5568	6523	Rail UK Ltd	Stored at Blackpool C
5569		Rail UK Ltd	Stored at Blackpool C
5574		Ridings Railtours	
5585		Ridings Railtours	
5586		ABB Transportation Ltd., Derby Carriage Works	
5590		East Lancashire Railway	
5595		Ridings Railtours	
5600		Steamtown Railway Centre, Carnforth	WDS99322 Carnforth Maroon S
5603	6500	RFS Engineering Ltd, Doncaster	

Lot No.: 30822. **Builder:** Derby. **Ordered:** 10/1969 **Completed:** 01/1972.
Diagram: 107. **New diagram:** AC209. **Seats:** 62S. **Bogies:** B4.

Mark 2D.

5642	Steamtown Railway Centre, Carnforth	
5645	Steamtown Railway Centre, Carnforth	
5704	Steamtown Railway Centre, Carnforth	WDS99323 Carnforth Maroon S
5709	Steamtown Railway Centre, Carnforth	
5712	Steamtown Railway Centre, Carnforth	
5714	Steamtown Railway Centre, Carnforth	WDS99324 Carnforth Maroon S
5727	Steamtown Railway Centre, Carnforth	WDS99325 Carnforth Maroon S

Lot No.: 30837. **Builder:** Derby. **Ordered:** 03/1971 **Completed:** 06/1972.
Diagram: 108. **New diagram:** AC210. **Seats:** 64S. **Bogies:** B4.

Mark 2E.

5756	Steamtown Railway Centre, Carnforth

Lot No.: 30844. **Builder:** Derby. **Ordered:** 04/1972 **Completed:** 02/1973.
Diagram: 108. **New diagram:** AC210. **Seats:** 64S. **Bogies:** B4.
Mark 2E.

5809	ABB Transportation Ltd., Derby Carriage Works

OPEN BRAKE SECOND BSC

Lot No.: 30757. **Builder:** Derby. **Ordered:** 04/1965 **Completed:** 08/1966.
Diagram: 185. **New diagram:** AE203. **Seats:** 31S. **Bogies:** B4.

9383/89/401 converted to BSOT, new diagram AE211, seats 23S in 1986. 9400 Air-braked.

9382		East Lancashire Railway
9383	9102	Northampton & Lamport Railway
9384		Buckinghamshire Railway Centre
9389	9103	The Great Central (Nottingham) Ltd.
9390		Watercress Line
9391		East Lancashire Railway
9392		South Devon Railway
9393		Great Eastern Railway
9394		Peak Railway, Darley Dale
9396		Llangollen Railway
9400		Errol Station Museum, Tayside
9401	9104	Watercress Line
9409		Great Eastern Railway
9410		Chinnor & Princess Risborough Railway

Lot No.: 30798. **Builder:** Derby. **Ordered:** 05/1969 **Completed:** 06/1970.
Diagram: 186. **New diagram:** AE205. **Seats:** 31S. **Bogies:** B4.
Mark 2C.

9440		Rail UK Ltd	Stored at Blackpool C
9444		Ridings Railtours	Stored at Norwic
9448		Rail UK Ltd	Stored at Blackpool C

CORRIDOR FIRST FK

Lot No.: 30550. **Builder:** Swindon.   **Ordered:** 11/1958   **Completed:** 01/1963.
Diagram: 120.   **Seats:** 42F.   **Bogies:** B4.
Prototype Mark Two coach.

13252	National Railway Museum	Stored at MoD Kineton

Lot No.: 30774. **Builder:** Derby.   **Ordered:** 01/1967   **Completed:** 06/1968.
Diagram: 123. **New diagram:** AA106.   **Seats:** 42F.   **Bogies:** B4.

Mark 2A. 13454/62 declassified to SK in 1985, new diagram AA206, 19462 reclassified to FK in 1986. 13435/36/37/38/40/42/44/46/47/50 Vacuum-braked.

13435	Pleasure Island, Lytham St. Annes	
13436	Chinnor & Princess Risborough Railway	
13437	Midland Railway Centre	
13438	Gloucestershire-Warwickshire Railway	
13440	East Lancashire Railway	
13442	Gloucestershire-Warwickshire Railway	
13444	South Yorkshire Railway	Stored at Basford Hall Yard
13446	Great Eastern Railway	
13447	Great Eastern Railway	
13450	Watercress Line	
13453	Pleasure Island, Lytham St. Annes	
13454 19454	Gloucestershire-Warwickshire Railway	
13462 19462 13462	The Railway Age, Crewe	Stored at Basford Hall Yard

Lot No.: 30785. **Builder:** Derby.   **Ordered:** 05/1967   **Completed:** 11/1968.
Diagram: 124. **New diagram:** AA106.   **Seats:** 42F.   **Bogies:** B4.

Mark 2A. 13464 declassified to SK in 1985, new diagram AA206. 13470/74/75 Vacuum-braked.

13464 19464	Gloucestershire-Warwickshire Railway	
13467	The Railway Age, Crewe	Stored at Basford Hall Yard
13470	Rogart Station	
13474	East Lancashire Railway	
13475	Watercress Line	

Lot No.: 30789. **Builder:** Derby.   **Ordered:** 11/1967   **Completed:** 06/1969.
Diagram: 124. **New diagram:** AA107.   **Seats:** 42F.   **Bogies:** B4.

Mark 2B. 13479/84/504 declassified to SK in 1985, new diagram AA207, 19479 reclassified to FK in 1986.

13479 19479 13479	The Railway Age, Crewe	Stored at Basford Hall Yard
13482	The Railway Age, Crewe	Stored at Basford Hall Yard
13484 19484 DB977528	Midland Railway Centre	
13487 DB977529	North Downs Steam Railway	
13502	CAD Bramley Militay Railway	
13504 19504	Lancastrian Carriage & Wagon, Heysham	

19484/13487 converted to RTC Brake Force Runners in 1987.

Lot No.: 30797. **Builder:** Derby.   **Ordered:** 05/1969   **Completed:** 07/1970.
Diagram: 125. **New diagram:** AA108.   **Seats:** 42F.   **Bogies:** B4.
Mark 2C. 13540 declassified to SK in 1985, new diagram AA208.

13514	CAD Bramley Militay Railway
13540 19540	Watercress Line

CORRIDOR BRAKE FIRST BFK

Lot No.: 30756. **Builder:** Derby.   **Ordered:** 04/1965   **Completed:** 09/1966.
Diagram: 162. **New diagram:** AB102.   **Seats:** 24F.   **Bogies:** B4.

14031 17031	Avon Valley Railway	Stored at Long Marston
14041 17041	Didcot Railway Centre	CHEL99141 71000 Support Coach
14055 17055	The Great Central (Nottingham) Ltd.	

Lot No.: 30775. **Builder:** Derby.   **Ordered:** 01/1967   **Completed:** 02/1968.

Diagram: 163.   **New diagram:** AB103.   **Seats:** 24F.   **Bogies:** B4.

Mark 2A. Vacuum-braked.

14059 17059   Caledonian Railway
14060 17060   Peak Railway, Darley Dale

Lot No.: 30786. **Builder:** Derby.   **Ordered:** 05/1967   **Completed:** 09/1968.
Diagram: 163.   **New diagram:** AB103.   **Seats:** 24F.   **Bogies:** B4.

Mark 2A. 17092 declassified to BSK in 1985, new diagram AB204, subsequently reclassified to a BFK in 1988. 14092/101 Vacuum-braked.

14092 17092 35501 17092   Bodmin Steam Railway
14096 17096   Venice-Simplon Orient Express   Ocean Liner Express set
14101 17101   Strathspey Railway   SR No. 120
14102 17102   Steamtown Railway Centre, Carnforth MANC99680 'ATTENDANTS CAR'

14096 is on loan from South Western Train Unit.

Lot No.: 30796. **Builder:** Derby.   **Ordered:** 05/1969   **Completed:** 01/1970.
Diagram: 165.   **New diagram:** AB105.   **Seats:** 24F.   **Bogies:** B4.
Mark 2C. 17122 declassified to BSK in 1992.

14122 17122 35506   Rail UK Ltd   Stored at Blackpool CS
14124 17124   South Otterington Station

Lot No.: 30823. **Builder:** Derby.   **Ordered:** 10/1969   **Completed:** 01/1972.
Diagram: 166.   **New diagram:** AB106.   **Seats:** 24F.   **Bogies:** B4.
Mark 2D.

14168 17168   Steamtown Railway Centre, Carnforth WDS99319 Carnforth Maroon Set

MARK 3 SLEEPING CARS

The Mark 3 design first appeared in 1972, the principle difference from Mark 2s being the increased length of 75' and the fitting of BT10 bogies and other than a few vehicles scrapped following accidents or research use all survive. However, as all the preserved examples are sleeping cars built in the early 1980s it is only this derivative that is considered here.

During the 1970s it was becoming increasingly apparent that a decision had to be taken regarding the replacement of the ageing fleet of Mark 1 sleeping cars then in use. The first tentative step at developing a replacement took place in 1976 when a prototype Mark 3 sleeping car was ordered. The order was however subsequently cancelled. During 1978 further studies took place as to the viability of building new vehicles, refurbishing existing vehicles or withdrawing from the sleeper market entirely. The decision influenced by the disastrous Taunton sleeper fire of that year came out in favour of building new vehicles. Thus in 1979 an order was placed for 236 new sleeper cars, subsequently reduced to 210. Two types were built both utilising the same bodyshell, one with thirteen sleeping compartments and the other with twelve sleeping compartments and an attendants compartment. All sleeping compartments have folding upper berths thus giving greatest flexibility of use allowing each individual compartment to be used for first or second class passengers as required. The sleeping compartments were designed to give a light comfortable appearance and when the upper berth is folded away it blends into the partition. A vanity unit with wash basin and hot and cold taps was provided and the partition opposite the berths incorporated a hanging wardrobe. A communicating door allows two adjacent compartments to be made into a family unit. Berth light switches, an attendant call push button and berth environmental controls are located by the bedhead. The air-conditioning system was designed to provide individually controlled compartment environment to suit the occupants, the compartment temperature being selected by a variable thermostat offering a range of 60°-70°F. As on other Mark 3 vehicles compartment cooling and basic heating was provided from an air conditioning module mounted within the underskirt. A most noteable feature, certainly influenced by the Taunton fire, was the fitting of smoke detectors in each compartment, the vestibule ends and in the air-conditioning delivery and recirculation ducts. The detection of a fire resulted in an audible warning and also a visual indication on a panel at the end of the coach and in the attendants compartment. Waste water was fed into storage tanks which could be emptied either by gravity or by vacuum extraction.

The reality was that as the cars were being built the market for overnight sleeper travel was declining, one major influencing factor being the higher speeds of day time services with earlier provincial morning departures and later evening arrivals, thus reducing the need for overnight travel. Indeed the order was further curtailed when the final two cars to be built were transferred to the Royal Train fleet and fitted out accordingly. As no attempt was made to develop new long distance routes the fleet of 208 cars has never thus been fully employed and it was not surprising therefore that six cars severely damaged in the 1984 accident at Morpeth were scrapped, the cars being 10505/24/28, 10652/59, 10733, with no replacements being ordered. Attempts to find work for these expensive and surplus carriages included the transfer of several for use by the Inter City Charter Train Unit whom predominately utilised them on land cruise operations. Even after Danish Railways had borrowed ten cars there was still spare capacity in the fleet, thus several cars were put to store having seen little use. Nine of these ended up in secure storage at MoD Bicester were they had their BT10 bogies replaced with accommodation bogies and it is from these that the majority of those so far purchased have come. However they are only suitable for static use and it is believed the new owners intend to use them for volunteer accommodation, presumably running their complex systems from a shore supply. ABB at Derby have however purchased a car complete with BT10 bogies as part of its development program and it will be interesting to see what use they put it. Even now there remains considerable over-capacity in the remaining fleet and even after the sale of the ten cars to Danish Railways, the sale of three cars to SIG in Switzerland, the conversion of five cars to generator vans for European Passenger Services overnight trains and the transfer of one car to departmental stock, twenty seven cars remain stored.

CONVERTIBLE SLEEPING CAR WITH PANTRY SLEP

Lot No.: 30960. **Builder:** Derby 1983. **Ordered:** 08/1979 **Completed:** 09/1983.
Diagram: 7. **New diagram:** AS403. **Bogies:** BT10.

12 compartments with a fixed lower berth and a hinged upper berth, plus an attendants compartment. BT10 bogies removed by British Rail, now mounted on accommodation bogies.

10509	Didcot Railway Centre	
10511	Colne Valley Railway	
10517	Llangollen Railway	Stored at COD Bicester Military Rly
10518	Gloucestershire-Warwickshire Railway	
10521	Llangollen Railway	Stored at COD Bicester Military Rly
10525	North Norfolk Railway	
10608	Llangollen Railway	Stored at BRML Wolverton Works
10611	Llangollen Railway	
10618	Bodmin Steam Railway	
10619	Swanage Railway	To be confirmed

CONVERTIBLE SLEEPING CAR   SLE

Lot No.: 30961. **Builder:** Derby 1984. **Ordered:** 08/1979 **Completed:** 06/1984.
Diagram: 6. **New diagram:** AS404. **Bogies:** BT10.

13 compartments with a fixed lower berth and a hinged upper berth.

10671	ABB Transportation Ltd., Derby Carriage Works

NON PASSENGER CARRYING COACHING STOCK

A peculiarity is that the forty-one Kitchen Cars built are classified under this heading, but mention of these however has been given previously in the narrative concerning catering cars. Thus the only preserved example, 80030, is listed in this section.

To date only one travelling post office van has been preserved, this being a sorting van, 80307 on the Severn Valley Railway. This was one of only three such vans not built at the time with provision for fitting arms or nets. As with Gangwayed Full Brakes detailed below the design and construction methods were consistent with that of the passenger carrying types being built at the time. Few travelling post office vans have been withdrawn to date and as travelling post offices are set to continue for many years to come it is unlikely that any further vans will be preserved in the short term.

The more obvious non-passenger carrying vehicles were not given the priority of building that was afforded to the other standard coaches. Gangwayed Full Brakes however were included in the original series of designs and confirmed with the construction methods and specifications of the conventional passenger carrying types of the time although they were constructed on the short 57' frames. Examples from the majority of lots have been preserved with the opportunity existing for further examples to be preserved in the future. The majority of those preserved are used for storage or museum coaches, however 80736 on the West Somerset Railway and 80776 on the Severn Valley Railway have been specifically rebuilt for the use of disabled passengers. Although several major modifications were made to Gangwayed Full Brakes, a process which continues, the majority of those preserved were never modified. 80867, 81305 & 81533 are however examples of the many that were rebogied with B4 bogies and fitted with air brakes in order to allow them to run at up to 100 mph with more modern passenger carrying types. The most noteable Gangwayed Passenger Brake so far preserved is 81039 at the Gloucestershire-Warwickshire Railway. This is recorded by the Southern Region as being specially modified and was confined to working between Portsmouth, Eastleigh and Southampton.

Other types of non passenger carrying coaching stock did not reflect the design of passenger carrying types being devoid of corridor connections and with interiors uncluttered. The shape of British Railways thinking was seen in 1955-6 with the production of two prototypes. The longer of the two, 86500, was designated as a General Utility Van, though it had the features usually associated with a carriage truck. The standard short (57') underframe was employed with the addition of a hand brake applied externally by a wheel mounted centrally below the solebar. The body was to a much smaller cross section with flat steel panels on a steel frame and a lower flatter roof. End doors allowed vehicles to be driven directly into the van and the double fold of the 'cupboard' doors was arranged such that they could be opened even if a second similar van was coupled, so that a complete car carrying train could be loaded without shunting. This has recently been preserved and is stored at Basford Hall Yard, Crewe due to lack of capacity at The Railway Age, Crewe. Operating staff suggested more side doors would be an advantage and consequently production examples were given a third pair of doors each side. Examples have been preserved from all but one of the production lots so far with the opportunity of filling the gap at a later date existing. In later years the basic vans have undergone various significant modifications. To date only three of these converted vans have been preserved, these being from the twenty nine vans redesigned Newspaper Van in 1985, these had the end doors sealed and tables fitted for newspaper sorting. Not surprisingly the need for these ceased when the transportation of newspapers by rail ceased in 1988. As with the Gangwayed brakes the majority of GUVs preserved are used for storage purposes.

The second prototype, 94100, designated Covered Carriage Truck was virtually a half length version of the GUV. A four wheeled chassis was fitted having a 20' wheelbase. This shorter length meant that circular buffers could be fitted. The buffer guides of this and the GUVs had small castings on their top surfaces on which the fold down sections of the end doors could be supported. Regrettably, following a period of departmental use this prototype was sold for scrap. The increasing size of cars prompted a modified production version: two pairs of side doors and an extra window in each side were coupled with an increase in length to 37' through only a 3'6'' increase in wheel base. Although designated Covered Carriage Truck, the main use of these vehicles was for general parcels traffic. Examples of all the production lots have been preserved, many after a period of departmental use.

Three other types of four wheeled van were also constructed which could just as easily be defined as freight stock, these being Insulated Fish Vans, Fruit D's and Horse Boxes. The insulated Fish Vans were, basically, a pre-nationalisation design continuing the LNER tradition of express fish delivery from the many East Coast ports it served. Again they were wooden bodies and roofed though with double skin walls, heavily insulated. The body was 21'8'' on a 15' wheel base. The service for which these were designed involved considerable long distance, relatively high speed running and the original of axle boxes proved unsatisfactory. When the axle boxes were replaced by roller bearing types, this was marked by a large blue spot on the body side which gave them an instant nickname. Sadly changes in the fishing industry led to a very rapid traffic loss long before these vehicles were life expired. Some were transferred to freight stock but many, initially about 600, stayed on the passenger book. These were internally refurbished and painted in plain blue livery as parcels vans. In this guise labelled SPV and often with Express Parcels branding they put in more years work than they had as fish vans. Examples of three of the four lots built have been preserved, several of these however are incomplete.

Two lots of 'Fruit D's were constructed to a Great Western design at Swindon with 28'6'' wooden body and roof and a four wheel 18' wheel base. These owed nothing to current passenger stock design. One hundred and fifteen were built, but they had a fairly short life in a revenue earning capacity being withdrawn at the same time as the last of the GWR number series vehicles. They were popular departmental vehicles and many survived several more years. Examples of both lots are preserved many of which had seen departmental use prior to preservation. Increasingly these are being cosmetically restored and used in demonstration freight trains on which their design disguises their modernity.

The Horsebox design of British Railways allowed maximum use of Mark I coach building techniques Body work was to the C1 outline, incorporating standard size window units and doors but the whole vehicle was narrower to give greater operating flexibility and the roof needed a much less elliptical shape. The underframe was similar to, though rather shorter than, that of the four wheeled CCTs The rapid traffic loss caused them all to be withdrawn by the winter of 1971 after only 13 years in service. Fortunately several have been preserved albeit in the majority of cases after a period of departmental use when they were converted to mobile heating vans, thus giving an insight into former extensive traffic now completely lost from the railways.

The two other preserved non passenger carrying coaching stock vehicles are something of interlopers The first of these is a Bogie Covered Carriage Truck, 96202. This was one of four constructed in 196 utilising the frames and bogies of Gresley Composites. The new bodies had two pairs of side doors end doors, and, internally, folding shelves and wheelbars for car restraint. They were boldly lettered 'Anglo-Scottish Car Carrier' and used on the Kings Cross-Edinburgh train of that name. The preserved example has recently been externally restored in this style, it itself being a lucky survivor by way of seeing many years departmental service on the southern region. The second interloper is Exhibition Van 99629. This appears here by virtue of the rules explained in the introduction being one of five exhibition vans converted at Stewarts Lane Carriage & Wagon Workshop which was issued with new lot number. Interestingly it was originally one of the Corridor Seconds built with Commonwealth bogies which was rebogied by the southern region gaining BR Mark I bogies whilst its more modern bogies were used on an older carriage. It is currently stored at Long Marston along with several other carriages destined for the Avon Valley Railway.

KITCHEN CAR RK

Lot No.: 30585. **Builder:** Charles Roberts. **Ordered:** 02/1959 **Completed:** 03/1963.
Diagram: 702. **New diagram:** AK501. **Bogies:** BR Mk 1 h.d.
Rebogied with B5s.

M0030 Caledonian Railway

POST OFFICE SORTING VAN POS

Lot No.: 30487. **Builder:** Wolverton. **Ordered:** 06/1957 **Completed:** 11/1959.
Diagram: 721. **New diagram:** NS502. **Bogies:** BR Mk.1 h.d.

M0307 Severn Valley Railway

GANGWAYED FULL BRAKE BG

Lot No.: 30009. **Builder:** Derby. **Ordered:** 12/1950 **Completed:** 04/1953.
Diagram: 711. **New diagram:** NA501. **Bogies:** BR1.

M0501	Chinnor & Princess Risborough Railway
M0509 041997	Llangollen Railway
M0515	Pleasure Island, Lytham St. Annes
M0518	Llangollen Railway

Lot No.: 30039. **Builder:** Derby. **Ordered:** 03/1951 **Completed:** 10/1954.
Diagram: 711. **New diagram:** NA501. **Bogies:** BR1.

M0566 Diesel Traction Group, Old Oak Common

Lot No.: 30040. **Builder:** Wolverton. **Ordered:** 03/1951 **Completed:** 01/1955.
Diagram: 711. **New diagram:** NA501. **Bogies:** BR1.

M0580	Gloucestershire-Warwickshire Railway
M0590	Midland Railway Centre
M0591	Keighley & Worth Valley Railway

Lot No.: 30046. **Builder:** York. **Ordered:** 04/1951 **Completed:** 09/1954.
Diagram: 711. **New diagram:** NA501. **Bogies:** BR1.

M0653	R. Oakley, Brentford Rubbish Terminal	Stored at BRML Wolverton Works
M0654	Dean Forest Railway	
M0665	COD Bicester Military Railway	

Lot No.: 30136. **Builder:** Metro-Cammell. **Ordered:** 01/1954 **Completed:** 10/1955.
Diagram: 711. **New diagram:** NA501. **Bogies:** BR1.

| M0686 | Midland Railway Centre |
| M0702 | Bodmin Steam Railway |

Lot No.: 30140. **Builder:** BRCW. **Ordered:** 01/1954 **Completed:** 01/1956.
Diagram: 711. **New diagram:** NA501. **Bogies:** BR1.

M0736	West Somerset Railway	
M0741	Llangollen Railway	Rebuilt as Disabled Coach 'ENID'
M0742	West Somerset Railway	
M0753	Watercress Line	
M0776	Severn Valley Railway	Rebuilt as Disabled Coach
M0782	Midland Railway Centre	
M0785	Colne Valley Railway	
M0792	Colne Valley Railway	
M0796	North Yorkshire Moors Railway	
M0797	Tintern Parva Station Museum	

Lot No.: 30144. **Builder:** Cravens. **Ordered:** 01/1954 **Completed:** 12/1955.
Diagram: 711. **New diagram:** NA501. **Bogies:** BR1.

M0830 converted to Exhibition Van, diagram NY524 in 1983.

| M0827 | The Railway Age, Crewe |
| M0830 99650 | Embsay Steam Railway |

Lot No.: 30162. **Builder:** Pressed Steel. **Ordered:** 04/1954 **Completed:** 09/1957.
Diagram: 711. **New diagram:** NA501. **Bogies:** BR1.
80867 rebogied with B4s and dual braked.

80867 92004 92904	Venice-Simplon Orient Express	VSOE99554 Ocean Liner Express se
80892	Swindon & Cricklade Railway	
80905	South Yorkshire Railway	
80963 041570	RFS Engineering Ltd, Doncaster	

Lot No.: 30173. **Builder:** York. **Ordered:** 05/1954 **Completed:** 07/1956.
Diagram: 711. **New diagram:** NA501. **Bogies:** BR1.

80972	West Somerset Railway
80993	East Lancashire Railway
81013 84013	Severn Valley Railway

Lot No.: 30224. **Builder:** Cravens. **Ordered:** 03/1955 **Completed:** 06/1956.
Diagram: 711. **New diagram:** NA501. **Bogies:** BR1.

81039 was specially modified by the Southern Region and was dedicated for use in the Portsmouth and Southampton areas.

81020 84020	Midland Railway Centre
81025 84025	Southall Railway Centre
81031 84031	Northampton & Lamport Railway
81033 84033	North Norfolk Railway
81039 84039	Gloucestershire-Warwickshire Railway

Lot No.: 30228. **Builder:** Metro-Cammell. **Ordered:** 04/1955 **Completed:** 05/1958.
Diagram: 711. **New diagram:** NA501. **Bogies:** BR1.

81062	Rainhill Library Museum
81101 84101	Watercress Line
81107 84107	Llangollen Railway
81144 84144	Midland Railway Centre
81146 84146 024967	Swanage Railway
81156 84156	East Somerset Railway

Lot No.: 30323. **Builder:** Pressed Steel. **Ordered:** 11/1955 **Completed:** 10/1957.
Diagram: 711. **New diagram:** NA501. **Bogies:** BR1.

81305 rebogied with B4s and air braked.

81269 84269	North Norfolk Railway
81295	East Anglian Railway Museum
81305 92090 92990	Gloucestershire-Warwickshire Railway

Lot No.: 30400. **Builder:** Pressed Steel. **Ordered:** 05/1956 **Completed:** 01/1958.
Diagram: 711. **New diagram:** NA501. **Bogies:** BR1.

81343 84343	Great Central Railway
81428 84428	Battlefield Steam Railway

Lot No.: 30484. **Builder:** Pressed Steel. **Ordered:** 05/1957 **Completed:** 03/1958.
Diagram: 711. **New diagram:** NA501. **Bogies:** BR1.

81533 rebogied with B4s and Air-braked

81507 84507 041974	Colne Valley Railway
81533 92158	Peak Railway, Darley Dale
81554 84554	Peak Railway, Darley Dale

GENERAL UTILITY VAN   GUV

Lot No.: 30417. **Builder:** Pressed Steel. **Ordered:** 03/1958 **Completed:** 01/1959.
Diagram: 811. **New diagram:** NI501. **Bogies:** BR2.

93350 converted to Newspaper Van in 1985, new diagram NL502.

86105 93105	Severn Valley Railway
86178 93178	Birmingham Railway Museum
86183 93183	Peak Railway, Darley Dale
86226 93226	Spa Valley Railway
86253 93253	The Railway Age, Crewe

Above: Pullman Car 'ARIES', a parlour first with kitchen was photographed on 24th January 1987 at the Yew Tree Inn, Thornham, Rochdale, Lancashire. It was built in 1952 at Preston Park for the 'Golden Arrow' service, and still retains Gresley bogies. *Peter Hall*

Below: 1013 photographed at Oxenhope on 24th September 1994 is an example of a second class restaurant car. It was one of the first Mark 1 open coaches to be built and has no centre doors. It originally had 48 loose chairs and would have been coupled adjacent to an RK or an RF. The Keighley and Worth Valley Railway have converted it into a TSO with 62 seats, but it still has its 'Restaurant Car' branding. *Peter Fox*

Below: The most numerous type of catering vehicle was the RB which consisted of a kitchen, buffet bar and a buffet seating area with loose chairs. These vehicles were later refurbished with fluorescent lighting and fixed polypropylene chairs and classified RBR. Many RUs were also converted similarly and these were also classified RBR. 1695 is seen at Leicester North bearing a roofboard which states 'GREAT CENTRAL GRIDDLE CAR SERVICE', although it is not actually a griddle car.   *Peter Fox*

Left: For services where a large number of meals had to be served, the RKB was developed. These vehicles are kitchen cars with the addition of a buffet counter and have no seats. An RUO or an FO would normally be marshalled adjacent to the kitchen end. 1525, carrying the short-lived 'NE' prefix is seen at Leicester North, Great Central Railway on 9th October 1994 on the 'Silver Jubilee' Sunday lunch special. Two FOs were marshalled adjacent to this vehicle for dining passengers (see p. 68).

Peter Fox

For services which required only light refreshments the RMB or miniature buffet car was developed. This was basically a TSO with a quarter of the seating accommodation (16 seats) removed to provide a buffet bar. Another 8 seats were replaced by a lockable store in later builds and the earlier vehicles were modified retrospectively. The KWVR's 1836 in BR maroon livery is seen at Keighley (above) waiting to depart for Oxenhope. *Peter Fox*

The photograph below shows the buffet area of 1836, with stewardesses Alison and Denise waiting to serve passengers from what the KWVR claim is the only RMB in the country which serves hand-pumped real ale. *Peter Fox*

1806 (facing page bottom) is one of the earlier batch of RMBs that were built without store cupboards and modified retrospectively. It is in SR green livery and is seen at Ropley on the Watercress Line.

Chris Wilson

FO 3042 in use as a dining car on the 'Silver Jubilee' referred to on p. 66. This vehicle has been rebogied with B4s. The adjacent vehicle 3079 is one of a batch of 5 which were the first BR vehicles to receive Commonwealth bogies. *Peter Fox*

A large number of Mark 2 vehicles have recently been bought for preservation. SO 5235 is seen at the Peak Railway, Darley Dale on 2nd October 1994. It will presumably be used as a dining car in future. *Peter Fox*

TSO 4751 in use as a restaurant at the Marsden Rattler, South Shields. *Peter Hall*

BSO 9316 painted in chocolate and cream livery at Leicester North, Great Central Railway on 9th October 1994. This coach has been modified for use by disabled passengers. *Peter Fox*

Another two Peak Railway vehicles. Mark 2 BSO No. 9394 is seen above. This vehicle has first class seat spacing, as the same bodyshells were used for these vehicles as for the Mark 2 BFKs.. Mark 1 CK No. 16155 is shown below. *Peter Fox (2)*

Above: SK 26049 now at the Peak Railway, Darley Dale is one of nine vehicles originally bought fo the abortive main line 'Trains for Pleasure' set. All four SKs bought for this set are at the Peak Railway
Peter Fo

Below: BSK 34947 on the Watercress Line in SR green livery on 9th October 1994 bearing the rathe optimistic roofboards 'WATERLOO SOUTHAMPTON BOURNEMOUTH'. *Chris Wilsor*

above: The Keighley and Worth Valley Railway is one of the few railways operating suburban coaches. Lavatory composite (CL) No. 43003 is seen at Keighley on 24th September 1994. *Peter Fox*

BG No. 81343 in carmine & cream livery at Leicester North on 9th October 1994 where it is used as a booking office. *Peter Fox*

GUV 86183 in an odd faded red and white livery at Darley Dale on 2nd October 1994. *Peter Fox*

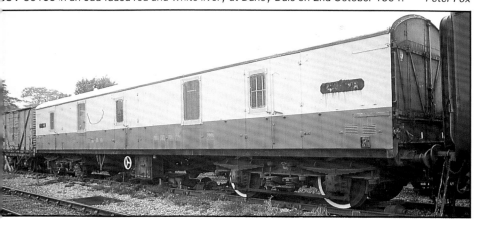

Above: These fish vans with roller bearings were passenger train-rated and carried a blue spot t denote this. Many were later reclassified SPV (special parcels van). 87582 is seen restored to origina condition at Oxenhope on 24th September. *Peter Fo*

Below: The enthusiast in search of preserved coaching stock vehicles has to travel far and wide t seek out his prey. Here two 'FRUIT D's built to a BR lots, 92047 and 92083 have ended up as grounde bodies in use as pigsties at Ashtree lodge; Chipping Warden near Banbury, Northants. *Peter Ha*

6283 93283	East Lancashire Railway	Numbered 93418
6350 93350 94066	South Yorkshire Railway	
6380 93380	Midland Railway Centre	
6383 93383	South Yorkshire Railway	
6450 93450	Buckinghamshire Railway Centre	
6460 93460	Watercress Line	
6470 93470	South Yorkshire Railway	

ot No.: 30188. **Builder:** York.   **Ordered:** 08/1954   **Completed:** 02/1956.
iagram: 810.   **Bogies:** BR2.

'rototype with two sets of doors each side.

| 6500 93500 DB977442 | The Railway Age, Crewe | Stored at Basford Hall Yard |

:onverted to CM&EE Stores Van in 1986.

ot No.: 30402. **Builder:** York/Glasgow.   **Ordered:** 07/1956   **Completed:** 07/1960.
iagram: 811.   **New diagram:** NI501.   **Bogies:** BR2.

6533 93533 024954	The Railway Age, Crewe	
6545 93545	North Yorkshire Moors Railway	
6558 93558	Orient Express Restaurant, Elsenham	¾ of body remains
6565 93565	South Yorkshire Railway	
6568 93568	The Railway Age, Crewe	
6622 93622	Llangollen Railway	
6639 93639	North Yorkshire Moors Railway	

ot No.: 30565. **Builder:** Pressed Steel.   **Ordered:** 01/1959   **Completed:** 10/1959.
iagram: 811.   **New diagram:** NI501.   **Bogies:** BR2.
 3802 converted to Newspaper Van in 1985, new diagram NL502.

6690 93690	Watercress Line	
6722 93722	Venice Simplon Orient Express	
6802 93802 94073	South Yorkshire Railway	
6813 93813	North Yorkshire Moors Railway	
6823 93823	Dean Forest Railway	

ot No.: 30616. **Builder:** Pressed Steel.   **Ordered:** 07/1959   **Completed:** 06/1960.
iagram: 811.   **New diagram:** NI501.   **Bogies:** BR2.

6847 93847	Dean Forest Railway	
6868 93868	Bristol Industrial Museum	
6869 93869	East Lancashire Railway	
6881 93881	Great Eastern Railway	
6918 93918	East Lancashire Railway	
6966 93966	Northampton & Lamport Railway	
6972 93972	South Yorkshire Railway	

=ISH VAN   FISH

ot No.: 30125. **Builder:** Earlestown.   **Ordered:** 08/1953   **Completed:** 02/1955.
iagram: 800.   **New diagram:** NR502.

7144	ABB Transportation Ltd., Derby Carriage Works	Body only remains
7194	ABB Transportation Ltd., Derby Carriage Works	Body only remains
7247 DB975642	Darlington Railway Preservation Society	

 7247 converted to Staff Changing Room in 1977.

ot No.: 30344. **Builder:** Faverdale.   **Ordered:** 01/1956   **Completed:** 01/1961.
iagram: 801.   **New diagram:** NR502.

7537	Nene Valley Railway	
7582 DB975377	Keighley & Worth Valley Railway	
7602 DB975359 041321	Great Eastern Railway	
7671	Southall Railway Centre	

 7582 converted to BTU Tool Van in 1973 and 87602 converted to a Parcels Storage Van in 1973.

Lot No.: 30384. **Builder:** Faverdale.　　**Ordered:** 04/1956　　**Completed:** 01/1961.
Diagram: 801.　　**New diagram:** NR502.

87807	Shaw's Metal Supplies Ltd, Derby	Body only remains
87888	Mangapp's Farm Railway Museum	Body only remains
87896	ABB Transportation Ltd., Derby Carriage Works	Body only remains
87905	Hull Museum of Transport	Part of National Collection
87921	ABB Transportation Ltd., Derby Carriage Works	Body only remains
87937 DB975306	Tanfield Railway	U/F used for NER Family Saloon
87940	ABB Transportation Ltd., Derby Carriage Works	Body only remains
87948 DB975957	Keighley & Worth Valley Railway	

87937/48 converted to Stores Vans in 1973/80. 87905 is currently under restoration at Steamtown Railway Centre, Carnforth.

Lot No.: 30442. **Builder:** Faverdale.　　**Ordered:** 11/1956　　**Completed:** 10/1961.
Diagram: 801.　　**New diagram:** NR502.

87990	ABB Transportation Ltd., Derby Carriage Works	Body only remains

FRUIT VAN　　　　　　　　　　　　　　　　FRUIT D

Lot No.: 30345. **Builder:** Swindon.　　**Ordered:** 01/1956　　**Completed:** 06/1958.
Diagram: 805.

92004	Gwili Railway	
92029	Coventry Railway Centre	Body only remains
92034	Tanfield Railway	No. 2 on underframe
92035 DB975335	South Devon Railway	
92060 DB975347 070888	Tanfield Railway	Body only, underframe not yet re-used
92061 DB975336	The Railway Age, Crewe	Stored at Basford Hall Yard

92035 converted to a CCE Stores Van, 92060 to a Parcels Storage Van and 92061 to a CCE Staff & Dormitory Van in 1973.

Lot No.: 30383. **Builder:** Swindon.　　**Ordered:** 04/1956　　**Completed:** 03/1959.
Diagram: 805.

92067 DB975307	South Devon Railway	
92069 DB975383	The Railway Age, Crewe	
92076	Birmingham Railway Museum	
92080	Severn Valley Railway	
92090	Severn Valley Railway	
92091	Paignton & Dartmouth Railway	
92095 DB975165	Avon Valley Railway	Body only remains
92096 DB975166 060947	Gloucestershire-Warwickshire Railway	Numbered 286?
92097	North Norfolk Railway	

92067/69/95/96 converted to CCE Stores Vans in 1973/74/71/71.

COVERED CARRIAGE TRUCK　　　　　CCT

Lot No.: 30549. **Builder:** Earlestown.　　**Ordered:** 11/1958　　**Completed:** 03/1960.
Diagram: 816.　　**New diagram:** NP501.

94109 041838	Mangapp's Farm Railway Museum	
94125	Great Central Railway	G.C.R. No. 9252?
94181	Venice-Simplon Orient Express	
94226 DB977154 061169	South Yorkshire Railway	
94259	Caledonian Railway	
94264 DB977357	East Lancashire Railway	
94286 041869	Great Central Railway	

94226/64 converted to CCE Stores Vans in 1983/86.

Lot No.: 30562. **Builder:** Earlestown.　　**Ordered:** 01/1959　　**Completed:** 07/1960.
Diagram: 816.　　**New diagram:** NP501.

94338 DB977303	Embsay Steam Railway	YDR No. 2?
94429 DB977140 024971	The Railway Age, Crewe	
94434	Colne Valley Railway	

94444 DB977200   Grimsby & Louth Railway, Lugborough

94338 converted to a CM&EE Electrification Section Stores Van in 1985, 94429 to a S&T Stores Van in 1983 & 94444 to a CCE Tool Van in 1984.

Lot No.: 30563. **Builder**: Earlestown.   **Ordered**: 01/1959   **Completed**: 12/1960.
Diagram: 816. **New diagram**: NP501.

94464	North Norfolk Railway	
94501 DB977097	Swindon & Cricklade Railway	
94502 DB977072	West Somerset Railway	
94518 DB977073	Dean Forest Railway	
94534 DB977707	East Lancashire Railway	
94536	Colne Valley Railway	
94578	Buckinghamshire Railway Centre	

94501 converted to a CCE Stores Van in 1982, 94502/18 in 1981 and 94534 to a S&T Stores Van in 1990.

Lot No.: 30564. **Builder**: Earlestown.   **Ordered**: 01/1959   **Completed**: 03/1961.
Diagram: 816. **New diagram**: NP501.

94597	Humberside Locomotive Group	
94600 DB977240	Grimsby & Louth Railway, Lugborough	
94605 024610	Great Central Railway	
94606	Great Central Railway	G.C.R. No. 96202
94620 041699	ABB Transportation Ltd., York Works	
94677	Llangollen Railway	
94691 DB977358	Llangollen Railway	

94600 converted to a CCE Staff Van in 1984 and 94691 to a CCE Stores Van in 1986.

Lot No.: 30614. **Builder**: Earlestown.   **Ordered**: 06/1959   **Completed**: 04/1961.
Diagram: 816. **New diagram**: NP501.

94707	Great Central Railway	G.C.R. No. 91427
94709 041870	Great Central Railway	
94737	Colne Valley Railway	
94796	Nene Valley Railway	
94817	South Yorkshire Railway	
94869 DB977222	Great Eastern Railway	
94889	Colne Valley Railway	

94869 converted to a Weedkilling train Stores Van in 1984.

Lot No.: 30651. **Builder**: Earlestown.   **Ordered**: 10/1959   **Completed**: 04/1961.
Diagram: 816. **New diagram**: NP501.

94917	West Somerset Railway

BOGIE COVERED CARRIAGE TRUCK CCTBOGIE

Lot No.: 30674. **Builder**: Doncaster.   **Ordered**: 05/1960   **Completed**: 05/1960.
Diagram: 817. **Bogies**: Gresley.

Converted from LNER CK 88030, originally 32480, built 1930, LNER diagram 50, Gresley bogies.

96202 082962	Great Central Railway

HORSE BOX   HB

Lot No.: 30146. **Builder**: Earlestown.   **Ordered**: 03/1954   **Completed**: 10/1958.
Diagram: 751.

96300 DB975056	Llangollen Railway	'CAVALL'
96327 DE321100 041554	Keighley & Worth Valley Railway	
96336 DE321099	Rutland Railway Museum	
96347 DE321101	Colne Valley Railway	
96369	National Railway Museum	
963xx	East Somerset Railway	Body removed - Numbered DW254
96403	Buckinghamshire Railway Centre	

96300 converted to a Cinema Coach Generator Van in 1971 & 96327/36/47 to Boiler Vans in 1966.

EXHIBITION VAN

EXHIBVAN

Lot No.: 30950.   **Builder:** Stewarts Lane.   **Ordered:** 07/1978   **Completed:** 05/1979.
New diagram: NY515. **Bogies:** BR1.

Rebuilt from SK 25972, lot 30686, built Derby, ordered 06/1960, completed 05/1962, diagram 147, new diagram AA202, built with Commonwealth bogies but rebogied with BR1s by Southern Region. Air-braked by Southern Region.

99629   Avon Valley Railway   Stored at Long Marston

COACHING STOCK BUILT TO WAGON LOTS

The four vehicles included in this section are strictly speaking not coaching stock at all, being built to wagon lots. However other than for this technicality they are for all intensive purposes coaching stock.

The first two vehicles covered in this section are based on the prototype GUV described earlier, these being two of four bogie ferry scenery vans built. Both of the preserved examples are owned by Sea Containers, 889202 is used on the mainline serving as additional luggage capacity for the Venice-Simplon Orient Express set whilst 889200 is used for storage purposes at Stewarts Lane. The other two bogie ferry vans remain in use, currently seeing internal use at Eastleigh. In addition thirty, four wheeled ferry vans were built, numbered 889000-889029, based on the prototype CCT. To date none of these has been preserved, however several remain active, thus the opportunity still exists to fill a gap in the ranks of preserved non passenger carrying coaching stock. Mention should also be made of the other two vehicles in the 889xxx series which continue in service, these being the two BR telecommunications vans 889301 and 889302 converted from Bullion Vans 99201 and 99204 which in turn were converted from Mark I Corridor Brake Seconds 34995 and 35201.

The other preserved vehicles are Inspection Saloons. Although built on a BR wagon lot these saloons were constructed to a LMS diagram and would arguably be better included in a book covering LMS design coaching stock. Between 1940 and 1947 the LMS built fourteen Saloons to diagram 2046, five of which remain in BR stock, a further seven have been preserved. The design was obviously successful for when British Rail constructed its first saloons in 1957 the design was continued with five being built numbered in the 9995xx BR saloon series as 999501-999505. Of the five, two remain in service, 999503 in the Manchester area and 999504 in the Derby area, whilst 999505 is believed to have been scrapped in the late 1960s following accident damage. The 9995xx series also contains a further three Inspection Saloons. These being 999506/8/9 which are similar being based on the successful Great Western Railway design of which seven examples were built in 1948. These three remain in service whilst all seven of their predecessors survive in preservation.

FERRY SCENERY VAN

Lot No.: 2849   **Builder:** Eastleigh   **Built:** 1958.
Diagram: 1/292   **New diagram:** YR025   **Bogies:** BR2.
889202 rebogied with Commonwealths.

889200	Venice-Simplon Orient Express	UIC No. 21 70 23-97 000-7
889202	Venice-Simplon Orient Express	VSOE99542. UIC No. 21 70 23-97 002-3

INSPECTION SALOON

Lot No.: 3093   **Builder:** Wolverton   **Built:** 1957.
Diagram: LMS 2046   **Bogies:** BR2   **Seats:** 13.

999501	The Railway Age, Crewe
999502	Caledonian Railway

BODIES OF NON PASSENGER CARRYING COACHING STOCK

In the section covering Non Passenger Carrying Coaching Stock details have been given of items at preservation and similar sites which have had the underframe and running gear removed and thus only a body remains. Normally these see use as store sheds or similar. In addition several scrap merchants have sold on the bodies of items being scrapped in particular to farmers and industrialists. It is normally only by chance that these are discovered by enthusiasts and those known to the authors are listed below along with their current locations. Few details are given about these bodies other than numbers they have carried. However reference to the list of non passenger carrying coaching stock lists in the appendix should suffice the curious.

With a few exceptions all bodies so far located are of two types, Fish Vans and Fruit Ds. It should be noted that in addition to the various BR design Fruit Ds a substantial number of GWR Fruit D bodies exist particularly in Warwickshire and surrounding counties. Fifty Fruit Ds were actually built by the Great Western Railway, numbered 2867-2916, whilst a further one hundred and twenty were built to the same design by British Railways, forty of these took vacant numbers in the series 2265-2400 whilst the remainder were numbered 3401-3480. Details of the bodies of these which survive and are known to the authors will be given in a future book in the series. Regrettably the authors have a list of several Fruit Ds of which the identities have not been established and are therefore currently excluded from this book until it can be established whether or not they are of BR design.

Obviously the authors would be very interested to here of further bodies which exist in order that details can be included in future editions of this book.

It is also worth adding that a number of non passenger carrying bodies are retained by British Rail at various locations on the Railtrack network. Regular up dates are given regarding these in the "Departmental Stock" section of "The Railway Observer", the monthly magazine of The Railway Correspondence and Travel Society.

Numbers	Use	Location	Grid Reference
86242 93242	Store shed	Tarmac PLC, Coates Gate Quarry, Coates Gate, Nr. Moffatt (Off A74)	NT 064053
87565	Store shed	Buckley & Sullivan LTD, Chaddesden, Derby, Derbyshire	SK 370361
87670	Farm store shed	Cinder Hill, Kilburn, Derbyshire	SK 372467
87685	Store shed	Alvaston & Boulton, Cricket & Tennis Association, Derby, Derbyshire	SK 383343
87696	Store shed	Outside Millwright Shop, Loco Industrial Estate, Horwich, Bolton, Greater Manchester	SD 638109
87702	Store shed	North British Maritime Shipping, Norbrit Wharf, Briton Ferry, West Glamorgan	SS 735948
87721	Farm store shed	Cinder Hill, Kilburn, Derbyshire	SK 372467
87729 975404	Store shed	Mayer Parry Recycling, Fordham Road, Snailwell, Cambridgeshire	TL 632625
87790	Store shed (derelict)	Loco Industrial Estate, Horwich, Bolton, Greater Manchester	SD 636108
87907	Store shed	Castle Cement Depot, Curzon Street, Birmingham, West Midlands	SP 082872
87966	Store shed	Mayer Parry Recycling, Fordham Road, Snailwell, Cambridgeshire	TL 632625
88000	Store shed	C&B Haulage & Excavation, Suez Street, Earlestown, Merseyside	SG 575951
88034	Store shed	C&B Haulage & Excavation, Suez Street, Earlestown, Merseyside	SG 575951
92003	Store shed	Manor Farm, Illmington, Warwickshire	SP 214443
92031	Farm workshop	Newstead Farm, Huntspill, Near Highbridge, Somerset	ST 321449
92047	Pig sty	Ashtree Lodge, Chipping Warden, Near Banbury, Northamptonshire	SP 484498
92058	Store shed	Construction & Engineering Services, Connah's Quay, Shotton, Clwyd	SJ 296697
92071	Store shed	Manor Farm, Lower Arncott, Bicester, Oxfordshire	SP 608183
92083	Pig sty	Ashtree Lodge, Chipping Warden, Near Banbury, Northamptonshire	SP 484498
92104	Stable	In a field at Bubbenhall Bridge, Bubbenhall, Warwickshire	SP 354726
92111	Store	Manor Farm, Illmington, Warwickshire	SP 214443
94768	Store	Fox Covert Dismantlers, Gateford Road, Worksop, Nottinghamshire	SK 575818
94787	Store	The Station House, Cheadle (CLC) Station, Manchester Road, Cheadle, Greater Manchester	SJ 856894

APPENDIX 1
BRITISH RAIL DESIGN CARRIAGES EXPORTED ABROAD

Four overseas railway administrations have purchased former British Rail carriages for further use, whilst a number of carriages have also been exported for preservation and similar purposes.

The first overseas railway to purchase carriages from British Rail was Coras Iompair Eireann, now known as Irish Rail, who purchased twenty two Corridor Brake Composites in 1972, these being converted to Brake Generating Steam Vans at Litchurch Lane Works, Derby prior to export. The majority of these have been confirmed as still in service in recent years, however several are now believed to be withdrawn from service and scrapped. During the late 1980s/ early 1990s Irish Rail along with Northern Ireland Railways purchased a considerable number of Mark 2 passenger carrying carriages when these became surplus to British Rail requirements. Those sold to Northern Ireland Railways are principally used on Cross Border services between Belfast and Dublin whilst those sold to Irish Rail see use throughout that system. In 1976 eight Mark 2C TSOs were sold to Israel Railways and are believed to remain in service to this day. As mentioned in the section covering Mark 3 Sleeping Cars ten such carriages have recently been sold to Danish State Railways.

Several Mark 1 carriages were exported to the Americas in the 1960s and early 1970s. The first of these was Tourist Open Second 3733 in 1965 which went to the East Kootenay Railway, Fort Steele, British Columbia along with Locomotive 'Dunrobin' and one of the Duke of Sutherland's carriages, Saloon 58A, the latter two items having been previously located at The Romney Hythe & Dymchurch Railway. In August 1969 locomotive 'Flying Scotsman' visited the United States of America along with its support coach Mark I Corridor Brake Composite 21177, Pullman Cars 114, 246 & 247 and LNER Gangwayed Brakes 104, 70497, 70632, 70636 & 70758. The story of how this visit ended in disaster is well known. However, although 'Flying Scotsman' was subsequently returned to Britain, the carriages remained in the U.S.A. It has proved extremely difficult for the authors to trace with certainty the subsequent history of the carriages, however it is believed that BCK 21177 is located at Victoria Station Restaurant along with three of the LNER Gangwayed Brakes. The other three Mark 1s in the States, Corridor Composite 15055, Corridor Second 24199, & Corridor Second 24551 were exported in 1971 along with a former industrial locomotive, initially going to the Boyne City Railroad, Michigan. Again it has proved difficult for the authors to trace these three carriages but it is believed they are now located as shown below.

In more recent times five carriages were exported to Israel with the intention being that they would be used as part of restaurant schemes. It is understood that this scheme has however foundered and the carriages have been dispersed away from Tel aviv. It is believed that two may be located near Ashdod whilst another two are in the Jordan Valley.

Details are given below of all the British Rail carriages exported. It should however be emphasised that there is no guarantee that the carriages either remain in use with the railway administration shown or are still located at the preservation sites shown. The authors would therefore be most grateful for any information which would assist in establishing the destinies of the carriages shown below.

Details have been split into two categories. Firstly those carriages exported for further use. For each country these are listed numerically in order of the numbers allocated by their new owners. Details then follow of their British Rail number(s), type, lot, builder and any further information regarding each individual carriage. Secondly those carriages exported for preservation or similar. For each country these are listed numerically in order of their British Rail numbers. Details then follow of their type, lot, builder and present owner/location.

CARRIAGES EXPORTED FOR FURTHER USE

DENMARK
DANISH STATE RAILWAYS

DSB Number	BR No.	Type	Lot	Builder	Comments
50 86 75-72 021-5	10721	SLE	30961	Derby	
50 86 75-72 064-5	10664	SLE	30961	Derby	
50 86 75-72 067-8	10667	SLE	30961	Derby	
50 86 75-72 069-4	10669	SLE	30961	Derby	
50 86 75-72 076-9	10676	SLE	30961	Derby	
50 86 75-72 077-7	10677	SLE	30961	Derby	
50 86 75-72 081-9	10681	SLE	30961	Derby	
50 86 75-72 094-2	10694	SLE	30961	Derby	
50 86 75-72 095-9	10695	SLE	30961	Derby	
50 86 75-72 098-3	10698	SLE	30961	Derby	

IRISH REPUBLIC
IRISH RAIL

IR No.	BR No.		Type	Lot	Builder	Comments
3171	21140		BCK	30187	Charles Roberts	
3172	21138		BCK	30187	Charles Roberts	
3173	21146		BCK	30187	Charles Roberts	
3174	21143		BCK	30187	Charles Roberts	
3175	21196		BCK	30425	Metro-Cammell	
3176	21137		BCK	30187	Charles Roberts	
3177	34227		BSK	30021	Ashford/Eastleigh	
3178	34590		BSK	30141	GRCW	
3179	34677		BSK	30156	Wolverton	
3180	34378		BSK	30032	Wolverton	
3181	34581		BSK	30095	Wolverton	Scrapped?
3182	34685		BSK	30156	Wolverton	
3183	34687		BSK	30156	Wolverton	
3184	34566		BSK	30095	Wolverton	
3185	34093		BSK	30003	Derby	
3186	34757		BSK	30157	Wolverton	
3187	34012		BSK	30003	Derby	
3188	34701		BSK	30156	Wolverton	
3189	34264		BSK	30021	Ashford/Eastleigh	
3190	34262		BSK	30021	Ashford/Eastleigh	
3191	34076		BSK	30003	Derby	Scrapped?
3192	34565		BSK	30095	Wolverton	
4101	5428		TSO	30787	Derby	
4102	5411		TSO	30787	Derby	
4103	3156	6406	FO	30810	Derby	
4104	3154	6405	FO	30810	Derby	
4105	3163	6401	FO	30810	Derby	
4106	3157	6413	FO	30810	Derby	
4107	3158	6403	FO	30810	Derby	
4108	5252		SO	30752	Derby	
4109	13512	19512	FK	30789	Derby	
4110	5306		TSO	30776	Derby	
4111	13521	19521	FK	30797	Derby	Scrapped?
4112	13533	19533	FK	30797	Derby	
4113	13469	19469	FK	30785	Derby	
4114	13471		FK	30785	Derby	
4401	13489	19489	FK	30789	Derby	
4402	13497	19497	FK	30789	Derby	

ISRAEL
ISRAEL RAILWAYS

I.R. No.	BR No.	Type	Lot	Builder	Comments
681	5575	TSO	30795	Derby	
682	5580	TSO	30795	Derby	
683	5612	TSO	30795	Derby	
684	5606	TSO	30795	Derby	

685	5567	TSO	30795	Derby	
686	5593	TSO	30795	Derby	
687	5588	TSO	30795	Derby	
688	5570	TSO	30795	Derby	

NORTHERN IRELAND   **NORTHERN IRELAND RAILWAYS**

NIR. No.	BR No.	Type	Lot	Builder	Comments
546	5970 1800	TSO	30860	Derby	
752	5516	TSO	30795	Derby	
753	5498	TSO	30795	Derby	
774	5521	TSO	30795	Derby	
902	13509	FK	30789	Derby	
903	3166	FO	30810	Derby	
904	3367	FO	30859	Derby	
911	14104	BFK	30790	Derby	
912	14108	BFK	30790	Derby	
913	14111	BFK	30790	Derby	
914	14110	BFK	30790	Derby	
915	14106	BFK	30790	Derby	
921	13490	FK	30789	Derby	
922	13495	FK	30789	Derby	
923	13496	FK	30789	Derby	
924	13508	FK	30789	Derby	
925	13503	FK	30789	Derby	
926	13498	FK	30789	Derby	
927	13506	FK	30789	Derby	
928	13510	FK	30789	Derby	
930	5573	TSO	30795	Derby	
931	5531	TSO	30795	Derby	
933	5577	TSO	30795	Derby	Originally NIR 929

SWITZERLAND   **SIG**

SIG No.	BR No.	Type	Lot	Builder	Comments
?	10581	SLEP	30960	Derby	For tilt bogie tests
?	10673	SLE	30961	Derby	For tilt bogie tests
?	10705	SLE	30961	Derby	For tilt bogie tests

CARRIAGES EXPORTED FOR PRESERVATION

CANADA

BR.No.	Type	Lot	Builder	Location
3733	SO	30031	Derby	East Kootenay Railway, Fort Steele, British Columbia

ISRAEL

BR Nos.	Type	Lot	Builder	Location
3947	TSO	30086	Ashford/Eastleigh	Apropo Ltd, Tel Aviv
5250	SO	30752	Derby	Apropo Ltd, Tel Aviv
5645 7645	CK	30158	Wolverton	Apropo Ltd, Tel Aviv
5768 18768	SK	30685	Derby	Apropo Ltd, Tel Aviv
81438 84438	BG	30400	Pressed Steel	Apropo Ltd, Tel Aviv

U.S.A.

BR.No.	Type	Lot	Builder	Location
15055	CK	30022	Ashford/Eastleigh	Harrods Creek & Westport Railway, Louisville, Kentucky
21177	BCK	30424	Charles Roberts	Victoria Station Restaurant, Universal City, Los Angeles
24199	SK	30015	Doncaster	Harrods Creek & Westport Railway, Louisville, Kentucky
24551	SK	30070	York	Harrods Creek & Westport Railway, Louisville, Kentucky

APPENDIX 2
LOT DETAILS OF LOCOMOTIVE HAULED COACHING STOCK

Details are given below of all Mark 1, Mark 2, Mark 3, Mark 4 and Non-passenger carrying locomotive hauled coaching stock built to British Railways lots. These are listed numerically by first number carried for the five designs in the same order as the preserved examples are covered in this publication. Many of the details included have been explained in 'Guide to Layout' but a few further notes covering the layout used below are given to assist readers.

Lot Number.

This is given in the first column. It should however be noted that in a few cases carriages built to a lot are not strictly in order. For example lot 30721 consists of 35407-35446 & 35450-35499, the number series being bisected by lot 30728 which consists of 35447-35449. This listing is however not given in lot number order but in numerical order of carriages constructed. Readers therefore requiring a list of lots in lot number order are referred to the book 'Departmental Coaching Stock' published by South Coast Transport Publishing which contains a full lot list in lot number order. Note: This book is distributed by Platform 5.

First Number/Last Number.

The order of these lists is dictated by the first number of each lot, or part lot, of carriages built to the particular design covered in each list. The first and last number of carriages included in a particular lot, or part of a lot (see above) are given, all numbers inclusive representing a carriage which has existed. In a few cases construction of carriages to a lot has been curtailed, usually resulting in the later allocated numbers not being taken up. Lot 30690 consisting of 4918-4966, 4973-5010 & 5023-5044 is however an example of this occurring when intermediate numbers have not been taken up. In such cases the various series of numbers used are shown. The numbers used in this section are those first carried by the carriage, it should however be noted that in a few cases carriages have been allocated other numbers prior to construction which were never carried. An example of this is Mk 3 11003 which was initially allocated number 3217. One peculiarity occurs however with Mark 4 stock. 12405 of lot 31049 was renumbered 12232 and converted to a TSOE early in its life. However 12221, at the time still under construction appeared as a TSO numbered 12405! Thus to avoid confusion in the list of Mark 4s this later carriage is recorded as 12221, a number which it never actually carried.

Type Code.

The type code is given rather than a description of the vehicle. A full list of these can be found in 'Guide to layout'.

Original Diagram/New Diagram.

These are given were applicable.

If the lot consists of carriages which are conversions from existing vehicles rather than being built from scratch the diagram(s) are followed by the letter 'C'.

Builder

The British Railways Workshop(s) or Private Contractor responsible for the construction of carriages of each lot is given.

Ordered/Completed

The full date on which the order for each lot was placed and officially completed is given.

MK 1 PASSENGER CARRYING COACHING STOCK

Lotnum	First	Last	Type	Dia.	New dia.	Conv	Builder	Ordered	Completed
30012	1	11	RFO	36			York	14/12/1950	19/05/1951
30013	301	305	RF	16			Doncaster	14/12/1950	01/11/1952
30511	306	309	RF	17	AL101		BRCW	10/06/1958	20/05/1961
30633	310	342	RF	17	AL101		Ashford/Swindon	06/10/1959	27/01/1962
30129	499	499	ROYAL	201	AT502		Wolverton	31/11/1953	06/10/1956
30014	1000	1013	RSO	56			York	14/12/1950	08/09/1951
30526	1014	1017	RSO	60			Wolverton	26/08/1958	16/07/1960
30647	1018	1057	RUO	61	AM403		Wolverton	22/10/1959	12/08/1961
30637	1100	1102	RG	30	AG401		Ashford/Eastleigh	13/10/1959	10/09/1960
30783	1106	1106	Booth	32	AG404	C	Derby	02/02/1967	20/04/1968
30514	1500	1526	RKB	25	AH502		Cravens	22/07/1958	28/01/1961
30635	1527	1529	RKB	25	AH502		Cravens	13/10/1959	09/09/1961
30346	1546	1546	RKB	20	AH501		Ashford/Eastleigh	23/01/1956	11/08/1956
30624	1547	1569	RKB	25	AH502		Cravens	30/07/1959	17/06/1961
30628	1644	1699	RB	24	AJ402		Pressed Steel	19/08/1959	02/12/1961
30347	1700	1700	RB	21	AJ401		Eastleigh	23/01/1956	21/04/1956
30512	1701	1738	RB	24	AJ402		BRCW	10/06/1958	28/01/1961
30527	1739	1754	RB	24	AJ402		BRCW	26/08/1958	15/07/1961
30636	1755	1772	RB	24	AJ402		Pressed Steel	13/10/1959	24/03/1962
30485	1801	1812	RMB	97	AN201		York	04/06/1957	22/03/1958
30520	1813	1837	RMB	99	AN203		Wolverton	24/07/1958	31/12/1960
30507	1838	1852	RMB	98	AN202		Wolverton	23/05/1958	18/06/1960
30670	1853	1864	RMB	99	AN203		Wolverton	28/03/1960	27/01/1962
30702	1865	1882	RMB	99	AN203		Wolverton	12/06/1961	19/05/1962
30784	1883	1883	Bar	100	AN206	C	Derby	02/02/1967	20/04/1968
30348	1900	1900	RU	22			Eastleigh	23/01/1956	11/08/1956
30401	1901	1912	RU	23	AL401		Ashford/Swindon	24/05/1956	30/11/1957
30476	1913	1924	RU	23	AL401		Ashford/Swindon	16/05/1957	27/12/1958
30513	1925	1943	RU	23	AL401		BRCW	10/06/1958	30/01/1960
30575	1944	1958	RU	23	AL401		Ashford/Swindon	19/01/1959	10/09/1960
30632	1959	1991	RU	23	AL401		Ashford/Swindon	06/10/1959	17/06/1961
30035	2000	2009	SLF	1	AS101		Wolverton	21/03/1951	14/08/1958
30159	2010	2019	SLF	1	AS101		Wolverton	07/04/1954	27/12/1958
30318	2020	2029	SLF	1	AS101		York	07/12/1955	04/10/1958
30377	2030	2063	SLF	1	AS101		York	20/03/1956	21/03/1959
30490	2064	2104	SLF	1	AS101		Metro-Cammell	19/07/1957	31/10/1959
30528	2105	2106	SLF	1	AS101		Wolverton	26/08/1958	05/09/1959
30590	2107	2120	SLF	1	AS101		Metro-Cammell	18/03/1959	03/08/1960
30650	2121	2125	SLF	1	AS101		Wolverton	22/10/1959	20/05/1961
30687	2126	2130	SLF	1	AS101		Wolverton	29/06/1960	15/07/1961
30722	2131	2132	SLF	1	AS101		Wolverton	17/08/1961	16/06/1962
30096	2400	2401	SLC	5	AS301		Wolverton	28/04/1953	05/10/1957
30161	2402	2403	SLC	5	AS301		Wolverton	07/04/1954	02/11/1957
30492	2404	2426	SLC	5	AS301		Metro-Cammell	19/07/1957	27/02/1960
30538	2427	2427	SLC	5	AS301		Metro-Cammell	17/09/1958	26/03/1960
30591	2428	2437	SLC	5	AS301		Metro-Cammell	18/03/1959	03/08/1960
30649	2438	2438	SLC	5	AS301		Wolverton	22/10/1959	25/02/1961
30688	2439	2442	SLC	5	AS301		Wolverton	29/06/1960	12/08/1961
30727	2443	2445	SLC	5	AS301		Wolverton	15/11/1961	26/01/1963
30736	2446	2454	SLC	5	AS301		Wolverton	04/09/1962	18/04/1964
30036	2500	2521	SLSTP	10	AS201		Doncaster	21/03/1951	02/11/1957
30160	2522	2526	SLSTP	10	AS201		York/Doncaster	07/04/1954	05/10/1957
30245	2527	2536	SLSTP	10	AS201		York/Doncaster	23/05/1955	30/11/1957
30379	2537	2573	SLSTP	10	AS201		York/Doncaster	28/03/1956	09/08/1958
30491	2574	2578	SLSTP	10	AS201		Metro-Cammell	19/07/1957	31/10/1959
30529	2579	2606	SLSTP	10	AS201		Wolverton	26/08/1958	30/01/1960
30586	2607	2658	SLSTP	10	AS201		Wolverton	16/02/1959	28/01/1961
30689	2659	2666	SLSTP	10	AS201		Wolverton	29/06/1960	12/08/1961
30723	2667	2681	SLSTP	10	AS201		Wolverton	17/08/1961	29/12/1962
30735	2682	2691	SLSTP	10	AS201		Derby	04/09/1962	21/03/1964
30130	2900	2900	ROYAL	200	AT501		Wolverton	03/11/1953	10/09/1955

30131	2901	2901	ROYAL	202	AT503	Wolverton	03/11/1953	23/02/1957
30010	3000	3002	FO	71		York	14/12/1950	21/04/1951
30008	3003	3019	FO	72		BRCW	14/12/1950	22/05/1954
30042	3020	3039	FO	73	AD103	Doncaster	21/03/1951	27/02/1954
30091	3040	3057	FO	73	AD103	Doncaster	27/04/1953	19/06/1954
30169	3058	3070	FO	73	AD103	Doncaster	31/05/1954	13/08/1955
30242	3071	3080	FO	73	AD103	York/Doncaster	23/05/1955	08/09/1956
30359	3081	3081	FO	77		BRCW	13/08/1956	13/07/1957
30361	3082	3082	FO	76		Cravens	13/08/1956	02/11/1957
30372	3083	3083	FO	74		Doncaster	02/05/1957	13/07/1957
30373	3084	3084	FO	75		Doncaster	20/03/1956	20/04/1957
30472	3085	3094	FO	73	AD103	BRCW	14/05/1957	08/08/1959
30576	3095	3100	FO	73	AD103	BRCW	19/01/1959	03/10/1959
30648	3101	3103	FO	73	AD103	Wolverton	22/10/1959	17/06/1961
30697	3104	3129	FO	73	AD103	Swindon	22/03/1961	23/02/1963
30717	3130	3151	FO	73	AD103	Swindon	10/08/1961	28/12/1963
30053	3500	3514	SO	90		Eastleigh	26/10/1951	11/07/1953
30011	3700	3705	TSO	92	AC203	York	14/12/1950	19/05/1951
30017	3706	3720	TSO	92	AC203	Cravens	14/12/1950	14/06/1952
30031	3721	3735	SO	94	AD201	Derby	21/03/1951	11/09/1954
30043	3736	3753	TSO	93	AC204	Doncaster	02/04/1951	26/12/1953
30079	3754	3772	TSO	93	AC204	York	24/02/1953	26/12/1953
30043	3773	3788	TSO	93	AC204	Doncaster	02/04/1951	26/12/1953
30079	3789	3823	TSO	93	AC204	York	24/02/1953	26/12/1953
30054	3824	3849	TSO	93	AC204	Ashford/Eastleigh	26/10/1951	19/06/1954
30080	3850	3885	TSO	93	AC204	York	24/02/1953	30/01/1954
30054	3886	3903	TSO	93	AC204	Ashford/Eastleigh	26/10/1951	19/06/1954
30086	3904	3969	TSO	93	AC204	Ashford/Eastleigh	21/04/1953	29/01/1955
30090	3970	3997	TSO	93	AC204	York	27/04/1953	27/03/1954
30149	3998	4097	TSO	93	AC204	Ashford/Swindon	17/03/1954	23/03/1957
30171	4098	4197	TSO	93	AC204	York	31/05/1954	28/01/1956
30172	4198	4257	TSO	93	AC204	York	31/05/1954	21/04/1956
30207	4258	4357	TSO	93	AC204	BRCW	03/01/1955	06/10/1956
30067	4358	4362	SO	94	AD201	Eastleigh	10/05/1952	26/02/1955
30121	4363	4372	SO	94	AD201	Eastleigh	29/04/1953	05/11/1955
30219	4373	4412	TSO	93	AC204	Ashford/Swindon	16/03/1951	17/09/1957
30226	4413	4472	TSO	93	AC204	BRCW	21/04/1955	26/01/1957
30227	4473	4487	SO	94	AD201	BRCW	21/04/1955	20/04/1957
30243	4488	4636	TSO	93	AC204	York	23/05/1955	26/01/1957
30360	4637	4637	SO	96		BRCW	13/08/1956	28/12/1957
30362	4638	4638	TSO	95		Cravens	13/08/1956	30/11/1957
30375	4639	4726	TSO	93	AC204	York	04/06/1957	05/10/1957
30739	4727	4729	TSO	91	AC202	Derby	25/01/1963	13/06/1964
30375	4739	4778	TSO	93	AC204	York	04/06/1957	05/10/1957
30376	4779	4809	SO	94	AD201	York	20/03/1956	28/12/1957
30473	4810	4829	SO	94	AD201	BRCW	14/05/1957	16/05/1959
30506	4830	4839	TSO	89	AC201	Wolverton	23/05/1959	26/12/1959
30525	4840	4899	TSO	89	AC201	Wolverton	26/08/1958	23/04/1960
30646	4900	4917	TSO	89	AC201	Wolverton	22/10/1959	20/05/1961
30690	4918	4966	TSO	89	AC201	Wolverton	29/06/1960	21/04/1962
30690	4973	5010	TSO	89	AC201	Wolverton	29/06/1960	21/04/1962
30690	5023	5044	TSO	89	AC201	Wolverton	29/06/1960	21/04/1962
30724	5045	5069	TSO	89	AC201	York	31/08/1962	28/12/1963
30170	9200	9276	BSO	183	AE201	Doncaster	31/05/1954	24/03/1956
30244	9277	9321	BSO	183	AE201	Doncaster	23/05/1955	11/08/1956
30443	9322	9362	BSO	183	AE201	GRCW	04/01/1957	30/01/1960
30698	9363	9380	BSO	184	AE202	Wolverton	04/04/1961	28/12/1963
30019	13000	13032	FK	116	AA101	Swindon	14/12/1950	14/06/1952
30052	13033	13035	FK	116	AA101	Eastleigh	01/06/1951	14/07/1951
30019	13036	13059	FK	116	AA101	Swindon	14/12/1950	14/06/1952
30027	13060	13064	FK	116	AA101	Swindon	10/05/1952	21/02/1953
30066	13065	13076	FK	116	AA101	Swindon	10/05/1952	31/10/1953
30083	13077	13084	FK	116	AA101	Swindon	26/03/1953	28/11/1953
30089	13085	13107	FK	116	AA101	Swindon	27/04/1953	06/11/1954
30107	13108	13125	FK	116	AA101	Swindon	28/04/1953	04/12/1954

30147	13126	13184	FK	116	AA101	Swindon	17/03/1954	03/12/1955
30217	13185	13219	FK	116	AA101	Ashford/Swindon	16/03/1955	21/02/1959
30355	13220	13220	FK	117		Metro-Cammell	13/08/1956	23/02/1957
30357	13221	13221	FK	118		GRCW	13/08/1956	13/07/1957
30370	13222	13222	FK	119		Doncaster	20/03/1956	20/04/1957
30381	13223	13238	FK	116	AA101	Ashford/Swindon	04/04/1956	11/07/1959
30432	13239	13251	FK	116	AA101	Ashford/Swindon	17/10/1956	28/11/1959
30578	13253	13302	FK	116	AA101	Metro-Cammell	23/01/1959	13/08/1960
30667	13303	13360	FK	116	AA101	Swindon	24/03/1960	08/09/1962
30738	13407	13409	FK	121	AA103	Derby	25/01/1963	13/06/1964
30148	14000	14001	BFK	161	AB101	Ashford/Swindon	17/03/1954	26/12/1959
30218	14002	14006	BFK	161	AB101	Ashford/Swindon	16/03/1955	30/01/1960
30382	14007	14012	BFK	161	AB101	Ashford/Swindon	04/04/1956	27/02/1960
30668	14013	14022	BFK	161	AB101	Swindon	24/03/1960	30/12/1961
30718	14023	14027	BFK	161	AB101	Swindon	10/08/1961	30/11/1963
30001	15000	15000	CK	127		Eastleigh	14/12/1950	23/03/1952
30004	15001	15020	CK	126	AA301	Derby	14/12/1950	27/12/1952
30022	15021	15064	CK	126	AA301	Ashford/Eastleigh	14/12/1950	26/11/1952
30005	15065	15270	CK	126	AA301	Metro-Cammell	14/12/1950	03/10/1953
30016	15271	15310	CK	126	AA301	Cravens	14/12/1950	21/02/1953
30033	15311	15349	CK	126	AA301	Derby	21/03/1951	05/09/1953
30075	15350	15424	CK	126	AA301	Derby	19/01/1953	17/07/1954
30076	15425	15435	CK	128	AA302	Derby	19/01/1953	03/10/1953
30081	15436	15442	CK	128	AA302	Derby	25/02/1953	24/04/1954
30062	15443	15532	CK	126	AA301	Metro-Cammell	05/03/1952	22/05/1954
30063	15533	15542	CK	128	AA302	Metro-Cammell	05/03/1952	14/08/1954
30134	15543	15562	CK	126	AA301	Metro-Cammell	11/01/1954	23/04/1955
30135	15563	15584	CK	128	AA302	Metro-Cammell	11/01/1954	16/07/1955
30138	15585	15596	CK	126	AA301	BRCW	11/01/1954	23/04/1955
30139	15597	15624	CK	128	AA302	BRCW	11/01/1954	16/07/1955
30158	15625	15694	CK	126	AA301	Wolverton	07/04/1954	06/10/1956
30179	15695	15770	CK	126	AA301	Metro-Cammell	13/07/1954	25/02/1956
30180	15771	15820	CK	128	AA302	Metro-Cammell	13/07/1954	28/01/1956
30221	15821	15860	CK	126	AA301	Metro-Cammell	22/03/1955	11/08/1956
30222	15861	15915	CK	128	AA302	Metro-Cammell	22/03/1955	06/10/1956
30317	15916	15985	CK	126	AA301	Wolverton	03/10/1955	26/01/1957
30351	15986	16057	CK	126	AA301	Wolverton	27/01/1956	20/04/1957
30471	16058	16092	CK	126	AA301	Metro-Cammell	14/05/1957	18/04/1959
30475	16093	16107	CK	126	AA301	Charles Roberts	15/05/1957	28/11/1959
30577	16108	16152	CK	126	AA301	Metro-Cammell	22/01/1959	21/05/1960
30665	16153	16197	CK	126	AA301	Derby	22/03/1960	17/06/1961
30666	16198	16225	CK	128	AA302	Derby	22/03/1960	17/06/1961
30729	16226	16240	CK	126	AA301	Derby	20/06/1962	07/09/1963
30730	16241	16267	CK	126	AA301	Derby	20/06/1962	28/12/1963
30006	21000	21019	BCK	171	AB301	Metro-Cammell	14/12/1950	06/11/1954
30034	21020	21024	BCK	172	AB302	Derby	21/03/1951	30/01/1954
30132	21025	21059	BCK	171	AB301	Metro-Cammell	11/01/1954	29/01/1955
30133	21060	21091	BCK	172	AB302	Metro-Cammell	11/01/1954	21/05/1955
30185	21092	21118	BCK	171	AB301	Metro-Cammell	16/07/1954	19/05/1956
30186	21119	21133	BCK	172	AB302	Metro-Cammell	16/07/1954	19/05/1956
30187	21134	21168	BCK	172	AB302	Charles Roberts	20/07/1954	16/06/1956
30424	21169	21194	BCK	172	AB302	Charles Roberts	01/10/1956	24/01/1959
30425	21195	21224	BCK	171	AB301	Metro-Cammell	02/10/1956	06/09/1958
30474	21225	21230	BCK	171	AB301	Charles Roberts	15/05/1957	21/03/1959
30574	21231	21235	BCK	171	AB301	GRCW	15/01/1959	13/08/1960
30669	21236	21251	BCK	171	AB301	Swindon	24/03/1960	24/02/1962
30731	21252	21262	BCK	171	AB301	Derby	22/08/1962	28/12/1963
30732	21263	21275	BCK	172	AB302	Derby	22/08/1962	22/02/1964
30002	24000	24179	SK	146	AA201	Derby	14/12/1950	01/12/1951
30015	24180	24219	SK	146	AA201	Doncaster	14/12/1950	12/07/1952
30026	24220	24301	SK	146	AA201	York	14/12/1950	12/07/1952
30020	24302	24331	SK	146	AA201	Ashford/Eastleigh	14/12/1950	17/05/1952
30007	24332	24396	SK	146	AA201	BRCW	14/12/1950	13/06/1953
30030	24397	24436	SK	146	AA201	Derby	21/03/1951	26/12/1952
30072	24437	24446	SK	146	AA201	Wolverton	19/01/1953	31/10/1953

30088	24447	24468	SK	146	AA201	Swindon	27/04/1953	17/07/1954
30070	24469	24538	SK	146	AA201	York	10/05/1952	01/01/1955
30068	24539	24548	SK	147	AA202	York	10/05/1952	27/12/1952
30070	24549	24556	SK	146	AA201	York	10/05/1952	01/01/1955
30044	24557	24568	SK	146	AA201	York	02/04/1951	01/11/1952
30070	24569	24575	SK	146	AA201	York	10/05/1952	01/01/1955
30057	24576	24675	SK	146	AA201	BRCW	05/03/1952	30/01/1954
30058	24676	24700	SK	146	AA201	Cravens	10/05/1952	03/10/1953
30059	24701	24720	SK	147	AA202	Cravens	05/03/1952	11/07/1953
30073	24721	24745	SK	146	AA201	Wolverton	19/01/1953	26/12/1953
30077	24746	24753	SK	147	AA202	Swindon	02/02/1953	30/01/1954
30078	24754	24795	SK	146	AA201	Swindon	02/02/1953	22/05/1954
30137	24796	24818	SK	146	AA201	BRCW	11/01/1954	29/01/1955
30153	24819	24944	SK	146	AA201	Derby	07/04/1954	16/06/1956
30154	24945	24974	SK	146	AA201	Derby	07/04/1954	16/06/1956
30208	24975	25044	SK	146	AA201	Derby	19/01/1955	01/12/1956
30155	25045	25164	SK	147	AA202	Wolverton	07/04/1954	19/05/1956
30230	25165	25247	SK	147	AA202	Metro-Cammell	27/04/1955	30/11/1957
30231	25248	25279	SK	146	AA201	Metro-Cammell	27/04/1955	19/04/1958
30494	25280	25282	SK	150	AA204	Metro-Cammell	23/01/1958	14/06/1958
30349	25283	25402	SK	146	AA201	Wolverton	15/02/1956	05/10/1957
30350	25403	25454	SK	146	AA201	Wolverton	15/02/1956	28/12/1957
30356	25455	25455	SK	148		Metro-Cammell	13/08/1956	23/02/1957
30358	25456	25456	SK	149		GRCW	13/08/1956	13/07/1957
30371	25457	25457	SK	151		Doncaster	20/03/1956	20/04/1957
30374	25458	25507	SK	146	AA201	York	23/05/1958	01/11/1958
30737	25508	25509	SK	152	AA206	Derby	25/01/1963	13/06/1964
30426	25558	25703	SK	146	AA201	Wolverton	12/10/1956	06/09/1958
30685	25704	25905	SK	146	AA201	Derby	29/09/1960	14/07/1962
30686	25906	25972	SK	147	AA202	Derby	29/06/1960	15/05/1962
30719	25973	26059	SK	146	AA201	Derby	17/08/1961	01/12/1962
30720	26060	26137	SK	147	AA202	Derby	17/08/1961	15/06/1963
30726	26138	26217	SK	146	AA201	York	27/09/1961	02/11/1963
40003	34000	34094	BSK	181	AB201	Derby	14/12/1950	04/10/1952
40025	34096	34224	BSK	181	AB201	Wolverton	14/12/1950	17/05/1952
40021	34225	34284	BSK	181	AB201	Ashford/Eastleigh	14/12/1950	29/11/1952
40032	34285	34289	BSK	181	AB201	Wolverton	21/03/1951	29/11/1952
40065	34290	34301	BSK	182	AB202	Wolverton	07/05/1952	31/10/1953
40082	34302	34315	BSK	182	AB202	Wolverton	02/03/1953	30/01/1954
40074	34316	34371	BSK	181	AB201	Wolverton	19/01/1953	19/06/1954
40032	34372	34388	BSK	181	AB201	Wolverton	21/03/1951	29/11/1952
40074	34389	34409	BSK	181	AB201	Wolverton	19/01/1953	19/06/1954
40032	34410	34412	BSK	181	AB201	Wolverton	21/03/1951	29/11/1952
40064	34413	34450	BSK	181	AB201	Wolverton	19/01/1953	05/09/1953
40060	34451	34500	BSK	181	AB201	GRCW	05/03/1952	27/02/1954
40061	34501	34520	BSK	181	AB201	Charles Roberts	05/03/1952	09/10/1954
40095	34521	34584	BSK	181	AB201	Wolverton	28/04/1953	23/04/1955
40141	34585	34612	BSK	181	AB201	GRCW	11/01/1954	18/06/1955
40142	34613	34630	BSK	182	AB202	GRCW	11/01/1954	10/09/1955
40143	34631	34654	BSK	182	AB202	Charles Roberts	11/01/1954	18/06/1955
40156	34655	34748	BSK	181	AB201	Wolverton	07/04/1954	08/10/1955
40157	34749	34808	BSK	182	AB202	Wolverton	07/04/1954	31/12/1955
40220	34809	34868	BSK	182	AB202	GRCW	22/03/1955	21/04/1956
40223	34869	34880	BSK	182	AB202	Charles Roberts	22/03/1955	11/08/1956
40225	34881	34930	BSK	182	AB202	Charles Roberts	14/04/1955	15/06/1957
40229	34931	35023	BSK	182	AB202	Metro-Cammell	27/04/1955	20/04/1957
40232	35024	35038	BSK	182	AB202	GRCW	27/04/1955	06/10/1956
40233	35039	35113	BSK	181	AB201	GRCW	27/04/1955	15/06/1957
40386	35114	35175	BSK	181	AB201	Charles Roberts	04/05/1956	04/06/1958
40427	35176	35273	BSK	181	AB201	Wolverton	12/10/1956	18/04/1959
40573	35274	35293	BSK	181	AB201	GRCW	15/01/1959	21/05/1960
40699	35294	35400	BSK	181	AB201	Wolverton	04/04/1961	26/01/1963
40700	35401	35406	BSK	182	AB202	Wolverton	04/04/1961	26/01/1963
40721	35407	35446	BSK	181	AB201	Wolverton	17/08/1961	07/09/1963
40728	35447	35449	BSK	181	AB201	Wolverton	16/04/1962	23/02/1963

30721	35450	35499	BSK	181	AB201	Wolverton	17/08/1961	07/09/1963
30071	41000	41014	C	311		Wolverton	21/08/1952	04/12/1954
30102	41023	41042	C	311		Wolverton	28/04/1953	29/01/1955
30103	41043	41048	C	312		Swindon	28/04/1953	16/07/1955
30102	41049	41059	C	311		Wolverton	28/04/1953	29/01/1955
30152	41060	41064	C	312		Swindon	17/03/1954	25/02/1956
30094	43000	43049	CL	313		Doncaster	27/04/1953	23/04/1955
30045	43100	43161	BS	371		York	02/04/1951	26/03/1955
30100	43360	43367	BS	371		Derby	28/04/1953	23/04/1955
30151	43374	43383	BS	372		Swindon	17/03/1954	28/01/1956
30028	46000	46018	S	326		Swindon	21/03/1951	04/12/1954
30037	46019	46062	S	327		Swindon	21/03/1951	26/02/1955
30051	46063	46108	S	326		Derby	01/06/1951	01/11/1955
30038	46109	46198	S	326		Wolverton	21/03/1951	06/11/1954
30098	46199	46259	S	326		Derby	28/04/1953	23/04/1955
30104	46267	46279	S	327		Swindon	28/04/1953	26/03/1955
30150	46280	46298	S	327		Swindon	17/03/1954	31/12/1955
30101	46299	46306	S	326		Derby	28/04/1953	21/05/1955
30092	48000	48027	SLO	330		Doncaster	27/04/1953	18/06/1955
30145	48028	48034	SO(NG)	328		Doncaster	10/02/1954	23/04/1955
30099	48035	48042	SO(NG)	328		Derby	28/04/1953	18/06/1955
30105	48043	48053	SO(NG)	329		Swindon	28/04/1953	10/09/1955
30047	53036	53051	BS	370		Swindon	19/04/1951	21/05/1955
30087	53078	53170	BS	371		York	24/04/1953	13/08/1955
30093	53171	53259	BS	371		Doncaster	27/04/1953	04/12/1954
30106	53268	53273	BS	372		Swindon	28/04/1953	18/06/1955

MK 2 PASSENGER CARRYING COACHING STOCK

Lotnum	First	Last	Type	Dia.	New dia.	Conv	Builder	Ordered	Completed
30755	500	507	PK	15	AP101		Derby	11/11/1964	23/04/1966
30754	540	553	PC	78	AQ101		Derby	11/11/1964	23/04/1966
30753	580	586	PB	85	AR101		Derby	11/11/1964	23/04/1966
30888	2905	2905	ROYAL		AT527	C	Wolverton	01/10/1974	17/05/1977
30889	2906	2906	ROYAL		AT528	C	Wolverton	01/10/1974	17/05/1977
31044	2920	2920	ROYAL		AT536	C	Derby/Wolverton	31/03/1987	08/10/1988
31086	2921	2921	ROYAL		AT541	C	Derby/Wolverton	14/01/1991	20/07/1991
30810	3152	3169	FO	80	AD104		Derby	07/05/1969	05/12/1970
30821	3170	3216	FO	81	AD105		Derby	17/10/1969	09/09/1972
30843	3221	3275	FO	82	AD106		Derby	26/04/1972	24/02/1973
30845	3276	3320	FO	83	AD107		Derby	26/04/1972	01/02/1973
30859	3321	3428	FO	83	AD107		Derby	10/01/1973	02/11/1974
30873	3429	3439	FO	83	AD107		Derby	27/09/1973	22/03/1975
30751	5070	5228	TSO	88	AC205		Derby	01/10/1964	17/06/1967
30752	5229	5256	SO	87	AD203		Derby	07/10/1964	08/10/1966
30776	5257	5345	TSO	86	AC206		Derby	10/01/1967	20/04/1968
30787	5346	5433	TSO	86	AC206		Derby	24/05/1967	28/12/1968
30791	5434	5497	TSO	105	AC207		Derby	10/11/1967	06/09/1969
30795	5498	5615	TSO	106	AC208		Derby	07/05/1969	07/11/1970
30822	5616	5743	TSO	107	AC209		Derby	17/10/1969	01/01/1972
30837	5744	5804	TSO	108	AC210		Derby	10/03/1971	17/06/1972
30844	5809	5907	TSO	108	AC210		Derby	26/04/1972	24/02/1973
30846	5908	5958	TSO	109	AC211		Derby	26/04/1972	29/09/1973
30860	5959	6170	TSO	109	AC211		Derby	10/01/1973	28/12/1974
30874	6171	6184	TSO	109	AC211		Derby	27/09/1973	25/01/1975
30757	9381	9416	BSO	185	AE203		Derby	20/04/1965	06/08/1966
30777	9417	9425	BSO	180	AE204		Derby	10/01/1967	04/11/1967
30788	9426	9438	BSO	180	AE204		Derby	24/05/1967	05/10/1968
30798	9439	9448	BSO	186	AE205		Derby	07/05/1969	20/06/1970
30820	9449	9478	BSO	186	AE205		Derby	17/10/1969	02/01/1971
30824	9479	9495	BSO	187	AE206		Derby	17/10/1969	06/11/1971
30838	9496	9509	BSO	188	AE207		Derby	10/03/1971	25/03/1972
30861	9510	9539	BSO	189	AE208		Derby	10/01/1973	08/01/1974
30550	13252	13252	FK	120			Swindon	06/11/1958	26/01/1963
30733	13361	13378	FK	122	AA105		Derby	22/08/1962	08/08/1964

30734	13379	13406	FK	122	AA105	Derby	22/08/1962	31/10/1964
30749	13410	13431	FK	122	AA105	Derby	01/10/1964	27/02/1965
30750	13432	13433	FK	122	AA105	Derby	01/10/1964	26/11/1964
30774	13434	13463	FK	123	AA106	Derby	10/01/1967	15/06/1968
30785	13464	13475	FK	124	AA106	Derby	24/05/1967	16/11/1968
30789	13476	13513	FK	124	AA107	Derby	10/11/1967	07/06/1969
30797	13514	13561	FK	125	AA108	Derby	07/05/1969	18/07/1970
30825	13562	13610	FK	129	AA109	Derby	17/10/1969	12/08/1972
30756	14028	14055	BFK	162	AB102	Derby	20/04/1965	10/09/1966
30775	14056	14077	BFK	163	AB103	Derby	10/01/1967	24/02/1968
30786	14078	14103	BFK	163	AB103	Derby	24/05/1967	07/09/1968
30790	14104	14112	BFK	164	AB104	Derby	10/11/1967	30/06/1969
30796	14113	14138	BFK	165	AB105	Derby	07/05/1969	18/01/1970
30823	14139	14172	BFK	166	AB106	Derby	17/10/1969	29/01/1972

MK 3 PASSENGER CARRYING COACHING STOCK

Lotnum	First	Last	Type	Dia.	New dia.	Conv	Builder	Ordered	Completed
30886	2903	2903	ROYAL		AT525	C	Wolverton	04/10/1974	17/05/1977
30887	2904	2904	ROYAL		AT526	C	Wolverton	04/10/1974	17/05/1977
31002	2914	2915	ROYAL		AT531		Derby/Wolverton	29/06/1984	14/07/1984
31059	2916	2916	ROYAL		AT536	C	Derby/Wolverton	16/11/1988	03/12/1988
31084	2917	2917	ROYAL		AT539	C	Derby/Wolverton	25/01/1990	26/05/1990
31083	2918	2918	ROYAL		AT538	C	Derby/Wolverton	07/12/1989	02/12/1989
31085	2919	2919	ROYAL		AT540	C	Derby/Wolverton	06/08/1990	10/11/1990
31035	2922	2922	ROYAL		AT534		Derby/Wolverton	16/04/1987	03/04/1989
31036	2923	2923	ROYAL		AT535		Derby/Wolverton	16/04/1987	03/04/1989
30890	10001	10028	RFB	43	AJ412		Derby	18/10/1974	14/10/1980
30960	10500	10619	SLEP	7	AS403		Derby	08/08/1979	10/09/1983
30961	10646	10733	SLE	6	AS404		Derby	08/08/1979	30/06/1984
30833	11003	11003	FO	665			Derby	11/09/1970	17/06/1972
30878	11004	11063	FO	69	AD108		Derby	20/11/1973	31/01/1976
30982	11064	11101	FO		AD110		Derby	20/06/1983	03/10/1985
30832	12003	12003	TSO	674			Derby	11/09/1970	17/06/1972
30877	12004	12168	TSO	111	AC212		Derby	20/11/1973	18/06/1977
30990	17173	17175	BFO		AE101		Derby	03/01/1984	16/06/1986

MK 4 PASSENGER CARRYING COACHING STOCK

Lotnum	First	Last	Type	Dia.	New dia.	Conv	Builder	Ordered	Completed
31045	10300	10333	RFB		AJ105		Metro-Cammell	25/03/1988	08/10/1991
31046	11200	11263	FO		AD111		Metro-Cammell	25/03/1988	10/09/1991
31046	11272	11276	FO		AD111		Metro-Cammell	25/03/1988	18/06/1992
31047	12200	12231	TSOE		AI201		Metro-Cammell	25/03/1988	23/07/1991
31048	12300	12330	TSOD		AL201		Metro-Cammell	25/03/1988	20/09/1991
31049	12400	12489	TSO		AC214		Metro-Cammell	25/03/1988	30/08/1991

NON PASSENGER CARRYING COACHING STOCK

Lotnum	First	Last	Type	Dia.	New dia.	Conv	Builder	Ordered	Completed
31049	12513	12538	TSO		AC214		Metro-Cammell	25/03/1988	30/03/1992
30018	80000	80009	RK	700			Doncaster	14/12/1950	19/05/1951
30524	80010	80021	RK	701			Charles Roberts	31/07/1958	21/04/1962
30539	80022	80027	RK	702	AK501		Charles Roberts	29/09/1958	11/08/1962
30585	80028	80039	RK	702	AK501		Charles Roberts	05/02/1959	23/03/1963
30634	80040	80040	RK	702	AK501		Charles Roberts	05/10/1959	18/05/1963
30486	80300	80305	POS	720	NS501		Wolverton	21/06/1957	05/09/1959
30487	80306	80308	POS	721	NS502		Wolverton	21/06/1957	28/11/1959
30661	80309	80314	POS	720	NS501		Wolverton	01/03/1960	30/05/1961
30662	80315	80317	POS	720	NS501		Wolverton	01/03/1960	30/05/1961
30663	80318	80318	POS	720	NS501		Wolverton	01/03/1960	17/06/1961
30778	80319	80327	POS	728	NS504		York	31/01/1967	15/02/1969
30779	80328	80338	POS	729	NS505		York	31/01/1967	08/02/1969
30780	80339	80355	POS	731	NS506		York	31/01/1967	15/03/1969
30839	80356	80380	POS	726	NS503		York	07/09/1971	24/03/1973

30900	80381	80395	POS	726	NS531	C	York	24/01/1975	13/08/1977
30488	80400	80402	POT	722	NT502		Wolverton	21/06/1957	28/11/1959
30781	80415	80424	POT	732	NT505		York	31/01/1967	02/11/1968
30840	80425	80430	POT	727	NT504		York	07/09/1971	24/03/1973
30901	80431	80439	POT	727	NT521	C	York	24/01/1975	31/12/1976
30489	80450	80455	BPOT	723	NU501		Wolverton	21/06/1957	28/11/1959
30782	80456	80458	BPOT	733	NU502		York	31/01/1967	05/10/1968
30009	80500	80529	BG	711	NA501		Derby	14/12/1950	18/04/1953
30023	80530	80535	BG	711	NA501		Eastleigh	14/12/1950	16/06/1951
30039	80536	80566	BG	711	NA501		Derby	29/03/1951	09/10/1954
30040	80567	80596	BG	711	NA501		Wolverton	29/03/1951	29/01/1955
30046	80597	80671	BG	711	NA501		York	02/04/1951	11/09/1954
30136	80672	80724	BG	711	NA501		Metro-Cammell	11/01/1954	08/10/1955
30140	80725	80802	BG	711	NA501		BRCW	11/01/1954	28/01/1956
30144	80803	80854	BG	711	NA501		Cravens	11/01/1954	31/12/1955
30162	80855	80964	BG	711	NA501		Pressed Steel	07/04/1954	07/09/1957
30173	80965	81014	BG	711	NA501		York	31/05/1954	14/07/1956
30224	81015	81054	BG	711	NA501		Cravens	22/03/1955	16/06/1956
30228	81055	81179	BG	711	NA501		Metro-Cammell	27/04/1955	17/05/1958
30234	81180	81204	BG	711	NA501		Cravens	10/05/1955	23/03/1957
30163	81205	81265	BG	711	NA501		Pressed Steel	07/04/1954	10/08/1957
30323	81266	81312	BG	711	NA501		Pressed Steel	03/11/1955	15/10/1957
30400	81313	81497	BG	711	NA501		Pressed Steel	17/05/1956	25/01/1958
30484	81498	81572	BG	711	NA501		Pressed Steel	31/05/1957	22/03/1958
30715	81573	81592	BG	711	NA501		GRCW	28/07/1961	03/11/1962
30716	81593	81612	BG	711	NA501		GRCW	28/07/1961	01/12/1962
30725	81613	81628	BG	711	NA501		GRCW	08/10/1962	23/02/1963
31042	82101	82152	DLV		NZ501		Derby	06/08/1987	23/05/1990
31043	82200	82231	DLV		NZ502		Metro-Cammell	01/12/1987	06/08/1991
31095	83301	83301	DLV		NZ503	C	RFS, Doncaster		14/02/1990
30826	85000	85000	PCV		NJ503	C	Derby	17/02/1970	17/01/1970
30922	85500	85507	PVG		NL501	C	Wolverton	14/06/1976	04/11/1978
30922	85508	85534	PVG		NL501	C	Doncaster	14/06/1976	04/11/1978
30417	86078	86499	GUV	811	NI501		Pressed Steel	21/03/1958	24/01/1959
30188	86500	86500	GUV	810			York	04/08/1954	25/02/1956
30343	86501	86520	GUV	811	NI501		Doncaster	05/01/1956	13/07/1957
30402	86521	86654	GUV	811	NI501		York/Glasgow	10/07/1956	16/07/1960
30565	86655	86834	GUV	811	NI501		Pressed Steel	08/01/1959	31/10/1959
30616	86835	86984	GUV	811	NI501		Pressed Steel	20/07/1959	18/06/1960
30125	87000	87499	Fish	800	NR502		Earlestown	13/08/1953	26/02/1955
30344	87500	87692	Fish	801	NR502		Faverdale	16/01/1956	28/01/1961
30384	87693	87957	Fish	801	NR502		Faverdale	06/04/1956	28/01/1961
30442	87958	88057	Fish	801	NR502		Faverdale	06/11/1956	07/10/1961
30345	92000	92064	FRUIT D	805			Swindon	16/01/1956	14/06/1958
30383	92065	92114	FRUIT D	805			Swindon	04/04/1956	21/03/1959
30189	94100	94100	CCT	815			Doncaster	04/08/1954	03/12/1955
30549	94101	94300	CCT	816	NP501		Earlestown	06/11/1958	26/03/1960
30562	94301	94454	CCT	816	NP501		Earlestown	06/01/1959	16/07/1960
30563	94455	94595	CCT	816	NP501		Earlestown	06/01/1959	03/12/1960
30564	94596	94692	CCT	816	NP501		Earlestown	06/01/1959	25/03/1961
30614	94693	94892	CCT	816	NP501		Earlestown	01/06/1959	22/04/1961
30651	94893	94922	CCT	816	NP501		Earlestown	22/10/1959	22/04/1961
30770	95001	95016	CARTIC-4	821			Pressed Steel	14/01/1966	17/06/1967
30770	95051	95066	CARTIC-4	821			Pressed Steel	14/01/1966	17/06/1967
30674	96200	96203	CCTbogie	817		C	Doncaster	19/05/1960	21/05/1960
30664	96286	96299	TCV	820	NV501		Newton Chambers	08/03/1960	21/04/1962
30146	96300	96414	HB	751			Earlestown	03/03/1954	04/10/1958
30831	99500	99503	BFB		NW501		Derby	29/07/1970	27/03/1971
30841	99602	99613	ExhibVan		NY503	C	Swindon	10/08/1971	21/04/1973
30842	99614	99614	ExhibVan		NY503	C	Swindon	10/08/1971	31/01/1976
30842	99620	99625	ExhibVan		NY503	C	Swindon	10/08/1971	31/01/1976
30950	99629	99629	ExhibVan		NY515	C	Stewarts Lane	04/07/1978	19/05/1979
30951	99630	99630	ExhibVan		NY504	C	Stewarts Lane	04/07/1978	18/04/1979
30952	99631	99631	ExhibVan		NY517	C	Stewarts Lane	04/07/1978	19/05/1979
30971	99641	99642	ExhibVan		NY517	C	Stewarts Lane	29/12/1980	30/06/1980

APPENDIX 3
BRAKE TYPES FOR BR MARK 1 PASSENGER CARRYING COACHING STOCK

All Locomotive hauled Mark I Passenger Carrying Coaching Stock was fitted with vacuum brakes when built except lot 30732 (BCK 21263-21275) which were built with air brakes. Various carriages were subsequently fitted with air brakes and are listed below:-(* - signifies carriages which retained their vacuum brakes after fitting with air brakes.)

Type	Carriages
RF	325
RUO	1006, 1018, 1020, 1021, 1023, 1024, 1025, 1027, 1028, 1029, 1030, 1031, 1032, 1033, 1034, 1035, 1036, 1037, 1038, 1039, 1040, 1042, 1043, 1045, 1047, 1049, 1050, 1051, 1052, 1053, 1054, 1055.
RG	1102
RKB	1501, 1502, 1503, 1504, 1505, 1506, 1507, 1508, 1509, 1510, 1511, 1512, 1514, 1515, 1516, 1517, 1518, 1519, 1520, 1521, 1522, 1523, 1524, 1525, 1527, 1528, 1529, 1547, 1548, 1549, 1550, 1551, 1552, 1553, 1554, 1555, 1556, 1557, 1558, 1559, 1560, 1561, 1562, 1563, 1564, 1565, 1566, 1567, 1568, 1569.
RB	1618, 1620, 1621, 1622*, 1623, 1625, 1626, 1627, 1628*, 1630, 1631, 1632, 1633, 1635, 1636, 1637, 1638, 1639, 1640, 1641, 1642, 1643, 1644, 1645, 1646, 1647, 1648, 1649, 1650, 1651, 1652, 1653, 1654, 1655, 1656, 1657, 1658, 1659, 1663*, 1665*, 1666*, 1667*, 1670*, 1671*, 1672*,1673, 1674, 1675*, 1678*, 1679, 1680*, 1681, 1683, 1684*, 1686, 1687, 1688, 1689, 1690*, 1691, 1692, 1693*, 1694, 1695, 1696, 1697, 1698, 1699, 1701*, 1702*, 1703, 1704*, 1705*, 1706*, 1707*, 1708, 1709*, 1710, 1711*, 1712*, 1713*, 1725*, 1727*, 1728*, 1729, 1730*, 1731*, 1732, 1734, 1735*, 1736, 1737, 1738*, 1739, 1740, 1741, 1742, 1743, 1744, 1745, 1746, 1747, 1748, 1749, 1750, 1751, 1752, 1753, 1754, 1755, 1756, 1757, 1758, 1759, 1760, 1761, 1762, 1763, 1772, 1774, 1775, 1776, 1780*.
RMB	1805, 1806, 1807, 1813*, 1814*, 1815*, 1816*, 1822, 1832*, 1833*, 1838*, 1842*, 1845*, 1848*, 1850, 1853*, 1854*, 1857*, 1859*, 1860*,1861*, 1863*, 1864*, 1867, 1868, 1869, 1870, 1871*, 1872, 1873, 1874, 1875, 1876, 1877, 1878, 1879, 1880, 1881, 1882.
BAR	1883.
RU	1917*, 1923*, 1924*, 1944, 1945, 1946, 1947*, 1948*, 1953*, 1954, 1956, 1959, 1961, 1962, 1963, 1964, 1965, 1966, 1967, 1968, 1969, 1970, 1971, 1972, 1973, 1975, 1976, 1978, 1980, 1981, 1982, 1983, 1984, 1985, 1986, 1987, 1988, 1989, 1990.
SLF	2013.
SLC	2441*, 2442*, 2453*.
SLSTP	2500*, 2501*, 2502*, 2503*, 2504*, 2505*, 2506*, 2507*, 2508*, 2509*, 2514*, 2515*, 2517*, 2518*, 2519*, 2520*, 2522*, 2523*, 2524*, 2525*, 2526*, 2527*, 2528*, 2529*, 2530*, 2537*, 2538*, 2544*, 2545*.
ROYAL	499, 2900, 2901.
FO	3009, 3011, 3013, 3014, 3015, 3016, 3017, 3018, 3048, 3049, 3050, 3051, 3052, 3054, 3055, 3059, 3063, 3064, 3065, 3066, 3067, 3068, 3069, 3070, 3071, 3072, 3073, 3075, 3085, 3086, 3087, 3088, 3089, 3090, 3091, 3092, 3093, 3094, 3097, 3098, 3100*, 3107*, 3111*, 3114*, 3115*, 3118*, 3119*, 3120*, 3121, 3122, 3123, 3124, 3127, 3128, 3131*, 3132*, 3133*, 3134*, 3135, 3136, 3137, 3138, 3139, 3140*, 3141, 3142, 3143, 3144, 3145, 3146, 3147, 3148, 3149, 3150, 3151.
TSO	3738, 3739, 3742, 3745, 3746, 3748, 3749, 3756, 3759, 3768, 3773, 3774, 3828, 3829, 3834. 3835, 3837, 3838, 3839, 3840, 3841, 3842, 3843, 3844, 3845, 3846, 3848, 3849, 3915, 3916, 3918, 3919, 3921, 3923, 3924, 3925, 3987, 3988, 3989, 3990, 3991, 3992, 3993, 3994, 3997, 4025, 4031, 4033, 4035, 4036, 4055, 4058, 4059, 4062, 4063, 4065, 4066, 4072, 4073, 4074, 4076, 4077, 4376, 4381, 4389, 4392, 4393, 4436, 4830*, 4831*, 4832*, 4834*, 4835*, 4836*, 4842*, 4849, 4854, 4856*, 4858*, 4860*, 4866, 4869*, 4873, 4875, 4876, 4880, 4902*, 4909*, 4915*, 4916*, 4917*, 4919, 4925, 4927, 4930, 4938, 4939, 4946, 4949, 4956, 4959, 4961, 4963, 4966, 4977, 4979, 4986, 4991, 4993, 4996, 4998, 4999, 5001,

	5002, 5005, 5007, 5008, 5009, 5010, 5023, 5025, 5027, 5028*, 5029, 5030, 5032*, 5033, 5035*, 5037, 5038*, 5040*, 5041, 5042*, 5044.
BSO	9208*, 9225*, 9226*, 9227*, 9229*, 9237*, 9343*.
FK	13143, 13215*, 13218*, 13225*, 13226*, 13227*, 13228*, 13229*, 13230*, 13265*, 13267*, 13318.
BFK	14015*, 14023*.
CK	15049, 15563, 15564, 15565, 15567, 15568, 15570, 15572, 15574, 15575, 15576, 15577, 15579, 15875, 15876, 15877,15878, 15881. 15891, 15896, 15898, 15899, 15902, 15908, 15909, 15915.
BCK	21246*, 21251.
SK	25906, 25907, 25908, 25909, 25910, 25912, 25913, 25914, 25915, 25916, 25917, 25918, 25920, 25924, 25934, 25942, 25944, 25946, 25948, 25953, 25972.
BSK	34637, 34638, 34640, 34641, 34642, 34643, 34644, 34647, 34648, 34652, 34964, 34965, 34971, 34988, 34989, 34990, 34991, 34999, 35006, 35007, 35010, 35011, 35016, 35017, 35023, 35452*, 35453*, 35469*.

N.B. 21272 had its air brakes replaced with vacuum brakes in 1973.

APPENDIX 4
MARK 2 CARRIAGE MODIFICATIONS
1. BRAKES

1.1. Mark 2

All Mark 2 built with vacuum except 13387-13406 which were air.

1.1.1. 13387 subsequently converted to vacuum.

1.1.2. 5126/30/34/37/42/44/46/47/52/53/60/69/76/82/85/87/89/90/92/95/97, 5202. 9387/95/ 97, 9400/03/11/12. 13411/15/16/23/24/27/31. Converted to air for Edinburgh-Glasgow push/pull service in 1971.

1.1.3. 5245/46/47/48/51/52/53/54/55/56. Converted to air for West Coast services.

1.1.4. 14042. Converted to air for Motorail use.

1.1.5. 504/06/46/48/49/50/51/52/53/86. Converted to air for Charter Train use.

1.2. Mark 2A

All Mark 2A built with air.

1.2.1. 13434/35/36/37/38/40/41/42/43/44/46/47/50/70/74/75. 14059/60/61/62/64/66/68, 14083/85/87/89/90/91/92/94/95/99, 14101/03. Converted to vacuum.

2. DECLASSIFICATION

2.1.   Mark 2A

2.1.1.   13452/54/55/57/58/60/62/64/65/66/69/73, 14057/63/69/75/79/80/88/89/90/92/94/97. Declassified to SK/BSK and renumbered.

2.1.1.1.   13462/73, 14092. Subsequently reclassified to FK/BFK, former numbers reinstated.

2.2.   Mark 2B

2.2.1.   13476/78/79/81/83/84/85/86/88/89/91/97, 13500/01/04/05/07/11/12/13. Declassified to SK and renumbered.

2.2.1.1.   13479/88, 13507/13. Subsequently reclassified to FK, former numbers reinstated.

2.3.   Mark 2C

2.3.1.   3152/53/54/55/56/57/58/59/60/61/62/63/64/65/67/68/69, 13515/18/21/22/23/29, 13533/34/35/36/37/38/40/41/42/43/44/45/46/47/48/49/55/56/57/60, 14118/22/23/28, 14130/38. Declassified to SO/SK/BSK and renumbered.

2.3.1.1.   13542. Subsequently reclassified to FK and former number reinstated.

2.3.2.   13550/51/53/58/61 Partially declassified to CK and renumbered.

2.4.   Mark 2F

2.4.1.   3276/81/82/83/87/88/89/94/97/98, 3301/06/07/10/11/15/16/17/20/23/24/27/28/29/39, 3342/43/49/55/57/61/65/76/80/94/96, 3403/04/05/10/22/23/27/30/35/36/37. Declassified to SO and renumbered.

2.4.1.1.   3403. Subsequently reclassified to FO and former number reinstated.

3. CONVERSIONS

3.1.   Mark 2

3.1.1.   9383/89/98, 9401/04/05/06/07. Converted to BSOT and renumbered.

3.2.   Mark 2C

3.2.1.   5499, 5503/06/10/11/13//18/28/34/37/38/44/47/51/53/56/58/63/64/68/78/79/87, 5592/98/99, 5602/03/08/11. Converted to TSOT and renumbered.

3.3.   Mark 2D

3.3.1.   5622/27/35/41/44/49/55/56/88/91/96/97/98, 5702/20/21/25/33/36/41. Converted to TSOT and renumbered.

3.3.1.1.   5622/27/41, 5721/36. Subsequently converted to RMBT and renumbered.

3.3.2.   3170/71/73/75/76/77/79/80/83/84/85/89/90/91/93/94/95/96//97/98/99, 3200/01/03/04/05/06/07/08/09/10/11/12/13/15/16. Converted to TSO and renumbered.

3.4.   Mark 2E

3.4.1.   3236/38/53/54/55/71. Converted to FO (Pantry) and renumbered.

3.5.   Mark 2F

3.5.1.   6420/23/24/25/27/28/29/31/34/35/36/37/39/40/42/43/46/47/48/49/51/52/54/55/58, 6460/61/63/64/65. Converted to TSO and renumbered.

3.5.2.   3280/84/91/96, 3302/05/19/22/32/71/72/77/78/83/91/93, 3401/18/19/32/39, 6422/32/33/38/44/45/53/56/57/59/62. Converted to RFB and renumbered.

3.5.3.   3308/41/46/47/70, 3421, 6418/21/30. Converted to RLO and renumbered.

3.5.4.   9510/11/12/14/15/17/18/19/28/30/32/34/35/36. Converted to DBSO and renumbered.

3.5.5.   5970. Converted to RSS and renumbered.

APPENDIX 5
SOUTHERN REGION AIR BRAKED MARK 1/MARK 2 COACHING STOCK

From 1963 onwards the Southern Region instigated a program of air-braking much of its locomotiv
hauled coaching stock fleet. The Mark 1s included in this program are included in Appendix 3 above
The Southern Region air-braked fleet of the 1970s and early 1980s is detailed below, it being spl
into three distinct groupings.

Group one consists of 100 mph stock, this being principally used on the South Western Division fc
Boat Trains to both Weymouth Quay for the Channel Islands and Southampton Docks for Ocean Line
sailings. This stock also saw occasional use on the West of England line, particularly on summe
weekends, and on relief and excursion workings. This group includes the forty seven Mark 1s whic
received Commonwealth bogies from newer carriages in the late 1960s and the batch of early Mar
2 FKs built with air-brakes. The most significant change to this group took place in 1974 when fiv
RBs were swapped for five RMBs. The remaining RB, 1759, being the one fitted for use with multipl
unit stock and formed as part of 8-Vab unit 8001 at the time. This carriage was withdrawn a coup
of years later. Two of the RMBs, 1872 & 1873, were subsequently modified to work with multipl
unit stock. In 1976 several of the FKs were transferred for use on Oxted line duties displacing CK
in sets otherwise consisting of stock from group two. In the early 1970s a few carriages left this grou
for other regions. FK 13387 was transferred to the Eastern Region, where it later had its air-brake
replaced with vacuum brakes, FK 13396 became the prototype air conditioning coach at the Railwa
Technical Centre Derby numbered DB975290 and BCKs 21269 & 21272 were transferred to th
Scottish Region, principally seeing use as the 'Carstairs spare brake'. This was a carriage kept a
Carstairs for attachment to portions of trains from the south arriving without a brake vehicle. For thes
duties 21272 was converted to vacuum braking for use with vacuum braked trains, whilst 2126!
retained its air brakes for use with air braked trains. The CKs were the first carriages of this grou
to be withdrawn, all being condemned in the mid 1970s. In the early 1980s several TSOs wer
withdrawn for EMU conversion whilst quite surprisingly the FOs which had become synonymous wit
'Ocean Liner' trains were withdrawn in 1982 along with RMBs 1806, 1807 & 1822. Other than
few withdrawals for departmental conversions the remainder of this group survived in service unt
the late 1980s, whilst many of the BCKs remain in service today with the Special Trains Unit. Th
early 1980s saw a gradual infiltration of TSOs & BSKs on to Oxted line workings where they replace
90 mph equivalents, this coinciding with the increased deployment of Oxted line sets at weekend
on West of England workings. Locomotive haulage ceased on the Oxted line in 1984, by which tim
the remaining sets had been completely formed of this stock for a couple of years.

Group two consists of 90 mph stock, this being principally used for Oxted line duties, the locomotiv
hauled trains on the Tonbridge-Reading route, relief & special workings and in the early 1970s
Newhaven boat trains. The withdrawal of locomotive-hauled Newhaven Boat Trains and a reductio
in the requirement of carriages for special workings etc in the early 1970s resulted in man
condemnations of TSOs, CKs, BSKs and the FK, this was followed by the condemnation of th
remaining CKs in 1976 following their replacement with FKs from group one on Oxted line trains. Th
majority of locomotive hauled trains ceased on the Tonbridge-Reading route in 1977 with one diagran
surviving a further year, this resulting in further withdrawals of TSOs & BSKs. As mentioned abov
the early 1980s saw an infiltration of 100 mph TSOs & BSKs from group one on to Oxted line services
This resulted in the final BSK from this group being withdrawn in 1981 whilst the SKs and remainin
TSOs saw several more years service on relief & special workings.

Group three consists of stock used principally in connection with the 'Night Ferry', a train runnin
between London Victoria and Dover which conveyed through Wagon Lits sleeping carriages t
European destinations. These carriages were fitted with heaters to UIC standards which had an eart
return via the track allowing them to be used in conjunction with Class 71 locomotives. For workin
'Night Ferry' trains RUOs 1006 & 1018 were fitted with adaptor gangways which allowed them t
be coupled to the Wagons Lits sleeping cars. When dining facilities were removed from the train o
22nd May 1977 the adaptor gangways were switched to BCKs 21270 & 21273 which up to this tim
had found use on the South Western Division with carriages in group one when not required for th
'Night Ferry'. Passengers not partaking of the sleeping accommodation were conveyed on the trai
until 31st May 1975 after which they were conveyed separately by EMU. This resulted in th
remaining CKs being condemned and TSOs transferred to other duties. By this time BCKs 21263 &
21264 had already been displaced, 21263 passing to the Railway Technical Centre at Derby for us
as a Laboratory Coach numbered DB975280 and 21264 to the Scottish Region for use as a 'Carstair

pare brake'. The withdrawal of dining facilities resulted in RBs 1755 & 1772 being transferred to the Western Region and the other catering carriages being condemned. However RUO 1006 found further use as EMU translator vehicle DB975867 whilst RUO 1018 became Exhibition Van 99631. The 'Night Ferry' last ran on 31st October 1980, 21270 & 21273 thus had their adapter gangways removed and again saw use with carriages in group one.

The presence of air-brakes has made the Corridor Brakes particularly suited to departmental conversion following withdrawal, this having happened to four of the BCKs covered in this appendix. Indeed only one of the BCKs has been scrapped, this being 21264 which was scrapped at W.F. Smith, Ecclesfield in the late 1970s. All of the 100 mph BSKs were converted for departmental use, regrettably two of these, 34638 (DB977509) and 34641 (DB977495) having now been scrapped, the former by Gwent Demolition & Construction at Margam Yard and the latter on site at Stratford TMD. This later coach was initially purchased for preservation, the intention being that it would be used as a support coach for locomotive 69621 based at the East Anglian Railway Museum. Regrettably however vandals put a stop to this project. Nine of the nineteen 90 mph BSKs were converted to departmental use although two of these have subsequently been scrapped. Carriages in these three groups during the 1970s and 1980s are shown below:-

1. EH/AB 100 mph Commonwealth bogies (*B4 bogies)

RB	1758, 1759, 1760, 1761, 1762, 1763. (Total = 6) *1758/60/61/62/63 Removed 1974.*
RMB	1806*, 1807*, 1822, 1872, 1873. (Total = 5) *Added 1974.*
O	3064*, 3065*, 3066*, 3067*, 3068, 3069*, 3070*. (Total = 7)
TSO	3749, 3828, 3829, 3837, 3840, 3844, 3846, 3916, 3918, 3919, 3921, 3923, 3924, 3988, 3990, 3991, 3992, 3993, 3994, 4058, 4059, 4062, 4063, 4065, 4066, 4072, 4076, 4376, 4381, 4389, 4392, 4393, 4436. (Total = 33)
K	13387*, 13388*, 13389*, 13390*, 13391*, 13392*, 13393*, 13394*, 13395*, 13396*, 13397*, 13398*, 13399*, 13400*, 13401*, 13402*, 13403*, 13404*, 13405*, 13406*. (Total = 20)
CK	15563, 15567, 15568, 15570, 15572, 15891, 15896. (Total = 7)
BCK	21251, 21265, 21266, 21267, 21268, 21269, 21271, 21272, 21274, 21275. (Total = 10)
SK	25906, 25924, 25934, 25942. (Total = 4)
BSK	34638, 34641, 34642, 34971, 35010, 35011. (Total = 6)

2. EH/AB 90 mph BR1 bogies

TSO	3738, 3739, 3742, 3745, 3746, 3748, 3756, 3759, 3768, 3773, 3774, 3834. 3835, 3838, 3839, 3841, 3842, 3843, 3845, 3848, 3849, 3915, 3925, 3987, 3989, 3997, 4025, 4055, 4073, 4074, 4077. (Total = 31)
K	13143. (Total = 1)
CK	15049, 15564, 15565, 15574, 15575, 15576, 15577, 15898, 15899, 15902, 15908, 15909, 15915. (Total = 13)
SK	25907, 25908, 25909, 25910, 25912, 25913, 25914, 25915, 25916, 25917, 25918, 25920, 25944, 25946, 25948, 25953, 25972. (Total = 17)
BSK	34637, 34640, 34643, 34644, 34647, 34648, 34652, 34964, 34965, 34988, 34989, 34990, 34991, 34999, 35006, 35007, 35016, 35017, 35023. (Total = 19)

3. EH(BR & UIC)/AB 90 mph (*100 mph) BR1 bogies (*Commonwealth bogies)

RUO	1006, 1018*. (Total = 2)
RB	1755*, 1756*, 1757*, 1772*. (Total = 4)
TSO	4031, 4033, 4035, 4036. (Total = 4)
CK	15579, 15875, 15876, 15877, 15878, 15881. (Total = 6)
BCK	21263, 21264, 21270*, 21273*. (Total = 4)

APPENDIX 6
LOCATION ORDER LISTING

Details are given below of the principal locations where preserved carriages included in this book are normally found. Readers are however recommended to check the individual carriages entry earlier in the book to ensure that the particular carriage is not located elsewhere. Carriages are listed for each location in the same order as detailed earlier in the book, that is Pullman Cars, Mark 1s, Mark 2s, Mark 3s and Non-passenger carrying coaching stock whilst the locations are in alphabetical order. It should be mentioned that smaller sites where very few vehicles are located, such as public houses, are not included here. The number shown is the original number which may not be the number now carried by the vehicle.

Avon Valley Railway

Mk 1: 1933, 2599, 3089, 3745, 3746, 3749, 3815, 3991, 4035, 4058, 9208, 13231, 24800, 25040, 25299, 25735, 34111, 34531, 35174, 35255
Mk 2: 14031
NPCCS: 92095, 99629

Battlefield Steam Railway

Mk 1: 301, 1981, 3785, 4824, 4918, 13125, 21031, 34953
NPCCS: 81428

Bo'ness & Kinneil Railway

Mk 1: 1730, 1859, 1866, 2612, 2613, 3096, 4215, 4224, 4422, 4466, 4529, 4831, 4832, 4836, 4844, 4856, 4871, 5028, 9227, 9237, 13228, 13229, 13230, 15834, 16201, 35123, 35197, 35304, 35328, 35405

Bluebell Railway

Mk 1: 1566, 1818, 1838, 1987, 2108, 2110, 2442, 3116, 4921, 4941, 4957, 5034, 16210, 16263, 21238, 25728, 25752, 25769, 25776, 25778, 25795, 25853, 25856, 25871, 25994, 26169, 26208, 35448

Birmingham Railway Museum

PULLMAN: 310
Mk 1: 3045, 3736, 4508, 14018
NPCCS: 86178, 92076

Buckinghamshire Railway Centre

Mk 1: 4867, 15319, 16235, 24993, 25500, 35192, 53190
Mk 2: 5324, 9384
NPCCS: 86450, 94578, 96403

Bodmin Steam Railway

Mk 1: 1873, 1874, 16012, 16065, 16068, 16237, 25560, 25572, 34620, 34627, 35130
Mk 2: 5136, 5181, 14092
Mk 3: 10618
NPCCS: 80702

Chinnor & Princes Risborough, Railway

Mk 1: 1845
Mk 2: 9410, 13436
NPCCS: 80501

Caledonian Railway

Mk 1: 4249, 4495, 4676, 4809, 4864, 9315, 34539, 46142
Mk 2: 5145, 5188, 14059
NPCCS: 80030, 94259, 999502

Cheddleton Railway Centre

Mk 1: 4354, 4392, 4795, 15207, 15208, 35343, 35473, 53086, 53111

Colne Valley, Railway

PULLMAN: 305
Mk 1: 1809, 4512, 4628, 4810, 15939, 15981, 15984, 25697, 34623, 35169
Mk 3: 10511
NPCCS: 80785, 80792, 81507, 94434, 94536, 94737, 94889, 96347

Cholsey & Wallingford Railway

Mk 1: 15849, 24918

Dean Forest Railway

Mk 1: 1803, 1917, 4218, 4300, 4316, 4472, 4614, 4729, 4862, 9369, 13407, 21129, 21247,
    25509, 34665
NPCCS: 80654, 86823, 86847, 94518

Didcot Railway Centre

Mk 1: 15565, 15577, 34671, 35276, 35322, 35333
Mk 2: 14041
Mk 3: 10509

Elsecar at Barnsley, Elsecar

Mk 1: 3958, 4903, 35305

East Anglian Railway Museum

Mk 1: 3779, 21027, 24959, 43157
NPCCS: 81295

East Kent Light Railway

Mk 1: 21234, 43140

East Lancashire Railway

Mk 1: 1703, 1816, 1833, 1837, 1848, 1875, 1880, 2586, 3771, 4199, 4232, 4350, 4371, 4647,
    4762, 4767, 4784, 4885, 4895, 4928, 4933, 4937, 4992, 5031, 9356, 13333, 15916,
    15928, 16153, 25385, 25828, 34624, 34666, 34949, 35070, 35314, 35455
Mk 2: 5199, 5216, 5238, 5526, 5590, 9382, 9391, 13440, 13474
NPCCS: 80993, 86283, 86869, 86918, 94264, 94534

East Somerset Railway

Mk 1: 4378, 4562, 4584, 4641, 4907, 9241, 25917, 53049, 53100
NPCCS: 81156, 963XX

Embsay Steam Railway

Mk 1: 1826, 1857, 1969, 2573, 4406, 4460, 4575, 4666, 4799, 5003, 9370, 15952, 16165,
    21261, 25472, 34558, 46235
NPCCS: 80830, 94338

Foxfield Light Railway

Mk 1: 25225, 25231, 25607, 25891

Gloucestershire-Warwickshire Railway

Mk 1: 1808, 1811, 1876, 1946, 3091, 3727, 3960, 4331, 4440, 4787, 4790, 4798, 4806, 5054,
    13089, 13326, 13329, 13337, 15989, 16166, 16195, 16221, 21092, 24421, 24778, 24949,
    25020, 25341, 25451, 25501, 25618, 25631, 25646, 25743, 34548, 34676, 34929, 35006,
    35201, 35308, 46116
Mk 2: 13438, 13442, 13454, 13464
Mk 3: 10518
NPCCS: 80580, 81039, 81305, 92096

Great Central Railway

PULLMAN: 315, 337
Mk 1: 1012, 1525, 1526, 1695, 1852, 1962, 3042, 3079, 3092, 3095, 3126, 4362, 4610, 4630,
    4662, 4758, 4788, 4857, 4914, 4922, 4948, 4965, 4982, 9316, 13313, 14026, 15096,
    15611, 15960, 16025, 16070, 21184, 21242, 25189, 25312, 25366, 25711, 34393, 34738,
    35334, 43043, 46139, 48001
NPCCS: 81343, 94125, 94286, 94605, 94606, 94707, 94709, 96202

Great Eastern Railway

Mk 2: 5211, 5219, 5536, 9393, 9409, 13446, 13447
NPCCS: 86881, 87602, 94869

Gwili Railway

Mk 1: 1106, 3060, 4420, 4906, 15829, 21187, 24825, 24843, 35012, 46132, 53051
NPCCS: 92004

Kent & East Sussex Railway

Mk 1: 1955, 3753, 4037, 4640, 9254, 9269, 15927, 15961, 25446

Keighley & Worth Valley Railway

Mk 1: 1013, 1824, 1836, 1963, 4306, 4467, 4588, 4774, 4840, 4900, 4955, 9273, 14019,
    35451, 43003, 43128, 43145, 46145, 46157, 48011, 48018, 53156
NPCCS: 80591, 87582, 87948, 96327

Lakeside Railway

Mk 1: 1812, 3881, 3962, 4255, 4410, 4760, 9218, 25337, 25364, 35309, 35330

Lavender Line, Isfield

Mk 1: 3125, 4668, 4830, 21249

Llangollen Railway

Mk 1: 1651, 1657, 1665, 1829, 1864, 1869, 1878, 2132, 2574, 3950, 4236, 4243, 4484, 4503,
    4643, 4702, 4779, 4789, 4796, 4808, 9380, 13340, 15626, 15667, 15674, 15931, 16071,
    25417, 25421, 25807, 34537, 34538, 34584, 35188, 35340, 35342, 46130, 53182
Mk 2: 5220, 9396
Mk 3: 10517, 10521, 10608, 10611
NPCCS: 80509, 80518, 80741, 81107, 86622, 94677, 94691, 96300

Mangapp's Farm Railway Museum

Mk 1: 13324
NPCCS: 87888, 94109

Midland Railway Centre

Mk 1: 334, 499, 1802, 1862, 3809, 4366, 4480, 4534, 4537, 4804, 4816, 4904, 5045, 9281,
    9300, 21059, 21232, 26014, 34255, 34625, 35131, 35297, 35476, 46097, 48004, 53186
Mk 2: 3168, 5333, 5461, 13437, 13484
NPCCS: 80590, 80686, 80782, 81020, 81144, 86380

National Railway Museum

PULLMAN: 326
Mk 1: 1100, 4286, 35362, 35468, 43046
Mk 2: 5455, 13252
NPCCS: 96369

Nene Valley Railway

Mk 1: 1872, 4200, 4615, 4627, 4635, 4667, 4686, 4919, 13328, 24997, 25347, 25639, 26193,
    34935, 35043, 35239, 35248
NPCCS: 87537, 94796

North Norfolk Railway

Mk 1: , 3868, 4355, 4521, 4651, 4843, 15997, 21103, 35148, 43034, 43041, 46147, 48026,
    53168, 53170
Mk 3: 10525
NPCCS: 81033, 81269, 92097, 94464

North Yorkshire Moors Railway

PULLMAN: 318, 327, 328
Mk 1: 324, 1823, 3798, 3801, 3805, 3860, 3872, 3948, 4198, 4207, 4252, 4290, 4425, 4455,
    4597, 4728, 4786, 4817, 4839, 4990, 5000, 9235, 9267, 9274, 13043, 15709, 15745,
    16156, 16233, 21100, 21240, 24804, 24808, 24984, 25142, 25488, 25508, 25700, 34699,
    35089, 35299, 35449, 35457, 35464
Mk 2: 3161, 3167

NPCCS: 80796, 86545, 86639, 86813

Northampton & Lamport Railway

PULLMAN: 321
Mk 1: 3919, 9225, 13092, 16019, 24576, 34712, 43012, 43147
Mk 2: 5229, 9383
NPCCS: 81031, 86966

Paignton & Dartmouth Railway

Mk 1: 1694, 4081, 4205, 4233, 4507, 4642, 4665, 4756, 4763, 4772, 9275, 25307, 34535, 34550, 35072
NPCCS: 92091

Peak Railway, Darley Dale

Mk 1: 1835, 1970, 2080, 3825, 4372, 4476, 4623, 4974, 9276, 15663, 15943, 16155, 26025, 26043, 26049, 26157, 35193, 35200
Mk 2: 5235, 9398, 15541t 86183

Plym Valley Railway

Mk 1: 16204, 25591, 34756, 34945

Pontypool & Blaenavon, Railway

Mk 1: 1854, 4046, 4654, 4677, 25444, 35494

Severn Valley Railway

Mk 1: 1682, 1855, 1856, 1883, 3083, 3103, 4345, 4399, 4509, 4545, 4550, 4593, 4690, 9220, 16169, 16202, 16232, 16267, 21254, 24839, 24845, 25346, 25498, 25594, 25686, 25771, 34562, 35315, 35316, 35467, 46141
NPCCS: 80307, 80776, 81013, 86105, 92080, 92090

South Devon Railway

Mk 1: 3081, 4496, 4785, 4802, 4805, 4962, 15644, 24458, 25032, 25355, 25693, 35326
Mk 2: 9392
NPCCS: 92035, 92067

South Yorkshire Railway

Mk 1: 4976, 25362, 25562, 34675, 35129
Mk 2: 13444
NPCCS: 80905, 86350, 86383, 86470, 86565, 86802, 86972, 94226, 94817

Southall Railway Centre

Mk 1: 2013, 3769, 3961, 14007, 14013, 14021, 35204, 35327, 35447, 35466
NPCCS: 81025, 87671

Spa Valley Railway

Mk 1: 21214, 25832, 25843, 25845, 25857
NPCCS: 86226

Steamtown Railway Centre, Carnforth

PULLMAN: 311, 316
Mk 1: 1860, 1863, 1882, 1926, 1929, 1949, 2131, 2500, 3016, 3105, 3113, 3117, 3128, 3130, 3766, 4912, 4931, 4932, 4954, 4958, 5033, 5044, 5067, 13317, 13320, 13321, 13323, 14025, 16168, 16187, 16190, 16191, 21096, 21256, 25729, 25756, 25767, 25806, 25808, 25837, 25862, 25893, 25955, 26013, 35073, 35459, 35461, 35463
Mk 2: 504, 506, 546, 548, 549, 550, 551, 552, 553, 586, 3155, 3260, 5299, 5600, 5642, 5645, 5704, 5709, 5712, 5714, 5727, 5756, 14102, 14168

Steamport Railway Museum

Mk 1: 1839, 1879, 4886, 35128

Stephenson Railway Museum

Mk 1: 43010, 48015, 53172

Strathspey Railway

PULLMAN: 325
Mk 1: 1928, 1936, 4079, 4127, 4477, 4777, 5053, 5055, 5057, 5060, 9362, 15401, 35069, 43024, 53160
Mk 2: 5149, 5228, 14101

Swanage Railway

Mk 1: 1865, 1908, 1937, 1947, 2564, 3090, 3764, 4055, 4074, 4349, 4416, 4803, 4899, 4945, 9229, 13308, 13314, 15673, 21205, 24127, 25424, 35059
Mk 3: 10619
NPCCS: 81146

Swansea Vale Railway

Mk 1: 46137

Swindon & Cricklade Railway

Mk 1: 1569, 1805, 4764, 4766, 13233, 13303, 13316, 25869, 34540, 34634, 34941
NPCCS: 80892, 94501

Telford Railway Centre

Mk 1: 13349

Watercress Line

Mk 1: 302, 1668, 1806, 1807, 1840, 1851, 1961, 1973, 3065, 3067, 3070, 3738, 3748, 3906, 4423, 4549, 4600, 4656, 4712, 9377, 16083, 21208, 21252, 34618, 34947, 35329
Mk 2: 5125, 5141, 5171, 5200, 5222, 5236, 5237, 5239, 5243, 5249, 9390, 9401, 13450, 13475, 13540
NPCCS: 80753, 81101, 86460, 86690

West Somerset Railway

Mk 1: 1804, 1909, 3058, 3108, 4039, 4260, 4346, 4419, 4435, 4449, 4493, 4599, 4602, 4660, 4814, 4884, 4911, 5024, 9278, 15632, 21034, 21174, 24006, 24307, 24985, 25308, 25323, 25454, 34769, 35257
Mk 2: 5344
NPCCS: 80736, 80742, 80972, 94502, 94917

LIST OF LOCATIONS

The following is a list of UK locations where the carriages included in this book can be found, together with Ordnance Survey grid references where these are known. At certain locations, particularly the larger private railways, carriages may be dispersed at several sites. In such cases the principle site where carriages can normally be found is the one given. Enquiries at this location may reveal the whereabouts of other carriages. Details of carriages stored on a long term basis away from their home location are generally given in the text of this book.

Location	OS Grid Ref.
ABB Transportation Ltd, Derby Carriage Works, Litchurch Lane, Derby, Derbyshire (Private Site)	SK 364345
ABB Transportation Ltd., York Works, York, North Yorkshire (Private Site)	SE 587516
Alf Hall, Delph Station, Oldham, Greater Manchester (Private Site)	SD 987074
Albert Looms Ltd., Spondon, Derby, Derbyshire (Private Site)	SK 390354
The Anglers Arms, Weldon Bridge, Northumberland	NZ 137988
Army Dogs School, Defence Animal Centre, Welby Lane Camp, Melton Mowbray, Leicestershire (Private Site)	SK 734206
Audley End Miniature Railway, Audley End, Saffron Walden, Essex	TL 523379
Avon Causeway Hotel, Hurn, Christchurch, Dorset	SZ 136977
Avon Valley Railway, Bitton Station, Bristol, Avon	ST 670705
Battlefield Steam Railway, Shackerstone Station, Shackerstone, Leicestershire	SK 379066
Bekonscot Model Village, Warwick Road, Beaconsfield, Buckinghamshire	SU 939914
Bere Ferrers Station Museum, Bere Ferrers, Devon	SX 452635
Bideford Station Museum, Bideford, Devon	SS 458264
Birmingham Railway Museum, Tyseley Depot, Tyseley, Birmingham, West Midlands	SP 105841
Bluebell Railway Company, Sheffield Park, Uckfield, East Sussex	TQ 403238
Bo'ness & Kinneil Railway, 'Forth Valley Line', Bo'ness Station, Bo'ness, West Lothian	NT 003817
Bodmin Steam Railway, Bodmin General Station, Bodmin, Cornwall	SX 073664
Bogie Chain Public House, Western Road, Wallsend, Tyne & Wear	NZ 318666
Bristol Industrial Museum, Princess Wharf, City Dock, Bristol, Avon	ST 585722
Buckinghamshire Railway Centre, Quainton Road Station, Aylesbury, Buckinghamshire	SP 736189
The Buffers Resturant, Scholes, Leeds, West Yorkshire	SE 376374
Bulmers Railway Centre, Hereford, Herefordshire (Private Site)	SO 505402
CAD Bramley Military Railway, Bramley, Hampshire (Private Site)	SU 658589
COD Bicester Military Railway, Bicester, Oxfordshire (Private Site)	SP 581203
Caerphilly Railway, Harold Wilson Industrial Estate, Caerphilly, Mid-Glamorgan	ST 113865
Caledonian Railway, Brechin Station, Brechin, Angus, Tayside	NO 603603
The Carriages Of Moy, Invermoy House Hotel, Moy, Invernesshire	NH 763345
Casterton Taverner Motor Inn, Stamford, Lincolnshire	TF 007083
The Cedar Tree Resturant, Nutbourne, Bosham, West Sussex	SO 782055
Cheddleton Railway Centre, Cheddleton Station, Cheddleton, Leek, Staffordshire	SJ 983519
Cheriton Exhibition Centre (Eurotunnel), Folkestone, Kent	
Chinnor and Princess Risborough Railway, Chinnor Cement Works, Chinnor, Oxfordshire	SP 756004
Cholsey & Wallingford Railway, Hithercroft Industrial Estate, Wallingford, Oxfordshire	SU 599891
Colne Valley Railway, Castle Hedingham Station, Halstead, Essex	TL 774362
Conwy Valley Railway Museum, Old Goods Yard, Betws-y-Coed, Gwynedd	SH 796565
Coventry Railway Centre, 'The Airfield Line', Rowley Road, Baginton, Coventry, Warwickshire	SP 354751
Dalriada Steam Packet Company, Station Pier, Loch Avenue, By Dalmally Argyll, Strathclyde	NN 124274
Darlington Railway Preservation Society, North Road Goods Shed, Darlington, County Durham	NZ 290156
Dawlish Warren Camp Site, Dawlish Warren, Devon	SX 979785
Dean Forest Railway, Norchard Steam Centre, Lydney, Gloucestershire	SO 629044
Didcot Railway Centre (Great Western Society), Didcot, Oxfordshire	SU 524906
Diesel Traction Group, BR Old Oak Common CARMD., Acton, London	TQ 218823
Directors Saloon, Wymondham Station, Wymondham, Norfolk	TG 113009
Donnington Park Race Track, Castle Donnington, Leicestershire	SK 421258
East Anglian Railway Museum, Chappel and Wakes Colne Station, Essex	TL 898289

East Kent Light Railway, Shepherdswell, Kent	TR 258483
East Lancashire Railway, Bolton Street Station, Bury, Greater Manchester	SD 803109
East Somerset Railway, 'The Strawberry Line', Cranmore Railway Station, Shepton Mallet, Somerset	ST 664429
Elsecar at Barnsley, Wath Road, Elsecar, Barnsley, South Yorkshire	SE 390003
Embsay Steam Railway, Embsay Station, Embsay, Skipton, North Yorkshire	SE 007533
Eureka, National Childrens Museum, Halifax, West Yorkshire	SE 097247
Eastleigh Railway Preservation Society, BRML Eastleigh Works, Eastleigh, Hampshire	SU 457185
Errol Station Museum, Errol, Tayside	NO 254246
Euroclad, Wentloog Corporate Park, Rumney, Cardiff, South Glamorgan (Private Site)	
Fire Service Training Centre, Moreton-in-Marsh, Gloucestershire (Private Site)	SP 216329
Flying Scotsman Railways, Bounds Green T&RSMD., London (Operating Home Base)	TL 302907
Foxfield Light Railway, Blythe Bridge, Stoke-on-Trent, Staffordshire	SJ 976446
Foster Yeoman, Isle of Grain, Rochester, Kent (Private Site)	TQ 875743
Glenfinnan Station Museum, Glenfinnan, Highland	
Gloucestershire-Warwickshire Railway, Toddington Station, Gloucestershire	SP 020323
Great Central Railway, Loughborough Central Station, Leicestershire	SK 543194
The Great Central (Nottingham) Ltd., Nottingham Heritage Centre, Mereway, Ruddington, Nottinghamshire	
Great Eastern Railway, County School Station, North Elmham, Norfolk	TF 990227
Great Scottish & Western Railway Company, Millerhill Royal Scotsman Siding, Edinburgh (Operating Home Base)	NT 327690
Greater Manchester Museum of Science & Industry, Liverpool Road Station, Manchester, Greater Manchester	SJ 831978
Grimsby & Louth Railway, Lugborough Station, Lugborough, Lincolnshire	TF 308961
Gwili Railway Company, Bronwydd Arms Station, Carmarthen, Dyfed	SN 417236
214 High Street, Burbage, Wiltshire (Private Residence)	SU 230610
Humberside Locomotive Preservation Group, Dairycoates Depot, Hull, Humberside	TA 068269
Hull Museum of Transport, 40 High Street, Kingston upon Hull, Humberside	TA 103284
Keighley & Worth Valley Railway, Haworth Station, Haworth, Keighley, West Yorkshire	SE 034371
Kent & East Sussex Railway, Tenterden Town Station, Tenterden, Kent	TQ 882336
Kingdom of Fife Railway Preservation Society (Site still to be established)	
Lakeside Caravan Park, Exbridge, Devon	SS 933241
Lakeside Railway, Haverthwaite, Cumbria	SD 349843
Lancashire Fire Brigade, International Training Centre, Washington Hall, Chorley, Lancashire (Private Site)	SD 570188
Lancastrian Carriage & Wagon, Bay Close, Port of Heysham Industrial Park, Heysham, Lancashire (Private Site)	SD 408604
Lavender Line, Isfield Station, Isfield, East Sussex	TQ 452171
Leadburn Inn, Leadburn, Peebleshire	NT 235556
Llangollen Railway, Llangollen Station, Llangollen, Clwyd	SJ 211423
London Underground Ltd., Various locations within Greater London	
Long Marston Military Railway, Long Marston, Warwickshire (Private Site)	SP 153473
Mangapp's Farm Railway Museum, Mangapp's Farm, Burnham-on-Crouch, Essex	TQ 944980
Markinch Goods Depot (J.B. Cameron), Markinch Station, Markinch, Fife	NO 299013
Marsden Rattler Restaurant, Sea Road, South Shields, Tyne & Wear	NZ 377673
Madame Tussaud's, Royalty & Railways Exhibition, Windsor & Eton Central Station, Windsor, Berkshire	SU 966769
Midland Railway Centre, Butterley Station, Ripley, Derbyshire	SK 403520
Mod Cad Kineton, Warwickshire (Private Site)	SP 37352.
National Railway Museum, Leeman Road, York, North Yorkshire	SE 594519
National Rifle Club, Bisley Camp, Bisley, Surrey (Private Site)	SU 938577
Nene Valley Railway, Wansford Station, Peterborough, Cambridgeshire	TL 093979
Nomix-Chipman, Horsham Goods Yard, Horsham, West Sussex (Private Site)	TQ 179313
North Downs Steam Railway, Stone Lodge Centre, Dartford, Kent	TQ 562745
North Eastern Locomotive Preservation Group, ICI Wilton, Cleveland (Private Site)	NZ 564218
North Norfolk Railway, 'The Poppy Line', Sheringham Station, Norfolk	TG 156430
North Yorkshire Moors Railway, Pickering Station, North Yorkshire	NZ 828049
Northampton and Lamport Railway, Pitsford & Brampton Station, Pitsford, Near Northampton, Northamptonshire	SP 736660
Once Upon A Time, Woolacombe Station, Woolacombe, Devon	SS 484438
Orient Express Restaurant, Elsenham, Cambridgeshire	TL 53227
Paignton & Dartmouth Railway, Queen's Park Station, Paignton, Devon	SX 889060

Peak Railway, 'Peak Rail', Darley Dale Station, Derbyshire SK 273626
Peco Modelrama, Beer, Devon SY 225894
Platform Three Restaurant, Colwyn Bay Station, Colwyn Bay, Clwyd, North Wales SH 852793
Play Train, Huddersfield Station, Huddersfield, West Yorkshire SE 143169
Pleasure Island, South Promenade, Lytham St Annes, Lancashire SD 368269
Pleasurewood Hills Park, Lowestoft, Suffolk TM 545965
Plym Valley Railway, 'The Woodland Line', Marsh Mills Station, Marsh Mills,
Plymouth, Devon SX 521566
Pontypool & Blaenavon Railway, Furnoe Sidings, Big Pit, Blaenavon, Gwent SO 237093
Pullman Lodge Hotel and Restaurant, Seaburn, Sunderland, Tyne & Wear NZ 406595
Queen of Scots Train, St Leonards Depot, Hastings, East Sussex
(Operating Home Base) TQ 778086
R. Oakley, GLC Rubbish Terminal, Brentford, London, (Private Site) TQ 166779
RFS Engineering Ltd., Doncaster Wagon Works, Doncaster, South Yorkshire
(Private Site) SK 569031
Rail Uk Ltd., Steamtown Railway Centre, Carnforth, Lancashire SD 496708
The Railway Age, Crewe, Cheshire SJ 708552
Railway Inn, Whittlesea, Cambridgeshire TL 277964
Rainhill Library Museum, View Road, Rainhill, St Helens, Merseyside ST 493912
Ridings Railtours, Neville Hill T&RSMD, Osmondthorpe, Leeds, West Yorkshire SE 328330
Rogart Station, Rogart, Highland, Scotland
Rushden Station Museum, Rushden, Northamptonshire SP 957672
Rutland Railway Museum, Cottesmore Iron Ore Mines Sidings, Cottesmore, Oakham,
Leicestershire SK 887137
Schering Agricultural, Chesterton Junction EY, Chesterton, Cambridge,
Cambridgeshire (Operating Home Base) (Private Site) TL 474608
Scottish Industrial Railway Centre, Minnivy Colliery, Dalmellington, Strathclyde NS 475073
Severn Valley Railway, The Railway Station, Bewdley, Worcestershire SO 715926
Shaw's Metal Supplies Ltd, Haydock Park Road, Ascot Drive, Derby, Derbyshire
(Private Site) SK 373336
Sidings Hotel and Restaurant, Shipton By Benningborough, North Yorkshire SE 552580
Solent Rigging Services, Shamrock Quay, William Street, Southampton (Private Site) SO 438125
South Devon Railway, 'The Primrose Line', Buckfastleigh Station, Buckfastleigh,
Devon SX 747633
South Otterington Station, South Otterington, Northallerton, North Yorkshire SE 381879
South Yorkshire Railway, Meadowhall, Sheffield, South Yorkshire SK 383890
Southall Railway Centre, Old Southall Diesel Depot, Southall, Middlesex
(Including Main Line Depot) TQ 131798
Spa Valley Railway, Wealdon Railway Company Ltd, Tunbridge Wells West Station,
Tunbridge Wells, Kent TQ 542346
Steam Rock Cafe, 256 The Broadway, Muswell Hill, London
Steamport Railway Museum, Derby Road, Southport, Merseyside SD 341170
Steamtown Railway Centre, Carnforth, Lancashire SD 496708
Stephenson Railway Museum, North Tyneside Steam Railway, Middle Engine Lane,
West Chirton, North Tyneside, Tyne & Wear NZ 323693
Strathspey Railway, The Station, Boat of Garten, Inverness-shire NH 898131
Swanage Railway, 'The Purbeck Line', Swanage Railway Station, Swanage, Dorset SZ 028789
Swansea Vale Railway, Llansamlet, Swansea, West Glamorgan SS 660928
Swindon & Cricklade Railway, Blunsdon Station, Swindon, Wiltshire SU 110897
Tanfield Railway, Marley Hill Engine Shed, Sunniside, Tyne & Wear NZ 207573
Telford Railway Centre, Old Locomotive Shed, Horsehay, Telford, Shropshire SJ 675073
Tintern Parva Station Museum, Tintern Parva, Gwent SO 537004
Train Now Standing Restaurant, Pannel Station, Pannal, Harrogate, North Yorkshire SE 307514
Venice-Simplon Orient Express, Sea Containers Ltd, Stewarts Lane T&RSMD,
Battersea, London TQ 257798
Vic Berry Ltd, Western Boulevard, Leicester, Leicestershire
(believed to be relocated elsewhere) SK 580035
Watercress Line, New Alresford Station, New Alresford, Hampshire SU 588325
Welshpool & Llanfair Railway, Llanfair Caereinion, Powys SJ 107069
West Somerset Railway, The Railway Station, Minehead, Somerset SS 975463
Window Tech Systems Ltd, Kirk Sandall, Doncaster SE 613077
Yew Tree Inn, Thornham, Rochdale, Lancashire SD 908104
Ystwyth Valley Railway, Llanilar, Aberystwyth, Dyfed

UNDERSTANDING ECONOMICS

UNDERSTANDING ECONOMICS

Ken Cole

Illustrated by
Phil Evans

Pluto ◖◗ **Press**
LONDON - BOULDER, COLORADO

For JENNY and ALEX

First published in 1995 by Pluto Press
345 Archway Road, London N6 5AA
and 5500 Central Avenue
Boulder, Colorado 80301, USA

British Library Cataloguing in Publication Data
A catalogue record for this book is available from the British Library

Library of Congress Cataloging in Publication Data
A catalog record for this book is available from the Library of Congress

ISBN 0 7453 0894 5 hardback

Printed in EC by J W Arrowsmith Ltd

CONTENTS

"Annual income twenty pounds, annual expenditure nineteen nineteen six, result happiness. Annual income twenty pounds, annual expenditure twenty pounds ought and six, result misery"

Mr Micawber.
DAVID COPPERFIELD

ACKNOWLEDGEMENTS

This book has been a longtime coming.

The journey began in the late 1970s. John Cameron, Chris Edwards and myself began work on designing a new Principles of Economics course for the School of Development Studies (DEV) at the University of East Anglia, Norwich, England. The aim was to develop a course more appropriate for understanding the debate and controversy that surrounds every economic issue than traditional 'micro'/'macro' courses.

Students found this course - based on a comparative analysis of alternative analyses of economic experience - relevant, topical and interesting. The course was subsequently written up as a text book, Why Economists Disagree (see Cole, Cameron and Edwards 1983 and 1991).

In my experience of nearly 20 years teaching, this programme was the most vibrant and dynamic course I have been associated with. The comparative analysis of current economic issues stimulated students creativity and captured their imagination. Indeed, at one time, faculty became as much facilitators of a joint research programme with students, as teachers. And students could write of the course: 'Economics is, without doubt, the gem of DEV ... it is worth coming here to do Economics, if for no other reason' (UEASU 1982:26).

The creative edge of the course has been dulled in recent times, but student demand for plausible, coherent explanations of contemporary issues is the spark that reignites passionate debate over the appropriate way to teach economics. Since this time my own teaching, thinking and research has been guided by this comparative framework. I owe a debt to John Cameron, for his commitment to the initial project and for his insights into the implications of economic theory, and to the generations of DEV students by whom I have been stimulated to extend my thinking, the results of which are written up as this book.

In my teaching practice I have developed the idea of 'flow charts' to present concepts and theories in lectures, a technique based on Tony Buzan's 'mind maps' which was refined for this book. The impetus to publish in this form came from a number of students, particularly Chris Peters, and from a valued colleague and friend, Phil O'Keefe. To them I owe thanks for the confidence they inspired to explore the possibilities of publication. Thanks also to Roger van Zwanenberg of Pluto Press for being willing to chance a new direction and the staff at Pluto, especially Anne Beech and Duncan Blackie, for helping turn my draft into this book. Ray Addicott also gave me invaluable technical advice.

Parts of the text have been read by Pete Dwyer, Ian Yaxley and John Cameron. Alan Duhs, Alan Whiteside and Shaun Hargreaves-Heap were kind enough to read the whole text. All the comments and insights were helpful and stimulating, even though, at times, I did not agree with their advice.

The writing of this book, in this format, is only possible because of sophisticated desk-top publishing computer programmes, and I have been helped immeasurably by Ian Yaxley in being able to make sense of, and become proficient at, using computers to this end. His insights into 'human nature' (see Chapters 6 and 7) were also invaluable.

In spite of all this positive experience and good advice this book is the result! However, it is not entirely my fault. The illustrations can be blamed on Phil Evans, whom I thank for his good humour and patience.

Last, but not least, my thanks go to Jenny and Alex for living with, and being understanding of, someone often preoccupied with obscure theoretical issues, or with the nuances, pressure and discipline of writing.

Ken Cole
Norwich
December 1994

INTRODUCTION

ABOUT THIS BOOK

THE STRUCTURE OF THIS BOOK

This book is very different from most economics texts.

First, the argument is presented in the form of 'flow charts', or 'mind maps', explained below.

Secondly, the book is illustrated by Phil Evans, who tries to bring out the funny side of economics. The intention is not to deny the importance of economic argument, as peoples' lives are often fundamentally affected by economic policy. But learning can be fun and academic work should be a pleasure rather than toil.

Thirdly, the substantive argument of the book approaches economic theory in a context of trying to understand differences <u>between</u> economists, rather than attempting to assert economic 'truths'. More on this in the next section.

To benefit from study, effectively to understand and learn, academic work has to be personally fulfilling. This can only be achieved if our reading engages with our intuitions, helping us to be aware of the particular way in which we interpret human activity, making us conscious of our prejudices and bias. Treating alternative approaches to understanding as serious options and attempting to make explicit the ideological and moral implications of different points of view, allow readers to make their own minds up on where they stand on the social implications of economic analyses. We have to develop as creative beings. In this regard, it is incumbent on authors not to forget the readers' right to assert their individuality. This book is structured towards that end.

THE ARGUMENT OF THIS BOOK

The argument of this book does not presuppose any previous knowledge of economics, although readers who have had some exposure to economics might find the text easier, if only because they have confronted the 'jargon' of economists before. However, every term is explained when it first appears.

At appropriate places in the text there are suggestions for further reading in shaded boxes. These suggestions are not meant to be exhaustive but point to texts I have found useful in developing my own ideas and understanding.

This book is based on the premise that the only reason for studying economics is to understand economic argument. This may seem obvious, but few economics text books and courses are structured to achieve such understanding. <u>Every</u> economic issue can be approached and understood from different points of view. Economic issues are <u>always</u> controversial. Alternative analyses conceptualise economic problems differently, and consequently theorise the sequence of events differently. The assumed <u>dynamic</u> of economies is distinct. Consequently perspectives on economic analysis quite logically and coherently arrive at different policy conclusions on essentially the same economic issue. The resultant policy prescriptions have distinct political implications and in every economic strategy there are winners and losers.

There is an unavoidable political, and necessarily an ideological, dimension to economic debate.

Different political movements, parties and institutions have their <u>own</u> economic advisers. Their advice is invariably framed within political parameters, interpreting economic issues in keeping with particular priorities and objectives. Different economic strategies are legitimated by an associated, if often implied, ideological agenda. The conclusions are ultimately <u>morally</u> justified as being consistent with a belief in 'human nature'. This book concludes by situating economic debate in such a political, ideological and moral context.

To be able to understand economic argument it is essential that the student is aware of the distinct intellectual basis which gives meaning to economic analysis. Once we are conscious of such parameters, alternative analyses can be meaningfully compared and contrasted. Only then can the relative merits and deficiencies of economic perspectives be appreciated, enabling people to choose which approach they find most acceptable (or least objectionable).

In economics it is important to separate the conceptual wood from the intellectual tree and from the theoretical forest. For instance, economics courses and text books will address the concept of the 'price elasticity of demand'. But I have yet to see a book which asks the intellectual question, 'How must prices be conceived for the concept of elasticity to have any significance?' And different theoretical conceptions of price are not highlighted, making a comparative analysis of economic analyses (and policies) impossible. The concept of elasticity is described, not explained. This book aims to be explanatory rather than descriptive.

Indeed, it might appear that this book goes too far the other way. Detailed description of concepts and theories is often not attempted, though references are given where such descriptions might be found. Rather, my concern is to show the significance of particular concepts and theories in supporting and expounding particular beliefs in how economies function. In other words I wish to show the role played by intellectual argument in justifying specific policies with regard to particular economic problems. It is one of the purposes of study in general, and this book in particular, to help people theorise their intuitions and to make people aware of the significance and implications of their beliefs. People acquire these beliefs in order to make sense of their experience and therefore exercise some control over their lives.

Such concerns are not on the intellectual agenda of most economics courses and text books. To assess and meaningfully compare alternative economics perspectives is not, usually, judged to be important.

Rather, the emphasis is to present one approach as the only 'correct' approach, and to examine the logical implications of a particular conception of economic motivation. Usually it is assumed that people, as individuals, are 'endowed' with particular tastes and talents, and that they exchange, through markets, so as to maximise their own, individual pleasure. Economic difficulties, then, are thought to derive from individuals not being free to express the unique preferences which reflect their tastes and talents. And economic policy prescriptions are intended to emphasise free exchange, it being assumed that an environment of free trade will tend to 'equilibrium', a state in which there is economic harmony, and people's pleasure, or 'utility', is maximised.

This book is not so limited. The analysis is not restricted to the implications of how economies ought to operate; the logical implications of assumptions about how life ought to be. Rather the concern is with debate between economists, economists' disagreements, and how economists' policy conclusions affect people's lives. To be economically 'literate', to understand the significance of economic argument, requires an awareness of the social implications of economic analyses and policies.

To be so aware requires that the political, ideological and moral implications of economic analysis are made explicit, and the relative bias of economists, a bias which is justified by appeal to a theory of science and knowledge, is acknowledged. This is what this book sets out to do.

We begin in Chapter 1 by taking disagreements between economists seriously. The extent of the disagreement is noted. Then we consider if economists disagree what is it that defines them all as 'economists' rather than, say, geographers, or philosophers. We can only compare the differences if we identify where economists agree. We need a common standard by which to judge the relative strengths and weaknesses of alternative economic strategies. The common agenda that underlies all economic analysis is concern with a particular aspect of social existence - 'what determines the rate of exchange, or value, of commodities exchanged between consumers and producers'. This raises the question as to the determinant of value; the <u>dynamic</u> of economies.

Is the dynamic of economies provided by the preferences of consumers purchasing particular commodities in accord with their tastes? Does value reflect the technical conditions of production? Or perhaps the choices of consumers and the exigencies of production processes interact in the determination of value. It is the social context in which people produce and consume that is important - the citizen is the economic dynamic. Thus, is the determinant of value, the dynamic of economies, the consumer, the producer, or the citizen?

Economies can be analysed quite coherently, but differently, from each of these perspectives. We end Chapter 1 by considering the problems of comparing alternative, logical and coherent analyses. This is an issue addressed in more detail and with regard to the scientific, ideological, moral and political implications of social analysis at the end of the book in Chapters 6 and 7.

Having identified what unites economists - the study of relations of exchange between consumers and producers - we can begin to understand their differences. In Chapter 2 we begin to compare and contrast alternative economic analyses according to different under-standings of <u>value</u>. To illustrate distinct theoretical perspectives we consider what is often thought to be a 'basic' concept in economics: the market 'forces' of demand and supply, and how these are variously understood to affect market prices, identifying distinct approaches to the same phenomenon.

Chapters 3 through 5 then analyse in greater detail the way in which each theory of value conceives of and analyses economic experience. Concepts, theories and policies, which are almost invariably presented as the <u>only</u> way to analyse economies in most text books are discussed, situated in a comparative context, and their relative merits, significance and implications highlighted.

In Chapter 6, we look at how we might choose between alternative

4

analyses which we have hitherto only compared. Economics attempts to understand a particular aspect of human social experience. If we are to address and explain human behaviour we must somewhere, at least implicitly, have a conception of what it is to be human - what is 'human nature'. It is argued throughout this book that economic concepts and analyses have an ideological, political and moral dimension. And this bias reflects the particular, implicit, conception of human nature that underlies the analysis.

Chapter 7 concludes by reemphasising the importance, for economic 'literacy', of a comparative analysis of economic theory, summarising the links between the assumed economic dynamic, the theory of value, the nature of economic relations, policy emphasis, implied conceptions of human nature, the associated conception of scientific knowledge, and the political and ideological bias of economic analyses.

Hence we can decide which analysis, in our opinion, is more plausible, relevant and important. That choice is made by being conscious of the unexamined and unexpressed assumptions about human nature upon which economic analyses are founded, and by comparing these to our own intuitions and beliefs.

We all have beliefs about what it is to be human, though these are normally ascribed to 'common sense' and not given the status of theory. But we are <u>all</u> potential theorists if, as pointed out above, we acquire the intellectual skills to articulate our intuitions as theory. Theorisation allows us to be aware of the social implications of particular beliefs, beliefs which are built on individuals' experience.

It is in this sense that this book respects readers' own attitudes and individuality. The intention is to highlight the <u>social</u> implications of often deeply held beliefs. And raising individuals' consciousness allows people greater control over their own, social, activity. Personal understanding and self-control permit purposeful action to better society - individual creativity is fostered and stimulated.

To understand economic theory and policy, to be economically 'literate', it is essential to be aware of the likely social implications of alternative policy implications and economic strategies. This is the project of this book.

HOW TO USE THIS BOOK: A STUDENTS' GUIDE

Apart from this introduction, the book is written in the form of 'flow charts'. The idea comes from the work of Tony Buzan, an educational psychologist, who has made excellent studies into how the human mind most easily understands, accumulates and remembers information. His findings were first published in the book <u>Use Your Head</u>, published by the BBC in 1974 (though there have been a number of subsequent editions), which I recommend to all the students I come into contact with.

He developed the idea of 'mind maps', by which arguments are most efficiently understood and remembered if recorded in the form of 'key words'; words which succinctly summarise the theme at issue. These words are then <u>spatially</u> organised to recreate the logic of the argument. If a text is presented in the traditional linear form then the reader has to make these links for him/herself and the meaning of the argument is not immediately clear. Of course the mental images implied by certain words will differ from person to person, and so the idea of 'mind maps' only applies to how people learn and inform <u>themselves</u>.

However, my purpose is to <u>communicate</u> with the reader, and hence I use what might be called 'key paragraphs'. Each paragraph is a step in the logic of the argument, and because, logically, a number of implications might follow from any one idea, the paragraphs are presented so that the logic of the argument is, again, represented <u>spatially</u>.

The central point here is that the mind works by <u>associating</u> words and concepts to each other. These associations are highlighted through 'key paragraphs' organised into 'flow charts'. This has the advantage of making the sequence of ideas obvious, but the disadvantage of being very concentrated. The significance of the argument is not embellished with assiduous description, mellifluous turns of phrase or amusing anecdotes. It is intended to be unaffected logic.

This means we cover a lot of theoretical ground very quickly. The book requires application, it takes time, and sometimes repeated reading, to internalise and understand the logic of new arguments or of different points of view. But the book is ideal for those who are prepared to concentrate and achieve a rapid insight into complex arguments.

Every paragraph is there for a reason. It is a logical step in the argument, and each step builds upon previous points.

HOW TO USE THIS BOOK: A TEACHERS' GUIDE

The idea of presenting arguments in 'flow chart/key paragraph' format, while being based on Tony Buzan's work, was developed to aid my own teaching practice.

A problem with lectures is that students, preoccupied with taking notes, are too busy to absorb the logic of the argument. Often (usually?) questions arise when students are rereading/revising their notes: the traditional lecture format is not conducive to meaningful discussion or intellectual debate.

To address this problem, for every one of my lectures I hand out 2/3 pages of flow charts (not quite as comprehensive as the pages of this book), and the lecture is a process of explaining the logic of these handouts. Students can add their own points to further elaborate the argument, concept or theory. And the flow charts act as a reference point for questions, drawing out of students their own opinions and helping them frame meaningful questions.

Teachers might find the pages of this book useful or suggestive of lecture content. Between two and four pages should suffice for the average lecture.

HAPPY READING!

I hope that this attempt to make both the significance of economic debates clear, and the mode of presentation through 'flow charts' to aid understanding, works for you.

Readers who wish to further explore the implications of economic analysis are welcome to write to me at, The School of Development Studies, University of East Anglia, Norwich NR4 7TJ, England.

I hope you enjoy the book.

CHAPTER ONE

ECONOMISTS' ARGUMENTS

ECONOMISTS' EXPLANATIONS

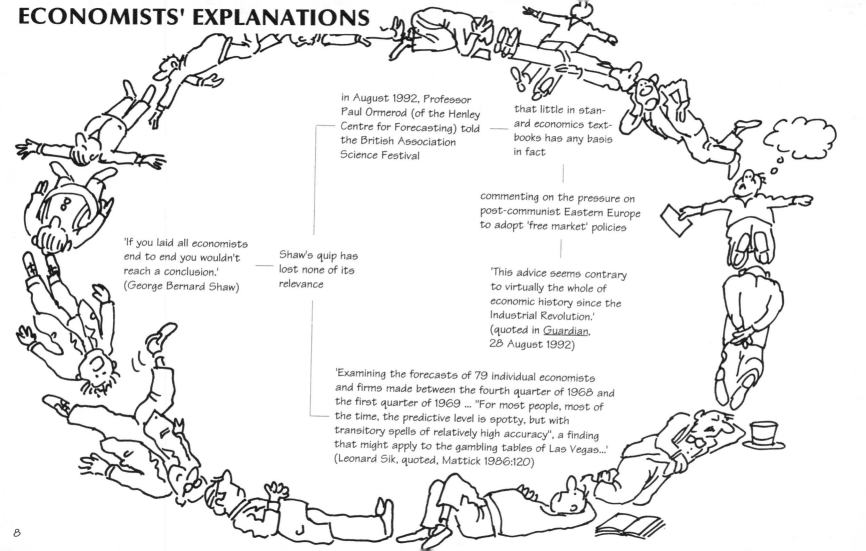

in August 1992, Professor Paul Ormerod (of the Henley Centre for Forecasting) told the British Association Science Festival

that little in stanard economics text-books has any basis in fact

commenting on the pressure on post-communist Eastern Europe to adopt 'free market' policies

'If you laid all economists end to end you wouldn't reach a conclusion.' (George Bernard Shaw)

Shaw's quip has lost none of its relevance

'This advice seems contrary to virtually the whole of economic history since the Industrial Revolution.' (quoted in <u>Guardian</u>, 28 August 1992)

'Examining the forecasts of 79 individual economists and firms made between the fourth quarter of 1968 and the first quarter of 1969 ... "For most people, most of the time, the predictive level is spotty, but with transitory spells of relatively high accuracy", a finding that might apply to the gambling tables of Las Vegas...' (Leonard Sik, quoted, Mattick 1986:120)

8

Christopher Huhne, financial journalist of <u>Independent</u> (2 May 1993) surveyed 43 economic forecasts of the British economy, no two of which agreed

— and internationally

'...economic forecasts are the subject of open derision ... their accuracy is appalling. Within the past 12 months [1993/4] ... forecasters have failed to predict the Japanese recession, the strength of the American recovery, the depth of the collapse in the German economy, and the turmoil in the European ERM [exchange rate mechanism].'
(Ormerod 1994:3)

'Forecasting is still essentially a souped-up extrapolation of the recent past...'
(Huhne, <u>Independent</u>, 2 May 1993)

trends are correlated according to a particular conception of economic causation - how different economic phenomena influence each other

but alternative conceptions of the economic dynamic (the causative mechanism in economies - why people behave in particular ways) are not addressed

identifying the often implicit assumptions that underlie economic analyses, making explicit the conception of the economic dynamic, and comparing alternative analyses based upon different assumptions, is central to the argument of this book

<u>all</u> economic analyses are based upon assumptions about why people behave in particular ways

assumptions which, as we shall see in Chapter 6, have ideological, political and moral dimensions

and <u>every</u> economic event, issue or problem can be, and usually is, analysed quite coherently according to different sets of assumptions

economists disagree, and the root of these disagreements is political, ideological and moral in content

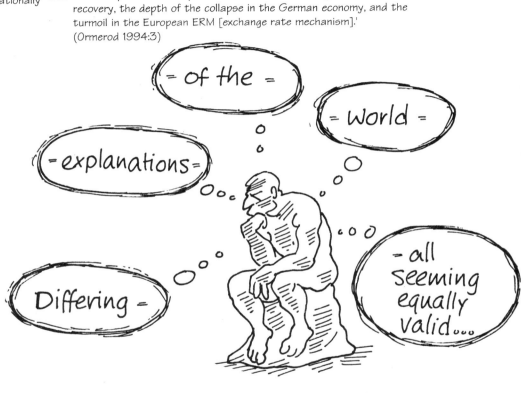

= of the =

= World =

= explanations =

Differing =

= all seeming equally valid...

be as happy as possible

address economic issues such as value, inflation, trade, development, etc., as if there is only one 'correct' analysis

usually assuming that the motivation to exch- ange is merely explained by personal gratification

economic relations are understood in terms of individuals attempting to maximise utility

basic text books, and courses in economics

but this is only one possible way to explain economic behaviour

although on the one hand there is fierce intellectual debate between economic theorists on the relative merits of alternative, analytical approaches

very rarely is the student of economics made aware of these controversies

'We all talk about the same things, but we have not agreed what it is we are talking about.' (Robbins 1984:1)

for instance see;
Campbell, Hardy & Healey (1989)
Pheby (1989)
Chalmers (1982)
Glass & Johnson (1989)
Caldwell (1984)
Cole, Cameron & Edwards (1991)
Diesing (1982)
and see Appendix 1, Chapter 2

Do you think our author is saying economic explanations vary according to how rich you are?

Yes

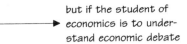

but if the student of economics is to understand economic debate — if s/he is to be <u>economically literate</u> — then it is essential to be able to compare and contrast alternative analyses — and to be aware of the relative merits and significance of each

ECONOMIC DISSENT

25 years ago there seemed to be a consensus between economists — there was a reconciliation between

- Adam Smith's 'invisible hand' of free market forces
- Keynes's heresy of the need for the state to intervene in the working of market forces

this consensus is known as the <u>neoclassical synthesis</u> — which divides economics into

- <u>micro</u> economics — addressed in Chapter 3
- <u>macro</u> economics — addressed in Chapter 4

and while economic orthodoxy appeared to explain economic experience (in the 1950s and 1960s)

writers outside the mainstream could be dismissed as being 'ideologically inspired'

and beyond the pale of economic 'science'

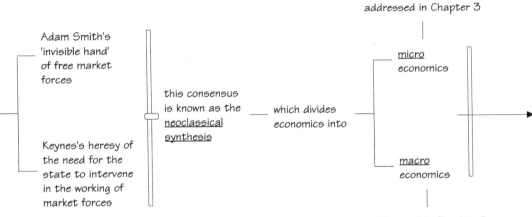

Smith's free market — or Keynes's state intervention — which is better?

Depends whether you control the market or the state!

the neoclassical syn-
thesis held that the
principal concerns for
economic policy were

unemployment

inflation

if there was insufficient purchasing power in the economy

if there was too much purchasing power in the economy

too <u>little</u> effective demand

too <u>much</u> effective demand

people would be unable to
buy all the goods produced

people would compete to
buy the goods available

there would be
<u>excess</u> <u>supply</u>

there would be
<u>excess</u> <u>demand</u>

and there would
be unemployment

and there would
be price inflation

the economic problems of inflation
and unemployment were alternatives

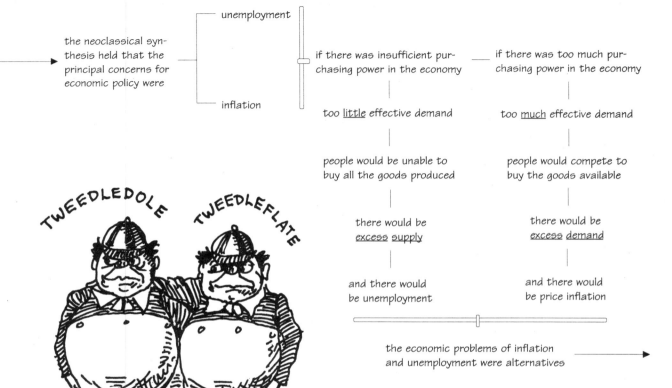

TWEEDLEDOLE   TWEEDLEFLATE

after Tenniell

but with the onset of <u>stagflation</u> in the 1970s ___ rising unemployment <u>with</u> rising prices

mainstream economics was at a loss to explain how economies function

'The famous "neoclassical synthesis" which developed over the next three decades [since the 1930s] ... foundered ... ' (Romer 1993:5-6))

'...the textbook "neoclassical synthesis" simply juxtaposes Keynesian macro-economics and neoclassical micro-economics in the hope that no one will bother to ask any awkward questions.' (Bleaney 1985:1)

the economic consensus of the 1960s fragmented into a plethora of competing schools of thought

monetarists, post-Keynesians, rational expectations theorists, institutionalists, neo-Ricardians, etc...

'...there is a flowering of epistemological doubt... [but] resistance to real diversity within faculty ranks and classroom curricula is fiercer than ever. The debates are for the college of cardinals, not for the parish flock...' (Kuttner 1985:83)

stressing the importance of 'free' market forces unhindered by state intervention

though there has been a shift of emphasis towards <u>micro</u> economics

the economic orthodoxy of 'micro' and 'macro' economics is still the basis of many economics courses and text books

we shall highlight the logical incompatibility of micro and macro economics when we address the <u>capital controversy</u> in Chapter 4 (pp 105-8)

I wish some of this cooking was theoretical!

in the 'flowering of epistemological doubt' between economists — each school of thought competed to fill the theoretical vacuum left by the lack of theoretical consensus — and each claims to offer a coherent, logical analysis of economic experience — but then they differ over the definition of <u>economic</u> activity — '...most controversies in economic theory involve a clash of assumptions about the structure of economic reality.' (Bell & Kristol 1981:viii)

ECONOMISTS' QUESTIONS

'Scientists, like other intellectuals, come to their work with a world view, a set of preconceptions that provides the framework for their analyses of the world. These preconceptions enter at both an explicit and an implicit level, but even when invoked explicitly, unexamined and unexpressed assumptions underlie them.'
(Levins & Lewontin 1985:267)

HOW EARLY ECONOMIC DEBATES WERE RESOLVED

we shall return to the 'unexamined and unexpressed assumptions' in Chapter 6 when we consider the moral, political and ideological dimensions of economic theory — but at this point in the argument it must be emphasised — that although theoretical analyses of economic experience are different — the choice between theories cannot be made merely on the basis of which is empirically 'right' and which is empirically 'wrong' even though analyses are of the same economy

and reach different conclusions on the same economic issue

each analysis is potentially

realist — an explanation of economic experience is offered — and evidence cited to validate theoretical conclusions

rationalist — the analysis is logically coherent — arguing from assumptions to conclusions

activist — policy prescriptions are proposed to address economic problems

see Cole, Cameron and Edwards 1991:Chapter 1

'Each point(s) to an area of experience as matching its description, carefully displays the logic of its arguments, and arrives at appropriate policy conclusions.' (Cole, Cameron and Edwards 1991:5)

and each approach asks legitimate questions

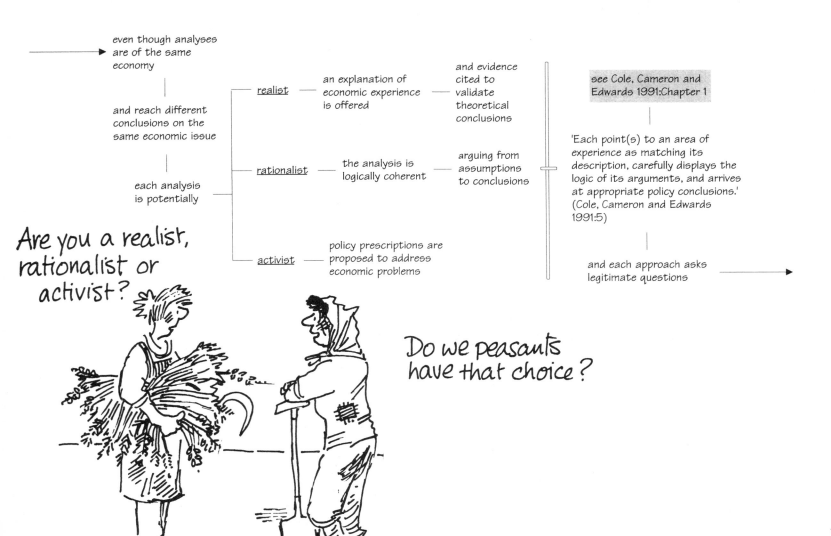

Are you a realist, rationalist or activist?

Do we peasants have that choice?

every economic transaction can be variously considered as

- an independent <u>event</u>
- a component part of a <u>system</u>
- a moment in a <u>process</u>

for instance: analyses of Ken Cole buying a bar of chocolate

the fact that I am willing to exchange some of the money I earn for chocolate

indicates my preferences as a consumer

and this approach suggests that if markets are 'free'

then I will earn what I am 'worth'

there is no state interference

and the price of chocolate will be forced to the minimum

so that my utility (pleasure) is maximised

economic phenomena are independent <u>events</u> reflecting individuals' preferences, this approach is addressed in detail in Chapter 3

to p. 17

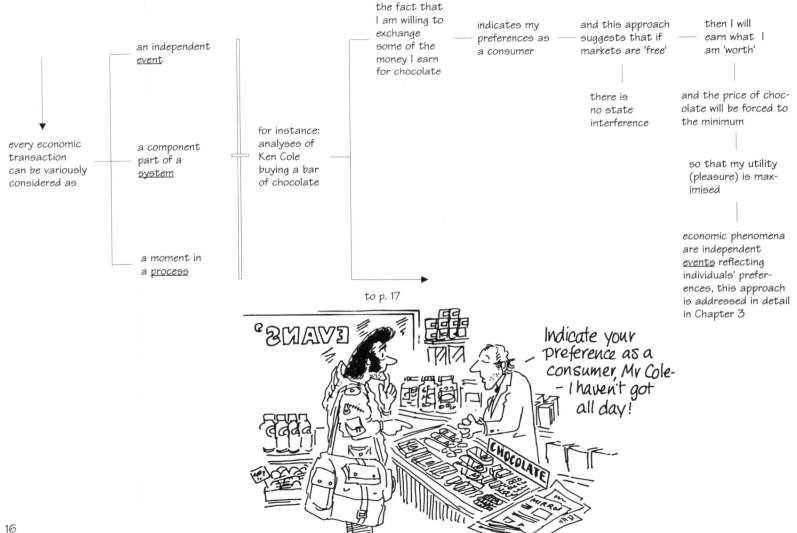

EVANS'

Indicate your preference as a consumer, Mr Cole — I haven't got all day!

CHOCOLATE

another approach considers my buying chocolate in terms of creating incomes for producers

and the fact that I can afford to purchase the chocolate means that I also have received an income

people are not now considered as mere consumers, but as producers

societies are characterised by a technical <u>division</u> of <u>labour</u>

people do not produce what they consume

Yesterday I worked out one person's expenditure is another's income. So I won't be coming tomorrow

economic specialisation requires people to cooperate and exchange their products

and where there is cooperation through markets, one person's expenditure is another's income

from another point of view, my behaviour as a producer and a consumer are related

individuals are not <u>independent</u> consumers, but <u>dependent</u> producers

what I am able to consume is crucially limited by the income I receive as a producer

people are component parts of a technically defined economic <u>system</u>, analysed in Chapter 4

which does reflect my role in the technical division of labour

but somebody controls technology

giving them social power, which leads to economic inequality

17

economic activity cannot be explained without taking into account power in society — the dynamic of economies is not independent consumers — or dependent producers — but interdependent citizens

and society changes as the powerless challenge the extent to which they are exploited to the advantage of the powerful

and in as far as my buying chocolate maintains the income of the chocolate workers

it is one moment in the process of maintaining a social system — economic behaviour is understood as one dimension of social existence — economic relations between citizens are considered

addressed in detail in Chapter 5

where the power of the privileged derives from the control of the social process of production

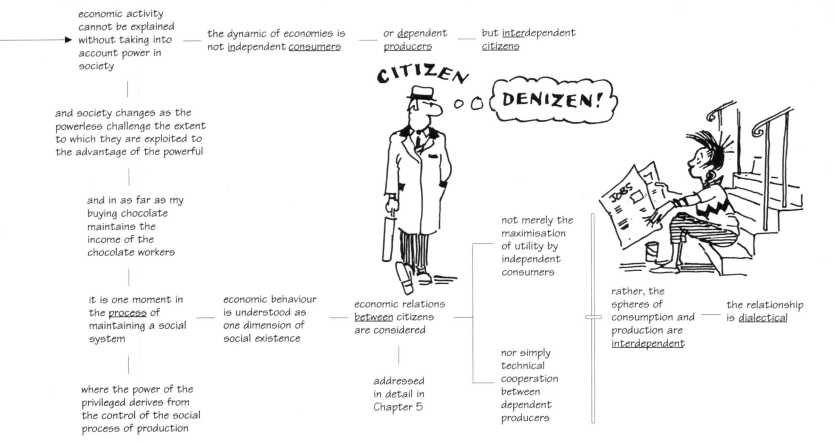

CITIZEN oo DENIZEN!

not merely the maximisation of utility by independent consumers

nor simply technical cooperation between dependent producers

rather, the spheres of consumption and production are interdependent — the relationship is dialectical

DISTORTED COMMUNICATION

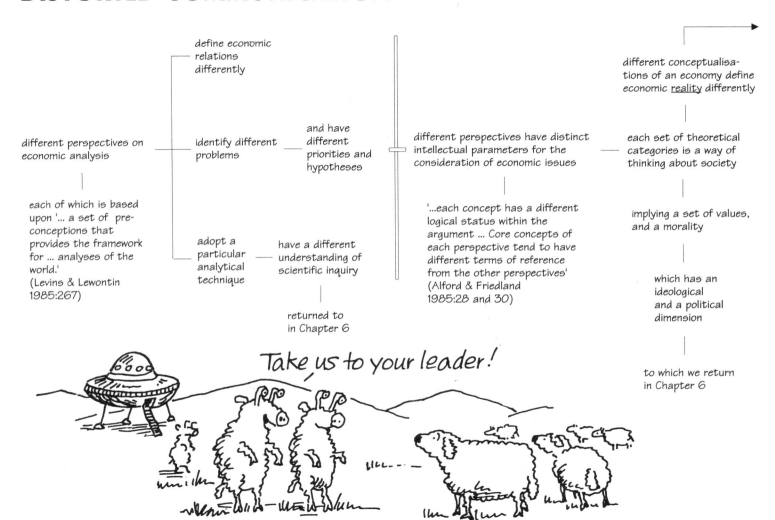

define economic relations differently

different perspectives on economic analysis

identify different problems

and have different priorities and hypotheses

each of which is based upon '... a set of pre-conceptions that provides the framework for ... analyses of the world.' (Levins & Lewontin 1985:267)

adopt a particular analytical technique

have a different understanding of scientific inquiry

returned to in Chapter 6

different perspectives have distinct intellectual parameters for the consideration of economic issues

'...each concept has a different logical status within the argument ... Core concepts of each perspective tend to have different terms of reference from the other perspectives' (Alford & Friedland 1985:28 and 30)

different conceptualisations of an economy define economic reality differently

each set of theoretical categories is a way of thinking about society

implying a set of values, and a morality

which has an ideological and a political dimension

to which we return in Chapter 6

Take us to your leader!

there are '... controversies between neoclassicists, Keynesians, and institutionalists ... Very little intelligent discussion occurs in these controversies ... Sometimes there are debates, in which the two sides talk past each other ... monetarists are convinced that all the evidence confirms their theory, and their opponents are equally convinced of the opposite.'
(Diesing 1982:12, 13)

addressed in Chapter 6

the differences, apart from being methodological are also moral, political and ideological

'...ideologies produce distorted communication, allowing some concepts to be communicated but blocking and distorting others.'
(Diesing 1982:5, emphasis added)

for such an analysis of the monetarist-Keynesian debate see Wilber, 1979

and for further comparable analyses of economic debates in which either side employs distinct conceptual approaches, see:

Diesing 1982, especially Chapters 1, 11, 13 and 14

Ward 1979, especially Book 1 Part 1, Book 2 Part 1, and Book 3 Part 1

Coates & Hillard 1986, especially Part V

Coates & Hillard 1987, especially Part .

Cole 1993

and Professor Wilber reaches the following conclusion:
'...the reasons for theory selection must be sought elsewhere than in empirical verification ... theories are chosen because they yield policy implications that are compatible with one's vision of the economic process.'
(Wilber 1979:978, emphasis added)

reflecting the analysts' '...set of preconceptions that provides the framework for their analyses of the world...'

perspectives on economic
analysis are defined by the
<u>preconceptions</u> that
underlie the explanation

preconceptions
which define a
<u>vision</u> of the
economic process

and the vision of the
economic process
defines what is
thought to be the
economic <u>dynamic</u>

why do people
relate through
exchanging
commodities?

what
determines
the price?

and what is the
economic relation
between people?

all these questions
relate to the <u>causation</u>
of economic relationships

which determines
the interpretation
of economic data

'Yet in reality, what reasoned
debate does take place is
about <u>means</u> not ends.'
(Lal 1983:xi, emphasis added)

'The state of confusion in
policy, and indeed amongst
academic theorists, stems
from a sharp disagreement
over the real <u>causes</u> of ...
phenomena, and the ways they
can best be addressed.'
(Colclough 1982:490,
emphasis added)

THE STORY SO FAR...

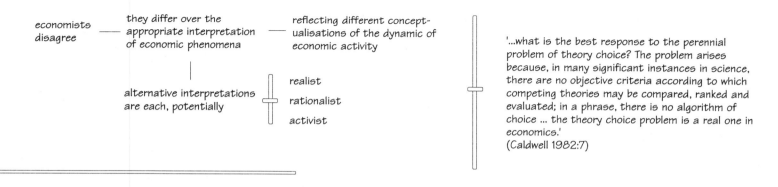

economists disagree — they differ over the appropriate interpretation of economic phenomena — reflecting different conceptualisations of the dynamic of economic activity

alternative interpretations are each, potentially —

realist

rationalist

activist

'...what is the best response to the perennial problem of theory choice? The problem arises because, in many significant instances in science, there are no objective criteria according to which competing theories may be compared, ranked and evaluated; in a phrase, there is no algorithm of choice ... the theory choice problem is a real one in economics.'
(Caldwell 1982:7)

THE REAL WORLD AND REAL EXPERIENCE

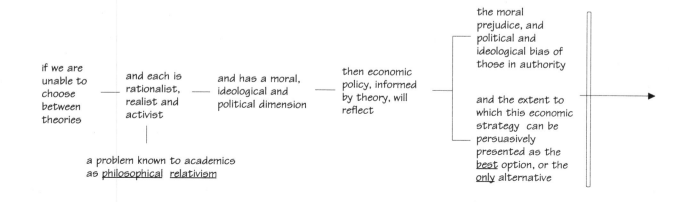

if we are unable to choose between theories — and each is rationalist, realist and activist — and has a moral, ideological and political dimension — then economic policy, informed by theory, will reflect —

the moral prejudice, and political and ideological bias of those in authority

and the extent to which this economic strategy can be persuasively presented as the <u>best</u> option, or the <u>only</u> alternative

a problem known to academics as <u>philosophical</u> <u>relativism</u>

theory choice is, ultimately, politically inspired, reflecting particular economic interests

for instance, even though the inequality gap in 1993 between the top and bottom earners is the widest in Britain since records began over 100 years ago

and in the 13 years up to 1992, of the £13 billion tax reductions, 27% went to the richest 1%, and the bottom 50% received only 15%

at the time of writing (autumn 1994) the government is looking to cut further the Social Security, Health and Education budgets

and the economic policies which have led to (in 1993):

data from Dean, 1993

the poorest 10% surviving on £54 per week while the directors of the top 100 firms earn on average £10,000 per week

top 10% of households paying 32% of their income in tax, whereas the bottom 10% pay 43%

those with earnings over £50,000 pay £15,000 less in tax, while the bottom 10% (£2,700 per annum) receive 14% less in income

were all justified by economic theorists in the name of the enterprise culture (addressed in Chapter 3)

but economists working within different perspectives were just as adamant that these policies were theoretically misguided

I've come to raise the rent.

Thank goodness— because I can't!

THEORY...

the moral prejudice and political bias by which particular theories inform economic policy

is not simply a cynical expression of economic advantage, perpetrated by the rich

but reflects a particular <u>vision</u> of economic motivation

visions of the real <u>world</u> evolve to help people understand their particular <u>experience</u>

and different experiences generate different visions

<u>why</u> people behave in certain ways

what the <u>dynamic</u> of economic activity is

'It is part of conventional wisdom that you should believe the evidence of your eyes ... But in our world you cannot see the most important things, for they are abstractions, concepts. You cannot <u>see</u> "Britain" or "China", the population of Zambia, a gross national product or a steel industry. You may see illustrative details of each ... You may see a steel plant, a line of workers queuing to clock on, the glow of the furnaces in the night sky, but it is only a detail of the "German steel industry", a detail meaningful because we have joined three concepts - "Germany", "steel" and "industry". It is a "theory" ... it allows us to understand ... [and] understanding ... allows us to act.' (Harris 1983:10, emphasis in original))

the real world is a <u>theoretical</u> reality

an abstraction

for social life to be possible people have to feel they can explain their experience

and visions of what the real world is like are derived from experience

but as we have seen, there are different visions of the economic process

visions which become <u>common sense</u>

but, 'Common sense is ... inadequate ... All everyday experience is partial, and reflects the social location of the person both in the range of knowledge it confers and the perspective that it gives ... it is highly questionable, for instance, whether ideas about balanced budgets which work well for families have the same effects for national economies.' (Loney et al 1993:341)

which, if we are to resolve, we have to find something general to all economic perspectives by which the alternative analyses can be <u>compared</u>

leading to distorted communication

implying different conceptions of the economic dynamic

if we are to under-stand the differences <u>between</u> economists

we have to discover what they agree about

what is the 'lowest common denominator' that can be used as a yardstick to compare differences between economic analyses

more specifically, what defines economics, relative to, say, sociology, geography or psychology

Columbus will sail off the edge - it's Common Sense!

THE MEANING OF ECONOMICS

economic analyses focus on a particular dimension of social behaviour

— people live in societies which are characterised by a <u>division</u> of <u>labour</u>

— they have particular skills and specialise in particular economic roles

— initially the division of labour was within the household or immediate locality

— but as standards of living rise with an increase in technical efficiency

— the division of labour goes beyond the household, homestead or village

people do not consume what they produce, and vice versa

there has to be some form of exchange <u>between</u> consumers and producers

and economists are concerned to explain this exchange process

in particular they are concerned to explain the <u>rate</u> of exchange, or price

and exchange is regulated by other than social values and obligations, customs and traditions

market forces are born, and commodities have an <u>exchange</u> <u>value</u> and a <u>price</u>

Here, Oogi – you paint the antlers in !

EARLY DIVISION OF LABOUR

26

in adapting to new ways of surviving socially

people now produce things for other people, rather than for their own consumption

people become more and more specialized as technical efficiency improves

and progressively, producers serve larger, and ever more distant markets

people's understanding of social life changes

technical improvements lead to higher living standards

the culture through which people socially interact evolves

Left: Adam Smith after an accident with Crompton's 'Spinning Mule'

there are new social priorities to be taken into account

producing commodities for exchange (rather than for personal use) becomes fundamental to social existence

the evolving social context of survival has to be understood

economics as an intellectual discipline appeared at a particular point of historical development

'With the Scientific Revolution and the Enlightenment [of the seventeenth and eighteenth centuries], critical reasoning, empiricism and individualism became the dominant values, together with a secular and materialistic orientation that led to the production of worldly goods and luxuries, and to the manipulative mentality of the Industrial Age. The new customs and activities resulted in the creation of new social and political institutions and gave rise to a new academic pursuit: the theorising about a set of specific economic activities - production, exchange, distribution, money-lending - which suddenly stood out in sharp relief and required not only description and explanation but also rationalisation.'
(Capra 1982:202-3, emphasis in original)

changes in how
people socially
produced their
livelihoods

|

went hand-in-hand with
changes in the organisa-
tion of society

|

which were justified and legitimated   economics as a
by cultural norms and values which   discipline, is a
rationalised the changed social order   ——   battle in the realm
                                              of ideas in the
| cause of particular
                                              economic interests
survival requires that people
have an understanding of
their (social and natural)
environment

|

they must have a   a <u>theory</u>
'working knowledge' —— of their
of the <u>real</u> <u>world</u>   universe ——

'Feudal society, characterised by a hierarchical structure of control over
land where lords maintained their control over the producers, the serfs, by
threat of physical coercion, was primarily a system of production for use
rather then for exchange. However, with the separation of towns (manufacturing) from the countryside (agriculture) [consequent upon higher levels of
efficiency and economic specialisation] and the establishment of a market
economy, new interest groups emerged and economics developed as a
"science" of valuation, replacing systems of valuation founded on morality
and power.'
(Cole, Cameron & Edwards 1991:19)

'This view of the universe permeates all
aspects of our life. All communities in all
places at all times manifest their own view
of reality in what they do. The entire
culture reflects the contemporary model
of reality. We are what we know. And when
the body of knowledge changes so do we.'
(Burke 1985:11)

CHAPTER TWO

ECONOMISTS'
ARGUMENTS
COMPARED

THEORIES OF VALUE

we ended the last chapter with the conclusion

to understand differences between economists

we first have to establish what unites economists

economics is the study of relations of exchange between producers and consumers

the agreement that value is associated with exchange is the 'lowest common denominator' of economists' analyses, and the baseline for comparing different perspectives

but economists differ over the determination of the rate or exchange, the price (or value) of commodities

over the dynamic of economic activity

what causes value

does the value of a commodity reflect the needs and pleasure of individual consumers?

is it the use of natural resources (including people's time and skills) by producers that gives something value?

is the exchange between consumers and producers a social relation, and is it people as citizens who are the economic dynamic?

I produce beans-

THE PRODUCER

I consume beans-

THE CONSUMER

and I vote for people who tell me to produce and consume beans!

THE CITIZEN

the subjective
preferences of
consumers? ——— the <u>subjective</u>
<u>preference</u>
<u>theory</u> of <u>value</u>

analysed in
Chapter 3

how and why consumers
and producers interact

the ultimate
<u>determinant</u> of
economic activity

does
value
reflect

the costs of
production?

the <u>cost-of-</u>
<u>production</u>
<u>theory</u> of <u>value</u>

analysed in
Chapter 4

<u>all</u> theories of
value offer an
explanation for
the activities of
consumers <u>and</u>
producers

but they differ
over the definition
of the economic
<u>dynamic</u>

and each approach
asks legitimate
questions
(see p.15, above)

the social pri-
ority of things
produced and
consumed?

the <u>abstract</u>
<u>labour</u> <u>theory</u>
of <u>value</u>

analysed in
Chapter 5

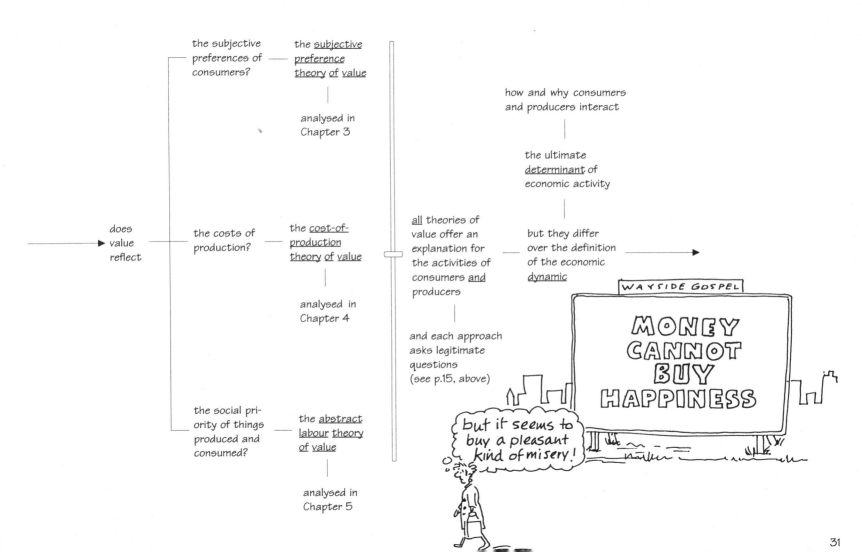

WAYSIDE GOSPEL

MONEY
CANNOT
BUY
HAPPINESS

but it seems to
buy a pleasant
kind of misery!

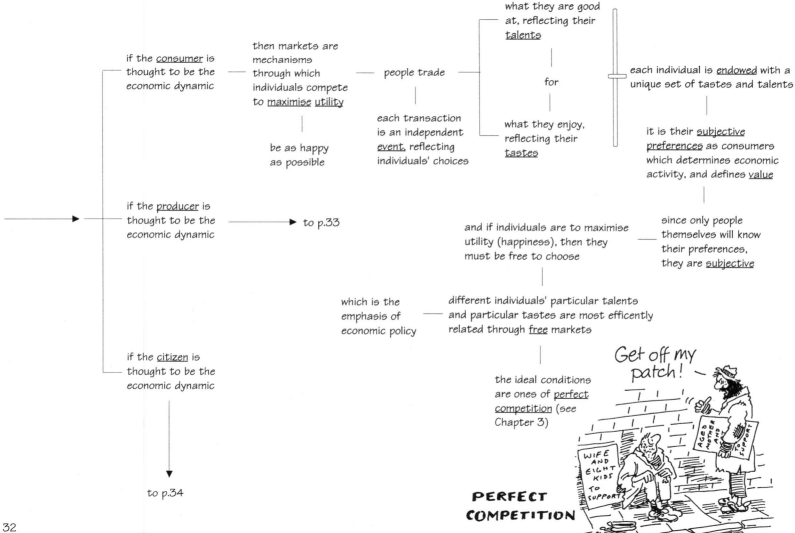

if the <u>consumer</u> is thought to be the economic dynamic

then markets are mechanisms through which individuals compete to <u>maximise</u> <u>utility</u>

be as happy as possible

people trade

what they are good at, reflecting their <u>talents</u>

for

what they enjoy, reflecting their <u>tastes</u>

each transaction is an independent <u>event,</u> reflecting individuals' choices

each individual is <u>endowed</u> with a unique set of tastes and talents

it is their <u>subjective</u> <u>preferences</u> as consumers which determines economic activity, and defines <u>value</u>

if the <u>producer</u> is thought to be the economic dynamic

to p.33

and if individuals are to maximise utility (happiness), then they must be free to choose

since only people themselves will know their preferences, they are <u>subjective</u>

which is the emphasis of economic policy

different individuals' particular talents and particular tastes are most efficently related through <u>free</u> markets

if the <u>citizen</u> is thought to be the economic dynamic

the ideal conditions are ones of <u>perfect</u> <u>competition</u> (see Chapter 3)

Get off my patch!

to p.34

WIFE AND EIGHT KIDS TO SUPPORT

AGED MOTHER AND TO SUPPORT

PERFECT COMPETITION

individuals' economic activity depends upon their place in the technical division of labour

and individuals socially interact through institutions

and as technology evolves to higher, more technically efficient forms

then social institutions must evolve as appropriate so that individuals can cooperate efficiently

and with technical evolution, production is less and less an individual operation and requires technical coordination

from p. 32

markets are institutions through which individuals cooperate to produce

and markets have to be managed to reflect a general social interest

and now value does not reflect the preferences of consumers, but the activity of producers

free markets, reflecting the preferences of individual consumers, only lead towards stagnation and unemployment

value is determined by the cost of production, which reflects:

the economy is a system, not a series of independent events

the amount of resources used in production

the cost of those resources

reflecting the management and technology of production

reflecting the distribution of income in society

the emphases of economic policy

as individuals' incomes are paid out of the revenue received for products

see Chapter 4

Production is less and less an individual operation and requires technical coordination

from p. 32

market activity reflects the relative social power of the transactors

which derives from the <u>control</u> of the process of production

hence, the most important transactions are those concerned with the production process

in a capitalist, private enterprise economy, the <u>owners</u> of the means of production (the owners of factories, raw materials, etc...), or capital, are in a strong position

ultimately they can decide who to hire and fire, and thus who can earn their subsistence

but the means of production only become <u>capital</u> when they earn a return

that is when labour works with the means of production to produce <u>commodities</u> to sell to consumers

labourers can only defend their interests by combining in trade unions

but whereas capitalists can hire and fire individual workers

the relationship between labour and capital is one of <u>interdependence</u>

and the economy is part of a social <u>process</u>

You're fired - but on second thoughts...

and the ability to work, labour power, is <u>itself</u> a commodity

capitalism is fundamentally a system of <u>commodity</u> <u>production</u>

the value of which reflects the <u>socially</u> <u>necessary, abstract labour</u> <u>time</u> embodied in each commodity - explained in Chapter 5

34

PERSPECTIVES AND SCHOOLS OF THOUGHT

economic activity is understood through theories of value —— that there are <u>three</u> theories of value

is a reflection that <u>every</u> economic transaction involves consumers and producers (and citizens)

and hence can <u>always</u> be interpreted in terms of different economic dynamics

the assumed <u>causative</u> mechanism of economic activity

you can't <u>see</u> causation, experience has to be <u>interpreted</u> to explain why it happened

'...intellectuals come to their work with a world view, a set of pre-conceptions that provides the framework for their analyses of the world...'
(Levins & Lewontin, quoted p. 14 above)

ECONOMISTS AT WORK.

and while there are 3 theories of value there are more than three schools of thought ——→

perspectives in economic analysis are <u>theories</u> of <u>value</u>

the 'world view' that underlies an analysis defines the theoretical <u>perspective</u>

a <u>school</u> <u>of</u> <u>thought</u> applies a perspective on causation to the analysis of actual experience

— for instance, as we shall see in the next chapter, the subjective preference theory of value when applied to the experience of inflation is expressed as the school of monetarism

— each theory of value includes a number of schools of thought, and the major schools of each theory of value will be specified in Chapters 3, 4 and 5

A TIME OF TREMENDOUS SOCIAL CHANGE

L-look in the air! Is it a bird? Is it a plane?

No, Adam — it's a balloon!

THE HISTORY OF ECONOMIC ANALYSIS

in Chapter 1 (p.27) we argued that economics as a discipline appeared at a particular point in history

— when exchange between producers and consumers became fundamental to social existence

— and the writings of the early economists (the Mercantilists, Physiocrats, Adam Smith, etc.) were confused and sometimes contradictory, as they tried to understand an emerging social order

see:
Cole, Cameron & Edwards 1991:Chapter 2

— they were writing at a time of tremendous social change

— a whole new conception of reality was emerging

see:
Burke 1985

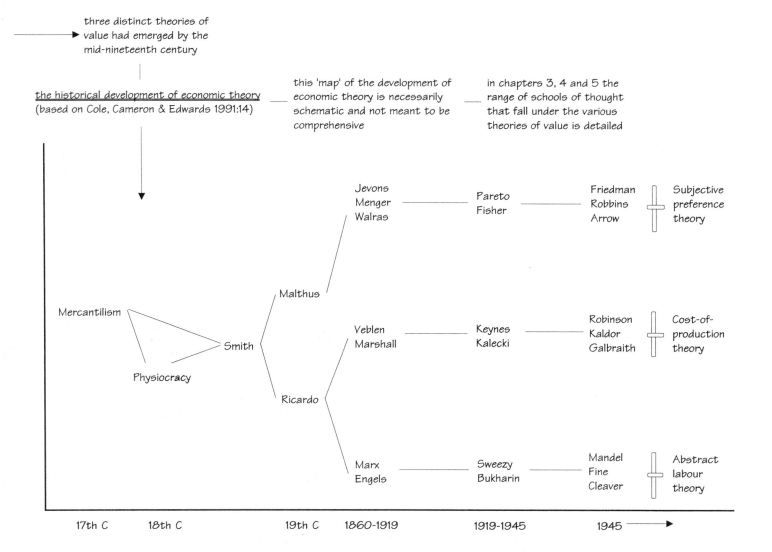

three distinct theories of
value had emerged by the
mid-nineteenth century

the historical development of economic theory
(based on Cole, Cameron & Edwards 1991:14)

this 'map' of the development of
economic theory is necessarily
schematic and not meant to be
comprehensive

in chapters 3, 4 and 5 the
range of schools of thought
that fall under the various
theories of value is detailed

Mercantilism

Physiocracy

Smith

Malthus

Ricardo

Jevons
Menger
Walras

Pareto
Fisher

Friedman
Robbins
Arrow

Subjective
preference
theory

Veblen
Marshall

Keynes
Kalecki

Robinson
Kaldor
Galbraith

Cost-of-
production
theory

Marx
Engels

Sweezy
Bukharin

Mandel
Fine
Cleaver

Abstract
labour
theory

17th C   18th C   19th C   1860-1919   1919-1945   1945 ⟶

it is beyond the scope of this book to address the various writings of those economists cited on the previous page

but since the latter half of the nineteenth century three distinct perspectives have offered alternative economic analyses

and the issues addressed have evolved with the need to explain and rationalise changed social experience, reflecting economic and social development

for instance, the theory of market equilibrium resulting from the interplay of the 'forces' of supply and demand, often thought to be the basis of modern economics

developed out of a particular historical context

for readers who wish to study the history of economic thought there is no substitute for reading the works of great thinkers as close to the original as possible

'...the so-called law of supply and demand is the fundamental tool of economic analysis.'
(Baumol & Blinder 1991:50)

so as to be able to situate the work in the context of contemporary intellectual culture as nearly as possible

of the many studies of economic thought see:

Cole, Cameron & Edwards 1991:Chapter 2
Gray & Thompson 1980
Roll 1973
Routh 1975
and the very much underrated
Stark 1944

OK- throw in the mirror and you can have the Bronx as well!

"MARKET EQUILIBRIUM"

the Industrial Revolution fundamentally changed people's experience

with the development of manufacturing, increasingly in workshops and factories, since the mid-sixteenth century

people's livelihoods were ever more under the control of and at the behest of capitalist employers

and throughout Europe there was revolt and opposition from the disadvantaged, culminating in a revolutionary wave as a result of the economic crisis of 1847

see:
Stark 1944
Abendroth 1972, Chapters 1, 2 and 3
Clarke 1982 Chapters 5 and 6

TRADE UNIONISM 1833.

but the 1850s (up until 1857) was a period of prosperity, strengthening industrial, capitalist, development

a development which was complemented by the emergence of trades unions and the political organisation of the working class

and economists turned their attention to the maintenance of social and economic order

the prospects for social and economic _equilibrium_

three economists, in different parts of Europe, independently, arrived at a similar theoretical interpretation of economic activity

common to all three was a theory which can be described as the mechanics of self-interest

individuals' economic activity is the result of personal self-interest

Leon Walras (pronounced Valras), (1801-1866), published in 1831 in Switzerland, De la Nature de la Richesse et de l'Origine de la Valeur

William Jevons, (1835-1882), published in 1871 in England, Theory of Political Economy

Karl Menger, (1840-1921), published in 1871 in Austria, Grundsatze der Volkswirthschaftslehre

individual people were considered as independent of society, and the economy operated according to the '...laws of the pre-social psyche of the individual.' (Stark 1944:55)

Why do I deserve to be rich? Because my great, great grandfather came over with William the Conqueror!

and by focussing on the individual as a consumer, the claim was that a theory based on individuals' utility maximisation (trying to be happy) was '...independent of any specific social order' (Roll 1973:372)

a characteristic which was extremely important for this approach to become the dominant ideology of economics in the twentieth century

as long as there are 'free' markets economic inequality is not an economic problem

by only focussing on independent individuals maximising utility, the theoretical con-clusions (and hence economic policies) only call for greater freedom for individuals to maximise utility (see Chapter 3)

the political implication of which is, in market societies the rich deserve to be rich, see Chapter 3, p.76

THE ECONOMICS OF SUPPLY AND DEMAND

economic theory as the <u>mechanics</u> of <u>self-interest</u> (the subjective preference theory of value) will be examined in Chapter 3

but at this point in the book your attention has only been drawn to the emphases of this perspective

in order to compare alternative analyes of the 'law of supply and demand' as an example of how, at any point in historical time, pervasive social priorities are differentially explained

there are <u>competing</u> analyses

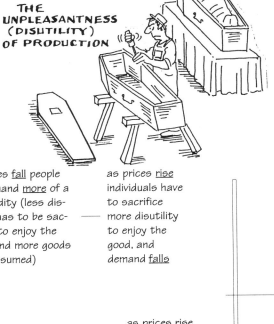

PLEASURE (UTILITY) OF CONSUMPTION

THE UNPLEASANTNESS (DISUTILITY) OF PRODUCTION

for orthodox economists (and the subjective preference theory of value), the economic dynamic is the consumer

as prices <u>fall</u> people will demand <u>more</u> of a commodity (less dis-utility has to be sac-rificed to enjoy the good, and more goods are consumed)

as prices <u>rise</u> individuals have to sacrifice more disutility to enjoy the good, and demand <u>falls</u>

this simplified analysis will be expanded in Chapter 3

individuals trade the <u>disutility</u> of work (which is <u>unpleasant</u>) for the utility (the pleasure) of consumption

and typically

'...to <u>maximise pleasure</u>, is the problem of economics' (Jevons 1970:101, emphasis in original)

the disutility of production is rewarded with an income, and the utility derived from consumption is reflected in the price of the good

as prices <u>fall</u> individuals are rewarded less for the disutility involved in production, and the supply of goods for sale <u>declines</u>

as prices <u>rise</u> individuals receive higher rewards and are prepared to suffer more disutility and supply <u>increases</u>

and individuals' willingness to exchange commodities reflects the <u>pain</u> associated with production and the <u>pleasure</u> of consumption

'The theory ... is entirely based on the calculus of pleasure and pain; and the object of economics is to ... (purchase) pleasure ... at the lowest cost of pain.' (Jevons 1970:91)

although neoclassical economics also includes the economics of Alfred Marshall, working within a different theory of value

so that eventually supply equals demand and there is economic <u>equilibrium</u>

price

supply

demand

with the birth of <u>neoclassical economics</u>

hence the standard 'supply and demand' diagram

quantity

such an emphasis became pervasive in the late nine-teenth century

in this analysis the <u>price</u> paid reflects the utility enjoyed in consumption by individuals - consumers' <u>demand</u> determines <u>value</u>

and for the subjective preference theory of value the dynamic is <u>assumed</u> to be the utility maximising, independent consumer

now, since price and quantity, and demand and supply change <u>simultaneously</u>

the <u>dynamic</u> of the relationship, the <u>causative</u> <u>mechanism</u>, has to be assumed

'... <u>value</u> <u>depends</u> <u>entirely</u> <u>upon</u> <u>utility</u>.' (Jevons 1970:77, emphasis in original)

and at the price consumers are willing to pay, producers decide <u>how</u> <u>much</u> to supply at that price - producers' <u>supply</u> determines <u>quantity</u>

we saw above (p.40) that
for the subjective pref-
erence theory of value,
as long as free markets
obtain, inequality is <u>not</u> a
problem

his major work, <u>The Principles</u>
<u>of Economics</u>, was first
published in 1890

however, for Alfred Marshall
(1842-1924), who was also writing at
the end of the nineteenth century

poverty <u>was</u>
a problem

'...there are vast numbers of people ... who are brought up with
insufficient food, clothing and house room; whose education is
broken off early in order that they may go to work ... and have no
chance of developing their higher mental faculties ... the study of
the causes of poverty is the study of the <u>degradation</u> <u>of</u> <u>a</u> <u>large</u>
<u>part</u> <u>of</u> <u>mankind</u>'.'
(Marshall 1947:3, emphasis added)

so for Marshall
individuals were
<u>not</u> independent
of society

individuals are not simply
endowed with tastes and
talents, but the
potential of their mental
faculties develops in
society

Pity I can't
afford it!

BOOKS

PRINCIPLES
OF
ECONOMICS
Alfred
Marshall

'Economics is thus taken to mean a
study of the economic aspects and
conditions of man's political, social and
private life; but more <u>especially</u> of his
<u>social</u> life.'
(Marshall 1947:42, emphasis added)

and, '...the answer (to poverty) depends
in a great measure upon facts and
inferences, which are within the province
of economics: and this it is which gives
to economic studies their <u>chief</u> and
<u>highest</u> interest.'
(Marshall 1947:4, emphasis added)

Marshall approaches economics with a different 'world view' and 'set of preconceptions'

'And in reply to Jevons a catena rather less untrue than his can be made by inverting his order and saying:- Utility determines the amount that has to be supplied. The amount that has to be supplied determines cost of production. Cost of production determines value because it determines the supply price which is required to make the producers keep to their work.' (Marshall 1947:818-19, emphasis added)

producers decide how much they can profitably supply

for Jevons (and the subjective preference theory of value) demand determines value and supply determines quantity

the consumer is the economic dynamic

with regard to the forces of supply and demand

for Marshall (and the cost-of-production theory of value) supply determines value and demand determines quantity

the producer is the economic dynamic

consumers decide how much they can afford to purchase

How much can I afford to buy?

How much can I profitably supply?

TOFFEE

CRISPS

The real inner laws of capitalist production cannot be explained by the interaction of supply and demand — can you lend me five pounds Fred?

KARL MARX   FRIEDRICH ENGELS

for Marx the economy is only one dimension of social life

and people's economic activity and motivation will reflect <u>all</u> of the social experiences and influences, which through <u>praxis</u>, go to develop the human character

explained in Chapters 5 and 6

and so, people's behaviour as consumers reflects their experience as producers, and vice versa

the relationship between supply and demand is <u>dialectical</u>

each <u>determines</u> the other

'The real difficulty in formulating the general definition of supply and demand is that it seems to take on the appearance of a tautology ... If supply equals demand they cease to act, and for this very reason commodities are sold at their market-values ... (But) if supply and demand balance one another, they cease to explain anything, do not affect market values, and therefore leave us so much more in the dark about the reasons why the market-value is expressed in just this sum of money and no other. It is evident that the <u>real</u> <u>inner</u> <u>laws</u> <u>of</u> <u>capitalist</u> <u>production</u> <u>cannot</u> <u>be</u> <u>explained</u> <u>by</u> <u>the</u> <u>interaction</u> <u>of</u> <u>supply</u> <u>and</u> <u>demand</u> .'
(Marx 1972:186 and 189, emphasis added)

while supply and demand not being equal might explain <u>changes</u> in price and quantity, with the trend towards equilibrium (where at a certain price the amount demanded and supplied are equal)

however the 'forces' of supply and demand cannot explain why a certain price is the <u>equilibrium</u> <u>price</u>

when supply and demand '...balance one another, they cease to act...',

and hence a deeper analysis of the '...inner laws of capitalist production...' is called for to understand the exchange process

the economy is a dimension of social life, and the <u>citizen</u> (who is both consumer <u>and</u> producer) is the dynamic

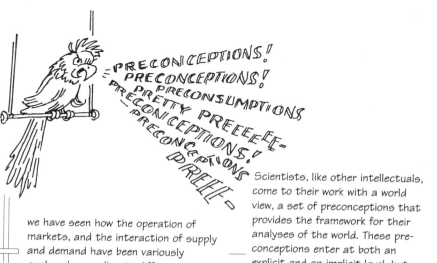

we have seen how the operation of markets, and the interaction of supply and demand have been variously analysed according to different <u>assumed</u> economic dynamics

Somebody shoot that economist!

Scientists, like other intellectuals, come to their work with a world view, a set of preconceptions that provides the framework for their analyses of the world. These preconceptions enter at both an explicit and an implicit level, but even when invoked explicitly, unexamined and unexpressed assumptions underlie them.' (Levins and Lewontin 1985:267, also quoted on p.14 above)

to <u>understand</u> economics we have
to identify these '...unexamined and
unexpressed assumptions...'

and ask the question <u>why</u> has the economist
theorised economic behaviour with respect
to a particular, assumed, economic dynamic
(the consumer, producer, or citizen)

economics, as a social science,
aims to explain an aspect of
human behaviour

and therefore must, at
least <u>implicitly</u>, be
based on a notion of
what it is to be <u>human</u>

implying a conception of
the economic <u>dynamic</u>

discussed
in detail in
Chapter 6

biasing the
analysis

implying a
<u>morality</u>

'In economics there is nothing more elementary
than the most complex of mathematical formulae,
nor anything more complex than the most
elementary of concepts. While the former is wholly
without content, the latter contains, latent within
it, the system of economic relations in its
entirety.'
(Levine 1977:ix)

the next three Chapters aim to
explore the complexity of the
elementary concepts of: the
<u>subjective</u> <u>preference</u> <u>theory</u> <u>of</u>
<u>value</u> , the <u>cost-of-production</u>
<u>theory</u> <u>of</u> <u>value</u>, and the
<u>abstract</u> <u>labour</u> <u>theory</u> <u>of</u> <u>value</u>

Economics is - of course -
a **social science**!

APPENDIX 2:1
CHARACTERISATIONS OF THE TRI-PARTITE DIVISION OF ECONOMY THEORY

in Chapter 1 we saw that to avoid 'distorted communication' between economists

and allow alternative analyses to be compared and contrasted so that the relative merits of each perspective can be made explicit

we had to find a standard of comparison, common to each perspective, to which they could all be compared

a standard which is independent of the particular interpretation of economic experience characteristic of each perspective

that standard is the implicit concept of value through which economists explain relations of exchange between producers and consumers

the theories of value - the subjective preference, cost-of-production, and abstract labour theories of value - each imply and assume different economic dynamics - the consumer, the producer and the citizen

three theoretical perspectives can commonly be identified in analyses of economic issues, problems and themes

in the table that follows, authors have found it necessary to identify three perspectives if they are to understand particular economic debates

in column III the economic dynamic is the citizen

in column II the economic dynamic is the producer

in column I the economic dynamic is the consumer

I have arranged the various categorisations of economic perspectives into three columns the references at the end of the table will indicate the topic or issue which is under consideration — in each case the author characterises the competing perspectives _differently_ — and the categories have been arranged here in terms of the implicit theory of value that structures the analysis — providing the common theoretical standard by which they might be compared

	I	II	III
Atkinson (1989)	supply side/free market	Keynesian/interventionist	Marxist
Axline (1979)	laissez-faire	dirigiste	dependency reducing
Barbier (1989)	descriptive	functional	evolutionary
Bardham (1988)	neoclassical	structuralist-institutionalist	Marxist
Brett (1985)	orthodox	reformist	Marxist
Coates & Hillard (1986)	right	centre	Marxist
Cole, Cameron & Edwards (1991)	subjective preference theory	cost-of-production theory	abstract labour theory
David (1986)	orthodox paradigm	mid-range perspectives	radical heterodox paradigm
Evans (1989)	neoclassical	neo-Ricardian	Marxian
Gill & Law (1989)	liberalism	realist-mercantilist	Marxism
Gilpin (1975)	liberalism	mercantilism	Marxism
Glass & Johnson (1989)	falsificationism	inductivism	instrumentalism
Hart (1988)	neoclassical	Keynesian	structuralist
Helburn (1986)	neoclassical/Keynesian synthesis	Keynes	Marx
Hirschman (1981)	orthodox economics	development economics	neomarxist economics
Honeywell (1983)	market forces	economic management	political interest
Hutchinson (1981)	Austrian	Keynesian	Marxian

	I	**II**	**III**
Jansen (1986)	monetarist	post-Keynesian/structuralist	Marxist
Kirkpatrick (1987)	neoclassical	structuralist	radical
Kitromilides (1983)	technocratic	pluralist	Marxist
Kristol (1981)	neo-Austrian	post-Keynesian	radical-humanistic
Kuttner (1985)	neoclassicism	post-Keynesian	neo-Marxism
Lal (1976)	neoclassicism	structuralist	dominance/dependency
le Roux (1990)	free market	social democratic	socialist
McGrath (1990)	liberal orthodoxy	political reformist	Marxist revisionist
Magnum et al (1987)	neoclassicism	institutionalism	radicalism
Mohun (1989)	market optimists	market pessimists	Marxists
Pearce (1989)	knowledge based	procedure based	needs based
Redclift (1987)	neoclassical economics	'deep' ecological positions	Marxist thoery
Reynolds (1971)	capitalist	less developed	socialist
Rowthorn (1974)	neoclassical	neo-Ricardian	Marxist
Smith & Toye (1979)	evolutionist	technocratic	Marxist
Staniland (1985)	behavioural	interactive	deterministic
Stiglitz (1988)	neoclassical/rational peasant model	information/theoretical approach	institutional/historical approach
Stiles (1990)	fuctional	neo-functionalist	political dominance
Toye (1988)	neoclassical	classical political	political economy of class
Ward (1979)	conservative	liberal	radical

REFERENCES TO APPENDIX 2:1

Arestis P & Skouras T (eds.), (1985), Post-Keynesian Economic Theory, Brighton, Wheatsheaf.

Atkinson G, (1989), Economics: Themes and Perspectives, Ormskirk, Causeway Press.

Axline W A, (1979), Caribbean Integration, London, Frances Pinter.

Barbier E A, (1989), Economics, Natural-Resource Scarcity and Development, London, Earthscan.

Bardham P, (1988), Alternative Approaches to Development Economics, in Chenery & Srinivasan (1988).

Bell D & Kristol I (eds.), (1981), The Crisis in Economic Theory, New York, Basic Books.

Brett E, (1985), The World Economy Since the War, London, Macmillan.

Chenery H & Srinivasan T (eds.), (1988), Handbook of Development Economics Vol 1, New York, North-Holland.

Coates D & Hillard J, (1986), The Economic Decline of Modern Britain: the debate between left and right, Brighton, Harvester-Wheatsheaf

Cochrane A & Anderson J (eds.), (1989), Politics in Transition, London, Sage.

Cole K, Cameron J & Edwards C, (1991), Why Economists Disagree, London, Longman.

David W L, (1986), Conflicting Paradigms in the Economics of Developing Nations, New York, Praeger.

Evans D, (1989), Comparative Advantage and Growth: trade and development in theory and practice , London, Harvester-Wheatsheaf.

Gemmell N, (1987), Surveys in Development Economics, Oxford, Blackwell.

Gill S & Law D, (1989), The Global Political Economy: perspectives, problems and policies, London, Harvester-Wheatsheaf.

Gilpin R, (1975), U.S. Power and the Multinational Corporation, New York, Basic Books.

Glass J & Johnson W, (1989), Economics: progression, stagnation or degeneration, London, Harvester.

Hart P, (1988), Youth Unemployment in Great Britain, Cambridge, Cambridge University Press.

Helburn S, (1986), Economics and Economics Education, in Hodkinson & Whitehead (1986).

Hirschman A O, (1981), Essays in Trespassing - economics to politics and beyond, Cambridge, Cambridge University Press.

Hodkinson S & Whitehead D (eds.), (1986), Economics Education: research and development issues, London, Longman.

Honeywell M (ed.), (1983), The Poverty Brokers: the IMF and Latin America, London, Latin America Bureau.

Hutchinson T W, (1981), The Politics and Philosophy of Economics, Oxford, Blackwell.

Jansen K (ed.), (1986), *Monetarism, Economic Crisis and the Third World*, London, Frank Cass.

Kirkpatrick C, (1987), Trade Policy and Industrialisation in LDCs, in Gemmel (1987).

Kitromilides Y, (1983), The Formation of Economic Policy, in Arestis & Skouras (1985).

Kristol I, (1981), Rationalism in Economics, in Bell & Kristol (1981).

Kuttner R, (1985), The Poverty of Economics, in Atlantic Monthly, February 1985.

Lal D, (1976), Distribution and Development: a review article, in World Development, Vol 4, No 9.

le Roux P, (1990), The Case for a Social Democratic Compromise, in Nattrass & Ardington (1990).

McGrath M, (1990), Economic Growth, Income Distribution and Social Change, in Nattrass & Ardington (1990).

Magnum G, Magnum S & Phillips P, (1987), The Three (at least) Worlds of Economic Theory, in Challenge, March/April 1987.

Mohun S, (1989), Continuity and Change in State Economic Intervention, in Cochrane & Anderson (1989).

Nattrass N & Ardington E (eds.), (1990), *The Political Economy of South Africa*, Cape Town, Oxford University Press.

Pearce I, (1989), Putting Perspectives in Perspective, in Economics, Vol XXV, Part 1.

Redclift M, (1987), *Sustainable Development*, London, Routledge.

Reynolds L G, (1971), *The Three Worlds of Economics*, New Haven, Yale University Press.

Rowthorn B, (1974), Neo-Classicism, Neo-Ricardianism and Marxism, in New Left Review, No 86.

Smith S & Toye J (eds.), (1979), *Trade and Poor Economies*, London, Frank Cass.

Staniland M, (1985), *What is Political Economy?*, New Haven, Yale University Press.

Stiglitz J E, (1988), Economic Organisation, Information and Development, in Chenery & Srinivasan (1988).

Stiles K, (1990), I.M.F. Conditionality: coercion or compromise, in World Development, Vol 18, No 7.

Toye J, (1988), Political Economy and the Analysis of Indian Development, in Modern Asian Studies, Vol 22, No 1.

Ward B, (1979), *The Ideal Worlds of Economics*, New York, Basic Books.

CHAPTER THREE

THE CONSUMER AS ECONOMIC DYNAMIC

THE SUBJECTIVE PREFERENCE THEORY OF VALUE

economics is the study of relations of exchange between consumers and producers

this is given a particular interpretation where the consumer is assumed to be the economic dynamic

this is by far the most common approach to economics

'Economists proceed on the fundamental article of faith that the economy is a structure that exists for the benefit of the individuals in it as human beings and, therefore, for consumers.' (Lancaster 1974:216, emphasis added)

the value of an object reflects the pleasure or need of consumers

that the consumer is the economic dynamic is an 'article of faith', an assumption

'Valuation is a subjective process. We cannot observe valuation.' (Robbins 1984::87, emphasis in original)

value reflects the preferences of consumers

'The preferences of consumers are held to be revealed through their choices of goods and services.' (Ormerod 1994:26, emphasis added)

see, Krepps 1990:63

the theory of revealed preference →

LAWNMOWERS

Think of it as a woman!

£19⁹

"THE VALUE OF AN OBJECT REFLECTS THE PLEASURE OF CONSUMERS"

and consumers' preferences reflect their own <u>tastes</u> and hence are <u>subjective</u>

and the analysis is presented as <u>obvious</u> and <u>universal</u> to all human beings

'...the nature of economic analysis ... consists of deductions from a series of postulates ... which are almost universal facts of experience present <u>whenever</u> human activity has an economic aspect...'
(Robbins 1984:99-100, emphasis added)

for the basic philosophy of the subjective preference theory of value see:
Friedman 1951
Stigler 1965
Cole, Cameron & Edwards 1991: Chapters 3 and 4

'...general principles can be derived from <u>simple</u> statements about how individuals behave in various circumstances ... we examine economic questions by first looking at <u>individual</u> decisions.'
(Craven 1984:6-7, emphasis added)

the analytical development of this theory of value forms the basis of most <u>microeconomics</u> text books, though there is a tendency to slip into a 'common sense' argument, sacrificing theoretical rigour

this economic perspective includes the following schools of thought:
Neoclassical economics (except Marshallian economics, see Chapter 4, pp. 88-90)
Austrian economics
Monetarism
New Classical Macroeconomics
Rational Expectations Theory
Chicago Economics
Supply-Side Economics
Disequilibrium Keynesianism (see Chapter 4, pp. 100-108)

and those 'simple', 'elementary' facts are:

one of the better texts is still,
Kelvin Lancaster 1974,
but see also,
Sloman 1991:Chapters 1-5

The consumer is the economic dynamic!

INDIVIDUALS -

individuals are different —— each is <u>endowed</u> with a unique set of tastes and talents —— that individuals are endowed with characteristics, determined either by biology (genetics) or God, is crucial to understanding the subjective preference theory of value, as we will see in Chapter 6

- ARE DIFFERENT.

can only be defined as more or less

|

utility is an <u>ordinal</u> concept

individuals like to enjoy themselves —— they attempt to <u>maximise utility</u> —— as we have already seen what gives people utility (pleasure) is <u>subjective</u> —— '...the consumer can communicate only relative preferences ... we can tell whether ... utility is higher or lower ... but not by <u>how</u> <u>much</u>.' (Lancaster 1974:231, emphasis in original) —— cannot be quantified

|

it is not a <u>cardinal</u> concept

individuals choose between alternatives —— human beings suffer from a condition known as <u>diminishing marginal utility</u> —— that is, the more any particular source of utility is consumed, at some point each extra (marginal) unit consumed gives less (diminished) pleasure (utility) —— individuals therefore prefer to choose different quantities of a range of alternative sources of utility

|

'...moderation in all things...'

because each individual has his/her own unique set of tastes and talents, the real cost of anything consumed differs between people

everything has an opportunity cost

everything you want to do - eat, sleep, run, watch television - involves a choice

you don't do something else

the pleasure you forego is the real cost: the opportunity cost

and people always want more pleasure (utility)

individuals are assumed to be insatiable

even if that is just to have an extra hour in bed in the morning

and because of 'diminishing marginal utility' individuals always want a selection of pleasant experiences (sources of utility)

the opportunity cost of which is, say, the pleasure from spending the extra hour's wages you would have earned had you gone to work

and where the consumer is assumed to be the economic dynamic

the economic problem is how to allocate productive resources so as to maximise utility

'The economist studies the disposal of scarce means ... Economics is the sceince which studies human behaviour as a relationship between ends and scarce means which have alternative uses.' (Robbins 1984:16, emphasis added)

and economic efficiency is defined in terms of the satisfaction of consumers' subjective preferences

Shall I be the "economic dynamic" -

- or shall I have another hour in bed?

THE MAXIMISATION OF UTILITY

how should individuals behave so that, given their unique set of tastes and talents, they can be as happy as possible - <u>maximise</u> <u>utility</u> ?

if individuals are endowed with tastes and talents, are motivated to maximise personal pleasure, suffer from diminishing marginal utility, and are insatiable, then,

in the sphere of consumption

using the <u>indifference curve</u> analysis

<u>all</u> any individual has to know to be as happy as possible are the prices of the alternative sources of utility that can be bought

explained in detail in any basic economics textbook, for example see:
Begg, Fisher & Dornbush 1991:Chapter 6.1
Cole, Cameron & Edwards 1991:Chapter 3.3
Kreps 1990:Chapter 2.1
Lancaster 1974:Chapter 7.3
Sloman 1991:Chapter 3.2

PRODUCTION.

CONSUMPTION.

some individuals have a special talent for anti-cipating consumer demand, and organising disparate individuals, with particular talents, to produce together

in the sphere of production

the technical division of labour implicit in any production process requires individuals with different talents to cooperate (specialise) in the production of a product

this key role is fulfilled by the <u>entrepreneur</u> → again it can be shown, through the <u>isoquant</u> analysis → that, <u>if</u> people are as assumed, then <u>all</u> the entrepreneur has to know to maximise output → are the prices of alternative productive inputs, known as <u>factors</u> of <u>production</u>

similarly addressed in any basic economics textbook, see for example:
Begg, Fisher & Dornbush 1991:Chapter 11(appendix)
Cole, Cameron & Edwards 1991:Chapter 3.5
Krepps 1990:Chapter 7.1
Lancaster 1974:Chapter 4.4
Sloman 1992:Chapter 4.2

FACTORS OF PRODUCTION

Why use expensive brushes to clean chimneys when you can save money by using boys like young Alex here, Mr Grimes?

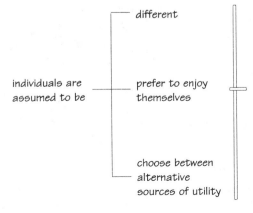

THE STORY SO FAR...

individuals are assumed to be
— different
— prefer to enjoy themselves
— choose between alternative sources of utility

and they only have to know market prices for
— for utility to be maximised in the sphere of consumption
— for output to be maximised in the sphere of production

in both spheres individuals <u>choose</u> what to do according to their subjective preferences →

in the sphere of consumption individuals _enjoy_ utility

in the sphere of production individuals _suffer_ disutility

the pleasure of consumption is equated to the pain of production

the set of prices that brings equilibrium to the sphere of consumption (utility is maximised)

is the same set of prices that guide entrepreneurs' decisions in buying factors of production to maximise output

consumers and producers are responding to the _same_ stimuli

individuals' behaviour is guided by sensual expediency

SUFFERING DISUTILITY

and so the equilibria in each sphere (the maximisation of utility and output) are brought into _general equilibrium_

ENJOYING UTILITY

see:
Krepps 1990:Chapter 15
Lancaster 1974:Chapter 7.10
Gee 1991

and it can be demonstrated through the _Edgeworth-Bowley Box_ that a set of prices exist such that both transactors in any exchange are better off (their utility is increased)

but for there to be _general equilibrium_ not only must exchanges be voluntary, and therefore to the advantage of _both_ parties

but all of an individual's income must be purposefully used

individuals do not suffer the disutility of production for no purpose

in economists' jargon;

'For general equilibrium, we require that the excess demand for each and every traded good be equal to zero, that is, the market supply of, say, bananas must equal its market demand ... [and] it can be shown that there exists a particular price configuration that results in the excess demands for each and every good and factor to be equal to precisely zero.'
(Gee 1991:85, emphasis in original)

known as Walras's Law, after the economist Leon Walras (1834-1910)

so that, given their income, everyone can purchase as many commodities as they wish at market prices

and nobody has any excess commodities they cannot sell (including factors of production)

in general equilibrium each individual is in equilibrium with every other individual

so nobody can become better off without someone else becoming worse off

Oi - Pareto - what about your Welfare Criterion?

sometimes referred to as, the Pareto Welfare Criterion, Pareto Superiority, or the Pareto Efficiency Criterion

a condition known as Pareto Optimality

after the economist Vilfredo Pareto (1848-1923)

see any basic economics textbook, for instance:
Begg, Fischer & Dornbush 1991:Chapter 19 (difficult)
Cole, Cameron & Edwards 1991:Chapter 4.3
Sloman 1991:Chapter 10.1

PERFECT COMPETITION

the concepts and theories of:
the indifference curve
the isoquant
Edgeworth-Bowley box   are defined
Walras Law   — in terms of
Pareto Optimality   utility
etc.

which is subjectively
defined and peculiar
to each individual

such a condition
exists where ——————————▶

which raises the question 'how do
individuals participate, socially, in
markets so as to achieve 'Pareto
Optimality' ?

such an equilibrium state is
achieved in conditions of
<u>perfect</u> <u>competition</u>

How much
for the snake?

because of the crucial role
played by entrepreneurs,
sometimes this concept
is subsumed under the
general heading of <u>the</u>
<u>theory</u> <u>of</u> <u>the</u> <u>firm</u>

the theory and concept of perfect competition is
addressed with varying degrees of rigour in every
economics textbook, but see:
Begg, Fischer & Dornbusch 1991:Chapter 9
Cole, Cameron & Edwards 1991:Chapter 3.8
Lancaster 1974:Chapter 6
Sloman 1991:Chapter 5

THE MARKET

in any market transaction there are so many buyers and sellers that no one individual can affect the market price — so that any commodity is the same price in any market — and no matter how much is bought and sold by any individual the price remains unchanged — this is, of course, impossible

markets are characterised by lots of small firms who are all in competition — and production is such that, as the amount sold, and therefore the amount produced, increases, the costs of production and the selling price do not decrease — in economists' jargon, there are no economies of scale — this is, of course, impossible

everyone has perfect knowledge of all transactions, so that they can buy (sell) in the cheapest (dearest) markets — this is, of course, impossible

all individuals have the freedom to be a producer, and to enter any market — this is, of course, impossible

I've believed as much as six impossible things before breakfast.

~ Like perfect competition "

'In a famous passage in Alice in Wonderland, the Red Queen declares that she often believes six impossible things before breakfast. The model of competitive equilibrium [perfect competition] appears to be requiring us to move into this kind of world.'
(Ormerod 1994:71)

[in fact it is in the sequel to Alice in Wonderland, Through the Looking Glass, both by Lewis Carroll, that the White Queen thinks of impossible things - KC]

-after Tenniell...

63

entrepreneurs play a crucial role in the functioning of the perfectly competitive economy

— having identified an unmet consumer demand

the available productive inputs (factors of production) are organised to produce as efficiently as possible

and this is achieved because there are so many sellers and buyers, and each buyer is motivated to maximise utilty and thus buy as cheaply as possible, that sellers have to compete to offer the lowest price possible

'The world of marginal economics ... is a world of many small firms ... [and] sophisticated mathematics applied ... to the competitive equilibrium model often makes the assumption of a "continuum" of firms. In other words, of an infinite number of companies!' (Ormerod 1994:52)

and such an 'equilibrium' state has the following characteristics

the consumer demand, reflecting individual subjective preferences, determines price and therefore value

the cost of the last unit produced (the marginal cost) equals the revenue from the sale of the last unit (the marginal revenue)

production is at minimum cost

and so prices cannot be lower

we saw earlier (p. 60) that individuals, to maximise utility, trade the disutility of production (work) for utility from consumption

and the conception of an equilibrium where the marginal cost (pain) equals the marginal revenue (pleasure), expresses this utility trade-off in terms of prices

giving the theory of perfect competition a superficial plausibility

but as we will see, the concept of 'perfect competition' is conceived of as an ideal, and not meant to describe the 'real world'

"Perfect competition"– has superficial plausibility

on p. 63 the assumptions that underlie the theory of perfect competition were specified, each of which is a practical impossibility

it might be thought that being so removed from the real world is a handicap in understanding economic experience

but, as we shall see in Chapter 6, such an abstraction from reality is considered to be a strength

though economists working within the other two theories of value see this as a fundamental weakness

if people are as assumed, then a perfectly competitive economy would be the ideal

the theory is not meant to describe any actual economy

the model of perfect competition becomes a 'benchmark' for economic policy

the actual economy is compared to perfect competition

and economic policy is intended to make the real economy more like the ideal

'The Utopian theoretical construct of perfect competition ... becomes relevant as a reference point by which to judge the health of an economy, as well as the remedies suggested for its amelioration.' (Lal 1983:15)

Perfect competition is a Utopian ideal!

it being 'common sense' → that the closer we tend to the 'ideal' the better

the problem of the 'second-best'

'Unfortunately, common sense is not always a good guide ... forty years ago, an important contribution to the literature demonstrated that serious problems exist for the model if <u>any</u> of its assumptions are breached.' (Ormerod 1994:83, 82)

in the absence of <u>all</u> the conditions for perfect competition, each policy proposal which is intended to make the economy more competitive may <u>not</u> in fact move the economy towards 'Pareto Optimality'

see: Lancaster and Lipsey 1956

any potential improvement is an empirical question which faces insuperable methodological problems

it is <u>impossible</u> to measure individuals' 'subjective preferences'

utility is an <u>ordinal</u> concept

the appropriateness of the subjective preference theory of value as a way of understanding economic experience remains an <u>article</u> <u>of</u> <u>faith</u>

SUBJECTIVE PREFERENCE THEORY

THOU SHALT

ARTICLE OF FAITH.

MARKET FORCES

for the subjective preference theory of value —— economic equilibrium is established by the operation of market forces

consumer demand determines value, or price —— individuals' subjective preferences determining how much they are 'willing to pay'

at this price producers then decide how much they can profitably supply

the paradox is, while it is asserted (assumed) that price reflects individual preferences

price determination through perfect competition (the ideal) assumes that no one individual can affect market price

'The free market argument ... [holds] that all social action must be sanctioned by the will of rational individuals composing society. Under this view society is nothing more than the aggregate of the individuals composing it ... norms should not be imposed upon society by a government ... [and] people have an inviolable right to keep what they have earned...'
(Schotter 1990:1/2)

" THE INVISIBLE HAND OF MARKET FORCES "
Adam Smith

as we shall see in Chapter 6, that markets require no <u>conscious</u> control to reach 'equilibrium' is central to the ideological power of the subjective preference theory of value

as long as there are 'free' markets inequality and poverty are not a problem!

an economist working within this perspective has to be able to describe market forces to be able to say anything about economic activity

which is assumed to tend towards equilibrium

a methodology has to be employed which can focus on <u>individual</u> economic transactions

herein lies the importance of <u>marginalism</u>

in any exchange, the last unit bought/sold is held to indicate individuals' priorities in the maximisation of utility

and can be considered <u>independently</u> of all other relations of exchange

marginal analysis is amenable to mathematical handling

giving the illusion of scientific exactitude

the technique manipulates <u>given</u> variables, it is assumed that the determination of economic variables is locked in the unfathomable individual human psyche

utility is an <u>ordinal</u> concept

" THE UNFATHOMABLE INDIVIDUAL HUMAN PSYCHE "

independent individuals essentially relate through markets

and economists have to be able to 'measure' market activity

this is done by calculating the <u>elasticity</u> of demand and supply functions

through which individuals' preferences are <u>revealed</u> by what they choose to buy

prices are assumed
to be determined by
the interaction of
supply and demand

where demand determines
value (price) offered for any
quantity, and supply determines the quantity sold

if there is a change in the
price that consumers will
pay for an amount of a
commodity

and at the 'equilibrium' price
the amount bought by con-
sumers equals the amount
that producers wish to sell
to maximise profits

or if the conditions of
production change such
that the amount that
producers are willing to
produce changes

Our prices are
elastic, Madam

CORSETRY

then the equilibrium price and quantity, to which market prices and the
volume of sales tend, will change

and the extent of the
change will reflect the
responsiveness of price
paid to quantity sold

how elastic a
relationship is

the concept of elasticity is addressed in basic
textbooks, see, for instance:
Begg, Fisher & Dornbusch 1991:Chapter 5
Hardwick, Kahn & Langmead 1994:Chapters 3 & 5
Lancaster 1974:Chapter 2
Sloman 1991:Chapter 2

see, for instance:
Begg, Fisher & Dornbusch 1991:Chapter 3
Cole, Cameron & Edwards 1991:Chapter 3
Hardwick, Khan & Langmead 1994:Chapters 3, 5, 6.
Sloman 1991:Chapter 2

THE CONSUMER AND ECONOMIC POLICY

economics is the study of relations of exchange between consumers and producers

in the market forces of demand and supply consumers' demand is assumed to determine value (see pp. 41-6)

and total 'utility' can be maximised, achieving the ideal of 'Pareto Optimality' (see pp. 58-61), as long as individuals, each of whom has a unique set of preferences, respond to 'free market' prices

and invariably policy prescriptions of the subjective preference theory of value rationalise economic issues to justify a move towards 'freer' markets

as an example the following themes will be addressed

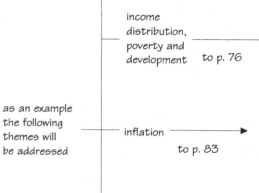

Hello Ms Hathaway - we want to build a motorway over your cottage!

the concept of 'perfect competition' (see pp. 62-6) is an idealised model of market exchange, used as a 'bench-mark' for policy formulation, which would reach the 'equilibrium' position implied by 'Pareto Optimality'

economic problems, at root, imply market failure, the Utopian conditions of 'perfect competition' not obtaining, leading to 'sub-optimal' economic performance

public goods and environmental economics to p. 71

income distribution, poverty and development to p. 76

inflation to p. 83

employment to p. 85

PUBLIC GOODS AND ENVIRONMENTAL ECONOMICS

Don't pick him up before you've been through his pockets

a commodity is a <u>public good</u> when, even though it is consumed by one individual, it can still be consumed by someone else

— and hence resources cannot be allocated so as to maximise the utility of individuals

it is not possible to exclude other individuals from consuming the same commodity

and the marginal adjustment of supply and demand in free markets is ineffectual in achieving 'equilibrium'

for instance, street lighting, policing, public broadcasting, roads, etc.

in the absence of 'market forces' automatically reconciling different individuals' tastes and talents, and tending towards 'equilibrium'

thus, potentially, there is a problem in ensuring that the pleasure (utility) of consumption is paid for in effort expended (disutility) in production

— known as the <u>free rider</u> problem —

individuals escaping having to contribute to the cost of providing a utility

economists now have to estimate the value of the marginal utilities (disutilities) enjoyed (suffered) by individuals

making the achievement of 'Pareto Optimality' impossible

estimate individuals' 'willingness to pay' for utilities, and the compensation they would accept for disutility endured

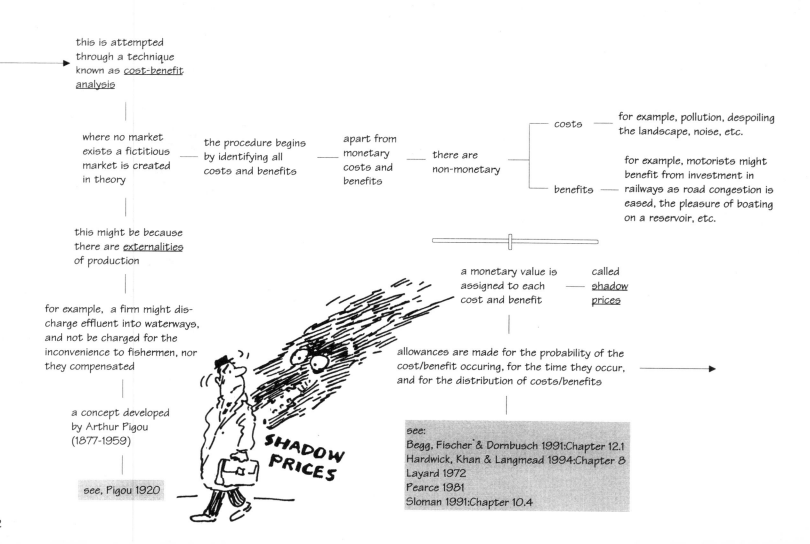

this is attempted through a technique known as _cost-benefit analysis_

where no market exists a fictitious market is created in theory — the procedure begins by identifying all costs and benefits — apart from monetary costs and benefits — there are non-monetary

costs — for example, pollution, despoiling the landscape, noise, etc.

benefits — for example, motorists might benefit from investment in railways as road congestion is eased, the pleasure of boating on a reservoir, etc.

this might be because there are _externalities_ of production

for example, a firm might discharge effluent into waterways, and not be charged for the inconvenience to fishermen, nor they compensated

a concept developed by Arthur Pigou (1877-1959)

see, Pigou 1920

a monetary value is assigned to each cost and benefit — called _shadow prices_

allowances are made for the probability of the cost/benefit occuring, for the time they occur, and for the distribution of costs/benefits

SHADOW PRICES

see:
Begg, Fischer & Dornbusch 1991:Chapter 12.1
Hardwick, Khan & Langmead 1994:Chapter 8
Layard 1972
Pearce 1981
Sloman 1991:Chapter 10.4

the costs and benefits are then compared, and if the benefits exceed the costs the project goes ahead

the approach of the subjective preference theory of value to the economics of the environment is essentially similar to the economics of 'externalities'

the concern is to 'commoditise' the environment as much as possible so as to encourage a cost/benefit, economising rationality in the management of environmental resources

resources are 'squandered', or there is pollution or other 'externalities' because it is not in any individual's financial interest to do otherwise

individuals have great ingenuity and can be motivated to solve environmental problems as long as the appropriate (price)incentives exist

REAL ESTATE AGENTS

I'm Sorry – South America's been sold already!

'...capacities for and commitment to economic development and control over our external and internal environment and concomitant systematic, technological innovation, application, and diffusion, of these capacities are increasing seemingly without forseeable limit.' (Khan & Wiener 1967:116)

'The basic general argument is that the present form of economic expansion poses no threat to the viability of the environment but, on the contrary, contains the key to the solution of any environmentally related problems.' (Mellos 1988:43)

and the '...key to the solution...'

is that the '...present form of economic expansion...' is one of individual, market incentives

so that where economic expansion leads to shortages of raw materials, prices will rise, reducing consumption and giving incentives to entrepreneurs to develop substitutes

'...estimates of reserves at any moment of time never represent true reserves in the sense of being all that can ever be found ... the known reserves represent the reserves that have been <u>worth</u> finding, given the <u>price</u> and the prospects of demand and the costs of exploration.' (Beckerman 1974:218, emphasis added)

and where environmental utilities are not commodities to be bought and sold because they are 'common property' (for example, common land, the oceans, etc.), they should, where possible, be 'privatised' and traded

'...overgrazing of pastures and pollution of the oceans and atmosphere result from the fact that common land, seas and air are not owned. If they were, then the resolution of damage levels and payments would be organized through the valuation and enforcement of the relevant property rights.' (Helm and Pearce 1991:8)

–then, after one really bad day out in the bay, I thought - maybe it's time we moved back to the land!

POLLUTION

indeed the whole question of environmental sustainability can be meaningfully addressed by determining appropriate 'shadow prices' and appraising alternatives through cost-benefit analysis

see:
Pearce, Barbier & Marakandya 1990
Pearce 1991
Dasgupta 1991

Remind me when pollution has reached optimum`

and economists working within this perspective can even talk of an 'optimum' level of pollution

for instance, where pollution is an 'externality' of production (for example, carbon dioxide emissions), the costs of reducing pollution should be compared to any improvement in individuals' lives from less carbon dioxide while accountng for individuals' utility from consuming the final product

indeed in the United States, the (1955) Clean Air Act amendments of the 1970s established the right for firms to trade licences to emit certain pollutants

firms are issued with a license permitting a certain level of pollutants to be produced, and if firms are able to operate such that less pollution is produced, then the spare pollution capacity can be sold to other firms, allowing them to pollute the atmosphere

and if the benefits exceed the costs, then pollution can be justified

there is a market in <u>emission reduction credits</u>, intended to act as an incentive for firms to develop more environmentally friendly production techniques so that they can sell their permits

see:
Beckerman 1991

see: Tietenberg 1991

75

INCOME DISTRIBUTION, POVERTY AND DEVELOPMENT

where there are free markets (the ideal being 'perfect competition')

then issues of economic inequality and improving living standards are questions of individual responsibility

in the state of 'Pareto Optimality' individuals receive an income equal to what they are 'worth' to society

there is <u>consumer sovereignty</u>

the prices of commodities reflect what consumers are 'prepared to pay'

which reflects the utility derived from consumption according to their subjective preferences

which determines the incomes of individuals (as producers)

hence there is an incentive to work hard, and those endowed with talents which are much sought after are particularly lucky

'Simple though this view is, its appeal derives from its political message which is that those who have money got it by dint of merit and effort and those who do not have only themselves to blame for it.' (Desai 1982:293)

so in a 'free market' economy, being wealthy is a sign that a lot of pleasure has been given to a lot of consumers

I buy - you exist!

POOR

which raises
two questions

inheritance ——— when individuals' fortunes
derive from the efforts of
their ancestors rather
than their own hard work
- how is this justified?

individuals should be
free to dispose of
their income accord-
ing to their subjective
preferences

how they choose to
dispose of their assets
is entirely their business

if they choose not to consume their
wealth but to bequeath it, then the
beneficiaries are very fortunate

when a 'free
market' economy
does not obtain

when the economy
is not perfectly
competitive

for instance, 'perfect information'
does not exist (this is an ideal
rather than an actuality) and
individuals are unable to use
information to their best
economic advantage

it might be thought that a
possible response would be
to tax those who have
benefited from 'imperfect'
competition and to
compensate the losers

leading to some people
being able to benefit
(become richer) through
market imperfections

for instance 'insider trading' on
the stock markets of the world,
when stockbrokers are able to buy
shares cheaply before priviledged
information which inflates the
share price is generally known

and the same applies when
all the other ideal conditions
of 'perfect competiton' fail
to obtain

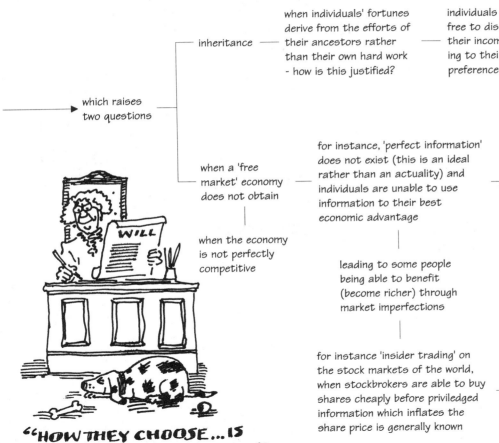

WILL

"HOW THEY CHOOSE...IS
ENTIRELY THEIR BUSINESS"

77

but for subjective preference theorists such a response would only <u>compound</u> the problem

'...a tax/subsidy system based on <u>income</u> difference which aimed at legislating for a desired income distribution ... would affect the choices individuals make at the margin between work and leisure. By distorting the initial, <u>ex</u> <u>hypothesi</u>, efficient allocation, the income-based tax/subsidy system, though improving the distribution of income, would impair the productive efficiency of the economy.' (Lal 1983:14, emphasis in original)

Of course the better-off I am, the worse off you are - have you never heard of Pareto Optimality?

what this quote is trying to say is that although imperfections in the market may have created 'undeserved' wealth

the state intervening to penalise the 'winners' and compensate the 'losers'

would create <u>even</u> <u>more</u> distortions, making the achievement of 'Pareto Optimality' even more remote

'Pareto Optimality' is said to apply where no one individual can be made better off without someone else being worse off

that is, <u>total</u> utility cannot be increased

the correct government response is to tighten up market regulation so that 'imperfect' competitive behaviour is less and less an option for the unscrupulous

of course, 'perfect competition' (and 'Pareto Optimality') is an impossibility

and as we saw in the discussion of the 'second-best' (p. 66), the belief that moving closer to perfection is an improvement, is just that, a <u>belief</u>, an <u>article</u> <u>of</u> <u>faith</u>

who enjoys that
pleasure (utility)
is not a meaning-
ful question for
subjective prefer-
ence theorists

this perspective on
economics (the consumer
as economic dynamic)

the subjective
preference
theory of value

Let's look at ourselves as **individuals**!

has nothing to say
about distribution,
inequality and poverty

only questions of market
perfection/imperfection
can be considered

— or in economists' jargon —

'Given an initial distribution of resources, each
individual entering the market may be conceived to
have a scale of relative valuations; and the interplay
of the market serves to bring these individual scales
and the market scale as expressed in relative prices
into harmony with one another. Prices, therefore,
express in money a grading of the various goods and
services coming on the market. Any given price,
therefore, has significance only in relation to the
other prices prevailing at that time. Taken by itself
it means nothing.'
(Robbins 1984:55, emphasis added)

which remains an article of faith

to which we will return in Chapter 6

just as the only room for policy
initiatives in addressing economic
inequality and poverty is to create
the conditions through which individuals can exploit their <u>own</u> potentials

trying to make economies
as 'perfectly competitive'
as possible

the efficacy of
which is an 'article
of faith'

the same belief in the benign
effects of market forces, and
the importance of individual
responsibility, characterises
the subjective preference
theory of value understanding
of development

development is <u>economic</u>
development, synonimous
with economic growth and
achieved through free
markets

development
is a question
of individual
initiative

development is a
process in which
individuals adopt
a 'cost-benefit'
type, economic
rationality

"MODERNISATION OF THE MIND "

this theme is developed in
Bauer 1976, but see also:
Bauer 1981 and 1991

'Economic development requires modernisation
of the mind. It requires revision of the attitudes, modes of conduct and institutions
adverse to material progress. The attitudes,
mores and institutions of large parts of the
underdeveloped world differ radically from those
which have promoted material progress in the
west...'
(Bauer 1976:84)

and contact with western 'developed' societies can only help the 'Third World' escape the cultural bonds that tie them to poverty

such an approach to development underlies <u>modernisation theory</u>

Let them eat cake!

MARIE ANTOINETTE

'...what we have been looking at are dead-end societies; in other words there is no prospect of change in the Third World that would substantially improve the lives of more than a few people ... A semblence of development ... was possible as long as Western economic growth remained vigorous enough to stimulate and sustain it.'
(May 1981:226)

for a discussion of contemporary writing in the modernisation theory vein see: So 1990:Part 1

but of course, such western-generated 'economic incentives' can only take effect if people have the 'appropriate' attitudes

and Brian May draws a logical conclusion from Bauer's position, that the poverty (of all) and the violence of (many) Third World societies is evidence of 'irrationality'

'Assuming that certain mentalities are not conducive to socio-economic development ... It is clear that the balance of reason and emotion varies from society to society ... It is apparent that irrational pressures in the Third World are increasing and that a sane leader may be quickly overthrown by one whose actions are unpredictable ... The West's wilful blindness to even the possibility of psychic differences between societies - perhaps of biochemical origin - could make the Third World calamity a calamity for us all.'   (May 1981:251, 255)

a racial (genetic) explanation of poverty

development is under-stood to be a transition from <u>traditional</u> to <u>modern</u> society

where the standard of 'modernity' is taken to be the 'developed' cap-italist economies of the West

a key work in this approach is W. W. Rostow's <u>Stages</u> of <u>Economic Growth</u> (Rostow 1960)

in the evolution from 'traditional' to 'modern' societies, economies <u>take</u> <u>off</u>

which occurs when scientific knowledge begins to be applied to production, increasing productivity and efficiency

and crucial to this eventuality is appro-priate economic incent-ives to encourage such a calculating approach to production

Hello - you look like someone open to new ideas - what's your name?

Rostow!

'It is evident that the take-off requires the existence and the successful activity of some group in the society which is prepared to accept innovations ... Whatever ... the motives which have led men to under-take the constructive entrepreneurial acts of the take-off period ... these motives have varied greatly from one society to another ... In non-economic terms, the take-off usually witnesses a definitive social, political and cultural victory of those who would modernise the economy...'
(Rostow 1960:50, 52, 58)

INFLATION

'...long-continued inflation is always and everywhere a monetary phenomenon that arises from a more rapid expansion in the quantity of money than in total output - though ... the exact rate of inflation is not precisely or mechanically linked to the exact rate of monetary growth.'
(Friedman 1974:10)

economies are conceived of as mechanisms through which individuals, as consumers, maximise utility

and to tend towards 'Pareto Optimality' and 'General Equilibrium' requires individuals to move between markets, trading their talents for a multiplicity of sources of utility to consume

money makes the different sources of utility/ disutility commensurable, and relative prices reflect 'strength of preference' or the 'degree' of pleasure

money then is an essential economic lubricant which makes the achievement of economic 'equilibrium' possible

'The information that is important for the organization of production is primarily about relative prices - the price of one item compared with another. High inflation ... drowns that information in meaningless static.'
(Friedman M & R 1979:37, emphasis in original)

and inflation, steadily rising prices which diminish the purchasing power of money, leads to the economy coming unstuck

'Money is demanded essentially for transactions purposes. The role of money is to bring buyers and sellers together with a minimum of fuss: it is the glue that links supply and demand.'
(Harrigan & McGregor 1991:110)

monetarism, the understanding that inflation is a 'monetary' phenomenon, being generated by an increasing availability of money for transactions purposes

became theoretically and politically important in the 1970s, as the prevailing economic orthodoxy could not adequately explain rising prices and rising unemployment: stagflation (see Chapter 4)

see: Smith 1987: Chapters 4, 5 & 6.

as more money circulates in the economy, there is more money available to buy goods, and as individuals attempt to maximise utility, there is competition for the available goods and prices rise

'...there is no single ... definition of money. In the ten years from 1976, at least seven different definitions of money were measured and monitored in Britain...' (Smith 1987:4)

Your monetarist theory doesn't seem to operate here, Friedman!

'The cure for inflation is simple to state but hard to implement ... a reduction in the rate of monetary growth is the one and only cure for inflation ... The problem is to have the political will to take the measures necessary...

The initial side effects of a slower rate of monetary growth are painful: lower economic growth, temporarily high unemployment, without, for a time, much reduction in inflation...' (Friedman M & R 1979:317)

and because there is no 'mechanical' link between the rate of monetary growth and the rate of inflation, there is no way of predicting, except in very broad terms, the effect of monetary restraint on economic activity

indeed, monetarist economists cannot even agree what 'money' is

and monetarist economic policy, like the subjective preference theory of value, becomes an article of faith

there is a huge literature on monetarism. On the theory of monetarism see: Friedman 1956, 1970 and 1974; M & R Friedman 1979; Harrigan & McGregor 1991; Chrystal & Price 1994:Chapter 3. On the underlying philosophy see: Graham & Clarke 1986. On the rise to political prominence see: Smith 1987; Keegan 1984. For some of the critics see: Healey 1989; Kaldor 1982; Nell & Azarchs 1984.

EMPLOYMENT

the market for labour is like any other market —— the price of labour (the wage rate) equates supply and demand

the utility derived from labour (the pleasure of consuming the products of labour) is equated to the disutility of labour

the wage (and the pleasure derived from spending it) has to be enough to compensate for the effort (pain) of work

if the wage rate is not high enough people won't work

there is a <u>natural</u> <u>rate</u> <u>of</u> <u>unemployment</u>

'The "natural rate" is "natural" only in the sense that actual unemployment tends to move automatically towards that rate.' (Harrigan & McGregor 1991;121)

and not specifically 'full employment'

the emphasis of economic policy should be 'free' markets and the 'correct' relative prices

there is a point below which unemployment cannot be reduced, indeed, it is asserted that for some people unemployment benefit and welfare relief are <u>more</u> than the wage rate which would induce them to work and the first step in employment policy is to reduce any employment benefit so as to stop the undeserving from receiving state benefit

— it being an <u>article</u> of <u>faith</u> that the market price of labour (the wage rate) is all that people are entitled to

the second step is to remove any constraints which might 'artificially' increase the cost of employing labour

— generally called '<u>supply-side</u>' policies

any trades union priviledges which might force wages above the market rate must be removed (for example, minimum wage legislation)

'...emphasis is placed on "pricing the unemployed into jobs" both by reducing wage rates and by lowering the range and level of benefits to increase work incentives.'
(Ditch 1991:33)

the cost of employing labour should be reduced by such action as limiting the health and safety standards of workplaces to the minimum

Listen, Friday - if you tidy up the stockade I'll pay you two cowries

CHAPTER FOUR

THE PRODUCER AS ECONOMIC DYNAMIC

THE COST OF PRODUCTION THEORY OF VALUE

we return again to the study
of economics as the study of
relations of exchange between
consumers and producers

only this time the
<u>producer</u> holds
the whip hand

'Most people think of themselves first of
all not as consumers but as producers.'
(Galbraith & Salinger 1981:164)

and the value (price) of
commodities does not now
reflect the preferences of
consumers

but the costs faced by
producers in providing
these commodities for
consumers

'Utility determines the amount that has to be supplied,
The amount that has to be supplied determines the cost of production,
Cost of production determines value,
Because it determines the supply price which is required to make the producers
keep to their work.'
(Marshall 1947:819)

placing the producer in the key
role in economic relations leads
to a fundamental re-evaluation in
the understanding of economic
experience

productive processes imply
a <u>technical</u> <u>division</u> <u>of</u> <u>labour</u>

there is economic
specialisation

and technical specialisation requires that producers with different skills cooperate to produce

|

people are not independent *of* each other, but dependent *on* each other

|

they are not 'free to choose'

|

schools of thought within this economic perspective include;
Fundamentalist Keynesians
Hydraulic Keynesians
(but <u>not</u> Disequilibrium Keynesians, see pp. 100-8)
Post Keynesians
New Keynesian Economics
New Cambridge Economics
Institutionalists
Structuralists
Neo-Ricardians
Evolutionary Economics

markets are now <u>systems</u> through which individuals cooperate to maximise output

|

not <u>mechanisms</u> through which individuals maximise utility

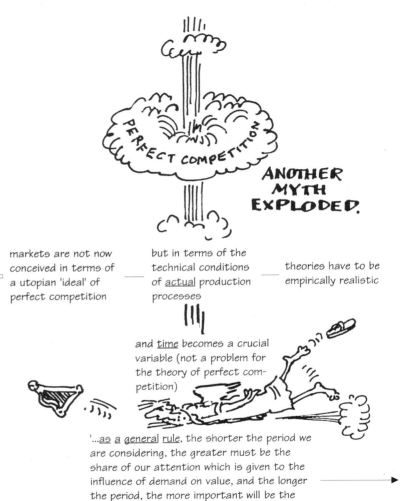

ANOTHER MYTH EXPLODED.

markets are not now conceived in terms of a utopian 'ideal' of perfect competition

but in terms of the technical conditions of <u>actual</u> production processes

theories have to be empirically realistic

and <u>time</u> becomes a crucial variable (not a problem for the theory of perfect competition)

'...<u>as a general rule</u>, the shorter the period we are considering, the greater must be the share of our attention which is given to the influence of demand on value, and the longer the period, the more important will be the influence of cost of production on value.' (Marshall 1947:349, emphasis in original)

it takes time for production processes
to adapt and produce at the technical
optimum (most efficient) - which is
when the 'equilibrium' price is reached

see:
Marshall 1947:book V, chapter III

'...Marshall [and cost-of-production theorists in general] did not see
that any optimization procedure - that is any problem of combining
factors in the "best" way - depends essentially on a system of prices ...
[but] could ... as a rule be formulated in purely technical terms...'
(Frisch 1950:59, emphasis added)

and the concern is with
how the market system
functions, not with
independent individuals'
decisions

the concern with
individuals' decisions is
known as microeconomics

the concern with economic
systems is known as
macroeconomics

'Macroeconomics is the study of how whole economic
systems function. What is utlimately at issue are
such things as the determination of national income,
output, inflation and unemployment...'
(Godley & Cripps 1983:13, emphasis added)

the economy is more
than the individuals
that comprise it

the whole is more than
the sum of the parts

IMPERFECT COMPETITION

there is a <u>social</u> interest above and beyond that of individuals' preferences

and economic problems occur when individuals' interests conflict with the wider social interest

the state has to intervene so that the social interest prevails over individuals' preferences

and cost-of-production economists' analyses are invariably focussed on how the economy might be better organised to limit the malign effects of individuals' independent choices

'No doubt men ... are capable of much more unselfish service than they generally render: and the supreme aim of the economist is to discover how this latent social asset can be developed most quickly...'
(Marshall 1947:9)

'short-term' market prices reflect individuals' consumption preferences

it takes time for price to adjust to the minimum, defined by the lowest cost of production

value, then, does not equal market price, but 'long-run' market price, after production techniques have had time to adjust to the level of demand (the quantity demanded) and to produce most efficiently (lowest price)

and competition is important in forcing producers to adopt the cheapest method of production

even though competition, driven by individual gain, can be against the broader social interest

The state has to intervene now, because you've been so selfish !

the utopian ideal of 'perfect competition' then is not relevant to the theoretical priorities of cost-of-production theorists

and alternative models of markets have been developed that focus on the power of producers to affect prices:

the theory of <u>natural</u> <u>monopoly</u> developed by Alfred Marshall (1890) - see Marshall 1947:Chapter XIV

the theory of <u>monopolistic</u> <u>competition</u> developed by Edward Chamberlain (1933) - see Chamberlain 1933

the theory of <u>imperfect</u> <u>competiton</u> developed by Joan Robinson (1933) - see Robinson 1933

the theory of <u>oligopoly</u> developed by Paul Sweezy (1939) - see Sweezy 1939

these models of markets, in all of which producers have a degree of 'monopoly' power to affect prices (the assumption of 'perfect competition' - that there are, potentially, an infinite number of firms - is discounted as unrealistic) are handled in most textbooks under the title of 'imperfect competition'

see:
Begg, Fischer & Dornbusch 1991:Chapters 9 and 10
Cole, Cameron & Edwards 1991:Chapter 6.3
Hardwick, Khan & Langmead 1994:Chapter 10
Sloman 1991:Chapters 6 and 7

although these altern-ative conceptions of how markets function challenged the idea of 'perfect competition'

markets are still seen to function as institutions through which <u>individuals</u> exch-ange

only now markets have to be regulated to avoid the excesses of individuals' greed

however, these models did not lead towards positing an alternative conception of how the whole economy might work

in models of imperfect competition firms' responses follow a similar logic to those in a supposedly perfectly competitive environment

it wasn't until the work of John Maynard Keynes (published in 1936), who focussed on the decisions of producers in determining 'macro' economic activity, that there was a fully worked out alternative framework to the subjective preference general equilibrium model

'...the importance of ... [Keynes's] <u>General</u> <u>Theory</u> lay in its presentation of both a consolidated critique of the then orthodox view and an alternative set of relationships which proved a rationale for a policy of government intervention.'
(Love 1991:169)

HE ECONOMICS OF KEYNES

that production is carried out with the most advanced <u>technology</u>

the efficient use of resources in the production process

that resources are <u>fully</u> <u>utilised</u> (employed)

if value is determined by the cost of production then there are two pre-eminent concerns of theorists

'The outstanding faults of the economic society in which we live are its failure to provide for full employment and its arbitrary and inequitable distribution of wealth and income.'
(Keynes 1936:372)

the price paid for productive resources

which reflects the earnings of the suppliers of productive resources

the <u>distribution</u> of the technical product

economic analysis has to be <u>historically</u> <u>realistic</u>

reflecting the actual use of resources and the distribution of the product

and not by comparison to an 'ideal' (perfect competition)

and subjective preference analyses are rejected for their lack of 'realism'

rather the emphasis is upon the problems faced by producers

and Keynes, concerned with the problems of unemployment in the 1920s and 1930s

'Our criticism of the accepted classical theory (essentially subjective preference theorists) of economics has consisted not so much in finding logical flaws in its analysis as in pointing out that its tacit assumptions are seldom or never satisfied, with the result that it cannot solve the economic problems of the <u>actual</u> world.' (Keynes 1936:378, emphasis added)

focused on the nature of decisions taken by producers, who he called <u>entrepreneurs</u>

'...<u>enterprise</u> ... the activity of forecasting the prospective yield of assets over their whole life...' (Keynes 1936:158, emphasis in original)

to p. 95

'...orthodox economics is in many ways an empty box. Its understanding of the world is similar to that of the physical sciences in the Middle Ages. A few insights have been obtained which will stand the test of time, but they are very few indeed, and the whole basis of conventional economics is deeply flawed.' (Ormerod 1994:ix)

94

the decision to produce creates jobs

and Keynes thought that in this endeavour entrepreneurs were frustrated by the individual interests of <u>rentiers</u>, people who speculate on the future value of assets

'...<u>speculation</u> ... the activity of forecasting the psychology of the market...' (Keynes 1936:158, emphasis in original)

to p. 96

from
p. 94

in deciding to produce entrepreneurs have to take a long view over the life-time of the equipment

estimating and comparing the costs and returns from production, and only proceeding if they are confident of making a profit

but there is such uncertainty that enterprise is '...partly a lottery...' (Keynes 1936:150)

ENTREPRENEURS

'...our [entrepreneurs'] decisions to do something positive, the full consequences of which will be drawn out over many days ... [are] a result of animal spirits ... not as the outcome of ... quantitative probabilities ... if the animal spirits are dimmed and the spontaneous optimism falters leaving us to depend on nothing but a mathematical expectation, enterprise will fade and die...' (Keynes 1936:161-2)

to encourage enterprise (and therefore job creation) it is essential to create an economic environment of business confidence

entrepreneurs must expect to sell their products

therefore people must have incomes to buy goods

people must have jobs

and job creation is a cumulative process (which Keynes called the multiplier), as one employed person buys another's product and therefore creates more employment

so the government can create full employment by directly employing relatively few people through public works or giving people incomes through state expenditure

from
p. 94

entrepreneurs have
to borrow money to
invest in production

money is raised on the financial market
(the stock exchange, commercial banks,
finance houses, financial intermediaries,
etc.)

and the cost of borrowing
money (the interest rate)
reflects the valuation (the
estimated future return
from) of the investment

Put it all on RTZ, GM, and Exxon!

'A conventional valuation which is established as
the outcome of the mass psychology of a large
number of ignorant individuals is liable to change
violently as the result of a sudden fluctuation of
opinion due to factors which really do not make
much difference to the prospective yield...'
(Keynes 1936:154)

'When the capital development of a country
becomes the by-product of the activities of
a casino, the job is likely to be ill done.'
(Keynes 1936:159)

for Keynes the malign influence of
rentiers' speculation had to be
abrogated for there to be a recovery
from the 1930s economic depression

rentiers are only concerned with the
'current' value of their financial assets,
which fluctuates with opinion in the
finance markets as to the supposed
future prospects of the firm or even
the whole economy

hence the cost of borrowing
money may not reflect the
anticipated return of the
actual investment itself

and the cost of borrowing may
be so high as to increase the
costs of the investment, making
the project non-profitable

in the past four pages we have considered the kernel of Keynes's analysis — emphasising the 'animal spirits' that drive entrepreurs (willingness to gamble and take a risk) to organise production — hence the imperative of <u>creating</u> an environment of 'business confidence' to encourage investment and job creation — rather than the 'free market' emphasis of the subjective preference theory of value

in this he was writing firmly in the tradition of Alfred Marshall (who was one of his teachers at Cambridge University)

crucialy market forces do not equate

'Keynes's notion of economic activity is essentially Marshallian ... it recognises <u>production</u> as the essential economic activity ... the concept of entrepreneurial economy is applied to an economy where agents are organized to produce...' (Carvalho 1992:43, emphasis added)

the demand for investment funds from entrepreneurs

the supply of funds for investment from savers (via rentiers)

for subjective preference theorists the price of money, the interest rate, equates the demand and supply of funds for investment

but for Keynes the interest rate reflects the sectional interests of rentiers rather than the interests of independent individuals →

there is a social interest above and beyond that of individuals' preferences

GOOD GUY (ENTREPRENEUR)

BAD GUY (RENTIER)

it is incumbent on the state to protect and assert the general social interest over the vested economic interests of individuals

for Keynes the state should intervene in the economy to

create an economic environment of optimism to encourage investment

there must be sufficient <u>effective demand</u> (individual preference backed by purchasing power)

maintain interest rates at a level low enough to encourage investment to achieve full employment

for Keynes (and cost-of-production theorists in general) individuals' interests are defined by their technical role in the production process

individuals' subjective preferences to consume are no longer sufficient

because their incomes no longer merely reflect their 'talents' and individual motivation

to this end Keynes called for the '...euthanasia of the rentier...' (Keynes 1936:376)

individuals are not 'free to choose'

Put it down as 'euthanasia of the rentier'!

so that the supply of investment finance could more nearly reflect the <u>productive</u> potential of an investment rather than the 'casino' mentality of the suppliers of investible funds

rather they are <u>dependent</u> on the economic 'system' and their incomes reflect their place in the 'technical division of labour'

Keynes, and cost-of-production theorists in general, do not share the 'faith' that economies can be mechanisms through which independent individuals, as consumers, maximise utility

You ask God to intervene in the economy - I'm going to ask the state!

KEYNESIANISM.

rather economies are conceived of as systems upon which people <u>depend</u> for their livelihoods

the whole (the economy) is <u>more</u> than the sum of the parts (individuals)

indeed, Keynes's analysis is often conceived of positing a <u>circular</u> <u>flow</u> <u>of</u> <u>income</u>

they have 'faith' that there is a general social interest and that the state is capable of managing economic systems in that interest

where one person's expenditure is another's income, and it is a government function to balance income and expenditure

to organise and engender economic cooperation between dependent people

and all economic analyses within this theoretical perspective focus on, and justify, purposeful economic intervention by the state to ensure the smooth working of the economic system

through balancing:
government expenditure & taxation
imports & exports
savings & investment
domestic consumption expenditure & incomes

a technique known as <u>demand</u> <u>management</u>

see:
Vines, Maciejowski & Meade 1983

see:
Begg, Fischer & Dornbusch 1991:Chapter 21
Craven 1984:Chapter 5.7
Sloman 1991:Chapter 13.2
and most economics text books

THE ECONOMICS OF KEYNES AND KEYNESIAN ECONOMICS

we have only been able to approach Keynes's economics very generally — understanding the analysis in terms of assumptions about the nature of the economic dynamic: the producer

'...the set of preconceptions that provides the framework for ... analyses of the world.' (Levins & Lewontin 1985:267, quoted p. 14 above) — 'preconceptions' that set parameters for the definition and consideration of the 'real world'

Keynes's conception of economic reality not only saw economic management as a political imperative

but also gave economic concepts a distinct meaning, different from that of the subjective preference theory of value. Concepts such as: production costs, demand for money, interest rate, marginal efficiency, value, inflation, etc. have a different significance — leading to '...distorted communication...' between economists (see p. 19 above)

the same <u>words</u> are different <u>concepts</u>

Down!

Walkies!

" THE SAME WORDS CAN BE DIFFERENT CONCEPTS "

Keynes was very well aware that his analysis would face problems in being accepted because of the redefinition of economic reality

'The difficulty lies, not in the new ideas, but in escaping from the old ones, which ramify, for those brought up as most of us have been, into every corner of our minds.'
(Keynes 1936:viii)

TOO LATE ...

THE GENERAL THEORY

an observation that proved to be prophetic: 'It [Keynes's <u>General</u> <u>Theory</u>] is a badly written book ... the Keynesian system stands out indistinctly, as if the author were hardly aware of its existence ... until the appearance of the mathematical models of Meade, Lange, Hicks and Harrod, there is reason to believe that Keynes himself did not truly understand his own analysis.'
(Samuelson, quoted in Bell 1981:62/3))

the 'mathematical models' Samuelson refers to came to be known as the 'Hicks-Hansen' <u>neoclassical synthesis</u>

often referred to as the <u>IS/LM</u> <u>analysis</u>

Hicks's book <u>Value</u> <u>and</u> <u>Capital</u> '... would have been very different had I not had the [Keynes's] <u>General</u> <u>Theory</u> at my disposal...'
(Hicks 1935:4)

proceeded to reinterpret Keynes "...under assumptions of <u>perfect</u> <u>competition</u> ... [deriving] laws of market conduct ... which deal with the reaction of the <u>consumer</u> to changes in market conditions.'
(Hicks 1935:6, 23 emphasis added)

led to Hicks's 'IS/LM' formulation (Hicks 1937) which followed the precepts of 'perfect competition' in ignoring production time, and therefore expectations and confidence about the future, so central to Keynes's analysis

in keeping with the 'set of preconceptions' that underlies the subjective preference theory of value

which, as we will see in Chapters 6 and 7, has distinct <u>political</u> implications

Keynes's message, for it to be understood by economists, had to be translated into the intellectual parameters of the prevailing orthodoxy which assumed the consumer to be the economic dynamic

emphasising competitive market forces, with the analysis conducted in terms of prices

yet the basis of Keynes's analysis was that. '...the concept of the general price-level [is] ... very unsatisfactory for the purposes of causal analysis...' (Keynes 1936:39)

'...distorted communication...' — see pp. 19-21

'Keynesianism' became a particular interpretation of the 'neoclassical synthesis'

the alternative interpretation being the 'neoclassical model'

these emphases were intellectually compatible as they were both based on the intellectual parameters of the subjective preference theory of value

Keynes's thought was absorbed into economic orthodoxy though the IS/LM formulation (sometimes called the <u>money</u> <u>augmented</u> <u>expenditure</u> <u>system</u>)

THE MARKET

The problem isn't only here - it's here!

NOW READ ON...

the problem became one of achieving 'macro market equilibrium'

in particular two markets had to be 'managed' to achieve equilibrium

the 'goods' market

the 'money' market

for a comprehensive analysis of the IS/LM model see: Levacic & Rebmann 1982 Chrystal & Price 1994:Chapter 1

the supply of money is determined by government policy

GOODS   BANK →

in the 'simple' IS/LM model money is demanded by consumers for transactions (purchases) and there is also a precautionary demand (helping to give people a degree of security)

there will also be a speculative demand by rentiers, worried about the changing value of their assets and it being safer to hold cash

aggregate supply is defined by output produced under full employment

and in the 'simple' IS/LM model, aggregate demand reflects consumer demand and entrepreneurs' investment

which in turn reflects aggregate income (Y) and the interest rate (i)

and there are a number of combinations of (Y) and (i) such that aggregate supply equals aggregate demand

the 'IS' function

the 'LM' function

the transaction and precautionary demand are held to vary with income (Y), and the speculative demand with the interest rate (i)

and there are a number of combinations of (Y) and (i) such that the money supply equals the demand for money the IS and LM functions are plotted onto a graph where the axes are aggregate income (Y) and the interest rate (i)

similar to the supply and demand diagram on page 42, with the IS function being the demand curve and the LM function the supply curve

the goods (IS) and money (LM) markets can be brought into equilibrium, avoiding the problems of unemployment and inflation

by taking action to adjust (Y) and/or (i) to alter the demand for goods and/or money

the choice of policy instruments, fiscal (expenditure) or monetary (interest rate)

reflects the perceived responsiveness (elasticity) of the dependent variables (expenditure/investment) to the independent variables (income/interest rate)

'With reference to the different schools of thought, Keynesians generally <u>believe</u> the demand for money to be fairly elastic ... [and] they cast doubt on the responsiveness of investment to interest rate changes ... Monetarists [neoclassicals], on the other hand, <u>believe</u> that the demand for money is fairly interest-inelastic and that changes in the money supply have a more direct effect on aggregate spending than is envisaged by Keynesians.'
(Hardwick, Khan & Langmead 1982:413, emphasis added)

once again it is a question of beliefs, of assumptions

Why do I have to wear a frock?

ABOVE: FIRST DOUBTS ABOUT ARTICLE OF FAITH

for our purposes we do not need to understand the preceding argument precisely, only to be aware that the effectiveness of economic policy in achieving full employment and avoiding inflation rests upon the elasticity of the relationship between the independent and dependent variables in IS/LM relationship

which interpretation is accepted is an 'article of faith'

'Considerable leeway is ... afforded to subjective judgement in evaluating a whole body of econometric evidence on any given economic relationship. This leaves ample room for intuition and the casual empiricism of personal observation, intermingled with the influence of political preferences in choosing between rival hypotheses.'
(Levacic & Rebmann 1982:7)

'Unfortunately, these elasticities are extremely difficult to measure in practice ... [and] the available evidence leaves us in doubt as to which is the more effective policy.'
(Hardwick, Khan & Langmead 1982:413)

CONTRADICTIONS IN THE NEOCLASSICAL SYNTHESIS

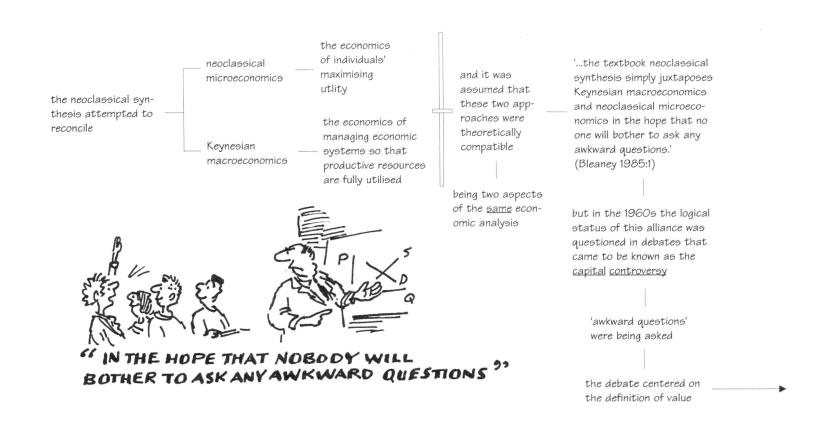

the neoclassical synthesis attempted to reconcile

— neoclassical microeconomics — the economics of individuals' maximising utlity

— Keynesian macroeconomics — the economics of managing economic systems so that productive resources are fully utilised

and it was assumed that these two approaches were theoretically compatible

being two aspects of the <u>same</u> economic analysis

'...the textbook neoclassical synthesis simply juxtaposes Keynesian macroeconomics and neoclassical microeconomics in the hope that no one will bother to ask any awkward questions.' (Bleaney 1985:1)

but in the 1960s the logical status of this alliance was questioned in debates that came to be known as the <u>capital</u> <u>controversy</u>

'awkward questions' were being asked

the debate centered on the definition of value

" IN THE HOPE THAT NOBODY WILL BOTHER TO ASK ANY AWKWARD QUESTIONS " for neoclassical (subjective preference) theory, price (value), reflects the utility enjoyed by individual consumers

'...attention is focussed on the equilibrum set of factor prices which optimises resource allocation by maximising utility.' (Burkitt 1984:164)

see:
Baumol & Blinder 1991:Chapter 35
Dolan & Lindsey 1988:Chapter 28
Hardwick, Khan & Langmead 1994:Chapters 16 and 17
Sloman 1991:Chapter 8

and the price (income) paid to productive inputs (factors of production) depends upon the pleasure (utility) given to consumers of the final product

known as the <u>marginal productivity theory of distribution</u>

the marginal product of capital (the marginal utility, enjoyed by consumers of the product, which derives from the contribution of 'capital' to the production process) determines the price of capital

there is a <u>derived</u> demand for factors of production, reflecting consumers' 'willingness to pay' for the final product

the wage rate is determined by the utility resulting from the productive activity of labour

and the interest rate on capital loans reflects the utility produced by capital (investment)

strictly, profit is the reward to entrepreneurs for the exercise of their managerial talents

What's profit?

The reward to the entrepreneurs, stupid!

as with any price which is determined by the market forces of supply and demand

as the supply is reduced the price should rise

the price (interest rate) moves inversely with the quantity of capital

106

thus, the <u>price</u> of capital is logically separable from the <u>quantity</u> of capital

but, the <u>quantity</u> of capital <u>is</u> the <u>value</u> of capital

price and quantity are not separable

to add such items of capital as typewriters, airliners and warehouse space, to determine the return to capital is impossible without a common index

items of capital are made commensurable through prices

Half a pound of capital please...

and in equilibrium the price of capital will equal the ability, at the margin, to provide utility for consumers – its <u>marginal productivity</u>

but the marginal quantity can only be conceived of in price terms

now, rewards to factors of production (and the incomes of their owners) are held to be determined by the forces of supply and demand (price and quantity)

the quantity of capital determines the marginal productivity of capital which determines the price

the logic breaks down

but as we have already seen (p. 66) inconsistency is not an obstacle to having 'faith' in market forces

but such a justification does not hold with the rewards to capital

and 'faith' in free markets is based on the belief that the market determines people's 'just rewards'

more importantly, the idea of there being a 'micro' and a 'macro' economics

rests on the assumption that the microeconomics of individual utility maxmisation

and microeconomic equilibrium is explained through choices by consumers made at the 'margin'

and the capital controversy challenges the logical basis of such a marginal analysis

for an introduction to this very complex debate see:
Burkitt 1984:Chapter 10
Cole, Cameron & Edwards 1991:84-5
Harcourt & Laing 1971
Harcourt 1972

microeconomics is the basis of the macroeconomic analysis of the economic system

but the capital controversy shows that, logically, there can be no micro foundations (based on individual utility maxmimisation) to macro analyses

and yet it is extremely common for economics texts and courses to be divided into 'macro' and 'micro' economics

with the implicit assumption (and sometimes the explicit assertion) that these are two aspects of the same analysis

DEAD SEA SCROLLS

"POOR QUALITY OF TEXTBOOKS"

'This can be partly explained by plain ignorance fomented by the poor quality of textbooks that avoid questions about fundamental concepts...'
(Carvalho 1992:29)

'Macroeconomics is the branch of economics that tries to explain how and why the economy grows, fluctuates and changes over time ... The other branch of economics is microeconomics - the study of the behaviour of individual consumers, firms and markets ... macroeconomics is only as good as the microeconomics that underlies it.'
(Hall & Taylor 1991:4, emphasis in original)

THE REGENERATION OF THE COST-OF-PRODUCTION THEORY OF VALUE

central to economics post-1945 — has been the management of economics to avoid the twin dangers of inflation and unemployment

for the Keynesian economic orthodoxy of the 1960s these were alternatives

unemployment implied that 'effective demand' was insufficient

price inflation implied that 'effective demand' was excessive

and Alban Phillips described an inverse, non-linear, statistical relationship between

using UK data between 1861 and 1957

see: Phillips 1958

the annual rate of change of money wages

the annual per-centage change in unemployment

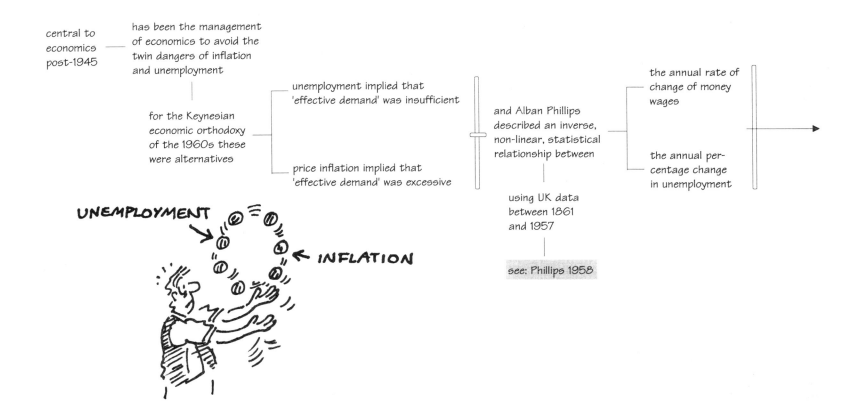

UNEMPLOYMENT

INFLATION

by allowing for long run changes in labour productivity

this relationship can be considered to be between

the rate of change of prices - _inflation_

the rate of change of employment - _unemployment_

apparently confirming received theory that inflation and unemployment _are_ alternative consequences of effective demand either being too high or too low (and not equating aggregate demand and aggregate supply)

from the large literature, see:
Begg, Fischer & Dornbusch 1991:Chapter 28.3
Bleaney 1985:Chapter 5
Cole, Cameron & Edwards 1991:Chapter 7.3
Levacic & Rebmann 1982:Chapter 18
Smith 1987:Chapters 2, 3 and 4

known as the _Phillips curve_

'Following Phillips's paper, researchers looked for, and found, similar kinds of relationships in the data for the period after the Second World War, both in Britain and in other countries.'
(Ormerod 1994:119)

Oh well - back to the drawing board...

by the purposeful management of 'effective demand' (aggregate income), through fiscal policy (managing government spending and income)

which implied that governments could make policy decisions to 'trade off' reduced employment for a higher rate of inflation (and vice versa)

UNEMPLOYMENT   INFLATION

see: Levacic 1982:342

see: Freidman 1968

but in the 1960s the apparently stable statistical relationship between inflation and unemployment predicted by the Phillips curve started to break down

however, Milton Friedman preferred an explanation that apparently could explain the emergence of 'stagflation'

this interpretation of economic experience was based on the assumption that individuals were independent, economic agents, free to make meaningful choices

'The Keynesians could neither predict accurately what was going to happen, nor offer a convincing way out of the morass into which Western economies were sinking. The nightmare of stagflation - simultaneous rising prices and unemployment - had arrived.' (Smith 1987:45)

a denial of the Marshallian (cost-of-production) basis of Keynes's thought, though in keeping with the emphasis of the 'neoclassical synthesis'

'The majority view in the economics profession ... was that Friedman's ideas could be perfectly well fitted into the conventional interpretation of Keynesian economics, as presented in the IS-LM diagram...' (Bleaney 1985:137)

STAGFLATION

it was assumed that economies had strong self-righting tendencies of there own - if left 'free' there would be a 'natural' tendency towards 'equilibrium'

and unemployment was not to be explained by an <u>organisational</u> 'failure' of the economic 'system', requiring economic management to utilise all available productive resources rather it was a question of 'individual responsibility'

there was a return to the notion of a 'natural rate of unemployment'

the 'victims' (the unemployed) were to blame (for being lazy)

and governments could only reduce unemployment below this 'natural' level

by increasing the rewards for the 'disutility' suffered in work by paying the 'naturally unemployed' more than they were really 'worth' to society (as indicated by market prices/wage rates)

such a policy emphasis was part and parcel of 'monetarism', touched upon in Chapter 3 (see pp. 83-8)

crucially, unemployment could only be affected by government if wages (and therefore prices) kept rising, giving the temporary illusion to individuals that they are being paid more than they really are (and more than they are 'worth')

and the resulting inflation had to be controled by 'monetary restraint' - reigning back the government expenditure that had created this false sense of well-being

the 1960s and 1970s saw a powerful theoretical reaction against the Keynesian orthodoxy, which in all its forms, world wide, had recommended a degree of state intervention in economies

but as the bias shifted towards free markets and against economic manage-ment with the rise of the monetarist 'counter-revolution'

Why don't you pull yourself up by your bootstraps?

I haven't got any boots!

unemployment and economic inequality increased consequent upon 'monetary restraint'

and job creation and poverty are now back on the economic policy agenda

in July 1993 at the Tokyo world summit, US President Clinton emphasised job creation as a policy priority

in September 1992 the World Bank explicitly refocused attention upon the alleviation of poverty in developing countries

at the end of 1993 the European Commission published a discussion document on unemployment in the EC

changing emphasis away from 'free markets', the central feature of the 'structural adjustment' programmes that had been imposed on indebted, developing economies

'Worldwide the intellectual and political pendulum is swinging. The passion for deregulating, tax cutting, let-the-financial-markets-rule ... is in decline; the interest in the regulated market, the state-as-partner ... is growing.'
(Will Hutton, Guardian 6 April 1992)

in March 1994 the Director General of the Confederation of British Industry called upon the British government and employers to address problems of inequality and poverty

THEORETICAL RESTITUTION

apart from changing political priorities, which are placing the theoretical priorities of the cost-of-production theory of value back on the policy agenda

there has been an ongoing theoretical critique of the economic orthodoxy of the 1950s and 1960s - a critique of the neoclassical synthesis

such critical thought has been inspired by the intellectual emphases of the cost-of-production theory of value, though in the guise of a number of apparently distinct schools of thought.

we saw in Chapter 1 (pp. 19 -22) how theorists, to make sense of the world, have to work with a set of preconceptions - a 'world view'

and these 'intellectual parameters' of the real world define the meaning and significance of theoretical concepts - the explanatory <u>language</u> of the analysis

as a consequence, little meaningful debate occurs between theoretical per-spectives because of this language barrier

PRECONCEPTIONS

but there can be, and is, fruitful discussion, producing new insights and understand-ings of economic behaviour, between the various schools of thought that go to make up economic perspectives (theories of value) much of the critique of economic orthodoxy has been labelled <u>post-Keynesian</u>

'Post Keynesian theory was born of a critique of neoclassical theory in its beginnings, the label served as a portmanteau for several schools of thought that had little in common besides their rejection of neoclassical economics and their dissatisfaction with marxism as an alternative...'
(Carvalho 1992:218)

Joan Robinson began the critique and set the tone: 'It is easy enough to make models on stated assumptions. The difficulty is to find the assumptions that are <u>relevant to reality</u>.'
(Robinson 1971:141, emphasis added)

'faith' is now placed in empirically accurate, economic analyses - focusing on productive imperatives - being able to reveal the 'dynamic' of relations of exchange

it is assumed that there is a common social interest, defined by the need to technically cooperate to produce, where production is based upon a technical division of labour - economic specialisation

CLOUD NINE

markets in competitive economies are understood to be inherently unstable

people are only aware of their immediate experience and naturally operate in their own interests, which if left unchecked lead to individuals' preferences overriding the technical, cooperative, imperatives of productive systems

REALISM

and there is no necessary trend towards economic 'equilibrium'

economic relations appropriate to the prevailing technical context have to be managed to achieve appropriate degrees of cooperation

central to post Keynesian theoretical emphases are problems of economic coord- inaton reflecting uncertainty

and in this regard the state, having the authority to create money, influence interest and exchange rates, encourage technical development through educational and regional policy, etc.

has the power to influence, and within limits determine economic activity, which no individual or firm has

and priority is placed on appropriate institutional management and reform to promote economic cooperation

for reviews of the scope and method of Post-Keynesian economics see:
Arestis 1988
Arestis & Skouras 1985
Carvalho 1992
Eichner 1979, and 1987
Lavoie 1992
Pheby 1989

Now - just show me which one 'Keynesianism' is under..

through:
the regulation of aggregate demand, aid for technical research and development, regulation of personal income redistribution

the problems of non-market clearing prices, with no tendency to move towards 'equilibrium'

see:
Colander 1988
Special Issue of the Journal of Economic Perspectives, Vol 7, No 1, Winter 1993

the New Keynesians on the other hand, return to the problems of imperfect competition

emphasise the technical bases of relations of exchange

see:
Fine 1986
Sawyer 1989:Chapter 8
Steedman 1977
Steedman & Sweezy 1981

the Neo-Ricardians, following the work of Pierro Sraffa

see:
Sraffa 1960

there are other schools with different theoretical emphases in the cost-of-production revival

see:
Hamouda & Smithin 1988
Mair & Miller 1991:Chapters 6-9

CHAPTER FIVE

THE CITIZEN
AS ECONOMIC
DYNAMIC

DIALECTICS

for the third perspective
on economic analysis

neither the consumer nor the
producer is considered to be
determinate in relations of
exchange

rather, consumers
and producers are
interdependent, each
is the condition and
cause of the other

the subjective preferences of
individual consumers structure
the environment within which
people as producers cooperate
in a technical division of labour

the social context of
such cooperation
influences people's
attitudes, personalities
and preferences,

people as citizens
are considered to
be the economic
dynamic

the relationship is dialectical,
one of mutual causation

social relations also structure
the distribution of income, and
hence the 'effective demand'
(purchasing power) of individuals

the perspective includes the
following schools of thought;
philosophic Marxists
materialist Marxists
structuralist Marxists
deductive Marxists

the relationship between
individuals and society is
dialectical, which will be
addressed in Chapter 6

see;
Vaillancourt 1986:10-1

DIALECTICS

'The properties of individual human
beings do not exist in isolation but
arise as a consequence of social life,
yet the nature of that social life is a
consequence of our being human.'
(Rose, Kamin and Lewontin 1984:11)

the analytical interrelation between individuals' behaviour and the social context of that action is enlightening, but as we shall see, if not handled carefully can be confusing

crucially, the analysis is concerned with the interactions <u>between</u> people

it is the relation between concepts that really counts rather than the concepts themselves

and relationships have to be <u>inferred</u> from actual behaviour, they exist in theory - you cannot <u>see</u> a relationship

and a word of warning to anyone attempting to read Marx in the original, because of the dialectical method the beginning presupposes the ending!

but they are no less real for that

people really do exist in relation to other people

'To understand the concepts fully requires that we understand the inner logic of capitalism itself. Since we cannot possibly have that understanding at the outset, we are forced to use the concepts without knowing precisely what they mean.' (Harvey 1982:1-2)

the analyst has to ask the question - 'what must the relationship be for people to behave in the way observed?'

for readers who wish to understand the complex, dialectical logic of Marx's economic analysis, see: Harvey 1982, especially Chapter 1

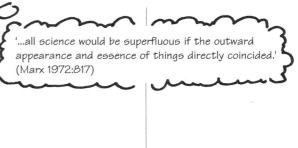

the theorist has to look 'behind' the evidence to understand its significance

'...all science would be superfluous if the outward appearance and essence of things directly coincided.' (Marx 1972:817)

the analysis is of relationships, which are in constant flux — individuals, fundamentally, are <u>creative</u> <u>beings</u> — they are also <u>social</u> beings — people only express, and indeed are only aware of, their individual creative potential through social interaction

addressed in detail in Chapter 6

people as social individuals are <u>inter</u>dependent — not <u>independent</u> nor <u>dependent</u>

'...all history is nothing but a continuous transformation of human nature.' (Marx 1936:124)

consequently people develop and change because of their experience - a process known as <u>praxis</u>

and people's creative individuality is a product of their genetic inheritance <u>and</u> their social experience

we shall return to this theme in Chapter 6, but at this point in the argument it must be emphasised

that the analysis is concerned with relationships - not with what people do, but how their behaviour affects <u>other</u> people

and as people respond to each other in soc- iety there is a constant dialectical <u>process</u> of social change

hence the historical context of social (and there- fore economic) behaviour is of crucial importance

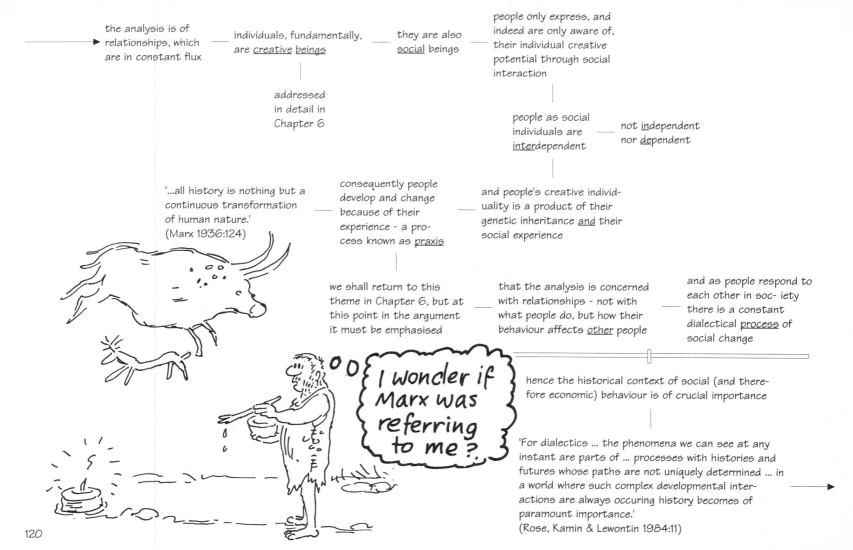

I wonder if Marx was referring to me?

'For dialectics ... the phenomena we can see at any instant are parts of ... processes with histories and futures whose paths are not uniquely determined ... in a world where such complex developmental inter- actions are always occuring history becomes of paramount importance.' (Rose, Kamin & Lewontin 1984:11)

the analysis is intended to reveal how people socially cooperate in order to fulfill individuals' needs

and the purpose of theorising relationships is to reveal the social context of individual existence

contradictions between individuals and society are identified, contradictions which particularly affect the disadvantaged, the 'powerless'

'Men make their own history, but they do not make it just as they please, they do not make it under circumstances chosen by themselves, but under circumstances directly encountered.'
(Marx 1950:255)

contradictions which potentially generate social conflict, possibly leading to social change

Men make their own history –

Aha! – but not under circumstances chosen by themselves!

hence, the thrust of the analysis is to identify the social constraints faced by people trying to fulfill their individual potentials

and suggesting possible strategies for the disadvantaged to overcome their shared frustrations in collective action

'The dialectic, as such, explains nothing, proves nothing, predicts nothing, and causes nothing to happen. Rather, dialectics is a way of thinking that brings into focus the full range of changes and interactions that occur in the world.'
(Ollman 1993:10)

THE MODE-OF-PRODUCTION

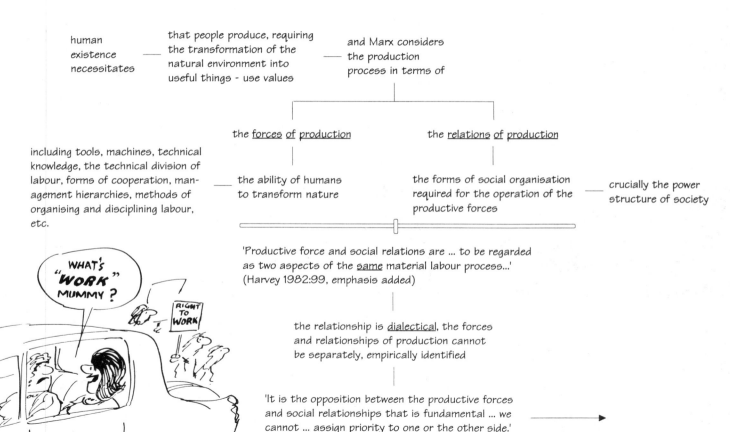

human existence necessitates — that people produce, requiring the transformation of the natural environment into useful things - use values — and Marx considers the production process in terms of

the <u>forces</u> of <u>production</u>

the <u>relations</u> of <u>production</u>

including tools, machines, technical knowledge, the technical division of labour, forms of cooperation, management hierarchies, methods of organising and disciplining labour, etc. — the ability of humans to transform nature

the forms of social organisation required for the operation of the productive forces — crucially the power structure of society

'Productive force and social relations are ... to be regarded as two aspects of the <u>same</u> material labour process...' (Harvey 1982:99, emphasis added)

WHAT'S "WORK" MUMMY?

RIGHT TO WORK

the relationship is <u>dialectical</u>, the forces and relationships of production cannot be separately, empirically identified

'It is the opposition between the productive forces and social relationships that is fundamental ... we cannot ... assign priority to one or the other side.' (Harvey 1982:196)

as we shall see this opposition
is fundamental to the analysis
of societies and social change

'...as men develop their productive forces, that
is, as they live, they develop certain relations
with one another and ... the nature of the
relations is bound to change with the change
and growth of these productive forces.'
(Marx 1975:34)

and in this process
people change
themselves

'By thus acting on the external
world and changing it, he [humans]
at the same time changes his own
[human] nature.'
(Marx 1974:173)

the process of <u>praxis</u>
addressed in Chapter 6

the dialectical unity of
the forces and relations
of production makes up
the <u>mode-of-production</u>

a fundamental concept
in the marxist analysis
of social life

'The mode of production of
material life conditions the
social, political and intellectual
life-process in general.'
(Marx 1976:3)

'The materalist conception of history starts
from the proposition that the production of
the means to support human life and, next to
production, the exchange of things produced,
is the basis of all social structure.'
(Engels 1970:57)

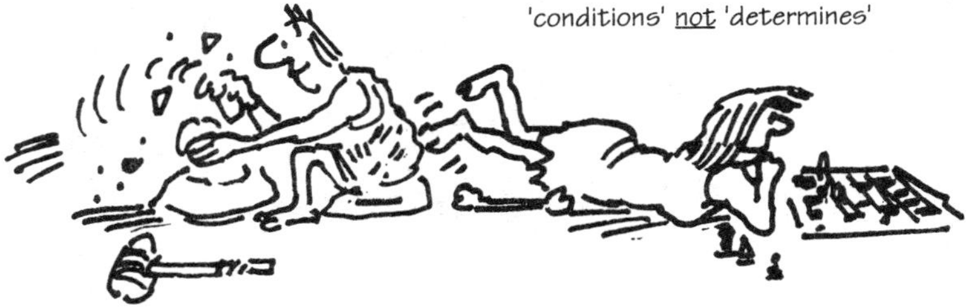

'conditions' <u>not</u> 'determines'

LEFT : BEFORE ECONOMICS
WAS INVENTED.

for Marx production is the basis of social organisation, but as we shall see in Chapter 6 (pp. 163-6), this does not mean that society is technically determined

the degree to which individuals control the social 'means of production' - which reflects the character of the mode-of-production - invests people with social power, the ability to exercise control over other peoples' lives

such control defines the class structure of the mode-of-production

and making explicit the contradictory class interests which underlie economic relationships is central to economic analyses which see the citizen as the economic dynamic

'...Marx wrote Capital to put a weapon in the hands of workers. In it he presented a detailed analysis of the fundamental dynamics of the struggles between capitalists and the working classes.'
(Cleaver 1979:3)

see:
Bell & Cleaver 1982
Cleaver 1979
Wright 1975

TOUCHÉ.

THE CAPITALIST MODE-OF-PRODUCTION

the mode-of-production most pervasive in the modern world is <u>capitalism</u>

fundamental to the way in which production influences social, political and cultural behaviour in capitalist society

is <u>commodity exchange</u>

within the capitalist mode-of-production individuals engage in useful labour without any central direction or coordination of their efforts

'Yet [capitalist] commodity production is ultimately social in nature; it is production not for private use but for exchange with others.'
(McNally 1993:162)

every technical division of labour has to be organised so that people with different skills and specialisms can cooperate to produce

there must be some form of coordination if individuals are to produce commodities that are wanted by other people

'What I proceed from is the simplest social form in which the product of labour in contemporary society manifests itself, and this is the "commodity".'
(Marx, quoted Dragsted 1976:44)

'The central characteristic of the capitalist mode of production ... is that the private labour of individuals is not directly social, but must be rendered social by the exchange of products as commodities.'
(Weeks 1981:29)

social coordination is achieved through competitive markets: the 'forces' of supply and demand

because the products of individual labourers are exchanged on the market they are 'valued' relative to each other which determines the <u>rate</u> of exchange

for qualitatively different products (use-values) to be exchanged, there must be a common quality in terms of which they can be rendered commensurable and quantified - so that, say, 1 table equals 2 car tyres (in <u>value</u> terms)

the one common quality of all commodities is that they are <u>all</u> products of labour

individual, useful, <u>concrete</u> labour becomes social, exchangeable <u>abstract</u> labour

market exchange establishes how much any <u>particular</u> labour (plumbing, driving, typing, accounting, etc.) is worth relative to labour in <u>general</u>

actual, useful, concrete labour time, is expressed as <u>socially</u> <u>necessary</u> <u>abstract</u> labour time

'Every product of labour is, in all states of society, a use-value; but it is only at a definite historical epoch in a society's development that such a product becomes a commodity ... when the labour ... becomes expressed ... as its value.' (Marx 1974:67)

I say, Holmes - found any abstract labour yet?

'Concrete labour refers to the unique production process undertaken by an individual, while abstract labour describes the <u>social</u> <u>value</u> of that labour as it is expressed through the exchange of commodities on the market ... Thus 10 hours of concrete labour expended in producing a commodity may be worth only 8 hours of average social labour when it comes to exchanging with other products on the market. The market, in other words, translates concrete (individual) labour into abstract (social) labour...' (McNally 1993:177-8, emphasis in original)

THE ABSTRACT LABOUR THEORY OF VALUE

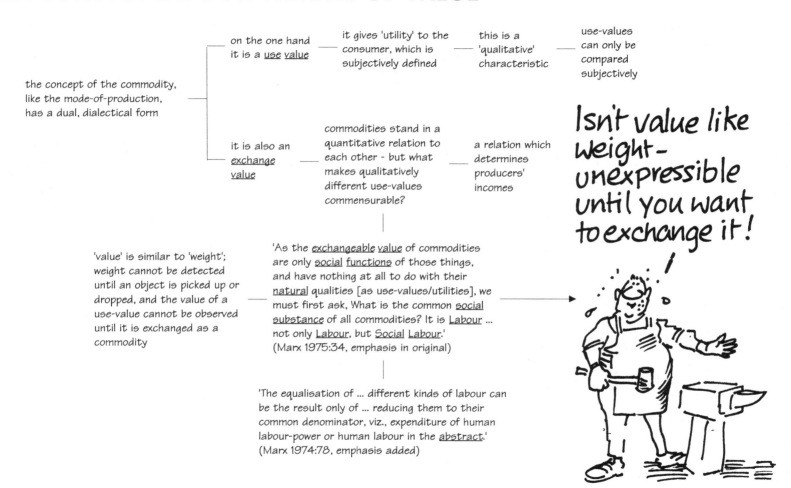

the concept of the commodity, like the mode-of-production, has a dual, dialectical form

on the one hand it is a <u>use</u> value

it gives 'utility' to the consumer, which is subjectively defined

this is a 'qualitative' characteristic

use-values can only be compared subjectively

it is also an <u>exchange</u> <u>value</u>

commodities stand in a quantitative relation to each other - but what makes qualitatively different use-values commensurable?

a relation which determines producers' incomes

'value' is similar to 'weight'; weight cannot be detected until an object is picked up or dropped, and the value of a use-value cannot be observed until it is exchanged as a commodity

'As the <u>exchangeable</u> <u>value</u> of commodities are only <u>social</u> <u>functions</u> of those things, and have nothing at all to do with their <u>natural</u> qualities [as use-values/utilities], we must first ask, What is the common <u>social</u> <u>substance</u> of all commodities? It is <u>Labour</u> ... not only <u>Labour</u>, but <u>Social</u> <u>Labour</u>.' (Marx 1975:34, emphasis in original)

'The equalisation of ... different kinds of labour can be the result only of ... reducing them to their common denominator, viz., expenditure of human labour-power or human labour in the <u>abstract</u>.' (Marx 1974:78, emphasis added)

Isn't value like weight - unexpressible until you want to exchange it!

social labour is abstract labour, which can only be conceived of 'theoretically' ——— what is the magnitude of the "abstract labour" contained in commodities which determines their rate of exchange? ——— it is the socially necessary abstract labour time contained in commodities that determines their rate of exchange ——— reflecting social supply

reflecting social demand

I'm sorry the price has gone up - supply has gone down!

YAMS
1 EMALANGANI EACH

MARKET TRENDS IN SWAZILAND.

'For a commodity to be sold at its market value ... the total quantity of social labour used in producing the total mass of the commodity must correspond to the quantity of the social want for it, i.e. the effective social want. Competition, the fluctuation of market prices which correspond to the fluctuations of demand and supply tend to reduce to this scale the total quantity of labour devoted to each kind of commodity ... If the demand for ... [a] particular kind of commodity is greater than the supply, one buyer outbids another ... and so raises the price ... If conversely, the supply exceeds the demand, one begins to dispose of his goods at a cheaper rate and the others must follow ... which reduces the socially necessary labour to a new level.'
(Marx 1972:192)

'...the quantity of labour necessary for its production in a given state of society, under certain average conditions of production, with a given social average intensity, and average skill of labour employed ... if with modern means of production, a single spinner converts into yarn in one day, many thousand times the amount of cotton which he could have spun during the same time with a spinning wheel, it is evident that every single pound of cotton will absorb many thousand times less of spinning labour than it did before ... The value of yarn will sink accordingly ... The greater the productive powers of labour ... the smaller the value of this produce. The smaller the productive powers of labour ... the greater its value'.
(Marx 1975:38-39, emphasis in original)

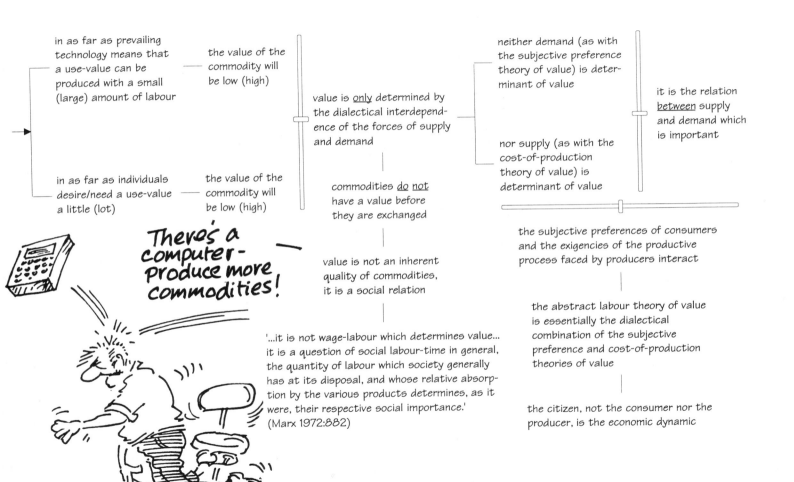

in as far as prevailing technology means that a use-value can be produced with a small (large) amount of labour

the value of the commodity will be low (high)

in as far as individuals desire/need a use-value a little (lot)

the value of the commodity will be low (high)

value is only determined by the dialectical interdependence of the forces of supply and demand

commodities do not have a value before they are exchanged

value is not an inherent quality of commodities, it is a social relation

There's a computer – Produce more commodities!

'...it is not wage-labour which determines value... it is a question of social labour-time in general, the quantity of labour which society generally has at its disposal, and whose relative absorption by the various products determines, as it were, their respective social importance.' (Marx 1972:882)

neither demand (as with the subjective preference theory of value) is determinant of value

nor supply (as with the cost-of-production theory of value) is determinant of value

it is the relation between supply and demand which is important

the subjective preferences of consumers and the exigencies of the productive process faced by producers interact

the abstract labour theory of value is essentially the dialectical combination of the subjective preference and cost-of-production theories of value

the citizen, not the consumer nor the producer, is the economic dynamic

129

VALUE, EXCHANGE-VALUE AND PRICE

value is a social relation —— what is a (qualitatively defined) use-value to an individual is only revealed to have social value when someone buys it

it is only evident that, say, a table has value when someone is prepared to exchange, say, a bicycle for it

and the value of the table can only be expressed as an equivalence to something else, in this case the bicycle

the value of the table, the socially necessary abstract labour time embodied in the table, can only be expressed as being equal to the socially necessary abstract labour time embodied in the bicycle, which is the exchange-value of the table

I'll only get one table for it now!

the need for an equivalent by which to express the value of commodities explains the purpose of money

a much neglected area of study is Marx's theory of money, see:
Marx 1973:the chapter on money
Weeks 1981:Chapters IV and V
Harvey 1982:Chapters 9 and 10

people with tables to exchange and who want bicycles do not have to search out people with bicycles who want tables

'For it is in the nature of the commodity form that the translation of use-value into exchange -value, of concrete into abstract labour may not occur ... It is an ever present posibility that some producers will fail the test of the market, they will be unable to find a buyer for the use-values they have produced.'
(McNally 1993:178)

and herein lies the possibility of economic crises

they can both, independently, exchange their products against money

value, then, is manifested as exchange-value, which appears as a price

while value can <u>only</u> be expressed as an exchange-value, exchange-value <u>is</u> <u>not</u> the same thing as price

the question of the significance of prices is addressed below when considering capital accumulation, see pp. 136-9

at this point in the argument we should make explicit the importance of value only being manifested as exchange-value, which is a relation <u>between</u> values

and exchange-values only <u>appear</u> as prices

the value of a commodity expressed as a price, is its value <u>compared</u> to the value of all other commodities against which it might be exchanged

TECHNICAL DEVELOPMENTS

with economic development, technical efficiency is generally rising

there may be producers who fail to keep up with technical developments, and still produce according to outmoded processes. Consequently they have not kept pace with the trend of progressively less and less labour time being required to produce the same use-value

so, even though they work just as hard - the <u>concrete</u> labour time expended has not changed - the exchange-value of the use-value (and hence the price and their income) will decline, as the socially necessary <u>abstract</u> labour time has fallen

in the context of declining incomes in Africa see:
Sender & Smith 1986:Chapter 5

THE LAW OF VALUE

exchange, then, is governed by the relative, socially necessary abstract labour time, embodied in commodities

the exchange-value of a commodity is determined <u>after</u> production, beyond the control of the direct producer

so as to earn profits, clearly capitalist producers try to estimate at what price they can sell a commodity, and compare this to the costs expended in production, the surplus of sales revenue over costs of production being profits

'The restless never-ending process of profit-making alone is what ... [the capitalist] aims at. This boundless greed after riches, this passionate chase after exchange-value, is common to the capitalist and the miser; but while the miser is merely a capitalist gone mad, the capitalist is a rational miser.'
(Marx 1974:151)

and where there is an assured social demand for the commodity producers may be able to increase prices by limiting production, or other ways of controlling market exchange

I need some house-keeping money, dear

ABOVE: KARL MARX CONFRONTS REALITY.

but the paremeters within which such 'imperfectly competitive/monopolistic' activity is possible are beyond the control of producers

an external discipline is imposed on producers who are apparently exchanging within 'free' markets

'...the value of a commodity is determined objectively, independently of the perception or knowledge of the exchanging parties, and this objectification is achieved through the money form.'
(Weeks 1981:39)

capitalists invest in production - advance money to undertake production

in the expectation of making a profit - the sales revenue will exceed the costs of produciton

and each capitalist has to compete with all other capitalists to maintain an adequate rate of profit

'It is the compelling force of anarchy in social production that turns the limitless perfectability of machinery under modern industry into a compulsory law by which every individual industrial capitalist must perfect his machinery more and more under penalty of ruin.'
(Engels 1970:65)

why?

capitalists' investment in production means that they purchase commodities (raw materials, technology, labour power) with which to produce

and yet the product is sold for <u>more</u> <u>than</u> the cost of the inputs into the productive process

where does this surplus come from?

to p. 134

'Where in short does profit come from under conditions of fair exchange?'
(Harvey 1982:22)

which is perhaps the most fundamental question to be asked of capitalist economies

that capitalists have to compete to be profitable

suggests that individual capitalists are struggling for a share of a social surplus

to p. 136

'Morning, Dave!'

'CAPITALISTS HAVE TO COMPETE.'

instruments of labour:
tools/equipment

means of production

objects of labour:
raw materials

capitalists purchase
commodities with which
to start production

labour power

Society calls me
Labour Power, but
actually I'm
called
Susan!

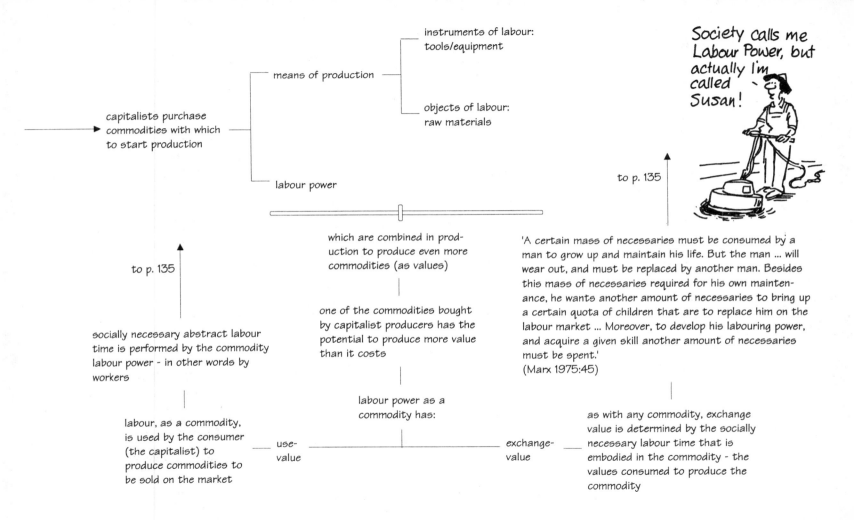

to p. 135

which are combined in production to produce even more
commodities (as values)

to p. 135

one of the commodities bought
by capitalist producers has the
potential to produce more value
than it costs

'A certain mass of necessaries must be consumed by a
man to grow up and maintain his life. But the man ... will
wear out, and must be replaced by another man. Besides
this mass of necessaries required for his own maintenance, he wants another amount of necessaries to bring up
a certain quota of children that are to replace him on the
labour market ... Moreover, to develop his labouring power,
and acquire a given skill another amount of necessaries
must be spent.'
(Marx 1975:45)

socially necessary abstract labour
time is performed by the commodity
labour power - in other words by
workers

labour power as a
commodity has:

labour, as a commodity,
is used by the consumer
(the capitalist) to
produce commodities to
be sold on the market

use-
value

exchange-
value

as with any commodity, exchange
value is determined by the socially
necessary labour time that is
embodied in the commodity - the
values consumed to produce the
commodity

the use-value and exchange-value are both conceived in terms of abstract labour time

the use-value of labour power is defined by the abstract labour time that <u>is</u> produced

the exchange-value of labour power is defined by the abstract labour time that <u>went</u> <u>to</u> produce the ability to work

and labour power is only employed because its use-value is greater than its exchange-value —— the difference is surplus-value

'It must never be forgotten that the production of ... surplus value ... is the immediate purpose and compelling motive of capitalist production.' (Marx 1972:243-4)

labourers are paid the exchange-value of their —— so there is no cheating labour power

but they produce <u>more</u> <u>than</u> their exchange-value (for which —— and hence are <u>exploited</u> they are not paid

'Why is the capitalist interested in buying labour power from the proletariat under conditions of "equal exchage", i.e. at the real value of that labour power ... Here appears Marx's main economic discovery, his <u>theory</u> <u>of</u> <u>surplus</u> <u>value</u>.' (Mandel 1983:190-1, emphasis in original)

Don't go home yet - you haven't produced your surplus value!

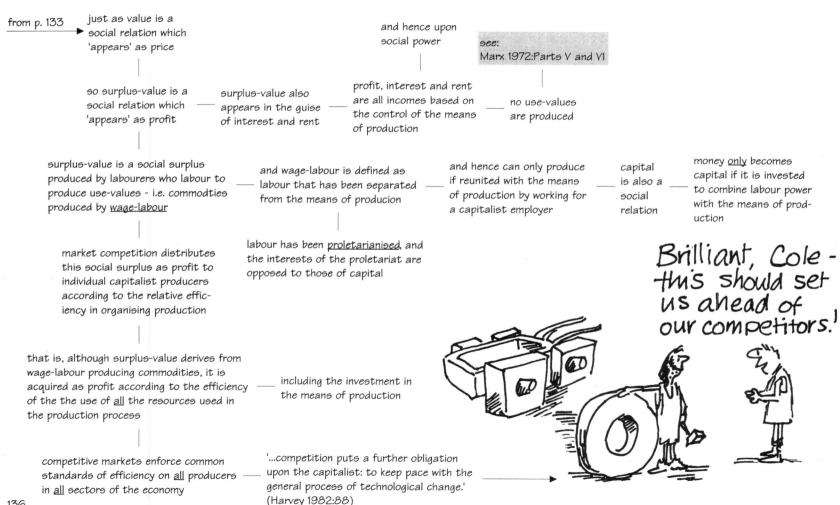

from p. 133 → just as value is a social relation which 'appears' as price

and hence upon social power

see:
Marx 1972:Parts V and VI

so surplus-value is a social relation which 'appears' as profit — surplus-value also appears in the guise of interest and rent

profit, interest and rent are all incomes based on the control of the means of production — no use-values are produced

surplus-value is a social surplus produced by labourers who labour to produce use-values - i.e. commodties produced by <u>wage-labour</u>

and wage-labour is defined as labour that has been separated from the means of producion

and hence can only produce if reunited with the means of production by working for a capitalist employer — capital is also a social relation — money <u>only</u> becomes capital if it is invested to combine labour power with the means of production

market competition distributes this social surplus as profit to individual capitalist producers according to the relative efficiency in organising production

labour has been <u>proletarianised</u>, and the interests of the proletariat are opposed to those of capital

Brilliant, Cole - this should set us ahead of our competitors!

that is, although surplus-value derives from wage-labour producing commodities, it is acquired as profit according to the efficiency of the the use of <u>all</u> the resources used in the production process — including the investment in the means of production

competitive markets enforce common standards of efficiency on <u>all</u> producers in <u>all</u> sectors of the economy — '...competition puts a further obligation upon the capitalist: to keep pace with the general process of technological change.' (Harvey 1982:88)

136

individual <u>concrete</u> labour only becomes social labour when it becomes <u>abstract</u> labour through exchange

socially necessary abstract labour time denotes the magnitude of value, and is a social relation

individual capitalist producers are obliged to produce to these social standards by the <u>law of value</u>

capitalists receive profits, a share of the social surplus (surplus-value)

'...exchange is ruled by the law of value, a law which has two clauses: competition forces all producers to produce with the minimum input of concrete labour time, and forces a tendency toward a normal rate of profit in all industries.'
(Weeks 1981:40)

according to the efficiency, relative to all other capitalist enterprises, of employing <u>all</u> the inputs into production (means of production <u>and</u> labour power)

either directly, or giving a credit rating on which to borrow money

profits (a share of surplus-value) are the source of funds for reinvestment to maintian relative technical efficiency

'...commodity producers experience the law of value - external exchange governed by socially necessary labour time - as an external pressure. Should they fail to produce efficiently enough, the prices which rule the market will be insufficient to redeem their actual costs of production. The result will be a failure of self-reproduction of the producing unit (bankruptcy).'
(McNally 1993:179)

outside any <u>particular</u> act of production

which is established through competition

and the social standard of efficiency is set by the <u>average rate of profit</u>

to receive this rate of profit producers have to produce at a level of efficiency at least as high as the social average

'The law of the equalization of the rate of profit, an aspect of the law of value, is a law of the distribution of surplus value among capitalists.'
(Weeks 1981:76)

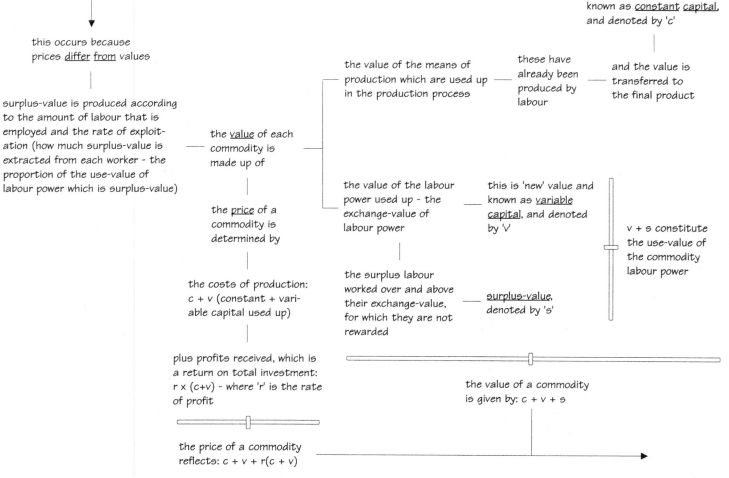

this occurs because
prices <u>differ</u> <u>from</u> values

surplus-value is produced according
to the amount of labour that is
employed and the rate of exploitation (how much surplus-value is
extracted from each worker - the
proportion of the use-value of
labour power which is surplus-value)

the <u>value</u> of each
commodity is
made up of

the <u>price</u> of a
commodity is
determined by

the costs of production:
c + v (constant + vari-
able capital used up)

plus profits received, which is
a return on total investment:
r x (c+v) - where 'r' is the rate
of profit

the price of a commodity
reflects: c + v + r(c + v)

the value of the means of
production which are used up
in the production process

these have
already been
produced by
labour

and the value is
transferred to
the final product

known as <u>constant</u> <u>capital</u>,
and denoted by 'c'

the value of the labour
power used up - the
exchange-value of
labour power

this is 'new' value and
known as <u>variable</u>
<u>capital</u>, and denoted
by 'v'

the surplus labour
worked over and above
their exchange-value,
for which they are not
rewarded

<u>surplus-value</u>,
denoted by 's'

v + s constitute
the use-value of
the commodity
labour power

the value of a commodity
is given by: c + v + s

'The discrepancy between price and value ... is an essential feature of any system of commodity production ... This is not a defect, but, on the contrary, it makes this form the adequate one for a mode of production whose laws can only assert themselves as blindly operating averages between constant irregularities.'
(McNally 1993:163-4)

'Surplus value originates in the production process by virtue of the class relation between capital and labour, but it is distributed among individual capitalists according to the rules of competition.'
(Harvey 1982:61)

the distinction between values and prices is perhaps the most difficult paradox in Marxist theory to understand

for further clarification see:
Harvey 1982:especially Chapters 1 and 2
McNally 1993:Chapter 4
Weeks 1981:Chapters 1, 2 and 3

value is <u>essentially</u> a social relation and is not directly observable/measurable

price is <u>apparently</u> the basis of individuals' economic behaviour

'...all science would be superfluous if the outward appearance and essence of things directly coincided.'
(Marx 1972:817)

on p. 119 the point was made that the purpose of the analysis is to ask the question - 'What must the (social) relationship be for people to behave in the way observed?'

and in the capitalist mode of production there are a number of paradoxes to be explained — for instance ⟶

what is a cynic, Wilde?

A man who knows the <u>price</u> of everything and the <u>value</u> of nothing

-same as a capitalist!

even though, formally, there is <u>equality</u> between people

— there is an iniquitous social and economic order

even though, formally, people are free to act independently

— people are coordinated to act in concert by 'market forces'

the analysis in terms of values is intended to reveal the social relations which give purpose and rationality to competitive behaviour in capitalist society

even though, apparently, the capitalist mode of production is 'competitive'

— there is a constant tendency towards centralisation and concentration of capital (see p. 150)

and yet competitive pressures apparently increase

Hey guys - I don't see last years winner here anywhere!

even though, apparently, market forces tend to 'equilibrium'

— the capitalist mode of production moves from economic crisis to economic crisis (see pp. 142-9)

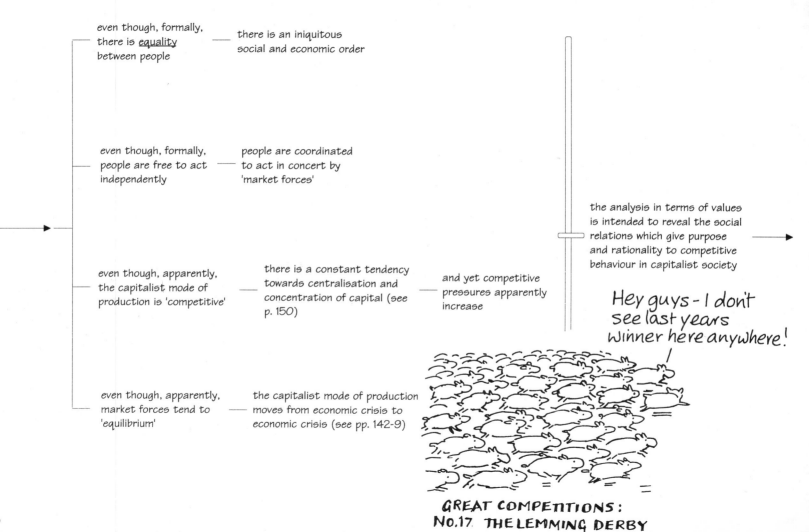

GREAT COMPETITIONS:
NO.17 THE LEMMING DERBY

the only way independent commodity producers can produce according to consumers' demands and preferences — is for their individual concrete labour, producing use-values — to be translated into socially necessary, abstract labour, producing exchange-values — people's labour is performed according to a social norm, therefore justifying their level of income (consumption), by competitive market exchange

which establishes an average rate of profit between competing capitalist producers

'The necessity of translating concrete into abstract labour, of exchanging commodity for money, makes competition an essent-ial feature of the relations between individual producing units ... [and] [T]here can be no market regulation ... without a labour market, the wages system, and the unplanned drive to accum-ulate for the sake of further accumulation.' (McNally 1993:179 and 183)

with an inevitable trend towards economic crisis

GREAT COMPETITIONS:
No.18 THE FIRST WORLD WAR

CONTRADICTION AND CRISIS

the logic of commodity production, then, implies ___ and to stay in the competitive race capitalists <u>must</u> earn profits

'With the separation of labour from the means of production, production becomes socially isolated, with each capitalist arriving at his or her production decisions in a formally independent manner ... This anarchy is both reflected in and rendered into an orderly anarchy through exchange. Conceptually, the first consequence of this exchange is that each capitalist is forced to produce in an efficient way.' (Weeks 1981:47)

which necessitates exploiting labour power (rewarding labour according to what it is 'worth' - the exchange-value of labour power: but less than what labour produces - the use-value of labour power)

and the exigencies of inter-capitalist competition compel employers to maximise profits, and hence minimise the payment to labour, and maximise production from labour

'The antagonism between each individual capitalist's interests and those of the capitalist class as a whole ... comes to the surface.' (Marx 1972:253)

there is a fundamental conflict of class interest between capital and labour

precipitating class conflict

which is a <u>positive</u> force for progressive social change - change tending towards higher material standards of living with enhanced individual freedom - see Chapter 6, pp. 163-7

'...the classic Marxist thesis [is] that class struggle is a positive force in the progressive development of [capitalist] production...' (Fine & Harris 1985:36)

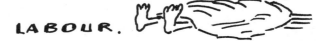

the dialectic of:
intra-capitalist competition, and,
inter-capital/labour class interest
contradiction

tends towards
economic and
social crisis
(a decisive
turning-point)

which, paradoxically, leads to the
progressive development of the
capitalist mode-of-production

'...just as the most fundamental contradiction of capitalism is between the
classes, so the most fundamental role of
crisis-as-solution is restoring the balance
of class forces such that capital can
resume its growth...'
(Bell and Cleaver 1982:257)

'The real barrier of capitalist production is capital itself. It is
that capital and its self-expansion appear as the starting
and the closing point, the motive and purpose of production...'
(Marx 1972:250, emphasis in original)

what is meant by:

the self-expansion of capital?

the starting and closing
point of production?

capitalists accumulate surplus
value as profits, through a
process of production

it is a social process, in which the social
relation of capital assumes different forms

which exhibit contradictory
class interests and give
rise to distinct forms of
class struggle

'...no worker known to historians ever has
surplus-value taken out of his hide without
finding some way of fighting back ... and ... by
his fighting back...the "forms of development"
were ... developed in unexpected ways.'
(Thompson 1978:345-6)

BERLIN WALL

Let's tear
it down

OK!

'UNEXPECTED
WAYS'

143

'Capital, recall, is defined by Marx as a
process in which value undergoes an expansion, and he therefore sought definitions that reflected the flow of this
process.'
(Harvey 1982:129, emphasis in original)

the purpose of this process is to
accumulate capital - surplus-value
acquired as profit is reinvested to
continue the process of capitalist
production

initially capitalists invest money
(M) in the production process
(P) by buying the commodities
(C) labour power (LP) and means
of production (MP)

M → C

LP

MP

→ P

Capitalism is a
Process

I think I know
that already!

and crises occur
when accumulation
is interrupted

in the production process (P)
even more commodities (as
values) are produced (C ') -
this is the point in the
process where the use-value
exceeds the exchange-value
of labour power, leading to
the 'self-expansion of value'

— P → C '

'The difficulty is that there is not one
Marxist theory of economic crisis, but
several ... all Marxist perspectives on economic crisis tend to see crisis as growing
out of the contradictions inherent in the
process of capital accumulation ... understood as the reproduction of capitalist
social relations on an ever-expanding scale
through the conversion of surplus value into
new constant and variable capital...'
(Wright 1975:5-6)

the commodities produced now have to be sold and converted into money, or <u>realised</u>, into more money (M') than the capitalist originally started with, and this money has to be invested, starting the whole process again, with capitalists buying more commodities (C') with which to produce (P)...

and the process continues

a process called the <u>circuit</u> <u>of</u> <u>capital</u>

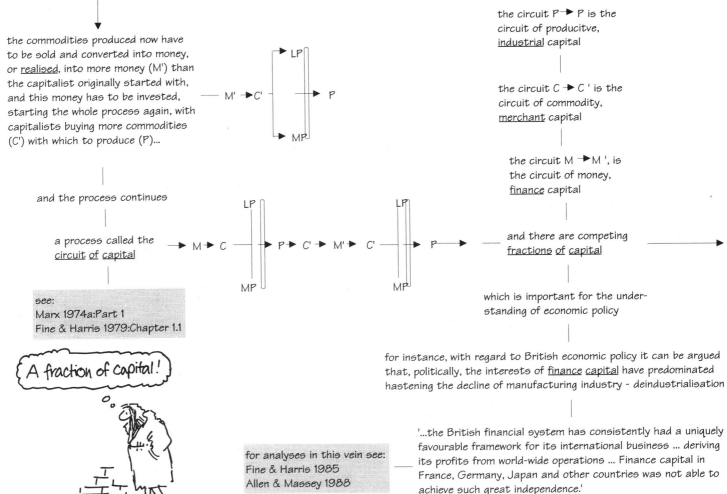

the circuit P → P is the circuit of producitve, <u>industria</u>l capital

the circuit C → C ' is the circuit of commodity, <u>merchant</u> capital

the circuit M → M ', is the circuit of money, <u>finance</u> capital

and there are competing <u>fractions</u> <u>of</u> <u>capital</u>

which is important for the under-standing of economic policy

see:
Marx 1974a:Part 1
Fine & Harris 1979:Chapter 1.1

A fraction of capital!

for analyses in this vein see:
Fine & Harris 1985
Allen & Massey 1988

for instance, with regard to British economic policy it can be argued that, politically, the interests of <u>finance</u> <u>capital</u> have predominated hastening the decline of manufacturing industry - deindustrialisation

'...the British financial system has consistently had a uniquely favourable framework for its international business ... deriving its profits from world-wide operations ... Finance capital in France, Germany, Japan and other countries was not able to achieve such great independence.'
(Fine & Harris 1985:45)

145

→ in the process M → C

the commodities which
capitalists wish to buy
may not be available,
or too expensive

which might be linked to
disproportionality crises

or to struggles
for higher
wages, etc.

for instance see:
Glyn and Sutcliffe 1972

and there might also be problems in
being able to borrow investment finance at a low enough interest rate

see:
Harvey 1982:Chapter 6, part II
O'Connor 1984:Chapters 3 & 4
O'Connor 1987:Chapter 2

see: Weeks 1981:Chapter 5

in the production process,
in which more values are
produced than enter
production, P → C'

production must be such that the surplus-value produced by labour realises a sufficient rate of profit for
firms to reinvest and stay relatively efficient

and where capitalists respond to
inadequate profits by increasing the
technical efficiency of the production
process, cutting back on the input of
labour into production - increasing the
'capital intensity' of production

then potentially this sets off a process
by which the average rate of profit falls

generalising the economic crisis to
the capitalist system as a whole

known as the tendency for
the rate of profit to fall →

**TENDENCY OF RATE
OF PROFIT TO FALL**

when technical efficiency is raised through investment in constant capital (machines, etc. - produced means of production)

then relatively less variable capital is used in the production of commodities

labour is replaced with machinery

when this change in the technical composition of capital is translated into values it becomes the organic composition of capital

but in the production process it is labour power (variable capital) that produces the surplus-value (a social surplus) which is distributed to individual capitalists as profit

'Each capitalist contributes to total aggregate surplus value in society according to the labour power each employs, and draws upon the aggregate surplus value according to the total capital each advances.'
(Harvey 1982:63)

leading to the paradox

see pp. 148-9

the social 'pool' of surplus-value decreases

for those firms that invest in relatively more constant capital

with less surplus resources to be paid out as profits

efficiency and profitability rises

and the least technically efficient firms experience difficulty in realising the commodities (values) produced at a price high enough to earn an adequate rate of profit

We've worked out a a scheme to make your **ears** productive, Smithers!

the firms that 'generate' the problem of falling profitability are precisely those who experience rising profitability

and falling profitability appears to be caused by the falling productivity of labour

'The rate of profit does not fall because labour becomes less productive, but because it becomes more productive ... The rate of profit does not sink because the labourer is exploited any less, but because generally less labour is employed in proportion to the employed capital.' (Marx 1972:240 and 246)

but of course if the remaining labour is required to work harder, or if wages are cut

'...the gradual growth of constant capital in relation to variable capital must necessarily lead to a gradual fall of the general rate of profit so long as the rate of surplus value, or the intensity of exploitation of labour by capital, remains the same.' (Marx 1972:212, emphasis in original)

there is an increase in the rate of exploitation

for other counter-vailing tendencies see:
Marx 1972:
Chapter 14

then the tendency for the rate of profit to fall might be offset, indeed surplus value and profits might even rise

'...what is rational from the standpoint of the system as a whole is not rational from the standpoint of each ... firm taken seperately, and vice versa ... The naive conviction that the "common interest" is perfectly served if each individual pursues his "private interest" turns out to be manifestly illusory...' (Mandel 1978:178-9, emphasis in original)

that is why the falling rate of profit is only a tendency, the realisation of such a tendency relies on the ability of people to defend/prosecute their class interests

the falling rate of profit is not an inevitability but crucially reflects class consciousness, and the mobilisation and organisation of people in class struggle

exacerbating the problem

a tendency which is a consequence of competitive pressures to raise the social, organic composition of capital

which is why it is a contradiction of the capitalist mode-of-production

in the face of competitive pressures capitalists have to economise on labour time, and hence the organic composition of capital rises

and the resultant pressure on firms' profits compels further economising on the employment of labour (variable capital)

the tendency towards the rate of profit to fall, and the countervailing tendencies, are <u>social</u> trends and pressures,

social contradictions analysed in terms of <u>values</u>, which appear as price movements

empirical data has to be interpreted to reveal the (value) essence beneath the (price) appearance

an analysis which is complicated by conflicting tendencies, such that, even if <u>actual</u> profits are rising

'The growing incompatibility between the productive development of society and its hitherto existing relations of production expresses itself in bitter contradictions, crises, spasms. The violent destruction of capital, not by relations external to it, but rather as a condition of its self-preservation, is the most striking form in which advice is given to it to be gone and to give room to a higher state of social producton.'
(Marx 1973:749-50)

PROFIT.

the rising organic composition of capital/tendency for falling rate of profit thesis is not invalidated

'...the ... empirical evidence existing against the theory of the falling rate of profit is partly irrelevent, partly contradictory, and partly supportive of the main propositions of the theory.'
(Castells 1980:39)

and having reached C' in the circuit of capital, these commodities as values have to <u>be realised</u> as money, sold to consumers, so that M is transformed into M'

and commodities may not be sold for a price high enough to earn sufficient profits, and this will appear as there being an over-supply of commodities that forces the price down

this might be a crisis of 'effective demand' (an underconsumptionist theory of crisis) or an effect of the falling rate of profit

'Historically, if there is a secular tendency of the organic composition of capital to increase and the rate of profit to decrease, this can only be proved by studying, in terms of value, the process of accumulation at a world level.'
(Castells 1980:40)

'...capitalist crises are crises of <u>over-production</u> of <u>exchange values</u>. It is not because there are too few products that economic life is upset. It is because it is impossible to sell commodities at prices guaranteeing the average rate of profit - that is because there are "too many commodities" - that economic life is disorganised.'
(Mandel 1978:167, emphasis in original)

on the theory of the tendency for the rate of profit to fall see: Castells 1980:Chapter 1

149

CHANGE AND TRANSFORMATION

in the capitalist mode-of-production, individual producers have to abide by a social division of labour by the regulatory pressures of the law of value

society is not organised for the satisfaction of needs (use-values), but for the earning of profits (exchange-values)

creating social tensions and individual frustrations that exert pressure towards a socialisation of society - addressed in Chapter 6

for capitalists to remain capitalists they have to earn profits, and hence strive to maintain efficiency to ensure they share in the pool of social surplus labour (surplus-value)

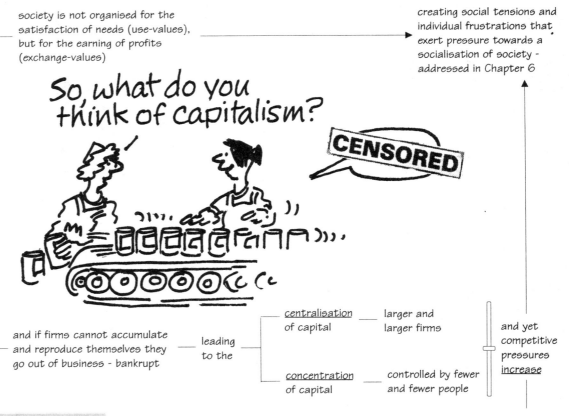

So, what do you think of capitalism?

CENSORED

capitalists must accumulate

and accumulation is a <u>process</u> described by the 'circuit of capital' (see pp. 143-9)

a process which can, and does, break down at a number of places, depending on the social effects of individuals' action to defend their interests

and if firms cannot accumulate and reproduce themselves they go out of business - bankrupt

leading to the

<u>centralisation</u> of capital — larger and larger firms

<u>concentration</u> of capital — controlled by fewer and fewer people

and yet competitive pressures <u>increase</u>

see:
Weeks 1981:Chapter VI
Bryan 1985
Capital and Class 1986
Semmler 1982
Wheelock 1983

'Monopoly produces competition, competition produces monopoly ... the more the mass of proletarians grows as against the monopolists of one nation, the more desperate competition becomes between the monopolists of different nations. The synthesis is of such a character that monopoly can only maintain itself by continually entering into the struggle of competition.'
(Marx 1936:128)

CHAPTER SIX

ECONOMIC BEHAVIOUR

AND

HUMAN MOTIVATION

ECONOMISTS' PRECONCEPTIONS

'Scientists, like other intellectuals, come to their work with a world view, a set of preconceptions that provides the framework for their analyses of the world.'
(Levins & Lewontin 1985:267, quoted on p. 14 above)

'The preconceptions enter at both an explicit and an implicit level, but even when invoked explicitly, unexamined and unexpressed assumptions underlie them.'
(Levins & Lewontin 1985:267)

This is my set of Preconceptions!

the argument of this book has been intended to make explicit the fundamental preconceptions (assumptions) which underlie all economic analyses

see p. 155

revealing the logic of economic analyses - why economists identify particular features of economies as being more or less important in determining economic experience

arriving at different policy conclusions for essentially the same economic problem

and if we are to be economically literate, to understand the implications and importance of alternative economic policy proposals

then we have to understand why analyses which arrive at different conclusions can each be realist, rationalist and activist

there are no objective criteria according to which different theories can be judged to be more or less adequate or accurate than each other

see p. 15 above

see p. 22 above

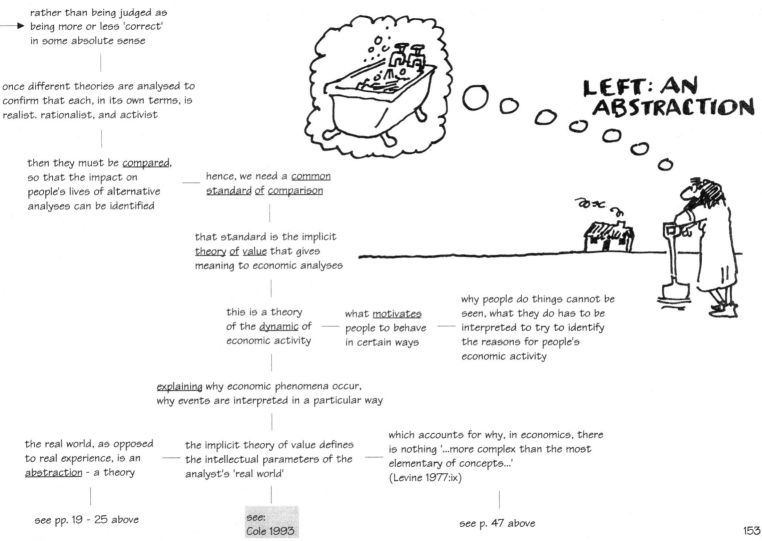

rather than being judged as
being more or less 'correct'
in some absolute sense

once different theories are analysed to
confirm that each, in its own terms, is
realist. rationalist, and activist

then they must be compared,
so that the impact on
people's lives of alternative
analyses can be identified

hence, we need a common
standard of comparison

that standard is the implicit
theory of value that gives
meaning to economic analyses

this is a theory
of the dynamic of
economic activity

what motivates
people to behave
in certain ways

why people do things cannot be
seen, what they do has to be
interpreted to try to identify
the reasons for people's
economic activity

explaining why economic phenomena occur,
why events are interpreted in a particular way

the real world, as opposed
to real experience, is an
abstraction - a theory

the implicit theory of value defines
the intellectual parameters of the
analyst's 'real world'

which accounts for why, in economics, there
is nothing '...more complex than the most
elementary of concepts...'
(Levine 1977:ix)

**LEFT: AN
ABSTRACTION**

see pp. 19 - 25 above

see:
Cole 1993

see p. 47 above

153

HUMAN NATURE AND ECONOMIC BEHAVIOUR

the 'world view', or preconceptions, of economists — determine the assumptions that are made in interpreting economic experience

the economists' 'real world'

the <u>axioms</u> of the analysis

where axioms are self-evident propositions requiring no proof; they '...mark the stage beyond which one does not seek to explain.' (Hahn 1984:6)

but if we are to identify the intellectual parameters of the economist's real world, and hence compare alternative economic analyses, we have to go beyond the statement of an axiom - Frank Hahn is too complacent

axioms, assumptions, have to be compared

economic assumptions, the axioms of economic analyses, are essentially assertions about <u>why</u> people behave in particular ways

statements about human motivation, <u>human</u> <u>nature</u>

which structure the way economic theories explain economic experience

and economic policy is intended to organise economies such that people's (assumed) 'natural' economic proclivities are exploited to their full potential

What's a preconception, Dad?

Er, something to do with sex, I think – ask your teacher!

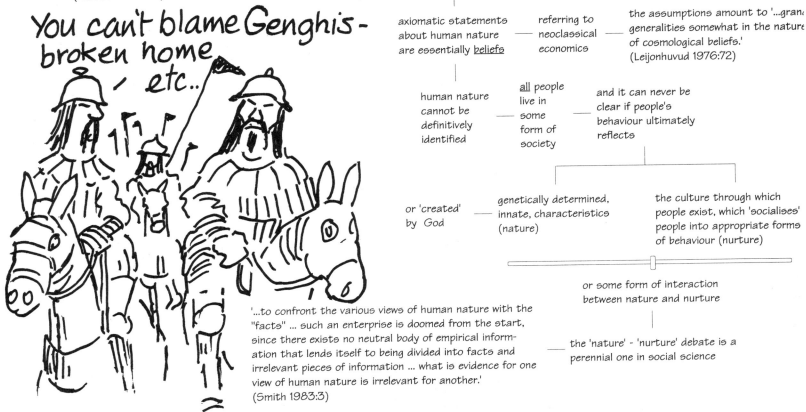

'Questions about what man should strive to be, the structure of the good society, the meaning of justice, the distinction between political right and wrong, and how to bring about a better society can have no adequate answers until one has some idea about what what man is in the first place.'
(Harbour 1982:52)

You can't blame Genghis-broken home etc...

axioms about <u>human nature</u> are '...the unexpressed and unexamined...' assumptions that underlie economic analyses - see p. 153 above

axiomatic statements about human nature are essentially <u>beliefs</u> — referring to neoclassical economics — the assumptions amount to '...grand generalities somewhat in the nature of cosmological beliefs.' (Leijonhuvud 1976:72)

human nature cannot be definitively identified — <u>all</u> people live in some form of society — and it can never be clear if people's behaviour ultimately reflects

or 'created' by God — genetically determined, innate, characteristics (nature)

the culture through which people exist, which 'socialises' people into appropriate forms of behaviour (nurture)

or some form of interaction between nature and nurture

the 'nature' - 'nurture' debate is a perennial one in social science

'...to confront the various views of human nature with the "facts" ... such an enterprise is doomed from the start, since there exists no neutral body of empirical information that lends itself to being divided into facts and irrelevant pieces of information ... what is evidence for one view of human nature is irrelevant for another.'
(Smith 1983:3)

'NATURE' AND ECONOMIC ANALYSIS

if it is believed that people reflect their innate capacities and drives, then behaviour is <u>biologically</u> <u>determined</u>

society, and the economy, is merely the sum of the individuals that compose it

'...to an [subjective preference theory] economist ... there is no such thing as society, only the individuals who constitute it.'
(Ormerod 1994:34)

'The ends of human behaviour (the relative degrees of satisfaction to be gained from consuming various commodities) are taken to be metaphysically given and fixed, and all human beings are imagined to be rational, calculating maximizers ... exchanging ... commodities and productive resources with which they have been "endowed" (the source and propriety of the endowment is beyond the purview of the analysis).'
(Hunt 1977:23)

that people are <u>endowed</u> with productive resources (essentially 'talents') is crucial to understanding the moral, ideological and political dimension of the subjective preference theory of value (see pp. 171-80, and Chapter 7)

people are also endowed with preferences

it is this 'endowment' (with tastes and talents) which defines people as <u>independent</u>, utility maximising, individuals

a dimension which justifies the policy conclusion that 'free market exchange' is desirable (the ideal being perfect competition)

so that independent individuals can maximise the full potential from their unique endowment

Could be a bright kid if you can get that thing off his head!

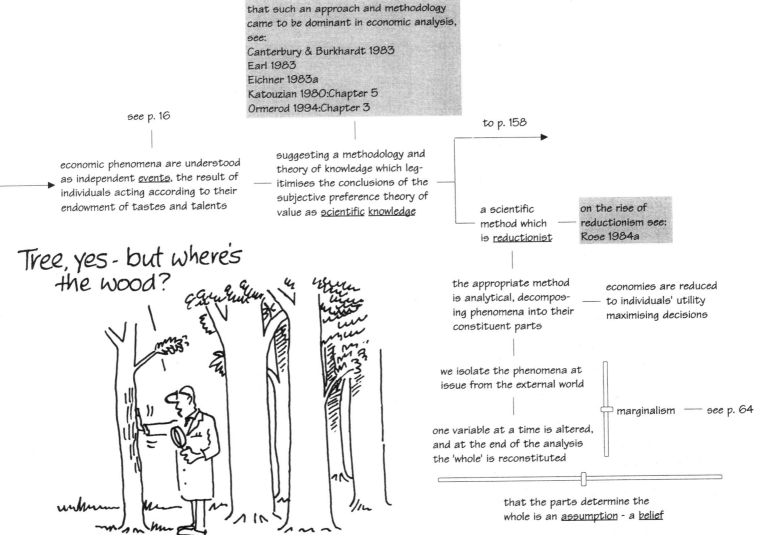

see p. 16

economic phenomena are understood as independent <u>events</u>, the result of individuals acting according to their endowment of tastes and talents

that such an approach and methodology came to be dominant in economic analysis, see:
Canterbury & Burkhardt 1983
Earl 1983
Eichner 1983a
Katouzian 1980:Chapter 5
Ormerod 1994:Chapter 3

suggesting a methodology and theory of knowledge which legitimises the conclusions of the subjective preference theory of value as <u>scientific</u> <u>knowledge</u>

to p. 158

a scientific method which is <u>reductionist</u>

on the rise of reductionism see: Rose 1984a

Tree, yes - but where's the wood?

the appropriate method is analytical, decomposing phenomena into their constituent parts

economies are reduced to individuals' utility maximising decisions

we isolate the phenomena at issue from the external world

one variable at a time is altered, and at the end of the analysis the 'whole' is reconstituted

marginalism — see p. 64

that the parts determine the whole is an <u>assumption</u> - a <u>belief</u>

the appropriate theory of scientific knowledge is the <u>positivism</u> of Karl Popper ——

see:
Magee 1975
Popper 1959

data are considered as independent events

individuals' consumption behaviour is the appropriate scientific economic data

theories are not regarded as reliable scientific knowledge if they fail to predict forthcoming events ——

theories can never be proven to be scientifically 'correct', once it is never known what might happen in the future, nor what past events failed to be noticed or recorded ——

'...no theory [can] ever be relied on to be the final truth. The most we can say is that it is supported by every observation so far, and yields more, and more precise, predictions than any known alternative. It is still replaceable by a better theory.' (Magee 1975:29)

'...without a carefully protected free market, the whole economic system must cease to serve its only rational purpose, that is, <u>to</u> <u>satisfy</u> <u>the</u> <u>demands</u> <u>of</u> <u>the</u> <u>consumer</u>...' (Popper 1962:348, emphasis in original)

<u>only</u> the ability to predict forthcoming events matters

the 'realism' of the assumptions is not an issue

OUTLOOK

The dry weather is expected to continue ...

'A hypothesis is important if it "explains" much by little, that is, if it abstracts the common and crucial elements from the mass of complex and detailed circumstances surrounding the phenomena to be explained and permits valid predictions on the basis of them alone. To be important, therefore, a hypothesis must be descriptively false in its assumptions...' (Freidman 1953:14)

hence, that the theory of 'perfect competiton' is patently unrealistic is not seen as a weakness, but a strength - see p. 63 above

'NURTURE' AND ECONOMIC ANALYSIS

alternatively, if it is believed that people's character and their behaviour essentially reflect their environment (both natural and social)

people are 'socialized' into adopting appropriate forms of behaviour

then individuals' biological endowment is no longer the sole determinant of economic activity

'Man is innately programmed in such a way that he needs a culture to complete him ... Man is like one of those versatile cake mixes that can be variously prepared to end up as different kinds of cake ... just as a cake has to be baked, so a baby has to be exposed to a specific, already existing, culture.' (Midgely 1978:286)

and hence, in their economic interaction, the <u>consumer</u> is no longer the economic dynamic

individuals are no longer <u>independent</u> utility maximisers

"EXPOSING A BABY TO AN EXISTING CULTURE" (ABOVE- WRONG.)

rather, people are <u>dependent</u> on society, and the basis of their economic inter- action is common interest

and 'nurture' rather than 'nature' is important in affecting economic behaviour

economic relations are essentially between <u>producers</u>

and the source of that common interest in economic activity is the technical division of labour that underlies <u>all</u> production - requiring <u>cooperation</u>

economies should not now be 'free' so as to allow individuals to utilise their full, endowed, potential, so as to maximise utility

rather, economies should be managed in the common interest so as to maximise output and the full utilisation of economic resources

improving technical cooperation is now the purpose of economic policy

159

and poverty is not now a conseq-uence of personal inadequacy (as for the subjective preference theory of value) —— but the result of a person's place in the technical division of labour allied to the degree of their control over technology —— hence the importance of 'monopoly power' (imperfect competition) for the cost-of-production theory of value - the extent to which <u>producers</u> can affect market prices —— see pp. 91-93 above

'We need to abandon the economist's notion of the economy as a machine, with its attendant concept of equilibrium. A more helpful way ... is to imagine it as a <u>living organism</u> .' (Ormerod 1994:151, emphasis added) —— for the economy to function efficiently as a <u>system</u> requires cooperation

PRAGMATISM...

see quotes from Alfred Marshall, pp. 43-4 above —— and to this end economic inequality is dysfunctional, engendering unrest, work stoppages (strikes) and economic disruption

and the appropriate economic policy evolves with technology in a 'pragmatic', realistic, way

'It is certain that the world will not much longer tolerate the unemployment which ... is assoc-iated ... with present-day capitalistic individualism.' (Keynes 1936:381) —— it is the purpose of economic and political institutions to achieve compromise between technically defined economic interest groups

markets have to be more effectively managed to achieve technical effic-iency through economic cooperation

and with the evolution of technology towards ever higher levels of efficiency, economic interest groups are continually adjusting to the changing exigencies of the technical division of labour —— and with the evolution of technology towards an ever more extensive div-ision of labour (greater and greater economic specialisation)

requiring a step-by-step, pragmatic, approach to the design of economic policy, which goes hand in hand with the reform of economic and political institutions —— economic theory and policy must be <u>realistic</u> —— '...the major criticism of post-Keynesians [cost-of-production theorists] against neoclassical theory [subjective preference theory] is that it lacks <u>realism</u>.' (Lavoie 1992:8, emphasis added) since the operation of the economy as a 'system' is beyond the experience of any one individual

that the analysis starts with the whole and works down to the parts is as much an assumption as the contrary reductionist strategy of seeing the parts as the fundamental building blocks of scientific analysis

economic policy has to be left in the hands of experts, economists, with the necessary technical training

and we also need a scientific methodology which addresses the analysis of systems

the approach has to be <u>holistic</u>

the nature of the 'whole' determines the character of the 'parts'

not the reductionist, marginalist, positive approach to economics which is the hallmark of the subjective preference theory of value, and which only looks at the behaviour of independent individuals

scientific inquiry now proceeds through <u>paradigms</u>

see:
Kuhn 1970
Glass & Johnson
1989:Chapter 9

'The universe [social and natural] is not longer seen as a machine, made up of a multitude of separate objects, but appears as a harmonious indivisible whole...'
(Capra 1982;32)

a paradigm is essentially a 'world view', a perspective on the world which explains how it functions

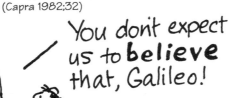

as an explanation of the world, paradigms define the parameters of 'normal science'

'...researchers <u>implicitly</u> <u>accept</u> [that is it is a question of <u>belief</u>] the worldview embodied in the basic assumptions of the paradigm's theoretical framework...'
(Glass & Johnson 1989:157, emphasis added)

until there are 'anomalies' - discrepancies between observation and theory which cannot be explained within a paradigm

there then follows a period of 'revolutionary science'

in which a new paradigm emerges which conceptualises systems in such a way that the 'anomalie' is explained

however, Kuhn can only account for competing theories (paradigms) in times of 'revolutionary science', and hence is unable to account for '...economics as being characterized by competing research programmes rather than by one paradigm.' (Glass and Johnson 1989:168)

Imre Lakatos, building on Kuhn's concept of 'paradigms', explains the development of science through competing Scientific Research Programmes, and that programme which explains the most is superior, and defines current 'scientific' knowledge

see:
Lakatos 1970
Glass & Johnson 1989: Chapters 5 & 6

research programmes are not 'refuted' by the failure to predict 'individual' facts or events, but are replaced when an alternative, 'progressive' research programme explains the system better

INCORRECT PARADIGM.

'...economists are always considering a temporal sequence of groupings of hypotheses rather than a temporal sequence of individual hypotheses, this in turn means that we require a methodology that not only explicitly deals with groupings of hypotheses but also attempts to explain why one grouping of hypotheses is preferred to another.' (Glass & Johnson 1989:85)

NATURE, NURTURE AND ECONOMIC ANALYSIS

<u>all</u> theories of economic behaviour have to be based on a conception of human motivation, <u>why</u> people behave in particular ways

in this chapter it has been argued that, ultimately, the subjective preference theory of value assumes that individuals' behaviour reflects their biological (genetic) 'endowment' of tastes and talents

alternatively, the cost-of-production theory of value understands people's behaviour as a reflection of their environment

hence, individuals can be assumed to be 'independent' of society, and their activity is purely motivated by sensuous expediency - maximising utility

human nature is malleable, people adapt to the exigencies of technical cooperation in order to survive

I'm determined not to be a, well -

economies now have to be 'managed' so as to create an institutional environment which is conducive to technical cooperation

and a policy strategy emphasising 'free' markets (ideally perfect competition) can be justified as providing the economic environment which allows independent individuals to best fulfil their innate potentials

fully employing available resources as efficiently as possible to maximise output

- a determinist!

in both of these perspectives the source of human motivation is beyond people's control

implying a determinist economic analysis

either economic policy is intended

to harness individuals' innate proclivities (nature), through a <u>competitive</u> environment, to encourage economic specialisation and a division of labour

to maximise utility in consumption

to create an economic environment (nurture) in which people are able to <u>cooperate</u> most efficiently in a technical division of labour

to maximise output in production

but the environment within which people live and their biological potentials can also be conceived of as mutually reinforcing

and rather than being 'independent' (the subjective preference theory of value), or 'dependent' (the cost-of-production theory of value), people, within the abstract labour theory of value, are <u>interdependent</u> in their economic relations

people are fundamentally <u>creative</u> beings

while being born with innate biological potentials

humans are also social beings, fulfilling their potentials through social interaction - and hence priority is not now a question of maximising utility or output, but of ensuring that people's social existence allows them to fulfil their individual potentials

see pp. 118-21 above

potentials which <u>change</u> with experience

through experience people become aware of what they are capable of, and having achieved an ambition or objective, as creative beings, people widen their horizons and become aware of new potentials

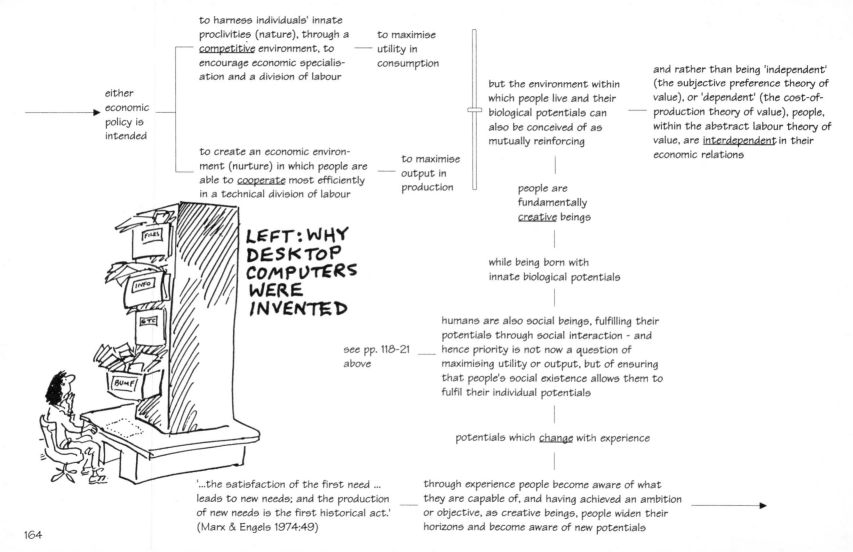

LEFT: WHY DESKTOP COMPUTERS WERE INVENTED

FILES

INFO

ETC

BUMF

'...the satisfaction of the first need ... leads to new needs; and the production of new needs is the first historical act.' (Marx & Engels 1974:49)

164

so people change themselves through their own experience

'The materialist doctrine that men are products of their circumstances ... forgets that it is men who change circumstances...' (Marx, Theses on Feuerbach, quoted in Vazquez 1977:123)

there is a dialectic between people's 'objective' (material) circumstances and their 'subjective' (ideal) ambitions, priorities and expectations

while people have to adapt to society, and adjust to objective circumstances, which are beyond their control, in order to survive

people are not socially determined in some simplistic, mechanical sense

people's biological potentials, their experience and their awareness of what they are capable of temper the dominance of social conditions

Not only men, Marx!

and people, uniquely, feed back and deter-mine society, just as social existence sets the parameters of their own development

'In the social production of their existence, men inevitably enter into definite relations, which are independent of their will, namely relations of production appropriate to a given stage in the development of their material forces of production.' (Marx 1976:20, emphasis added)

though, as individuals, they do not directly control their circumstances

people are not determined by circumstances beyond their control

there is a subjective/objective (idealist/materialist) dialectic in Marx's thought

'...just as society itself produces man as man, so is society produced by him. Activity and mind, both in their content and their mode of existence, are social: social activity and social mind.' (Marx 1973a:137, emphasis in original)

but people are able to **change** those relations

if, as individuals, they <u>want</u> change; if they are aware of other people similarly motivated; and if they are mobilised and organised to <u>socially</u> prosecute their demands

people will want to change society, if, as creative individuals they are frustrated from fulfilling their potentials - for instance they may become unemployed, be low paid, denied the opportunity for training/education, discriminated against, etc.

the concept of <u>class</u> is addressed on p. 174

though to be aware of, and motivated by, the need to combine with other, similarly frustrated people, requires a <u>theoretical</u> awareness of the nature of social existence - it requires <u>class</u> <u>consciousness</u>

'...material force must be overcome by material force; but theory, too, becomes a material force once it seizes the masses. Theory is capable of seizing the masses once it demonstrates <u>ad hominem</u>, and it demonstrates <u>ad hominem</u> once it becomes radical. To be radical is to grasp matters by the root. But for man the root is man himself.'
(Marx 1970:137)

experience is 'real' for people, but the idea of a 'real world', a 'society' beyond their immediate experience is a conception, a 'theory'

see pp. 22-5 above

so people, <u>themselves</u>, have to understand the social context of their own existence

indeed, individuals are the only people that can be aware of their own potentials, fully understand their frustrations and anger, and their priorities for social change - the reasons for combining with others to change society

I just **hate** class consciousness!

and the theory of knowledge/scientific methodology appropriate to prioritising individuals' needs in a social context is the theory of <u>praxis</u>

'...the conception of praxis is central to Marx's thought, since it provides the starting-point for understanding both the activity of men and knowledge itself ... Marx's philosophy ... is the philosophy of human praxis.'
(Vazquez 1977:137)

'praxis' is often confused with 'practice' - while practice is what people <u>do</u>, praxis is how what they do, their experience, affects their understanding, their consciousness, their awareness

defining 'relevant' knowledge

raising the question - how do we translate the philosophy of 'praxis' into scientific 'practice'?

data only has meaning in a particular social and historical context, and everybody, potentially, might have a different interpretation and emphasis

the only methodology of which I am aware which explicitly addresses the context specificity of data is <u>naturalistic inquiry</u>

'...naturalistic researchers ... assume that human beings must operate within realities they themselves have constructed. Further, the constructed realities of no two human beings are identical ... [naturalistic inquiry] deal[s] with the processes by which realities are constructed, communicated, and verified...'
(Erlandson, Harris, Skipper & Allen 1993:21)

on 'naturalistic inquiry' as a theory of knowledge and an approach to scientific enquiry, see:
Erlandson, Harris, Skipper & Allen 1993
Guba 1990
Lincoln & Guba 1985

PRACTICE COURSE

PRAXIS COURSE

"OFTEN CONFUSED"

SCIENTIFIC ENQUIRY AND ECONOMIC ANALYSIS

we have seen how different perspectives on economic analysis —

— conceive of the economic dynamic - which determines the rate of exchange between consumers and producers - differently

— highlight distinct priorities for economic policy

— embody particular conceptions of 'scientific knowledge'

and all of these distinctions are based upon different <u>beliefs</u> in human nature

either the consumer, the producer, or the citizen being identified as the causal mechanism

the maximisation of utility, the maximisation of output, and creating an environment in which people can fulfil their potentials

reductionism/positivism: holism/paradigms-research programmes: dialectics/praxis

changing economists' perceptions of the 'real world'

'Facts then are collected to be placed in the kaleidoscope of theory, and our perceptions of them are constantly transformed by the shaking of that kaleidoscope.' (Rose 1984:4)

'...scientific propositions are not stable in meaning, but are reinterpreted as they move from one social context to another.' (Mulkay 1979:120)

ECONOMISTS' KALEIDOSCOPES

Mummy, Mummy - can I have one to reinterpret scientific propositions!

there are
distinct
scientific
practices

concerned with
the identification
of individual data

through statistical
techniques, economists
are concerned to est-
ablish correlations
between independent
events

it being assumed that
a correlation between
variables indicates a
relationship

from an economics stat-
istics textbook: 'This book
is intended for students of
economics. It is concerned
primarily with the estim-
ation and measurement of
relationships between
economic variables.'
(Fox 1968:1)

concerned with systematising
aggregate data to explain a
sequence of events

devising 'realistic'
models to explain the
working of economic
systems

'Economics is a science of thinking in
terms of models joined to the art of
choosing models which are relevant to
the contemporary world.'
(Keynes, quoted Moggridge 1976:26)

an in depth inquiry establishing
the different social contexts of
individuals' experience

addressing
different
realities

different under-
standings of
the same social
process

'...there is, in a sense, no
final truth or final telling.
There are only different
tellings of different stories
organized under the head-
ing of the same tale...'
(Denzin 1992:124)

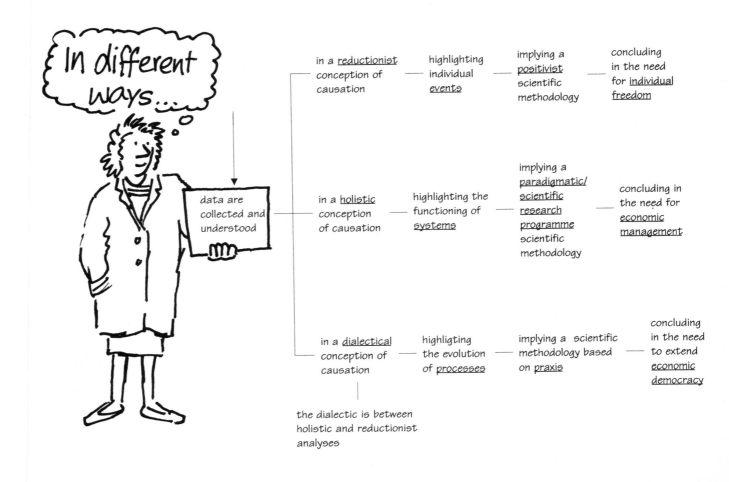

In different ways...

data are collected and understood

in a <u>reductionist</u> conception of causation — highlighting individual <u>events</u> — implying a <u>positivist</u> scientific methodology — concluding in the need for <u>individual freedom</u>

in a <u>holistic</u> conception of causation — highlighting the functioning of <u>systems</u> — implying a <u>paradigmatic/scientific research programme</u> scientific methodology — concluding in the need for <u>economic management</u>

in a <u>dialectical</u> conception of causation — highligting the evolution of <u>processes</u> — implying a scientific methodology based on <u>praxis</u> — concluding in the need to extend <u>economic democracy</u>

the dialectic is between holistic and reductionist analyses

EOLOGICAL BIAS AND ECONOMIC ANALYSIS

different perspectives on economic analysis — conceptualise economic reality distinctly — and each implies a particular vision of what economic relat-ions should be like — justifying a particular social order — a justification which ultimately derives from a belief in human nature — beliefs which structure political practice

see Appendix 6.1

and economic policy is the political articulation of economic theory

Whose interests does a theory serve?

'Let me first dispose of the question whether any economic theory is, or can be, "correct". Students often ask me which theory is right? This is an inappropriate question because there is no objective way of assessing whether any theoretical school is right ... the main ones are self-contained systems, perfectly logical on their own premises ... Empirical tests are not very relevant ... because the objectives ... are derived from the theories ... The crucial questions are: whose interests does a theory serve? How does it serve them?'
(Seers 1983:33)

'...[economic] policymakers generally engage in economic, political and other types of transactions that tend to shape the evolution of the social order.'
(David 1988:6)

Not me, pal!

'Theory is always for someone and for some purpose. All theories have a per-spective. Perspectives derive from a position in time and space, specifically social and political time and space ... There is ... no such thing as a theory in itself, divorced from a standpoint ... When any theory so represents itself, it is the more important to examine it as an ideology...'
(Cox 1981:444, emphasis in original)

the subjective preference theory of value — addresses the economic activity of independent individuals — who should be democratically represented by politicians — whose function it is to maintain an environment of individual liberty — it being reassuring to the rich and priviledged that they <u>ought</u> to be rich and priviledged — leading to a politics intended to preserve the 'status quo' in market societies - political conservatism

'There is no such thing as society. There are individual men and women and there are families.'
(Margaret Thatcher, the then British, Conservative Prime Minister, reported in <u>Observer</u>, 27 December 1987)

'The nation as a whole is not equivalent to <u>one</u> large decision maker, but is rather composed of a complex <u>collection</u> of individual decision makers.'
(Littlechild 1978:18, emphasis in original)

'Conservative governments [in Great Britain] in the years following 1979 have been inspired by ... a belief that markets should be allowed to operate freely without any intervention from government, whose function should largely be limited to <u>maintaining</u> the framework of law and order and national security which makes this possible.'
(Donaldson & Farquhar 1988:277, emphasis added)

on the appropriate organisation of political institutions to ensure free markets and individual economic liberty, see:
Littlechild 1978
Menger 1960

the cost-of-production theory of value — to p. 173

the abstract labour theory of value — to p. 174

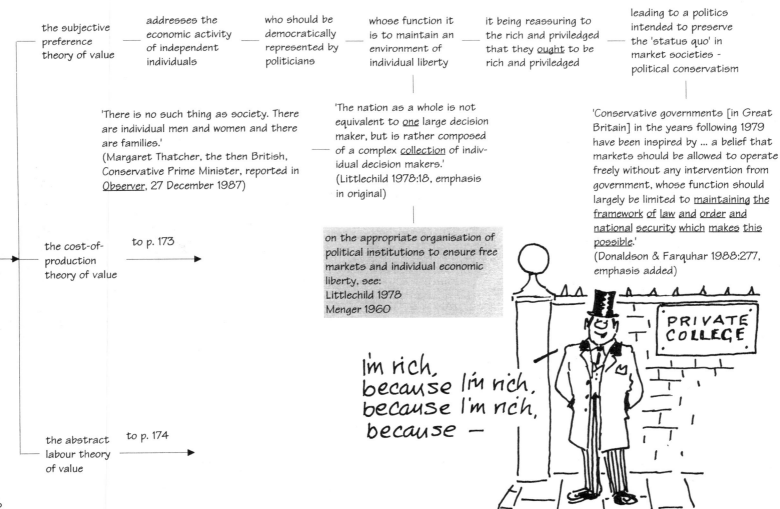

I'm rich, because I'm rich, because I'm rich, because —

PRIVATE COLLEGE

from p. 172 conceives of economic
activity as between
dependent individuals

whose motivation and interests
reflect the technically defined
economic interest group to
which they belong

it is the function of pluralist
political institutions to achieve
compromise between such
groups, providing the basis for
(technical) economic cooperation

'At a minimum, economic policy
becomes far more dependent on
political skill than on economic
wisdom.'
(Galbraith & Salinger 1981:120)

institutions which are staffed by 'experts'
(economists), who are trained to understand
the workings of the economic system

We have joint discussions
about everything
important - right!

Right!

though individuals may be
consulted, the final policy
(in the general interest)
is decided by the experts

'In practice governments begin with consultation.
They seek agreement from the principal groups in
the economy ... However, having done everything
possible to reach consensus, the government
must also retain the power to enforce the result.'
(Galbraith & Salinger 1981:121)

implying (in market societies)
a social democratic political
system

But I'm still in
control, pal!

economic policy and pluralist politics is
a matrix where each connects with the
other, in pursuit of discovering, through
negotiation and bargaining, the common
interest (which is constantly changing
with the evolution of technology)

and the policy emphases
are with socio-economic
issues such as: full
employment, economic
growth, price stability,
balance-of-payments
equilibrium - but not to
the exclusion of each
other, each is the cond-
ition of the other

from p. 172

people are econom-
ically interdependent

Give the rabble bread
and circuses - that
will shut them up.

but they do not have equal power
to determine the course of events

where economic, and
ultimately political,
power is held to derive
from the control of
the social means of
production

— power which
enables people
to better fulfil
their creative
potentials

— greater economic security,
higher incomes and a better
standard of living, more
control over what they do in
work, more leisure time to
follow their own pastimes,
etc.

and with the
inevitable trend
towards capitalist
economic crises

class is defined
by control over
the means of
production

it is the powerless who suffer the most: unemployment, prices
rising faster than incomes, deteriorating and demoralising
working conditions, declining social services (health, pensions,
housing, education), the denial of trade union rights, etc.

and for people to defend their economic, class interest

even though the manifestation of
their disadvantage (powerlessness)
might be very different: including
racial, sexual and religious discrim-
ination, etc.

— they have to be aware of a shared
interest with others who are disadvantaged for being 'property-
less' (wage labour not controlling
the means of production) - that is
<u>class</u> <u>conscious</u>

people are motivated to
struggle for social change,
when, as individuals, they
are frustrated from
fulfilling their creative
potentials

— and need to
mobilise and
organise, and
combine their
disparate
struggles into
a 'class'
movement

progressive social change derives from a broad class movement oriented toward changing the social, economic and political priorities of capitalist society

emphasising the production of 'use' values (concrete labour) and the fulfillment of people's creative potentials, overturning the 'law of value' and the drive to accumulate exchange values (abstract labour)

see:
Collective Design 1985

it is the denial of peoples' human potential which is the seedbed for discontent

leading to pressure to challenge capitalist priorities

'Capitalism is not regarded as consonant with [changing] human nature. The negation of capitalism, communism, is held to represent humankind's full flowering.' (Heyer 1982:91))

which is fundamentally a process of cultural change, people intuitively believing in the value and priority of people's creative fulfilment, rather than the competitive, individualist culture of capitalist society

Unfortunately, O mighty Emperor, the bakers and the gladiators seem to be supporting the rabble!

the cultural hegemony of capital has to be challenged and transformed

'The struggle for socialism [a movement towards communism] is thus not just, or even principally, about the struggle against a certain group of capitalists ... More impotant, it is about overturning capital - the system of wage-labour and its basic dynamic, competitive accumulation...' (McNally 1993:181)

'...the oppressed must demystify the ideological armour of the status quo and create their own "integrated culture" prior to and within the process of achieving economic and political control ... Since every hegemonic world-view is so deeply-imbued in the individual consciousness, ideological struggle must above all confront the most concrete issues of personal and social existence.' (Boggs 1976:123)

'...theory ... to be radical ... grasp[s] matters by the root. But for man the root is man himself.' (Marx, quoted p. 166 above)

175

socialism, then, is an evolutionary process in which people change their natures

'...the communal production by society as a whole ... will both require and generate an entirely different kind of human material. Communal operation of production cannot be carried out by people as they are today...' (Engels 1977:19-20)

but '...communist society ... _emerges_ from capitalist society ... [and] is thus in every respect, economically, morally and intellectually, still stamped with the birth marks of the old society from whose womb it emerges.' (Marx 1972a:15, emphasis in original)

it is only really with Lenin that the term 'socialism' is seperated from 'communism'

'What is usually called socialism was termed by Marx the "first", or lower, phase of communism.' (Lenin 1969:90)

socialism (or communism) is an evolutionary _process_ - not a _system_

'...socialist revolution should be conceived of as an organic _process_, not as an event (or series of events), and the _consciousness transformation_ is an inseparable part of structural change, indeed ... it is impossible to conceptualise them as distinct phenomena.' (Boggs 1976:17-8, emphasis in original)

as a consequence of people being denied their creative 'essence' in the functioning of capitalist society

through 'praxis' human nature changes towards more communal attitudes and beliefs, paradoxically increasing individual freedom

since, '...freedom really begins ... only where labour determined by expediency and external necessity ends; it lies by its very nature beyond the sphere of material production proper.' (Marx 1972:958-9)

Revolution is an **organic** process!

for individual freedom, for the potential for people to fulfil their innate, unique, creativity, society must be organised to minimise <u>necessary</u> labour

necessary labour, which is minimised for the individual, and made more (technically) efficient by being collective

'...this central goal of socialism - the free development of the individual - has an essential precondition: the subjection of economic life to collective and democratic control.'
(McNally 1993:188)

what does a real revolution need?

Us, I suspect!

see:
Ollman 1993:Part 1

with the concomitant shift in Marxism's meaning from an analysis of human existence under capitalism, to an organising ideology for a 'socialist' state

but this vision of socialism/communism is very different to the experience of 'actually existing socialism' in Eastern Europe, the Soviet Union, and elsewhere, culminating in the collapse of the Soviet Bloc in the late 1980s

where the concept of 'praxis', and people working towards a future where they have greater control of their livelihoods (socialism as an extension of democracy) was hardly accurate

for Lenin, contrary to Marx, people did not construct their own reality, but adapted to a material reality beyond their control

see: Cole & Yaxley 1991

commenting of the collapse of 'communist' states; 'The break with Marxism came with Lenin ... If there had been no Lenin ... if the separate Soviet Republics hadn't been deprived of all power, there could have been no Stalin.'
(Gunter Grass, quoted Conquest 1972:134-5)

but it is in society, the dialectic being between the forces of production (technology) and the relations of production (class structure)

the dialectic of change is not in people's consciousness, that is between people's awareness of their potential and the degree to whch they are socially frustrated from fulfiling themselves

people's human nature does not creatively evolve but is <u>determined</u> by society

'Marx treats the social movement as a process of <u>natural</u> <u>history</u>, governed by laws not only <u>independent</u> of human will, consciousness and intentions, but, rather, on the contrary, <u>determining</u> the will, consciousness and intentions of men.'
(Lenin 1963:166, emphasis added)

APPENDIX 6:1
CHARACTERISATIONS OF THE TRI-PARTITE DIVISION OF SOCIAL THEORY

in Appendix 2:1 (pp. 48-52), some economic analyses where three theoretical perspectives had been identified were listed

and these characterisations were arranged, in my understanding, according to the implicit economic dynamic underlying the alternative perspectives

the consumer - column **I**
the producer - column **II**
the citizen - column **III**

allowing distinct perspectives (theories of value) to be compared

it has been argued in this chapter that beliefs in human nature underlie perspectives in economics

assumptions which complicate '...elementary concepts...'

the '...unexamined and unexpressed assumptions...'

assumptions which define the 'intellectual parameters' of the real world and the conception of 'valid knowledge'

and the ideological bias of the analysis

that 'intuitive link' is an implicit, shared, conception of human nature

a 'conservative' or 'socialist' economist will intuitively be drawn to analyses by conservative or socialist philosophers, sociologists, ecologists, or psychologists, even though they may know little of the detail of these disciplines

a bias which is shared by social analyses in general

for a more comprehensive list see:
Cole 1993:43, table 2

in the table that follows some examples from other disciplines of social analysis, including sociology, development studies, ecology, philosophy, politics, etc. are cited

in each example three perspectives are identified, which I have arranged into three columns

column **I** - biological determinism

column **II** - cultural adaption

column **III** - biological/cultural dialectic

	I	II	III
Alford & Friedland (1985)	managerial	pluralist	class
Applebaum (1976)	equilibrium	evolutionary	conflict
Atkinson (1991)	intellectual crisis	environmental crisis	social crisis
Bhaskar (1979)	Weber	Durkheim	Marx
Chenery (1975)	neo-classical	structuralist	neo-Marxist
Cox, Furlong & Page (1985)	elite	pluralist	Marxist
Crook, Pakulski & Waters (1992)	Weberian	Durkheimian	Marxian
Habermas (1987)	empirical science	historico-hermeneutic science	critique of ideology
Hermassi (1978)	liberal	managerial	neo-Marxist
Johnston (1983)	positivist	structuralist	humanistic
LeShan & Margeneau (1982)	one-dimensional reality	two-dimensional reality	three-dimensional reality
Levins & Lewontin (1985)	conservative	radical	revolutionary
Mellos (1982)	neo-malthusianism	eco-development	radical ecology
Preston (1982)	positivist	radical	Marxist
Reason & Rowan (1981)	naive inquiry	old paradigm research	new paradigm research
Rose (1973)	reductionist	holistic	interactive
Smith (1983)	conservative	liberal	Marxist
Stinchcombe (1978)	narrative sequences	causal sequences	epochal interpretations
Wallerstein (1979)	conservative	liberal	Marxist
Weiss (1988)	neoclassical	structuralists	radical

REFERENCES TO APPENDIX 6:1

Alford R & Friedland R, (1985), Powers of Theory, Cambridge University Press, Cambridge.

Applebaum R, (1976), Theories of Social Change, Rand McNally, Chicago.

Atkinson A, (1991), Principles of Political Ecology, Belhaven Press, London.

Bhaskar R, (1979), The Possibility of Naturalism, Harvester, Brighton.

Chenery H, (1975), A Sructuralist Approach to Development Policy, in American Economic Review, Vol 65, no 2.

Cox A, Furlong P & Page E, (1985), Power in Capitalist Society, Harvester, London.

Crook S, Pakulski J & Waters M, (1992), Postmodernism: change in advanced societies, Sage, London.

Habermas J (1987), Knowledge and Human Interests, Polity Press, Cambridge.

Hermassi E, (1978), Changing Patterns of Research in the Third World, in Annual Review of Sociology, No 4.

Johnston R, (1983), Philosophy and Human Geography, Edward Arnold, London.

LeShan L & Margeneau H, (1982), Einstein's Space and Van Gogh's Sky, Collier, New York.

Levins R & Lewontin R, (1985), The Dialectical Biologist, Harvard University Press, Cambridge Mass.

Mellos K, (1982), Perspectives on Ecology, Macmillan, London.

Preston P W, (1982), Theories of Development, Routledge and Kegan Paul, London.

Reason P & Rowan J (eds.), (1981), Human Inquiry, John Wiley, New York.

Rose S, (1973), The Conscious Brain, Weidenfeld and Nicholson, London.

Smith S, (1983), 'Introduction', in Forbes I & Smith S (eds.), (1983), Politics and Human Nature, Frances Pinter, London.

Stinchcombe A, (1978), Theoretical Models in Social History, Academic Press, New York.

Wallerstein I, (1979), The Capitalist World Economy, Cambridge University Press, Cambridge.

Weiss J, (1988), Industry in Developing Countries, Croom Helm, London.

CHAPTER SEVEN

THE COMPLEXITY OF ELEMENTARY CONCEPTS

UNEXAMINED AND UNEXPRESSED ASSUMPTIONS

'In economics there is nothing more elementary than the most complex of mathematical formulae, nor anything more complex than the most elementary of concepts. While the former is wholly without content, the latter contains, latent within it, the system of economic relations in its entirety.'
(Levine 1977:ix)

this quote from David Levine was first cited at the end of Chapter 2 (p. 47), and I expect at that stage of the argument it seemed contradictory rather than paradoxical

learning how to manipulate variables in a mathematical equation has absolutely <u>no</u> economics content

economics is important in deciding <u>which</u> variables to include in the relationship, and whether or not it is meaningful to quantify these variables and/or to understand the relationship with mathematical certainty and exactitude

that is, how do economic variables affect each other - what is the economic dynamic

conceptions of the economic dynamic are the most elementary of economic concepts, and contain, latent within them, 'the system of economic relations in its entirety'

though every chapter in this book could have been extended to a book in its own right

hopefully, by now the complexity of elementary concepts should be clearer

I have tried to restrict the argument to making the essential differences between perspectives (theories of value) explicit

it has been argued that perspectives on economic analysis in particular, and social science in general

implicity, yet fundamentally, are based upon <u>beliefs</u> in human nature

revealing the '...unexamined and unexpressed...' assumptions that underlie <u>all</u> economic analyses

and without theorising these assumptions, we tend to accept those understandings of economic behaviour where the underlying, implicit beliefs are similar to our own

assumptions which are usually accepted naively, learnt by rote authoritatively, and held dogmatically (reflecting a lack of understanding)

and, where the axioms of economic analysis are adopted in ignorance of their implications

see p. 46 above

economic analyses have the status of prophecies

sustaining interpretations which the credulous justify as 'common sense'

and scholarship is reduced to an 'intellectual game of chess'

examining the logical possibilities of alt-ernative, arbitrary, 'a priori' assumptions

FORTUNES TOLD

COMMON SENSE

FOR THE CREDULOUS

183

all of us organise our lives based upon
a belief structure: a structure which
makes sense of our experience

Today we have
the Gospel
– according to
Adam Smith

though rarely are these beliefs
given the status of a 'theory' -
they are obvious, common sense,
they are how we intuitively understand the world

it was argued in the
Introduction (p. 4),
that a purpose of
education is to help us
acquire the skills to
theorise our intuitions

the first requirement of any student
of economics, or any social science,
is to try and understand <u>themselves</u>

try to answer the questions: 'Why do I find that
<u>particular</u> theory or policy plausible, relevant or
pragmatic?' - 'What is <u>my</u> interest and bias?'

students (and readers)
deserve more respect

there are <u>no</u> 'neutral' economic theories or
policies, all we can try to do is to understand
the bias and decide where we stand

there is
no 'fence'
to sit on

and it is incumbent on teachers
of economics not to treat their
students as 'disciples'

uncritically teaching <u>an</u>
approach to economics
as <u>the</u> approach to
economics

as a teacher it is not my function to impose my intuitions, masquerading as 'science', on the student or reader

rather, my job is to help people to understand the range of economic analyses on any particular issue as coherently as possible

and then the student/reader can decide for him/herself on the organisation of economic activity

certainly I have my preferred analysis, as does every other economist

and hence this not a recipe for 'philosophical relativism' (see p. 22 above), since people have a reference point by which to choose between theories

theories which are compared by reference to the implicit theory of value that underlies all economic analyses

but this reflects my own priorities, attitudes and beliefs

a reference point born out of 'self-understanding' (see p. 184 above)

a self-consciousness which makes people aware of their priorities

Not good enough, Frisby - write out a hundred times -

"Economics is not boring!"

it is appropriate to end this book by summarising the intellectual, political and moral implications of the alternative approaches to understanding economics

economic dynamic	theory of value	economic relations between	policy emphasis	conception of human nature	conception of scientific knowledge	political bias
consumer	subjective preference	independent individuals	free markets	biological determinism	positivism	conservative
producer	cost-of-production	dependent individuals	managed markets	cultural adaption	paradigms/ research programmes	social democratic
citizen	abstract labour	inter-dependent people	economic democracy	biological/ cultural dialectic	praxis	socialist

economic activity is the relation of exchange between producers and consumers

REFERENCES

Abendroth W, (1972), <u>A Short History of the European Working Class</u>, New Left Books, London.

Alford R and Friedland R, (1985), <u>Powers of Theory</u>, Cambridge University Press, Cambridge.

Allen J & Massey D (eds.), (1988), <u>The Economy in Question</u>, Sage, London.

Arestis P (ed.), (1988), <u>Post Keynesian Monetary Economics: New Approaches to Financial Modeling</u>, Edward Elgar, Aldershot.

Arestis P & Skouras T (eds.), (1985), <u>Post Keynesian Economic Theory: A Challenge to Neo-Classical Economics</u>, Wheatsheaf, Brighton.

Bauer P T, (1976), <u>Dissent on Development</u>, Weidenfeld and Nicolson, London.

Bauer P T, (1981), <u>Equality, the Third World and Economic Delusion</u>, Weidenfeld and Nicolson, London.

Bauer P T, (1991), <u>The Development Frontier</u>, Harvester-Wheatsheaf, London.

Baumol W J & Blinder A S, (1991), <u>Economics: Principles and Policy</u>, Harcourt Brace Jovanovich, London.

Beckerman W, (1974), <u>In Defense of Economic Growth</u>, Jonathan Cape, London.

Beckerman W, (1991), 'Global Warming: A Sceptical Economic Assessment', in <u>Helm (1991)</u>.

Begg D, Fischer S & Dornbusch R, (1991), <u>Economics</u>, McGraw Hill, London.

Bell D, (1981), Models and Reality in Economic Discourse, in <u>Bell & Kristol (1981)</u>.

Bell D & Kristol I (eds.), (1981), <u>The Crisis in Economic Theory</u>, Basic Books, New York.

Bell P & Cleaver H, (1982), 'Marx's Crisis Theory as a Theory of Class Struggle', in <u>Research in Political Economy</u>, Vol 5.

Blaug M, (1975), <u>The Cambridge Revolution: Success or Failure?</u>, Institute of Economic Affairs, London.

Bleaney M, (1985), <u>The Rise and Fall of Keynesian Economics</u>, Macmillan, London.

Boggs C, (1976), <u>Gramsci's Marxism</u>, Pluto, London.

Bryan R, (1985), 'Monopoly in Marxist Method', in <u>Capital and Class</u>, No 26.

Burke J, (1985), <u>The Day the Universe Changed</u>, British Broadcasting Corporation, London.

Burkitt B, (1984), <u>Radical Political Economy</u>, Wheatsheaf, Brighton.

Buzan B, (1974), <u>Use Your Head</u>, British Broadcasting Corporation, London.

Caldwell B, (1982), <u>Beyond Positivism: Economic Methodology in the Twentieth Century</u>, George Allen and Unwin, London.

Campbell M, Hardy M & Healey N (eds.), (1989), <u>Controversy in Applied Economics</u>, Harvester-Wheatsheaf, London.

Canterbury E & Burkhardt R, (1983), 'What Do We Mean by Asking Whether Economics is a Science', in <u>Eichner (1983)</u>.

Capital and Class, (1986), <u>Competition and Monopoly</u>, a complete issue of <u>Capital and Class</u>, No 30, Conference of Socialist Economists, London.

Capra F, (1982), <u>The Turning Point</u>, Flamingo, London.

Carvalho F, (1992), <u>Mr Keynes and the Post Keynesians</u>, Edward Elgar, Aldershot.

Castells M, (1980), <u>The Economic Crisis and American Society</u>, Princeton University Press, Princeton.

Chalmers A, (1982), <u>What is this Thing Called Science?</u>, Open University Press, Milton Keynes.

Chamberlain E H, (1933), <u>The Theory of Monopolistic Competition</u>, Harvard University Press, Cambridge Mass.

Chrystal K A & Price S, (1994), <u>Controversies in Macroeconomics</u>, Harvester-Wheatsheaf, London.

Clarke S, (1982), <u>Marx, Marginalism and Modern Sociology</u>, Macmillan, London.

Cleaver H, (1979), <u>Reading Capital Politically</u>, Harvester, Brighton.

Coates D & Hillard J (eds.), (1986), <u>The Economic Decline of Modern Britain</u>, Wheatsheaf, Brighton.

Coates D & Hillard J (eds.), (1987), <u>The Economic Revival of Modern Britain</u>, Edward Elgar, Aldershot.

Colander D, (1988), 'The Evolution of Keynesian Economics: From Keynesian to New Classical to New Keynesian', in Hamouda & Smithin (1988a).

Colclough C, (1982), 'Lessons from the Development Debate for Western Economic Policy', in Foreign Affairs, Vol 58.

Cole K, (1993), The Intellectual Parameters of the Real World, Discussion Paper No 234, School of Development Studies, University of East Anglia, Norwich.

Cole K, Cameron J and Edwards C, (1983), Why Economists Disagree, Longman, London.

Cole K, Cameron J and Edwards C, (1991) (2nd edn.), Why Economists Disagree, Longman, London.

Cole K & Yaxley I, (1991), The Dialectics of Socialism, Discussion Paper No 220, School of Development Studies, University of East Anglia, Norwich.

Collective Design (eds.), (1985), Nice Work If You Can Get It: the socially useful production debate, Spokesman, Nottingham.

Colletti L, (1972), 'Some Comments on Marx's Theory of Value', in Schwartz (1977).

Conquest R, (1972), Lenin, Fontana, London.

Cox R, (1981), 'Social Forces, States and World Orders: beyond international relations theory', in Journal of International Studies: Millenium, Vol 10, No 2.

Craven J, (1984), Introduction to Economics, Blackwell, Oxford.

Cullenberg S, (1994), The Falling Rate of Profit, Pluto, London.

Dasgupta P, (1991), The Environment as a Commodity, in Helm (1991).

David W L, (1988), Political Economy of Economic Policy, Praeger, New York.

Dean M, (1993), Will it be tax-man or axe-man?, in Guardian, 11 September 1993.

Denzin N K, (1992), Whose Cornerville Is It Anyway?, in Journal of Contemporary Ethnography, Vol 21, No 1.

Diesing P, (1982), Science and Ideology in the Policy Sciences, Aldine, New York.

Ditch J, (1991), 'The Undeserving Poor: Unemployed People, Then and Now', in Loney, Bocock, Clarke, Cochrane, Graham & Wilson (1991).

Dolan E & Lindsey D, (1988), Economics, Dreyden Press, Chicago.

Donaldson P & Farquhas J, (1988), Understanding the British Economy, Penguin, Harmondsworth.

Dragsted A (ed.), (1976), Value: Studies by Marx, New Park, London.

Earl P E, (1983), 'A Behavioural Theory of Economics', in Eichner (1983).

Eichner A S (ed.), (1979), A Guide to Post Keynesian Economics, Macmillan, London.

Eichner A S, (1978), The Macrodynamics of Advanced Market Economies, Sharpe, London.

Eichner A S (ed.), (1983), Why Economics is Not Yet a Science, Sharpe, Armonk (NY).

Eichner A S, (1983a), 'Why Economics is Not Yet a Scienne', in Journal of Economic Issues, Vol 17, No 2.

Engels F, (1970), Socialism: Utopian and Scientific, Progress Publishers, Moscow.

Engels F, (1977), Principles of Communism, Foreign Languages Press, Peking.

Erlandson D A, Harris E L, Skipper B L & Allen S D, (1993), Doing Naturalistic Inquiry, Sage, London.

Fine B (ed.), (1986), The Value Dimension, Routledge and Kegan Paul, London.

Fine B & Harris L, (1979), Rereading Capital, Macmillan, London.

Fine B & Harris L, (1985), The Peculiarities of the British Economy, Lawrence and Wishart, London.

Forbes I & Smith S (eds.), (1983), Politics and Human Nature, Frances Pinter, London.

Fox K A, (1968), Intermediate Economic Statistics, Wiley, New York.

Freidman M, (1953), Essays in Positive Economics, Chicago University Press, Chicago.

Freidman M, (1956), 'The Quantity Theory of Money - A Restatement', in Freidman (1956a).

Freidman M (ed.), (1956a), Studies in the Quantity Theory of Money, University of Chicago Press, Chicago.

Freidman M, (1968), 'The Role of Monetary Policy', in <u>American Economic Review</u>, Vol 58.

Friedman M, (1970), <u>The Counter-Revolution in Monetary Theory</u>, Institute of Economic Affairs, London.

Freidman M, (1974), <u>Monetary Correction</u>, Institute of Economic Affairs, London.

Freidman M & R, (1980), <u>Free to Choose</u>, Penguin, Harmondsworth

Frisch R, (1950), 'Alfred Marshall's Theory of Value', in <u>Townsend (1971)</u>, originally published in the <u>Quarterly Journal of Economics</u>, Vol 64.

Galbraith J K & Salinger N, (1981), <u>Almost Everyone's Guide to Economics</u>, Penguin, Harmondsworth.

Gee J A, (1991), 'The Neoclassical School', in <u>Mair & Miller (1991)</u>.

Glass J & Johnson W, (1989), <u>Economics: Progression, Stagnation or Degeneration</u>, Harvester, London.

Glyn A and Sutcliffe B, (1972), <u>British Capitalism, Workers and the Profits Squeeze</u>, Penguin, Harmondsworth.

Godley W & Cripps F, (1983), <u>Macroeconomics</u>, Fontana, London.

Graham D & Clarke P, (1986), <u>The New Enlightenment</u>, Macmillan, London.

Gray A & Thompson A E, (1980), <u>The Development of Economic Doctrine</u>, Longman, London.

Guba E G (ed.), (1990), <u>The Paradigm Dialog</u>, Sage, Newbury Park Calif.

Hahn F, (1984), <u>Equilibrium and Macroeconomics</u>, MIT Press, Boston.

Hall R E & Taylor J B, (1991), <u>Macroeconomics</u>, Norton, New York.

Hamouda O F & Smithin J N (eds.), (1988a), <u>Keynes and Public Policy After Fifty Years: Economics and Policy</u>, Edward Elgar, Aldershot.

Hamouda O F & Smithin J N (eds.), (1988b), <u>Keynes and Public Policy After Fifty Years: Theories and Method</u>, Edward Elgar, Aldershot.

Hansen A, (1953), <u>A Guide to Keynes</u>, McGraw Hill, New York.

Harbour W, (1982), <u>The Foundations of Conservative Thought</u>, University of Notre Dame Press, London.

Harcourt G C, (1972), <u>Some Cambridge Controversies in the Theory of Capital</u>, Cambridge University Press, Cambridge.

Harcourt G C & Laing N F (eds.), (1971), <u>Capital and Growth</u>, Penguin, Harmondsworth.

Hardwick P, Khan B & Langmead J, (1982), <u>An Introduction to Modern Economics</u>, Longman, London.

Hardwick P, Khan B & Langmead J, (1994) (4th edn.), <u>An Introduction to Modern Economics</u>, Longman, London.

Harrigan F and McGregor P, (1991), 'The Macroeconomics of the Chicago School', in <u>Mair & Miller (1991)</u>.

Harris N, (1983), <u>Of Bread and Guns</u>, Penguin, Harmondsworth.

Harvey D, (1982), <u>The Limits to Capital</u>, Blackwell, Oxford.

Healey N, (1989), 'Has Monetarism Failed?', in <u>Campbell, Hardy & Healey (1989)</u>.

Helm D (ed.), (1991), <u>Economic Policy Towards the Environment</u>, Blackwell, Oxford.

Helm D and Pearce D, (1991), 'Economic Policy Towards the Environment: An Overview', in <u>Helm (1991)</u>.

Heyer P, (1982), <u>Nature, Human Nature and Society</u>, Greenwood Press, Westport Conn.

Hicks J R, (1935), <u>Value and Capital</u>, Cambridge University Press, Cambridge.

Hicks J R, (1937), 'Mr Keynes and the Classics, a suggested interpretation', in <u>Econometrica</u>, Vol 5.

Hunt E K, (1977), 'The Ideological Foundations of Welfare Economics', in <u>Schwartz (1977)</u>.

Irvin G, (1978), <u>Modern Cost-Benefit Methods</u>, Macmillan, London.

Jevons W S, (1970), <u>The Theory of Political Economy</u>, Penguin, Harmondsworth, (edition edited by R D Collinson Black).

Kaldor N, (1982), <u>The Scourge of Monetarism</u>, Oxford University Press, Oxford.

Katouzian A, (1980), _Ideology and Method in Economics_, New York University Press, New York.

Keegan W, (1984), _Mrs Thatcher's Economic Experiment_, Penguin, Harmondsworth.

Keynes J M, (1936), _The General Theory of Employment, Interest and Money_, Macmillan, London.

Khan H, (1979), _World Economic Development: 1979 and Beyond_, Westview Press, Boulder Col..

Khan H & Wiener A, (1967), _The Year 2000: A Framework for Speculation on the Next Thirty-three Years_, Macmillan, London.

Kreps D, (1990), _A Course in Microeconomic Theory_, Harvester-Wheatsheaf, London.

Kuhn T, (1970), _The Structure of Scientific Revolutions_, University of Chicago Press, Chicago.

Kuttner R, (1985), 'The Poverty of Economics', in _Atlantic Monthly_, February.

Lakatos I, (1970), 'Falsification and the Methodology of Scientific Research Programmes', in _Lakatos & Musgrave (1970)_.

Lakatos I & Musgrave A (eds.), (1970), _Criticism and the Growth of Knowledge_, Cambridge University Press, Cambridge.

Lal D, (1983), _The 'Poverty' of Development Economics_, Institute of Economic Affairs, London.

Lancaster K, (1974), _Introduction to Modern Microeconomics_, Rand McNally, Chicago.

Lancaster K & Lipsey R, (1956), The General Theory of the Second Best, in _Review of Economic Studies_, December.

Latsis S (ed.), (1976), _Method and Appraisal in Economics_, Cambridge University Press, Cambridge.

Lavoie M, (1992), _Foundations of Post-Keynesian Economic Analysis_, Edward Elgar, Aldershot.

Layard R (ed.), (1972), _Cost Benefit Analysis: Selected Readings_, Penguin, Harmondsworth.

Leijonhufvud A, (1976), 'Schools, Revolutions and Research Programmes in Economic Theory', in _Latsis (1976)_.

Lenin V I, (1963), _Collected Works_ Vol 1, Progress Publishers, Moscow.

Lenin V I, (1969), _The State and Revolution_, Progress Publishers, Moscow.

Levacic R & Rebmann A, (1982), _Macroeconomics: An Introduction to Keynesian-Neoclassical Controversies_, Macmillan, London.

Levine D P, (1977), _Economic Studies: contributions to a critique of economic theory_, Routledge and Kegan Paul, London.

Levins R & Lewontin R, (1985), _The Dialectical Biologist_, Harvard University Press, Cambridge Mass..

Lincoln Y S & Guba E G, (1985), _Naturalistic Inquiry_, Sage, Beverley Hills Calif..

Littlechild S, (1978), _The Fallacy of the Mixed Economy_, Institute of Economic Afairs, London.

Loney M, Bobock R, Clarke J, Cochrane A, Graham P & Wilson M (eds.), (1991), _The State or the Market_, Sage, London.

Love J, (1991), 'The Orthodox Keynesian School', in _Mair & Miller (1991)_.

McLellan D (ed.), (1983), _Marx: The First 100 Years_, Fontana, London.

McNally D, (1993), _Against the Market_, Verso, London.

Magee B, (1975), _Popper_, Fontana/Collins, London.

Mair D & Miller A (eds.), (1991), _A Modern Guide to Economic Thought_, Edward Elgar, Aldershot.

Mandel E, (1978), _The Second Slump_, Verso, London.

Mandel E, (1983), 'Economics', in _McLellan (1983)_.

Marshal A, (1947), _Principles of Economics_, Macmillan, London.

Marx K, (1936), _The Poverty of Philosophy_, Lawrence and Wishart, London.

Marx K, (1950), _Marx and Engels Selected Works_ Vol 1 [18th Brumaire], Lawrence and Wishart, London.

Marx K, (1970), _Critique of Hegel's Philosophy of Right_, Routledge, London.

Marx K, (1972), _Capital_ Vol III, Lawrence and Wishart, London.

Marx K, (1972a) _Critique of the Gotha Programmme_, Foreign Languages Press, Peking.

Marx K, (1973), _Grundrisse_, Penguin, Harmondsworth.

Marx K, (1973a), _The Economic and Philosophic Manuscripts of 1844_, Lawrence and Wishart, London

Marx K, (1974), _Capital_ Vol I, Lawrence and Wishart, London.

Marx K, (1974a), _Capital_ Vol II, Lawrence and Wishart, London.

Marx K, (1975), _Wages, Price and Profit_, Foreign Languages Press, Peking.

Marx K, (1976), _A Contribution to the Critique of Political Economy_, Lawrence and Wishart, London.

Marx K & Engels F, (1974), _The German Ideology_, Lawrence and Wishart, London.

Mattick P Jnr, (1986), _Social Knowledge_, Routledge and Kegan Paul, London.

May B, (1981), _The Third World Calamity_, Routledge and Kegan Paul, London.

Mellos K, (1988), _Perspectives on Ecology_, Macmillan, London.

Menger C, (1960), _Problems of Economics and Sociology_, University of Illinois Press, Chicago.

Midgely M, (1978), _Beast and Man_, Harvester, Brighton.

Moggridge D E, (1976), _Keynes_, Fontana/Collins, London.

Mulkay M, (1979), _Science and the Sociology of Knowledge_, George Allen and Unwin, London.

Nell E J (ed.), (1984), _Free Market Conservatism_, George Allen and Unwin, London.

Nell E & Azarchs A, (1984), 'Monetarism: Conservative Policy and Monetary Theory', in _Nell (1984)_.

O'Connor J, (1984), _Accumulation Crisis_, Blackwell, Oxford.

O'Connor J, (1987), _The Meaning of Crisis_, Blackwell, Oxford.

Ollman B, (1993), _Dialectical Investigations_, Routledge, London.

Ormerod P, (1994), _The Death of Economics_, Faber, London.

Pearce D, (1981), _The Social Appraisal of Projects: a Text in Cost-Benefit Analysis_, Macmillan, London.

Pearce D, (1991), 'An Economic Appraisal of Saving the Tropical Forests', in _Helm (1991)_.

Pearce D, Barbier E & Markandya A, (1990), _Sustainable Development_, Earthscan, London.

Pheby J, (1988), _Methodology and Economics: a critical introduction_, Macmillan, London.

Pheby J (ed.), (1989), _New Directions in Post Keynesian Economics_, Edwards Elgar, Aldershot.

Phillips A W, (1958), 'The Relation Between Unemployment and the Rate of Change in Money Wage Rates in the UK 1957-1986', in _Economica_, Vol XXV.

Pigou A, (1920), _The Economics of Welfare_, Macmillan, London.

Popper K R, (1959), _The Logic of Scientific Discovery_, Hutchinson, London.

Popper K R, (1962), _The Open Society and its Enemies_, Vol 2, Routledge, London.

Robbins L, (1984), _An Essay on the Nature and Significance of Economic Science_, Macmillan, London.

Robinson J, (1933), _The Economics of Imperfect Competition_, Macmillan, London.

Robinson J, (1971), _Economic Heresies_, Macmillan, London.

Roll E, (1973), _A History of Economic Thought_, Faber, London.

Romer D, (1993), 'The New Keynesian Synthesis', in _The Journal of Economic Perspectives_, Vol 7, No 1.

Rose S, (1984), 'Introduction', in _Rose & Appignanesi (1984)_.

Rose S, (1984a), 'The Limits to Science', in Rose and Appignanesi (1984).

Rose S & Appignanesi L (eds.), (1984), Science and Beyond, Blackwell, Oxford.

Rose S, Kamin B & Lewontin R, (1984), Not in Our Genes, Penguin, Harmondsworth.

Rostow W W, (1960), The Stages of Economic Growth, Cambridge University Press, Cambridge.

Routh G, (1975), The Origin of Economic Ideas, Macmillan, London.

Sawyer M C, (1989), The Challenge of Radical Political Economy, Harvester-Wheatsheaf, Hemel Hempstead.

Schotter A, (1990), Free Market Economics, Sage, London.

Schwartz J (ed.), (1977), The Subtle Anatomy of Capitalism, Goodyear, Santa Monica.

Seers D, (1983), The Political Economy of Nationalism, Oxford University Press, Oxford.

Semmler P, (1982), Theories of Competition and Monopoly, in Capital and Class, No 18.

Sender J & Smith S, (1988), The Development of Capitalism in Africa, Methuen, London.

Sloman J, (1991), Economics, Harvester-Wheatsheaf and Prentice Hall, London and New York.

Smith D, (1987), The Rise and Fall of Monetarism, Penguin, Harmondsworth.

Smith S, (1983), 'Introduction', in Forbes & Smith (1983).

So A, (1990), Social Change and Development, Sage, London.

Sraffa P, (1960), Production of Commodities by Means of Commodities, Cambridge University Press, Cambridge.

Stark W, (1944), A History of Economics in its Relation to Social Development, Kegan Paul Trench & Trubner, London.

Steedman I, (1977), Marx After Sraffa, Verso, London.

Steedman I & Sweezy P (eds.), (1981), The Value Controversy, Verso, London.

Stigler G, (1965), Essays in the History of Economics, University of Chicago Press, Chicago.

Sweezy P, (1939), Demand Under Conditions of Oligopoly, in Journal of Political Economy, Vol 47.

Thompson E P, (1978), The Poverty of Theory and Other Essays, Merlin, London.

Tieterberg T, (1991), 'Economic Instruments for Environmental Regulation', in Helm (1991).

Townsend H (ed.), (1971), Price Theory, Penguin, Harmondsworth.

UEASU, (1982), Alternative Prospectus 1982-83, University of East Anglia Students' Union, Norwich.

Vaillancourt P, (1986), When Marxists Do Research, Greenwood, Westport Conn.

Vasquez A S, (1977), The Philosophy of Praxis, Merlin, London.

Vines D, Maciejowski J & Meade J E, (1983), Demand Management, George Allen and Unwin, London.

Ward B, (1979), The Ideal Worlds of Economics, Basic Books, New York.

Weeks J, (1981), Capital and Exploitation, Edward Arnold, London.

Wheelock J, (1983), Competition in the Marxist Tradition, in Capital and Class, No 21.

Wilber C, (1979), 'Empirical Verification and Theory Selection: The Keynesian-Monetarist Debate' in Journal of Economic Affairs, Vol 13, No 4.

Wright E O, (1975), 'Alternative Perspectives in the Marxist Theory of Accumulation and Crisis', in Insurgent Sociologist, Fall 1975.

INDEX

The **UNDERSTANDING** Series

Edited by Ken Cole

Knowledge and understanding continually change. People's interpretations of how the world functions evolve with changing experience and there is always a conflict of ideas between those eager to embrace and foster change and those wedded to the status quo and to tradition.

Distinct perspectives on explanation and understanding implicitly reflect different political interests. This book explores such ideological battles in the realm of economics, but similar approaches to understanding underlie conflicting ideas in other intellectual disciplines and subjects.

The **UNDERSTANDING** series of books explores parallel approaches across a broad spectrum of knowledge, examining the hidden political and ideological agenda behind arguments, theories and concepts and providing students with a clear, understandable grasp of cross-disciplinary perspectives on understanding.

Each volume in the series analyses competing perspectives, presenting the material in the form of 'flow charts'.

ALREADY PUBLISHED

UNDERSTANDING ECONOMICS
- KEN COLE

FORTHCOMING

UNDERSTANDING WORLD AFFAIRS
- RALPH PETTMAN

UNDERSTANDING SOCIAL POLICY
- TOM BURDEN

SOMERSET
Tales

SOMERSET
Tales
Shocking & Surprising

JACK WILLIAM SWEET

AMBERLEY

To my family and to my many ancestors who lived, loved and passed away in this
County of Somerset – the Land of Summer.

O' who would trust this world or prize what's in it,
That gives and takes and chops and changes every minit.

An epitaph at Saint George's church, Bicknoller, of a member of the Slocombe family,
dated 1649.

Front cover illustration: 'A peep into Ilchester Prison' (from Hunt's Investigations, April 1821).
Reproduced in *The Western Gazette Almanac and Diary 1913*.

All the illustrations and images in this book are taken from the author's collection.

Every effort has been made to contact copyright holders, but in the event that you have
been overlooked, please get in touch so that appropriate credit can be included in future editions.

First published 2011

Amberley Publishing
The Hill, Stroud
Gloucestershire, GL5 4EP

www.amberleybooks.com

Copyright © Jack Sweet, 2011

The right of Jack Sweet to be identified as the Author
of this work has been asserted in accordance with the
Copyrights, Designs and Patents Act 1988.

British Library Cataloguing in Publication Data.
A catalogue record for this book is available from the British Library.

ISBN 978 1 4456 0651 4

Typesetting and Origination by Amberley Publishing.
Printed in Great Britain.

Contents

Acknowledgements

My many thanks to the staffs of the Yeovil Reference and Somerset Studies Libraries, and the Heritage Team of South Somerset District Council, for their help during the preparation of this book.

My thanks to Mr M. Shorter, ARPS, for photographic help and advice.

Thanks also to the National Archives, Kew, Richmond, for permission to quote extracts from Document WO71/677, relating to the court martial of Private Ernest Horler.

My great appreciation and thanks to Lynne Fernquest, the editor of the *Western Gazette*, for permission to reproduce the articles acknowledged in the sources.

And finally, a very special thank you to my wife Margaret for her great patience and tolerance.

About the Author

Jack Sweet was born in Yeovil and has lived most of his life in the town and county of many of his ancestors. An old boy of the former Yeovil School, he joined the staff of the Yeovil Borough Council on leaving the Royal Air Force in 1958. After working as a professional local government administrator, he took early retirement following thirty-four years' service with the Borough Council and its successor, the South Somerset District Council.

Jack has a great love of history, and for many years has been writing articles for local publications, including the former *Yeovil Times* and the *Western Gazette*. In 1997, his first book, *Shocking Somerset Murders of the Nineteenth Century,* was published by Somerset Books, followed in 1999 by *Shocking and Surprising Somerset Stories* and *More Shocking and Surprising Stories* in 2002, both by Somerset Books. In 2002, Jack and Robin Ansell compiled *Yeovil Then and Now* for Tempus and in 2009, again with Robin Ansell, compiled *Yeovil Through Time* for Amberley Publishing. *Yeovil's Years* is Jack's latest book, published by Amberley in 2010.

In addition to his writing, Jack is interested in local and family history, photography, and has travelled widely in Europe and visited many former battlefields from South Africa to the Crimea, via the United States of America and North West Europe. He is married to Margaret and they have three daughters, two grandsons and a granddaughter.

Introduction

This is my third book on the theme of *Shocking and Surprising Somerset Stories*, but I have extended the contents to include some strange tales with a touch of the unknown. My new book of *Somerset Tales – Shocking and Strange* spans the one hundred and fifty years from 1800 to 1950, and from a time when witchcraft could still loom large in the minds of town and country folk to the fatal crash of a Spitfire fighter aircraft. Once again I tell of events and personal stories which could have shocked, surprised and perhaps sent a shiver down the backs of the folk who lived in this, not so quiet, Land of Summer. So please read on, and I hope you will enjoy this modest work as much as I enjoyed writing it!

Upholders of Somerset law and order – five constables of the Yeovil Division of the Somerset Constabulary during the early 1900s. From left to right: Number 55 – Constable Percy Powis; Number 77 – Constable Albert Culliford; Number 274 – Constable Arthur Brice; Number 287 – Constable Summers; Number 288 – Constable Stevens. (With thanks to the Somerset Archives and Local Studies Service for supplying this information.)

A Sad Death by Drowning

Mary Grace Hewitt, nineteen years of age, was described as 'A very spirited, self-willed girl, but of an amiable disposition, and beloved by all who knew her.' She was an apprentice to Messrs Chapman, drapers, of Taunton. Her widowed mother lived at Sampford Peverell, but tragically she drowned in the River Tone at Firepool on a warm summer Wednesday evening, 21 June 1871. What began as a jolly row on the river with four young friends ended in tragedy when their small boat sank in eight feet of cold, dark water.

The events of that fateful summer evening were recounted at the inquest into the death of Mary Grace Hewitt, which initially opened on Friday 23 June at the George Inn, where the coroner and his jury viewed the body of the young woman which 'appeared as calm as in life and having a smile on the countenance, fitting emblems surrounding her narrow bed, the choicest flowers being strewn upon her'. The proceedings were then adjourned and jury proceeded to Firepool, where they inspected the fatal spot and the boat, before moving on to the Railway Hotel to resume the inquest.

The first witness was Charles Bartlett, who stated that he resided at Firepool, where he was the lock-keeper and proprietor of rowing boats and canoes for hire. He said that at about a quarter to ten on the Wednesday evening, Miss Hewitt, in company with three young men, Messrs Parris, Batten and Bright, and the Misses Hellings and Wickenden, had arrived at Firepool. Mr Parris had asked to hire a boat, and although it was getting dark Mr Bartlett had let them have a 'dinghy', which they boarded from the landing place. Mr Batten and Miss Wickenden sat in the after part of the boat, Miss Hellings on the next seat and Miss Hewitt on the one at the front. With all four seated, Mr Parris paid the fee, but as the boat started off he had stepped into the stern behind Mr Batten and Miss Wickenden. Miss Hewitt and Miss Hellings had taken an oar each and began to row steadily up the river towards the town.

Charles Bartlett stated that shouts and screams had brought him racing back to the landing place, from where to his horror he could see in the failing light the boat upturned about 30 yards away in the middle of the river and several young people struggling in the water. Stripping off his waistcoat and cap, he jumped in and, reaching the boat, righted it. As he did so, Miss Hellings surfaced beside him and he caught hold of her neck, placed her chin of the side of the boat and, still holding her, began to guide the craft towards to river bank. The lock-keeper recalled that when they were within a yard of safety, the young lady had slipped back under, and in the struggle which followed she had gone down twice more and would have perished but for the help of a man standing on the bank. After Miss Hellings had been lifted onto the bank, he was told that the other young people were accounted for and he helped carry the half-drowned young lady to the nearby Sun Inn, where she was attended to.

Following a change into dry clothes, Charles Bartlett stated that he had gone back to the river, where a crowd had collected on both banks, and was told by Police Constable Perry that one of the young ladies was missing. Despite his enquiries, no one knew who it was because it was assumed that the young people involved had left the scene. However, Mr Chapman, the draper, arrived and told him that he had heard of the accident but Miss Hewitt had not returned home. With this information to hand, Charles Bartlett stated that with a man by name of Joe Virgin he had taken a boat out and with the aid of a boat hook soon located a body, which was recovered and identified as Mary Grace Hewitt.

In reply to a question from one of the jurors, Charles Bartlett replied that the boat was only suitable for four persons and suggested that the effect of Mr Parris stepping into the boat was sufficient to upset or swamp it. Indeed his wife had said to Mr Parris when he had got in that he had better get out or it would get upset. Either Mr Parris or Mr Batten had replied that they would not; they would be alright, and if they got upset they would be able to scramble out somehow. Furthermore, he had told the party that if they took the boat away it was their responsibility and if they got upset not to blame him.

The next witness was Thomas Watkin Parris, a chemist's assistant, who told the jury that he had left his shop in company with fellow assistant Frederick Bright, intending to go for a row on the river at Firepool, and as they walked along Fore Street, they met Henry Batten, who agreed to join them. Shortly after, they met up with the three young ladies, who accepted their offer of a row on the river, and the party walked down to Firepool. When a boat became free, Henry Batten and the three young ladies had got in, and after paying the lock-keeper, he had boarded at the stern and they pushed off. As the boat moved away, Thomas Parris recalled hearing Mrs Bartlett say to her husband that he had better not let them go, to which he had replied that if they pulled steady they would be alright.

With Miss Hewitt and Miss Hellings rowing, they had travelled less than 30 yards when Mr Batten became concerned that the boat was sitting very low in the water and suggested than they turn back. Thomas Parris recalled that no sooner had the words left his mouth than water began to pour over the stern and the boat started to sink. The boat suddenly tipped and, shouting for help, they were all thrown into the river. As it was nearly dark he could not see what was happening to the others, but as he began to swim for the bank Miss Wickenden surfaced and grabbed his right arm and legs. He managed to struggle to the bank with the young lady still holding him and she was helped out. Thomas Parris stated that, despite being exhausted, wet and cold, he remained on the scene to see what he could do to help and was told that Henry Batten and Miss Hellings had been saved, but no one knew the whereabouts of Miss Hewitt.

Replying to a question from a juror, Thomas Parris denied hearing the lock-keeper tell them that they went at their own risk but argued that Mr Bartlett had said that if they pulled steadily they would be alright.

A peaceful boating scene on the River Tone is shown in this early postcard, but an evening's row near this spot in June 1871 ended in tragedy.

Thomas Batten, a baker's son, was the next witness, and confirmed his friend's account up until the boat sank. He had been in the middle of the three young ladies and when they had caught hold of him they all sank. He felt one of the young ladies let go but the other two still held him tight. Thomas Batten stated that somehow he had managed to struggle free but when two of the young ladies grabbed his coat tail they all went down again. He lost count of the number of times they sank and then struggled back to the surface, but finally all three reached the side of the boat. However, as they seized it and tried to get in, the boat turned over and they were back in the water. One of the young ladies then let go and disappeared and shortly after so did the other. By now he was completely exhausted but as he struggled towards the river bank someone held out a long pole which he grabbed and was hauled to safety. Thomas Batten stated that he made his way to the Sun Inn, where Miss Hellings was thereby shortly after brought in and was revived, followed later by Thomas Parris. Henry Batten stated that he had heard no warnings from Mr or Mrs Bartlett.

The next witness was Frederick Bright, who stated that he had seen his friend Thomas Parris pay and get in the boat when the others were seated, and had turned down his invitation to join the party. He had heard Mrs Bartlett ask her husband not to let them go but did not think the lock-keeper's reply that they did so at their own risk could have been heard by his friends. However, Frederick Bright confirmed that he had heard Charles Bartlett call out that if they kept the oars steady they would be alright. He further stated that he could not recall anyone in the boat saying that if they sank they would be able to scramble out.

Charles Bartlett was recalled and swore that he was certain that he had told the party that they had better get out but if they took the boat out it would be at their own risk. Asked why he had allowed five persons to get into the boat when he knew it could not carry so many, the lock-keeper replied that Mr Parris had jumped into it. This was denied by Thomas Parris and Henry Batten, but Charles Bartlett continued and said that Mr Parris had jumped in when the boat was starting and he had heard him call to Mr Bright to join them.

Thomas Parris was recalled and confirmed that they had all had called to Frederick Bright to join them, but he had refused, and the boat was not in motion when he stepped in.

At this stage, the coroner stated that if the jury desired he would take evidence from Miss Hellings and Miss Wickenden, but if they were satisfied with the evidence so far presented, he would rather spare the young ladies' feelings. The jury confirmed that they were perfectly satisfied with the evidence, but before asking them to return a verdict the *Taunton Courier* reported that the coroner observed:

> There could be not be the slightest doubt but that the unfortunate young woman died from drowning by the sinking of a boat. It would be for the jury to say whether the accident happened through the carelessness or negligence of anybody, or whether it was the result simply of an accident. The boat certainly was not fitted to carry so many persons. The persons in the boat acted properly, and the young ladies themselves were perfectly calm and collected. The boat, however, capsized, and it was unfortunate to say the least, that Bartlett should have allowed so large a number to get into it, and he ought not to have done so, knowing that it was over-laden. After the accident had happened he did all he could to save life, for which he deserved great credit. The conduct of Mr Batten, too, was especially deserving of praise, and by his presence of mind, his own and Miss Hellings' lives were saved. He only wished there was a law to prevent those boats being used, for they were decidedly dangerous in the hands of unskilled persons. When the jury returned their legal verdict, they might make what remarks they chose, and he trusted the attention of the Board of Health would be drawn to the subject of licensing boats. The boats used were full of danger and those persons who were in the boat were greatly to blame for overloading it.

The jury returned the verdict that Mary Grace Hewitt was 'Accidentally Drowned', and appended a rider that the boat was overloaded, the construction was such as to be dangerous except to persons experienced in the management of boats, and the attention of the Board of Health ought to be called to the necessity of licensing pleasure boats for hire within their jurisdiction.

Violent Death in Crewkerne

The past could be a very violent place and reading the spoken words can give a fascinating glimpse back to a time quite often so different from ours, and yet in some ways quite familiar. The trial for the manslaughter of a young woman called Jane Holland, by Charles Savidge, in the Greyhound Inn at Crewkerne in 1852, is a good example.

Briefly, the facts are that thirty-seven-year-old Charles Savidge (also spelt Savage), a butcher from Hinton St George, and Jane Holland, with whom he was cohabiting, were drinking in the Greyhound during the evening of Tuesday 26 October 1852. Slightly the worse for drink, Jane began flirting with a couple of customers, with the result that Charles Savidge lost his temper, pushed Jane over a table and beat her about the face. The landlord, William Bishop, quickly removed Jane from the bar and into his kitchen, leaving Savidge arguing with the two customers who had tried to prevent the assault. A fight started, which resulted in Savidge being thrown out of the pub, and he made his way back to widow Elizabeth Holland's house, where he was living with her daughter Jane.

Let Elizabeth Holland, in her words reported in the *Western Flying Post*, describe what happened next when she recounted the events of that evening before the coroner at the inquest into the death of Jane Holland:

The deceased is my daughter. On Tuesday evening last, she left my house at half past six. I do not know where she went to, she came home at half past eleven o'clock and said 'Mother, mother open the door for the rogue have almost killed me,' and before I could open the door, she burst the door open, and before I could lock the door Savidge came into the house. I said 'Savidge, whatever is the matter', he looked up at me and said 'look and see what a face the b--- w--- have given me'. He then struck her over the chair that she was sitting in. I said you go and pick your clothes up for here you sha'nt stop. He told me to go and pick it up for him. I said I sha'nt for you know where it is. He picked up the candle and picked up his clothes, and when he came down he said you b--- w--- I never killed my child. My daughter then said nor didn't I and nobody can say so. She jumped up and tore her frock off her back and threw it on the floor. She said now I'll let thee know whether I killed my child or not, and she catched him hold by the hair of his head with both hands. I said to her, Jane, my dear child, do thee let go of his hair. I then unclenched her hands from his hair. He said if you catch hold of my hair again, I will knock thy head off. I pulled her away from him and said Jane don't you go near him any more. He then went round me and struck her over my left shoulder and knocked her down on the floor.

The Market Square, Crewkerne, in the mid-nineteenth century. Charles Savidge was charged with the manslaughter of his partner, Jane Holland, in the town on 26 October 1852.

She laid about two or three minutes on the floor groaning. I went and lifted her up. I then saw blood. She said – Lord have mercy on us, do let me lie down. Savidge then took her on his knee on the chair and asked me to fetch some water. After I had washed the blood off her head, I asked him to carry her up stairs. He then sat down in a chair with her on his knee and she got very sick. I told him to lay her down on the bed and he done so. My candle got very short and I went down for some more. He followed me downstairs and tied up his clothes. I heard some groans upstairs, I said, oh dear, she got the fits. I ran upstairs and he followed me. He took her up in his arms and told me to fetch some water and he washed her face, he looked up and said to me do fetch somebody for she is a dead woman. Then I went and called Ann Furzer, and she came in and she was quite dead in his arms. I said you murderous rogue, you have murdered my child. I then called the woman again, and when she came she said, Charles what has thee done, thee has killed the woman. He said I have done nothing. She then went for the doctor, Mr. Morse and Mr. Webber attended.

Mr John Webber, the surgeon, testified that Jane Holland had been a healthy young women and the cause of death was a clot on the brain produced by her skull coming into 'contact with some hard body'.

Charles Savidge was sent for trial at the Somerset Assizes, and six months later in April 1853 he was found guilty of the manslaughter of Jane Holland, and sentenced to seven years' transportation to Australia.

As the author's late father used to say, 'When the drink's in, the wits are out,' and how true this proved to be for Jane Holland and Charles Savidge one October evening at Crewkerne over a century and a half ago.

Tragedy on the Barnstaple Mail Coach

At about twenty minutes past ten o'clock, on the morning of Saturday 16 August 1828, the Barnstaple mail coach drew up outside the Lion Inn at Wiveliscombe to change the four-horse team. The coachman and guard climbed down to supervise the change of horses, and, with the exception of Mrs Abigail Slowly, who remained on one of the outside seats of the coach, the passengers alighted and went into the hostelry for a quick break.

What happened next was described by John Featherstone, the Surveyor of the Wiveliscombe roads, at the inquest, held a few days later in the Lion Inn, into the death of the said Mrs Abigail Slowly. The witness told the coroner and his jury that he had been standing near the inn when the Barnstaple mail coach arrived and had watched the horses being changed. The two rear wheels of the coach were plugged to hold the vehicle steady as the horses were taken out of their harness and replaced by the fresh team. The horses appeared calm as they were being harnessed, but as one of the inn's two horse-keepers was adjusting the reins, the 'off-leader' of the first pair became restless, and the coachman came forward to quieten the animal. Suddenly, the horses started, but despite the efforts of the horse-keepers and the coachman to hold them, they moved off. The guard's attempt to place the drag shoe in front of the near-side rear wheel failed, the plugs could not hold against the power of the horses, and the coach was away. John Featherstone told the inquest that 'The coachman and the two horse-keepers held on as long as they were able, which was more than halfway down the street, until they were in imminent danger of their lives.' He watched the coach career down the High Street, disappear around the bend, and then he heard the sound of a crash. The witness stated that he had run after the coach and on turning the corner saw it overturned.

Blacksmith John Harris, told the inquest that he saw the coach coming down the High Street at full speed and around the bend. The leading pair of horses broke free from the props of the main bar of the coach, and the vehicle turned over on its side throwing Mrs Slowly from her seat, followed by a large trunk, which fell on the unfortunate lady. John Harris told the inquest that he had found Mrs Slowly lying unconscious under the trunk, which weighed nearly a hundredweight (50 kg), and helped carry her back to the Lion Inn.

The inquest was informed that medical assistance was called and Dr Henry Sully, from Taunton, and his pupil Mr West, had struggled to save the injured lady but to no avail,

High Street, Wiveliscombe.

The horses drawing the Barnstaple mail coach bolted from outside the Lion Hotel, shown here in this early postcard, down the High Street at Wiveliscombe, carrying Mrs Abigail Slowly to her death in 1828.

and she died a few days later. Dr Sully stated that there were marks on Mrs Slowly's chest caused by the blow from the trunk; she had suffered a fractured arm, and a bruised and lacerated eye. He had ascertained that Mrs Slowly had suffered from a chest complaint for some time prior to the accident, and although the blow to her chest was the main cause of death, her decease had been accelerated by the weakness in her lungs.

In his summing up, the coroner told the jury that he was perfectly satisfied from the evidence, that no blame could be attributed to the coachman, guard, horse-keepers, or proprietors of the mail coach, and the jury returned the following verdict:

> The Jury are all unanimously of the opinion that Mrs Abigail Slowly died in consequence of an injury sustained by the overturning of the Barnstaple mail-coach, which happened by mere accident, and without the slightest inattention of the coachman, guard or any other person.

Now followed an age-old legal discussion and decision, namely the levying of a deodand. And what was a deodand? This was an old English law (abolished in 1848) which required any animal or thing causing the death of a human being to be forfeited to the Crown and applied for pious uses – this was the deodand, which over time developed a monetary value. Having concluded the inquest, the coroner pronounced that it would be necessary to levy a deodand, but whether it should be declared on the horses, the mail coach or trunk would be for the jury to decide. James Waldron, the foreman of the jury, quoted an old proverb – 'Whatever moves and strikes one dead, is deodand and forfeited' – and his fellow jurors decided to levy a deodand of one shilling on the trunk, the immediate cause of Mrs Slowly's death.

Shooting Tragedies

Firearms, whether in the hands of the experienced or inexperienced, are very dangerous unless treated with great respect. There was a motto hammered in during the author's limited service in Her Majesty's armed forces that warned, 'Never, never let your gun pointed be at anyone!'

The following three tragic shootings bear out the extreme caution which must be exercised when firearms are present.

Mr Wilfred Keirle of Welham Farm, Charlton Mackrell, climbed up onto the horse-drawn self-binder reaping machine and sat down next to the driver, Mr Herbert Bown. The afternoon of Saturday 25 August 1917 was warm and the reaping had gone well in the oat field by Charlton Lane. The farmer had been shooting rabbits as they ran to escape the reaping machine and, having taken a reasonable bag, he decided to ride back to his farm. Herbert Bown started the horses and set off down the lane. Farmer Keirle placed his double-barrelled shotgun on the bed of the machine, holding the barrels between his legs and resting the muzzles against his stomach as he lit his pipe. Suddenly there was a bang as the shotgun went off and the contents of one barrel of shot tore into Wilfred Keirle's abdomen. The noise startled the two horses, but before Herbert Bown could render assistance to his employer, he had to fight to bring them under control. With the help of Mr Herbert Crossman, one of Mr Keirle's cowmen who had been helping with the reaping, the terribly injured farmer was laid in the shade at the side of the lane, and Dr Ingle was sent for from Somerton.

On receiving the message, Dr Ingle set out for Charlton Mackrell and some twenty minutes later reached the scene, and found the farmer curled up on the grass bank. The doctor packed the gaping wound and Farmer Keirle was conveyed home to Welham Farm, but despite Dr Ingle's best efforts the terrible injuries proved fatal, and Mr Wilfred Keirle passed away the next morning.

At the inquest which followed, the jury were informed that death was caused by haemorrhage and shock, and it was established that both barrels of the gun had been loaded and the hammers cocked. From the evidence it was concluded that the jolting of the machine had caused one of the barrels to be fired with the fatal consequences.

The jury returned a verdict of death from shock following injuries caused by the accidental discharge of a gun, which the deceased was carrying while riding on a reaping machine.

Roland Raymond left his home in Brunswick Street, Yeovil, for a day's rabbiting on 26 August 1922, but tragically would not return alive. Most of the houses shown in this photograph of Brunswick Street were demolished in the 1960s.

A day's rabbiting on Mr Denning's farm at Pavyott's Mill, East Coker, ended in tragedy with the accidental death of a thirty-two-year-old glover, Roland Raymond of Brunswick Street, Yeovil.

Roland was rabbiting with three friends, coal merchants William and Percy Dalymount, and labourer Benjamin Druce, on the afternoon of Saturday 26 August 1922, when, picking up a shotgun, he accidentally shot himself.

At the inquest before the coroner, Mr W. Wintergoode, the first witness was William Dalymount, who testified that the friends had been ferreting for rabbits for about two hours along both sides of a hedgerow, when his brother Percy called out from the other side that there was a rabbit in their net. He had placed his double-barrelled shotgun against the hedge – fully cocked, there being no half-cock – but in the excitement did not put the two hammers down before running around to his brother. William Dalymount stated that the rabbit was caught, the net re-laid, but as he returned he saw Roland pick up the gun by the barrels. His shouted warning that the gun was cocked was immediately followed by a shot and, still holding the gun, the deceased cried out 'Bill, I'm shot!', collapsed, and died within a few moments. Assistance and the police were summoned but nothing could be done. William Dalymount stated that he had used a gun for twenty years, and went shooting nearly every week. To his knowledge, Roland Raymond had never fired a gun and it was not intended that he should touch this one.

The *Western Gazette* reported the following exchange between the coroner and the witness:

The Coroner: Don't you think it was very careless to leave a gun like that?
Witness: Well. May be. But may I ask how many do on the spur of the moment when they are out.

The Coroner: Did you do it very quickly?

Witness: I put the gun against the hedge and had to run.

The Coroner: There was no particular hurry was there; the rabbit would have stayed there.

Witness: It might have got away.

The Coroner: Your idea was to act quickly?

Witness: Yes.

The Coroner: You have done a good deal of rabbit shooting?

Witness: Yes.

The Coroner: You know it is the most dangerous form of sport.

Witness: There is nothing like a bit of sport is there?

The Coroner: But it is, isn't it?

Witness: Yes but I've never had a spill before.

Superintendent Williams, of the Yeovil Police, suggested that the gun might have become entangled in the hedge, and this was the reason the deceased had pulled the gun towards himself. It was possible that a twig had caught the trigger and one barrel was discharged.

Dr Clayton, of West Coker, who had conducted the post mortem, stated that there was a large gaping wound in the deceased's lower abdomen, his clothes were singed, and death had been almost instantaneous.

The verdict was returned that the deceased had died from the effects of a gunshot wound in the stomach, caused accidentally, and the coroner remarked that,

It was an extraordinary thing that greater care was not taken in rabbit-shooting. People seemed to forget the most ordinary precautions when they put down a gun. It was surprising that there were not five times as many accidents. It was by far the most dangerous form of sport.

Roland Raymond left a widow and four young children.

Eighteen years later in the summer of 1940, following the evacuation of the British Expeditionary Force from Dunkirk, there were thousands of armed troops in the country, and even if many of them were experienced in the use of firearms, tragedies were inevitable.

On Tuesday 9 July 1940 an inquest opened at the Yeovil Law Courts, into the death of twenty-one-year-old Driver John Harper of the Royal Army Service Corps, who had died at Houndstone Camp from a gunshot wound in his chest. Witness Driver Davidson told the inquest that he had asked his pal, John Harper, if he knew how to load a rifle after it had been fully cocked. Replying in the negative, Davidson told him it was easy, and was demonstrating the technique when the rifle went off and John Harper fell dead.

The coroner asked Driver Davidson who had taught him this 'silly trick' with the rifle and the witness replied that he had learnt it during his recent service in France.

Summing up, the coroner said that this was a case of 'familiarity breeding contempt'. There was no doubt that the tragedy was an accident but it had been caused by orders being disobeyed. He knew that in the last war men used these kinds of tricks, but it was wrong to do so. A verdict of Accidental Death was recorded.

Witchcraft

It is all too easy in the first decades of the twenty-first century, when we have instant light at the turn of a switch, together with all our modern conveniences, to dismiss the fears and superstitions of our not too distant forbears. In those times, when darkness fell, for most people it was close the doors, put up the shutters or draw the curtains, light a candle or an oil lamp, and keep out whatever was wandering abroad during the night. Witches, spirits, ghosts and spells were thought commonplace. Such fears could lead sometimes to brutal assaults on innocent people, and the contemporary records contain many cases of such attacks, many of which were on elderly women, usually eccentric and living alone.

One such case occurred at Wiveliscombe in November 1822, when Elizabeth Bryant, together with two of her daughters, launched a vicious assault on a seventy-year-old widow by name of Ann Burge after accusing her of bewitching another of her daughters.

The circumstances were revealed at the Somerset Assizes at Taunton in the following March, when the court was told that for some twelve months leading up to the assault, one of Elizabeth Bryant's daughters had been afflicted with fits, and for some reason the mother believed that Ann Burge had bewitched the girl. Elizabeth Bryant had sought the assistance and advice of a 'cunning man' known locally as 'Conjuror' Baker, and following the consultation, she began telling friends and neighbours that Ann Burge had bewitched her daughter. Cunning men and women could be found in many neighbourhoods, especially in the more rural parts of the country, and were often called upon, for a fee, to heal humans and animals, foretell the future, tell fortunes and many other strange and peculiar things. Furthermore, the cunning men and women could be called up to diagnose witchcraft, identify the witch and cast or recommend counter-spells. One of the counter-spells was to draw the blood of the witch by scratching or cutting, and perhaps such advice from 'Conjuror' Baker was the reason for the vicious assault, now to be related.

Ann Burge, having heard the allegations, went to the Bryant house and said to the accused, 'Betty Bryant I come to ask you a civil question, whether I bewitched your daughter?' To which the reply was, 'You damned old bitch, you have bewitched my daughter for twelve months past, and I be ten pounds' money the worst for it!' Then shouting that she would kill her, Elizabeth Bryant attacked the defenceless widow, and while two of her daughters held Ann Burge, beat her and scratched her arms with a

William Hyam, believing that he had been put under a spell by Ann Green, stabbed her in a shop at Bruton on 7 June 1871.

nail, yelling out, 'Bring me knives to cut the old bitch's flesh from her bones for she shall never go home alive!' The struggle carried on into the street, where a crowd was gathering to watch the proceedings until finally the poor widow was rescued and taken home suffering from extensive lacerations to her arms and the effects of the severe beating, from which it took over a month to recover.

Elizabeth Bryant and her two daughters were found guilty of assaulting and beating Ann Burge, and were sentenced to four months' imprisonment in the county gaol. In his summing up of the case, the judge, Mr Justice Burrough, recommended that the magistrates seek the arrest of 'Conjuror' Baker under the Vagrancy Act for the deceptions he practised, but he had left the neighbourhood and his whereabouts were unknown.

Thirty-two years later, in September 1854, the *Western Flying Post* reported the following curious incident in Yeovil at Ram Park, now an ornamental town park called Sidney Gardens:

MODERN WITCHCRAFT
A singular case of vulgar superstition came to light here last week. Some men were cleaning out the Ram Park pond, and on Thursday last at the bottom of the pond a workman named George Swatridge picked up a pickle-bottle containing figures and signs, which was at once stamped as a device of witchcraft. Three figures of the human body, fashioned out of gutta-percha and some other substance, and stuck all over with black pins, were in the bottle. There was writing at the back denoting that the figures were intended to represent persons named Roan, Mary Millard, (Mrs Roan, to wit) and Trimby, and the artist consigned them to 'sudden destruction, legal and moral' &c. The sign of the planet Saturn was made on the breasts of these unfortunates. There was also a flat piece of lead in the bottle, with cyphering and other marks on it,

no doubt of great significance, but we don't know what. The men whose effigies were treated in this way are police constables, and have probably in that capacity rendered themselves obnoxious to some one who determined to serve them out with the devil's aid. Roan has for some time been very ill, but has recovered since the finding of the pickle-bottle; which we understand Mrs. R. and some other people think marvellous and not to be laughed at. We must, however, do P.C. Roan himself the justice to say that he assured us, – when he brought the apparatus to our sanctum for the further elucidation of its importance which we were unable to give – that he did not consider himself to have been in such jeopardy on its account.

In June 1871, labourer William Hyam was brought before the Wincanton magistrates, charged with stabbing Ann Green, who told the Bench that on the evening of 7 June she had called at Mrs Vigar's shop in Bruton to purchase a candle. At Mrs Vigar's invitation she had gone into the kitchen, but shortly after William Hyam had come into the shop asking who was in there. When Mrs Vigar had said no one in particular, he pushed past her and opened the kitchen door. Ann Green stated that the prisoner had shouted 'Hello, is that thee you bitch!' and, rushing into the room, stabbed her twice in the shoulder with a clasp knife. When she cried out in pain and pleaded that she had done him no harm ,William Hyam suddenly calmed down and, after saying he was so sorry, 'offered her 5s. "to make it up"'.

The blood-soaked dress and undergarments worn by Ann Green were produced and the prisoner was asked why he had attacked the woman. William Hyam told the Bench that Ann Green had 'overlooked' him with a spell and he had heard people say that 'if you can draw blood, that will stop it'. The Chairman of the Bench enquired whether he had found any relief since the stabbing but the prisoner replied 'No Sir'.

Mrs Vigar gave evidence and corroborated Ann Green's testimony and PC Parsons stated that when he took William Hyam into custody, the prisoner said that he had carried out the stabbing because 'she had overlooked him'.

The prisoner's mother told the Bench that during the previous fortnight her son was constantly muttering that Mrs Green was overlooking him and the spell was killing him. Police Superintendent Shepherd stated that he understood William Hyam had injured his head in an accident a little while ago.

All the evidence had now been presented and the magistrates told the prisoner that had they believed he had been in his right mind when he committed the offence, they would have inflicted a very severe sentence. However, they remanded William Hyam in custody for a week to find if any Bruton householder would be willing to stand surety for his future good behaviour, failing which, he would be sent to prison for three week's hard labour. I have not discovered whether the surety was found or whether William Hyam went to gaol.

On 7 July the *Western Gazette* reported that the Wincanton case had 'Furnished a text for comments on Somersetshire Superstition to every journalist between Lands End and John o' Groats,' and quoted from the *Birmingham Daily Mail*:

Everybody who is acquainted with Somersetshire knows that it is one of the most benighted counties in England. Ignorance rides rampant there, and one has only to study the Assize calendars to show that it is ignorance of the most debasing kind. As one of the accompaniments of a crass and widespread ignorance, superstition exists to a great extent. A belief in witches, and 'evil eyes' and spells, and all such nonsense is more common in some villages in Somersetshire than the belief in a Deity, or a Saviour, or a heaven or a hell. We state these facts from a familiar acquaintance with the locality. Horse-shoes nailed to the door to keep away witches are the rule and not the exception. We frequently have to record instances of gross superstition in Somersetshire; and now we have to add another case to the long black list.

It seems, however, that only a few months later, in September 1871, ignorance was still riding somewhat rampant in Somerset following an inquest held in the Volunteer Inn, North Street, Crewkerne, into the sudden death of George Lynham, a forty-two-year-old foreman at Messrs T Lye and Son's brickyard, on Saturday morning, 8 September.

Hannah Lynham told the jury that her husband had gone to bed as normal on the Friday evening at their home at Ashlands, but at six o'clock the next morning he had jumped out of bed saying that it was time to go to work, immediately fell back and expired without a word. Dr Wills, the family doctor, stated that death arose from heart disease, for which he had been treating the deceased for some nine months.

The jury returned a verdict of 'Died by the visitation of God', but on 27 September 1871, the *Taunton Courier* reported:

There is a belief in the neighbourhood that the deceased had been 'bewitched.' About two years since the deceased, his brother and a man named Prue left Bridgwater and entered the employment of Messrs. T. Lye and Son, as brick makers. Rumour says that the 'witch' was once heard to threaten to 'do' for the men. No notice was taken of the threat, but within a very few months Prue died. About twelve months since one of the brothers died suddenly of heart disease. This awakened the suspicion, and the 'witch' is said to have stated that 'the other (George) would soon follow.' Moreover, deceased recently took a house for eight years, and the 'witch' is said to have declared that he would not live half so long as that. The sudden death of poor Lynham is thus satisfactorily accounted for. As a rider, comes the assertion that on the day before the funeral, deceased opened his eyes in the morning and closed them again at night – an act which those versed in witchcraft declare to be a sure proof of having been 'overlooked,' and it is said that the deceased himself with two fellow workmen, a few nights before his death, had their attention attracted from their work at midnight by a continual shrill whistling, and that when they looked about the yard to ascertain the cause thereof they saw the excellent lady dancing a dance of defiance upon the burning lime kiln!

All very strange indeed and, so far as I can tell, the identity of the 'witch' was never publicly disclosed in the local press.

The Disappearing Bank Manager

Mr William Robertson Lidderdale was the highly respected manager of the Ilminster branch of Stuckey's Bank. Aged forty, Mr Lidderdale had been engaged to Miss Elizabeth Chapman for two years, and the marriage ceremony would be held at Newbury on 14 January 1892. The couple were said to be ideally matched.

On 8 January, Mr Lidderdale drew £1,020 in notes and gold from his current account with Stuckey's Bank, and departed on the train to Paddington after telling his fiancée that he was travelling up to London to purchase a property in the city for a gentleman in Australia, and would be returning to Ilminster on the next morning's mail train.

Mr Lidderdale did not return on the following morning's mail train, nor any morning that week, and enquiries revealed that he had not notified his employers of his visit to London.

Mr Lidderdale did not keep his appointment at the altar and, after 8 January 1892, was never seen again in Ilminster, nor, as it turned out, anywhere else – at least not under the name of William Robertson Lidderdale.

To continue with my tale – on 10 January 1892, Miss Elizabeth Chapman received the following letter sent from the Great Western Hotel, Paddington:

> Am sending this to Raby in case I do not see my darling tomorrow. I promised you that if I ever saw Miss Vining again I would tell you, and I do so dear, at once. She has found out that her old lover is dead, and those old duffers and lawyers must tell her they expected me up. So the first person I ran against on getting out of the train was her. I soon told her what she wanted to know, and got rid of her. She knows we are to be married, but does not seem to know the date of the wedding. Now, my sweet darling, just be happy about this. It will be all right. Excuse this haste as I want to start off. – Yours for ever.   Willie

Some weeks later, on 10 February, there appeared in the London newspapers the following announcement: 'Lidderdale – On Feb 3, on Miss B. H. Vining's yacht, Foresight, Wm. Robertson Lidderdale of Ilminster, as the result of an accident on Jan. 8, alighting from a carriage in motion.'

Subsequently Miss Chapman received a package containing a visiting card bearing Miss Vining's name and on which was written in Mr Lidderdale's hand the message 'Was true to you', £500 in banknotes, a Jubilee sixpence, and a Christmas card in the

Mr William Robertson Lidderdale, who mysteriously disappeared in January 1892, was the manager of the Ilminster branch of Stuckey's Bank – the large building shown right centre of this photograph.

form of a cheque drawn on the Bank of Love, both of which she had previously given him.

Enquiries into the fate of Mr Lidderdale were made both privately and through the police at New Scotland Yard. An advertisement was inserted in London newspapers asking Miss Vining to contact Mr Lidderdale's relatives regarding his death, and a £25 reward offered to the Registrar who provided an authentic death certificate. No information was forthcoming, nor could any reason be found for his disappearance as his business and personal affairs appeared to be in order, and nothing more was heard of Mr Lidderdale, Miss Vining or the yacht *Foresight*.

Fifteen years later, in November 1907, an application was made before Mr Justice Bargrave Deane, in the Probate Division of the High Court, to presume the death of Mr William Robertson Lidderdale and to grant probate for his will. In March 1890, Mr Lidderdale had made a will making Miss Chapman the beneficiary of his estate for life and his nieces and nephews in the remainder. There were three life insurance policies in his name for £1,000 each, a substantial sum both in 1890 and 1907. Mr Lidderdale's executor applied for the judgement but this was opposed by the insurance companies on the grounds that every possible effort to trace his whereabouts or confirmation of his decease had proved unsuccessful.

The case, which was known as 'The Kidnapped Bridegroom Case', was considered on a number of occasions during the following six years, but despite the judge finally accepting that the mysterious Miss Vining and her yacht *Foresight* might not be figments of imagination, all enquiries had failed to establish the fate of Mr Lidderdale; the fact remained that Mr William Robertson Lidderdale, Miss Vining and the yacht *Forsight* had disappeared.

It would seem that the mystery of the disappearing bank manager may well remain unsolved.

It Was a Perfectly Hopeless Case

Mary Jane Saunders was the eldest daughter of George and Mary Saunders and she died at her home at Lufton, near Yeovil, on Wednesday 8 June 1892. Mary Jane had been taken ill in October 1891 with 'chronic inflammation and softening of the brain' and was attended by Dr Walters of Stoke-sub-Hamdon. Because of her worsening condition in the following month, Mary Jane was taken into Yeovil Hospital, but because family visits were refused, her parents brought her home. During the last six weeks of her life, Mary Jane 'had not had her reason' and Dr Walters told the father and mother that there was no hope of her recovery.

On Thursday 9 June 1892, the local coroner, Mr W. Muller held an inquest into the death of Mary Jane Saunders before a jury at the house of Mr Edwin Laxton, a Lufton dairyman, and with Superintendent Self of Yeovil police in attendance. The coroner explained that the inquest was being held because he had received information that the deceased's parents, believing that their daughter's illness was due to her being 'overlooked' by a malignant spell, had called in a quack doctor to remove it.

The first witness was Bessie Saunders, who described her sister's illness, and stated that on Tuesday 31 May her parents had called in a herbalist doctor by name of Stacey from South Petherton because her mother believed Mary Jane's illness was caused by a 'bad wish'. Bessie could not explain what a 'bad wish' was, and did not know whether or not her sister was suffering from one. However, she had heard that a herbalist doctor had cured two cases in Montacute. In reply to a question from the coroner, Bessie said that because she had heard people talk of 'bad wishes', she could not help but believe in such things. However, she could not say who might have wished her sister ill or 'overlooked' her. Bessie went on to relate that Stacey, the herbalist, had come to their house on Thursday evening, 2 June, remained the whole of Friday, and left on Saturday morning. He had brought some dried herbs from which he made some tea that he put in a black bottle. Her mother had told her that Stacey had claimed he could get rid of the 'wish' and he had been paid for his services. Her mother had given some of the tea to Mary Jane and then taken some herself; a cousin had also drunk some of the mixture.

More questions followed from both the coroner and Superintendent Self. Had Stacey put pins in a heart and hung it up, mentioned drawing blood, broken up some playing cards and put them under a flower pot, claiming these actions would remove the 'wish'? Bessie denied everything. She confirmed, however, that Dr Walter had always

Despite her rapidly failing health, Mary Jane Saunders was taken home by her parents from Yeovil Hospital, where she had been receiving treatment in November 1891, and a few days before her death a 'quack doctor' was called in.

been kind to her family and had told her parents that there was no hope of Mary Jane's recovery.

Next to appear was George Saunders, who confirmed that Dr Walters had been very attentive to his daughter and five weeks ago had told him that she would not get better. Under rigorous questioning by the coroner, he admitted that despite the doctor's advice, the herbalist had been called in as they thought a bad spell had been cast on their dying daughter, and Stacey had been paid for the medicine but not for breaking the spell.

Mary Saunders testified that she had paid the herbalist eleven shillings (a labourer's weekly wage) because at the time she believed her daughter had a 'bad wish' cast on her. When asked by the coroner whether she would be likely to believe this in future, Mary Saunders replied 'No', leading the coroner to comment, 'If this enquiry has been the means of disabusing from your mind this belief it will have done good and I will say to you, as I have to your husband and daughter: Don't be so silly as to believe anyone can cast a spell on anyone else.'

Dr Walters told the inquest that he had attended Mary Jane for two or three years and she had suffered from chronic inflammation and softening of the brain. He last saw her about five weeks ago and had informed the parents that it was a perfectly hopeless case. The doctor had carried out a post-mortem that morning and found that death was caused by extensive softening of the brain. He had examined the herbal tea and found it to be harmless, with a slight tonic value.

The *Western Gazette* reported the coroner's summing up:

> He hoped in addressing a great many working men that there was not one who had even got a suspicion in his mind that there was any truth in witchcraft. He could assure them that it was absolutely imagination. No one could have any influence over another person except, he hoped, it was for good; and no person had the power of removing any influence of that kind. In that nineteen century, when all the educational advantages they possessed in the county of Somerset, this belief was more extensive than he could credit. He hoped that it would gradually die out. They had great educational advantages, and their children would not be so silly as to believe anyone could influence another in this manner.

The jury returned a verdict of 'Natural Death' in accordance with the medical testimony.

'I'll Blow Your Brains Out!'

At about ten o'clock on Friday evening, 24 January 1817, James Watts, described as 'a stout young man', and employed by Mr Isaac Wilkins, of Chapmanslade, just over the border in Wiltshire, left the village with a two-horse wagon, to collect a load of coal from a colliery at Writhlington, near Radstock.

Some time after midnight he arrived outside Norton St Philip and decided to stop and have a short nap before completing the rest of his journey. After looking to the needs of the horses, James clambered back onto the wagon and made himself comfortable against a truss of hay, but just as he was falling asleep a harsh voice rasped in his ear, 'Deliver your money and be quick, or I'll blow your brains out!' Opening his eyes he was horrified to find a large horse pistol pushed against his chest. The stout young man's first reaction was to make a grab for the whip lying beside him, but as he did so there was a brilliant flash of light. The blast of the shot did not come: the pistol had misfired, and in the flash from the priming pan James clearly saw the face of the robber; it would remain seared in his memory.

Undaunted by the shock, James leapt from the wagon, grappled with his assailant, and a savage fight took place. His opponent was big and strong and had almost overcome the young man when James managed to take hold of the pistol and, with the butt end, delivered a fearsome blow to his assailant's left temple, sending him crashing to the ground and, with several more hefty blows, rendered him senseless.

Recovering from the fight, James Watts found that his horses had strayed down the road and, still holding the pistol, went to retrieve them. On the way he met another carter with whom he was acquainted, and together they returned to the scene of the fight only to find that the villain had disappeared. However, he had left behind his hat and an unusually shaped stick.

Within hours the news of the attempted murder and robbery had spread, and at Farleigh Hungerford, a few miles from the scene, Mr Greenhill, a farmer, was wondering why one of his men by name of John Bodmin had not turned up for work. Early that evening, the farmer went to Bodmin's house to enquire, and found several of his children at the door. When asked about their father, the children replied that he was bad, but then one of the youngsters blurted out that 'I must not tell what's the matter'. With this intelligence, Mr Greenhill's suspicions were aroused and, going in, he found Bodmin prostrate with a badly injured and bloody head. The farmer had heard the story of the attempted robbery and here was the culprit.

THE GEORGE INN, NORTON ST PHILIP, FROME

In the early hours of 25 January 1817, just outside the village of Norton St Philip, famed for the historic George Inn, there was a desperate fight Between James Watts and a robber.

John Bodmin was taken into custody and brought before three local magistrates. James Watts identified him as the man he had seen in the flash from the pistol's misfire, and the hat and the unusually shaped stick were confirmed as belonging to Bodmin. A Mr Noad, of Farleigh Hungerford, swore that one of Bodmin's sons had tried to buy the pistol from his servant and shortly after it had been stolen. During the magistrates' examination, Bodmin was said to have 'appeared in great pain but manifested a most hardened indifference'.

On 30 January, the *Taunton Courier* reported that 'About 13 years ago, Bodmin was one of the London patrols, and his beat was from Hyde Park corner to Kensington during which time he stated at Farleigh not long ago, that he and another faithful guardian of the night, robbed a man of 7 pounds and his watch.'

John Bodmin was committed to take his trial at the forthcoming Lent Assizes in Taunton and on 11 April he was found guilty of discharging a pistol at James Watts, with intent to rob and murder him, and sentenced to death.

The *Western Flying Post* reported that at eleven o'clock in the morning of Wednesday 30 April 1817, fifty-three-year-old John Bodmin, Abraham Slade and Thomas Langdon (both convicted of burglaries in the Yeovil area), Joseph Pitts (sheep stealer), and Joseph Turner (house-breaker) were led onto the platform erected above the lodge of Ilchester Gaol, all appearing very devout and, after acknowledging their crimes, were hanged before 'an immense number of spectators who attended the awful spectacle'.

A Burglary at Langport

On the night of 22 July 1827, Henry Parry, butler to Mr Vincent Stuckey, of High House, Langport, locked up his master's house and went to bed. At about five o'clock the following morning he was rudely woken by one of the servants and told that the house had been broken into during the night. It was quickly established that a considerable amount of silver plate had been stolen, including the spoon from a mustard pot, and a charity box containing twenty shillings in halfpenny pieces.

The alarm was raised in Langport and the surrounding countryside, and during the succeeding days the robbery was the main subject of conversation in the town. A villain by the name of William Kerslake was soon taken into custody and, early in the following September, appeared before Lord Chief Justice Best at the Somerset Assizes, indicted for burglary and stealing from Mr Vincent Stuckey upwards of £200 of plate and 'sundry other articles' specified in the indictment – if found guilty the sentence would be death for the theft of goods of this value.

Following the evidence of the butler, Henry Parry, giving details of the burglary, and Mr Vincent Stuckey describing the articles and cash stolen, the next witness testified that he had seen Kerslake at an inn near Mr Stuckey's house at about half past midnight on the night of the robbery.

The landlord of another Langport inn deposed that during the following morning Kerslake was drinking on his premises and paid for several pints of beer with halfpennies. However, when the robbery and the theft of the charity box with its halfpennies were mentioned, Kerslake paid for the next pint with a sixpence piece.

The next witness was the landlord of Street Inn. He testified that Kerslake had come into his taproom carrying a large trunk and bought everyone a drink before leaving and taking the road to Bristol. Some time after Kerslake had left, news of the robbery at Langport arrived and, with his suspicions aroused, the landlord had saddled his horse and hurried up the Bristol road in pursuit. The landlord described how he caught up with Kerslake and found him arguing, with the driver of the cart who had given him a lift, over the payment of a shilling extra for the carriage of the trunk. The witness demanded to see what was in the trunk and ordered Kerslake to open it. In the trunk was a quantity of silver plate matching the description of the stolen articles and so the witness took Kerslake into custody.

The court was told that, initially, only half the stolen plate was recovered, but the rest was subsequently found in a field near Mr Stuckey's house.

On 12 September 1827, William Kerslake was executed at Ilchester Gaol, shown here in a contemporary print, for burglary at Langport and 'appeared to suffer much'.

With all the prosecution witnesses heard, and William Kerslake offering no defence or calling witnesses on his behalf, the jury took less than a minute to return a verdict of guilty and the dramatic scene in the court was described in the *Western Flying Post* on 8 September:

> The Chief Justice then directed the usual proclamation to be made previous to his passing sentence of death, and then addressed the prisoner thus:– 'Wmn. Kerslake, you having been convicted by the jury, nothing remains for me now to do but to pass on you the awful sentence of the law, which is, that you be taken from here to the place from whence you came, and thence to the place of common execution, and there be hanged by the neck until you are dead; and may God of all mercy have mercy on your soul!'
>
> The prisoner was then borne out of the dock by four men, moaning rather than uttering sounds, which prayed for mercy to be shown to him. The whole court was in the most profound silence during this scene, and most persons present were evidently affected by the dreadful manner in which the prisoner received the passing of the sentence.
>
> Kerslake is a native of the neighbourhood of Beaminster, the only worthless member of a large and industrious family. From his youth he has been given to vicious habits, and has already undergone a sentence of seven years transportation, for robbing a cloth manufactory, near Ilminster.

Justice was swift in 1827, and at noon on Wednesday 12 September, thirty-three-year-old William Kerslake, in company with capitally convicted felons John Burton (for assaulting and robbing a man at Priddy Fair), Thomas Wilshire (convicted of burglary in Bath), and William Latcham (for burglary at West Pennard) were hanged at Ilchester Gaol. The *Western Flying Post* reported that 'Latcham and Wilshire died almost immediately without a struggle but Burton and Kerslake appeared to suffer much'.

There is a story that John Burton's father was standing by the gallows and called out to his son, 'Jack, die like a man – Jack, die like a man', and after replying 'Yes, father' Jack did, albeit after appearing 'to suffer much'.

Two Aircraft Down

At about half past ten on the morning of Monday 3 September 1917, Flight Sub-Lieutenant John Emyr Thomas of the Royal Naval Air Service, an Air Department ferry pilot, took off in his Avro 504E two-seater biplane from the Westland Aircraft Company's airfield en route for the Royal Naval Air Station Hendon. Accompanying the Flight Sub-Lieutenant in the observer's seat behind him was Mr Robert Norton, the company's commercial director, on his way to a meeting with the Air Board in London.

The take-off to the west was normal, but at about 300 feet the aircraft banked sharply to the left and nosedived into a field near the bridge over the Yeovil to Taunton railway line at Bunford Lane. Rescuers from the factory arrived at the crash within minutes and found Mr Norton pinned under the aircraft's fuel tank, still alive but badly injured. Mercifully the plane had not caught fire. The injured man was carefully extracted from the wreckage and rushed to Yeovil Hospital in the Red Cross ambulance which had now arrived on the scene. Sadly the young pilot was found to have died in the crash.

The inquest into the death of twenty-three-year-old Flight Sub-Lieutenant J. E. Thomas before Mr E. Q. Louch, the coroner, and his jury, was held on 5 September. The first witness was Mr Percy Warren, the Westland assistant manager, who stated that the Avro biplane had flown down to the factory from Hendon on the Monday previous to the accident. The officer had taken a new plane back, and left instructions for the Avro to be returned by another pilot. Flight Sub-Lieutenant Thomas had arrived at the works early on Monday morning for this flight, and the witness stated that he had accompanied the officer and Mr Norton to the aircraft. There had been some trouble starting the engine, but it was running well when the Avro taxied out and took off. Mr Warren stated that the aircraft had flown some 600 yards and risen to a height of about 300 feet when it banked to the left and got into a vertical spin until about 100 feet off the ground when it took a nosedive. With other employees he had rushed to the scene of the crash and found the aircraft a total wreck. Mr Warren went on to say that at no time had the Flight Sub-Lieutenant expressed any doubts about the condition of the aircraft prior to take off.

Squadron Commander Evill, DSC, Royal Naval Air Service, representing the Air Board, testified that the deceased officer was fully qualified to fly the Avro 504E biplane and was in fact flying an aircraft easier to handle than those he was used to. The Squadron Commander believed that the pilot had been overconfident with the machine and had made an error, which if he had been flying higher he might have corrected. Flight Sub-Lieutenant Thomas had been used to more powerful aircraft, and had been too low when he banked. The witness went on to say that Mr Norton, the passenger, who was too ill to attend to give evidence, had told him that the engine was running perfectly at the time, and thought the aircraft had been banked too steeply.

John Hardie, an engine mechanic employed by the Royal Aircraft Factory at Westland, took the stand and testified that when the engine had failed to start, a short circuit had been found and rectified, after which it had run smoothly. On the morning concerned, Flight Sub-Lieutenant Thomas had asked if anyone knew anything about the engine because he had flown in similar machines but had no experience of this one. Mr Hardie stated that:

> Lieutenant Thomas had no doubt flown this type of machine, but with a different engine – one of lower power. Deceased got out two fire extinguishers from the hangar – an unusual thing for a pilot to do – he having heard no doubt, that the type of engine sometimes caught fire. He also asked for the seat to be packed so that his feet could more easily reach the rudder-bar, and some sacks were brought, which brought his feet forward. When he got off the engine was running well. He told witness that he did not like the type of engine. Witness had seen a good many of this type of engine in that particular type of machine. When it left the ground the machine seemed all right, and in witness's opinion, deceased 'pushed up the nose' of the machine too much in climbing. He had seen the machine arrive at the works and the engine had been running well. It was of the rotary type.

John Hardie was the last witness. In his summing up, the coroner stated that in flying an aeroplane a good deal must be left to the skill of the pilot upon whom everything depended:

> When a man was in the air at a considerable altitude, it was impossible to tell what he was doing, or whether he came to grief through an error of judgment or a temporary stoppage of the engine, or defect in the engine or machine. There was the opinion of the commander that the sub-lieutenant was flying in over-confidence, and any evolution he could have made in a more powerful machine might not have come off in the one he was flying. They were assured that the machine ascended well. What caused the accident was a matter of speculation, but the machine came into a position which brought about a nose dive, and crashed to earth, causing injuries to the sub-lieutenant which cause his immediate death.

The jury delivered a verdict of 'accidental death, sustained while flying a Service biplane, which fell, the accident being probably due to over-confidence of the deceased in flying'. They also added that they were of the opinion that officers should not be called upon to fly machines with the engine of which they were not conversant.

The coroner stated that he would send the jury's opinion to the Air Board, and closed the inquest by expressing his sympathy to the relatives of the late officer who had lost his life in the execution of his duty just as much as a soldier or sailor of the King lost in direct action.

The wreckage of the Westland Walrus single-engine biplane, in which Pilot Officer James Rose, RAF, was killed when it crashed near Yeovil on 14 June 1923.

The body of Flight Sub-Lieutenant John Emyr Thomas was taken, under the escort of the Yeovil Volunteers and two Royal Naval Air Service officers, from the hospital to the town station on its last journey home to rest in the Rhewl Calvanistic Methodist Chapel Yard, near Ruthin in Denbighshire. After twelve months recovering from his serious injuries, Mr Robert Norton returned to work.

The Walrus, the Westland-designed three-seat naval reconnaissance single-engine biplane, was not the most successful of the company's aircraft; in fact it was described by Derek N. James in his book *Westland – A History*, published by Tempus in 2002, as 'the most ugly aeroplane ever supplied to the Royal Air Force', and by Captain Stuart Keep, MC, Westland's Chief Test Pilot, in his first flight test report of the prototype in 1921, as being somewhat vicious in its behaviour.

Thirty-six of the ungainly Walrus, with its unpleasing bulges and projections, were supplied to the RAF, and remained in service with coastal reconnaissance units until 1925.

Early on the afternoon of Thursday 14 June 1923, a Walrus Mark II, serial number N9510, was prepared for take-off on the Westland airfield following extensive reconditioning of the two-year-old machine, the installation of a new Rapier engine and new pattern wings. Following a successful test flight by Captain Stuart Keep, MC, the machine was signed off as fit for duty by the Air Ministry's resident aeronautical inspector at the works, and handed over to Pilot Officer James Rose, RAF, to fly down to Royal Air Force Gosport.

At about two o'clock, the Walrus, with James Rose at the controls, took off westwards, climbed straight up to about 500 feet, banked hard left back towards the airfield, appeared to stall, began to spin and nosedived into a field near Bunford Lane in the approximate location of the present Brympton Way. Sadly, when the would-be rescuers arrived at the scene of the crash a few minutes later, they found Pilot Officer Rose dead in the wreckage – the second fatal crash at Westland since aircraft production began eight years before in 1915 and, by a tragic coincidence, near the site of the first fatal crash in September 1917.

At the inquest into the death of James Rose, held two days later in the town hall, Mr W. Winter Goode, the deputy coroner for South East Somerset, was given details of the fatal injuries suffered by the pilot, and proof of identity from the dead man's father. The inquest was told that Pilot Officer Rose had qualified as a pilot some five months previous to the crash and had flown from the Westland airfield on four occasions. The relevant documents and records were produced by Mr W. G. Gibson, Supervisor of the Westland Works (who in addition to being a qualified ground engineer was also a licensed pilot), showing that the aircraft and its engine had been tested and were in perfect working order. Mr Gibson stated that the Walrus had taken off, climbed to about 500 feet and while climbing had executed a left-hand turn. The aircraft had completed the turn back towards the airfield with its nose at an angle of some 45 degrees to the ground and immediately went into a spiral dive, completing one turn of the spin before crashing into the field. In Mr Gibson's opinion, the machine had stalled and got into a spin before the pilot realised what was happening. The deputy coroner asked what would cause the aircraft to stall, and Mr Gibson replied that in the act of turning while in a climb, a much greater strain was placed on the engine, causing it to slow and lose air speed, and this would result in the stall. The engine installed in the Walrus was sufficiently powerful and the machine was in perfect trim. Mr Gibson told the deputy coroner that he had flown a number of these aircraft and in his opinion the crash was the result of a pure error of judgement and one which any pilot could make – once.

The deputy coroner returned the verdict that Pilot Officer James Rose had died from injuries accidentally received on 14 June while acting as the pilot of a Westland Walrus Mark II aeroplane, having nosedived from an altitude, but there was not sufficient evidence to show what caused the nosedive. Expressing his deep sympathy to the dead pilot's father, the deputy coroner stated that he was absolutely satisfied that, as far as was humanly possible, the machine was in perfect working order and all precautions had been taken to see that it was in perfect working condition before it left the works.

Twenty-year-old Pilot Officer James Rose was buried with full military honours in Yeovil Cemetery on 20 June, three volleys were fired over the grave and the Last Post was sounded.

On 22 June, the *Western Gazette* printed the following letter of tribute sent to *The Times*:

We read in 'The Times' on Friday, 'Airman Killed at Yeovil' Jim Rose's machine, a new one, he was taking to Gosport, crashed down just a mile from the town, and that was all. Looking back over the memories of his short, happy life, one thing stands out – how greatly he was loved. Tall, graceful, boyish-looking, his twenty-first birthday was due in a month's time. After his private school came Malvern. Then, the difficult problem of a profession. Jim's choice was the Air Force. He was sensitive and nervous; over anxious as to passing his tests. But he stuck to his guns, and by sheer grit conquered his air-sickness which had been a trouble to him. He received his wings and became a pilot officer. The pride and energy he put into his training was equalled by his modesty in all he had achieved. The treasured holidays in Scotland; the fishing and shooting; the snatches of leave spent in his home on Harmer Green in Hertfordshire, are over now for ever, but his memory remains with us.

Highway Robberies in 1872

During the winter of 1872, there was an outbreak of highway robbery in the area of Stoke-sub-Hamdon which prompted *Pulman's Weekly News* to comment, 'One would almost think by the following robberies, we were going back to the days of Dick Turpin.'

The newspaper went on to report that at about ten o'clock on the night of Saturday 30 November, seventy-five-year-old Montacute shoemaker James Stagg was returning home from Stoke when he was attacked near Hatchcock Lane by a man who struck him a violent blow on the head and then robbed him of fifteen shillings and sixpence in cash, plus his walking stick and lantern.

Earlier that evening, seventy-year-old Widow Cook, of Percombe Hill, was returning home in her donkey cart when she was held up by a man near the Three Cross Roads and robbed of two baskets containing bread, butter, tea and other articles she had purchased at a shop in Bower Hinton. The robber also took her umbrella, which she had just had mended.

Pulman's sarcastically commented that the police were 'much engaged in watching those inhuman wretches who see no more harm in drinking a glass of ale at 11.10 than at 10.50, that the detection of highway robbery is hardly, we suppose, thought worthy of consideration'. In 1872, prosecutions under a new Licensing Act for after-hours drinking was a very 'sore point' among many, including the editor of *Pulman's Weekly News*.

However, three days later, on Tuesday 3 December, David Long, a reporter on *Pulman's Weekly News*, was the victim of an attack near Stoke, and the newspaper had an exclusive. On 10 December *Pulman's* reported with relish its scoop:

We have to report another daring highway robbery, accompanied with brutal violence. On Tuesday evening, shortly after seven, David Long of Huish, near Crewkerne, one of the newsmen of the *Weekly News*, was proceeding on a velocipede along the turnpike road, on his road home from Stoke. After going about a quarter of a mile he met a man who asked him the road to Ilminster. Long told him and received in return a violent blow upon the nose with a bludgeon, followed by several severe blows on the head. Long moved away and the ruffian searched the velocipede. Finding that it contained nothing of value, he again went towards Long, and demanded a shilling. While Long was feeling for the

Shoemaker James Stagg was attacked and robbed on his way home to Montacute on the night of Saturday 30 November 1872.

money, the ruffian threatened again to knock him down if he did not be quick. After receiving the shilling he made off in the direction of Stoke. Long, bleeding profusely, managed to get as far as Norton Gate. The gatekeeper saw that he was unable to proceed further and assisted in removing him to the Nelson's Arms, Norton. A message was despatched for Dr. Walter, of Stoke, who promptly attended and found Long suffering severe injuries about the head and face. This is the third highway robbery near here within the last few days. It is rumoured that a man has been apprehended on suspicion.

However, no one was arrested for the robberies, which then appear to have stopped, but suspicion had fallen on a forty-year-old labourer, William Gully, who found himself before the magistrates some four months later in April 1873 on an unrelated charge. The *Western Gazette* reported on 2 May that 'William Gully, of Norton-sub-Hamdon, who was supposed to have committed the highway robberies in the neighbourhood of Stoke in December last, was charged with stealing a bag of potatoes, the property of Mr. Jesse Pattemore, Landlord of the Nelson Inn, Norton-sub-Hamdon'.

The Bench heard that Mr Pattemore had found that a quantity of potatoes were missing from an outhouse and William Gully became the principal suspect, having been seen by the landlord's servant girl looking in at the outhouse window on the evening before the robbery. The village constable, PC James, went to the suspect's house, where he found half a bag of potatoes downstairs and the rest in the bedroom. William Gully was not at home and so the constable went looking for him. He found his man standing by a hayrick between Norton and Stoke, but as soon as Gully saw the constable he took to his heels. The chase over fields and hedges went on for nearly a mile when Gully suddenly stopped, turned and faced his pursuer, waving the hoe he was carrying, and threatened to kill the constable. Undaunted by the threats, PC James closed, and after a brief but desperate struggle in which the constable received a black eye, he snapped the handcuffs on his prisoner. William Gully was taken to Yeovil police station, and charged with the theft of Mr Pattemore's potatoes.

The magistrates were told that marks of hobnailed boots on the window ledge of the outhouse matched those of the prisoner's, and shreds of leather, used to manure the ground where the potatoes were grown, were found attached to the potatoes found in William Gully's house.

William Gully was sent for trial at the Somerset Quarter Sessions, where he was found guilty, and after a long list of his previous convictions was read out, he was sentenced to seven years' penal servitude.

The perpetrator of the highway robberies was never brought to justice for these crimes, but no more were reported.

In Time of War

During the summer of 1940, the nation was facing the threat of Nazi invasion following the evacuation of British troops from Dunkirk and the fall of France, and the country's state of extreme tension saw the rigid enforcement of wartime emergency legislation.

On 21 June 1940, the *Western Gazette* reported that at the Yeovil county sessions a Canadian aircraft fitter, lodging at Barwick, appeared charged with photographing a military tank contrary to the Defence Regulations. Police Constable Stevens testified that the defendant admitted photographing the tank and that he was aware of the regulations and knew that he should not have done so. The film was seized and destroyed. When asked to account for his actions, the fitter said that photography was a strong hobby with him and more or less a passion. The Chairman of the Bench, imposing a fine of £15 and ordering the camera to be confiscated, said, 'You can consider yourself extremely fortunate not to go to prison. It was touch and go whether you did or not. You knew you were doing wrong and you persisted in it.'

During that long and very tense summer of 1940, you had to be very careful what you said because it could land you in trouble and possibly gaol.

A Dorset special constable, employed by a firm of mineral water manufacturers, appeared at the Yeovil county sessions in August charged with publishing 'a statement connected with the war likely to cause alarm or despondency'.

An East Coker housewife told the court that the defendant had said that it would be the last time he called, adding that next time we shall have to see what Hitler has to say and the Germans would land within a week. He had been ready to bet her that the King and Queen would go to Canada, the Duke and Duchess of Windsor would be in London and the Duke would be the dictator for the Germans.

The housewife's mother testified that the accused had told her that there would be no unemployment when Hitler got here. There would be plenty of work but wages would be low and Ireland would be the next place the Germans got into.

The accused denied mentioning the Duke and Duchess of Windsor, and when the housewife had complained about not being able to get certain drinks, he had told her to blame Hitler.

A second housewife stated that when she had asked for some grapefruit the defendant had told her that 'You cannot have grapefruit. You can have it when we are under German rule. I will make you any bet we are under German rule in a fortnight's time.'

In August 1940, a Dorset special constable was found guilty of publishing 'a statement connected with the war likely to cause alarm and despondency' in the picturesque village of East Coker.

Police Sergeant Bundy told the Bench that the defendant made a statement to the effect that he was at East Coker for about two hours on his round but had no recollection of saying anything about the war. He also stated that he had been a special constable since 1939. He imagined the people must have made up the statements against him.

In his defence, the accused swore on oath that he had said nothing about the Duke and Duchess of Windsor or the King and Queen. When customers complained to him of not calling more often, or because he could not get certain drinks, he told them they must blame Hitler.

Inspector Morris stated that the accused was a native of Hampshire and had been residing in Dorset for about three years. He had been employed by the firm of mineral water manufacturers for twelve months.

The Chairman of the Bench said that they took a very serious view of this case. The very nature of his employment gave the accused the opportunity for taking the action he did. They considered the reports were spread maliciously and made with the idea of causing alarm and despondency among women. The Bench believed the evidence of the witnesses entirely. The fact that he was a special constable made the offence infinitely worse.

The defendant was found guilty, sent to prison for one month and fined £5 plus twelve shillings and sixpence costs.

Rumour and gossip are always present at a time of war, and 'Silentium' wrote to the *Western Gazette* on 31 May 1940, suggesting that 'Could not the Mayor, or some other responsible person, follow the example of the Mayor of Southampton and institute an "anti-gossip" week in Yeovil. It is badly needed. The amount of gossip regarding Westlands, where troops are &c., would keep any "Fifth Columnist" busy recording it. Also the amount of "scare gossip" which is also very prevalent must be doing a lot of harm.'

There were spy scares galore and Mrs Knight of 52 West Hendford, Yeovil, went so far as to insert the following notice in the *Western Gazette* on 31 May denying that 'Miss Fordham who has recently lived with her, has masqueraded as a man, or has acted as a spy, while staying at her house. The lady has been proved to be a highly-respected British retired business woman of Grays, Essex.'

Spy scares continued throughout much of the war, and one that comes to mind is the rumour that during several nights in the autumn of 1942 an unnamed woman was seen signalling with a torch, near the Houndstone military camp on the outskirts of Yeovil, to enemy aircraft passing overhead. I can find no official record of the incident and it would appear to be one of the many rumours and myths generated by over-inflamed imaginations.

During the Second World War you could be prosecuted for being persistently late for work. A week before VE Day in May 1945, a girl was fined £2, with the option of a month in prison for non-payment, following her plea of guilty to being persistently late for work at Westland Aircraft between November 1944 and January 1945. The magistrates were told that in forty-six days the girl had only been punctual on two days and her lateness amounted to 33 hours and 33 minutes. In her defence the girl stated that she had been unwell and had also stayed at home to look after her married sister, who could not get help during her confinement.

Three Country Fires

Fire broke out in one of the sheds on Mr Chapman's Dillington Farm, near Ilminster, on Sunday 5 July 1857. The shed housed a large threshing machine run by water power and subsequent investigations indicated that the friction of the machinery caused the outbreak. The fire was discovered by Mrs Chapman, but by the time help arrived an extensive group of sheds, outbuildings and a large barn were well alight with flames roaring through the roofs. Despite the strenuous efforts of Mr Chapman's workpeople, neighbours and amateur firefighters, all the buildings were completely destroyed. The large barn contained the contents of three mowings of corn, of which two had been threshed for immediate delivery. Although it was reported that the stock and machinery were insured, it was believed Mr Chapman would suffer a serious loss from the fire.

The prompt arrival of the Martock fire brigade at Mr William Peach's farm at Witcombe in the morning of New Year's Eve 1905 saved his barns and hayricks from becoming one of the biggest fires in the district.

Just after eight o'clock on the Saturday morning, one of Mr Peach's sons was working in the new cow shed, when the oil lamp he was using tipped over and fell onto a large pile of dry straw, which immediately burst into flames. The cows were quickly turned out, but despite every effort to extinguish the blaze with buckets of water, it was soon burning out of control and a messenger was dispatched to Martock for the fire brigade. On receipt of the call, the fire bell was rung; horses to pull the fire engine were secured from Mr Paull; and at twenty to nine, the brigade, commanded by Captain Yandle and accompanied by the Revd Preb. Wickham, the Brigade President, left at full speed to cover the two miles to Witcombe.

By the time the brigade arrived, the cow shed was a mass of flames, and despite the firemen's efforts it could not be saved. Captain Yandle and his men then turned their attention to hosing down a nearby thatched barn with water pumped from the farm pond. Thus the blaze was contained, but had the brigade arrived fifteen minutes later, all the thatched barns and hayricks would probably have been destroyed.

The First World War was less than three weeks old on Saturday 21 August 1914, when fire broke out in a block of three thatched cottages on the top of Primrose Hill on the road to Hardington Mandeville. Two were completely gutted, the third badly damaged, and the occupiers – Edward Stevens, Arthur Grainger and Charles Helyar and their families – rendered homeless.

The Martock fire engine was driven along North Street at full speed to the fire on Mr William Peach's farm at Witcombe in the morning of 31 December 1905.

At about seven o'clock on the Saturday morning, Edward Stevens was leaving for work when he saw flames coming from the roof of the middle cottage occupied by Arthur Grainger. He quickly raised the alarm with his neighbours and as Arthur Granger went into his children's bedroom the flames burst through the ceiling, but thankfully the three youngsters and their father escaped unhurt. The Yeovil fire brigade had been summoned, but in the meantime the three families and their friends salvaged as much of the furniture and possessions as they could.

In Yeovil the volunteers of the fire brigade assembled at the fire station and within a few minutes were on their way, commanded by Lieutenant Wallbridge. As an experiment, the manual pump was attached to a large and powerful motor car supplied by Mr Swaffield, and with the firemen packed into the vehicle, the brigade set off for Primrose Hill. Although the experiment resulted in the brigade arriving much sooner than would have been the case if the usual horses had been used, by the time they reached the scene two of the cottages were blazing fiercely. Now came the problem of finding a suitable water supply. The nearest stream was at Hew Mill and over half a mile of hose had to be laid up to the fire, but even now, the problems were not over. The pump was manually operated and to begin with there were not enough helpers to pump the water up the hill and more time was lost in finding more hands. Finally pumping began in earnest, but even now, with the full complement of pumpers, the pressure was only sufficient to provide a fairly low jet of water. However, the efforts of the firefighters and helpers to save two of the cottages were unsuccessful and they were totally destroyed; the blaze was finally contained and Edward Steven's home was saved, although badly damaged by water. The cause of the fire could not be established. The Yeovil fire brigade took delivery of its first motor fire engine in 1922.

Big Cats on the Loose

A ferocious animal on the loose is the stuff of nightmares, but this actually happened on a dark Wednesday evening in November 1895.

The Wednesday afternoon's performance of Messrs Haslam and Anderton's Menagerie at Martock on 13 November 1895 was over, the animals had been fed, their vans cleaned out, and the attendants had just sat down to tea. Suddenly, one of the elephants began trumpeting wildly and, rushing to find out the reason, the attendants were horrified to see that one of the menagerie's four lions had escaped from its van and was running around inside the main enclosure. Captain Rowland, the lion tamer, and Mr Anderton were summoned immediately, but decided that the lion would have to be shot as they considered it would be too dangerous to try and return the frenzied animal to its van, and they feared what could happen if it broke out of the enclosure. Captain Rowland climbed onto the roof of one of the caravans and killed the lion with a single shot.

The dead lion had been one of four bought some six months before from the Crystal Palace, and enquiries established that the animal had escaped when the door of its van was left unsecured. However, the show must go on, and *Pulman's Weekly News* reported that a large number of people attended the Menagerie's evening performance – 'the dead lion being, no doubt, an extra attraction'.

Believe it or not, on the same Wednesday evening, a lion escaped during the performance of Crecraft's Menagerie at Queen Camel. One of the main attractions of the show was 'Captain' Marco's performance with his four-year-old lion 'Wild Prince' in a large cage in the main tent, but on this evening, as the 'Captain' opened the door to leave the cage, the lion suddenly sprang forward and burst out to freedom. Chaos and panic reigned as the audience scrambled to escape the beast, which in turn seemed more intent on trying to escape than attacking humans. However, during the failed attempt to capture Wild Prince in the tent, Joseph Crecraft, the Menagerie's proprietor, was badly clawed, and the lion was away out into the dark November night.

Recovering from their surprise, the Menagerie's attendants, accompanied by a large party of villagers armed with an assortment of weapons, including guns, pitchforks, and a couple of old swords, set out to track down the runaway with the aid of powerful Naptha lamps.

Wild Prince had not gone far, no doubt confused in the dark and unused to freedom, and was soon spotted in the beams of the lamps. At the approach of the 'hunting party',

The escape of 'Wild Prince', the lion from 'Captain' Marco's Menagerie at Queen Camel, caused panic throughout the village in November 1895.

the lion made off and bounded into a garden, one side of which was enclosed by a high wall and other two by a cottage and outbuildings. Cornered and blinded by the powerful lamps, the lion took refuge in the outhouse of the cottage. Once inside the building the door and windows were barricaded, and steps taken to secure the animal alive. A large box was brought from the Menagerie, and after three anxious hours under the barrels of assorted firearms, Wild Prince was coaxed from his refuge and into the box by means of a large piece of meat. Thus secured, the box and its live contents were conveyed back to the Menagerie. Wild Prince's bid for freedom was over.

In concluding the story of 'The Hazardous Chase and Capture' of Wild Prince, *Pulman's Weekly News* wrote:

Intelligence of the animal being at large spread like wild fire through Queen Camel and for some hours a state of panic prevailed. When at two o'clock on Thursday morning it became known that the lion had been secured there was a feeling of general relief, and those who had assisted in the capture, as well as many who had anxiously awaited, were afterwards treated to a gratuitous performance by the trainer 'Captain' Marco.

The Death of Private Ernest Horler

Among the 306 British soldiers executed in the First World War and granted posthumous pardons by Parliament is a Yeovil man, Ernest Horler, and this is his story.

At 6.46 a.m. on the morning of Sunday 17 February 1918, twenty-six-year-old Private Ernest Horler of B Company, 12th (S) Battalion, West Yorkshire Regiment (Prince of Wales Own), died by rifle fire at a place called Boisleux-Au-Mont in France, a few kilometres south of Arras, and his 'death was instantaneous'. Private Horler did not die going into action, but this instantaneous death came from the barrels of .303 Short Lee Enfield rifles fired by British soldiers – Ernest Horler had been shot for desertion.

And how did Private Horler come to the place called Boiseleux-Au-Mont on that February morning in the year 1918?

Nearly three weeks earlier, on 30 January, a Field General Court Martial was convened at the Headquarters of the 9th Infantry Brigade, 3rd Division, to try 46127 Private Ernest William Horler on three charges – two for desertion while on active service and one for escaping from lawful custody; to all three he pleaded not guilty

The proceedings of the court martial are briefly recorded in pencil on five sheets of paper and can be examined in the National Archives at Kew under reference WO71/677.

The President of the four member court was Major E. L. Thomson, of the 3rd York and Lancashire Regiment, attached 12th West Yorkshire Regiment, and the other members were Captain J. Young, 2nd Royal Scots, Captain C. M. Hadden, 1st Royal Scots Fusiliers (he would be killed in action two months later) and Second Lieutenant H. H. Harding, of 7th Gordon Highlanders. Lieutenant J. Thurgood of the 12th Battalion, West Yorkshire Regiment, was the prosecuting officer, but there was no officer or 'prisoner's friend' acting for Private Horler.

Opening the prosecution on the charge of desertion, Lieutenant Thurgood called the first witness, Corporal J. Russell of B Company who testified that unit was in the support line in the Lagnicourt sector of the Front, and that the accused, Private Horler, was a member of his section. At 3 p.m. on 3 December 1917, the accused had been present when the Company were told that they were going to wire in front of the support trenches and were instructed to parade for this work at 7 p.m. that evening. However, at 7 p.m. the accused was absent.

The next witness was Private Gilbert, also of B Company, who stated that the Company was paraded by the Sergeant-Major at 7 p.m. and had brought wire cutters and gloves for the work. The witness told the Court that he was in the accused's platoon and when his name was called out there was no answer; he did not see him that night or the next day.

Private Horler did not exercise his right to cross-examine the witnesses but in his defence stated that:

> I was present on the parade at 3 p.m. on 3 December. We were told to parade again at 7 p.m. I left the battalion because I was a sick man when I was sent to it. (He had joined the 12th Battalion on 2 October 1917, possibly with the '80 untrained men from the Labour Battalion' recorded in the Battalion Diary.) My heart is in a very bad state, the arteries poisoned by an injection. My stomach is poisoned, also I have reported sick on different occasions for these ailments. I have been ill for a good many months and done duty the whole time in the line and out. When I left the battalion I did not know that the wiring party was going up to the support line. I left because my condition had been getting worse.

The prosecution presented no further witnesses, none were called by the accused and he made no further statement. The court now closed to consider its findings on the first charge of desertion; this was guilty, and the sentence was death.

It appears that after leaving his unit on 3 December, Ernest Horler had made his way to Boulogne, where he surrendered to the Military Police on the following day. He was then taken to the large Base Depot at Etaples, where he waited to be returned to his unit and a probable disciplinary charge.

The court martial reconvened to consider the charge of escaping from lawful custody. Private Illingworth of the 12th Battalion testified that at the Base Depot, Etaples, on 14 December, he had been a member of a draft of men being returned to the Front in the charge of Sergeant Bevan, and saw the accused join them. However, when the draft reached the railway siding to entrain, he could not see the accused and he was not with them when they reached the 12th Battalion. Under cross-examination by the court, Private Gilbert could not confirm that Private Horler was under escort at this time. He stated that Sergeant Bevan had since been killed.

Once again Ernest Horler had disappeared, and remained absent somewhere in the Etaples area, to re-emerge several weeks later when he was stopped by Lance-Corporal Pryce of the Military Police, who testified that 'At Etaples on 12 January at about 10.50 p.m. I was on duty and met the accused in the street. I stopped him. He could not produce a pass so I arrested him. Accused had no identity disc, pay book or tunic.'

In response to this charge Ernest Horler produced no witnesses but stated that: 'I was supposed to be on my way to join the Battalion without escort. I admit that I disappeared from the party. I had no intention of deserting. I had lost my disc, pay book up at the camp at Etaples. I do not mean the military prison.'

The proceedings on the charge of escaping were now complete and after due deliberation the court found the prisoner not guilty. The finding on the second charge of desertion was guilty and once again the sentence was death.

With the findings on the charges now given, the prosecuting officer, Lieutenant Thurgood, produced Ernest Horler's conduct sheet and this was not very good. He had been absent from his previous unit for twenty-four hours on 25 July 1917 and forfeited seven days' pay. Three days later on 28 July he disobeyed a lawful command and was sentenced by a Field General Court Martial to fifty-six days of No. 1 Field Punishment. On 8 November a Field General Court Martial had sentenced him to two years hard of labour for escaping and being absent without leave, but this was reduced to ninety days No. 1 Field Punishment; Ernest Horler was still under this sentence when he deserted on 3 December. No. 1 Field Punishment was designed to humiliate as well as punish the offender, and usually involved the soldier being secured by ropes or manacles to a fixed object, such as a cart wheel, for up to two hours a day followed by hard labour and other demanding work in the vicinity of the front line.

Ernest Horler was now afforded the opportunity to plead mitigation and to call evidence of character. No character witnesses were called but he sought mitigation of the sentence, stating that, 'I have been ill. I have been deprived of pay and am sure there is a lot due to me. (This is the response of a man just sentenced to death!) I should like to apply for a medical board on my physical and mental condition. Before joining the Army I had a fine character. I have an aged mother and make her an allotment. My illness has told against me all the time. I appeal to the Court to see that my health is inquired into.'

With this statement the court closed and Private Ernest Horler was taken away into the custody of the Third Division's Assistant Provost Marshal to await his fate; would the sentence of death be confirmed, or a term of imprisonment substituted?

The death sentence required the confirmation of the Commander in Chief, Field Marshal Sir Douglas Haig, and the wheels of military justice were turning rapidly as the findings were passed up the chain of command.

On 31 January, Lieutenant Colonel R. C. Smythe, Officer Commanding the 12th Battalion, West Yorkshire Regiment, transmitted the findings of the Court Martial to the Headquarters of 9th Infantry Brigade accompanied by the following statement:

Re 46127, Private ERNEST WILLIAM HORLER, 12th Bn. West Yorks Regt.
Herewith particulars required under SS 412a. 66.
- He has been in one action only whilst serving with this Battalion. Most of his time has been spent under arrest or as an absentee.
Enlisted 23.5.16
Joined 12th Battn. West Yorkshire Regt., 2.10.17.
Struck off the strength as a deserter, 14.12.17.
Apprehended by M.P., 12.1.18
Rejoined Battalion under escort 20.1.18.
- Discipline in the Battalion is good.
- I am of the opinion that the crime was deliberately committed.
- Age: 27. Married.
R.C. Smythe
　　Lieut.-Col.,
- Commanding 12th (S.) Battn. West Yorkshire Regt.

The statement that Ernest Horler was married is a puzzle. There is no record of his marriage and as later events will show, this information is almost certainly inaccurate.

On 1 February, the prisoner was medically examined by the Deputy ADMS of the

Ernest Horler, who was shot for desertion in the First World War, is remembered on the north side of his family's headstone cross in Yeovil Cemetery by the words 'Ernest Horler killed in France Feb. 17 1918 aged twenty six years'.

Third Division who could 'find him suffering from no appreciable disease', and on the same day the Battalion's Medical Officer reported that he had seen him on five occasions:

> Firstly with Bad feet
> Secondly 'Rheumatic' – which did not exist
> Thirdly Chill – easily remedied
> Fourthly during Field Punishment stomach required purge
> Fifthly Prior to disappearance reported that his heart was bad.
> I examined him and found his heart normal.
> On the morning of the trial he made no complaint of illness and on examination I found him to be suffering from no appreciable disease.

The papers were proceeding up the chain of command and on 1 February landed on the desk of Major-General C. J. Deverell, Commanding, Third Division, who wrote in his own hand,

> I recommend that the sentence be put into execution. The crime was apparently deliberate to avoid service as a soldier and to avoid going out with a wiring party. The prisoner has been previously convicted of absence without leave. From his previous record and the opinion given by his CO the prisoner appears to be a

worthless man who has continually endeavoured to evade service. I can find no extenuating circumstances.

The recommendation was sent on with the papers to the Corps Commander, Lieutenant General A. Haldane, who concurred, as did General Byng, Commanding Third Army, and on 3 February the proceedings were presented to the Adjutant-General for scrutiny at General Headquarters prior to their submission to the Commander-in-Chief. When the papers were read, a Captain Dowson, on behalf of the Deputy Judge Advocate General, noted that the words 'as a deserter (or absentee without leave)' in the certificate of surrender put in evidence relating to Ernest Horler's arrest in Boulogne were not strictly admissible, but they were merely formal and could not have affected the finding on the first charge.

On 12 February, Field Marshal Sir Douglas Haig, the Commander-in-Chief, confirmed the sentence of death and Private Ernest Horler's fate was sealed – he had five days left.

Four days later on 16 February, the following order was given by the Commander of the Third Division;

> No.46127. Private E. W. HORLER, 12th Battalion, West Yorkshire Regiment, having been sentenced to Death by shooting and the sentence having been confirmed, I direct that it be carried out in the neighbourhood of BOISLEUX-AU-MONT, FRANCE, on February 17th, 1918, at an hour appointed by, and under supervision of, the A.P.M. 3rd Division.

How Ernest Horler spent his last days, or how he went to his death, is not recorded; all that is known is that he was shot to death at 6.46 a.m. on Sunday morning 17 February 1918, as certified by the Assistant Provost Marshal, who confirmed that 'Death was instantaneous'.

On 9 March 1918, the court martial papers were sent to London by the Deputy Judge Advocate General with the added note 'No further action required'.

So ended the life of Private Ernest Horler, a former grocer's assistant, born in Yeovil on 30 March 1892, the second son of Yeovil police constable Edmund Horler and his wife Sarah, who sadly had been a widow for nineteen years at the time of her son's death. Ernest lies in peace in Bucquoy Road Cemetery, Ficheux, 9 kilometres from Arras. Tragedy had struck the Horler family some seven months previous, when Sarah Horler's elder son, George, had been fatally electrocuted in an accident at the electricity generating station at Back o'th Bank, Bolton, Lancashire on 1 July 1917. George lies buried in Bolton Cemetery.

However, this is not the end of this sad story, because two months later on 17 April, a Member of Parliament asked a question in the House of Commons and the *Western Gazette* reported the outcome:

> The recent death of a Yeovil soldier has raised a good deal of local interest. The case was raised in the House of Commons on Wednesday last by Mr Athlestan Rendall, MP who asked the Pensions Minister whether he has now considered the question of the awarding of a pension to the mother of Priv. E. H. No. 46127, West Yorkshire Regt, who was shot for desertion, and, who prior to her son's death, was receiving 8s 9d

weekly; if such pension has been refused, is it because although the widow of a soldier who has been shot is entitled to a pension a mother under similar circumstances is not; and how he justifies such a distinction?

The Minister of Pensions (Mr Hodge): The regimental paymaster reports that separation allowance will be paid in this case till the 16th September next. The question of pension will therefore be dealt with in August, and any pension admissible will be paid from 17th September. No distinction is drawn in these cases between widows and other dependants.

Mr Rendall asked whether any and what enquiries were made as to the past history of Private E. H. No. 46127, West Yorkshire Regiment, before he was sentenced and shot for desertion on 17th February last: whether it was known that this man was considered by his employers and townspeople, previous to his becoming a soldier, to be mentally weak, and that whilst a soldier he gave considerable anxiety and trouble to the doctors and his officers; whether such doctors had made any report and if so, what report of his mental condition; whether, after he deserted, he wrote his mother several letters, the envelopes of which she sent on to his regiment to enable them to discover his whereabouts, and that it was by means of these that he was found, and, as a consequence, shot; and will he call for a full report on this man's health and conduct record previous to his death?

Mr. Macpherson: I have made enquiry, and find that this man was specially examined by the medical authorities both before and after his trial by court-martial, with the result that he was found to be in a perfectly normal state of health. I have no information as to the other suggestions raised by my hon. friend.

Mr. Rendall asked whether information to the effect that the man had been shot for desertion and no other information and no preliminary letter was sent on 16th March to his mother by the Infantry Record Office at York and whether he will explain why such method was adopted in view of the pledge given by him?

Mr Macpherson: It is much regretted that an error was made at the Record Office, and steps have been taken by the officer in charge to prevent a recurrence.

Mr. Rendall: As this has caused very great pain and also injury to the health of the mother of this young man, will the War Office send some recognition of their error to this woman?

Mr. Macpherson: I think that is a very reasonable suggestion, and if the officer in charge of the battalion has not done so I will see that it is done.

Someone at the Infantry Record Office had made a serious blunder, because in 1917 the government had directed that pensions were not to be denied in such cases and the cause of death was not to be disclosed to the next of kin. Mr Rendall's question relating to the envelopes is puzzling because no mention was made of this at the Court Martial, and from the evidence of Lance-Corporal Pryce, his meeting with Ernest Horler appears to have occurred by chance. There is also no mention of a widow.

The author's late father, who served on the Western Front in 1918 with the Wiltshire Regiment, and was awarded the Military Medal as an eighteen-year-old, occasionally mentioned the death of Ernest Horler, but never condemned him, commenting that , 'He was a simple chap who should never have been a soldier.' Perhaps this says it all!

The Simple Life

Dr Charles A. Fox was a retired medical practitioner and member of the Royal College of Surgeons. He came from an old West Country family, and at sixty-four years of age was the founder member and practitioner of 'The Simple Life' and 'Health Culture' at his home in The Birdcage, South Petherton. According to a set of four pictorial cards featuring Dr Fox and a lady (presumably his wife), he explained at great length that both these movements 'now interesting so many of both Sexes, tend to a return to the more natural conditions'. The cards announced that the doctor was the author of a large number of tracts and books on a wide range of subjects, including 'The Interpretation of the Great Pyramid and Fairy Tales', 'Royal Family', 'Disasters', 'Small pox', 'Epidemics', 'Baptism', 'The Salvation Army', 'Hiawatha', 'Anglo-Israelism', and 'Canaan', to name but a few.

On 11 May 1913, *The New York Times* wrote an account from a Special Correspondent in Taunton, published by the *Daily Mirror*, on a day spent in the company of Dr Charles Fox at his South Petherton home:

> Dr Fox, who is a member of the Royal College of Surgeons, is no mere theorist. In the secluded fields and orchards round his cottage he puts his ideas into practice. Jumping and skipping and frisking like a high-spirited schoolboy. This for instance, is a typical day in his simple life:
>
> Rises soon after dawn; pole twirling exercises; dew bath, or ordinary bath in pool; vegetarian breakfast about seven o'clock; running, cycling, reading, and writing during the morning; plain vegetarian meal about midday; more pole twirling in the afternoon; running and other exercises during the remainder of the day.
>
> 'To meet Dr. Fox for the first time,' says the correspondent, 'is a surprising experience. His sudden appearance when he left his cottage to receive me was startling. It was a lovely Spring morning, and only the singing of the birds could be heard. Suddenly a soft and jaunty step sounded behind me. A twirling pole narrowly missed my head. Then I turned and saw the strangest figure of a man to be found on any country road'.
>
> Dr. Fox was dressed in the costume that he generally wears. His body was draped with a white cotton wrapper, leaving the arms bare. A pair of white calico knickers and brown stockings covered his legs, and on his feet were sandals. Long, gray-brown curls reached to his shoulders, and his hat was a curious round piece of brown felt.

Dr Charles A. Fox enjoying 'The Simple Life', in the garden of his home at South Petherton in 1911.

'It is very good of you to come and see me,' he cried. 'I am just going to have my exercise and bath in the orchard! Come with me.'

He started skipping off down the road gaily twirling a pail over his head. Under the blossoming trees, Dr. Fox went through the weirdest evolutions. He ran to and fro, hopped, jumped, skipped and flung his arms about in graceful circles.

'Grace!' he said, during a pause. 'That is what Englishmen lack to-day. It is a quality which seems to have died out in modern civilization. Grace and beauty are almost lost to-day owing to our frightful rectangular form of dress.'

He continued talking rapidly. 'We want to see people as they really are – the human form is full of beauty – yet men and women make their figures un-natural and hideous by their clothes. Why do men wear coats which make their shoulders square? Did Nature ever intend that man should make himself look so awful? The true and only existence is the simple life of the savage.'

Dr. Fox then took his morning dew bath. The thick grass was drenched in dew, and this most ardent simple-life apostle revelled in the moisture.

'In the summer I bathe in a pool here five times a day,' he said. 'I never feel the cold. All the year round I dress like this.'

After Dr. Fox had dressed he walked briskly about the orchard, explaining his views. One of his favourite exercises – one which he frequently performs every day – is that of pole-twirling – twisting a light pole with the fingers above his head. 'It is a splendid method,' he says, 'for keeping in good health.'

Hanging John William Beale

John William Beale, butler to Captain Watkins of Badby House, near Daventry, murdered Charlotte Pugsley, a thirty-year-old cook, by shooting her in the head and cutting her throat in Leigh Woods, near Long Ashton, Bristol, on Thursday 10 September 1857.

Beale, it would appear, may have been facing an age-old classic problem and, as in so many tragic cases, it ended in disaster for both parties. He was a married man who, because of his employment as a single servant or a butler, was required on occasion to live apart from his wife.

It was during the time that John Beale was employed at Bristol as a servant to the Hon. Mrs Hutchinson of Dorset House, Clifton Down, that he began an affair with Charlotte Pugsley, the cook. He had subsequently left the Hutchinson household and in September 1857 Beale was butler to Captain Watkins at Badby House, with his wife living in a cottage nearby. However, the affair had continued until the autumn of 1856, when Charlotte took a position as cook in Mr Bythesea's household at Freshford, near Bath. What triggered the events which terminated in Charlotte's demise in Leigh Woods seem to have been lost as the years have passed, but one thing is certain: Beale was a man who almost certainly feared the loss of his apparent respectable reputation and future employment. Whatever the problem, Beale hatched a plot to resolve it.

On Saturday 5 September 1857, John Beale obtained a week's leave of absence under the pretence that his father, a pork butcher at Bath, had been seriously injured in a fall from a scaffold and that the shock had killed his sister. Travelling down to Bristol, he stayed on the Monday and Tuesday, visiting friends and telling them that he was going to visit his parents. On Wednesday he went to Mr Bythesea's house to collect Charlotte Pugsley, as it seems that Beale had previously arranged with her to surrender her place and leave with him for marriage at Southampton, and onward travel for a new life in America. This is what he told Charlotte's friends and fellow servants; he also informed everyone that he had been discharged from Captain Watkins' service because his employer and family had gone to India. That evening the couple were back at Bristol, where Charlotte spent the night in a hotel and Beale with a cousin. The following morning they took her luggage to Bristol Station, to be collected later, and on the Thursday afternoon the couple were seen going towards, Leigh Woods and then in the woods, by several boys.

On Friday afternoon under gamekeeper George Warren found the body of a woman in the Nightingale Valley, shot in the head and with her throat cut. The corpse was

On 10 September 1857 John William Beale murdered his lover, Charlotte Pugsley, in the Nightingale Valley at Leigh Woods, near Bristol, shown here in an early postcard.

identified to be that of Charlotte Pugsley, and Bristol police enquiries resulted in John Beale's arrest at the house of Captain Watkins. It transpired that he had returned on Saturday 12 September with the luggage containing Charlotte's clothes, which he then gave to a female friend, saying they were his late sister's. The search of Beale's room produced a knife, two pocket pistols, one of which fitted the ball removed from Charlotte's head, and a Bible given to her by a great friend in service at Freshford.

Thirty-year-old John William Beale was charged with murder of Charlotte Pugsley, and at his trial on 22 December at Winter Assizes in Taunton, it took the jury only three minutes to find him guilty, and he was sentenced to death by a public hanging at the front of the county gaol at Taunton on Tuesday 12 January 1858.

On New Year's Day, Beale's wife paid her farewell visit, followed a few days later by his mother and sister. During the last Sunday before his execution, Beale was reported to appear to be more depressed than at any time since sentence was passed and he was exceedingly devoted in his religious duties throughout the day.

The *Western Flying Post*, of Tuesday 19 January describes in graphic detail John William Beale's last day:

The execution of the culprit took place exactly three weeks after his conviction. The drop was constructed between three and four o'clock in the morning, the cross beam having an iron loop and short chain affixed to render it unnecessary for the hangman to tie the rope to the beam, as heretofore; all that was required was to pass a hook attached to the fatal noose in the piece of suspended chain. Calcraft [William Calcraft, the public hangman] reached Taunton the day previous by train, and his arrangements were promptly made for carrying the last sentence of the law into effect. Towards the grey dawn of morn upwards of 7000 spectators were collected beneath the drop. There were perhaps few persons in the throng belonging to what is termed the better class of persons; among them might be described the aged and blear-eyed drunkard of either sex; slip-shod mothers without their babes; unwashed and unkept urchins for the most part shoeless and in rags; the incipient boy smoker just entering on that important epoch in his history, his teens and his first 'cutty pipe'; the cadaverous-looking factory girl and the gaping rustic, each and all anxious to bear personal testimony to the bearing of the unhappy fellow mortal about to be suspended in mid-air for a revolting and hideous murder.

The culprit was visited on Monday night by the Chaplain, who spent a considerable time with him in the condemned cell; subsequently the Rev. Mr Liddon saw him, and remained at prayer and earnest conversation with the convict until after eleven o'clock. During the night Beale slept but very little, and his slumbers were of a fitful and perturbed character. From 2 till 3 he slept soundly, and continued dozing at intervals during the rest of the night. The Governor of the Gaol visited his cell about a quarter before six o'clock this morning when the convict was asleep; he however awoke before Mr Oakley left him and in the course of some conversation the unhappy man expressed great gratitude to Mr Oakley, the Governor, to the Chaplain and the officers generally, for the kindness and consideration with which he had been treated. Soon after he awoke, the Governor reminded Beale that Mr Liddon was coming by appointment at six o'clock, on which he promptly replied, 'I am quite prepared for him and my fate.' Mr Liddon accordingly came and stayed with him in fervent prayer until about 7.15. After Mr Liddon had left him Beale had breakfast of the ordinary prison diet, with the exception of the addition of a little tea which he asked for and he ate but sparingly. Mr. Mast, the chaplain then saw him, and remained with the convict until he proceeded to the chapel shortly after 9, where Divine service was celebrated, the whole of the prisoners, debtors excepted, being present and the culprit again joined the Holy Communion. The procession was then formed, the Chaplain reading the burial service, followed by the convict who walked with a firm and measured step between two turnkeys, the Governor, the Rev. Mr Liddon, and the surgeon bringing up the rear. From the chapel the procession moved across the Governor's garden to the court leading to the steps. On the first landing the culprit was received by Calcraft, who proceeded to pinion him, and the procession moved on to the scaffold. At the foot of the drop, the Chaplain asked Beale if there was anything he wished to communicate and he replied in the negative. Calcraft first mounted the scaffold, next came the culprit, followed by Sulley, the chief turnkey and an assistant. Beale gave a vacant look around and turned his back on the spectators, the executioner place him in position, adjusted the rope, placed a cap over his face and retired and in less than a minute the drop fell. His struggles were severe and continued for about two minutes and a half. After hanging an hour, the body was cut down and after a caste of the head had been taken by a gentleman from Liverpool, was placed in a shell in the clothes Beale had worn at his trial, and buried within the precincts of the gaol.

A Murder and a Suicide

The elderly captain had lodged in comfortable circumstances on his army half pay at Fivehead House, near Taunton, for some five years, but events would take a shocking turn on the afternoon of Sunday 12 April 1817, when seventy-four-year-old Captain Fleming killed an old brother officer and then committed suicide.

Fivehead House was described in the *Taunton Courier* of 24 April 1817 as a Lunatic Asylum where, five years before, the captain had been placed in the care of the proprietor, Mr Gillett. The captain had been a patient in the establishment for some three years, but when pronounced sane he had preferred to remain as a private lodger because 'he received great civility and respect there, and knew of no place where he could be more happy'. For the previous two years, Captain Fleming had been regarded as a perfectly normal house guest, with freedom to come and go as he pleased, and enjoyed his large, east-facing, light and airy room with its feather bed, comfortable chairs, table and personal possessions, including a deal case placed on a shelf near the window.

Some time prior to 12 April, Mr Gillett had received an invitation from friends at Exeter to pay them a visit in company with Captain Fleming and another gentleman lodger. However, the captain made an excuse not to go, and Mr Gillett and the gentleman left for Exeter without him.

Following Mr Gillett's departure, Captain Fleming wrote to a Captain Miller, an old brother officer and former paymaster and agent to the Staffordshire Militia, now residing in London, asking him to come down to Fivehead as a matter of urgency. The captain told his acquaintance that because he was getting on in years, he proposed to make his will, which he wished him to witness, and also to grant Captain Miller, a power of attorney to transact business on his behalf.

Captain Miller arrived at Fivehead House at about midday on Sunday 12 April, and after a friendly exchange of greetings the two old soldiers, Captain Miller being sixty-five, sat down to a convivial dinner with Mrs Gillett and her family, recalling their campaigning years. The two were in a cheerful mood and because Mrs Gillett knew that the visitor had arrived on business, she left them alone and was not concerned when they went up to the captain's room. About ten minutes later, just after half past two, the keeper employed by Mr Gillett at the Asylum heard noises coming from an upstairs room and, thinking it was a patient who was sometimes very 'high', went to find out what was happening. However, as he climbed the stairs there was the sound of

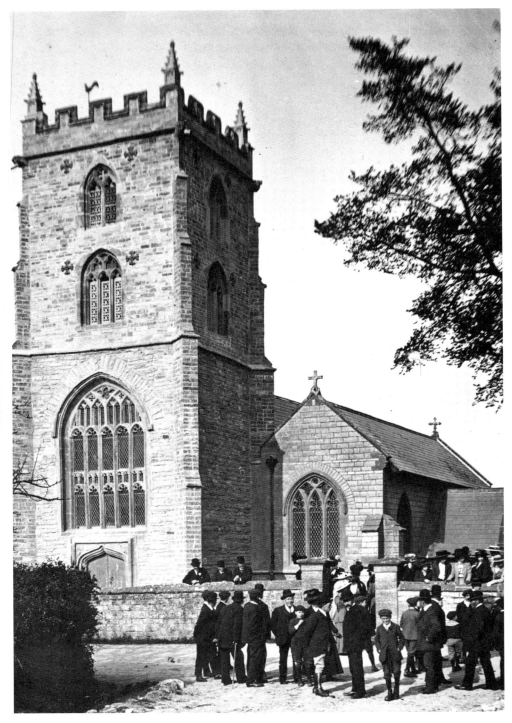

Parishioners are shown here are at the ceremony marking the restoration of the tower of St Martin's church, Fivehead. In 1817, the apparently restored sanity of a resident in the Asylum at Fivehead House failed, and the result was murder and suicide.

a gunshot, followed a few moments later by another, coming from Captain Fleming's room.

Bursting into the room, the first thing the keeper saw through the haze of powder smoke was Captain Miller lying on the floor on his back, dead, still wearing his glasses and gripping a quill pen in his hand; at the far end of the room, Captain Fleming was sprawled face down, also dead. A discharged pistol lay near the corpse of Captain Miller and a few feet away was another by the body of Captain Fleming; a bloodied three-bladed sword had been thrown down on the bed. On the table was a printed form of will, with blanks for names and sums of money to be added, two uncompleted powers of attorney in the deceased Captain Miller's handwriting, and the deal case standing open on the shelf.

A local surgeon, Mr Rich, was called, and following an examination of the room and the position of the bodies, it was concluded that Captain Miller had been sitting at the table in the act of writing when Captain Fleming had come up behind and shot him in the back. The pistol ball had entered below the dead officer's left shoulder but apparently, as this had not killed him outright, he had been stabbed fatally, seven or eight times, in the chest. Captain Fleming had thrown the sword onto the bed and then placed the second pistol against the right side of his head, pulled the trigger and blown his brains out.

Further enquiries established that when Captain Fleming had been admitted to Fivehead House, his trunks and the deal case, which, it transpired, held the sword and two pistols, had been kept unopened in the custody of Mr Gillette and had been returned with the keys after the patient had been pronounced sane. Two letters were found in a drawer in the captain's room, dated 12 April and addressed to the Reverend John Gale, one of the visiting magistrates appointed to inspect the Asylum at Fivehead House, and the contents were considered sufficient for the jury at the subsequent inquest to return verdicts of murder against Captain Fleming and insanity.

The contents of the letters were not disclosed in the local newspapers and therefore it is unlikely that, nearly two centuries later, we will ever know why Captain Fleming shot and fatally stabbed Captain Miller at Fivehead House on the afternoon of Sunday 12 April 1817.

Poachers

In 1825, the year of my story, poachers could be divided (generally speaking) between poor countrymen struggling to exist and feed their families on a pauper's wage and gangs, (organised or otherwise) who poached game for profit or gain and who could be ruthless in pursuing their objectives. Whatever the reason, the illegal hunting and trapping of game attracted severe penalties and extreme measures on the part of landowners determined to protect their living property. In addition to the chance of capture by gamekeepers and the authorities, the poacher could suffer maiming in the jaws of a vicious mantrap, or death or severe wounding from the contents of a spring gun fired by a hidden tripwire. However, despite the penalties and the risks, poaching was not diminished to any great extent, and as many of the participants were known and often highly regarded as local heroes, the authorities could not expect too much cooperation in bringing poachers to justice.

In the winter of 1825, a gang of poachers was at large in the countryside around Shepton Mallet, and in the early hours of a January morning they clashed with the gamekeeper of Edward Berkeley Portman, Esquire, by a wood on his estate at Pylle.

Gamekeeper Meshach Read was roused from his sleep at Pylle House at about one o'clock in the morning of 10 January by Bishop, the live-in labourer, and told that he had heard people in the nearby wood. Meshach Read quickly dressed, loaded and primed a large flintlock pistol which he slipped into the pocket of his greatcoat, pocketed a copper powder flask in his waistcoat, picked his large, heavy stick, and followed Bishop out into the bright moonlight. The events which followed were recounted three months later at the Somerset Lent Assizes before Mr Justice Bourrough, when twenty-two-year-old Charles Gray from south Brewham and Henry Austin, aged thirty-three years, of Upton Noble, near Bruton, stood indicted for being in a wood of Edward Berkeley Portman, Esquire, with intent to kill game in the night time, armed with bludgeons. One Joseph Edwards should have accompanied them in the dock, but he had gone on the run and was still at large.

Meshach Read, the gamekeeper, was the first and principal witness for the Crown and recounted how, in company with Bishop, he had gone down the road into the wood, where, in the bright moonlight, he could see two men standing under a tree. One of them was pointing a gun at something in the tree, and when it was fired, the gamekeeper had heard the clatter of a pheasant's wings as it flew away.

Read stated that he had concealed himself, but in doing so had lost sight of the two men and, hearing no further movement or shots, had returned to the road, hoping to

In 1825, a gang of poachers was active in the countryside around Shepton Mallet and one of the measures taken by landowners to protect their game was a mantrap. Joseph Lewis of the South Somerset District Council's Heritage Team inspects an early nineteenth-century mantrap from the collection of the Museum of South Somerset.

apprehend the men as they left the wood. He had not waited long, when two men came out of the wood onto the road, but neither appeared to be carrying a gun; however, they were both carrying large bludgeons. As they came closer, he recognised the pair as Charles Gray and Henry Austin despite the blacking they had applied to their faces. When he called out, demanding to know what they were doing in the wood at this hour of the night, one had shouted back 'Damn thy limbs, I'll let thee know in a minute!' and the two intruders began hurling stones at him. Read stated that he had walked towards the pair, brandishing his heavy stick, but as he did so five more black-faced men came out of the wood carrying bludgeons.

Meshach Read stated that the newcomers immediately attacked him and began beating him, in his words, 'most dreadfully'. Answering the gamekeeper's call for help, Bishop came running up, only to be set upon, knocked down and beaten insensible. One of the labourer's attackers picked him up and threw him into the stream which crossed the road, exclaiming 'Damn thy limbs, there's a watery bed for thee!' The court was told that the stream had been deep enough to have drowned Bishop if he had fallen face down, but fortunately he had landed on his back, with his upturned face in the shallows.

The gamekeeper went on to tell that when Bishop had been disposed of, all seven men had turned their attention back to him, and a blow from Austin's bludgeon had knocked the stick from his hand. Defenceless, Read threatened to bore a hole through Austin with a pistol, and his reply had been, 'Damn thy pistol, I don't care for thee or thy pistol either!' Now fearing for his life, Meshach Read stated that he had drawn the pistol from his pocket, but when he pulled the trigger it had misfired. However, using the weapon as a club he had given Austin two heavy blows to his stomach, knocked another man down, and taking hold of a fellow he recognised as Joseph Edwards, threw him to the ground, smacked the pistol into his face and fell on him. Edwards was dragged from under the battling gamekeeper, who went on to describe how he was held on the ground and kicked and beaten. A struggle then took place for the pistol, but Read stated that as the weapon was torn from his grasp, his hand had been badly cut by the lock flint.

Meshach Read stated that by now he had been so badly beaten that he was unable to move, but as his assailants walked away, he summoned enough the energy to call after them, 'You cowardly rascals, there's not a man among you!' One of the men turned and shouted to another of the gang, 'Damn his limbs, go back and leg him!' With that, Joseph Edwards came back with a bludgeon in one hand and a gun barrel in the other, striking the gamekeeper three savage blows across his legs with the bludgeon and a heavy blow to his chest with the gun barrel, which hit with such force that the copper powder flask in his waistcoat pocket was badly dented.

The gamekeeper described how, despite being covered in blood from the many head wounds and severe bruising, he had recovered sufficiently to crawl to the stream and drag out the still unconscious Bishop. When Bishop finally regained his senses, the two men had managed to stumble back to Pylle House. Both had been so badly injured that for some days they remained dangerously ill.

Charles Gray and Henry Austin had been arrested on the information of Meshach Read, but Joseph Edwards had disappeared and the gamekeeper could not identify the four remaining members of the gang.

Meshach Read's evidence was corroborated by Bishop, and it did not take long for the jury to find Gray and Austin guilty and Mr Justice Burrough sentenced them to seven years' transportation to Australia.

For Those in Peril

Those who go to sea are only four inches from death.
(Anacharsis)

The sea, calm and serene in the beauty of a setting sun, can turn into an ugly fearsome beast which devours without mercy, and those who ignore its power do so in mortal peril. One such man ignored the warnings,and paid the supreme penalty, tragically taking others to their doom.

Early on the morning of Friday 15 November 1822, Captain John Maunder Gill, late of the 46th Regiment of Foot, arrived at Watchet harbour, having sailed from Cardiff to meet his wife of four years, Anna Maria, her sister Sarah Tanner, and the maidservant, and return the same day to his house at Llandaff. Anna Maria and maid servant had been staying with her father, the Reverend Mr Thomas Tanner, at Sampford Brett, near Williton, as the captain was seeking to purchase an estate in the neighbourhood.

However, when Captain Gill and his party arrived back at Watchet later that morning, the brisk westerly wind had increased in strength and a rough sea was running. Before the party embarked, several local seafarers advised against setting out in these conditions, but the advice was rejected and the captain, his wife, sister-in-law, maidservant, together with the two experienced members of the crew, set out in his small sail boat. The vessel was nearly halfway home when a full gale blew up with driving rain squalls, and as the tide had turned and was running hard down the Bristol Channel against the westerly wind, the sea was whipped up into large, steep waves.

A labourer working on the cliffs above Watchet had watched the small boat leave the harbour and, because of the rough sea, was curious to follow its progress. The onslaught of a squall of wind and heavy rain sent him running for shelter, but when he returned to the cliff top about half an hour later: there was no sign of the boat just an empty, storm-tossed sea.

Across the bay at Minehead, the passage of Captain Gill's boat was being observed through telescopes by a number of people on the harbour wall and it had soon become evident that the vessel was in serious trouble. A white handkerchief could be seen tied to the mast head, and several occupants were waving white drapery. Attempts to launch rescue boats were prevented by the gale and the strength of the falling tide flowing down the channel.

The boat, with Captain John Maunder Gill, his wife Anna Maria, her sister Sarah, the maidservant and the two experienced seamen, disappeared into the blinding rain and raging sea, not to be seen again until a part of the vessel was washed up a few days later on the Somerset coast; there was no sign of the occupants.

For millennia, people from this Land of Summer have gone down to the sea and have travelled far and wide in peace and war. Most have returned, but sadly, some have not, and the following three stories tell of those who did not come back to this beautiful county of Somerset, the Land of Summer.

The Loss of the *Mohegan*

The Atlantic Transport Company's new fast ocean liner *Mohegan* left London bound for New York on her second transatlantic crossing during the afternoon of Thursday 13 October 1898. The *Mohegan* was a modern and extremely luxurious 'all first class' ship of some 7,000 tons, 482 feet in length and capable of a top speed of 13 knots from her triple expansion steam engines. On 13 October she was carrying fifty-three first class passengers and ninety-seven crew under the command of Captain Griffiths, the Commodore of the Atlantic Transport Company line.

The voyage down the English Channel was in the teeth of a strong south-westerly wind and steep seas, but these conditions could be easily handled by the liner. Just before seven o'clock on the Friday evening, the *Mohegan* was approaching the Lizard; it was dark but clear, and the passengers were assembling in the saloon for dinner. Without warning the liner, now travelling at full speed, crashed onto the treacherous Manacles Reef; the *Mohegan* was some 10 to 15 miles off course. The huge gash torn below the waterline was so devastating that the watertight compartments were useless. The engine room was immediately flooded and the electric lights failed, plunging the liner into darkness.

The passengers rushed on deck to find it being swept by breakers as the stricken *Mohegan* rocked to and fro on the reef and began to list. Captain Griffiths managed to fire several distress flares but only two of the ship's life-boats could be launched before the liner lurched and sank, throwing the crew and those passengers who had not escaped in the boats into the boiling surf. All that remained of the *Mohegan* was the top of her funnel and the tops of her four masts, into which sixteen survivors managed to scramble.

The distress rockets were answered by the Porthoustock lifeboat which first came upon an upturned ship's lifeboat (one of the two launched) and on turning it over found two ladies still alive. Shortly after, the Porthoustock lifeboat found the other ship's boat, water-logged and drifting helplessly with twenty-two survivors on board.

After landing the survivors, the lifeboat set out again and, arriving on the scene of the disaster, spent the rest of the night rescuing the sixteen cold and desperate survivors from the masts in a perilous and exhausting operation.

The total loss of life was 106 passengers and crew. Captain Griffiths and all his deck officers went down with the *Mohegan*. The inquiry which followed never established why the *Mohegan* was so far off course; all who could have thrown light on the tragedy had perished.

Captain John Maunder Gill, his wife, sister-in-law and maidservant set out from Watchet Harbour with two experienced seamen, on their fatal voyage in November 1822.

On 18 October 1898, *Pulman's Weekly News* reported that:'In the list of those drowned from the steamship Mohegan appears the name of Nelson Yeaxlee, described as a baker on the ill-fated ship. He is the son of Mr. Yeaxlee, who for some years carried on a baker's and pastry cook's business in Middle Street and subsequently Earle Street, Yeovil. The father left the town about four or five years ago and went to reside at Misterton, near Crewkerne, where he still lives. The son married a Miss Phillips of Yeovil, and he went to sea some years ago, living in London. He leaves a widow and one child, aged about four years.'

In St Kevern's churchyard on the Lizard Peninsula, over forty victims of the tragedy were buried in a mass grave marked by a cross, on the base of which is engraved the word *MOHEGAN*.

The Loss of the *Titanic*

On Friday 12 April 1912, the *Western Gazette* reported that,

The great liner Titanic of the White Star Fleet sailed from Southampton on Wednesday on her maiden voyage to New York ... The ship is really like a seagoing holiday resort, so many are the opportunities for recreation and amusement on board. Band concerts are frequent from morning to night. For passengers who want a strenuous life there is a deep sea water swimming pool, a rackets court and a gymnasium. The gymnasium is also equipped with appliances whereby the pleasure of cycling, horse and camel riding, and rowing may be enjoyed.

The story of the loss of *Titanic* with 1,500 lives, following the collision with an iceberg two days later on 14 April, is too well known to be recalled in detail in these pages, but the tragedy affected the lives of a number of people with Somerset connections or birth.

Forty-nine-year-old farmer Mr Samuel Hermon, his wife Jane, twin daughters Alice and Kate, and George Sweet, their adopted son, were travelling second class from Castle Cary to Bernardsville in New Jersey, where Jane had a brother. Samuel had been born in Galhampton and had been a butcher and the proprietor of the Britannia Hotel at Castle Cary. Tragically, both Samuel Herman and fourteen-year-old George Sweet did not survive, but Jane and her two daughters were rescued from lifeboat 9 by the liner *Carpathia* and spent the rest of their lives in the United States.

Henry John Spinner, a thirty-two-year-old Yeovil glove cutter, was travelling alone as a third class passenger to Gloversville, New York. Originally from Worcester, Henry had been a Royal Marine and served on HMS *Orion* in the China Seas during the Russo-Japanese War. He had worked as a glove cutter in Worcester, and was a member of the Yeovil Town football team from 1907 until 1910/11. Tragically, Henry Spinner did not survive the disaster and left a widow and daughter back home. On 30 April, the proceeds and a collection from the Dorset League match between Yeovil and Longfleet St Mary, amounting to £30, were presented to his widow.

Mr William Elsbury was born at Stanmoor, near Burrow Bridge, and in 1884 had emigrated to Illinois, where he acquired a farm at Gurnee, Lake County, married a local girl and raised a family of three boys and a girl. In 1911 he had returned alone to Somerset to help his brother wind up their late father's estate and planned to return home in March 1912. However, his departure was deferred so that he could travel back on the maiden voyage of the *Titanic*. Sadly, this was a fateful decision because William Elsbury did not survive the sinking.

Bound for a new life in Elmira, New York, carpenter Mr Arthur Ford was travelling as a third class passenger, having paid £8 1s for his ticket, but tragically Arthur from Bridgwater was one of the 1,500 passengers and crew who lost their lives.

The need to return to Canada to settle his affairs cost thirty-seven-year-old Mr Frank Maybery his life. Following the death of his parents, young Frank, his two brothers and two sisters, together with an aunt, had emigrated to Moose Jaw, Saskatchewan, where they grew up, and the three brothers had gone into partnership as real estate agents. Frank's wife, Frances, developed a severe eye complaint and it was decided to return to England to obtain up to date treatment. Accompanied by their two young daughters, the Mayberys settled in Weston-super-Mare, and Frank was travelling second class back to Canada to settle his affairs; tragically, he would not be one of the survivors.

Mr Edwin Wheeler, also known as 'Fred', was born at Bath in 1888 and was the personal valet to the wealthy Mr George Washington Vanderbilt. Mr Vanderbilt and his wife Edith had booked a first class cabin on the *Titanic,* but at the last minute changed their minds, and instead sailed to the United States on the liner *Olympic.*

However, most of their luggage, accompanied by Fred Wheeler, was sent on the *Titanic*, and tragically he did not survive the disaster.

One Somerset man who did survive the sinking was the *Titanic*'s Third Officer, thirty-four-year-old Mr Herbert John Pitman from Castle Cary. He had been off duty when the Titanic struck the iceberg which sealed the liner's fate and launched lifeboat 5, which was rescued by the *Carpathia*. Mr Pitman continued to serve with the merchant marine for the next thirty-four years, including sea time during both world wars, until his retirement in 1946, when he was awarded the MBE (Member of the British Empire) for long and meritous service at sea during the war. He retired to Pitcombe, near Bruton, where he passed away in December 1961 and lies at peace in the parish churchyard of St Leonard.

The Sinking of Submarine *B2*

A brass plaque in St Mary's Minster church, Ilminster, remembers the drowning of twenty-year-old Able Seaman Aeneas Lee in the loss of the Submarine *B2* in the English Channel on 4 October 1912. The *B2* was a Coastal Class submarine completed in 1905, the second of eleven built by Vickers. The boat was 142 feet long with a complement of two officers and fourteen crew, powered by a petrol engine for surface running and an electric motor when submerged. The B-Class submarines were fitted with a pair of hydroplanes at the forward end of the conning tower to improve underwater handling and this was not to be repeated in subsequent boats for another fifty years, when it was re-introduced in the United States' nuclear submarines. On Friday 4 October 1912, the *B2* was taking part in naval exercises of the destroyer and submarine flotillas attached to the Home Fleet off the south-east coast and in the English Channel. Between 4.30 and 6 a.m., the destroyers left Dover and, forming up line abreast, swept down the Channel with the thirteen submarines involved setting independent courses east-south-east towards the French coast. The Hamburg–America Line SS *Amerika*, outward bound for the United States vessel was steaming at 20 knots into the English Channel from the north-east, and at about 6 a.m. the *B2*, running on the surface, crossed the path of the 22,000-ton liner. The great bow rode over the *B2*, slicing a huge gash in the pressure hull just in front of the conning tower and virtually tearing the submarine in half. In an instant water poured into the doomed submarine and the boat sank like a stone, taking the crew to the bottom, including Able Seaman Aeneas Lee from Ilminster and Leading Stoker Frank Russell of Crewkerne. However, one man had a miraculous escape. The Second Officer, Lieutenant Pulleyne, was below when the collision occurred and described how he had been taken down in the stricken submarine and felt the *B2* touch bottom. Somehow he found himself on the surface, but despite two steamers passing within 50 feet and several submarines in the area, he was not spotted for nearly an hour until he was picked by the submarine *C16*. Following the inspection of the wrecked submarine by divers, the Admiralty decided the *B2* was too badly damaged to be recovered. She was the first submarine lost and not salvaged, and her crew were left undisturbed.

'We Shall All Be Hanged, Shan't Us!'

Following the French Emperor Napoleon Bonaparte's disastrous defeat in Russia during the winter of 1812/13, and again by a coalition of European nations at the Battle of Leipzig in October 1813, there was much celebration, and in Bristol the Mayor ordered a Grand Illumination of the city on the evening of Monday 29 November, 'in honour of the late splendid victories'.

The Mansion House, King William IV's statue in Queen Square, the Merchants' Hall, the Post Office and the Commercial Rooms were brilliantly lit with lamps of all colours and descriptions. The many other illuminations or 'Transparencies' included effigies of the King and Queen with the Duke of Wellington in pride of place, Britannia and tableaux of a patriotic nature, including one showing the feats of great warriors, and another showing Bonaparte being thrown into Hell with the Devil on his back. At four o'clock in the afternoon, soldiers from the Bristol garrison fired volleys in a 'feu de joie' on Brandon Hill, accompanied by the boom of cannon.

People travelled into Bristol from the surrounding countryside to enjoy the spectacle, one of whom was a wealthy widow from Brislington by name of Mrs Frances de la Moliere. At about three o'clock on the Monday afternoon, Mrs de la Moliere set out with some friends to travel the short journey into Bristol, leaving her live-in servant of some four months, Sarah Ovens, alone in the house to lock up and follow her into the city.

However, with her mistress gone, Sarah Ovens had other plans: the perfect robbery. As darkness fell on that late November afternoon, Sarah admitted her lover, George Long, accompanied by Elizabeth Hill, and the trio began to strip the house of silver plate, jewels and watches, candlesticks and every other valuable piece they could lay their hands on, including a silk parasol. The plan worked perfectly; there was no trouble, no one was hurt or interfered, they took their time forcing open locked cupboards and drawers and the goodies were carefully packed away in a couple of boxes, a leather portmanteau and a hair trunk. Thus satisfied with the haul and leaving the back door open as if forced, George Long and Elizabeth Hill departed with the loot, and Sarah Ovens made her way innocently to meet her mistress in Bristol.

Later that evening Mrs de la Moliere and Sarah Ovens returned to the house in Brislington to find the back door damaged and the place ransacked. No doubt Sarah appeared as horrified as her mistress at the scene which met their gaze; perhaps she comforted her, ran to the parish constable to report the crime, helped to clean up the

Mrs Frances de la Moliere's home at Brislington was robbed in the late afternoon of 29 October 1813, while she was attending the 'Grand Illumination' in Bristol.

damage and made herself generally useful. At no time could this willing servant be placed under suspicion.

However, there is no guarantee that the perfect plan will remain perfect, and by the following Saturday, the lovers George Long and Sarah Ovens and their accomplice, Elizabeth Hill, found themselves lodged in Ilchester Gaol, and in deep trouble.

Four months later, in April 1814, thirty-two-year-old George Long, Sarah Ovens (twenty-eight) and Elizabeth Hill (twenty-two) appeared at the Somerset Lent Assizes, indicted for entering the house of Mrs de la Moliere at Brislington, and stealing sundry articles of plate etc., the property of the said Mrs de la Moliere. If found guilty, all three could hang.

Mrs de la Moliere was the first witness for the Crown and stated that she had gone to see the illuminations at Bristol, leaving Sarah Ovens alone to lock up the house and follow her into the city. The widow described how she had returned to find the doors open and many of her valuables stolen.

The next witness was Mrs Elizabeth Gallop, who recalled that at about seven o'clock on the evening of Monday 29 November, George Long had come to her home in the Parish of St Philip and St Jacob (near Bristol) accompanied by two boxes and enquired whether he could leave them at the house. He told the witness that he was about to part from his wife because they had quarrelled and he would be leaving shortly for London. Long had left, but some ten minutes later returned with a leather portmanteau and a hay hair trunk.

Mrs Gallop told the court that Long had called the following evening and again on Thursday morning, when he said, 'If you hear of any outcry or rumpus about two boxes, don't say I brought'em here.' Then he left, promising to return to fetch the articles that evening.

The witness stated that during the course of Thursday she had heard about the robbery at Brislington and later that day, when her husband returned home, told him of the conversation with Long. Her husband had gone to report their suspicions to the parish constable, and when the prisoner came to fetch the boxes and the other articles that evening, he had been arrested.

Next witness was James Gallop, who confirmed his wife's testimony and stated that when Long was arrested he had exclaimed, 'I shall be hanged, I see!'

The constable of the Parish of St Philip and St Jacob, George Arnold, entered the witness box and described going to James Gallop's house, where he found the two boxes and the other articles which fitted the description on the handbills circulated by the Brislington parish authorities. When he was arrested, James Long had readily confessed to the robbery and freely admitted that Sarah Ovens and Elizabeth Hill were his accomplices.

George Arnold stated that Elizabeth Hill had been arrested at her mother's house, where he found some of the stolen goods, including the silk parasol and several candlesticks hidden away in a box. On being arrested Elizabeth Hill had blurted out: 'We shall all be hanged, shan't us!'

Constable Arnold testified that Sarah Ovens had been arrested shortly after, and when all three were brought before Mr Ireland, the magistrate at Brislington, they had confessed to the robbery and were committed to Ilchester Gaol to await trial at the Somerset Lent Assizes.

John Coxlee, another constable, told the court that during the journey from Brislington, Sarah Ovens had confessed to him and related how she had opened the door and let in the two accomplices. She told the constable that she had broken open the sideboard and bent a large silver salver, so that it could be better packed away, and had taken other articles.

Witness Thomas James testified that at Ilchester Gaol, Sarah Ovens had confessed to him the details of the robbery and said that Elizabeth Hill had not known what was intended until she was let into the house.

As all three prisoners had already confessed their guilt, the jury found them guilty and they were sentenced to death by hanging.

On 22 April 1814, George Long and his lover Sarah Ovens paid the supreme penalty at Ilchester for the crime which seemed so perfect, both dying 'pentitently and acknowledged the offence for which they suffered'; Elizabeth Hill was reprieved at the last minute and transported to Australia for life.

Yeovil Town Hall Burns Down

The commotion in the street below his bedroom awoke Mr Clement White, his immediate thoughts were that this was 'another London party' and he wished they would be quiet. Climbing out of bed, he pulled back the curtains and was amazed to see flames leaping from the roof of the town hall across the road from his High Street jeweller's shop. 'It was a wonderful sight chiefly on account of the cloud of sparks flying across King George Street. Although the clock tower was a mass of flames the clock itself continued to keep time for at least half an hour before the movement fell out,' he recounted to a *Western Gazette* reporter the following day.

In the early morning of Sunday 22 September 1935, Police Constable Udall was on the night beat and as he walked along High Street, he looked up to check the time on the illuminated clock on the town hall nearly 100 feet above him; it was 3.40 a.m. and smoke was pouring from the ventilators under the clock turret. As the constable went through the archway under the town hall to investigate the cause, he heard the crackle of flames and realised that the building above him was on fire.

The Yeovil Fire Station in South Street was not far away, but by the time the brigade arrived, led by Chief Officer Charles Mitchell, smoke was billowing from the windows and within about five minutes the roof began to fall in, sending sheets of flame roaring into the night sky.

One of the first to witness the fire, Mr A. E. Waddleton who worked at the nearby Mermaid Hotel, recalled that he had woken up and saw flames,

> at one end of the roof. Within a short time the clock tower was on fire and from that point the flames spread like wild fire. The Yeovil Brigade made a very smart turn out, the escape was run up within a few minutes and firemen were playing on the blazing roof. Very soon the roof fell in with a terrible crash and there was a series of explosions. The clock tower was like a blazing furnace.

The town hall could not be saved and all the brigade's efforts were directed to prevent the fire from spreading to Messrs Clements' shop next door in the High Street, the King George Street Municipal Offices and the shops and offices under the blazing building. Fearing that his men would not be able to contain the fire, Chief Officer Mitchell telephoned the Sherborne Brigade for back up. Five hoses played on the blaze from High Street and George Court at the rear, a sixth supplied by a mobile pump was

The fire which broke out in the clock tower of Yeovil Town Hall, pictured in the centre of this postcard, destroyed the whole building in September 1935.

directed at the clock tower, and another jet was aimed into the centre of the inferno from the top of the Brigade's recently acquired escape ladder. A group of gas meters under the flight of stairs leading up to the town hall had been smashed by falling debris, and the blazing gas ignited from four large pipes was endangering the wall of Messrs Clements' shop. If the gas from the ruptured pipes could not be stopped the shop would be in danger, and Mr Herbert Swetman of the Corporation Gas Works was called out to turn off the supply. Undaunted, he entered the blazing building and in the smoke and heat, with debris falling around him, managed to turn off the four taps after three attempts, but in doing so Herbert Swetman was badly overcome by the heat, smoke and gas and only prompt artificial respiration saved him from serious injury.

Gradually the brigade gained the upper hand and was finally able to get though the main door to the Hall and tackle the seat of the blaze. By the time the reinforcements arrived from Sherborne the fire was well under control and they stood by to give support if required.

By breakfast time, crowds of Yeovilians had gathered in High Street to see their once-proud town hall reduced to a smouldering shell, open to the sky and surmounted by the skeletal girders of the clock tower. Although the clock mechanism had been destroyed, the three bells which struck the hours still hung from the badly burnt stout oak beams.

Apart from Mr Swetman, no one was hurt in the blaze, but the town hall was completely gutted and two valuable paintings were destroyed; one was of King George IV by Sir Thomas Lawrence and the second, a modern one by Mr Francis Newberry, depicted the muster of the Earl of Bedford's troops in St John's Churchyard before the Battle of Babylon Hill in 1642.

Underneath the town hall were Messrs Moffat's showrooms, Mr Luffman's confectionery shop, 'The Chocolate Box', a second-hand bookshop and newsagents owned by Mr O'Hagan and the local office of the *Express and Echo*. Although the premises escaped the fire, they suffered considerable damage and loss from the huge volume of water used to douse the blaze above them.

The cause of the fire has always remained a mystery but Mr Clement White had a theory which he explained to the *Western Gazette* reporter,

> One dial of the clock had a piece broken out in last Monday's storm and the wind was blowing that way last night. I think it is probable the wind would blow cobwebs over the gas light inside the clock face or might have blown in leaves or scraps of paper. That might catch alight and fall down and start the fire. The large amount of smoke might be accounted for by the accumulation of dust, leaves, bits of paper, and bits carried by birds, which it is likely would collect in the open lattice work under the clock since it was erected in 1912.

The ruins of the town hall were pulled down and the shops known as the Arcade were built on the site. A scheme was prepared for a new town hall and municipal offices to be built at Hendford Manor, but Second World War intervened and the plans were put on the shelf. For some years after the war the Borough Council had more urgent matters to deal with and the great debates during the 1950s and 60s on the relocation of the civic offices were finally resolved by the building of Johnson Hall and the reorganisation of local government.

The Crash of a Spitfire

Reginald White and Charles Saunders were busy hedging in Hill Ground at Yeovil Marsh during the afternoon of Thursday 16 February 1950, when seemingly out of nowhere came a roaring scream low overhead. Seconds later, the startled pair watched in horror as a Spitfire fighter plane with its engine running at full speed ploughed nose first into the side of the hill a few hundred yards away and exploded in flames. Rushing to the scene they found the smashed aircraft in a smoking crater several feet deep with debris scattered across the ground; there was no sign of the pilot.

About a mile away in Yeovil, at the top of Coronation Avenue, Mr F. G. Foote saw the Spitfire coming from the west, flying fast but normal. As the aircraft passed overhead he watched it roll to the left, remain steady for a moment then suddenly disappear in a dive in the direction of Yeovil Marsh.

Mr W. F. Snell was working in his office at Marsh Farm when he heard a loud bang but, thinking it was an aircraft backfiring, took no further notice until his wife rushed in, telling him that a plane had crashed in Hill Ground near Pear Tree Cottage. While Mrs Snell rang for the fire and ambulance, her husband, accompanied by several of his farm hands, hurried to the crash site, where they found Reginald White and Charles Saunders standing helpless near the crater, there was nothing anyone could do. If the pilot had not bailed out (which was the case), he was dead somewhere in the wreckage. In the distance came the sound of the bells of the fire engines and ambulance racing to the scene, followed by the curious.

Less than a week later, on Tuesday 21 February, the inquest opened into the death of twenty-six-year-old Mr Keith Butler, a Westland Aircraft test pilot, who had perished in the crash.

The inquest was told that Mr Butler was an experienced pilot with over 2,000 flying hours to his credit and had served in the Royal Air Force as a flying instructor and with a Photo Reconnaissance Unit until the end of the war. Since then he had been a civilian test pilot at the Royal Aircraft Establishment, Farnborough, before joining Westland, only a fortnight before the crash.

The reconditioned Spitfire which he was testing had been airborne for about fifteen minutes and its final moments were described by Westland's chief test pilot, Mr Harald Penrose, with the aid of a metal scale model of a Westland Whirlwind twin-engine fighter. He told the inquest that he had briefed the pilot and later, from Westland's airfield, saw the aircraft travelling from west to east about 1,500 feet above the

The Spitfire flown by Mr Keith Butler crashed into the hillside at Yeovil Marsh in the afternoon of 16 February 1950.

northern skyline of Yeovil. Mr Penrose stated that it proceeded to carry out a left-handed slow roll with ample speed in hand – probably 300 mph – and ample height. Suddenly a recovery movement was initiated and the nose dropped. The plane was doing a left hand turn, dropping at the same time, before disappearing over the hill. Mr Penrose described the whole recovery as 'abnormal' and said that it conflicted with what he would have expected of an experienced pilot such as Mr Butler. He discounted a suggestion that the pilot had suffered a blackout and could offer only two explanations: firstly, that the pilot had made a fatal error of judgement, which Mr Penrose considered most unlikely, or secondly, that there might have been some jamming or failure of the controls.

Another witness, Kenneth Evans, a member of Yeovil Model Aircraft Society, stated that he had been near Johnson Park, Ilchester Road, on the afternoon in question and had heard an aircraft diving from about 2,000 feet. Easing out of the dive, he watched the Spitfire bank slightly at about 250 feet and then perform, in his words, 'a vicious turn' to the north, in the direction of the Yeoviliton Naval Air Station. The aircraft seemed to stall, and appeared to be in trouble from then on.

Mr Bertram Morris of the Accident Investigating Branch stated that all the pre-flight inspections and reconditioning was in order, but as the aircraft had disintegrated on impact it was impossible to discover what caused the crash. However, the remains of the propeller indicated that the engine was running at speed.

Westland test pilot Squadron Leader Derek Colvin, stated that he had flown the Spitfire on three previous occasions and he had found it smooth in flight. He went on to say that Mr Butler was flying the aircraft for the second time when it crashed.

Further statements were given by the eyewitnesses, Reginald White and Charles Saunders, together with medical evidence which indicated that Keith Butler had died instantly from multiple injuries and could only be identified from the medical card recovered from his wallet.

The deputy assistant coroner for South-East Somerset, Mr C. Jowett, recorded a verdict of misadventure, and stated that in fairness to the deceased pilot, one could reasonably conclude that the personal factor did not enter into it. He accepted also that the aircraft had been airworthy and any failure or fracture in the controls could not now be established. In extending his sympathy to the relatives, Mr Jowett observed that it was well known that test pilots had a dangerous job to perform and accepted the risks it entailed.

Arson at Templecombe

A house fire is terrible and frightening, but when caused deliberately it is a heinous crime. In the 1830s, there was general unrest across the nation; there was the struggle for political and parliamentary reform which spawned riots in the cities and towns, and widespread discontent in the countryside with the burning of hayricks, barns and the destruction in their scores of the newly invented threshing machines by country folk seeking to protect their already meagre livelihoods. The response of the authorities was harsh, with hangings, imprisonments and transportation to Australia of those found guilty of such crimes.

In 1830 there was a serious outbreak of arson in Bridport; a large number of buildings, including houses and workshops, were deliberately set on fire and on one occasion seventeen families were left homeless. In those days, when many houses and buildings were close together, with thatch roofs, and fire fighting was primitive or non-existent, once a blaze started it could be disastrous. Two years later, a number of unexplained fires broke out again in Bridport and early in 1833 a young man called Sylvester Wilkins was found guilty of setting fire to a flax combing shop and hanged outside Dorchester gaol.

Despite the hangings, imprisonments and transportations, cases of arson were reported from across the West Country in the succeeding years, and during the spring of 1836 there were a number of unexplained fires in the neighbourhood of Templecombe, culminating in the destruction of three cottages near the Parish Church on 18 May.

Three local men, Charles Avis, Daniel Case and Samuel Hall, were quickly taken into custody and charged with the capital offence of arson. If found guilty they could expect little mercy and an appointment with the hangman. No doubt terrified at the prospect, Charles Avis, with the rope staring him in the face, confessed his part and turned King's Evidence, thus implicating his two partners in crime and saving his neck.

The trial of Daniel Case and Samuel Hall, indicted for maliciously setting fire to a dwelling house at Templecombe on 18 May 1836, with intent to injure the occupier, Nancy Oliver, opened in the following August at the Somerset Assizes, before Mr Baron Alderson. Charles Avis was the principal witness for the prosecution. He told the court that on 18 May, the three men had met in an orchard and agreed to set fire to the houses next to the church the same evening. However, his wife had turned up and had taken him home, so he had not gone with Case and Hall. Avis stated that when he

Three men were arrested for setting fire to cottages next to the church at Templecombe on 18 May 1836, but only one was found guilty and hanged.

heard the cry of fire, he had gone to the scene and saw the two prisoners in the crowd. The following day Case had told him that he had started the fire but as no one had seen him do it, he could not be caught.

Charles Avis's wife, Maria, stated that she had seen her husband talking to Case and Hall but he had come home with her and not gone with them.

Witness Charles Read testified that he had been a prisoner in Shepton Mallet gaol and occupied the bed next to Daniel Case, who had told him that before Charles Avis had gone home with his wife, he had given Samuel Hall the tinder to be used to set the houses on fire. When asked why they had done it, Case replied 'for fun, because the rest of the folks set fire to houses about the country'.

Following their arrests, Case and Hall had been examined by the Wincanton magistrates and their statements were read to the court. Hall stated that,

Avis had asked him to keep a secret and said that he and Case had agreed to set some houses on fire, and they thought they could burn down three parts of the parish. They had afterwards met at Avis's garden but that his (Hall's) wife came and collared him and would not leave him. He then went home to bed and did not get up until he heard the cry of fire and Avis had told him that he had set fire to several houses.

In his examination statement, Case stated that he saw Avis and Hall together on the night of the fire, but he had left them and gone down to the river and set some eel hooks. On his return he saw the houses on fire.

At the end of the case for the prosecution, the judge stated that he did not think there was sufficient evidence to continue with the case against Samuel Hall and he directed the jury to acquit him, which they did.

Eighteen-year-old Daniel Case remained alone in the dock to face the verdict of the jury, who, after retiring for three quarters of an hour, returned a verdict of guilty. However, in delivering the verdict, the foreman of the jury, with tears running down his face, said that his fellow jurors would recommend mercy as they believed Charles Avis was 'a great accessory' – they were probably sickened at the duplicity of Avis and perhaps the direction to acquit Hall.

The trial was immediately followed by Case and Hall being arraigned on four further indictments of setting fire to buildings in the area, but no evidence was presented and they were acquitted on all four counts.

Daniel Case was then sentenced to death by hanging and was removed from the dock in tears. The *Western Flying Post* reported that 'the learned Judge was very much affected, and many of the jury sobbed aloud'.

At six minutes past eleven on the morning of Saturday 1 September 1836, Daniel Case 'was launched into eternity at Ilchester gaol and died with scarcely a struggle'. It was reported that prior to his execution, Daniel Case had made a full confession that he had been concerned with Avis and Hall in all the fires in the vicinity of Templecombe.

On 3 September, the *Western Flying Post* reported that, 'After the execution, it being discovered that the wife of Avis (who is said to have made the tinder for the fire) had witnessed the execution of Case, a mob of persons got round, and after tearing the clothes from her back and otherwise ill treating her, by stoning, she was with difficulty rescued from the infuriated people and placed in a state of safety.'

There is a story that the people were infuriated when Mara Avis shouted as Daniel Case was being hanged, 'Thank God, I've done for thee at last!' and she was thrown in the river.

A Tumultuous Suffragette Meeting

In the early 1900s, although many women could vote at local council elections, women could not vote at parliamentary elections, and they were pressing for this right to vote (the suffrage). The word 'suffragette', first coined by a national newspaper in 1906 as an insult to describe the more militant women activists, as opposed to those who sought the vote by moderate and constitution means, remained in common use and was used generally in the media to describe any woman engaged in seeking the right to the vote. To promote their aims, some groups of suffragettes were involved in demonstrations, marches and acts of civil disruption, leading to many women being jailed and often violently mistreated; one suffragette, Emily Davidson, was fatally injured when she threw herself in front of King George V's horse at the Epsom Derby in 1913.

Meetings of suffragettes and their supporters, both male and female, no matter how peaceful, were often broken up by mobs (mainly male), and on 30 November 1909, the first suffragette meeting to be held in Yeovil began peacefully enough in the town hall but finished in uproar and near riot.

The ticket-only meeting opened at 7.30 on the Tuesday evening, but for some time a crowd had been gathering in High Street outside the town hall. When the doors opened there was an 'ugly rush for admission', but the valiant efforts of the two police constables on duty at the entrance managed to keep the crowd at bay and ticket holders only were admitted.

The principal speaker of the evening was the Hon. Mrs Evelina Haverfield of the Women's Social and Political Union, the daughter of the Third Baron Abinger, and a national figure in the movement for women's suffrage. As she began to address the audience of over 100 men and women, the Hon. Evelina had to battle against the roar of the crowd outside the building and the noise of rattles and chanting from a gang of young men at the back of the hall. Battling on despite the din, she explained that the movement's aims were modest; all they sought were equal voting rights with men – they expected no privileges and wanted none.

The next speaker, a Miss Naylor, was subjected to an outburst of booing and catcalls, accompanied by explosions from fireworks at the back of the hall. However, she would not be deterred and pressed on to finish her address by saying that they wanted the right to vote for the same reasons as men. Suddenly, the meeting descended into chaos. The mob of men and youths in the High Street rushed the doors, brushing aside

UNREPORTED UTTERANCES.

3. Miss Tinkabel Spankhurts.

" Dear suffering sister suffragettes, our day of triumph is at hand. The fight has been uphill and we have had to tread the hollow-way—pardon me, I mean narrow way. Whether we were peeling the humble potato in our obscure suburban kitchen or dining at the Ritz or heckling dear Winston at Dundee, did we not drone or shriek or yell or howl or roar our bloodcurdling battle-cry of VOTES FOR WOMEN."

* * * * * * * * * * *

" Now that the tremendous applause has subsided, I will disclose to you my scheme for the subjection of that tyrant, man. What could be more simple than to attack him in his weakest spot, lure him on by feeding him with Ivelcon and all the other St. Ivel dainties you know so well, and thus make him so pleased and satisfied that he will grant us anything—especially votes. Historians of the future will write about the ' Ivelconquest of the Commons.' "

No Trouble, No Waste!

An advertisement (*c.* 1908) for IVELCON, a meat extract drink manufactured by the Yeovil firm of Aplin and Barrett, satirizing Mrs Emmeline Pankhurst, a leading campaigner for Women's Suffrage, which nearly resulted in a riot at a meeting in Yeovil Town Hall on 30 November 1909.

the two constables, and poured into the town hall. The *Western Gazette* graphically described what happened:

> Like wild animals the people scampered up the staircases and into the hall, which in a few moments became crowded almost to suffocation. The precincts of the Municipal Buildings, too, were also crowded and hundreds of people were unable to get in. The scene which followed almost baffles description, and a remarkable feature was that the coolest of the whole assembly were the Suffragettes themselves. A lady of the audience was carried out in a fainting condition. It was 'Bedlam let loose' with a vengeance, and the noise out rivalled any menagerie. Following a brief pyrotechnic display at the back of the hall, several of the spectators thought they would vary the fun by making the Suffragettes the target for pieces of coal, apples, bundles of wet paper, and even rotten eggs, which no doubt would have disfigured the portrait of King George but for the fact that, anticipating trouble, it had been covered with canvas. The skilful way the Suffragettes dodged the missiles showed that they had been in similar wars before.

Several of the Hon. Mrs Haverfield's male supporters on the platform tried to calm the mob, but they came under a renewed hail of missiles. Things now got really ugly as an attempt was made to storm the platform; chairs were thrown and broken, but in the words of the *Gazette* 'some of the besiegers were beaten back with sticks by the ladies' male supporters'. Two young men managed to catch Miss Naylor by her legs while a third rushed from the back of the platform and pushed her into the crowd. She was rescued, however, by a burly man who 'clasped her in his arms – quite a picture for the gods – and lifting her again onto the platform saved her from a severe mauling'.

With the meeting now completely out of control, and with the few gentlemen stewards and two constables helpless to maintain order, police reinforcements arrived and were welcomed with cheers. However, when asked to clear the hall, the superintendent in charge said that he had no power to do so, but agreed to clear the platform. As the Hon. Mrs Haverfield and her supporters were descending from the platform, some of the crowd tried to 'hustle' them, but fell back when the superintendent loudly ordered his men to draw their staves.

The general disorder continued into the High Street as the police and local supporters escorted the suffragettes to their lodgings in nearby Hendford, but by eleven o'clock peace had returned and the town was quiet.

Despite the near riot, both in the town hall and outside, there was only one reported casualty, Mr Sam Willie, one of the suffragettes' supporters, who was slightly injured on the forehead by a piece of coal when the platform was bombarded. Ironically, Mr Sam Willie was a local coal merchant!

During the following weeks the columns of the *Western Gazette* contained many letters of support for the suffragettes, expressing disgust at the actions of the crowd, which were considered to have reflected badly on Yeovil and its townspeople.

Women had to wait another nine years until 1918 before the Parliamentary vote was given to women over thirty years of age (men could vote at twenty-one), and they had to wait another ten years until 1928 before the voting age was lowered to twenty-one, finally giving women equal rights with men.

Dangers of Ponds

Deep ponds can be very dangerous places, yet they have always been a attraction to children – your author spent many happy hours as a boy fishing for sticklebacks and tadpoles with a jam jar on the end of a length of string in a pond at Yew Tree Close in Yeovil, which sadly long ago succumbed to the advance of the suburbs.

On the afternoon of Thursday 21 April 1808, sixteen-year-old Simon Rousell was killed when he fell from a horse owned by Mr William Ham at West Coker. A headstone in Merriott churchyard records his death but his epitaph includes the following words and an unanswered question:

'Twas through a horse I lost my breath
and cruel hands which caused my death

Whose were the cruel hands? The record is silent.

And what has this got to do with ponds? The following will explain.

Two days after Simon's death, Mr Ham's nephew was walking by the mill pond at West Coker, when he slipped, fell in and was drowned.

An inquest was held into both lads' deaths and verdicts of accidental death were recorded.

Ninety-nine years later, a pond in a field near St Michael's Road in Yeovil held a fatal fascination for eleven-year-old Ivy Fox. On 6 September 1907 Ivy, who lived in St Michael's Road, was playing in the field when she fell in the pond and tragically drowned before help could be found. At the inquest the following day in St Michael's Parish Room, the full story was told to the coroner's jury and recorded in the *Western Gazette*:

The scene of the accident which occurred on Friday evening, is a pit or pond from which clay or other substances have been worked, and which is surrounded by thick bushes and stands in a clump of trees in a field off St Michael's Road. From the top of the banks, which on more than one side of the pond slope inwards to the edge of the water, is about six or seven feet, and the depth of the muddy water in it is stated to be about 15 feet or more. On Friday evening some children, of whom the deceased was one, went playing near the pond, and she then tried to reach a piece of wood floating on the surface. To do this she supported herself with a bough of a

Teddy Rendell met three friends in The Square at West Coker, which can be seen in the centre of this photograph, before heading off to his tragic demise in a local pond in May 1910.

bush, and this suddenly breaking, the child fell headlong into the pit. She was one of the children given a free pass to the Corporation Baths by the Education Committee for regular attendance at school, and it is said that she was able to swim a little. On falling into the water she swam a few strokes and disappeared, and her companion failing to reach her ran and fetched the deceased's mother. Assistance was at hand, but by the time it reached the pond the girl had disappeared and was not seen alive again. The body was recovered by the means of large nails driven through a scaffold pole procured from an adjoining building, and which was let down to the pit, and when at last the deceased was brought to the bank after being immersed for 20 minutes, life was apparently extinct. However, artificial respiration was actively practised for a long time, without avail.

Statements were given by Ivy's friend, Laura Trevett, who described what had happened; a Mr Partridge who happened to be passing in St Michael's Road, described the rescue attempts; and finally Dr Colmer, who was involved in the unsuccessful attempts to resuscitate the child. In his summing up the coroner suggested that although this was an unfortunate accident, it might be said that the dangerous pond should have been fenced, but the owner of the field could in turn argue that children had no business being there; the accident might, however, induce him to better fence the field. One of the jurors suggested a notice should be put up warning people to keep out, another believed the pond would be filled in within the next twelve months and a third recalled pulling a man out of the pond twenty-one years before.

The jury returned a verdict of Accidental Drowning, and the *Western Gazette* disclosed that Ivy's father had once saved someone from drowning in the pond.

Whitsun Bank Holiday in May 1910 was a fine warm day, and the four lads who met in The Square, West Coker, decided to go for a ramble across the fields. Arriving at the pond in a field at Barton Farm, the youngsters played about and then twelve-year-old Teddy Rendell decided to have a bathe. Stripping off his clothes, the boy entered the water, ignoring the warnings from his friends that the pond was deep and dangerous. Non-swimmer Teddy paddled around in the shallows up to his knees, but suddenly he went under. Resurfacing, he screamed for help and Cecil Brown, stripping off, rushed into the pond, even though he could not swim, and managed to grab hold of Teddy as he came up for the second time. Tragically, the lad slipped from Cecil's grasp and disappeared. Now the non-swimmer Cecil Brown was in trouble but the two younger boys, also non-swimmers, joined hands and pulled him to safety.

The shocked youngsters ran for help and village policemen, PC Hollard, recently returned to duty following a serious illness, and George Parsons, rushed to the scene and into the deep water. Sadly they were too late and all they could do was recover Teddy's body, at no small risk to themselves.

The verdict at the inquest held the next day in the New Inn was 'Accidentally Drowned in a pond on Barton Farm' and both the coroner and his jury praised the pluck of young Cecil Brown in trying to save his friend, and PC Hollard and George Parsons in going into the pond knowing it to be a very dangerous place.

The Dowlish
Wise Woman's Mistake

Mrs Sarah Palmer was 'suffering a low state of mind' following the death of her three-week-old son Benjamin from acute diarrhoea in July 1857. Today, her condition would probably be diagnosed as acute depression and Sarah would have received the appropriate treatment, but in Stoke-sub-Hamdon, where she lived with her carter husband William and their large family, this was a condition little understood by the local medical men at the time.

Sarah Palmer had been attended by two local surgeons, Mr Walter Winter Walter of Stoke and Mr Stuckey of Martock, but the medicine they had prescribed for her 'low state of mind' had not affected a cure. As often happens when conventional treatments fail to produce the desired result, the patient may turn elsewhere for relief.

It was to Esther Peadon of Dowlish Wake that Sarah turned, in view of the 'wise woman's' claims to have cured people suffering from 'low spirits', but tragically the 'cure' was to have fatally consequences and Esther Peadon found herself appearing before Mr Justice Crowder at the Somerset Assizes in Taunton on 24 March 1858, indicted with the manslaughter of Sarah Palmer.

Selina Palmer, Sarah's sixteen-year-old daughter, testified that, apart from complaining of a lowness of spirits, her mother had been quite well previous to the few days before her death on 1 January last. About twelve weeks before her mother died, she had visited Esther Peadon and asked if she could cure her of her low spirits. The prisoner had said that she could and after paying four shillings (a small fortunate for a carter's wife), her mother had been given some medicine in a bottle, told to cut her finger and toe nails and wrap the clippings, together with a portion of her hair, in a piece of paper, tie it to the neck of the bottle and leave them until they 'perished'. Her mother had been given a box of pills and instructed that on no account should she see a doctor. Selina told the court that the medicine had the effect of 'sending her mother out of her mind'.

William Palmer, Sarah's husband, followed his daughter into the witness box and said that his wife had complained about the effects of the medicine, but Esther Peadon had told her to persevere as it would do her good. However, after taking the last bottle of medicine bought from the prisoner, Sarah had become delirious and told him she felt she would get no better. His wife had died shortly after on 1 January.

Walter Palmer, Sarah's son, corroborated his father's evidence and said that on the last Sunday in December, he had gone with his mother to visit Esther Peadon and when

Mrs Sarah Palmer died at Stoke sub Hamdon in 1858, but was it caused by medicine supplied by a 'wise woman' from Dowlish Wake? This photograph of the village shows the war memorial unveiled on Ham Hill in 1923.

the prisoner asked how she was, his mother had replied that she was still feeling very poorly. His mother had bought two more bottles of medicine one was for raising her spirits with three teaspoons each day, but no detail was given of the purpose of the second. Soon after taking the medicine, his mother had collapsed, and his father sent for Mr Walter.

Mr Walter, the surgeon, took the stand and told the court that he had attended Sarah Palmer during her last confinement and again some two or three weeks before her death, when he had given her some medicine for constipation and a 'deranged' stomach. He had been called to attend Sarah Palmer shortly before she died, when he had found her nearly insensible and had prescribed a dose of calomel but her condition had deteriorated. The surgeon said that he had been called again and found his patient lying on the floor, barely conscious, her feet cold and her body rigid, teeth clenched. She had died shortly after.

Mr Walter stated that he had carried out a post-mortem examination of the deceased woman, and had come to the conclusion that death was not from natural causes but occasioned by the effects of an acro-narcotic poison of a vegetable origin which could cause stupor, paralysis and convulsions. He understood that the medicine supplied to Sarah Palmer contained the herb mandrake, which was an acrid poison and slightly narcotic, and which in his opinion had been the cause of her death. The surgeon stated that someone in the dead woman's bedroom had handed him a nearly empty bottle which he had sealed and given to Superintendent Smith of the Yeovil police, together with the stomach of the deceased, directing that they be sent to Bristol for examination by Mr William Herapath, the analytical chemist, who had gained a formidable reputation as an expert witness in criminal cases involving poisoning.

Cross examined by Mr Cole, counsel for the defence, Mr Walter stated that there were a great many narcotic poisons and their effects were not the same.

At this point, the judge asked the prosecuting counsel, Mr Edwards, if he had any means of proving that the medicine found in the bottle sent to Mr Herapath was the same as that prescribed by Esther Peadon, because the deceased appeared to have been attended by two medical practitioners and both had given her medicine. The judge suggested that it was just possible that the contents of the bottle might not have been prescribed by the prisoner. Mr Edwards replied that that the surgeon, Mr Stuckey, was not in court but he could recall William Palmer and endeavour to clear up the doubt. However, when recalled to the witness box, William Palmer could not identify the bottle as one received from the prisoner.

At this stage the judge brought the trial to an end, saying there was no proof that the bottle had been obtained from Sarah Peadon, and neither was there proof that the medicine it contained had been supplied by her. He directed the jury to acquit the prisoner and a verdict of Not Guilty was returned. However, before discharging Esther Peadon, Mr Justice Crowder 'bestowed upon her a caution as to her future dealing in medicines, the nature and effects of which she was profoundly ignorant of, otherwise she might place herself in a very awkward predicament'.

A Gallant Airman

When I was a boy (how often do men of a certain age find themselves saying this!) I often went for a stroll around Yeovil with my father on warm summer Sunday evenings. Sometimes we would visit the cemetery on Preston Road and he would point out headstones and tell me stories about them. My father was born in 1899, and one of the pastimes enjoyed by our Victorian and Edwardian forebears was a walk around the local cemetery, and of course my father, as a boy, would join his parents in a Sunday evening perambulation to the one on Preston Road.

On our occasional perambulations, one headstone always seemed to fascinate me, I don't know why, but we usually ended up at the 'airman's grave'. The stone, now showing signs of weathering, is 'In memory of Lawrence Pratt Openshaw, Major, RAF. A gallant airman who lost his life while flying on the 6 June 1927, aged 35 years'. My father would tell me that Major Openshaw was killed in an air race but it was not until many years later that I gleaned the full story of the tragedy.

Major Openshaw, an Oxford University engineering science graduate, learned to fly just before the First World War broke out in 1914 and for a large part of the conflict he was engaged in the very dangerous occupation of test flying many prototype aircraft. In 1924, the major joined Westland Aircraft at Yeovil as Works Test Pilot, and on 12 April 1927 he married Alice Bruce, the eldest daughter of Westland's Joint Managing Director, Mr. R. A. Bruce. Following the ceremony in St John's church, the couple flew from the Westland airfield, with the bridegroom at the controls of the new two-seater Westland Widgeon III, bound for their honeymoon in Bournemouth and the major's participation in the Easter weekend air races at Ensbury Park.

Two months later, the Whitsun Bournemouth Flying Meeting was held at the 5-mile triangular course at Ensbury Park on 6 June and Major Openshaw, piloting the Widgeon III, was one of the twelve competitors in the first race of the afternoon. First to take off, in a Blackburn Bluebird, was Squadron Leader Walter Longton, a well-known RAF test pilot and stunt flyer, with a 46 second start on the three-lap course. As the aircraft flew up to the turning point at West Parley on the third and final lap, Squadron Leader Longton and Major Openshaw were lying fourth and fifth and banking sharply into the turn; the major began to overtake on the inside and slightly below the squadron leader. The machines began to straighten out but then, at 150 feet, the tips of their wings touched, interlocked, and the Widgeon and Bluebird crashed to the ground out of control and exploded in flames. Squadron Leader Longton was

Major Lawrence Openshaw, RAF, lost his life piloting a Westland Widgeon III at the Whitsun Bournemouth Flying Meeting on 6 June 1927.

killed outright, but Major Openshaw was trapped, alive and conscious in the blazing tangle of wreckage.

Rescuers were on the scene in minutes and, with scant regard for their safety, managed to pull the badly burned Major from the inferno. Although every effort was made to save his life, Lawrence Openshaw died in the ambulance on the way to Boscombe Hospital.

Tragically, both airmen's wives were at the race meeting and witnessed the aircraft collide.

Following the crash, the race officials decided to continue with the meeting but at the insistence of the pilots, restricted the number of entrants in each heat to three. The disaster also had little or no effect on the number of passengers on the pleasure flights.

The result of the inquest laid no blame, and the coroner's jury returned verdicts on the two men of accidental death while flying.

Major Openshaw was buried on 10 June, and the mourners accompanied the coffin on foot and in cars from the simple service in St John's church through streets lined with hundreds of local people to the Preston Road Cemetery. The grave was surrounded by a mass of floral tributes and on a nearby mound a model of an aircraft, made from clusters of white lilies, red roses and blue irises, lay nose down. Among the letters of condolence was one from King George V and Queen Mary.

Fatal Fights

Two hundred years ago, many sentences of the courts were extremely savage by today's standards. Hanging was the ultimate punishment in a large variety of crimes, ranging from murder to the theft of goods valued at a few shillings. Although many death sentences were recorded, few were carried into effect, and the guilty prisoner, male or female, would be transported to Australia for life; for some this could be a death sentence.

However, the courts seem to have been somewhat more lenient when it came to dealing with deaths caused by fighting. Take, for example, the death of John Burge in Shepton Mallet on a Sunday night in November 1814. A squadron of North British Dragoons rode into Shepton Mallet on 27 November and were quartered in the town for the night. One of the corporals, by the name of John Brash, and a fellow dragoon spent the evening drinking with 'some lower orders of the towns-people'; it appears that everyone got drunk, a fight broke out, and three of the 'lower orders' began to beat up the dragoon. Stripping off his regimental coat, Corporal Brash went to the aid of his comrade, but was in turn attacked by the three townsmen and severely beaten. The corporal managed to extricate himself from his assailants, but lost his regimental coat in the process, and ran back to the squadron baggage guard.

Enraged at the beating, John Brash collected two of his fellow dragoons and, arming themselves with bayonets, went looking for the three attackers. They soon found two of them, John Yeates, a shoemaker, and weaver John Burge, the latter carrying the corporal's regimental coat. The dragoons piled into the two men, beating them with the sockets of their bayonets, but in the melee John Burge was stabbed in the chest and died a few days later from the wound.

The verdict of the inquest into the death of John Burge was wilful murder against some persons unknown, but enquiries quickly established that men of the North British Dragoons had been involved in the fight. Corporal Brash and his two companions were returned to Shepton Mallet. The corporal was identified as the man who had struck the blow, and he was sent for trial at the next Assizes, charged with the wilful murder of John Burge.

John Brash appeared at the Somerset Lent Assizes in April 1815, but despite some doubt as to which of the dragoons struck the fatal blow, the evidence pointed to the corporal. In his summing up, the judge commented that the crime had been committed by the prisoner 'under the influence of passion, excited by the very ill-treatment he had received'. The jury found John Brash guilty of the lesser charge of manslaughter and he was sentenced to three months in Ilchester gaol and fined ten shillings. In reporting the case, the *Bath Journal* noted that the corporal had served sixteen years in the North British Dragoons and 'bore a good character'.

Lansdown Fair was held on the Downs above Bath on 10 August each year and in 1817, the day was a wash out. It poured with rain; in fact the rain fell in torrents, which caused the *Bath and Cheltenham Gazette* to comment that,

> The rain descended in torrents, and the booths being incapable of affording shelter for the majority, they exhibited a most ludicrous and grotesque appearance; the loose soil being trodden by an immense number of cattle and sheep, and dissolved in the abundance of rain which fell, formed a complete covering for the belles and beaux, many of whom appeared as if they had been drawn through a horse pond, and afterwards rolled in fullers' earth!

The Fair was famous for the sale of horses, cattle, sheep, pigs and huge quantities of cheese, and thousands of people came from near and far to enjoy the food and amusements provided in the scores of stalls and side-shows; the Fair was also notorious for bare knuckle fighting by local 'heroes'. It was in this atmosphere that two men arrived to settle a long running grudge by indulging in the 'too-prevalent but barbarous custom of *pugilism*'.

William Davies, described as 'a boxing butcher of Bath', had agreed to fight Samuel White, a sedan chairman working at the Bath General Hospital, and both met in one of the booths, where the butcher challenged the chairman to go outside and fight. However, when Samuel White suggested that they wait for the rain to stop, Davies struck him a tremendous blow on the side of his head and left for the 'usual spot for pitched battles', followed by the furious chairman. The bare-knuckle fight lasted a slogging, bloody and punishing forty minutes, at the end of which Samuel White had beaten the 'boxing butcher of Bath' unconscious. With the fight finished, the *Western Flying Post* reported that Samuel White 'rode down the hill in tolerably plight, but in the course of the night severely felt the effect of the blows he had received and died the next morning'.

The inquest into the decease of Samuel White, who had left a widow and a blind child, returned a verdict of manslaughter against William Davies, but the 'boxing butcher' had fled the city and a warrant was issued for his arrest. He was not long on the run, and at the Lent Assizes at Taunton in April 1818, William Davies was sentenced to nine months in gaol for 'killing Samuel White in a pitched battle on Lansdown'.

Thirty-year-old Edward O'Hare, a licensed hawker of Irish linen and drapery goods, got into a heated quarrel with a local man, James Bennett, at the beerhouse in which he lodged at Huntspill during the evening of Monday 2 November 1830. The reason for the quarrel does not feature in the record, but it would seem that both men were somewhat in liquor and they decided to settle the matter with a bare-knuckle fight on the following morning for a stake of five shillings, with George Toogood, a well-off farmer, acting as stakeholder.

It appears that when Tuesday dawned, and after a night sleeping on the issue, Edward and James decided not to fight, they ate a meal and drank together and shook

Edward O' Hare died of injuries following a fight in November 1830, and was buried in the churchyard of St Peter and All Hallows (formerly All Saints) church, Huntspill. The church was rebuilt following a serious fire in 1878.

hands. However, at the moment the two men shook hands, George Toogood arrived at the time agreed for the fight and refused to give up the stake money unless the two fought it out as agreed the previous evening.

O'Hare and Bennett walked to the nearby field where it had been decided the fight would be held, followed by 'a rabble', with James Bennett's brother William and Meschach Derrick as seconds, and George Toogood and John Searle, of Burnham, as stakeholders. The fight lasted for all of fifteen hard, brutal minutes until Edward O'Hare, suffering a fearful beating about the head, collapsed unconscious and was carried back to his lodgings at the beerhouse, where he died three hours later from his injuries.

The inquest into the death of Edward O'Hare was held in the Golden Lion at Huntspill and the jury of 'fifteen respectable yeomen' returned a verdict of Manslaughter against James Bennett, with Toogood, Derrick, Bennett and Searle as accessories. James Bennett and John Searle were in custody and were conveyed to Wilton gaol to await their trial at the next Assizes, but Toogood, William Bennett and Derrick had gone on the run and warrants were issued for their arrest.

Edward O'Hare was buried the day following the inquest, when 'an eloquent sermon appropriate to the occasion was delivered by the Reverend Mr Elliston who expatiated on the evils of beer-houses'.

Toogood and Bennett were quickly taken up but Derrick remained at large until the following March, when he surrendered on the morning of the trial.

The five men appeared at the Lent Assizes, indicted for killing and slaying Edward O'Hare on 2 November 1830, but it was soon evident that the fight was considered to have been a fair one and the deceased had been the most to blame. No evidence was brought against George Toogood and John Searle for aiding or encouraging the fight and the judge discharged the pair, but the jury found the other three guilty. However, the judge observed that this was not an 'aggravated case' and as the two Bennetts had been in prison some time, he sentenced them to pay a fine of one shilling, and then be discharged. The long-term absconder, Meschach Derrick, was sentenced to one week's imprisonment.

Gangs of Old Somerset

For centuries, until the establishment of a regular police force in Somerset in 1856 and its subsequent amalgamation with several town forces, the administration of justice lay with various authorities, from county magistrates to the lowly, elected parish constable, and on the whole was fairly ineffective. This state of affairs was nationwide and to compensate the criminal law was fierce and likewise were the punishments. By the beginning of the nineteenth century over 200 offences, from theft to murder, carried the death penalty, but as the eighteenth century passed into the nineteenth juries had become less willing to find persons charged with less serious capital offences guilty, and transportation to Australia became more commonplace.

Despite such draconian sentences, violence, robberies, thefts and such like were widespread in a society driven by great affluence for the few and great poverty for the many. Somerset was no exception and early in the nineteenth century, gangs of thieves and 'hard men', often family affairs, roamed the county, generally unchecked until they committed crimes which could not be ignored or overreached themselves.

The Pearce Family

On 23 January 1817, the *Taunton Courier* reported with evident satisfaction that 'another gang of robbers has been taken into custody at Chard'.

The gang comprised local stone mason William Pearce, his wife Ann, sons William junior, and George, and daughter Elizabeth, and all were accused of committing over a period of several months 'the most daring depredations'. Ann and her daughter Elizabeth had been engaged as letter carriers around Chard, and no doubt used the information gained during their perambulations for the series of 'daring depredations'.

The Pearce family were accused of burgling a large number of houses and business premises in and around Chard, including Mr Mitchell's watchmaker's shop, Messrs Forsey and Dean's factory, from which a large quantity of cloth was stolen, fifty bushels of wheat were removed from Mr Willie's farm at Langdon, and a wall of Mr Hancock's house was broken through and a number of clocks and watches was taken. A search of the family's residence produced nearly a cartload of stolen goods, and it was suggested that the loot was destined for a gang of house breakers at Bristol.

Three months later, the Pearces appeared at the Lent Assizes in Taunton, charged with various robberies, which resulted in William senior being given two years in the county gaol, his wife Ann being discharged. Their son William was sentenced to death for stealing the clocks and watches from Mr Hancock, and his brother George was transported to Australia for seven years; William's death sentence was reprieved and he was transported to Australia for life. Daughter Elizabeth was charged with her brother George and an Elizabeth Wilkins with stealing cloth, and all three were sentenced to seven years' transportation to Australia.

In addition to the possibility of receiving the death sentence at the 1817 Lent Assizes, there was the risk of a premature capital fate before the accused even appeared in court as there was an outbreak of the deadly and highly contagious typhus fever at Ilchester gaol, which held most of the 100 prisoners to be tried. Typhus was commonly known as 'jail fever' because it was spread by body lice in the overcrowded and unhygienic prisons of the time, and a number of prisoners had already succumbed to the infection.

The *Taunton Courier* reported on 10 April that in order to prevent the spread of the disease outside the gaol, the prisoners were 'brought from Ilchester to Bathpool by water' instead of the usual route by road, and presumably travelled along the River Yeo to Langport, then down the River Parrett to the junction with the River Tone at Burrowbridge and along the Tone to Bathpool, near Taunton.

The Howarths

The Howarth family were described rather dramatically in the *Taunton Courier* on 19 September 1827 as 'The most extraordinary depredators of modern times, they are now about the age of fifty or upwards and a system of plunder has been the study and practice of their lives. George Howarth is the eldest and appears to have been the leader in the career of villainy they have pursued.'

The Howarths, originally from Cheshire, had been resident in the old Keyford Nunnery near Frome for a good many years during which time according to the *Taunton Courier*, sheep, calves etc had been stolen, butchers' shops robbed of meat, clothes and blankets taken from local factories, and even sacrilegious thefts from churches. It was further reported that the Howarths' apparent immunity from the law was achieved by playing 'Robin Hood' to many neighbours, who benefited from some of the spoils and lavish entertainments. George Howarth and his younger brother Ralph were in fact skilled millwrights, scarcely without employment and earning good money at their craft, but at night were 'prowling about like wolves for prey, with weapons of destruction secreted on their persons to use in case of any resistance being made to their depredations'. However, the fall of the 'House of Howarth' came from one too many robberies, and at the hands of a fearless Frome tradesman.

Late on the evening of Sunday 6 August 1827, John Furnell and Charles Gilbert were in Bath Street, Frome, waiting for the arrival of Wheeler's carrier's van, when they saw two men going furtively down the private road near the wood-house occupied by Mr John Oxley, a maltster and cooper. They followed the men down the road and saw them disappear into the wood-house. Creeping up to the building and looking through the half-opened door, the two young men saw in the dim light of a lantern a man whom Charles Furnell recognised as George Howarth and heard him say 'Bring up that board.' Hurrying to Mr Oxley's nearby house, they knocked him up and explained what they had seen. Only a few days before, ten good oak planks had been stolen from the wood-house, and now was the chance to catch the thieves 'red-handed'. Charles Furnell went back to keep the building under observation and some ten minutes later Mr Oxley arrived, armed with a carving knife and carrying a lantern, accompanied by Matthias Butcher holding a heavy stick, and Charles Gilbert. They hurried down to the wood-house where they found the door closed but the padlock broken. A search of the building revealed no intruders but two planks had been moved from the far end and placed by the door, apparently ready to be taken away.

It seemed that the rogues had fled, but as Mr Oxley and his companions began to search around the outside of the wood-house, a rustling sound was heard coming from the next door garden, belonging to a Mr Drewe, and on going to investigate the figure of a man could be made out crouching under a quince tree.

When challenged, the figure rose up and, in the glow of Mr Oxley's lantern, John Furnell saw that he was holding a sword. As the man tried to escape, Furnell grabbed his coat, but was forced to let go when he swung around and struck the young man's arm with the back of the sword. The man then turned to run, fell over a wheel barrow, and, scrambling to his feet, retreated towards a paling fence but, on being unable to climb over or break through, turned and lashed out with his sword. Mr Oxley closed with the desperate man and received a savage cut but, undaunted, came on and a brief, vicious sword and knife fight ensued. Both men were badly cut, but the contest ended when Matthias Butcher, getting behind Mr Oxley's opponent, felled him with a heavy blow to the back of his head.

Disarmed, the man was pinioned and marched to the Frome guardhouse, where he was identified as George Howarth, first seen by John Furnell in the wood-house, and a dark lantern, tin candle box, a tinder box and steel, a disguising cap and a large knife were found on his person.

After spending the night in the guardhouse, Howarth was taken to the Blue Boar Inn, where his wounds were cleaned and he was held pending his appearance before the magistrates. However, despite his wounds, Howarth escaped and remained at large for several weeks, during which time he made his way some 200 miles north to Cheshire and his brother Peter's rented house in the village of Mobberley, near Knutsford. A reward of £100 was offered for his capture, and having been once told that Howarth had been held in Middlewich goal and had relatives in that county, one of the Frome overseers despatched a wanted poster to the prison governor for circulation in the area.

George Howarth's bid for freedom was short-lived; by chance the owner of Peter Howarth's house met a local solicitor, Mr D. W. Gratrex, on the road to the Assizes at Chester, and told him that he had seen the wanted man at his house that morning. However, such was the fear of the Howarths in Cheshire that when the solicitor asked the informant to accompany him to secure the fugitive, the reply was 'Lord sir, if you'd give me 500 guineas I wouldn't venture'. But Mr Gratrex was made of sterner stuff and, riding to Mobberley, secured the services of the parish constable, albeit after much

The Howarth family were described as 'the most extraordinary depredators of modern times' in and around Frome in 1827, but their reign was soon put to an end.

persuasion, to assist him in capturing the wanted man. Arriving at the house, they found the door unfastened and, discovering George Howarth was alone, informed him that he was now under arrest. At that moment his brother Peter burst into the room and made to grab a large pitchfork, but was foiled by the parish constable, who seized it first.

A subdued George Howarth was taken to Knutsford gaol, where he was formally identified and returned to Somerset, shackled in heavy irons, to be lodged in Ilchester gaol.

In the meantime, a search of George Howarth's house revealed a large quantity of stolen goods, including twenty-eight blankets stolen from a Frome factory and the ten planks of wood belonging to Mr John Oxley. Brother Ralph had also been taken into custody; a search of his home produced a variety of stolen goods and he was sent for trial at the next Assizes, where he was found guilty of various thefts and sentenced to transportation for seven years.

At the Somerset Lent Assizes in April 1828, fifty-five-year-old George Howarth pleaded not guilty to a string of charges of theft, including Mr Oxley's ten oak planks, but the most serious charge brought against him was 'that on 6 August 1827, at Frome, being in a garden for an unlawful purpose and then and there in order to prevent his lawful apprehension, having maliciously cut and stabbed with intent to murder John Oxley'. This charge, to which Howarth pleaded not guilty, was brought under the Malicious Shooting or Stabbing Act 1803, commonly called 'Lord Ellenborough's Act', which carried the death penalty if the cutting and stabbing was carried out to resist lawful apprehension.

The prosecution related the events of 6 August and evidence was given by Mr John Oxley, John Furnell, who testified that the prisoner was the person whom he had seen in the wood-house, Charles Gilbert and Matthias Butcher. No statements were submitted in Howarth's defence.

The jury found George Howarth guilty, but his counsel then pleaded a point of law and judgement was reserved to the next Assizes. On the several charges for robbery, he was found guilty and sentenced to fourteen years' transportation.

George Howarth was brought before Mr Justice Park at the Summer Assizes in the following August to receive the decision of the court on the point of law. The original trial had proved that he had been found in the garden and Mr Oxley had been wounded by a sword in his attempt to lawfully apprehend him. However, Howarth's counsel had argued that his client had not been lawfully apprehended because being in the garden was not a felonious offence and therefore, in the circumstances, he was justified in defending himself and could not be convicted of cutting and stabbing under Lord Ellenborough's Act.

Mr Justice Park informed Howarth that the point of law had been considered by nine judges and the trial judge, and they had unanimously decided that the point could not be sustained. In their opinion, the time from which he was first seen in the wood-house until he was apprehended in the garden comprised an entire case and his apprehension was legal and the use of his sword to wound Mr Oxley to avoid being taken came within the meaning of Lord Ellenborough's Act. Mr Justice Park told Howarth that he had placed himself in the situation in which his life was forfeited, and from all he had ascertained from the catalogue of the prisoner's offences, he had been a wicked and desperate character very little deserving of mercy. The judge ordered sentence of death to be recorded, and stated that in the event of his life being spared he should expect removal from the country for life.

George Howarth's sentence was commuted to transportation for life, a possible death sentence in itself, and the Howarth gang would no longer trouble the good people of Somerset.

Burton and Brittan

Another gang, this one feared for violence as much as their other criminal activities, were led by a tinker by the name of John Burton and a powerfully built dealer called John Brittan, alias 'Gypsy Jack'. This gang of ruffians was said to have 'infested' the Wells area in the early 1820s; in the words of an article written some twenty years later in the *Western Flying Post* of 30 September 1843, they were 'from the general acts of violence which they committed, feared throughout this and the surrounding district'.

However, the gang's activities came to an abrupt end on 21 August 1826 at Priddy Fair, when a local tailor called James Bartlett was attacked and beaten almost to death and some of his clothes stolen. The culprits were named as John Burton and John Brittan and warrants were taken out for their arrest. Burton was soon taken with some stolen clothes in his possession, but of Brittan there was no sign; he had fled the district and despite a reward of £100 for his apprehension, he was not captured.

At the Summer Assizes in August 1827, John Burton was found guilty of assaulting and robbing James Bartlett and was sentenced to death, in the words of the judge, the Lord Chief Justice Best, 'for the purpose of furnishing an example to gangs of such desperate marauders'. Burton was hanged at Ilchester Gaol the following month.

Lionel Lambert, a sergeant with the City of London Police, was on duty at Smithfield Market early in September 1843 when he thought he recognised one of the horse dealers. In his younger days he had lived at Wells and after careful study he recognised the large, powerfully-built middle-aged dealer as Gypsy Jack Brittan. Enquiries established that the dealer was known as John Briton, he lived at East Langston near Leicester, and was a wealthy horse dealer, owning considerable property, and was fond of pugilistic encounters, with a reputation to match.

Recalling the events at Priddy Fair back in 1826 and wondering whether the man he recalled as Gypsy Jack Brittan was still wanted, Sergeant Lambert reported his suspicions to Inspector Charles Hodgson, and enquiries of the authorities at Wells confirmed that the warrant was still valid for Brittan's arrest. With the warrant in their possession, Inspector Hodgson and Sergeant Lambert travelled to Leicester and Brittan was arrested at Waltham Fair, near Melton Mowbray.

John Brittan appeared at the Somerset Lent Assizes at Taunton on 8 April 1844, charged with assaulting James Bartlett on 21 August 1826 and robbing him of a pair of boots and a pair of braces, the same crime for which John Burton had been hanged seventeen years before.

The case for the prosecution was that on 21 August James Bartlett had been at Priddy Fair, he was quite intoxicated, and between half past ten and eleven o'clock that evening had left the booth where he had been drinking with friends. He had then been set upon by a group of men, one of whom struck him to the ground, where he was severely beaten and knocked insensible. Bartlett remembered nothing but when he recovered his senses, he found his shoes and braces gone. Although he believed the man who struck the first blow was John Brittan, he could not positively identify him.

Two witnesses were called who saw the attack and swore that Brittan had struck the blow and had taken Bartlett's shoes. However, under cross examination their evidence was found to be contradictory.

The two London City police officers described the arrest, when the prisoner had confirmed that he was at Priddy Fair, but denied having assaulted and robbed James Bartlett.

Brittan's defence counsel, one Mr Cockburn, addressed the jury, complaining of the great hardship his client had suffered for an alleged offence perpetrated nearly twenty years ago. All the circumstances had been buried in the oblivion of the past and had now been dragged back into existence. Those who could prove his innocence were no longer in this world, and counsel detailed areas of discrepancy in the testimony of the prosecution's witnesses which were such that no jury could fairly convict and called for an acquittal.

Three witnesses were called for the defence who swore that Brittan was not near the place of the assault. One deposed that Bartlett had been knocked over by a large dog and two men had beaten and robbed him, neither of whom was the prisoner. Further witnesses were called to discredit one of the prosecution's as a man whom they would not believe on his oath.

Witnesses from Leicester, Staines, Newbury and Marylebone testified to Brittan's reputation for honesty and good conduct, one saying that 'No man ever bore a better character.'

The judge, Mr Justice Wightman, then summed up, going into every detail, and placed before the jury the contradictions in the evidence.

After a short consultation, the jury returned a verdict of not guilty and John Brittan was released, only to be re-arrested shortly after on a charge of highway robbery committed in 1821. However, the charge was dropped and John Brittan was finally released. After spending the night with his wife at a local inn, the couple left the following morning for Wells in a gig, 'In the presence of several hundreds of persons who were anxiously waiting to get a sight of the new opulent "Gypsy Jack"', reported the *Bath Chronicle*.

When the Beer's in, the Wits are Out!

Alcohol in its many guises has been a common cause of crime over the centuries, and all too frequently was the reason a man or woman would find themselves with a noose around the neck and about to be launched into oblivion. Some of the prisoners who met such a fate at Ilchester Gaol were hanged for a crime committed either under the influence of alcohol or on someone who was hopelessly drunk. The consumption of too much beer during a January day in 1824 led to one man being beaten to within an inch of his life, two young men losing theirs at Ilchester Gaol, and another dying in rather strange circumstances.

Farmer Samuel Wyatt placed the one pound banknote and the golden sovereign in his breeches pocket and set out on Thursday 15 January 1824 to walk the 14 miles from his home at Marksbury to Shepton Mallet and the Friday market. By the time he arrived in the cosy taproom of the George Inn at Shepton Mallet he was very inebriated and the rest of the evening was a blank until he fully recovered his senses at the Swan Inn, with his head covered in blood and hurting all over. Somewhere in the back of his befuddled mind, Samuel Wyatt remembered a blow to his head, felt someone feeling in his breeches pocket, and with his instinct for preserving his hard-earned cash looked for his money but found his pockets empty. The events of that January evening were recounted at the trial of three young men in the following April at the Somerset Lent Assizes.

Joseph Moon, John Beard and Thomas Lewis, all under twenty-one years of age, were on trial on the capital charge of assaulting and robbing Samuel Wyatt during the evening of Thursday 15 January 1824. The jury heard that Samuel Wyatt had walked to Shepton Mallet, having carefully pocketed the one pound banknote and the sovereign, but had become so drunk that he could give no coherent account of what had taken place before receiving the blow to his head, the hand feeling in his breeches pocket and his arrival at the Swan Inn to find his money gone. The court was told that his injuries had been very severe, with much bleeding. Samuel had received an extensive cut to his forehead which extended from his scalp to his eyebrows as well as extensive bruising.

The first prosecution witness was Mrs Frances Newman, who stated that her husband kept the tap of the George Inn, and on the evening in question she recalled Samuel Wyatt and the three accused being present. The farmer had treated the three young men to some beer, after which she heard them offer to take him to some lodgings for the night. However, before they left Samuel Wyatt, in his befuddled state, had shown them some of his money.

Benjamin Hutton told the court that the evening had been moonlit and as he was passing the Tennis Court Field, about a quarter of a mile from the town, he saw Joseph Moon trying to help Samuel Wyatt over the stile into the field.

The next witness, Francis Moody, stated that as he passed Tennis Court Field, he heard someone groaning, and on going to investigate found Samuel Wyatt trying to get to his feet. He managed to sit him up and, in the bright moonlight, could see that the farmer was covered in blood. With the help of several passers-by, Samuel Wyatt was taken to the Swan Inn and the town constable called out.

The court then heard from a lady shopkeeper from Shepton Mallet, who testified that later the same evening John Beard had come to her shop and purchased a pair of 'trowsers', a coat, waistcoat and breeches, and paid for them with a one pound banknote and a sovereign, which were later confirmed as being the money belonging to Samuel Wyatt. The witness went on to reveal that John Beard had been carrying a thick blackthorn stick with a large knob at the end and had left it by accident at her shop. However, the stick could not be produced for the jury's inspection because her husband had used it to light the fire on the following morning.

The testimony of the next witness, however, put the noose around the necks of Moon and Beard. Thomas Lewis, who had also been charged with the robbery and assault, had now turned King's Evidence to save his neck and testified that following the drinking session with Samuel Wyatt, the keeper of the George Inn had refused him a bed for the night and Moon had offered to take the drunken farmer to the Hare and Hounds, where he might be comfortably lodged. However, Moon had led him to the Tennis Court Field, where they were joined by Beard and the Crown's witness. Once in the field, Moon had beaten Samuel Wyatt to the ground, knelt on his stomach, and took the money from the farmer's breeches' pocket. At the same time Beard had hit the victim's head with two savage blows from his stick, leaving him completely insensible.

A local surgeon testified that the blows to Samuel Wyatt's head had been delivered by a blunt instrument.

The Crown's case was closed, but neither Moon or Beard made any defence, and following the Judge's summing up, the jury returned an immediate guilty verdict for each prisoner. In passing sentence of death on both men, the Judge told them that they had been found guilty of a 'most disgraceful transaction to maltreat a person in this case under the hand of friendship'. They could expect no reprieve and following the awful sentence, it was reported that they left the court in despair.

During what little time was left to Joseph Moon and John Beard as they awaited their fate at Ilchester Gaol, Moon appeared 'very sullen and hardened', whereas Beard was 'more resigned and penitent'. At eight o'clock on the morning of Wednesday 28 April, the two were administered the Sacrament and 'fervently' joined in the prayers, and at three minutes before eleven o'clock they climbed up onto the scaffold. Joseph Moon, on seeing some acquaintances in the crowd below, called out to them to take warning from his fate. The nooses were placed around their necks, prayers were intoned, the trap fell and, in the words of the *Western Flying Post*, 'Moon died almost without a struggle, but Beard appeared to suffer very much. They were both very bad characters though neither had reached the age of twenty one.'

On Thursday 15 January 1824, Farmer Samuel Wyatt left his home in the village of Marksbury to attend the Friday Market at Shepton Mallet, but that evening he was severely beaten and robbed.

The *Western Flying Post* went on to tell a very strange story. It appears that on his release and return to Shepton Mallet, the King's Evidence, Thomas Lewis, in company with 'another worthless character', hung effigies of Moon and Beard in the town. But retribution was soon at hand when, a few days later, it was reported that Lewis had been struck down with 'an inflammation of the brain' which was supposed to have been brought on by 'visitings of conscience' and died at about half past twelve on the day Moon and Beard met their end outside Ilchester Gaol.

The old total abstainers' saying, 'When the beer's in the wits are out', could never have rung truer and with such tragic results!

Illegal Coining at Somerton

Was the story I am about to tell the result of a set up or a sting? I leave you, dear reader, to decide, but this is the outline.

It was 22 December 1835 when a young labouring man, Charles Caines by name, called at the Bear Inn in the Square at Somerton. In conversation with the landlord, Robert Way, it transpired that the young fellow was on his way to Bristol to buy some 'shuffle' or counterfeit coins. Surprisingly, the landlord offered to provide some 'shuffle' or, on payment of a sovereign, to show him how to make some. Young Caines' credentials were tested and accepted when he told Way that his contact was someone called 'Smiler Poole'. During the following days, Charles Caines was initiated into the ways of the counterfeiter, but to the landlord's considerable surprise and shock, he found himself in custody facing trial at the next Lent Assizes, charged with making and issuing a counterfeit half-crown at Somerton. The crime of counterfeiting in the 1830s was taken extremely seriously, and the penalties were severe.

Robert Way appeared at the Somerset Lent Assizes in April 1836, when the jury was informed that the prisoner had kept an inn at Yeovil before moving to Somerton, which might explain the reason why he was standing in the dock.

The first and principal witness for the prosecution was Charles Caines, from whom the story unfolded. He told the court that on 22 December last he had called at the Bear Inn at Somerton, and Robert Way, the landlord, had asked him where he was going. When he said that he was on his way to Bristol to see about some 'shuffle', the prisoner replied that he could make him plenty at five shillings per pound, or for a sovereign would show him how to make some after dinner.

Following the meal, Way told his wife and family to leave the room, and then asked the witness the name of his contact at Bristol. When Caines replied that it was 'Smiler Poole', a name that he had made up, the prisoner said that he was only testing him. Way then said that he needed some metal and asked the witness to go back to Yeovil to purchase some old teapots, spoons and such like from Mr Hanham's shop. He had also given the witness a plaster of Paris mould.

After paying for his meal, Caines returned to Yeovil, bought the articles, and went back to the Bear Inn. On his return the prisoner stated that he needed more plaster of Paris but if he went to buy some at Yeovil, there might be some awkward questions. He therefore asked the witness to go back to Yeovil to make the purchase and bring back the mould he had given him. Charles Caines stated that he told Way that he had

The Bear Inn on the Market Square at Somerton, where Robert Way counterfeited coins in 1836, is shown on the right of this postcard and was later renamed the White Hart.

hidden the mould under his hat, but it had been broken when his hat fell off, and he had thrown the pieces in the river at Ilchester. However, the prisoner then melted the articles brought from Yeovil, and Caines was told to come back again on 29 December, by which time he hoped to have secured some plaster of Paris.

The witness went on to tell the court that on his return to Yeovil, he had gone to see Thomas Holt, a town constable, and told him what had occurred. On 29 December Charles Caines, accompanied by his father, travelled back to Somerton and remained at the Bear Inn for the next week.

The following day, the witness, his father and the prisoner went to an empty upstairs room and another mould was made. Way took a good half-crown and laid it on a looking glass, a piece of pasteboard was placed around it and some plaster of Paris poured on top; then they left and the room was locked. Two days later, on the Friday evening, the room was unlocked, a fire lit and manufacture began. Present were the prisoner, his wife, Charles Caines and his father. Mrs Way melted the metal for the second time and poured it into the mould, which was being held firm by the prisoner. After about a dozen had been so made, the prisoner's wife trimmed off the surplus metal. However, Way was not satisfied with the work and sent his wife downstairs for the servant girl who, on her arrival, melted more metal and trimmed the coins to his apparent satisfaction. Some thirty-six half-crowns were made, one of which Caines' father managed to slip into his pocket. The work was done and the prisoner took the mould downstairs to the bar and placed it under the 'beer engine'; the coins were put in a drawer.

Charles Caines stated that on his return to Yeovil he had gone with his father to Thomas Holt, informed him of the counterfeiting and showed him the coin.

This concluded his evidence, which was challenged by Robert Way in an endeavour to discredit the witness by pointing out that Charles Caines was only fifteen years old and a labourer who associated with gypsies. He also claimed that the witness had been guilty of a gross attack on a young woman on the highway and fined a sovereign. Furthermore, he had stolen her umbrella.

Replying to the allegation, Charles Caines stated that he had only borrowed the umbrella and intended to return it when he would be in church the next Sunday.

It was reported that this reply produced considerable laughter in the court.

The next witness was Caines senior, who supported his son's evidence and produced the counterfeit half-crown.

Thomas Holt, the constable, told the court that on receiving the information he obtained a warrant and had gone to the Bear Inn in company with Thomas Roskelley and Henry Fletch. Robert Way was arrested and the inn was searched. Seven half-crowns were discovered in a dresser drawer, and some more under the head of a bed, all of which the witness produced as evidence. Marks of plaster of Paris and pieces of metal were found in the upstairs room described by Charles Caines. The constable told the court that the prisoner had escaped from custody when the upstairs rooms were being searched, but he had re-arrested him on 8 January in his brother-in-law's house at Sherborne.

Henry Fletch testified that he had searched the upstairs rooms with the constable and found eight half-crowns, which he produced. On hearing a noise from downstairs, he had run down to find that the prisoner had escaped.

Thomas Roskelley told the court that he had found some half-crowns, which he produced. He stated that he had been asked to guard the prisoner while the constable and Henry Fletch searched upstairs, but Way had told him that he wished to have a clean collar to go to Yeovil, and when his wife went to fetch one, the prisoner followed and escaped.

Ann Dunkerton testified for the prosecution, stating that she was the prisoner's servant and was present in the upstairs room. She had poured the metal and trimmed the coins.

The Assistant Solicitor to the National Mint and Inspector of Counterfeit Coin was called and examined the half-crowns produced in evidence. He confirmed that they were counterfeit, cast from a good half-crown, and in such a mould as he had heard described by the witnesses.

The jury found Robert Way guilty of making and issuing a counterfeit half-crown, and he was sentenced to transportation to Australia for life.

Thomas Holt remained as a police officer at Yeovil and was superintendent of the small town force when it was amalgamated with the Somerset County Constabulary in 1859. In recognition of Thomas Holt's long service, the Yeovil Borough Council continued to employ him in the office of mace-bearer and town crier, and on his retirement in 1876 he had been employed by the council in various capacities for forty-one years. The long and faithful servant died in 1880, aged sixty-seven years.

Bigamy

On Monday 10 June 1895, twenty-eight-year-old Tom Bradshaw, the driver of the Mermaid Hotel horse bus, appeared before the Yeovil magistrates, charged with bigamously marrying Miss Adelaide Sarah Bullock on the island of Guernsey on 23 April 1894, his first wife 'being then alive'.

The wronged Adelaide was the first witness and testified that before the said 23 April she had been living with her father on Guernsey, but was now resident in Weymouth. She told the court that she had met Tom Bradshaw when he was working with the same firm as her father and, after a brief courtship, they had married on the island in the town church of St Peter Port. The prisoner had bought the wedding ring, and they had married at eight o'clock in the evening of the 23 April, a not unusual time for weddings in Guernsey. Adelaide went on to tell the Bench that, just before the ceremony, when the couple had been sitting in a coffee shop, Bradshaw had told her to go into the church first and he would follow, explaining that if seen by his friends 'he would be chaffed'. Bradshaw had also borrowed money from the witness and had not repaid her. Some three months later, Adelaide stated that she had received a letter from a lady who claimed to be Tom Bradshaw's wife, but when challenged and despite his denials, she had refused to let him read the contents. Bradshaw had said that if she made enquiries about his past she would find nothing except that he was the father of an illegitimate child, but on the following day Bradshaw disappeared and Adelaide had not seen him again until this morning in court.

Following Adelaide's testimony, the magistrates remanded the prisoner in custody to appear again on the coming Friday.

At the adjourned hearing, the court was packed with spectators eager to hear more of this 'juicy' case. Adelaide Bullock produced the marriage certificate signed by both parties and witnessed and Yeovil Police Sergeant Dicks told the court that he had arrested the prisoner in the yard of the Red Lion Hotel in Kingston. The sergeant stated that after the warrant had been read to him, Bradshaw had asked 'Are both here?', presumably referring to the two women whose names he had read out from the warrant. Sergeant Dicks had replied, 'not yet', and shortly after the prisoner had said, 'I shall own up to it. They led me into it through the drink. I was drunk at the time I married her, and she paid the money.' The officer told the Bench that he had known Bradshaw during the seven or eight months he had been the driver of the Mermaid bus and had been going under the name of William Costain.

17   GUERNSEY. — St. Peter Port. — Town Church and Quay.
Saint-Pierre-Port — L'Église Saint-Pierre et les Quais.

St Peter Port, Guernsey, and the town church, where Tom Bradshaw went through a ceremony of marriage with Adelaide Bullock on 23 April 1895.

Police Constable Williams produced a marriage certificate dated 23 September 1891 between Thomas Bradshaw and Edith Louisa Wilding, which he had obtained from the Revd J. S. Masters, Vicar of Christ Church, Shooter's Hill, London, and stated that he had seen the vicar copy it from the original in the church marriage register and swore under oath that it was correct.

As PC Williams gave his evidence, Bradshaw was seen to turn pale and faint, nearly falling over the side of the dock. A chair was produced and, following drinks of water, the prisoner recovered.

The proceedings were adjourned for a second time to 25 June, to enable the first wife and another witness to appear. Once again the court was packed with eager spectators, but only one witness was called. He was Henry Hodgin, the verger of Christ Church, Shooter's Hill, who testified that he was present at the marriage of Thomas Bradshaw and Edith Wilding on 23 September and, with his daughter Mary, had signed the register as witnesses. The verger then formally identified the Tom Bradshaw in the dock as the Thomas Bradshaw who had married Edith Wilding. It was reported that on a number of occasions during the proceedings, the prisoner was on the point of fainting.

Tom Bradshaw made no answer to the charge and the magistrates committed him for trial at the next Somerset Assizes, where he was found guilty of bigamy and sentenced to twelve months' imprisonment.

A Somerset Spy Scare in 1914

The outbreak of the First World War in August 1914 saw the whole nation caught up in a surge of patriotism, and in the imaginations of large numbers of the population there were German spies everywhere. On 13 August 1914, the 'spy scare' saw an Army officer on his way to join his unit stop off for refreshment in Shepton Mallett and during the course of his short stay he was accused of being a spy because his grey great coat was thought to resemble that of a German officer's.

Likewise, sensational reports in the national popular press of the discovery of a German arsenal of weapons near Dunster were reprinted in the *Western Gazette* on 21 August 1914:

A Somerset Castle owned by Count Conrad Hochberg, has been seized by the police, who discovered 300 rifles, 7,000 gallons of petrol, and plans of the coast and defences round Minehead. The mansion in question is Croydon Hall, near Dunster, and is perched on a headland in an almost inaccessible corner of Exmoor, overlooking the Bristol Channel.

The Count, who has used it as a hunting box, vanished on the eve of the war, and is said to have been arrested at Dover as a spy. He is described as a tall man of military appearance, cleanshaven with sallow features and saturnine expression.

He turned up in Minehead a few years ago, bought an estate on the cliffs, and astonished a local builder by giving him a contract to erect Croydon Hall, at a cost variously estimated at from £30,000 to £60,000.

When it was completed the Count surrounded himself with German friends, including army officers, and a staff of servants, mostly foreign, with a retired English officer as private secretary. Occasionally the Count hunted or played golf at Minehead; but for many months at a time he was absent from England.

When he disappeared the Count wired to a manservant left behind at Croydon Hall, ordering him to blow up the premises. This fell into the hands of the police, who immediately seized the castle. Interesting facts relating about the Count are related by Mr. H. S. Kearsley, a resident of Tooting, who spent the summer of 1912 in Somersetshire at the time when Croydon Hall was being laid out.

'The Count's doings were a continual source of wonder from the time he arrived,' said Mr. Kearsley to a Press representative. 'His mansion was built according to extraordinary plans and in an extraordinary place. Every window of its long front was so constructed that the inmates could observe the traffic in the Channel. The floors were packed with seaweed to make the house sound proof. The surrounding grounds were fenced in by high mounds with hedges planted on the summit. To reach the house one had to climb a steep ascent, and all three converging roads were equally rough and difficult, and each of them placed an approaching stranger within view from the windows long before he could reach the door. The house and outlying buildings were protected by about a dozen watch-dogs. A night watchman was employed – a stalwart ex-soldier. The Count's steward, valet and butler were foreigners – Germans, I believe. The maidservants, about five in number, and the gardeners were English. The Count's liberality to them, and especially his English secretary, was the theme of much gossip. At one time many men were employed in the grounds excavating a pit large enough to contain a house. The object of this was not disclosed. The Count put off enquiries by telling them it was a cesspool.'

However, it was just a sensational story, and a very tall one at that, as explained by the following letters tucked away in the *Western Gazette* on 18 September 1914.

To the Editor
   Dear Sir, I understand some time ago you republished from, I conclude, the 'People,' a calumnious story about Count Conrad Hochberg, an unfortunate and very harmless German gentleman resident in Somersetshire. He is a brother-in-law of my daughter Princess Pless. The Chief Constable of Somersetshire (Captain Metcalfe) writes: 'All I can say is there is not a word of truth in the cutting you send.' I now send you a copy of Lord St. Audries' letter to me, which speaks for itself. I feel sure you do not wish to be unjust, even to a man who has the misfortune to be a subject of the German Emperor. I am, yours obediently, W. CORNELIUS WEST.
 Ruthin Castle, North Wales, September 13th 1914.
 (COPY)
St. Audries, Bridgwater, August 29th 1914.
   Dear Colonel Cornwallis West, I am very sorry you have been worried with this nonsense. I have known Count Conrad Hochberg as a neighbour for some years. I have constantly met him on the hunting field, and he has lunched with me here. He is a very good neighbour and popular in the district. As to the raid on his house, all that was found was a pair of breech-loading 12 bore guns, a rabbit rifle and 211 No. 12 cartridges loaded with No. 6 shot, which is exactly what you would find in my own house at any time. He had also I believe, 800 gallons of petrol, which as he kept, I think four motor-cars, was not an excessive amount. As for his 'inaccessible castle' it is an old farmhouse, largely increased and modernised by Count Hochberg. The approach used to be by a very old and bad farm road which his predecessor, who kept a motor very much improved, and which he, himself further improved. As to the windows overlooking the Channel and the traffic, everyone in this district tries to get a view of the Channel, simply because it is one of the most beautiful views in England. There are no coast or other defences round Minehead and the traffic does not come up this side of the Channel. The whole story is absurd, and has been contradicted at length in our local papers by the Rector of the Parish in which the 'alleged castle' stands. Yours very truly, ST. AUDRIES

Sensational press reports following the outbreak of war in August 1914 claimed that an arsenal of German weapons had been seized at Croydon Hall.

So there you are. A very tall story indeed. And what do we know about Count Conrad Hochberg? It appears that he was a very popular figure in West Somerset, entertaining lavishly and supporting local shows, charities and events. He was a younger brother of Prince Henry of Pless, who had married Colonel Cornwallis West's daughter, a cousin of the German Kaiser and a captain in the White Cuirassiers of Potsdam; he was said to have had a great love of England. Before war broke out in August 1914, the Count had already returned to Germany, but despite being unfit for military service following an accident as a young man, he assisted his brother Fritz in running a field hospital. In 1917 he became an invalid and the Count is reported to have died in Berlin the early 1930s.

A Railway Mystery

A century ago, bird-batting involved finding a hedge with roosting birds, shining a light, beating the branches with sticks and then netting the birds as they tried to fly away. On the cold, clear evening of Friday 8 February 1901, the brothers Penny and Hodge were engaged in such an undertaking in a field by the Marston Magna railway station when in the gloom they saw a figure stagger along the side of the track and collapse just short of the platform. Rushing to render assistance, the brothers found a very distressed and dazed young man who muttered, 'They have taken my watch and chain and thrown me out of the train.' The man was helped to the Red Lion Hotel, where he was recognised as Herbert Pitman, a farmer of Merrilands Farm, Galmington, and was found to have suffered a badly bruised head and ribs, and crushed fingers on his right hand, two of which were subsequently amputated. Doctors Coombs of Castle Cary and Hurley of Queen Camel were called, and the young farmer was taken home to bed.

During the next few days, Herbert Pitman told a curious tale. He stated that he had been to the Yeovil Friday Market and that evening had caught the 8.20 Bristol train from Yeovil Pen Mill station with a ticket to Sparkford, the nearest station to his home, where a horse and trap was waiting for him. When he arrived at the station all the other passengers had already boarded and he got into a Third Class compartment where two well-dressed men were seated. The train started and he had got into conversation with the two men. They had questioned him on the price of stock in the Yeovil Market and shortly after produced some coins and commenced some tricks. Herbert went on to relate how the men had invited him to join in and try some sleight of hand tricks, but he had refused. The man sitting next to him had suddenly put his arm around his neck and placed a cloth over his head. Herbert then lost consciousness, but before he blacked out he remembered feeling a man's hands in his pockets. It was suggested that cloth had been chloroformed, and the doctors who had treated Herbert Pitman noted that he might have been drugged. The young farmer remembered nothing more until he recovered consciousness and found himself lying beside the railway track about a mile from Marston Magna station. He had made his way along the track but collapsed a short distance from the platform.

Herbert Pitman stated that when he had left Yeovil he had about £4 in his possession, together with his watch and gold chain. The latter had been taken, and the only money found on him was a golden half sovereign and 22 shillings in silver money. The two men were strangers to him and he could not give a detailed description other than to

Farmer Henry Pitman was found in a distressed and dazed condition at Marston Magna railway station on 8 February 1901, claiming that he had been robbed and thrown from the Bristol train.

say that they were of medium height, each had a moustache and both wore overcoats and felt hats.

The Somerset police immediately began their investigations under Superintendent Self, who discovered blood stains at the spot where Herbert Pitman stated that he had been thrown out, but as it was established that this part of the railway line was in Dorset, Superintendent Simpson of Sherborne took over the case.

It was quickly established that ten Third Class passengers were travelling on the train, which had no communicating corridors, and all had been traced; three alighted at Sparkford, one went on to Wells, two to Bristol, one to Trowbridge, another to Bruton, one to Warminster, and the tenth was presumed to be Herbert Pitman. All the passengers were interviewed, none fitted the description of the robbers, and all were reported to have been 'respectable'.

The police concluded that the young farmer's injuries were caused when he fell from the train, and although robbery appeared to have been the motive, curiously, all the money seemed to have been taken from one pocket but left untouched in the others.

On 17 February, a reporter from the *Western Gazette* visited Merrilands Farm and gained an interview with Herbert Pitman, who despite his injuries was well on the way to recovery. Asked whether he could throw any further light on the mystery, Herbert replied that he could not add anything to what he had already said, but then gave some more details of his movements in Yeovil prior to catching the Bristol train. It appeared that the young farmer had intended to catch the 6.32 train from Pen Mill station, but had missed it due to overstaying his visit to an eating-house in Wine Street. Finding the train gone, he had walked back into the town and tried, without success, to find someone who could drive him home. After buying some sweets and sausages from a shop he described as being next to a chemist's, he had returned to the station in time to catch the 8.20 train.

The police enquiries continued, but no further clues were revealed, the stolen watch and cash never recovered, and no suspects detained; the case, it seems, remains unsolved.

There is a footnote to the story – The *Western Gazette* reported that Herbert Pitman was soon to be married and had taken West End Farm at Marston Magna.

The Dancing Party at
East Chinnock

The 'dancing party' in the Hare and Hounds Inn at East Chinnock on Shrove Tuesday, 16 February 1858, brought young men and women from the village and those around to enjoy an evening's drinking, music and dancing. Despite the convivial atmosphere, there were tensions, which would build up as the drink flowed, and village rivalries and jealousies rose to the surface. Fights between rival village lads were not uncommon and rarely resulted in more than bruises, black eyes and sometimes lost teeth, but occasionally the result could be serious, if not fatal, such as the death of a West Coker man some twelve years before in a fight with Odcombe men at Pye Corner.

Some young men who had arrived from Haselbury Plucknett were not very welcome, especially for their attention to some of the East Chinnock girls, and Alfred Voisey from West Coker, who was playing a cornopean, had remarked to Sarah Bicknell that the Haselbury men should not 'come over here after the girls of Chinnock'. One Chinnock girl, who was enjoying the company of twenty-two-year-old Henry Hewlett from Haselbury, his brother and several friends, was Sarah's sister, and it was against Hewlett that Voisey's remarks were directed.

The dancing party came to an end shortly after midnight and the revellers, many of whom were far from sober, began to disperse to their homes and villages. The cornopean player, Alfred Voisey, set off home up Chinnock Hill in company with Mary Ann Cooper, Elizabeth Higgins and a young man called Withey. Back at the Hare and Hounds, as the Haselbury men were leaving, Henry Hewlett got into an argument with a man called Pike, who attacked him and knocked him to the ground. Recovering, Hewlett shouted that he was going to get the West Coker policeman and made off up Chinnock Hill. Henry Hewlett and Alfred Voisey would shortly meet on Chinnock Hill, and a few days later Henry Hewlett would find himself in Yeovil before the county magistrates, charged with cutting and wounding Alfred Voisey with intent to do him grievous bodily harm.

The events leading to Henry Hewlett's appearance in court are somewhat confused, as it would seem that all the main participants and some of the witnesses were, as we might say, 'well under the influence', and gave contradictory evidence. However, what can be established with some certainty is that as Hewlett went up Chinnock Hill he passed Voisey and his companions, and following their warning that some men, who had gone before, were waiting to give him a 'hiding', words were exchanged and in the scuffle which followed, Henry Hewlett stabbed Alfred Voisey in his left arm.

Chinnock, or Coker Hill, shown here in the early 1900s, was the scene of a stabbing in the early morning of 17 February 1858.

His brother and friends from Haselbury saved Hewlett from further assault. The bad feeling between the Haselbury men and Henry Hewlett in particular was recalled by Sarah Bicknell, who told the Bench that Voisey had threatened to waylay Hewlett on his way home. Other witnesses stated that the participants were drunk and Henry Hewlett had been attacked, beaten and kicked by Voisey and Withey.

The Chairman of the Bench, George Harbin Esq., summed up the case by saying that,

> There appears to have been a drunken row, and if the prisoner had only given a blow in return, the Bench would have perhaps dismissed the case; but the use of an instrument was so extremely dangerous, and so unlike the English practice, that it must be prevented by law. If an artery had been cut, the prosecutor might have bled to death or if the blow had been given in some more vital part of the body, he might have been killed instantly.

Henry Hewlett was sent for trial at the Lent Assizes, where perhaps the jury had some sympathy with the predicament in which he had found himself on Chinnock Hill and delivered a verdict of not guilty.

Three Suspicious Deaths

Butcher John Glyde, of North Newton, near Bridgwater, was not popular with many of his neighbours and had incurred their wrath by laying information with the magistrates against some of them for selling cider without a license. On Saturday 7 February 1823, Butcher Glyde appeared once more before the magistrates in Bridgwater Guildhall and presented further information naming several sellers of illegal cider. However, on this occasion the magistrates considered that there were a number of inconsistencies in the information which discredited the butcher's allegations, and dismissed the case.

Meanwhile, during the proceedings, a mob had collected outside the Guildhall and when John Glyde emerged, he was followed in a threatening manner with shouted threats and cat-calls until he was hurried out of the town.

Later that Saturday evening, John Glyde was nearing his home in North Newton when he was stopped by three 'notorious characters' by the names of William and Thomas Durham and John Treble. The record is silent as to what happened, but whatever it was, John Glyde did not survive the encounter.

At the inquest into the death of John Glyde, a neighbour, James Haines, deposed that late in the evening of Saturday 7 February, he was at his house when he heard someone calling for help and on going out to investigate, he found the deceased down on his knees with the two Durhams and Treble standing near him. As he tried to help the butcher to his feet, the three men hurled mud and stones at him and when one of them punched him several times in the face, he had retreated to his house. James Haines stated that when the men had left he went back to see if he could render assistance but found John Glyde lying dead on the road.

William Durham, Thomas Durham and John Treble were arrested soon after on suspicion of murder and remanded in goal. However, there were no marks of violence on John Glyde's body, and the two surgeons who opened the corpse found 'an effusion of blood in the pericardium', which they considered was the cause of death – he had died from a heart attack, probably brought on by the traumatic events of the day and from the fear of attack by the three 'notorious characters'.

The jury returned a verdict of 'Found Dead', but expressed the opinion that John Glyde's life might have been preserved had the three men not prevented James Haines from assisting the deceased. Subsequently, the three 'notorious characters' were released without charge.

Yeovil is the scene of the next suspicious death, where on Saturday 4 July 1857, an inquest was held at the Pen Mill Hotel, Yeovil, into the drowning of fourteen-year-

Young James Lanham ran away from his father and drowned in the River Yeo near Compton Mill, in July 1857, and the inquest jury returned an open verdict of 'Found Drowned'.

old James Lanham in the River Yeo, near Compton Mill, on the previous Thursday. James was the son of William Lanham, an umbrella mender living in Gore Knap, who testified that the youngster had left home shortly before six o'clock on Wednesday morning to walk to his work as an apprentice to Mr Colley, a local shoemaker.

William Lanham stated that his son had not returned home that evening, but at about half past eight the following morning, a neighbour told him that he had just seen James walking down Lyde Lane towards Compton Mill. Following this information, he had gone in search of James and saw him standing on the Wilts & Somerset Railway line. William Lanham stated that he had called out to the lad to come home and that he would not beat him if he did, but James began to run away. However, when he had shouted that a policeman would be sent to get him, James came back and the two began to make their way home.

William Lanham stated that as he climbed over the gate at the bottom of Lyde Lane, James turned and ran back towards the bridge near Compton Mill. Instead of crossing the bridge the lad turned left and, after running a little way along the side of a meadow, jumped down an embankment some 15 or 20 feet from the river. William Lanham had then lost sight of his son, but when he reached the spot he saw James lying on his back in the water. He ran to Compton Mill for help but when he returned with two men from the Mill, James' body could be seen on the river bottom. Ropes and drag lines were sent for and the body was recovered about half an hour later.

In reply to a question from a member of the jury, William Lanham denied that he was in the habit of beating or threatening his son, and although Mr Colley had often complained about his apprentice's idleness, he did not believe the shoe maker ill-used the lad. William Lanham also told the jury that James had run off to Portsmouth during the previous September, and he had taken him nearly three weeks to find him.

After deliberation the jury decided that James Lanham had jumped into the River Yeo trying to get to the other side to escape his father, but as there was no direct evidence of his motive or how he got into the water, they returned an open verdict of 'Found Drowned.'

Three months later, another suspicious death occurred near Frome, at Elm Fair, on Tuesday 6 October 1857. Robert Welch, a horse dealer from Shepton Mallet, had made several good deals at the Fair, and as a result he was in a very jolly mood. He was seen on several occasions in the company of 'some rather suspicious characters', and during the late afternoon, at about six o'clock, he collapsed outside a refreshment tent. The horse dealer was helped to his feet and taken inside the tent, where he stood leaning against the bar with his head in his hands. About ten minutes later, Robert Welch suddenly fell forward onto his face and, after being helped up, was placed on a stool. However, he fell off the stool and the landlord of the refreshment tent, assuming that he was the worse for drink, had the horse dealer carried to the far end, where he was laid down to sober up. Here Robert Welch remained until the tent closed for business some half an hour later, and one of the waiters was sent to see how he was. On lifting him, the waiter was horrified to find that Robert Welch was dead! A call was made to Dr Terry, a physician living nearby, who on arrival twice unsuccessfully attempted to bleed the horse dealer, and then pronounced him dead

The police were quickly on the scene, but a search of Robert Welch's person could only produce the sum of five shillings and six pence, whereas enquiries suggested that his successful day's trading had netted the horse dealer nearly £7, a large sum for the time.

The news of Robert Welch's demise was soon the talk of the district, and there was a strong rumour that a jockey had been observed following him about and while he was leaning against the bar in the refreshment tent, the jockey had come in and ordered the landlord to give Robert Welch a glass of gin. The landlord had refused as he considered the horse dealer had already had sufficient to drink. It was also being rumoured that shortly before Robert Welch collapsed he had appeared sober and there was a suggestion that the mysterious jockey had slipped a powerful drug into his drink, which had stupefied him, and in this state he had been robbed.

However, both the police and the medical gentlemen who carried out the autopsy on the corpse of Robert Welch were satisfied that he had died from natural causes, and the verdict returned by the jury at the subsequent inquest was death from 'Visitation from God'.

On Saturday 17 October 1857, the *Somerset and Wilts Journal*, writing on the death of Robert Welch, commented that, 'Although he should certainly have a larger sum of money in his possession, no steps can be taken for its recovery.' An interesting remark, which confirms that this was truly a suspicious death.

Two Fatal Fires

Fire is an ever-present menace and the consequences can be terrible and tragic, and none more so than when children are in involved. The two stories which follow, although separated by nearly half a century, are tragic, but in one, two men act with complete disregard of their own lives in trying to save young lives.

The fire in Mr Henry White's upholsterer's workshops in Union Street, Yeovil, broke out just after one o'clock on Monday afternoon on 23 May 1881. Feeding on the packing materials, dry wood and shavings, the fire soon took hold and within minutes smoke was billowing from the premises. However, the early arrival of the town's volunteer fire brigade, led by Lieutenant Damon, soon contained the fire to the ground floor and prevented its spread to adjoining buildings.

At about two o'clock, when the blaze had been subdued, a ladder was put up to a first floor window and Fireman T. W. Vincent climbed up to inspect the extent of the damage. He smashed the smoke-blackened glass, pushed in the frame, and peered into the room. To his horror, he picked out the form of a small child huddled by the wall under the window. Reaching in, Fireman Vincent lifted the child and, to cries of consternation from the watching crowd, carried it gently back down the ladder. The small victim was found to be dead, and quickly identified as Frederick White, the upholsterer's four-year-old son. Although the fire had seriously damaged the workshops, the boy had not been burnt, but had died from the effect of smoke. Frederick was carried to his home in Peter Street and his distraught parents. But people were asking, why was he in the building and why did nobody know?

On the morning of Wednesday, 25 May, the inquest into the death of young Frederick White opened in the Swan Inn, Park Street, before the coroner, Dr Wybrants, and a 'respectable jury'. The first witness was Mr John Conway, who said that he was employed by Mr White and knew the young deceased. Mr Conway stated that just before one o'clock on the day in question he had taken Frederick from the workshop to his home in Peter Street and left the child in the front passage of the house. He had then returned to the workshop and had gone for his dinner at about ten minutes past one. The fire had broken out after he had left, and he had not seen Frederick return to the workshop. The witness went on to say that there had been a stray cat and her kittens in the room above the workshops and Frederick used to go there to play with them. Mr Conway suggested that the boy had gone back to see the kittens after he had taken him home.

Fireman Vincent, the next witness, stated that within five minutes of the call, all members of the brigade were on the spot. The flames had been so fierce that at first they could not get near the buildings, but within less than an hour the fire had been subdued sufficiently to enable a ladder to be put up. He had climbed up the ladder and, after breaking the window, had looked in to see if the floor was safe enough to allow him to enter the room. Fireman Vincent then described how he saw the boy lying on his back below the window, apparently quite dead but not burnt. He believed that when the fire had broken out, the boy had been in the room above the workshop but, running to the staircase, he had found it blocked by flames and had gone back into the room where he was found. The child was not tall enough to be seen through the window and had been suffocated by the thick smoke. In reply to a question from one of the jurors, Fireman Vincent did not know whether the front door of the building had been locked, but Mr Henry White, who was present, told the jury that it was never locked during the day. The witness said that he had been the first fireman on the scene, and although people were saying that a boy was missing, he took this to mean one of Mr White's workshop boys, who would have been able to make his way out of the building.

At this point, sensing criticism of the fire brigade, Mr W. N. Thring, the foreman of the jury, stated that he had been present at the fire, and he thought the members of the brigade did well.

Fireman Vincent continued with his evidence and stated that had the brigade known that there was a child in the building, they would have played the hoses on the room concerned at the expense of the rest of the buildings, and taken the most strenuous efforts to get him out. They had only heard the vague rumour of a child being missing, but not who or where, and had not the remotest idea that there was anyone trapped in the blazing building. The fire was one of the fiercest he had seen in such a small space.

No more witnesses were called, and following his summing up, the coroner said that there was only one verdict open to the jury, and that was 'accidentally smothered'. The jury commented that the contents of the building were very combustible, and the child must have fallen as soon as he got to the window. They were unanimous in returning a verdict of 'accidentally smothered'.

Next door to Mr White's workshops was a private school run by Mr G. S. Stone which had been in danger from the fire. On 2 June 1881 the *Western Gazette* published the following letter from Mr Stone:

Will you allow me to correct a false report current in the town, concerning two country pupils who were in my schoolroom during the dinner hour on the day of the fire? It seems generally believed that three boys were locked in by way of punishment and when the fire broke out on the adjoining premises their lives were in jeopardy. Some also add that the door was broken open to liberate them before the key could be procured. The facts of the case are, however, that a couple of country pupils are allowed to stay in the room to take their dinner, by way of accommodation, as they had all asked for a half holiday (instead of the following Wednesday) to attend the rifle battalion drill in Barwick Park, and they were furnished with the key to liberate themselves when they chose, but were requested to leave it at my house on their way to the park. They tell me that they had taken their exit from the school before any

Park Street, Yeovil, the row of houses shown in the centre of this photograph was the scene of a tragic fire which claimed the lives of three young children in November 1927.

alarm of fire took place, and were on their way to deliver the key before they heard of it. The statements also prove that the boy one of the spectators saw at one of the schoolroom windows could not have been either of those in question, but must have been one of the solicited or unsolicited helpers in the removal of the furniture of the room after the door had been broken open by the Fire Brigade, before my arrival.

Forty-six years later, it was just after four o'clock on the afternoon of Friday 11 November 1927 and Mr Sidney Peaty, a member of the Yeovil Volunteer Fire Brigade, was at work in the Arnold Glove Company's factory, Addlewell Lane, when a workmate ran up and told him that there was a fire in nearby Park Street. The two men hurried out into the road and saw smoke pouring from the chimney and from under the corrugated iron roof of 9 Park Street, which overlooked Addlewell Lane. Running up onto Park Street, they found a number of local women crowding around the front door of the house, several having already been beaten back by the flames inside, and one was screaming that three of her babies were still inside in the kitchen.

Without hesitation, Mr Peaty entered the house, but as he opened the kitchen door flames roared out and he slammed it shut. He called for buckets of water and within minutes, neighbours, passers-by and men who had arrived from nearby factories formed a bucket chain, the kitchen door was opened and water thrown into the blazing room. Meanwhile, a call had gone to the volunteer fire brigade.

A few hundred yards away, in the yard of Messrs Clothier and Giles, glove factory, Mr Walter Hitchcox saw the chimney fire in Park Street, but when he saw smoke coming from the house he ran to see if he could help and joined Mr Peaty. With the flames slightly subdued Mr Peaty, followed by Mr Hitchcox, entered the burning room keeping as low as possible. Almost blinded by the smoke, Mr Peaty felt the body of a child behind the door and heard a baby crying from a chair a few feet away. Believing the first child to be dead, Mr Peaty located the baby, and picking it up with its clothes on fire rushed back out in a state of near collapse and with burns to his head,

Meanwhile, Mr Hitchcox had struggled through the smoke and flame to see any of the children were in a small room just beyond the kitchen, but finding it empty, returned through the burning kitchen. It was just after he left the kitchen that Mr Peaty emerged with the burning baby and, realising the other two children had not been rescued, Mr Hitchcox went back in. Groping around on his hands and knees in the smoke and heat, he found one child, which he carried out and, going back, quickly located the other on the floor halfway across the kitchen and brought the infant out into the road.

The three terribly burnt children of Mr and Mrs Bertram Rood, three-year-old Doreen, Kenneth, aged just under two, and six-week-old baby Dorothy, were all still alive and were rushed to Yeovil Hospital in private cars, where despite every attention, they mercifully died very quickly from their massive burns.

Less than half an hour had passed from the time the alarm was raised and the arrival of the volunteer fire brigade.

The inquest into the deaths of the three Rood children was held in the town hall three days later, when the circumstances of the tragedy were recalled. Mr and Mrs Rood, of 9 Park Street, had five older children who were at work or school on the day in question, and Mr Rood was at work as a foreman baker with Messrs Aplin and Barrett. Mrs Rood had been at home with the three infants and had been drying washing in front of the kitchen range, protected by a fire guard. She had just gone to her mother's house a few doors away to collect some washing when a neighbour rushed in, shouting that her house was on fire.

The inquest was given details of the rescues and several witnesses told of the events of that tragic afternoon. While the cause of the blaze could not be established with any certainty, it was generally thought that the clothes set out for drying had somehow caught fire, but this would remain a mystery.

The coroner felt that no blame could be placed on Mrs Rood, as there was no evidence of neglect, the range had been guarded and the facilities for washing and drying clothes in the small house were poor through no fault of the Rood family.

The jury returned a verdict of deaths by burns, and added that no blame whatsoever attached to the mother. They also commended Mr Sidney Peaty and Mr Walter Hitchcox 'for the heroic part they played'.

She Told Me Her Husband Was Very Ill

Mrs Elizabeth Dunn was sitting down to her evening meal in her house at Cross, near Axbridge, on Wednesday 2 March 1836, when one of her neighbours, Sophia Edney, hurried in and said that her sixty-one-year-old husband, John, had been taken very ill. He was being sick, could keep nothing down and was so ill she wished he was in Heaven. This news surprised Elizabeth, as only on the day before she had seen John Edney walking up the drove-way looking well, and with a basket full of watercress, which he gathered and sold with eggs and cheese in the Bristol markets.

At about nine o'clock the following morning Sophia Edney called again to say that her husband was still very ill, and asked Elizabeth Dunn to come and see him. She found John in bed looking very ill indeed, and he told her that he had never felt so bad in his life. However, he fancied a little mutton broth, which he felt would make him better, and he would then go out watercressing. Elizabeth told him that he was not well enough to get up and when he vomited some milk, she suggested that Sophia should call the doctor.

Elizabeth Dunn called again that afternoon and found John complaining of a bad pain in his stomach but saying he would still like some mutton broth. Elizabeth noticed that there was some gruel in a tea cup in the bedroom, and Sophia Edney said that she had called the doctor, who said that it was probably inflammation of the kidneys. She then asked Elizabeth to go to Axbridge to buy a piece of mutton, a quarter of sugar, some groats and a penny rushlight.

On her return Elizabeth Dunn went in to the sick room just as Dr Wade arrived and after examining the patient, the doctor gave him some medicine and left powders to be taken as necessary. Having prepared some mutton broth, Elizabeth left it with Sophia and went home.

Sophia Edney called again on Friday morning and told Elizabeth Dunn that her husband had suffered a very troubled night. He had taken some of the powders, but was much worse and she would be sending for Dr Wade. Going up to see John, Elizabeth thought he was looking very ill; he was complaining of severe pain in his stomach, his face was swollen, his eyes were very red and he was very thirsty. During the day he got worse; the pain in his stomach increased and the mutton broth, gruel and any drink given by his wife was immediately vomited. Furthermore, John Edney complained that his wife's gruel did not taste like Elizabeth's. As the afternoon passed and he got worse, John asked Elizabeth whether she thought he was going to die, because if so, he wanted his body to be sold to a doctor to ensure that Sophia could have some money, but she replied that this was a hard thing to tell.

By evening, the sick man's condition had become desperate; he was writhing in pain, vomiting and in a sinking state, and at about half past two on the Saturday morning John Edney's suffering came to an end and he passed away from this world.

Doctor Edward Wade, however, was suspicious, and despite Sophia Edney's opposition, he carried out an autopsy, and his suspicions were confirmed when he found evidence of a mineral poison which he believed to be arsenic. Chemical tests were carried out on the deceased's stomach and some fried potatoes left in a frying pan, and both stomach and potatoes were found to contain arsenic.

Sophia Edney was taken into custody and the jury at the inquest into the death of her husband returned a verdict of 'Wilful Murder against the Wife', and she was sent for trial at the next Assizes.

Twenty-three-year-old Sophia Edney appeared a month later at the Somerset Lent Assizes on 5 April, indicted for the wilful murder of her husband John Edney on 2 March 1836, in the parish of Compton Bishop.

The first and principal witness for the prosecution was Mrs Elizabeth Dunn, who described the events of 2 and 3 March and her account of John Edney's final hours was graphically reported in the *Western Flying Post* of Monday 11 April:

> In the evening prisoner called to me and said – come quick, I believe John is dying; I ran up as fast as I could; I went upstairs and found Mrs. Edney, her husband and Mrs Collins [another neighbour], deceased was in prayer; she asked me if I thought he was dying and I said it was a hard thing to say, 'He said he was thirsty and wanted something to drink'; she gave him a tea cup with some milk in it, and he said what have you got! His wife said a drop of milk; he said – have you put the powder in it? She said she had not; he said – light the candle over nearer; I took the candle and put in near him; he said – I can't see. I took the tea cup out of his hand and examined the cup; he put his finger in the tea cup and put it to the bottom; he said have you put it in! She said she had not; he drank a drop, and was sick after it; I then went home. I saw him again at eight o'clock the same evening, and he seemed more restless than he did before; prisoner gave him a little milk in my presence. I saw him again at about half past nine and found him worse than I had ever seen him (witness further described the symptoms of the deceased.) He died about half past two. She never complained to me of there being rats in the house.

Elizabeth Collins, the next witness, told the court that she had been with John Edney during the Friday evening and he had been in great agony, twisting and turning about in bed and telling her he was very ill. He had said that he had been ill since Wednesday dinner time and complained that the stuff the doctor had given him burned his insides and that all the way up to his throat was raw and felt on fire.

The reason for the comment about rats in the last sentence of Elizabeth Dunn's testimony became clear when the next witness, Axbridge druggist William Allen, told the court that Sophia Edney had bought some arsenic to kill rats. He stated that he had marked the packet 'Poison' and cautioned her regarding its use.

In the village of Cross near Axbridge, shown here in the early 1900s, Sophia Edney murdered her elderly husband by the administration of poison in March 1836.

Doctor Edward Wade now took the stand, and stated that he lived at Cross, that on the evening of Thursday 3 March he had been called to the Edney house for the first time, and had never seen the prisoner before her husband's illness. The deceased had complained of pains in his stomach which extended from the throat of his stomach, everything he took seemed to be burning him and there were similar pains in the lower part of his belly. The doctor had given him some powders and left some to be taken. He had been called again the next morning and found the deceased much worse and in a sinking condition, with his wife present at the bed side. Doctor Wade stated that he had asked the deceased whether he had eaten any poisonous food, or watercress which might have been poisonous, or any vegetables boiled in a copper pot, but he had replied that he believed not. However, Sophia Edney had told him that they had both eaten some greens she had boiled in a saucepan and they had not affected her. The doctor went on to say that he had returned on the Friday morning, and that the deceased said that he had experienced a little relief. He had administered some mixture and it was then that John Edney had disclosed that he had suffered a slight gnawing pain in his stomach for a long time, and also that he had eaten some fried potatoes on the day he was taken ill. On a further visit at mid-day on Friday, the deceased appeared about the same.

Doctor Wade explained that following the death of John Edney he had examined the body and described the results, and his further observations were reported in the *Western Flying Post*:

The examination was opposed by the prisoner – I believe he died from the effects of a mineral poison introduced into the stomach; I should think that from 4 to 10 grains of arsenic would be sufficient to destroy life; sometimes it occasions vomiting immediately, and at other times it remains some hours in the stomach; if a large quantity of arsenic was given, and he does no vomit, it would most likely prolong his life; the appearance of death would be as I have described in the case of John Edney. I never stated to the prisoner that her husband's disease was an inflammation of the kidneys.

The next witness was William Herepath, Professor of Chemistry and Lecturer at the Bristol Medical College and a respected expert in the field of poisons, having appeared at a number of prominent trials. The professor stated that he had examined and made six tests of the contents of the deceased's stomach, all of which showed the presence of arsenic, and any one of the tests would be infallible.

The jury took only a short time to find Sophia Edney guilty of killing her husband by the administration of poison, and she was sentenced to be executed by hanging at Ilchester Gaol on the following Thursday; justice moved swiftly in 1836, and especially for wives who poisoned their husbands.

The *Western Flying Post* reported that Sophia Edney had since 'confessed everything', and that tragically she had fallen subject to one of the oldest problems faced by a vibrant young woman,who, at the age of sixteen, had married a man old enough to be her grandfather. From her confession it emerged that John Edney had supplied the house at Bristol where she was living as a servant 'in a very humble position' with eggs, butter and poultry. It appeared that friends had persuaded the young woman to marry him and they had lived reasonably content until some two and a half years previous when Sophia became very attached to a young man and, in the hope that he would marry her when she was a widow, she had poisoned her elderly husband. It transpired that the subject of Sophia's affections had no knowledge of her desperate plan, which she had hatched after reading the story of Mary Burdock, executed at Bristol for poisoning her elderly lady lodger and stealing her money – not a very promising example, it must be said.

The tragic, love-torn Sophia Edney was publicly hanged at Ilchester gaol on Thursday 14 April 1836, and on 25 April the *Western Flying Post* wrote that 'Her execution, from the shortness of the interval since her sentence, was not attended by many persons. The body was buried within the prison.' And that was that.

Strange and Ghostly

Winter is the time for strange and ghostly tales and here are four which, dear reader, you may wish to enjoy on a night when the wind moans around the roof and the rain rattles on the window panes!

Firstly, some ghostly goings on at Montacute House, as recalled in the *Western Gazette* on 22 January 1932 by Mr A. F. Montacute, the former coachman to the Phelips family, and his brother-in-law, Mr C. Osborne:

> 'There was room they called John Scott the huntman's room, which was said to be haunted,' related Mr. Montacute. 'No one would sleep there for years because of the noises. I remember when it was furnished, and a valet, who came with some visitors, was put there, and at another time a housemaid, but they complained of the noises. I believed they were caused by the wind rattling on a doorway leading on to the roof. But if you took up a board in the floor you could find the oats he used to take down to his hunter in the morning. Some of the oats are there now, I suppose. I have seen them.'
>
> John Scott, a huntsman of long bygone days, when a pack of hounds was maintained at Montacute, was the subject of local legend whose name was used to frighten children. 'There use to be a story that he rode around the house with the pack in full cry.' Mr. Osborne, told the Western Gazette representative. 'The hounds had their tongues hanging out and afire. As children we were terrified. I use to be told that if I went near the wood John Scott would have me.'

Another Somerset ghost story is told in *Strange Things Amongst Us* by H. Spicer, published in 1864. The place of the haunting was not disclosed, other than that it was a mansion in Somerset described as B--House, near F--, and neither are the names of the narrator of the tale and his companion. However, the haunting is said to have taken place every night at midnight, when the sound of a lady's high-heeled shoes and the swish of her dress was heard along one of the corridors.

At a house party a few miles from the haunted mansion, our narrator heard of the remarkable phenomenon and, his curiosity aroused, arranged with the family of B--House for a midnight vigil in the corridor with a friend, referred to as Mr W. K--. The family were away from home on the night picked for the vigil and the two friends dined early at five o'clock so as to remain alert, and established themselves in the corridor.

There was a door at each end, one or two at the side, and to block all passage a card table and two chairs were placed in the middle of the corridor, with two lighted candles on the floor near the wall two or three feet from the table, on the side from which the sound of ghostly steps always came. Two revolvers and two life preservers (a large cosh) were placed on the table and the ghost hunters sat down to play cards and await events.

The house clock struck midnight and – but let our narrator relate what happened next:

Mechanically we dropped our cards, and looked along the dim corridor. No sounds, however, followed, and after pausing a minute or two, we resumed the game, which chanced to be near its conclusion.

'I say, it's nonsense sitting up,' yawned K--, 'this thing never comes, you know after twelve. What do you say? After this game?'

I looked at my watch, which I had taken the precaution to set by the church clock, as we entered the village. By this it appeared that the house clock was fast. It wanted yet three minutes of the hour. Pointing out the mistake to K--, I proposed that we should, by all means, wait another ten minutes.

The words were not fairly out of my mouth, when the door at the end seemed to open and re-close. This time the cards literally dropped from our hands, for, though nothing could be seen, the conviction was growing on both our minds, that something had entered. We were soon more convinced of it. The silence was broken by a tapping sound, such as would be caused by a light person, wearing high-heeled shoes, quietly coming towards us up the gallery, each step, as it approached sounding more distinct than the last; exactly, in fact, as would be the case under ordinary circumstances. It was a firm and regular tread – light, yet determined – and it was accompanied by the sound between a sweep, a rustle, and a whistle, not comparable to anything but the brushing of a stiff silken dress against the walls!

How K-- and I looked as the sounds advanced as it were to storm us, I will not pretend to say. I confess I was, for the moment, petrified with amazement, and neither of us, moved hand or foot. On-on-on came the tap and rustle; they reached the lighted candles on the floor, passed them, not even disturbing the flame, then the tapping ceased, but the invisible silken robe seemed to brush the wall on both sides, on a level with our heads, then the tapping recommenced on the other side of the table, and so, receding, made its exit at the other door!

As for making use of our revolvers or life preservers, the idea never once occurred to either of us. There was not even a shadow at which to strike; it was sound alone.

I feel that any attempt to explain this strange phenomenon at once to my own satisfaction and that of others, would be perfectly futile; I must of necessity content myself with simply narrating the fact as it occurred, and as it had been, and probably may yet be, witnessed by many others, as little predisposed as my friend K-- and I to be made dupe of any human artifice.

Where was B--House near F--? The author, H. Spicer, noted that the mansion remained in the occupation of the same family but was about to be wholly or partially demolished 'in order to effect certain modern improvements'.

Phantoms seen on the river near Langport during an evening in 1872 made a local man's 'hair stand on end'.

In September 1872, *Pulman's Weekly News* told the following strange story from Langport:

A man named Jeanes belonging to this town, had occasion to go to Thorney last Sunday afternoon, and returned in the evening along the river bank. He separated from his companions at Huish bridge between ten and eleven o'clock, and continued his journey along the towpath. When nearing the bridge leading into Hams, he says he distinctly saw a big woman and behind her a little man 'walking on the water.' He stopped but then went on a few steps, rubbed his eyes and looked again, but still the spectres were there, marching up the middle of the river. In another moment they were opposite to where he was, and stared him hard in the face. He was unable to turn his gaze to the right or to the left, big drops of perspiration exuded all over him, and his 'hair stood on end.' Gathering together as well as he could his bewildered faculties he momentarily turned his gaze in the opposite direction. And then, when he mustered enough courage to take another look, his phantoms had vanished. In an immense state of perturbation, he pursued his course at increased speed along the path, and, in his haste, he stumbled and fell headlong over the style at the end of the field, which separates the river from the catch water. Along he sped as fast as his legs could carry him, past the Whatley foundry and up The Hill, where he overtook a person who was going home and to whom he related his adventure. Whether the man, notwithstanding the restrictions of the New Licensing Act, had found the means to indulge in a little Sunday afternoon imbibification, deponent sayeth not. But if such was the case, and his organs of vision affected thereby, when he was met on The Hill he must have been frightened into a state of sobriety, and told his story in a way that proved he had no doubt in his own mind that he had witnessed a supernatural.

In 1886 a Mr G. P. R. Pulman recorded a ghostly incident which he experienced when walking with a companion from Yeovil to Yeovil Junction through Newton Copse on a late autumn Sunday afternoon.

It was of a Sunday afternoon in the late autumn of the year, when a crisp and clear air and a fine-looking sky induced my friend and me to take a walk to the Junction. For the information of those who are strangers to the town, I will at once state that the 'Junction' is an important halting place on the main line leading from Exeter to London, and situated almost a mile and a half from the Yeovil Town Station.

The walk from the town is a pleasant one and therefore is oft resorted to, and it is, moreover, a favourite retreat of lovers at the gushing period of life when they fancy all the world is theirs. Stately elms and chestnut trees overhang and form shady avenues which give relief in the summer and in the winter shield you from the icy blast.

For some reason or other, which I will not attempt to explain, avenues are always associated with romance, nature seems to be unrestrained there, and the trunks and branches of the neighbouring trees intermingle and form symmetrical arches in the effort to enfold each other in their arms. I do not mean to infer from this that if human nature is allowed to run wild, everything will be morally symmetrical. Experience teaches us differently. My business now is not to moralise but to relate facts and to allow the ever-curious public to use their own discretion as to whether they place credence therein.

I never believed in 'ghosts' until – well, perhaps I had better say no more about the subject before you have had a chance to read what I write.

We were walking together (my friend and I) to the Junction, smoking cigarettes and talking the common-place affairs of life. Our path was on the roadway through Newton Copse and we had passed what is locally known as 'the Devil's Drive' (that vacant space between the trees leading from the summit of Summerhouse Hill to Newton House) and were slowly ascending the little declivity leading to the Junction, when we heard behind us the distant trotting of a horse. As the sound approached us, the clattering of the hoofs became more and more rapid and distinct, and my friend and I went to the side of the hedge to allow the fast trotter to pass us.

'Surely,' I said, looking round, 'the horse must be near us, and at a deuce of a pace it seems to be going. Let us wait until it has passed us.'

Thus agreed, we stood still. Closer and closer to us came the clattering of the hooves, but no horse or horseman could we see, although we had full view of a least two hundred yards of the road. In another moment an overpowering and indescribable feeling of being in the presence of something we could not see stole over me, and my friend evidently experienced the same sensation; as the invisible horse seemed to be charging directly upon us! Instinctively we stood close to the hedge as we possibly could, and in another second the sound passed close to us, and the trotting soon afterwards broke into a canter, and the canter into a wild gallop, which gradually died away as the invisible cause of the phenomenon rushed on in the direction of Stoford!

The feeling of relief which we both experienced I shall never forget. With blank amazement we looked at each other for an explanation we could not find. 'What can it mean? We are not blind, yet we saw no horse, although,' my friend said, 'I felt I could have touched it if I had put out my hand!'

The Newton Farm Potato Robbery

At about two o'clock in the cold early morning of Friday 23 February 1870, East Coker Police Constable Perry was on duty, and as he walked past the entrance gate to Newton Surmaville House, just outside Yeovil, he heard footsteps coming quickly up the drive. Two hunch-backed figures loomed out of the night, and on closer inspection the constable observed two men, each carrying a large sack.

Constable Perry's suspicions were aroused immediately, as carrying large sacks at two o'clock in the morning was somewhat unusual, and he challenged the pair, enquiring what they were up to. One of the men, whom the constable thought he recognised as young George Hutchings from Hardington Mandeville, replied that they were on their way home with some potatoes which they had bought from Mr Bown the day before at Newton Farm. They had not gone earlier because they had been staying with the farmer's shepherd. Not being convinced, Constable Perry took hold of George Hutching's arm and demanded to inspect his sack, but as he did so, the other man, who had stood well back in the dark, suddenly turned and fled back down the drive into the night, still carrying his sack.

George Hutchings made no attempt to flee and set out quietly with Constable Perry along Newton Road towards Yeovil. They had not gone far when a figure appeared out of the night and, approaching the policeman, asked what was going on. Constable Perry explained the circumstances and accepted his offer to help carry the heavy sack. However, as he asked the newcomer to take one end of the sack while he took the other, the constable felt a violent blow on his face which knocked him to the ground and he was kicked unconscious.

On recovering his senses, Constable Perry found that he was still holding the sack with the contents intact, and managed (remarkably) to carry it to the police station in Union Street and report the attack. Later that morning, Sergeant Howell proceeded to Newton Farm, where, in company with Farmer Bown, he found the potato store broken into and two sacks missing. The farmer identified the sack recovered by Constable Perry as one of those stolen from the store, and during the afternoon the second was recovered by some anglers from the River Yeo at Newton Park.

Now recovered from the beating, Constable Perry identified the man who had offered to help carry the sack as George Sparks, a Yeovil leather parer, and he was quickly arrested and charged with stealing potatoes and assaulting a police officer. In the meantime, warrants were issued for the arrest, on suspicion of stealing potatoes

George Hutchings was arrested by Yeovil Police Constable Perry on the drive of Newton Surmaville House on suspicion of stealing potatoes on 23 February 1870.

and assaulting the police, of George (alias Peter) Hutchings and his older brother Giles, who was believed to be the man who had fled the scene.

A week later, the two Hutchings surrendered at the Yeovil police station and were locked up. *Pulman's Weekly News* reported that,

> It appears that both men were suspected of being concerned in the robbery and that the police had been scouring the country for several days in search of them. Their house at Hardington was completely 'blockaded' so they dare not return home and subsequently had to spend one or two nights in the open air. On Monday night they were seen in Clifton Wood, but escaped before the police got there. Doubtless, however, feeling the course of proceeding rather uncomfortable, they struck their flag, and surrendered.

George Sparks, together with George and Giles Hutchings, appeared before the county magistrates in Yeovil on 7 March, when Sparks and George Hutchings were sent for trial at the forthcoming Somerset Assizes but Giles was discharged through lack of evidence. However, he was immediately re-arrested by Superintendent Everitt of Ilminster and remanded in custody to answer a charge of burglary at Haselbury Plucknett. On Tuesday 8 March, *Pulman's Weekly News* reported that the two Hutchings brothers were, suspected of having been concerned in a burglary at Haselbury on Monday night at the house of a man named Clarke. They were in the house in the afternoon of that day and saw Clarke put away some money in a box. Clarke did not go to bed until three o'clock the next morning, but on coming down stairs a few hours afterwards found that the window on the ground floor had been broken open, the room entered, and a watch and £1 in money stolen. Strange to say, however, there was a drawer near containing over £3 10s which had not been touched. One of the parties engaged, left part of one of his braces behind, and this identical part is missing from the braces of one of the prisoners and corresponds exactly. On an examination of the prisoners' boots, it appears that they have had the precaution to get them 'tapped and heeled' in order, it is supposed, to destroy the means of identifying them with the footprints at Newton.

It would seem that fortune was smiling on Giles Hutchings because the county magistrates at Ilminster dismissed the charge of burglary at Haselbury Plucknett for want of evidence, and no charge was brought against his young brother George.

Thirty-five-year-old George Sparks and George Hutchings, aged eighteen, appeared at the Somerset Lent Assizes, where they were both found guilty of stealing two bags of potatoes valued at ten shillings and assaulting Police Constable Perry in the execution of his duty, and were sentenced to fifteen months' hard labour.

There is a sequel to this tale. Six years later in November 1876, Giles Hutchings, his brother George (alias Peter), their father George and Charles Baker were involved in a fight at Netherton Lane, when the East Coker police constable, Nathaniel Cox, was killed and his colleague from West Coker, Constable Henry Stacey, severely beaten. The case excited great interest across the West Country, which turned to anger when the verdicts of murder (which demanded the death penalty) were reduced by the jury to manslaughter. The Hutchings brothers, their father George, and Charles Baker,were each sentenced to twenty-four years' penal servitude, but George senior was granted a free pardon after sentencing, when Charles Baker testified that the elderly man had taken no part in the assaults.

Would things have turned out differently if Giles Hutching had received a long prison sentence for the burglary at Haselbury Plucknett?

Death on the Lines

It goes without saying that railways can be dangerous places when they are operational, and being constructed. On Tuesday 26 December 1846, the *Western Flying Post* reported that:

> On Saturday last an Inquest was held at the John Bull Inn of this town, on the body of Charles Baker, aged thirteen years when, from the evidence adduced, it appeared that the deceased was employed by the Wilts, Somerset and Weymouth Railway, near Yeovil; that in the afternoon of the Wednesday previous, the deceased was with others at work in a cutting when a large quantity of earth suddenly gave way and fell on him and caused his death – it was also proved to the satisfaction of the jury, that every possible care had been taken to guard against such dangers, and so to prevent accidents, that the state of the work had been examined, and so no blame could attach to anyone. In consequence the jury returned a verdict 'that the said Charles Baker came by his death by a large quantity of earth falling on him, while at work on the Wilts, Somerset and Weymouth Railway.' We understand that four men were working with the deceased at the time the accident occurred, but they fortunately escaped without the least injury.

Just over ten years later, on the evening of Monday 2 February 1857, Benjamin Riddle, a porter at Pen Mill station (which opened on 1 September 1856), was found lying across one of the rails near the station, fully conscious but with an arm and a leg cut off. Later that evening the desperately injured porter died, and on 5 February the inquest into his decease was held in the Pen Mill Hotel.

George Compton, the first to give evidence, described himself as a pilot man working on the Wilts, Somerset & Weymouth Railway and stated that he drove the train between Yeovil and Evershot. On the evening in question, the down train from Chippenham had arrived at about half past six and before it left for Weymouth, three horseboxes and a truck had to be taken off. The pilot man described how he had gone down with the red lights to stop the train when he heard his name called and found Benjamin Riddle lying on his belly, one arm across the metals, crying out, 'Oh George! I am a dead man! I have had my leg and arm cut off!' The gravely injured man was carried to the station waiting room. George Compton stated that he had then taken his train to Evershot.

George Roberts, the stationmaster, told the inquest that some horse boxes had arrived from Trowbridge by the 6.20 train and were to remain for the next day's traffic. It was Benjamin Riddle's duty to see they were properly shunted and in doing so, it seemed that the porter had got between the last carriage of the Weymouth train and the horse boxes to be left at Pen Mill in order to disconnect them. The station master stated that this was against the company's rules. He had found the deceased lying on his face between the rails with his left arm and leg lying across one of the metals. He was 'perfectly sensible, but made no remark to me how the accident occurred'. Surgeon Coles had been sent for and Benjamin Riddle was carried on a stretcher to his lodgings, where he died later that evening. George Roberts, described the deceased porter as a most trustworthy and zealous man in the discharge of his duties.

The cause of the accident was not established and a verdict of Accidental Death was returned.

Mrs John Shapcott of Exeter had a good day selling dyed cloth at Chard Market on Monday 30 December 1872, and before catching the last train home, she enjoyed a convivial dinner, finished off with threepenny worth of brandy and lemon, at the Railway Inn. In company with fellow market trader Mr William Moore, a Yeovil hatter, she walked to the London & South Western station at Chard, from which both would travel to the mainline Chard Junction and catch their respect trains to Exeter and Yeovil. On entering the station, Mrs Shapcott asked her companion to look after a large parcel and, saying she would be back in a few minutes, disappeared along the platform in the direction of the shed station some, 60 yards away.

The train for Chard Junction was about to depart, but as Mrs Shapcott had not returned, Mr Moore searched along the platform; finding no sign of her he hurried back and told Mr Bainton the station master that she was missing. Despite a search, there was no sign of the good lady, and after a few minutes' further delay, the train left for Chard Junction with Messrs Bainton and Moore on board.

As the engine passed the signal box a few hundred yards from the station, Driver John Shepherd shouted up, enquiring if the signalman had seen anyone pass, but following a 'No', he slowly increased speed from a walking pace to about 15 mph. About half a mile further on, Driver Shepherd saw a shape in the darkness in front of the engine; he blew the whistle and applied the brakes. Nothing was found following a quick search of the line and the train was taken on to Chard Junction, where the passenger coach was taken off. As the engine and guard's van returned slowly to Chard, the badly mutilated body of Mrs Shapcott was found lying between the rails near the spot where Driver Shepherd had first seen the shape in the darkness.

The inquest into the decease of forty-six-year-old Mrs John Shapcott heard that she had been in high spirits, but not intoxicated, and was well acquainted with Chard station. However, her umbrella and cloak, together with the parcel, were found left at the station, which only deepened the mystery of why she was found on the line nearly a mile away; no one could answer the question, and a verdict of accidental death was returned with the rider that 'there was no evidence given to show how she got on the line of the railway where the accident occurred'.

Spectating by the line can be fatal for the unwary. On 9 September 1878, workmen were laying gas pipes by the South Western Railway line near Yeovil Junction. Work

On 2 February 1857, Benjamin Riddle was carried from Yeovil Pen Mill Station, desperately injured having been run over during shunting operations. The station buildings show little change when this photograph was taken nearly 120 years later in 1972.

stopped at one o'clock for dinner, and one of the workmen, sixty-year-old labourer Elijah Pound, decided to cross the rails to visit a hut where men working on the track sometimes took their meals. Finding it empty, he returned and began to walk beside the track to join his fellow workmen for dinner. A Great Western Railway passenger train was approaching from the Yeovil direction and Elijah stopped to watch it pass. However, a South Western Railway engine was coming down the line from Yeovil Junction on the track by which he was standing, unnoticed by the labourer. Alfred Reader, who was working nearby, saw the engine and shouted to Elijah Pound to watch out. Too late, the front buffer plank which projected from the side of the engine struck the labourer's head. The unconscious man was loaded onto a trolley and taken down the line to Yeovil Town Station, from which he was conveyed to his home. Doctor Colmer was called but despite his efforts, Elijah Pound died at eight o'clock the following morning without regaining consciousness.

At the inquest, Mr Howell, the manager of the Yeovil Gas Works, stated that the men laying the pipes had been repeatedly told to keep watch for trains, but Elijah Pound had been 'an obstinate man, and did not like to be spoken to about it'. The jury returned a verdict of accidental death and added that no blame could be attached to anyone.

On 2 October 1895, Walter Nicholls, formerly of Yeovil, and an assistant guard, was found dead on the roof of a passenger carriage when the train arrived at Tavistock on its way to Exeter. What was he doing on the roof of the passenger carriage? Perhaps, by reading between the lines of the evidence given at the inquest as reported by the *Western Gazette*, we can hazard a guess. John Shute, the head guard, told the jury that:

At Bere Ferrers, as he did not receive the usual signal before starting the train, he went back to the deceased's van to look for him. Failing to find him, he entered the rear van and took charge of the train to Tavistock. Enquiries established that Nicholls had left St. Budeaux all right in his van. At Tavistock the deceased's body was found on the top of the carriage at the rear of the train. It was no part of the deceased's duty to go on to the top of the carriage. He had no idea what had induced the man to go to the top of the carriage. Nicholls was a sober, steady man. – Mr Tonkin, a juryman, asked whether it was possible to see from the top of the carriage through the ventilators or by the sides of the lamp into the compartments. – Shute replied that it was impossible to do so. Mr Tonkin said that there was a rumour that sometimes guards walked on the footboards to peer into carriages in which newly-married couples were travelling. Inspector Foster remarked that he had been twenty-five years in the service and travelled six days a week, and he had never known of anything of this kind being done. In this case there was no reason to suggest the deceased did so. The witness added that the door to the deceased's van was shut and his lamp inside. There were no steps between the van and the carriage, the steps to the top of the carriage were at the other end. It was a mystery how the deceased got onto the carriage. He believed that the deceased's head must had struck against one of the iron girders of the Tavy Bridge, where his cap was found. Ralph Hooper, porter, Tavistock, deposed to finding the body on the top of the carriage. The ventilation did not appear to have been disturbed. – The jury after considerable consideration, returned a verdict of Found Dead. – The coroner said he would have been satisfied if the jury had returned a verdict of accidental death.

I think the jury had an inkling that the assistant guard was up to something suspicious to have returned this verdict.

Bad Lads and Hooligans

Bad or stupid behaviour by youngsters is nothing new; for example, back in July 1854 four boys were summonsed for trespassing and stealing flowers from Harriett Rendall's garden in Chiselborough on Sunday 4 June. Harriett told the magistrates that on returning home from the morning Service she had found that every gooseberry bush in her garden had been stripped of fruit. That evening she saw the four boys in her garden picking flowers, and on seeing her they had fled, breaking the garden gate in the process. Harriett went on to say that these boys had caused her 'much annoyance and depredations', and described her situation as the 'worst of all the awful situations a lone woman was ever in'. The youngsters raised no defence and were each fined £1 plus one shilling in costs and damages – a large sum at the time when a farm labourer's weekly wage was about ten shillings.

Two boys appeared before the Yeovil magistrates in July 1860, summonsed for driving about some horses in Mr George Harbin's field below Summerhouse Hill. Police Constable Everly told the Bench that he had been on duty on Penn Hill when he saw about a dozen boys chasing two colts around the field and then making them jump over a gate. The constable stated that both colts were injured and the two boys before the Bench were the main culprits. The youngsters were given a severe reprimand and each fined ten shillings or two weeks in gaol in default – the fines were paid there and then.

In March 1861, five boys were brought before the magistrates, charged with trespassing on Mr Harbin's Newton Surmaville Estate. Constables Holwell and Hubbard told the magistrates that they had seen a large crowd of boys playing in the grounds, where there were no permitted footpaths, but had only been able to catch the five now before the court. The magistrates dismissed the case but ordered the boys to pay the costs.

In May 1900, two youngsters were brought before the county magistrates charged with breaking a window in an empty cottage in Marsh Hollow, Yeovil Marsh. Constable Smith testified that he had been summoned to the cottage and had found some buckets of whitewash and water overturned in several rooms. A number of upstairs windows had been broken, and in one room he found a large stone. The constable stated that he had discovered footprints in the rooms which, following enquiries in the neighbourhood, matched boots worn by one of the boys before the Bench. Both youngsters had admitted the offence, and carpenter Herbert Robbins,

Only one boy was caught from a crowd of over 100 youngsters throwing stones at passers-by in Wellington Street, Yeovil, in January 1903.

who was carrying out the renovations to the cottage, estimated the cost of the damage to be ten shillings. Both lads were fined ten shillings each.

A few years later there was an outbreak of stone throwing in Yeovil and in January 1903 a boy was brought before the magistrates, summonsed by John Baulch for throwing stones 'to the annoyance of passengers' in Wellington Street. Mr Baulch told the Bench that about 100 boys had been throwing stones in the street, but he had only succeeded in catching one of them, to which the Chairman commented, 'Where's the ninety-nine more?' The Chairman went on to note that there was a continuing nuisance from stone throwing and fined the lad one shilling.

In January 1940 *The Yeovil Review* declared 'War on Hooliganism',

It would be a pity if the war is going to mean an outbreak in Yeovil of that type of senseless and wanton hooliganism on a par with German 'frightfulness' from which this town has hitherto been almost completely free.

During the past week or so there have been glaring examples of malicious damage to cars, shop windows as well as to trees and shrubs in public parks.

Three motorists found their cars almost wrecked. Tyres were slashed, leads torn out, windscreens and windows smashed, and in addition to their damage the tanks were filled with gravel and mud.

Such senseless acts can only be described as the work of maniacs, while the wilful smashing of shop windows with beer bottles is hooliganism at its worst.

The trouble now appears to have spread to public parks, on Christmas day seats in Preston Park were overturned and some thrown in the pond.

So determined are the Council to stamp out this wrecking campaign that it has been decided to offer a reward for information that will lead to the apprehension of the culprits.

When they appear before the local magistrates, it is hoped that the punishment meted out will be of such a nature as to indicate in the clearest possible manner that Yeovil is not going to stand behaviour of a kind only to be found in the lowest part of Limehouse.

Following the outbreak of war in September 1939, many hundreds of evacuees from London had been brought to the Yeovil area, and much of the vandalism which was occurring was blamed on them – quite wrongly in most cases!

In March 1945, a thirteen-year-old boy admitted to the Yeovil County Juvenile Court that he had climbed onto a United States Army lorry, opened a weapons box, removed a Thompson sub-machinegun, and had taken it home. A few days later he swapped it with another lad for a .22 pistol, and the Court was told by this youngster that he had found the pistol on the floor of his school changing room. He had thought that both the pistol and the sub-machinegun were toys. The Court heard that the two lads had no ammunition for either weapon, and the Thompson had only been taken to 'muck about with'. Putting the thirteen-year-old on a year's probation, the Chairman suggested that he join a youth organisation.

Down on the Farm

Looking across a peaceful landscape of fields, woods and farms, it is easy to forget that the countryside at work and play can be a dangerous place, and sometimes lethal.

In March 1862, North Perrott farmer Adam Rendell of Whitevine Farm had a very narrow escape from death. Farmer Rendell was riding on his horse towards a field where some of his men were employed in drainage work, and carrying under his arm an implement described at the time by the *Western Flying Post* as 'an instrument used in draining work which he had just been sharpening'. As he passed through the gate to the field, the horse stumbled, but in trying to prevent himself from falling off, Farmer Rendell brought the sharpened instrument he was holding upwards with a jerk across his throat. The blade cut into the farmer's throat, but was miraculously prevented from severing the vital organs by his jaw bone. Surgeon Joliffe was immediately summoned from Crewkerne, and on arrival stemmed the bleeding and stitched the 4-inch gash. Farmer Adam Rendell was a very lucky man.

Hedge trimming can be a dangerous occupation, as Frank Maldron found to his cost one evening in August 1907. Frank was trimming a hedge at North Coker when his razor-sharp hedging hook slipped and, cutting through his clothes, severed an artery in his side. Luckily, help was at hand, and after immediate first aid he was rushed to Yeovil Hospital, where an operation was carried out to repair the damaged blood vessel and Frank Maldron was reported to be making satisfactory progress towards recovery.

Adam Rendell and Frank Maldron were fortunate to have survived their injuries but not so Joseph Hann and Charles Perry, who died on a February afternoon in 1895.

At approximately four o'clock in the afternoon of Saturday 22 February 1895, the boiler of the steam engine being used to drive a threshing machine at Messrs E. and F. Haine's Manor Farm, Yeovilton, exploded. Joseph Hann, the contractor, who was operating the engine, and Charles Perry, one of the farm workers at the threshing machine, were killed outright. The explosion hurled Joseph Hann's body, engulfed in flames from the contents of the engine fire box, into a nearby straw rick, which immediately caught fire, and Charles Perry's badly burnt and mutilated corpse was blown a distance from the wreck, his hat being found in a tree over 100 yards away. Three other farm workers, Charles Perry's son, William, William Gillard and Tom Gawler, were injured, two severely.

The force of the explosion, which was heard several miles away at Ilchester, completely wrecked the steam engine and badly damaged the threshing machine.

A field near the pleasant village of North Perrott, shown here in an early printed postcard, was the scene of a near fatal accident in March 1862.

William Holland had just left the threshing machine when he heard a loud explosion and was blown off his feet. Recovering his senses, William was horrified by the scene which met his eyes through the smoke and steam. Bodies were scattered everywhere; for Charles Perry he could do nothing, but he rendered what help he could to his injured workmates.

The sound of the explosion brought Simeon Bridle running to the scene, where he met Mr Edwin Haine, who sent him to get help from men living in nearby houses. On returning, Simeon found the fire spreading to several other ricks and assisted in moving the injured to safety. Neighbours and workmen did what they could to render first aid while others went for help.

The badly burned and partly dismembered body of Joseph Hann was dragged from the burning rick and, together with that of Charles Perry, was laid in a shed. A message was despatched to the Yeovil Fire Brigade, who could not respond as their fire engine was under repair, but urgent telegraphs to Sherborne and Martock brought their brigades at full speed to the farm, where they succeeded in preventing the blaze from spreading to nearby hay stacks and farm buildings,

William Perry and William Gillard were conveyed to Yeovil Hospital, but Tom Gawler's injuries were less serious, and he was taken to his home in Yeovilton.

The coroner's inquest into the deaths of Joseph Hann and Charles Perry began on 24 February at Manor Farm and lasted two days, during which it emerged that the steam engine, hired from Mr W. Sparrow of Martock, had been extensively repaired, and there was a difference of opinion between engineering witnesses regarding its safety. However, it also emerged that the pressure gauge, which had been attached when the engine had been hired out, was missing before the explosion, and the safety valve had been screwed down. The whereabouts of the pressure gauge and the reason for screwing down the safety valve had died with Joseph Hann, the contractor and sole operator of the engine.

At the conclusion of the inquest, the jury returned a verdict to the effect that the engine was not defective, that death was caused by shock and explosion, and that the safety valve was screwed down while in the charge of the late Joseph Hann. The jury gave their fee to the fund set up on behalf of the widows.

Death Down the Shaft

To be lowered, attached to the end of a rope, hundreds of feet down a narrow shaft some four to five feet in diameter into the black bowels of the earth to begin the day's toil must be counted as one of the most hideous ways to earn a meagre living, even if you had done so for all, or most of your working life. This was the 'hooker' system, in which a number of miners sat or stood in loops of rope, which in turn were hooked onto the end of the winding rope and lowered into the blackness. Such was the daily round for many miners working in the Somerset coalfield during the eighteen century and early decades of the nineteenth century. And there was the fear, probably pushed to the back of the mind, but still lurking there – what if the rope should break? Miraculously, this was a relatively rare tragedy, but it did happen (and the stories which grew from such an event would be remembered when the news travelled throughout the Somerset coalfield of another disaster when the rope broke) and the daily descent could turn into a nightmare.

The following terrible disasters would have resurrected such fears.

Wells Way Coal Pit - 8 November 1839

The morning shift at the Wells Way Coal Pit, near Radstock, assembled at four o'clock on Friday 8 November 1839 and the twelve men and boys prepared for another back-breaking day toiling deep under the Somerset hills. The oldest miner was forty-four-year-old Richard Langford with his two sons, sixteen-year-old Farnham and Alfred, thirteen; forty-one-year-old James Keevil and his lads, Mark and James, fifteen and fourteen; John Barnett, forty-one; William Summers, twenty-six; William Adams nineteen; James Pearce, eighteen, Amos Dando, thirteen and twelve-year-old Leonard Dowling.

The miners climbed on to the rope and settled in the loops, the boards covering the mouth of the shaft were removed, the steam engine driving the winding drum hissed and began to rumble as the brakes were released, the rope took the weight and William Summers, hooked on the top, yelled, 'What's the matter with the rope – look how it jumps!' There was crash as the rope flew over the top of the winding drum and hit the roof of the shed, and then followed the twelve men and boys hurtling down into the black hole – the rope had broken and all its human cargo went screaming to their deaths, 756 feet below.

The shock and horror of the disaster can only be imagined over a century and a half later, but soon there were rumours that something was not quite right with the breaking of the rope. There were cries of 'murder' as the broken ends of the rope were examined. It was made of flat, interwoven hemp cables, five inches wide and one and a quarter inches thick, and showed signs of being deliberately weakened; the ends of the severed outside fibres were seen to be fairly even and level as if cut, whereas those inside were torn, jagged and uneven.

The evidence given at the subsequent inquest into the deaths of the twelve miners pointed to an unknown hand deliberately damaging the rope, but despite the verdict of 'Wilful murder against some person or persons unknown', and the offer of a substantial reward for the apprehension of the perpetrator, no one was ever arrested, and neither was a reason established for the outrage, other than a suggested personal grudge against one of the deceased, and that someone sought to kill the manager of the mine, who often went down the pit alone on the rope.

All twelve victims were laid to rest in Midsomer Norton churchyard under a grave stone bearing the following words,

In this grave are deposited the remains of the twelve under mentioned sufferers all of whom were killed at Wells Way Coal Works on 8th November 1839 by snapping of the rope as they were on the point of descending into the pit. The rope was generally believed to have been maliciously cut.

Bray's Down Coal Pit - 23 June 1843

Thursday 23 June 1843 was just another working day at the Bray's Down Coal Pit, opened three years before near Radstock. During the afternoon, engineer William Evans accompanied by the mine owner, Mr William S. Waite, had been working on installing new parts in the steam engine manufactured by Acramans of Bristol, used for winding and pumping water. With the work completed, he handed the operation of the engine over to the night engineer, Job West, and left the coal pit at about half past five.

The night shift assembled at the pit at eight o'clock and, after being handed their candles by the bailiff, John Berryman, the miners prepared to descend the narrow shaft to the workings, some 600 feet below. What happened next was described by the *Bath and Cheltenham Gazette* on 28 June:

They are attached to the main rope by means of a noose, through which one leg is placed, and being lifted off the platform or 'runner' which is then removed, the rope gradually lowered them into the pit, in this instance, however, the regulating power of the drum-wheel was either not adjusted or became deranged; for, in a few seconds after the descent was commenced, the drum-wheel began to revolve with fearful rapidity, and the unfortunate men were precipitated on to a projecting stage, erected at a short distance from the bottom of the pit. Such was the force with which the wheel revolved that several of the 'cogs' were broken from it, and other damage to the engine to the amount of 5l. was sustained.

A view of Radstock, in the vicinity of which there were three coal pits where the rope lowering miners down the shaft broke with awful results.

Lying dead at the bottom of the shaft, were twenty-eight-year-old, Aaron Dando; Jeremiah Filer, sixteen; Jacob Richardson, thirty-six; Thomas Aylesbury, twenty-three; Job Richardson, thirty; and twenty-three-year-old Richard Aylesbury. Eleven-year-old John Ashman was recovered, desperately injured, but died within a few hours.

The following afternoon, the inquest into the deaths opened at the Red Post Inn before Mr R. Uphill, the county coroner, and a 'respectable Jury'.

William Evans, the engineer, told the inquest that, in company with Mr Waite, he had been putting some new works on the engine and it was in perfect working order when he handed over to fellow engineer Job West and left at about half past five o'clock. He had been at Mr Waite's house when news of the accident reached him and he had gone immediately to find out what had happened. Evans stated that Job West was at the works and, hearing of the runaway winding drum, had asked him if the 'plug' had been put in to keep the drum in gear. West had replied that he had, but when asked where it was, he said that he did not know. Evans had then enquired if he had screwed up the nut of the plate which was placed over the plug to keep it in place, but the reply was no. Leaving out the plug would have caused the accident, and if the plate had not been properly secured, the plug would probably have been driven out of its place. William Evans stated that Job West had not been drinking and believed he understood his work.

Next to testify was Job West, who stated that he had been working the engine pumping water, and at about six o'clock had put it into gear in readiness for the eight o'clock descent. He was quite sure that he had inserted the plug, but could not confirm whether he had put the plate over the plug. West stated that he had screwed down the back nut, but admitted that he could not remember if he had secured the front one. Before he let the men down, he had moved the engine two or three times to drive out the water and made everything safe. West went on to relate that when he had let the men down about half way, he saw the drum running and stopped the engine 'and ran out, for I knew there was danger'. He told the inquest that he worked the engine by night, and his brother did so by day. Job West stated that he had worked the engine for nearly twelve months and had not been drinking that day.

John Berryman, the bailiff, told the inquest how the miners had been made ready to descend, West had confirmed that the engine was in order, and the rope was slowly wound down the shaft. The bailiff stated that he had remained by the pit, but when the men were down about 100 feet, he heard them cry out and saw the drum running; all the rope fell down the shaft. Nothing like this had occurred before and Berryman believed the engine must have started in gear, otherwise it would not have let the men go down so far. He confirmed that West was quite sober. Following a short consultation the jury returned a verdict of 'Accidental Death'.

Welton Old Coal Pit - 1 October 1851

At about five o'clock on the afternoon of Wednesday 1 October 1851, some dozen miners were making ready to go down the Welton Old Coal Pit to start their shift. The mine bailiff, Isaac Bryant, was issuing candles to the men, and three miners, Samuel Taylor, George Dallimore and George Hill, clambered on to the winding rope and hooked up. The winding drum began to turn, and the three disappeared from sight down the narrow shaft to join the sixty men and boys already labouring some 400 feet underground.

The sudden sound of something falling brought the bailiff to the mouth of the shaft, but on receiving no reply to his calls, his fears were realised when he felt the slackness of the winding rope; the rope had broken and the silence would indicate that all three men were dead or badly injured. The rope was immediately drawn up and, to everyone's dismay, was found to have snapped some 100 feet from the bottom of the shaft.

Two very brave men, Joseph Chivers and James Jones, were let down on the second rope kept ready for emergencies, followed by several more in one of the metal buckets used to haul coal up the shaft. At the bottom they found Samuel Taylor and George Dallimore dead, but George Hill, despite his terrible injuries, was still breathing. Eighteen-year-old George Hill was hurriedly brought to the surface and carried the half mile to his home at Midsomer Norton, where he died some twenty minutes later.

The terribly crushed body of Samuel Taylor, followed by that of George Dallimore, the latter showing no outward signs of the massive internal injuries, were brought up and taken to Stone's Cross Inn to await the inquest into their deaths, where they were soon joined by the body of George Hill.

On Wednesday, the *Bath Journal* wrote that the three miners were 'all steady well-conducted men. Taylor has left a wife and two children; Dallimore, who was 23 years of age was on the eve of marriage, the banns having been published in the parish church the previous Sunday; and Hill was aged about 18'.

At the inquest in the Stone's Cross Inn into the deaths of Samuel Taylor, George Dallimore and George Hill, the events of that tragic afternoon were described and the jury were told that the rope was a round hempen one, 3 ¾ of an inch thick and capable of carrying a weight of 3 tons. It had been in use for some three years for the sole purpose of letting the men up and down the shaft, and not for hauling coal. Ropes of this type had been safely used at the pit for five years. There had been no complaints by the miners about the rope and the bailiff was under instructions to replace it with the new one kept ready by the winding drum if the one in use was found to be defective. There was some suggestion that the bailiff, Isaac Bryant, had some culpability for the state of the rope, but he had been employed at Welton Old Pit for twenty-six years, during which time he had 'always proved himself to be a careful steady man'. Indeed, the jury were told that it was the bailiff's daily practice to go down the pit on the rope with the last men on each shift, something he would not have done if there was any fear that the rope was defective.

After hearing all the evidence, the jury returned a verdict of 'Accidental Death.' The three miners lie at rest in the churchyard at Midsomer Norton.

Two Horrible Murders (and a Suicide) at Bath

James Beere was said to have been a hardworking man, a good and affectionate husband to Mary, and a loving father to Charles his infant son – yet he murdered the two souls closest to his heart, and then committed suicide at Bath during the early morning of Monday 24 November 1829.

James Beere, was employed as a foreman at Mr Davies' bakery off St James' Street and, with his small family, lodged in rooms at No. 1 William's Place. At about half past five o'clock on that November morning, the neighbour, Mrs Catherine Chappell, heard the Beeres' door open and someone hurry downstairs, followed by a strange gurgling noise coming from No. 1. Fearing that Mary Beere had been taken ill, Mrs Chappell quickly got out of bed and, going next door, knocked and enquired if everything was in order. Puzzled at receiving no reply, she became concerned and, returning with a lighted candle, cautiously pushed open the door. The scene which unfolded in the flickering candle light was one of horror.

Mary Beere was lying on the bed, covered in blood, with her throat cut from ear to ear and next to the dead woman was the baby, with its head almost severed from its tiny body.

The local law officers and a surgeon, Mr White, who lived nearby, were quickly on the scene, where they found a bloody razor lying open on a box beside the bed, and because the bedclothes were little disturbed, it was concluded that the murders had been committed when the mother and child were asleep; of James Beere there was no sign.

Immediately the hunt was on for the missing man, and within a short time a blood-stained baker's jacket was found on the bank of the River Avon near Bedford Street. Following the discovery of the jacket, Mr William Russell of Walcot, accompanied by two companions, took out a boat and they found James Beere's body floating in the river near the bottom of Bedford Street. The corpse was retrieved and, on being brought onto the river bank, a search revealed thirteen sovereigns, two guineas and five shillings in the dead man's pockets, following which the body was conveyed to the Walcot poorhouse.

The murders and suicide were soon big news in Bath, and so were the questions. Why had the seemingly hardworking and loving family man butchered his wife and infant son? James Beere had been born at Widcombe, and for several years had worked as an errand-boy for Messrs Barnard of Bridge Street, during which time he had saved

The Town Hall and Abbey in Bath would have been familiar to the deranged James Beere who murdered his wife and baby son in 1829.

enough money to apprentice himself to a baker. About eighteen months previously he had married Mary, a girl from Frome, and for a short while had been in business as a baker and confectioner on his own account near the Wells Road toll gate. However, for the past twelve months, James Beere had worked as foreman baker for Mr Davies, who 'had found him attentive to his business, a trustworthy servant in his master's absence, particularly obliging and apparently happy'. Both Mr and Mrs Davies declared that they had noticed nothing out of the ordinary in the foreman's recent conduct or on the Sunday evening, when he had prepared for the Monday morning's baking.

The inquests into the deaths of James Beere, Mary Beere and the infant Charles were opened in the Walcot poorhouse on Wednesday 26 November and firstly the jury proceeded to No. 1 William's Place at the back of St James' Street, where the two bodies lay undisturbed. The *Taunton Courier* reported that;

> The bodies of the latter presented a horrible spectacle, the mother having a large and deep gash completely across the throat and a smaller one just below the chin; the child's head was nearly severed from the body, the vertebra being quite cut through, and nothing but a small portion of flesh kept the head from complete separation. The bed was covered with blood. On a box which lay beside the bed was found a razor deeply notched and clotted with blood, and in the kitchen below was found a case, apparently the case of the razor, and a plasterer's hatchet or lathing hammer which appeared sharpened and newly ground.

On the jury's return to the Walcott poorhouse, the first witness was Mr William Russell, who described how the body of James Beere had been recovered from the River Avon.

He was followed by W. Muckleway, a servant employed by Mr Davies, the baker, who stated that he had known James Beere for some fifteen months and spoke of his general good character. The witness told the jury that during that time the deceased had exhibited no signs of insanity, but on the Saturday afternoon prior to the murders Beere had complained of illness in his head and left work at six o'clock that evening. Muckleway stated that he had seen him again on the Sunday morning at about nine o'clock, when he was still complaining about the illness and appeared to be agitated. At eleven o'clock, Beere had gone home feeling unwell and this was the last time the witness saw the deceased. Muckleway concluded by saying that he had always believed James Beere to have been a fond and affectionate husband and had never heard him speak of his wife other than in the best of terms.

The neighbour, Mrs Catherine Chappell, was the next witness and told of the events of the fateful Monday morning, and went on to say that she had heard no sounds of any quarrelling from the Beeres' lodgings. On the Sunday morning she had seen James Beere return home and then at lunch with his wife and child. There had never been any signs of insanity and the couple seemed happy and contented. Mr Chappell was called and confirmed his wife's testimony.

The evidence concerning the death of James Beere was now concluded but the jury deferred returning a verdict until the witnesses into the deaths of Mary and the infant, Charles, had been examined.

Mrs Catherine Chappell was recalled and repeated her previous evidence.

The next witness was Cottle, one of the local police officers, who stated that on being informed of the murders, he had gone to the home of James Beere's parents on the Upper Bristol Road to enquire whether they had seen their son that morning. The officer stated that he found Mrs Beere and her daughter, Jane, seated at breakfast, and on informing them of the reason for his call, Jane had exclaimed, 'Oh, mother then you are done!'

Jane Beere was called and denied using these words but the subsequent examination of Mr and Mrs Beere revealed, in the words of the court reporter, that, 'A great deal of jealousy and ill-will had existed between the female part of the family on account of a charge being made by the deceased against his sister of taking money.' The jury also heard that the parents had taken a strong dislike to their daughter-in-law, and because of this, frequently quarrelled with their son.

The jury returned a verdict of suicide in the case of James Beere, and in relation to Mary Beere and the infant, Charles, that he had murdered them.

As a suicide, James Beere was ordered to be buried in the night time without the usual burial service, but what caused this hardworking, loving husband and father to butcher his wife and infant son will remain a tragic mystery forever.

References and Sources

A Sad Death by Drowning
Taunton Courier, 28 June 1871.

Violent Death in Crewkerne
Western Flying Post, 2 November 1852 and 6 April 1853.
Western Gazette, 17 April 2008.

Tragedy on the Barnstaple Mail Coach
Taunton Courier, 27 August 1828.
Western Gazette, 13 September 2007.

Shooting Tragedies
Western Gazette, 31 August 1917, 1 September 1922, and 12 July 1940.
Taunton Courier, 27 August 1828.

Witchcraft
Taunton Courier, 9 April 1823.
Western Flying Post, 12 September 1854.
Western Gazette, 23 June and 7 July 1871.
Taunton Courier, 27 September 1871.

The Disappearing Bank Manager
Pulman's Weekly News, 2 and 16 February and 2 March 1892, 13 May 1913, 2, 8, 22 and 29 March 1910.
The People, 28 February 1892.
The Times, 26 November 1907, 11 June and 22 October 1912, and 7 and 8 May 1913.
Western Gazette, 20 July 2006.

It was a Perfectly Hopeless Case
Western Gazette, 14 June 1892, and 9 March 2006.

'I'll Blow Your Brains Out'
Taunton Courier, 30 January and 17 April 1817.

Western Flying Post, 5 May 1817.

Burglary at Langport
Western Flying Post, 8 and 15 September 1827.
Castle Cary Visitor, August 1901.
Western Gazette, 22 June 2006.

Two Aircraft Down
Western Gazette, 7 September 1917 and 15 and 22 June 1923.
Derek N. James, *Westland – A History*, Tempus (2002).

Highway Robberies in 1872
Pulman's Weekly News, 3, 10, 24 and 31 December 1872, and 6 July 1873.
Western Gazette, 2 May 1873.

In Time of War
Western Gazette, 31 May, 21 June and 16 August 1940, and 9 February 2006.

Three Country Fires
Western Flying Post, 12 July 1857.
Pulman's Weekly News, 8 January 1905.
Western Gazette, 27 August 1914, and 28 September 2006.

Big Cats on the Loose
Western Gazette, 19 November 1895, and 24 August 2006.

The Death of Private Ernest Horler
National Archives, Kew, Reference WO71/677.
Yeovil Leader, 22 April 1918.

The Simple Life
The New York Times, 11 May 1913.

Hanging John William Beale
Western Flying Post, 22 and 29 September, 6 October and 29 December 1857, 19 January 1859.

A Murder and a Suicide
Taunton Courier, 24 April 1817.

Poachers
Taunton Courier, 6 April 1825.

For Those in Peril
J. W. Sweet, Private papers.

Taunton Courier, 27 November 1822.
Pulman's Weekly News, 18 October 1898.
Western Gazette, 12 April 1912,

'We Shall All Be Hanged Shan't Us!'
The Bath and Cheltenham Gazette, 1 and 8 December 1813.
Taunton Courier, 7 April 1814.
Western Flying Post, 25 April 1814.

Yeovil Town Hall Burns Down
Western Gazette, 22 September 1935.
Yeovil Times, 19 February 1999.

The Crash of a Spitfire
Western Gazette, 17 and 24 February 1950.

Arson at Templecombe
Western Flying Post, 20 August and 3 September 1836.
Western Gazette, 9 October 2008.

A Tumultuous Suffragette Meeting
Western Gazette, 3 December 1909, and 29 November 2009.

Dangers of Ponds
Western Flying Post, 25 April 1808.
Western Gazette, 10 September 1907, 24 May 1910, and 20 April 2006.

The Dowlish Wise Woman's Mistake
Western Flying Post, 30 March 1858.
Western Gazette, 20 November 2008.

A Gallant Airman
Western Gazette, 10 June 1927, and 23 August 2007.

Fatal Fights
Taunton Courier, 15 December 1814.
Bath Journal, 10 April 1815.
Western Flying Post, 12 December 1814, 8 April 1815, 18 August 1817, 13 April 1818, and 15
  November 1830.
Taunton Courier, 6 April 1831.
Robin Bush, *Somerset – The Complete Guide*, p.119, Huntspill, The Dovecote Press Ltd
  (1994).

Gangs of Old Somerset
Taunton Courier, 23 January and 10 April 1817, 19 September 1827, 9 April and 13 August
  1828 and 10 April 1844.

Western Flying Post, 15 and 25 August, 8, 15 and 22 September 1827, 7 April and 18 August 1828, 30 September 1843 and 13 April 1844.
Bath Journal, 18 August 1828.
Bath Chronicle, 11 April 1844
News of the World, 1 October 1843.

When the Beer's in the Wits are Out!
Western Flying Post, 12 April and 3 May 1824.
Illegal Coining at Somerton
Western Flying Post, 11 April 1836.

Bigamy
Pulman's Weekly News, 18 and 25 June, and 5 November 1895, and 17 August 2006.
Western Gazette, 15 November 2007.

A Somerset Spy Scare in 1914
Western Gazette, 21 August, 4 and 18 September 1914, and 17 August 2006.
West Somerset Free Press, 5 September 1914.
Somerset County Herald, 24 June 1937.

A Railway Mystery
Western Gazette, 15 and 22 February 1901, and 8 March 2007.

The Dancing Party at East Chinnock
Western Flying Post 23 February 1858.
Pulman's Weekly News, 30 March 1858.
Western Gazette, 3 July 2008.

Three Suspicious Deaths
Taunton Courier, 12, 19 and 26 February 1823.
Western Flying Post, 7 July 1857.
Wells Journal, 10 October 1857.
Somerset & Wilts Journal, 17 October 1857

Two Fatal Fires
Western Gazette, 2 June 1881, 18 November 1927, and 25 March 2010.

She Told Me Her Husband was Very Ill
Western Flying Post, 21 March, 11 and 25 April 1836.

Strange and Ghostly
J. W. Sweet, Private papers.
Western Gazette, 22 January 1932.
H. Spicer, *Strange Things Amongst Us,* published 1864.
Pulman's Weekly News, 21 September 1872.

The Newton Farm Potato Robbery
Western Gazette, 4 and 11 March 1870, and 13 March 2008.
Pulman's Weekly News, 1, 8, 15 and 29 March 1870.

Death on the Lines
Western Flying Post, 26 December 1846 and 10 February 1857.
Pulman's Weekly News, 31 December 1872, 17 September 1878 and 18 October 1895

Bad Lads and Hooligans
Western Flying Post, 11 June 1854, 25 July 1860 and 15 March 1861.
Western Gazette, 15 May 1900, 23 January 1903, 17 January 1940, 23 March 1945, and 15
    Marc 2007.
Yeovil Review, January 1940.

Down on the Farm
Western Flying Post, 25 March 1862.
Western Gazette, 22 February 1895, 23 August 1907, and 20 March 2008.

Death Down the Shaft
C. G. Down and A. J.Warrington, *The History of the Somerset Coalfield,* David & Charles.
Shane Gould, *The Somerset Coalfield,* SIAS Survey Number 11 Series of Books, The Somerset
    Industrial Archaeological Society.
Wells Way Coal Pit
Jack W. Sweet, *Shocking Somerset Murders of the Nineteenth Century,* Somerset Books, 1997.
Bray's Down Coal Pit
The Bath and Cheltenham Gazette, 28 June 1843.
Bath Chronicle, 29 June 1843.
The Somerset County Gazette, 1 July 1843.
Welton Old Coal Pit
Somerset County Gazette, 4 and 11 October 1851.
Taunton Courier, 8 October 1851.
Bath Journal, 8 October 1851.
Bath Chronicle, 9 October 1851.

Two Horrible Murders (and a Suicide) at Bath
Taunton Courier, 2 December 1829.